ADMINISTRATION

SECOND EDITION

ADMINISTRATION

SECOND EDITION

Carol Carysforth
Maureen Rawlinson

NVQ level 3

Student Handbook

Heinemann Educational Publishers
Halley Court, Jordan Hill, Oxford OX2 8EJ
a division of Reed Educational & Professional Publishing Ltd

MELBOURNE   AUCKLAND
FLORENCE   PRAGUE   MADRID   ATHENS
SINGAPORE   TOKYO   SAO PAULO
CHICAGO   PORTSMOUTH (NH)   MEXICO
IBADAN   GABORONE   JOHANNESBURG
KAMPALA   NAIROBI

First published 1996
99 98 97 11 10 9 8 7 6 5

A catalogue record for this book is available from the British Library on request.

ISBN 0 435 451278

Designed by Ken Vail Graphics Design

Typeset by Wyvern Typesetting Ltd, Bristol

Printed and bound in Great Britain by
Biddles Ltd, Guildford and King's Lynn

Acknowledgements

The authors would like to acknowledge the co-operation, assistance and support of all those who have helped them in the writing of this book – particularly the assistance and patience of close friends and relatives who have helped them to cope with the last-minute deadlines.

Special thanks are due to the following people: David Williams, for patiently checking every word written about integrated computer packages, Kevan Boyle for giving us the benefit of his expertise on costing, Margaret Berriman for her support and encouragement as our editor and friend, Jan Nikolic who helped to pull the book together and Paul and Rebecca who are rapidly becoming expert index compilers!

Finally, we would like to thank all those whose enthusiasm and kind comments about the first edition encouraged us to revise and update it on this occasion. We would like to take this opportunity to thank personally Dorothy Harrison from Wigan College, who has been kind enough to promote our book on a variety of occasions. We hope she will find this edition even better and more useful than the first!

Contents

Introduction

The second edition of this book has been produced in response to the new NVQ 3 Administration syllabus which came into effect early in 1995 and also in response to requests from users of the first edition that we provide them with a similar text for the new scheme.

The new award has been designed to provide better progression from NVQ level 2 Administration and to reflect more accurately the work carried out by administrators in a variety of organisations. The award is now comprised of eight core units and one optional unit from a choice of seven.

In this new scheme there has been a noticeable shift towards a more distinct administration role. This role is defined by the Administration Lead Body as:

> The establishment, operation, maintenance and evaluation of systems, procedures and services to assist organisations to achieve their objectives.

The old standards included a great deal on the supervision of junior staff, but it has been recognised that this is not necessarily the role of senior administrators. The new standards have removed the supervisory element from individual units, although the development of staff is still an implicit function within the terms of the award. Therefore, the ability to operate with and through people is still a vital skill at all levels of administrative work and for this reason we have retained the 'Managing . . .' chapters which proved so popular in the first edition.

The role of the PA or secretary is now seen as one aspect of a wider administrative remit and tutors should consider carefully the suitability of secretarial candidates for this award.

Additionally, whilst the skills inherent in the scheme are useful for both administrators and PAs alike, basic office procedures – such as those concerning reprographics, mailroom procedures, filing or telecommunications – are covered in NVQ 1 or NVQ 2 awards and are not repeated at this level. There is an assumption that administrators operating at this level should be able to carry out these types of activities competently whether or not they have progressed from level 2.

This book has been designed to give level 3 candidates the knowledge and understanding they require – and must later demonstrate – to achieve the award. For that reason, each element follows the knowledge/understanding headings used in the scheme itself. The text has also been designed to give the candidates the information required to enable them to address each of the performance criteria and all aspects of the range statements.

It is hoped that both students and tutors will find this book as useful and valuable as the first edition in preparing for accreditation.

Assessing competence

It is clear that NVQ level 3 Administration will be difficult for full-time students unless they have the maturity and ability to cope with the role and have continuous work experience at an appropriate level built into the course.

It is likely that the vast majority of people undertaking the scheme will be in full-time or part-time employment, and attending college on a day-release or evening-only basis. A further, increasingly popular, method of gaining accreditation is by APA or APLE – often with the NVQ adviser visiting the workplace to give guidance on the scheme and the evidence requirements.

The majority of evidence will have to be collected in the workplace. Areas of the scheme which cannot be covered by the employee undertaking his or her normal job role may point to the need for 'top-up' training in a specific area. Often evidence can then be obtained simply by job rotation for a few days. If the employer cannot accommodate this request then simulation may be required. However, this must be a structured activity with the same constraints and pressures introduced as would occur in a working environment. In choosing option units, it is strongly recommended that candidates undertake an option which accurately reflects their own job role.

The companion book to this student text, Simulated Work Activities – which includes activities for level 3 students – can be used to assess whether the students are ready to claim competence. In addition it will be useful for those students who have 'gaps' which cannot be met in the workplace. Further, it provides guidance on the type of evidence which the students or employees can use to claim competence as well as including a section specifically designed to enable candidates to demonstrate their knowledge and understanding.

Our aim is to provide all students and tutors of NVQ 3 Administration with a comprehensive 'pack' which will be equally useful no matter which route is being followed to achieve the award.

Carol Carysforth-Neild
Maureen Rawlinson

October 1995

1 Contribute to the improvement of performance

Element 1.1

Develop self to enhance performance

The aim of this element is to focus on you – the candidate for an NVQ level 3 Administration award. It concentrates on your aims and objectives and the development you need in order to achieve them.

It is interesting to note that, generally, the older a person, the more defensive he or she becomes when faced with any type of self-assessment activity. Often experienced staff feel that they know all about the way in which they should do their job or deal with other people. In reality, of course, we should never stop learning. A closed mind is a handicap in every field of life. A mind which is open and receptive to new facts and new opinions and is constantly forming and re-forming its views leads eventually to something much valued in the elderly of many cultures – wisdom. A 'wise' person is someone to whom we all want to turn when we have a problem or dilemma. We hope for a measured, considered reply based on knowledge and experience. If we take heed of the advice we receive – and the rationale behind it – then we move forward ourselves.

The aim of this element, therefore, is to lead you through a process of self-assessment, to help you to identify opportunities for your own self-development and to assist you in reviewing and evaluating your progress. Although much of the element will be concerned with your own job role and career aspirations, we also think it is important to concentrate on your development as a person. In your job you are responsible for the self-development of others (see Element 2.2), so it is important that you can operate as a role model for those who wish to follow in your footsteps.

Throughout your course you should be reviewing your own progress with either your tutor or your adviser (if you are obtaining the qualification through the APA/APL route). It is also beneficial if you have someone at work with whom you can discuss your progress – especially if this person can act as your guide and mentor. An understanding person you can trust who has worked for the organisation for some time is ideal – however, we appreciate that this may not always be possible.

Start by making a few notes to discuss with your tutor or adviser later.

1 What, apart from a level 3 Administration qualification, would you like to get out of this course? How do you think you would know if you have achieved this?

2 Think of the leaders, managers or supervisors you know yourself. Who do you admire the most – and why? Who do you least admire – and why?

Your work role and responsibilities

Your work role and responsibilities are important because they will provide the focus for this qualification. They also largely provide the focus for your own self-development.

Jobs and work roles can be described in terms of 'best fit' – both in relation to an individual and in relation to the NVQ3 award. If your job fits you well as an individual then you will know this because you will have a fundamental feeling of well-being when you are at work. It should be stressed that this happens very, very rarely for anyone all the time! Everyone has 'good days' and 'bad days' – and so do the people with whom they work. At times, the systems and procedures you have to follow get in your way or seem incomprehensible. Things can go wrong – and in a big way. There are days when you may be constantly interrupted, expected to undertake complex activities to unrealistic deadlines or have to follow through a monotonous task to its eventual completion. However, whilst this may seem overwhelming or depressing to one person it may be seen as a welcome challenge by another. Judging how well you fit your job (or it fits you) is something only you can assess.

The factors which influence 'best fit' – you and the organisation

There are three basic factors which influence how well you fit in to the job you hold in your particular organisation. These are:

- the people with whom you work
- the tasks you have to do
- the organisation itself – its culture, values, environment, history and structure.

On top of these factors you have to 'overlay' yourself – a unique person with a special 'mix' of skills, abilities, aptitudes and personality. An added complication is the fact that the 'shapes' of all these factors are constantly changing (Figure 1.1.1).

- Employees in an organisation leave and new people are appointed. You may have related to the existing staff particularly well but struggle to cope with some of the new arrivals.

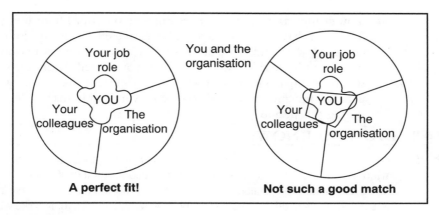

Figure 1.1.1

- Your job may change. A quick look at a job description a few years after the job holder arrived can show how easily this can become outdated! Today, not just the work may change but also where and how you do it. Teleworkers work from home, computerised systems do some of your work for you but create new tasks – and so on.
- The organisation changes – mainly because of outside forces in the environment. Government legislation, changes in suppliers or customer behaviour and increases or decreases in competition are all factors which can affect the output, responsiveness and tasks which are undertaken within an organisation.
- The structure of the organisation may change – many companies have gone through a period of slimming down or 'downsizing' because of the recession. This may mean the merging of some departments or a reorganisation of the staff at all levels. More staff may be employed on temporary or fixed-term contracts or on part-time hours. More services may be 'bought in' or 'contracted out'.
- The culture of the organisation can be, at one extreme, hierarchical, formal and procedural or, at the other, highly responsive, informal and subject to high or constant pressure – or anywhere in between. The culture manifests itself in many ways – from dress to language, from office furniture to staff conditions of service.
- Organisational values are often linked to the type of culture and can be identified if you think about which areas are given priority or accorded the greatest importance. For instance, in your organisation is there greater focus on task accomplishment or on interpersonal skills? If the values of the organisation are similar to your own views and beliefs, then you will have less personal conflict in linking your goals with the type of achievements valued by senior management.

● You change as new experiences impinge on your life or lifestyle. These can have both positive and negative effects. If you join a company at 18 and retire at 55 you are a very different person when you leave than you were when you started! Even if you stay in an organisation for only a short time, it is likely that your personal life and views will change – even if only marginally – during this period.

DID YOU KNOW?

The amount of impact any individual can have on an organisation is very limited, so it is important to recognise the restrictions you face (Figure 1.1.2). As you rise in the organisation then your influence will increase – but only in the specific areas relating to your own job role. When you leave, it is likely that the waters will close again fairly rapidly!

TEST YOURSELF

Do you match your organisation and does it fit with you and your style?

For each of the following statements below, give yourself a score between 0 and 5. A score of 5 indicates that you totally agree with the statement. A score of 0 indicates that you do not agree at all with the statement. Use the key at the bottom to see how you rate. Then discuss your individual responses with your tutor or adviser. In each case consider what you can do (other than resigning immediately!) if your 'fit' is distinctly poor.

1 I arrive at work most days feeling positive and cheerful.
2 I like the vast majority of the people I work with.
3 I relate well to my immediate superior.
4 I empathise with my boss and the problems he/she faces.
5 I find my job interesting.
6 I find my job challenging.
7 My boss praises me when I do a good job.
8 I am not expected to take the blame for problems which are not my fault.
9 I obtain regular feedback from my boss on the way I am performing – whether this is good or bad!
10 I relate to the 'style' of the organisation and the way in which it operates.
11 I know I have a future in the organisation – my 'style' suits them.
12 I socialise with the people I work with.
13 My boss encourages me to develop my personal and work skills.
14 The organisation rewards people like me.
15 I understand what the organisation is trying to achieve and agree with the methods it uses.
16 I understand what is expected of me.
17 I agree with the promotion policy.
18 I understand and agree with the systems I have to use and the procedures I have to follow.

Different organisational cultures	
Power culture (The Web) Usually a central figure in control – often started as a one-man/family business. Few rules – main ingredient is trust. Long-serving staff valued, often employed in key roles.	**Role culture** (Greek temple) Pillars identify specialist areas (finance, production, sales, etc.). Many procedures and rules coordinated by senior managers at the top. Usually specific job descriptions, predictable career path. Often a bureaucracy or public sector organisation.
The task culture (A net) Concerned with getting the job done – no overall boss. The right people are put together for a specific job or task. The outcome is the main issue – may be achieved by groups or project teams. Decision-making and control delegated downwards. Flexible and fast-moving enterprise.	**The person culture** (The cluster) Individuals are most important ingredient – often highly trained professionals (e.g. barristers, medical consultants). Each individual has power above and beyond the organisation. Each allowed to do his or her 'own thing' and further his or her own career.

Figure 1.1.2
(Adapted from Handy, *Understanding Organisations*)

19 My colleagues and my boss understand me.

20 I understand and agree with most of the decisions that are made.

Key

Score

80–100   You and the organisation were made for each other! You may struggle to find such a good fit again if you change jobs.

60–80   Although you are not always an ideal 'fit', most of the time you can cope quite easily with the differences. The longer you stay in the organisation the easier this is likely to become.

40–60   The situation is passable as it is – depending upon your personality you may have decided to leave things as they are or to argue every time you cannot see the reason for something! Try to identify those areas where you can effect change and come to terms with those you can't. That way you move yourself up the scale a little.

20–40   Fairly frequently you may feel undervalued or frustrated at your ability to make an impact. Bearing in mind that organisations usually *don't* change, the best strategy is to identify those areas which cause you the most problems and decide how you can adjust your work habits to minimise problems. If you feel this is impossible, it may be time to start looking around for alternatives.

0–20   Oh, dear! You are a very square peg in a very round hole. You have some serious thinking to do about your possible future in your current organisation. Look at Figure 1.1.2 and try to identify the type of organisation where you would be more likely to do well – keep this in mind if you start applying for different jobs!

The factors which influence 'best fit' – your job role and the NVQ3 Administration scheme

An ideal candidate for this scheme would be one who is employed in an administrative capacity and who regularly undertakes all the competencies included in the scheme as a regular part of his or her job role! In this case, most (if not all) of the knowledge, evidence and understanding has already been achieved and it is simply a matter of identifying which evidence should be used to confirm competence.

Of course, in most cases this ideal situation does not exist. This does not mean that you cannot achieve the award – unless your job is totally different or you work completely on your own all the time!

Your tutor or adviser is there to help you to obtain competence in any areas which you cannot achieve in the workplace. He or she will also help you to select the evidence you need to show the verifier. In some cases there may be a problem because the tasks you undertake at work do not match exactly the mandatory units of this award. For instance, you may not use a computer as part of your job. Or you may undertake all the tasks but have few dealings with other staff. In either of these situations you may need to negotiate with your employer. Job enhancement or rotation could be used to enable you to cover areas not normally associated with your own job. Alternatively, even though you are not formally responsible for a junior member of staff, your boss may welcome some assistance with a new employee. Flexibility and imagination can sometimes work wonders in helping you to 'plug any gaps'.

DID YOU KNOW?

The scheme consists of eight mandatory or compulsory units and then one optional unit. You should choose the optional unit which most nearly relates to your own job role and the tasks you carry out on a regular basis.

TEST YOURSELF

1   Make sure you know the scheme yourself! Read the information materials produced by your awarding body (as a quick check you could look at the contents page of this book).

2   The profiles of four NVQ3 students are shown in Figure 1.1.3.
    a   Who do you think would find it the easiest and who would find it the most difficult to undertake the award?
    b   What recommendations could you make to help each student to gain competency in any missing areas?

3   Obtain a copy of your own job description. Then attach a summary which indicates the accuracy of this job description – you may find it helpful to attach also a list of jobs you undertake on a regular and on an infrequent basis.

    Match up your own job with the scheme and discuss any 'gaps' you have identified with your tutor or adviser.

Suzanne works for an organisation which has a central office in London and branch offices all over the country. She is PA to the Regional Director and is responsible for 3 clerical/secretarial staff – one acts as receptionist and staffs the switchboard, the second is responsible for reprographics, mail and general typing and filing duties and the third is secretary to the Regional Manager. Suzanne undertakes the full range of secretarial/PA roles but is worried about the option units. Materials and equipment are allocated by head office. Meetings are held at the regional office – which also deals with all travel and accommodation requests. Finance is allocated centrally.

Ben works as a finance administrator in a large college. He is largely involved with processing accounts and student grants. His ambition is to become a chief administrative officer within the next 10 years – even if this means moving colleges. The college has a large computer network and he is a member of the college Safety Committee. Ben is worried about Element 3.3 as he has little to do with appointments. He is also unsure as to the best option unit to take. At present he has no specific responsibility for junior staff although the college does take on additional temporary workers in September of each year to cope with the influx of new students.

Sarah has always been involved in medical work. She started as receptionist in a health centre and then progressed to medical secretary. At present she is employed in general practice as deputy to the Practice Manager. Eventually she would like to become a Practice Manager herself. She has some authority for the reception staff when the Practice Manager is off-duty. Her major concerns are related to health and safety and developing procedures. Both of these areas are normally dealt with by the Practice Manager in consultation with the doctors.

Margaret works on a part-time basis for a firm of solicitors. She completed level 2 Administration at college before she obtained her present job and she has always wanted to gain level 3. The practice is very small, with only two partners, a legal secretary, a receptionist and Margaret herself. She can never remember receiving a formal job description! Her employers have so far ignored the computer revolution – the receptionist has an electronic typewriter and the legal secretary uses a PC, but only for word processing. Margaret has no specific responsibility for either of the staff but does give help and guidance to the receptionist who only left school last year.

Figure 1.1.3 Four student profiles

Ways of identifying development needs

You should now have achieved a more objective view of your own organisation and your own job – and related these to the scheme itself. You will also have talked through the main implications of your findings with your tutor or adviser.

The next stage is to identify your own development needs. These not only relate to your current work activities and the scheme itself but also to you, as a person. An area you should consider is your own career and potential.

The two main ways in which you can identify your own development needs are by:

- self-analysis and self-assessment
- discussions with others – your boss, tutor, adviser and colleagues. You may also want to include your partner – although this strategy may be a little risky!

DID YOU KNOW?

In some organisations staff are encouraged to prepare self-development plans or self-development diaries which include career plans. This can help human resource staff or line managers to identify activities which will help staff to achieve their ambitions.

Self-analysis/self-assessment

It is interesting that whilst we are all extremely self-critical in relation to our size and appearance, we are far less self-critical in relation to our personality traits and behaviour!

The reason for this may become clear in a moment. Basically we all need a certain amount of self-confidence to cope with life. If this is taken away from us then we may become psychologically disturbed and need professional help. In an extreme case we may become suicidal. There is therefore a 'no go' area in all of us which has to remain intact in order that we can survive. If other people move into this area and criticise us − or if life events force us into situations which are beyond our 'coping skills' − then we can suffer serious damage. In some cases, people have had to leave jobs, sometimes on the grounds of ill health, because they have been forced into situations with which they cannot cope.

Self-analysis is therefore often quite a difficult activity to undertake as we are, in effect, turning a mirror onto ourselves − though in a positive rather than a negative way. Several techniques have been developed in order to do this; three of these are outlined below.

The Johari Window

This is a well-known management exercise which identifies:

- the Arena − which contains the aspects of your own behaviour and personality which are in the public domain, i.e. known both to yourself and others
- the Facade − the areas in your private domain, i.e. known to yourself but not usually on public display
- the Blind Spot − the areas seen by others but not recognisable by yourself. Acknowledging these − or having someone point them out to you − may sometimes be a difficult or painful experience
- the Unknown − the hidden area formed by your experiences and up-bringing.

The size of the *arena* can vary depending upon the company we are in and the amount of trust between a group. With a stranger, the arena may be very small and the *facade* large. With someone we trust or know very well the reverse is likely to be true. The size of the *blind spot* can vary depending upon our willingness to be made aware of aspects of our personality and character of which we are normally in blissful ignorance! It is also affected by our willingness to change, adapt or modify our behaviour (Figure 1.1.4). (*Note:* the Johari Window is often used in relation to group interaction and seeking and exchanging information with colleagues – see Unit 4.1, page 195.)

THE ARENA Public domain – area known to self and others	BLIND SPOT Area seen by others but not known to self
FACADE Area known by self but deliberately hidden from others	UNKNOWN The 'hidden' area

Figure 1.1.4 The Johari Window

The repertory grid

Trying to find out how you think and why you think the way you do can be very difficult if not impossible. One way of approaching this is to look at your opinions of events or other people and use this information to reflect back on your own attitudes and values to find out *why* you think this way – and what this says about you. An example of how to do this is given in the exercise below.

TEST YOURSELF

1 Preferably (but not essentially) undertake this exercise with a colleague at work who knows the same people you do and who will respect your confidence.
2 Select five people at work (at random) who you know well. Write their names on five small cards.
3 Shuffle the cards and select any three.
4 Pair up two of the names and discard the third. Now say why you paired up the two you did and isolated the third member, i.e. what made you think the third person didn't fit. Repeat this four or five times.
5 Ask your partner to examine the three names you selected each time and to undertake the same exercise. You may find that the pairing and the reason given are different from your own.
6 Analyse your answers. This gives insight into how you view your colleagues and to what is important to you. For instance, if you isolated one member because he or she is aggressive or uncooperative then think about what this may tell you about your own views and your own identification of possible problems. You may find that your colleague saw the situation in a totally different way – not just because his or her perception of these people is different but because his or her own *needs* in relation to the working relationships are different from your own. (This is discussed more fully in Unit 4.)

The critical incident technique

This activity is best undertaken with your tutor or adviser. It involves thinking back over your life and career to date and identifying the incidents which were particularly influential in affecting your behaviour or thoughts. You should also think about difficult problems you have had to cope with and what you did about these.

You may find that recollection of some incidents is difficult – particularly if it is a long time since they occurred. If you go through the 'who, why, what, how, where, when' routine then this may help you.

The aim is to find some pattern in terms of situations in which you feel comfortable and those in which you don't – and to find areas where you feel that some personal development would be useful. If, for instance, you identify that you nearly always encounter difficulties when you have to stand up for yourself then you may decide that assertiveness training or self-confidence building would be good for you.

A key factor is to identify the cycle of repetition in relation to particular events or incidents. Those situations which tend to repeat themselves are those which should be 'flagged' as the most important – in terms of why they happen, their impact on you and the scope or limitations you have to effect change.

 DID YOU KNOW?

You can find additional useful information on self-assessment in the section on Managing Yourself (page 43). If you find self-analysis and self-development fascinating then you may also decide to visit your local or college library, which will have a range of books on this topic.

Career potential

The idea of 'jobs for life' is gradually fading. In 1975, the percentage of adults in full-time tenured employment was 55.5 per cent. In 1993 this had fallen to 35.9 per cent. Today more and more employees talk about 'a portfolio of work' based on a variety of experiences obtained in different companies or even on a freelance basis. Some may have more than one part-time job or work mainly on a succession of fixed-term contracts.

This does not mean that you should forget all about career prospects or career development. Even if you have different jobs with different companies there is nothing to stop you applying for higher level jobs each time. What it does mean is that the competition for these is likely to be fierce so that, at each stage, you will need to *prove* that you are well qualified and capable of doing the job. This often means taking additional training or studying on a higher level course and making sure that you keep up-to-date with the latest developments, especially in areas such as information technology. This type of training will give you 'portable' skills which you can transfer to another organisation or use to perhaps arrange a lateral transfer within your present organisation to a job which you think would be more interesting or challenging.

Today, more than ever before, identifying training needs and self-development opportunities is seen to be primarily the responsibility of the individual – hopefully with the help of a supportive organisation. This is actually a more appropriate approach than training requirements being dictated by the organisation – individuals' training needs can be so diverse that a corporate, or company-wide, approach may be inappropriate for many members of staff. In addition, a person can take his or her own personal development plan from one job to another, because it should focus on long-term aims or 'lifetime learning' – not just what could be undertaken in the next few months.

Of course, the degree to which you yearn for career progression will depend upon how ambitious you are. Before you cry 'Oh, not me!' bear in mind that many women, in particular, often undervalue their own potential in this area and, as a result, undersell themselves at an interview. They feel that to be thought of as ambitious is somehow unfeminine and 'something not very nice'. Yet if you *are* good, and know you could do well, why not recognise this and work towards fulfilling your own potential? You owe it to yourself to find out just how good you can be!

CHECK IT YOURSELF

1   Look at the structure of your own company and identify any possible progressive or lateral opportunities in which you would be interested. Try to decide objectively whether you can work towards progressing in your current organisation or whether you would probably need to move to a different company.
2   One useful tip to anyone wanting to get on is to look at those who *have* progressed in the organisation. They obviously 'fit' the company image and style – in appearance, behaviour and ability. Try to identify their key attributes and see if you can use one as a useful role model to guide your own career development.

Discussions with others

Needless to say, before you can consider moving on you need to make a success of your current job and to gain this award! Indeed, taking this award may have been suggested to you as a means of obtaining a nationally recognised qualification which links closely with your job. However, it is useful to be able to discuss and identify your development needs in a broader way and not just focus on one particular course. To do this you have to:

- identify where you are now and the development which has already taken place
- identify where you would like to be in, say, five years' time
- look at the development which would be useful both to you *and to your company* which will help you bridge this gap.

The only way, of course, to find out about the needs and expectations of your organisation and immediate boss is to talk to your manager and other colleagues. If your organisation has an active Personnel or Human Resources department then you may find you can obtain useful advice there. Some companies, particularly those working towards Investors in People or the ISO 9000 quality award, are very keen to encourage staff development activities. Usually this is also a key item of the annual appraisal interview and this is a golden opportunity for you to talk to your line manager about your future.

CHECK IT YOURSELF

1 Start by listing all the people you could consult about your development needs. Try to think of sources both inside and outside your organisation.
2 Identify where you are now by
    - listing the qualifications you have already gained
    - noting down the short courses and other training activities you have undertaken at work
    - considering the personal skills you possess – and those which you would like to improve
3 Identify where you want to be in a few years' time and find out the type of qualifications and experience you will need to acquire.
4 Obtain details on courses of training and higher education which interest you. Find out how much these are likely to cost – before you talk over your ideas with your boss (see below).

 ## DID YOU KNOW?

There are literally dozens of types of courses and training activities in which you can become involved. Some will be offered 'in-house' by your own organisation – particularly if it is a large company. Others will be offered in training establishments, colleges and universities. Some will require you to attend courses while others may be taken on a distance learning basis.

Today many organisations have their own open learning centre which contains CD-ROMs, learning packs and multimedia packages. In other cases it may be more appropriate for you to undertake work shadowing or develop a new skill by being coached at work by an expert (see Element 1.2, page 32). Figure 1.1.5 gives some idea of the range of courses available.

Short courses	Professional development – vocational
Assertiveness training	NVQ 3 Customer Service
Time management	NVQ 2/3 Information
Verbal communication skills/oral	Technology
presentations	LCCI Private and Executive
Public speaking	Secretary's Diploma
Project management	IPD Certificate of Personnel
Interpersonal skills (relating	Practice
to others)	Association of Accounting
Minute taking	Technicians courses
Managing your boss	Institute of Purchasing and
Health and safety training	Supply courses
Confidence building	Certificate/Diploma in
Team building	Marketing
Employment law	Language courses
First aid	Change Management
Stress awareness/management	Women into Management
Information technology training	Supervisory Management
Negotiating skills	(NEBSM)
Telephone selling	**Academic development**
Creative thinking	HND in Business Studies
Sign language	BA in Business Administration
Personal safety training	BA in Business Studies
Understanding equal opportunities	MBA (Master in Business
Leadership skills	Administration)
Managing change	
Problem solving	
Quality management	
Business writing skills	

Figure 1.1.5

 TEST YOURSELF

Add to this information by:

- visiting your local college or university and asking for a part-time course prospectus
- visiting your local library and reading a recent copy of one of the training journals available to find the names and addresses of the many private training companies. An example is CareerTrack, an organisation which produces videos and audio tapes and organises seminars on a variety of topics – including one for secretaries undertaking an administration role and others relating to women in management. Contact them for details at Sunrise House, Sunrise Parkway, Linford Wood, Milton Keynes MK14 6YA or phone 01908 354010.

- writing to the Open University for details of their courses (not just degree courses)
- contacting your local Training and Enterprise Council (their address and telephone number is in your phone book). They run a variety of short courses in conjunction with local training providers
- visiting your own human resources department and finding out what is available 'in-house'.

DID YOU KNOW?

Some private organisations run outdoor training courses to develop team building, communication, problem-solving and decision-making skills. They are usually run over one day or a weekend and can often be highly enjoyable as well as beneficial for employees.

TEST YOURSELF

As an administrator you have to be well-organised. Prove this by starting a filing system to store:

- the information on yourself – including the results of your self-analysis activities
- the information you have acquired on various courses and other self-development events.

This can provide the basis for your action plan. The documentation to help you to produce this is given in the accompanying tutor's pack.

Setting self-development objectives

Whereas a goal is a general aim, usually an objective is more specific. It is a statement of intent, often with a target date for completion. Therefore, your goal may be to update your IT skills and, at some date in the future, obtain a degree. These could translate into objectives as follows:

1 Take one-day Word for Windows course	Oct 96
2 Contact Open University for details of undergraduate courses	Nov 96

If you intend to take a degree and are going to finance yourself and study in your spare time, then it is not essential for you to discuss your ideas at work, let alone obtain agreement. If, however, you are hoping for financial support or time off work *or* if you want to please your boss to obtain support for promotion later, then you would be wise to talk through your proposed objectives and obtain agreement for your plans.

DID YOU KNOW?

Most awarding bodies which offer NVQ schemes also offer complementary Core Skills schemes. In this case you would also obtain accreditation for your skills in Communication, Application of Number, Information Technology, Managing your own Learning and Performance and Working with Others. A sixth core skill area is Problem Solving but this unit has not yet been accredited by the National Council for Vocational Qualifications.

Development opportunities and resource implications

Deciding that you need to expand your horizons, perhaps by taking a year out to work for an overseas branch of your organisation, may seem wonderful in theory. However, it is unlikely to be welcomed in practice unless your organisation would have much to gain by paying your airfare, covering your job for twelve months and then hoping you come back again!

Once you start costing out some courses of action you may find that you have to modify your ideas a little. Some one- and two-day courses run by experts or specialists can cost over £1000 – particularly if accommodation is also included.

Bear in mind that your organisation is only likely to finance something if it can see a direct benefit *or* if it can obtain support with the funding elsewhere. Sometimes companies can obtain assistance with staff development costs through their local Training and Enterprise Council – but you will need to find out which activities can be funded this way.

If you are paying your own way – either totally or in part – then you should be aware of two facts.

● If you are a taxpayer then you can pay your NVQ course fees at a level excluding tax if you make sure the local college knows your employer is not paying your fees. This means you will pay less than the normal fee.
● You can obtain a Career Development Loan to borrow between £200 and £8000 to put towards course fees, books and materials on any full-time, part-time, open or distance learning course. However, the course must relate to your job or the work you want to do and last no longer than two years. You must also be 18 years of age or over. If you are interested, telephone 0800 585 505 or ask for details at your local Jobcentre.

 DID YOU KNOW?

1   If you work for a small organisation and your manager says he or she cannot afford training, then obtain information on the Small Firms Training Loans scheme from your local Training and Enterprise Council and put the pack on your manager's desk!
2   Organisations who are working towards the Investors in People award can also obtain financial support from their local TEC. Investors in People is a national quality standard devised to encourage organisations

to invest in the training and development of their staff to help them to meet organisational goals. Again, details of the financial support available can be obtained from your local TEC.

Ways of implementing development activities

Do remember that you do not have to go on an official course to learn something! Not only can you develop yourself on a daily basis in dozens of different ways, but there are often cheaper alternatives than signing on to undertake a specific course of study. In other words, you do not have to go 'off the job' to undertake a development activity. Instead, think of all the more 'informal' options which may be available to you every day, such as:

- borrowing a book from the library on a topic which interests you
- reading 'quality' newspapers
- asking someone at work to show you how to do a job or use a particular computer package or a new type of equipment
- talking to your line manager about the different ways in which you can increase or enhance your skills and expertise
- finding out if there are any conferences, seminars, exhibitions or workshops you can attend to increase your knowledge
- asking for permission to 'work shadow' a colleague or someone in another department or organisation. This is often very valuable if you shadow someone who either has
  - a complementary role to yourself in your own organisation (which shows you both how you could liaise more effectively)
  - a similar role to yourself in your own or a comparable organisation (but not a major competitor!). This gives you an insight into different ways in which you can tackle your own job
  - a senior role to yourself – which will give you greater understanding of the pressures on your own line manager and your own potential for operating at that level
- training yourself with the help of a good handbook – preferably with someone available to help you if you get stuck
- using a computer-based training package (CBT) or CD-ROM or multimedia package
- reviewing with an adviser or mentor (see page 32) how you organised a task or came to a decision, talking through possible alternatives and deciding whether any of these may have been better
- discussing your own performance in staff development or appraisal interviews with your line manager.

Negotiating and agreeing your objectives

If possible, try to make sure that your personal development objectives contain a mixture of:

- formal and informal methods
- cheap (or free) and more expensive methods.

Before you make any arrangement to discuss your objectives with your boss, check that your ideas are sensible, would benefit both you and your company, your schedule isn't overloaded and that you are aware of the cost implications. Make sure also that you have a mental note of what you would be prepared to fund yourself if you had to.

The problem comes, of course, if your ideas don't coincide with those of your immediate line manager. You will need to think carefully about his or her motives in disagreeing – whether you are really being given sensible advice or whether he or she has some ulterior motive. Finance and resource implications will be a key consideration in the discussions. However, one office administrator had a 'hidden agenda' of never allowing staff to take courses which would mean they were better qualified than she was – which is a less valid reason for refusal!

If there is a conflict of ideas then try to negotiate a compromise – rather than have a row! Negotiating means not denying the other person his or her point of view. Accept it, talk it through and rationally discuss the strengths and weaknesses of each idea. Do not push the other person into a corner where he or she feels honour bound to defend his/her own ideas no matter what! Note also that volunteering information about funding, or being prepared to fund yourself, may often persuade the most difficult boss to support you.

If you need additional advice, have a word with your tutor or adviser in confidence.

handouts as you can – so that your own session will be as thorough as the one you originally attended!

Ways of assessing performance and progress

Do be aware that, to be effective, assessment of your performance and progress must be done regularly. It is not sensible to do a year-long course and only at the end of it find out whether you are on target to achieve your objective. By then it may be too late to rectify any problems.

This tenet is just as valid on an NVQ course, where you are assembling a portfolio of work, as it is on a course where you would be externally examined at the end of your studies. If you are trying to work towards a self-development plan, then your assessment should fall into two areas:

1 your performance and progress on each individual course or development activity
2 your performance and progress as a whole in relation to your development objectives.

Individual courses or activities

If you are being trained, in any way, then you have every right to expect your trainer to review your progress with you at regular intervals. Feedback is essential if you are to benefit from the experience. Of course, it is then up to you whether you take any notice of this feedback – particularly if you are told something you would rather not hear!

On some courses you will be scheduled to have regular tutorials with your tutor. If you do not, then request a discussion at a point which is appropriate for you. Discuss the structure of the course, your performance to date, and how much work still has to be done. Obtain help and advice on any aspects which are worrying you.

Your performance as a whole

This is something only you can really assess – although your line manager may show an interest, particularly if he or she is funding part or all of your development. Are you keeping to schedule in all areas, performing as well as you would have wished or are you slipping behind?

If the latter is the case then you need to assess:

● whether the plan is realistic
● what factors have impinged on your progress.

If the plan is unrealistic and was, say, over-ambitious then it should be reviewed in the light of your experiences. If there was nothing wrong with the plan but you have still fallen behind then try to assess objectively why this has occurred. Try to avoid creating a 'blame culture' where it is everyone's fault but your own! Unless you have had a major personal or professional change imposed upon you, most of the decisions made over the period in question will have been made by you! If you have chosen the wrong course of action you will learn more by acknowledging this than denying it.

Again, you may find that objective help and advice from an outside source is useful in clarifying any problem areas. Try to choose someone in whom you can confide with confidence and who knows you well enough to allow for both your strengths and weaknesses.

Of course, hopefully you will be surprised and delighted by the result of your assessment. In this case your findings will motivate you to continue to work hard and progress still further. As you hit your goals, try to reward yourself with a treat – even if it is only a takeaway from the local Chinese restaurant with a bottle of wine and the company of a very good friend!

Ways of evaluating and reviewing development activities

Ideally all staff should be given the opportunity of giving feedback on any staff development or self-development activities in which they have been involved (see also Element 2.2). Some organisations have a formal feedback process which can either involve a verbal feedback session to a training or human resources manager or the completion of a standard form for perusal by the training section. If the form is completed with particularly negative or contentious remarks then an interview may follow to investigate the activity more closely.

There are usually two ways in which you will be expected to evaluate a development activity:

a   objectively – in terms of its length, content, mode and quality of delivery
b   subjectively – in terms of its benefits to you in relation to your current job role and future prospects.

Your objective analysis tells the training section whether the activity has been good value for money. There is a huge difference between attending a professional short course which was lively, interesting and informative and included a variety of learning activities, and attending a boring lecture which told you nothing you didn't know already or was pitched a long way above your head. Do keep your analysis objective – don't be distracted by personal characteristics of the course leader!

Assessing the value of the course in relation to your own existing job role is normally easier – however, you may also be expected to evaluate the *degree* to which you think the activity was beneficial. This is more tricky as it involves more than a straight 'yes' or 'no' answer. As an example, many administrators and PAs are sent on desktop publishing (DTP) courses. If you regularly produce newsletters and other material which would benefit from being produced on a DTP package *and* you have access to the right equipment then the course is likely to be beneficial – not just to yourself but also to your organisation. If you rarely produce this type of material or the company you work for has only the most basic computer equipment then the course is likely to be of less value. Even if your job changed in the future or better equipment was bought, unless you had used your new skills regularly you would probably have forgotten most of what you learned by the time you needed it!

DID YOU KNOW?

The degree to which you use new information and ideas can, in many cases, depend almost totally upon yourself! All courses and activities will contain many new ideas – but it is often up to you whether you discard or practise them! This is one such course – if you consider the information you have already learned about self-development and that which will follow about dealing with other people. It is one thing to read a textbook, and quite another to put into practice some of the ideas you find in it!

Ways of recording achievements

Basically there are several different ways in which you can record your achievements.

- On an NVQ course such as this you will be building up a portfolio of evidence for your verifier. In the first section – which will correspond to this element – you will be expected to provide evidence of your self-development activities and achievements. This can be in the form of a list of your activities, certificates of attendance on courses, certificates of achievement and so on. A set of forms designed for this purpose is included in the tutor's pack which accompanies this book.
- If you left school in the last five years or so then you were probably involved in assembling your own National Record of Achievement containing a personal statement and records of your work experience, certificates of achievement and other qualifications. If you keep this up-to-date then you can also use this as evidence to show the verifier.
- Many organisations keep their own training and development records by asking staff to complete forms to request the activity in the first place and then to evaluate it afterwards. Copies of these, plus records of any discussions about your personal development, can also be included in your file.
- Probably the most comprehensive record is a **training or learning log**. This is your own personal record of each activity

you have undertaken which identifies the most interesting, significant or useful parts of the activity. It also ends with a miniature action plan for items you particularly want to learn more about or put into practice yourself. An extract from a log is shown in Figure 1.1.6. Again, blank forms are included in the tutor's pack which accompanies this book.

Figure 1.1.6 Extract from a training or learning log

Name . . . . Activity . . *Time Management Course* . . . . Date attended . . . *15 April 199–* . . . .
KEY EVENTS 1 Looked at time as an ever-decreasing resource, therefore very precious. 2 Need to identify best ways in which time can be spent – find out key areas – include personal areas. Maximum of 7 best. 3 Keep record of jobs to do. 4 Sub-divide main tasks. 5 Identify time-wasters (events or people) and own best time of day.
Name . . . . Activity . . . *Time Management Course* . . . . Date attended . . . *15 April 199–* . . . .
SELECTED ITEMS 1 Key events – identify up to 7 (e.g. for me – stock control/staff training/ reception records/sales reports/administration; personal – NVQ award and fitness club). 2 Keep record and identify time-wasting events and people (read up what to do about these).
Name . . . . Activity . . . *Time Management Course* . . . . Date attended . . . *15 April 199–* . . . .
MINI ACTION PLAN 1 Buy time planner. 2 Write up key areas. 3 Record main jobs under each area. 4 Keep log to identify where and when time wasted.

● You could create a personal development plan or write a personal development diary. Usually the former is a plan which you discuss regularly with a reviewer or your line manager whereas the latter may be personal and confidential. Some organisations encourage staff to write a PDP on a voluntary basis, in others it is part of the formal appraisal system, and in still more it is unheard of! This does not stop you discussing the benefits of doing this yourself with your own line manager.

ACTIVITY SECTION

1   Realistically assess your own attitude to self-development. Look at the scale in Figure 1.1.7 and decide the score which best reflects how you feel about it. Discuss your answer with your tutor or adviser. If you have a low score, try to analyse why – and what can be done about it. Remember that you will have quite a lot of work to complete in order to gain your award – and you do not need the encumbrance of battling against yourself and your own feelings at the same time!

10	Eager and positive – can't wait to start
9	Positive about the process – hope it proves to be worthwhile
8	One or two minor reservations but intend to make a go of it
7	Some reservations, but if I start it then I'll give it my best shot
6	Like the idea personally but want to talk more about the benefits
5	Mixed feelings – like the idea if it will benefit me overall
4	Need to be persuaded it's worth the effort
3	Possibly worth doing but seems to be a lot of work involved
2	Would need a lot of convincing that it's worth doing
1	Seems pointless – don't really want to know
0	No interest whatsoever

Figure 1.1.7 The range of views on self-development

2   Identify those people at work who have a positive attitude towards your own development and who will help you to achieve your goals. These are the people with whom it may be best to discuss your own plans and objectives. If you can, identify a person who is willing to act as your mentor.

3   You make an appointment with your line manager to discuss your proposed development objectives. Identify both how you would feel *and* how you would react in each of the following situations. Discuss your answers with your tutor or adviser.

   a   Your manager shows little, if any, interest in your plans.
   b   He or she argues that there is little that would match the company objectives – and asks you to rewrite them from scratch.
   c   You want to pursue a training and vocational route to increase your

job skills. Your manager obtained a degree in his thirties and thinks everyone should do the same.

d Your manager agrees to fund several activities but insists that he or she receives feedback from your tutor or adviser on your progress in each case.

4 Talk through with your tutor or adviser the forms you will use to record your activities and your achievements and how regularly this will be reviewed. Put these dates in your diary.

Element 1.2

Contribute to improving the performance of colleagues

If you have worked through Element 1.1, then you will not only have gained an insight into your own needs, but also into the support you would ideally like from your own line manager! Only you will know the extent to which this is forthcoming. However, you can use this information as a pointer as to how you should support those staff for whom you are responsible. In other words, do to others as you would be done by! If you do, then your actions may become the role model for your own line manager.

The benefits of assisting your colleagues to identify and achieve their own goals can be quite considerable.

- Working relationships will be improved between you and your colleagues.
- You will have a better understanding of how your section functions – and what can be done to improve it.
- Both you and your colleagues will be taking greater responsibility for new ideas and future developments.
- Training can be specifically linked towards the needs of your colleagues and your section.
- Your colleagues will have ownership of their own training and development and this will act as a motivator (see Element 4.2).
- Productivity should increase because your colleagues will have developed their skills.

Identifying training needs

You cannot help your colleagues to improve if you have no idea about their current performance, what they should be able to do or how well they need to do it. You also need to have some idea of their individual strengths and weaknesses, likes and dislikes. At first sight, it may seem a good idea to force a member of staff to take responsibility for the office petty cash even though he or she is very good with people but hopeless with figures! Occasionally, in a small office, this may be essential. However, it is usually much more successful to match the needs of the organisation with the needs of the staff, and, *as far as possible* take account of their individual strengths and weaknesses and their personal requirements.

Therefore the first step is to find out what training is required in a systematic and ordered way. This is usually done by undertaking a **training needs analysis**. When this is completed you can then decide the best way to help each person to improve his or her performance in the identified areas.

CHECK IT YOURSELF

Carry out a training needs analysis for one of your staff – or for yourself as a starting point. In each case decide your answers to the following questions. If you are deciding answers on behalf of other people for whom you are responsible then you *must* consult them as part of the process – or all the time you spend on this may be in vain. This is especially true if they do not perceive their problems in the same way that you do!

1 What are the key aspects of his/her job which must be carried out now?
2 What other roles
   a do you envisage for this person in the future?
   b would he/she like to undertake in the future?
3 What are his/her strengths and weaknesses?
4 Which weaknesses do not matter and which should or must be improved?
5 Which strengths could be enhanced with additional training?
6 What changes could occur/are occurring in his/her job?
7 What range of opportunities – both 'on' and 'off' the job are available for training?
8 Is the employee agreeable to training
   a in the identified areas?
   b by the identified means?

(*Note:* a training needs analysis form which you can use for this purpose is included in the tutor pack which accompanies this book.)

 ## DID YOU KNOW?

Everyone's training needs change the longer they remain in a job. In the early stages each person needs to concentrate on knowing the organisation, the jobs to be carried out, the systems to use and the skills which are required. After a while this becomes 'basic knowledge' and people want to enhance their skills or develop other areas – otherwise they become bored and stale. This is essential if the skills or technology they use are rapidly changing. After promotion, people need to start to develop their managerial, interpersonal and communication skills so that they can learn how to lead other people rather than just concentrate on their own personal development.

Assessing the competence of others

Training needs are, of course, affected by people's competence in different areas. You might recruit a school leaver who is a 'natural' on the telephone. Alternatively, another new employee might be terrified to lift the receiver. In this case one has a definite need for training – whilst the other could probably run the session! The first rule to remember is *not* to send people on training courses just for the sake of it, otherwise people will be bored, fail to see the benefit and, eventually, leave the company or at least subject you to their complaints. In addition, it is important that you remember that there are many other ways of training people besides sending them on courses (see Element 1.1 and below).

Identifying competence requirements

You should assess competence in different areas in a systematic and objective way. However, you might be surprised at the range of competencies required by people who seem to be carrying out a very simple task.

As an example, think of a switchboard operator handling incoming calls for an organisation. What skills are required to do the job *competently*?

1 Telephonist receives call. Listening skills required to assess nature of call. Background information required to assess importance of caller.
2 Telephonist responds to caller. Verbal skills required to communicate response clearly.
3 Telephonist finds out caller's requirements. Questioning skills and interaction required to find out information.
4 Caller states requirements. Telephonist needs knowledge of organisation, departmental functions, job roles and extension numbers to route call correctly. Also needs knowledge of equipment used.
5 Person not available. Written communication skills required to take clear, concise and accurate message.

In addition, you could also state that a telephonist must be able to

a find out information for internal extension users
b use other equipment (pagers, bleepers, answering machine, etc.) correctly
c cope with emergencies (bomb threats, fire alarms, etc.)
d deal with faults and report these accurately
e use reference books efficiently.

It is therefore possible to break down the components of most jobs into individual skill areas. A problem in just one area will affect overall performance. Therefore, if a temporary switchboard operator is employed, he or she may be able to operate the system and communicate with callers but have little knowledge of the organisation as a whole. Therefore the standard of service to callers will fall.

TEST YOURSELF

In many organisations staff need training to be able to deal with customers on a face-to-face basis, from the office receptionist to the staff on a customer services desk. How many skills can you identify that a member of staff would need to deal *effectively* with a difficult or problematic customer?

DID YOU KNOW?

You may like to note that when NVQ awards are being designed, they incorporate an analysis of the skills which are agreed to be required in a specific area. The NVQ standards can then be used as a basis for assessing training needs in a particular area. Acquired skills can be accredited and top-up training can be arranged for any other areas.

Assessing competence

It will soon be fairly obvious to the whole of the organisation if a switchboard operator is unable to write down a simple message or pass on a telephone number accurately! It may be less obvious that he or she cannot use a reference book accurately if all the enquirer hears is 'I'm sorry, there is no listing under that name.' Therefore you cannot just rely on your own immediate judgements – or those of other people – to assess competence. You need to obtain more detailed information, but this must be based on the **standards** which are considered acceptable. These standards determine the criteria required for a member of staff to be regarded as competent in a particular skill area.

There are standards which relate to the outcome of every job. The switchboard operator may be expected to answer every call within ten seconds, a word processor operator may be expected to type 30 A4 documents an hour and so on. In some cases these standards may be written down; in other cases we simply have a mental standard in our mind. If the new trainee takes an hour to photocopy four documents then he or she has no doubt breached our mental standard for that job – even though it isn't written down in a reference manual. You would be justified in thinking more training was needed to get the trainee up to a more acceptable standard.

Do bear in mind that standards involve both output and quality. The junior who takes two minutes to photocopy the same documents but produces unusable copies is just as incompetent as the new trainee. You therefore need to start with a good idea of the level of output and quality you consider denotes competency. Then you can start to obtain information which enables you to measure the reality of the situation against the standard for a task.

There are several ways in which you can assess quality and output, depending upon the role of the employee and how often you are in touch with him/her.

- **Observation** – preferably over a period of time to allow for nervousness at the beginning. It is unfair to sit next to someone keying in a document and time him or her with a stop watch. It is more sensible to have a job to do yourself in the vicinity and to keep a low profile over a period of time and on different occasions.

  Bear in mind, however, that observation is usually considered more suitable for lower level skills than higher level or more complex tasks.

- **Sampling** – obtain evidence of a person's work over a few days and assess it for output and quality. Do not be overly critical in relation to quality but do make sure you differentiate between important errors and minor faults which would not be noticed by an outsider. The basic principle should be whether the document(s) are usable at the first attempt in relation to why they were prepared. Therefore, you should have different standards in relation to a final report going outside the company than to a 'first pass' draft report prepared in the knowledge there will be further editing.

  So far as output is concerned, whilst you cannot allow even the most junior employee to spend all morning preparing one memo, you *should* make allowance for people's training and experience and the number of interruptions they might have had. If you have any queries in relation to the quantity of work, discuss these with the person concerned rather than speculate yourself.

- **Feedback from others** – be careful if you use this method and *never* give the impression that you are setting one person against another. Some people will love to run to you with gossip; others will protect their colleagues at all costs. If you receive constant complaints about the work output or quality of one person, however, then it is your job to assess the accuracy of the statement – and to take action if necessary. Equally, by the way, don't forget to praise your staff if feedback from other people is very good!

 ## DID YOU KNOW?

You can use the principle of triangulation to work out whether negative feedback (or complaints) is likely to be justified or not. This principle is based on the fact that:

- one person making a complaint may be causing trouble
- two people could be in collusion
- three people (the triangle) are probably correct! This is particularly true if

they have little or nothing to do with one another. If, therefore, you receive similar complaints about a member of staff from three different departments in a short space of time the situation is likely to be more serious than a moan in your ear from a colleague who never liked that person anyway!

Identifying development needs

People need training and development for several reasons. These may be because:

- they are new employees who need induction training
- they lack a basic skill which is required to do the job competently
- they lack basic knowledge which is required to do the job in such a way that they *understand* what they have to do and why
- their job or work role is changing
- the equipment they use is being updated
- the organisation has introduced new procedures
- they want to expand or extend their job
- they are ambitious and hoping for promotion.

Their reasons for needing training and the facilities and resources available will determine the development activities which can be undertaken.

The basic ways in which you identify a person's development needs are by:

a assessing competence
b keeping up-to-date with the needs of the organisation
c identifying the changes and targets which affect your own section
d finding out the needs of the person.

We have already discussed how you assess competence. You will only keep up-to-date with the needs of the organisation if you keep abreast with the changes of your job, new technology and organisational developments. Much of this may be received information from your own line manager. However, you will be expected to adapt this to the requirements of your own staff.

Finally, the only way to find out a person's own needs is to talk to him or her! This may be done formally through an appraisal interview or staff development sessions, by informal chats or team meetings (see Unit 4) or by carrying out a training needs analysis. A person who wants to get to the top in his/her profession and is willing to work hard to do so has very different needs from the person who is due to retire next year and wants a quiet life until then! It should be fairly obvious which of the two you would send on an outside course to learn how to operate Windows 95 or to cope with stress!

Methods of delivering training

There are basically two main ways in which training is delivered:

1 on-the-job
2 off-the-job.

A word of warning! Some people think that the term 'off-the-job' means that the training is received away from the workplace. This is not necessarily the case – some large organisations have specialised training centres for their staff where a range of external qualifications can be gained. The term 'on-the-job', though, should be taken quite literally. It means that training is received actually as part of doing the normal job role (or an extension of this). An example would be a trainee switchboard operator learning to use the equipment under the supervision of the experienced operator. 'Off-the-job' means learning away from your own desk or normal working environment – whether this is by attending a company training centre, a further education college or a seminar in a large hotel (Figure 1.2.1).

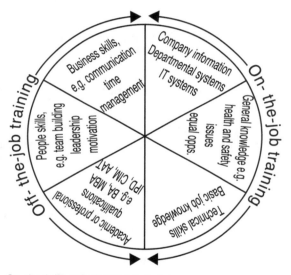

Figure 1.2.1 On-the-job and off-the-job training

On-the-job training

This often used to be known as 'sitting with Nellie' and implied that a trainee would be placed next to a more experienced worker to watch and learn. The problem was that if 'Nellie' had picked up any bad habits over the years then the trainee learned these too!

Today, on-the-job training has improved considerably and typical training activities can include:

- **induction programmes** – designed to familiarise new employees with the new workplace, basic systems and procedures
- **demonstration and practice** – particularly of new equipment or procedures. Often this can be done as **work mirroring** when one employee mirrors the way in which another, more skilled, member of staff undertakes a specific task
- **job rotation** – changing jobs with someone else for a particular period to learn new skills or gain a broader view of the job as a whole
- **work assignments** – giving staff responsibility for certain projects with a specific 'life' and seeing how they react. The complexity of the project would depend on the level of the employee
- **direct training activities** – undertaken to improve competence in a specific area, e.g. answering the telephone, using a fire extinguisher, dealing with paper jams in the photocopier.
- **advising** – giving specific assistance or suggesting recommended action to complete a task or undertake a more difficult job
- **coaching** – giving one-to-one assistance to improve performance in a specific area. Coaching can be used
  - if the employee is being asked to take on new duties and must learn them quickly
  - to consolidate other basic training or refresh skills which may have been forgotten
  - to improve competence quickly.

DID YOU KNOW?

Job enhancement is the term used when an employee is asked to take on additional tasks to stretch his or her abilities. It may be used to assess the potential for promotion. A person expected to take on more responsibility may welcome the assistance of a mentor – someone who has operated at that level for some time and can give confidential advice based on experience.

Off-the-job training

This type of training occurs away from the normal working environment. It is usually undertaken when the skill or knowledge being learned is such that constant workplace interruptions would disrupt training or when specialist expertise is required. Usually people learn as a group, rather than individually. **Work shadowing** is a form of training which is carried out 'off-the-job', but usually only one person is involved at once.

The benefits of off-the-job training are that:

- the learners can exchange information with other people – from other departments or organisations – to broaden their knowledge and expertise

- it gives staff the opportunity to stand back from their job and look at what they need to do more objectively
- staff can benefit from a professional programme and, often, obtain nationally recognised qualifications which will assist career progression either inside or outside the organisation
- a specialist can be employed to 'deliver' the session – whether this is a one-off session on fire training or a two-week course on employment legislation. This person will usually bring new ideas or techniques to the session which the learner can take back for implementation or further discussion.

The main disadvantages, of course, are that specialised training courses are more expensive than learning 'on-the-job' and employees asked to undertake training away from work may struggle to cope with their workload as well – unless some way can be found to reduce this.

DID YOU KNOW?

- All part-time vocational courses of further education are **free** to those aged 16–19.
- Young people **under 25** can usually undertake training for approved qualifications on a day release basis through regional variations of the Youth Training scheme. In addition, young people of 16 and 17 can obtain training through the Modern Apprenticeships scheme. Further details can be obtained from your local TEC.

TEST YOURSELF

Look back at the range of training courses and topics shown in Figure 1.1.5 on page 14. Identify:

a   which of these would be suitable for
  i   you
  ii   individual members of your staff
  iii   your line manager
b   which of these
  i   could be covered in your workplace
  ii   would require attendance on a specific course.

Advising and coaching methods

In case you think this may be the 'easy way out' to improve the performance of your staff, think again! The role of an adviser is a very responsible one and can be extremely time-consuming. Coaching requires specialist skills and – usually – a considerable amount of patience. Bear in mind that if you give someone the wrong advice, or try to teach someone to do a job you can't do properly yourself, then you are doing the opposite of helping them!

The skills required to be an adviser or a coach are broadly similar. Look at Figure 1.2.2 and identify the areas which you think apply to both jobs and those which apply to only one. Then decide those areas in which you are strong and those in which you are weak. If you are expected to advise or coach staff, making sure that you are qualified yourself may be part of your own staff development plan!

Advisory and coaching skills

Good listener

Thorough knowledge of the work/job role

Good communicator

Ability to empathise with another person

Patient

Objective (no 'personal agenda')

Ability to counsel, consult and persuade

Tact and diplomacy

Discretion

Ability to break down a task into component parts

Ability to give alternative explanations

Ability to see and explain the reason for something

Ability/imagination to suggest alternative courses of action

Knowledge of own self-limitations

Figure 1.2.2

 ## DID YOU KNOW?

Assessors and verifiers of NVQ awards have to undertake specific training and obtain certain national qualifications – known as the Training and Development Lead Body (TDLB) standards – before they can undertake these jobs. There are also specific NVQ training awards which can be gained by people who train staff within a company.

Acting as an adviser

A formal advisory or mentoring role usually implies an ongoing relationship between yourself and a member of staff. It is likely that you would arrange a series of confidential discussions over a period of time at which that person could discuss his or her problems, achievements and personal needs. The role of the adviser is usually to help the staff member to consider his or her own solutions to the problems and his or her own needs – and to work through these during an open discussion. This is why the skill of listening is so important. Being someone's adviser does not mean listening for five minutes, jumping to a conclusion and then offering your own suggestions based upon what you would do in that situation! However, what it can and should mean is that you can give the benefit of your experience to a member of staff and stop him or her making fairly basic mistakes. You can alert your protégé to the political situation in the organisation and give information on the procedures to follow to achieve certain ends.

However, if you are in a supervisory position then you should be an *informal* adviser to your staff all the time. You should not watch your staff making a fundamental mistake or going about something completely the wrong way without saying something! Hopefully, your relationship with your staff – and your communication skills – are such that you can do this without causing annoyance. Some basic rules to follow include:

Don't

- make sarcastic comments
- criticise anyone in front of a colleague
- discuss people's problems or failings with other members of staff.

Do

- have a sense of humour
- adjust fundamental aspects of behaviour *immediately* (even if it means taking someone on one side)
- work at having a good working relationship with your staff (see Unit 4)
- accentuate the positive, never the negative
- give the reasons for what you say and what you want your staff to do.

DID YOU KNOW?

You will help your staff to perform well if you always explain the reason why something needs to be done. Walking into the office and announcing, 'You'll never believe it, we now have to complete yet another form to record all the visitors we have' is likely to encourage a negative attitude in your staff. Even if that is your personal view you would be wise to keep it to yourself. Find out *why* the form must be completed and then explain this to your staff along with *how* it has to be completed. Often, when people understand the reason for doing something, they are less likely to treat it as just another chore.

TEST YOURSELF

What would you say to each of the following members of staff?

1 A junior who approaches you with the comment, 'I can't tell what you've wrote down here.'

2   A receptionist who is chewing gum whilst talking to a customer.

3   A reliable member of staff who says she is overloaded with work trying to cover for a sick colleague and cannot cope any longer.

4   The typist who sends a letter containing six awful typing or spelling errors.

Acting as a coach

The reasons why coaching may be necessary are given on page 31. Coaching usually implies a one-to-one relationship, though it is possible to coach a small group of people effectively in a discrete training session. In effect, this is what photocopier company representatives do when they install a new machine – they usually go through the main procedures with the staff concerned and then make sure they understand how to use the manual which comes with the machine. Coaching usually has more immediate results than standard training because there is constant feedback to the learner in relation to progress.

The methods to use will depend on what you are trying to coach someone to do.

- The 'tell, then show, then do' approach is often used to coach someone to learn or improve a specific skill. In this case you explain – step by step – what is required. You demonstrate it yourself, then watch someone else carry out the task. Immediate feedback on performance is vital and so is constant practice until the person can do the task well enough to be left alone.

- If you don't know the task well enough to coach someone yourself then you may decide to ask someone else who is more expert to undertake the specific training and then assess performance yourself.

- The length of individual coaching sessions must be determined in relation to the trainee's capabilities and previous knowledge.

- Confidential discussions are a better choice if you are trying to coach someone to remedy a basic weakness – such as in relation to written communication skills or to aspects of their behaviour or motivation. An action plan of coaching objectives can be drawn up with specific review dates. At each discussion you can review progress and identify further opportunities for development.

- Providing 'models' is the best method to use to give your staff an immediate view of the standards required. Examples include folders with housestyle documents, staff handbooks, filing and photocopying manuals, quality procedures, etc. Staff cannot perform to the standards you require unless they explicitly know these beforehand.

Key aspects in coaching

- Start with what the trainee already knows and build on this.
- Make sure the trainee understands the reason for the coaching.
- Start by giving an overview of what is going to be covered.
- Slow down if difficulties are being encountered – try explaining things a different way.
- Encourage the trainee to practise the areas causing specific problems.
- Make learning *active* – the trainee should be involved in a dialogue with you and practising the skill (but *not* at the same time!).
- Make certain the trainee sees how each individual skill fits into the sequence as a whole.
- Be prepared to lengthen or shorten the coaching sessions, as required.
- End the session with a review of what has been learned – preferably by questioning the trainee.

DID YOU KNOW?

Acting as a role model for your colleagues – in terms of your work output and quality, staff relationships and communications skills – is extremely important. They must be able to respect you both as a person and as an employee who holds a more responsible position. Consistency of approach is also vital. Your colleagues are not psychic – if you don't communicate your needs and keep to the same standards from one day to the next, they will soon give up trying to please you.

Designing and evaluating work assignments

Work assignments or work-based projects are a popular way of finding out whether staff have the potential you think they might have. At the same time, you have the added bonus of undertaking a developmental activity for your section. If it is done well, everyone benefits.

However, to be a fair method of assessing someone's potential, certain basic rules must be followed. Otherwise this method can cause more problems than it solves!

- The assignment should be well devised. It should:
  - be well structured and make sense to the employee undertaking it
  - have distinct tasks and objectives
  - be linked to the employee's job role
  - be designed to stretch the employee
  - not depend upon information which the employee cannot access or obtain

  If the employee can suggest ideas for the project this is even better as it is likely to lead to greater commitment to its success.

- There should be an agreed time limit for its completion.
- There should be support for the assignment by the line manager and, preferably, by the senior management of the organisation. It is not fair if no-one will cooperate with the employee in his/her attempts to obtain or analyse information.
- Adequate preparation time for the assignment should be given and ways found to ensure that the trainee has the skills and knowledge to undertake the tasks required.
- There should be regular review sessions to discuss progress with the employee.
- If the assignment is time-consuming and, particularly, if it will also be beneficial to the section or organisation, then sufficient time must be made available for the employee to carry it out.
- The aims and objectives of the assignment and the way in which it will be evaluated should be discussed with the employee at the outset. The employee must clearly know what he/she is expected to do and what he/she is not expected to do.
- The evaluation itself should be objective and fair and the outcome fully discussed with the employee.

There are, of course, several things which can go wrong even with the best-designed assignment. The employee may be unable to find out information everyone thought would be available, for a variety of reasons the assignment may not be able to be completed in time, the employee may be making a total mess of it – or disregarding it – and you don't know what to do to put things right.

Although there are no hard and fast rules for putting things right, you may like to bear the following in mind.

- Always be prepared to change the original design if it appears unworkable, unsuitable or is immediately out-of-date because of other developments.
- Keep the communication channels open at all times between yourself and person undertaking the project. Be sympathetic to genuine difficulties and make any adjustments that are necessary. Talk through problems which seem to stem through lack of motivation. If the assignment has become too cumbersome it may have to be shortened.

Key aspects of evaluation

Evaluation should be fair, and be seen to be fair. The method of evaluation will depend on the style of the assignment. If you have asked someone to design a new procedure then the key test is 'does it work?' If you have asked someone to investigate an issue, the key aspect to look for is a report which gives facts and not opinions, based on hard research. Something which tells you something you already knew, or only states an issue from one person's point of view (usually the writer's!) is useless. If the completed assignment is useful to the running or organising of your section and will improve or inform current working practices then you will have gained and so will the employee.

Finally – **the golden rule** – never take credit for someone else's ideas. If the procedures suggested by a member of your staff are put into practice then acknowledge this and make sure he or she receives due credit. You can be certain that the staff know who suggested it anyway and you will lose far more than you gain if you try to suggest you were the real originator of the plan!

TEST YOURSELF

Your own line manager is very concerned about the wastage of consumable materials in the office. Design a specific assignment which could be undertaken by a junior member of staff which would

a   help towards his or her own personal development
b   improve the situation in the office.

Providing feedback

Feedback can be formal or informal, subjective or objective, verbal or non-verbal. It is the opposite of advice or guidance in that it gives information *after* the activity has been undertaken. If your boss smiles and nods at you when you are speaking to someone you are receiving instant feedback that he or she approves of what you are doing and you will continue with more confidence. A glare and an immediate interruption by your boss may give you pause for thought!

Formal feedback is a key part of appraisal interviews and any mentoring or coaching activities. It should be a two-way process – you give feedback to your colleagues and they give feedback to you. Regular face-to-face meetings to discuss performance and critical incidents give your colleagues the outlet they need to put their own point of view and give you a better insight into what is happening in your section and why. It is important, therefore, that regardless of the official feedback mechanisms which may operate in your organisation you give regular, prompt and systematic feedback to your staff – and are prepared to listen in return.

You can see how well immediate feedback works – and how much people prefer this – by looking at the success of CBT packages and computer games. These are often popular because they immediately produce a 'score' for the user – who usually wants to try again to beat it! Conversely, everyone dreads the horrendous wait for examination results which seem to appear months later and are sometimes published for everyone to read. By then some people feel dissociated from the results because they wrote their answers such a long time ago. For that reason, if you want your feedback to your staff to have maximum impact, it must be as prompt as possible.

Prompt, positive feedback reinforces good behaviour and correct actions and is a learning experience in itself. Everyone knows this from when they were children. Praise for something done well was a far more powerful motivator than criticism for something done badly. Believe it or not, people don't change when they grow up. We all like praise and recognition for a job well done and we all find it difficult to accept criticism – whether or not it is accurate or justified. Feedback should contain enough information to enable people to use it to improve problem areas. It is useless saying to someone, 'that's not how to do it' unless you then show exactly how it should be done.

Your own attitude to feedback will have a direct impact on your colleagues. If you are critical and negative you will find that you are either disregarded or disliked. If you are positive, helpful and give praise where it is due you will soon find that your staff will try very hard indeed to win your approval. Even if you do have to criticise someone you should do this in private, outline the situation objectively and look for ways of solving the problem *in conjunction with* the member of staff concerned. If he or she needs help then it is your job to ensure it is available.

DID YOU KNOW?

Feedback can be received in a variety of ways. The photocopier which will not work no matter what you do to it, the telephone system which refuses to transfer a call for you and the computer printer which refuses to print are all telling you something! You should be long past the stage where you kick the machine in anger or throw all your papers on the floor. However, your junior employees may be less well controlled. A familiar emotional reaction to a machine which will not work is rage and then frustration. If you see this happening to one of your colleagues, step in quickly and use the problem as an opportunity to point out *why* knowing how to use something properly is usually very beneficial!

TEST YOURSELF

How would you give feedback to the following employees?

   a   A long-serving member of staff has been the target of five recent customer complaints.
   b   A junior annoys everyone by shouting across the office.
   c   A member of staff has just won a national award.
   d   A member of staff has made a suggestion for an improvement to the evacuation procedure – originally designed by your own line manager.
   e   A word processor operator has managed to produce a difficult document for you in record time.

DID YOU KNOW?

Positive feedback and praise are known in some management circles as 'positive strokes'. The belief is that we all need a number of positive strokes every day and that one thing we can all do for one another is to ensure our colleagues receive these. Small gestures done regularly are the most effective and give people the 'feel good' factor which helps them perform even better.

Legal and regulatory requirements

The provision of training and development within all organisations is subject to both statutory and non-statutory requirements.

Statutory requirements

Statutory requirements relating to training are those which are covered by **equal opportunities** legislation – e.g. the Sex Discrimination Act 1975 (as amended by the Sex Discrimination Act 1980) and the Race Relations Act 1976 (as amended by the Race Relations (Remedies) Act 1994). The aim of such legislation is to ensure that groups of people are not discriminated against on the grounds of gender or race.

Discrimination can be direct or indirect. Direct discrimination is easy to identify. It is the deliberate discrimination against a particular group of people. Therefore, a safety course run only for white employees would obviously be discriminatory as black workers are excluded. As there is an equal need for safety training amongst all employees, regardless of their colour, then the organisation could be prosecuted for practising direct racial discrimination.

Indirect discrimination occurs when a practice can result in unfair outcomes for different groups of people – whether or not this is intentional or unintentional. An example would be an organisation which devised a training policy stating that only staff on full-time contracts could attend training courses. Usually there are a higher number of women on part-time contracts than men. Therefore this policy would disadvantage female employees more than male employees and would be an example of indirect discrimination against women.

 DID YOU KNOW?

Further information on equal opportunities legislation and its application in relation to working practices is given in Element 3.1.

Non-statutory requirements

Whereas some organisations only do the minimum as required by law, others have a range of equal opportunities policies which include additional procedures in relation to access and opportunity for potential and existing employees. Therefore, if your organisation has an equal opportunities policy this is a non-statutory requirement but is one of which you must be aware.

Today many organisations employ what is called 'a diversity of employees'. This means that in any given workplace, staff may be of different ethnic origins, different genders, different ages and some may suffer from physical disabilities. Many equal opportunities policies clearly state that both potential and existing staff will not be discriminated against on any of these grounds. This does not just apply to recruitment but also to staff who are already employed.

Of course, some employees have a greater need for certain types of training than others. It would be silly to send young employees on retirement courses, for instance, or to insist that a course on 'women into management' or 'personal safety for women' should be open to all men as well. Whilst *individually* people's needs are different, what you should not do is to automatically exclude a whole group of people from training or development for a spurious reason. For instance, sexual harassment courses should be open to both men and women.

Sometimes, of course, legislation can almost dictate the type of training people require. Changes to health and safety legislation have resulted in people attending courses on fire training, risk assessment, manual handling and the use of display screen equipment (see Unit 2). Changes in employment law – such as that affecting part-time employees – or recommendations affecting groups such as the disabled require the attendance of human resource personnel on courses to keep up-to-date. Changes and recommendations in relation to consumer law would affect the training requirements of purchasing and sales staff and so on.

DID YOU KNOW?

- There is a difference between 'positive action' to encourage equal opportunities and 'positive discrimination'. Positive action aims at removing obstacles which may hinder the recruitment or progress of all groups of people equally – for example, provision of crèche places for young children, language training, extended leave and advertising campaigns to encourage job applications from those from minority groups to apply. Positive discrimination aims at deliberately ensuring that there is a fair distribution of all sectors in the workplace. This can be through imposing targets for recruitment which favour disadvantaged groups or being prepared to have different levels of entry qualifications and provide more top-up training for these groups.
- You may like to note that until people become aware that policies *on their own* do not automatically result in 'fair play' and until there is a greater awareness of the difficulties faced by certain groups, the situation will only change very slowly. This is one reason why many organisations are sending staff on racial awareness or racial equality courses to help them to examine their own attitudes and prejudices to members of staff who may have different backgrounds from their own.
- Recent studies have shown that companies and teams comprising diverse groupings, with a wide range of abilities, experience and skills,

are more apt to be successful and proactive than homogeneous groupings. Apparently the most complacent groups are those comprising all-white, middle-aged, male managers!

ACTIVITY SECTION

1   Discuss with your tutor or adviser the staff for whom you have the responsibility for training. Bear in mind that this does not have to be formal training but can be staff for whom you undertake a regular supervisory role.

Identify both the formal and informal methods you can use to improve their performance in your workplace.

2   If you carried out a training needs analysis for yourself on page 25, now undertake this for one member of your staff and make recommendations for future training. Make a note of any discussions you have with this member of staff. Discuss your completed documents with your tutor or adviser.

3   Find out your organisation's policy on training, to include
    ● the range of training available in-house
    ● the financial support available to staff
    ● the type of training you could do yourself and that for which you would need to get support for your plans.

4   Identify one task regularly carried out by a member of your staff and list the competencies required to undertake this satisfactorily. Make clear the standard of output and quality you require. State how you would assist an employee to improve his or her performance if this was required and how you would assess the competence achieved.

Discuss your findings with your tutor or adviser.

5   Draft a work-based assignment for one, identified, member of staff. Include a rationale stating why this assignment would be appropriate for this particular member of staff, how you would assess and evaluate it and the benefits to your section if it is completed satisfactorily.

6   Obtain a copy of your company's equal opportunities policy. Compare this with the minimum requirements of the law and discuss with your tutor or adviser the additional non-statutory requirements which affect training provision in your organisation.

Managing yourself

What do I really want out of life?

Before you can even think of 'managing yourself' you first need to know something about yourself. 'Know thyself'[1] (or in modern terms, self-awareness) is a concept which is over two thousand years old. In terms of your personal self-development it is critical; not knowing what you like to do, or what you want, is rather like going on a journey without knowing where you are starting from or where you want to end! From that point of view, you will also never know when you've actually arrived! So a little self-analysis and psychology is a good starting point.

People are often fascinated and intrigued by self-analysis. This is one reason why, especially in America, people pay a fortune to have their own analyst to help them to identify what they want out of life and what they can realistically hope to achieve.

> **RULE 1**
> Self-awareness helps you to promote a positive self-image and go forward in life.

You – your 'self'

We all regularly use the words 'myself' and 'yourself' in everyday conversation, but very rarely consider what these terms actually mean.

According to Freudian psychologists your 'self' has two parts – the unconscious self and the conscious self. As a whole your 'self' comprises all your values, needs, abilities, beliefs and feelings. Some of these you are not aware of, i.e. they are unconsciously held, inherited from your parents and others who influenced you when you were a child. Your conscious self is that part of yourself of which you are aware, i.e. your self-concept. This is the perception you have of yourself – how you would describe yourself to other people.

The reason why your description of your 'self' might not match their opinion is that they also see the behaviour which is determined by your unconscious self – of which you are not aware.

> **RULE 2**
> Because everyone's behaviour is determined by two factors – their unconscious and conscious 'self' – no-one is totally aware of how they appear to others or why they always act as they do.

[1]Variously attributed to Juvenal, Cicero and Diogenes Laertius, it is generally agreed that this inscription was written on the wall in the temple of Delphi in Ancient Greece.

Sigmund Freud was a famous Austrian psychologist who lived in the 19th century. Many consider him to be the father of psychoanalysis. Freud frequently referred to a person's 'ego', i.e. your ability to make rational decisions in order to make the most of what you have and what you want.

In addition, Freud considered that we also have an ego–ideal, or self-ideal. This comprises the goals and values we aspire to and the criteria we use to measure ourselves. These reflect the values our families taught us. If we undertake an activity which links with this, and are successful, then we enhance our self-esteem. Therefore, to help our self-development – and to increase our self-esteem – everything we try must be relevant to our needs and must make us feel successful. How this works is shown below.

	Activity fits with what you want for yourself	Activity doesn't fit with what you want for yourself
Success	Esteem increased – feel great	Feel OK but nothing more – activity tedious
Failure	Feel thwarted but can't wait to try again	Feel deflated and fed up – activity pointless

TEST YOURSELF

Think of several different activities you have undertaken in your life – tennis, golf, acting, car maintenance, etc. If you are still pursuing that activity today, it is probable that it falls into the middle box – it 'fits' your mental image of yourself and you have been successful. Now try to think of activities which fit the other boxes. What have you tried to do and then given up, regardless of how successful you have been?

RULE 3

You can develop your self-esteem by trying new things which 'fit' your self-perception. The only condition is that the goal you set yourself should be realistic and yet challenging.

Setting your goals

Usually if we identify the right goals then we can devote psychological energy to trying to achieve them. This is the energy which seems to come from nowhere when, after a hard day, we suddenly feel lively enough to go out with our friends or dance the night away!

To harness your psychological energy at work you need to consider the following.

1   What are the activities and interests on which I am really keen? What are my goals?
2   How can I strive for these realistically?
3   What are my strengths and weaknesses?
4   How can I build on my strengths and eliminate my weaknesses to help me to achieve my goal(s)?

Any form of personality quiz can be misleading, as it is apt to make you think in black and white categories and label yourself introvert or extrovert, sociable or shy, aggressive or defensive, patient or intolerant, when in fact most of us vary depending upon the circumstances.

However, if you have chosen to be an administrator or PA then there are undoubtedly certain attributes and abilities which will help you to do the job more easily. If you detest working with people, and like working in the open air, then it is hardly likely that you are tailor-made for the job!

Below is a list of questions you may usefully work through to discover a little more about yourself. Bear in mind there are no right and wrong answers; the questions are there purely to provide you with an opportunity to reassess yourself. You may find it interesting to answer the questions yourself, and then see if an honest and loyal friend can 'second-guess' your answers correctly. This will at least highlight areas where you do not give out the same 'signals' as perhaps you think! Consider what evidence you can offer to back up your answers – and be honest!

RULE 4

Remember that self-deception is exactly what it says – the only person you fool is yourself!

Have you the personality for the job?

Work profile

Do you like work which calls for accuracy and detail? Do you like thinking and planning out a job? Are you well organised? Do you like a known routine or do you like new challenges on a regular basis? Are you observant? Do you consider you have a good memory? Do you work quietly, or make a lot of fuss? Are you sometimes 'difficult' to work with – and in what way? Are you always punctual?

Achievement profile

Are you a hard worker or do you get tired easily? Are you highly competitive – or very laid back? Can you cope with constant interruptions? Do you enjoy responsibility? Are you constantly striving for something new or do you rest on past glories? Are the targets and goals you set yourself realistic? How do you react to failure? Do you ever blame someone (or something) else for your own failings? Do you give up easily? Would you cheat to get what you want?

Leadership profile

Do you like telling other people how to do things? Do you find it easy to get people to do what you want them to do? Do people consider that you are bossy? Does it annoy you if people disagree with you? Do you think before making a decision or are you impulsive? Do you change your mind frequently – or never? Do people often ignore you and/or your opinions? Can you make it clear to people what you want without causing any offence? Do you expect more from other people than you are prepared to do yourself? Can you motivate other people to work hard? Can you keep a secret?

Emotional profile

Do you get upset easily? Are you soon bored – if so, do you show it? Are you easily elated or depressed? Do you enjoy arguing or are you nervous if challenged by someone in authority? If someone 'takes you on' do you jump onto the defensive? Do you consider that you are tactful and/or diplomatic? Are you prepared to compromise with other people when necessary? Do you sulk or bear grudges? Do you ever lose your temper? Do you think before you speak?

Social profile

Do you value your close friends? Do you like a hectic social life? Do you always want to be 'in' with the crowd? Do you like working on your own? Do you consider you are always friendly? Do you share confidences easily? How do you cope if you find out someone doesn't like you? Could you make an unpopular decision if necessary? Do you mix with people easily? Are you a good judge of character or easily impressed?

Followership profile

Do you like to be told exactly what to do, or prefer to use your own initiative? Do you want to please people in charge of you? Do you follow rules to the letter – or ignore them? Are you a willing workhorse who finds it difficult to say 'no'? Could you cope with a moody or uncommunicative boss or do you need a lot of encouragement? Do you need constant supervision? Can you stick up for yourself without upsetting people?

Life profile

Are you always 'on the go' or in a rush? Do you burn the candle at both ends? Do you like to keep fit? Do you work quickly? Do you know what you want out of life? Do you quickly grasp what is required in a situation – or need it spelled out for you? Are you self-confident or a worrier? Do you find it difficult to relax or even harder to get started?

TEST YOURSELF

1   Under each profile area, discuss as a group the personal attributes you feel are essential for a first-class administrator.

2   Individually, highlight those attributes you feel you already possess and on which you could build quite easily.

3   Now highlight those qualities which you feel you are lacking. Divide these into:

   a   those which are essential (e.g. punctuality) and which you could adjust with a little self-discipline

   b   those which are important but are really not 'you', e.g. liking to meet new people.

Managing yourself

You are now on the way to learning to manage yourself. Under question 2 above you should have a list of your strengths – qualities you possess which are important to your chosen job. You have to 'manage' these by making sure that you continue to concentrate on these areas until they are second nature.

Under question 3a you have identified tougher areas – your weaknesses in relation to your chosen career. Come to grips with these one at a time over the next few months – if you normally fuss a lot when given something to do, try keeping quiet about it instead. Congratulate yourself as you achieve each goal. Don't give up if, at first, you slip back occasionally.

Under question 3b you have identified areas about which you feel unhappy and it is important for you to work in a job where these skills would not be essential.

In time, you will find that your areas of emphasis and your strengths and weaknesses will change. What is a problem one year may be of no significance the next, as you gain experience, knowledge and self-confidence.

> **RULE 5**
> Review your self-development profile at regular intervals throughout your career and adapt both this, and your goals, as necessary.

If you do this then not only will you come to know yourself better, but you will also gain greater satisfaction from your achievements than if you merely 'drift' through life. In this way you can be said to be truly 'managing' yourself.

2 Contribute to the maintenance of a healthy, safe and effective working environment

Element 2.1

Monitor and maintain a safe, healthy and secure workplace

As an administrator or PA you have to be prepared to take responsibility not only for your own actions but also for those of others. This is particularly true in the area of health and safety where, even though all employees are expected to contribute to maintaining a healthy, safe and effective working environment, a greater responsibility is placed on those who supervise the work of others or those who are in more senior positions. If, therefore, your remit includes organising a group of staff, you must ensure that not only do you comply with company safety rules and regulations but also that your staff do the same. The difficulty here, of course, is that many staff – office staff in particular – sometimes do not recognise the importance of safety.

TEST YOURSELF

Look at the following comments.

● 'I work in an office you know, not on a building site. It's common knowledge that the risk of an office worker being involved in an accident is very small.'

● 'What's dangerous about working here – I'm not going to electrocute myself with the word processor am I?'

● 'We're all adults – we're not likely to be found fighting near dangerous machinery or smoking in the stock room next to cans of cleaning fluids. We've more sense than that.'

● 'I've got more to worry about than the remote possibility that I might kill myself by tripping over a loose or trailing wire. The deadline for this report is 3 pm.'

Discuss as a group or with your tutor or adviser how you would respond to such comments if they were made to you by your staff. Note that you may have to read on if you think you need evidence to support your arguments!

Health and safety objectives

Suppose you have just been appointed, and part of your responsibility is to supervise a group of administrative staff. At your interview you will probably have been given information about:

- your terms and conditions of employment
- your job description
- where you will be working and for whom
- who will be working for you.

What you probably will not be told is anything about health and safety.

At your induction training session you will probably also have been given some information about the company, its management structure and its procedures and its policies – including those relating to health and safety. Unfortunately, health and safety is not the most exciting of topics and there is a danger that you might have lost a bit of concentration – or even nodded off – during the session given by the Health and Safety Officer. Consequently, you might find that when you actually start work back in your department, you have only a very vague idea of what has been said. If, therefore, an accident occurs – or there is an unexpected visit from the trade union safety representative – you may have a problem.

Remember that one of the attributes of a good administrator or PA is that of dependability. Another, is that of being calm in a crisis! You will be showing neither of these attributes, if you (a) shrug your shoulders and say you don't know what to do or (b) panic! Even if no-one else seems to know what they are doing, you must.

One of your first jobs therefore must be to check on your health and safety responsibilities not only in respect of you as an individual but also in relation to your staff.

Ways of monitoring the working environment

One of the first steps you should take is to check the extent of your working area and that of your staff, as that will be the area for which you will be responsible.

If you are working in a 'traditional' or closed area this will not prove too difficult. You will probably have your own office, your boss will have his or hers and there may also be an office for your staff. What is more difficult to determine is your area of responsibility if the office is designed on an open plan basis, i.e. where a large number of staff are accommodated in one area which is often landscaped with the use of acoustic screens, different seating arrangements, plants, etc. In such a case, you will have to consult your boss.

Risk assessment

Obviously, in whatever area you work, you will have to be alert to many potential health and safety problems and be prepared to report them either to your manager or, where appropriate, to the departmental safety representative. (See page 53 for the duties of the safety representative.) Although in many cases a brief report or memorandum may be sufficient, you should be aware that the law now requires that potential risks or hazards are recorded in a specific way and that the risks attached to activities are assessed in accordance with the Management of Health and Safety at Work Regulations 1992 (together with the Manual Handling Operations Regulations 1992).

These Regulations require every employer to make 'suitable and sufficient' assessments of the risks to the health and safety of employees and also other people who may be affected. Consequently you may be called upon to:

  a   analyse which work activities within your span of control *could* entail a certain risk, and
  b   carry out an assessment of each of them giving details of
      – the activity
      – the possible hazard
      – what control measures are in place, e.g. any personal protective or other type of specialist equipment
      – the level of risk, i.e. insignificant/low/medium/high, both to employees and other people
      – possible remedial actions.

Such a report will normally be submitted to the Health and Safety Officer who may arrange for the provision of any training or special equipment based on the results of the assessment. In most cases a re-assessment will be required at some future date to see if the risk has been minimised.

TEST YOURSELF

You work as the administrator for the Transport Manager of a local authority social services department, part of whose responsibility is to arrange transport of disabled people from their homes to day care centres. Your manager asks you to make a preliminary risk assessment of the work of the bus drivers involved in such duties. You watch them at work and also interview a number of them. You find out that a number of people are in wheelchairs and others have very limited freedom of movement. When you watch the drivers trying to manoeuvre the wheelchairs on to the buses you notice that some are much better than others at doing this. You also see instances where there have been near accidents both to the traveller and the driver – in one case a wheelchair was allowed to slip off the ramp because there were no restraints. Although the driver and his assistant managed to hold the wheelchair steady, the driver suffered a badly bruised foot in doing so.

Prepare a brief report to your manager using the headings outlined above and making what you consider to be the appropriate recommendations. Identify a time when you think there should be a reassessment of the situation.

(You may want to check page 69 for details of the provision of personal protective equipment.)

Safety policies

One of the requirements of the Health and Safety at Work Act (HSWA) is that employers of more than five employees should draw up and implement a safety policy to include:

- a statement of overall intent which should include an acceptance by management of a responsibility to apply and enforce current and future safety legislation
- an outline of the organisational structure including
  - the names, job titles and safety functions of the personnel involved
  - the chain of responsibility from top to bottom
  - the role of the supervisors
  - the functions of the safety adviser, occupational health personnel (if any), the safety representatives and the safety committee(s)
- the arrangements for ensuring that the policy is being implemented, e.g.
  - the training and instruction given
  - the company rules for safe systems of work
  - emergency arrangements (fire, first aid, etc.)
  - accident reporting and investigation
  - identification of risk areas
- the signature of the senior manager.

The statement must be revised when appropriate – when new legislation or new technology is introduced, when personnel changes occur, etc. – and must be drawn to the attention of all employees.

Implementing the safety policy

Most sensible employers want to make sure that working conditions conform to legal and regulatory requirements *before* their attention is drawn to them by a Health and Safety Executive (HSE) inspector. What can be difficult, however, is finding out where a problem exists! Some employees may be more than willing to conceal some very unsafe working practices from their boss even though they may be well aware that they are actually breaking the law. As an administrator or PA, you should not be willing to assist them – but you have to work with them and gain their trust and cooperation. That, of course, causes a problem for you.

 ## TEST YOURSELF

Despite a company rule that no unauthorised electrical equipment must be brought on to the premises, you have discovered that your staff are using a free-standing fan heater and also an electric kettle. Another member of staff has complained to you that they are breaking the rules. When you go to see them they protest that (a) it is always cold in their area of the department and

(b) the staff canteen is three floors away and it is virtually impossible for them to get there and back in time during their 20-minute morning and afternoon breaks. Discuss as a group or with your tutor or adviser what actions you should take.

Safety representatives and safety committees

You might be helped in your arguments if you work in an organisation which has a safety committee comprising a group of both management and employee representatives. Such a committee will form the basis of the company's monitoring system as it is its responsibility both to check that legal and regulatory requirements are being adhered to and also to alert management to any working conditions which do not conform to legal and regulatory requirements or to the company's stated codes of practice.

The Safety Representatives and Safety Committees Regulations 1978 give a legal right to trade unions to appoint safety representatives in the workplace provided that the union is recognised by the employer for negotiations. The representatives are elected by union members (not the employer). After the union has approved the election the name of the representative is submitted to the employer. The number of safety representatives varies from one workplace to another, depending on the size of organisation, type of work carried out, potential hazards, etc.

Duties of a safety representative

A safety representative's duties include:

- investigating potential hazards and dangerous occurrences at the workplace and examining the causes of any accidents (see further on page 62)
- investigating complaints by any employee relating to that employee's health, safety and welfare at work
- making representations to the employer on matters arising out of the first two points above and also on general matters affecting health, safety and welfare
- carrying out inspections (at least every three months)
- representing the employees in consultations at the workplace with inspectors of the HSE and any other enforcing body
- receiving information from those inspectors
- attending meetings of safety committees.

An amendment to these regulations passed in January 1993 also requires safety representatives to be consulted 'in good time' with regard to

- the introduction of any measure at the workplace which may substantially affect the health and safety of the employees
- the arrangements the employers make for appointing competent

persons to assist them in providing the measures necessary to protect the workforce

- any health and safety information the employer is required to provide for employees
- the planning and organisation of any health and safety training the employer is required to provide for the employees
- the introduction of new technologies into the workplace – especially at the planning stage.

 TEST YOURSELF

One of the problems many safety representatives face is that they are junior members of staff. However, when a health and safety problem occurs at work they may find themselves in the position of having to see a senior manager to tell him or her that some action *must* be taken. Discuss as a group or with your tutor how you would handle that situation.

The Safety Committee

The committee must:

- monitor local accident trends as shown by statistics and recommend preventive action
- consider reports of selected accidents and promote action to prevent recurrence (see further on page 64)
- consider suggestions and reports on safety matters and make recommendations to management
- promote local safety publicity and organise safety competitions and incentive schemes
- promote local applications of accident prevention techniques.

Legal and regulatory requirements relating to the working environment

Statutory requirements

Once you know the extent of your responsibility your next step should be to check first of all that you know what the law says about health and safety at work.

The major Act of Parliament – often referred to as statutory legislation – relating to health and safety is the Health and Safety at Work Act 1974 (HSWA) (now updated by the Workplace (Health, Safety and Welfare) Regulations 1992).

The Act is known as an 'enabling' or 'umbrella' act because it outlines the law in much more general terms than one of its predecessors, the Offices, Shops and Railway Premises Act 1963, which went into great detail about what employers should do to ensure safety in the workplace. The only problem with that Act, of course, was that it was almost *too* specific. It referred to the minimum temperature which must be reached within the first hour of work but didn't make a similar provision if the workplace was too hot in that hour. The HSWA, on the other hand, merely states that there must be a safe working environment – which obviously covers extremes of both heat and cold.

TEST YOURSELF

The phrase 'as far as is reasonably practicable' occurs throughout the HSWA. Discuss with your tutor why this phrase is necessary.

CHECK IT YOURSELF

Look at the Figures 2.1.1 and 2.1.2, which outline the main provisions of the HSWA and the Workplace (Health, Safety and Welfare) Regulations.

THE HEALTH AND SAFETY AT WORK ACT 1974

1   Applies to all work premises. Anyone on the premises is covered by and has responsibilities under the Act – whether employees, supervisors, directors or visitors

2   Requires all employers to:
  ● 'as far as is reasonably practicable' ensure the health, safety and welfare at work of their employees. This particularly relates to aspects such as
    –   safe entry and exit routes
    –   safe working environment
    –   well maintained, safe equipment
    –   provision of protective clothing
    –   safe storage of articles and substances
    –   information on safety
    –   appropriate training and supervision
  ● prepare and continually update a written statement on the health and safety policy of the company and circulate this to all employees (if there are five or more of them)
  ● allow for the appointment of safety representatives selected by a recognised trade union. Safety representatives must be allowed to investigate accidents or potential hazards, follow up employee complaints and have paid time off to carry out their duties

3   Requires all employees to
  ● take reasonable care of their own health and safety and that of others who may be affected by their activities
  ● co-operate with the employer and anyone acting on his/her behalf to meet health and safety requirements

---

Figure 2.1.1

WORKPLACE (HEALTH, SAFETY AND WELFARE) REGULATIONS 1992

Most of the Regulations cover specific areas of health, safety and welfare to supplement general duties on employers who have to ensure the workplace is safe and without risks to health under the HSWA 1974.

Employers and others in control of workplaces are required to comply with a set of requirements covering

1   **Work environment**, i.e.
    ● effective ventilation
    ● reasonable temperature
    ● adequate and emergency lighting
    ● enough space
    ● suitable workstations
    ● protection from adverse weather for workstations outside a building

2   **Safety**, i.e.
    ● traffic routes for pedestrians and vehicles to circulate in a safe manner
    ● properly constructed and maintained floors
    ● safe windows and skylights
    ● safely constructed doors, gates and escalators
    ● safeguards to prevent people or objects falling from a height

3   **Facilities**, i.e.
    ● sufficient toilets and washing facilities
    ● adequate supply of wholesome water
    ● adequate seating
    ● suitable accommodation for clothing
    ● rest areas – including provision for pregnant women or nursing mothers
    ● provision for non-smokers in rest areas
    ● adequate facilities for people who eat at work

4   **Housekeeping**, i.e.
    ● proper maintenance of all workplaces, equipment and facilities
    ● cleanliness of workplaces

Figure 2.1.2

● Obtain from your local Health and Safety Executive a copy of booklets HSC2, HSC3 and HSC5, which cover different aspects of the Health and Safety at Work Act
● Under the HSWA your employer has a duty to display details of the main terms of the Act in a notice for all employees to read.

Find this notice in your own workplace or college. Note down the name and address of your enforcing authority and what you should do if you think there is a health and safety problem in your workplace or college.

Regulatory requirements

In addition to Acts of Parliament there are a number of other ways in which health and safety at work is monitored. There are, for instance, a number of Regulations relating to health and safety which are published regularly as a supplement to the major statutory legislation. Reference has already been made to the Workplace (Health, Safety and Welfare) Regulations 1992. Other recent examples include:

- The Reporting of Injuries, Diseases and Dangerous Occurrences Regulations (1995) (RIDDOR)
- The Control of Substances Hazardous to Health (1994) (COSHH)
- The Electricity at Work Regulations (1989)
- The Noise at Work Regulations (1989)
- The Health and Safety (Display Screen Equipment) Regulations (1992)
- The Management of Health and Safety at Work Regulations (1992)
- The Manual Handling Operations Regulations (1992)
- The Provision and Use of Work Equipment Regulations (1992).

CHECK IT YOURSELF

If you are working as a group, decide who will check with their Health and Safety Officer or their college or local library to see whether they can obtain a copy of the range of HSE Health and Safety booklets listed in Figure 2.1.3. If you are on your own then see which booklets are kept in your workplace and then borrow or obtain the rest.

From the information you have obtained, compile a summary giving a short paragraph on each. Keep a copy for further reference.

Codes of Practice

Some Regulations can be difficult to understand, particularly if they are very detailed. Others may be less detailed but are still no easier to follow. What you, as an administrator or PA, should check on therefore is whether or not the organisation has copies of the relevant HSE Codes of Practice, some of which have already been mentioned above.

Management of Health and Safety at Work – Approved Code of Practice, 1992. ISBN 0 7176 0412 8

Personal Protective Equipment at Work – Guidance on the Regulations, 1992. ISBN 0 7176 0415 2

Manual Handling Guidance Regulations, 1992. ISBN 0 7176 0411 X

Workplace Health, Safety and Welfare – Approved Code of Practice, 1992. ISBN 0 7176 0413 6

Display Screen Equipment Work, 1992. ISBN 0 7176 0410 1

Noise at Work, 1989. ISBN 0 11 883529 7

Figure 2.1.3 Health and Safety booklets

 ## DID YOU KNOW?

Although employers will not break the law by failing to follow these Codes of Practice (as they would do if they failed to follow the regulations laid down in one of the statutes such as the HSWA), if an accident did occur and it was found that the relevant Code of Practice had not been followed, the court could take it as proof that the regulation itself had been broken. The onus is then on the employer to prove otherwise – which can be difficult!

Employer-devised codes of practice

Some employers institute their own codes of practice which are designed to let everyone know what procedures should be followed in certain situations such as fire, illness or accident. Some codes of practice extend even to how to operate a particular piece of machinery.

In the case of accident or illness, for instance, the code may contain details about:

- how to contact a named first aider when an accident or illness occurs
- where the nearest first aid box and facilities are kept
- how to send for the doctor or an ambulance in the case of major accidents or illnesses
- when an accident report should be completed in accordance with the company's policy (for details about the recording of accidents see page 62).

A code of practice in relation to a fire alarm may contain even more detailed provisions.

TEST YOURSELF

1   Look at the Figure 2.1.4, which shows an example of a fire precautions code of practice issued by one organisation. Although the majority of the procedures have been covered in it, individual responsibility for each of them has not been allocated. Assuming that you are an administrator or PA in the organisation, list those procedures which are

   a   the responsibility of every member of staff

   b   the responsibility of the Health and Safety Officer.

2   Which procedures do you think that **you** should be responsible for monitoring?

3   Discuss as a group, or with your tutor or adviser, the problems that may arise with (2) and (5). (Remember, for instance, that modern practice is not to encourage members of staff to endanger their own lives by trying to fight a fire rather than leaving the building immediately. On the other hand, expecting employees to do nothing is a practice which is generally discouraged.)

WAVERLEY ELECTRONICS LTD
CODE OF PRACTICE

FIRE PRECAUTIONS

1   Keep all fire exits clear in case of emergency

2   Make sure that you know what to do should a fire break out, i.e.
   ● how to operate the fire alarm
   ● how to use fire fighting equipment if required to do so
   ● where to assemble outside the building
   ● how to reach it

3   Display a fire/evacuation procedure notice in every relevant area and ensure it is constantly updated

4   Keep the fire doors closed at all times except where the Fire Brigade has given permission for the doors to be held open by an automatic device

5   Do not smoke in any part of the building where there is a risk of fire

6   Make sure that bulk quantities or large cans of highly flammable fluids are locked away in a well ventilated storeroom or metal cabinet when not in use

7   Make sure that all combustible materials such as paper and envelopes are put into metal waste bins and removed regularly

8   Ensure regular maintenance and checking of fire alarms and fire extinguishers

9   Arrange regular fire drills

Figure 2.1.4 An employer-devised code of practice

Consequences of breaching legal and regulatory requirements

The most serious consequence of an organisation breaching legal and regulatory requirements is the injury or even death of a member of the workforce. A secondary consequence is that, as a breach of a health and safety requirement is regarded as a criminal action, the organisation concerned may face either a large fine or some of its senior managers may even face a prison sentence.

However, there is little use in having a law – even a strict one – if there is no means of checking up to see that it is being followed. Prior to the HSWA, for instance, some unscrupulous firms, knowing that there were only limited checks on what they were doing, tended to ignore safety precautions. Under the HSWA a new enforcement agency was created called the Health and Safety Executive (HSE) with its own Inspectorate and Advisory Service. The HSE is directly responsible to the Health and Safety Commission (HSC) which comprises Advisory Committees on a variety of subjects and industries and whose responsibility it is to consider and reach agreement on proposals for new Regulations.

An inspector can visit any premises without warning either to investigate an accident or a complaint or simply to inspect the premises and question the employees. If dissatisfied with the working practices the inspector can issue an **Improvement Notice** requiring the employer to put matters right within a specified period.

Emergency reporting procedures and functions and powers of regulatory bodies

Sometimes when an accident has occurred – or even during the course of a routine visit – the HSE inspector will notice a practice which is so unsafe that immediate action must be taken. He or she is then in a position to issue a **Prohibition Notice** to stop operations immediately if the workers or the general public are felt to be in immediate danger.

On receiving a Prohibition Notice the company has the right to appeal to an Industrial Tribunal. If the appeal is lost and the company fails to comply with the terms of the notice then the organisation can be fined or the owner imprisoned.

DID YOU KNOW?

1   Whilst industrial premises are monitored by the HSE, offices and shops are the responsibility of the local council. This duty is usually undertaken by the Environmental Health Officer.

2   Another safeguard against the 'careless' employer is the introduction of the trade union or company safety representative who maintains close links with the HSE Inspectors and can alert them to any potential risks (see page 53).

Common types of emergency and organisational procedures for dealing with them

Dealing with the expected is well within the ability of a good administrator/PA whose organisational skills and training will assist him or her to implement company policy. What is less easy, even for the best organised person, is dealing with the unexpected – particularly when the unexpected concerns a health and safety issue.

You can take comfort from the fact that many companies now have procedures in operation to deal with the unexpected – no matter what it may be. Some companies call it their 'crisis' policy and lay down codes of practice which outline what levels of management should be called upon to deal with what types of emergency and what procedures should be followed. Obviously the more serious the crisis, the more senior the level of management involved.

Moreover, health and safety tend to come very near the top of every list of possible emergencies and you will probably find that there is a stated procedure to be followed as regards those types of emergency with which you may be faced.

Illness

When someone suddenly becomes ill it is not a good idea to try to treat the illness yourself. If you work in a large organisation you may have access to a medical unit staffed with either a doctor or nurse. This, however, may not be the case in smaller organisations. The Health and Safety (First Aid) Regulations require that staff trained in first aid are available, the number depending on the size of the organisation, the type of industry, the location of the employees and the situation of the organisation. 'Trained' first aiders are those who have been on an approved training course and awarded a certificate to prove they are competent at administering first aid. To remain first aiders, they must take a refresher course and be re-examined every three years.

An up-to-date list of first aiders should be easily accessible in every part of the organisation together with their contact telephone numbers.

TEST YOURSELF

If you worked for the Health and Safety Officer and had to make sure that every department of the organisation was covered by a trained first aider, what would you bear in mind when doing so – particularly if different hours are worked in different areas, different substances are used or varied types of work are carried out?

First aid boxes

Guidance notes to the Regulations give details of the contents of first aid boxes and the quantities required. Drugs should not be kept in first aid boxes or administered by first aiders because of the risk of adverse reaction by the patient.

In addition to the usual items of bandages, burn dressings, etc., larger equipment such as stretchers and blankets may also need to be stored nearby. All should be checked regularly and replenished as necessary.

DID YOU KNOW?

1   An 'occupational' first aider is someone who has received additional training to cover particular hazards which may occur in a specific workplace, e.g. electrocution, poisoning.
2   First aiders should be aware of any members of staff who suffer from diabetes or epilepsy. Such information should be given to them by the Human Resources Department.

Accidents

Accidents can range from the trivial, such as a trip over a loose carpet tile which doesn't cause any injury, to the very serious, such as a hand being caught in a cutting machine. In the former case a telephone call to the maintenance staff to repair the carpet as soon as possible plus a notice warning staff to be careful in the meantime should be sufficient. In the latter case, of course, there will have to be a full-scale investigation.

Recording of accidents

Companies are required by law to record accidents. Safety representatives have the right to investigate them and to make appropriate recommendations to management. All employers with more than ten workers must keep an accident book and records must be retained for at least three years. (See Figure 2.1.5 for an example of an accident report form.)

Employees must report accidents to their employer or they may find that they are debarred from any DSS benefits to which they would otherwise be entitled. Their report must include:

- their full name and address
- the date and time the accident happened
- the place where it occurred
- the cause and nature of the injury.

WAVERLEY ELECTRONICS LTD
ACCIDENT REPORT FORM

Report of an accident or injury to a person at work or on duty

This form must be completed in all cases of accident, injury or dangerous occurrence and submitted to the Health and Safety Officer

Name of injured person

Date of birth

Position held in organisation

Date and time of accident

Particulars of injury/accident

Activity at time of injury/accident

Place of injury/accident

Details of injury/accident

First aid treatment (if any) given

Was the injured person taken to hospital? If so, where?

Names and positions of persons present when the accident occurred

Signature of person reporting incident

Figure 2.1.5 An accident report form

Contribute to a healthy, safe and effective environment   63

If the person reporting the accident is doing so on another person's behalf then he or she must also give full name, address and occupation.

DID YOU KNOW?

1   Many organisations record both actual and 'near miss' accidents as these show potential hazards which need some attention to prevent them from turning into actual hazards.

2   An accident which causes serious or fatal injuries or leads to more than a certain period off work has to be notified to the HSE under RIDDOR (the Reporting of Injuries, Diseases and Dangerous Occurrences Regulations 1995). These regulations also require employers to keep records of all notifiable injuries, dangerous occurrences and diseases. Safety representatives and committees must also be given access to this information.

Investigating accidents

In the case of serious accidents, the Health and Safety Office and/or the safety representative will carry out an investigation. They should be alerted as soon as possible after an accident occurs so that they can have the opportunity of arriving at the scene of the accident in time to:

● ensure that nothing is moved until a representative from the insurance company arrives unless there is a danger of another accident occurring

● record details of the accident – including the taking of photographs, the drawing of sketches and the interviewing of witnesses whilst they can still remember the incident clearly

● carry out a detailed accident inspection in relation to
    – the working environment – lighting, noise, layout, etc. – at the time of the accident
    – the person involved, the level of supervision and the type of equipment being used.

The HSE or environment officer must also be informed and a check made that all appropriate records have been completed (such as the accident report form). The safety representative may also wish to advise any injured staff on their legal rights.

TEST YOURSELF

When recording details of an accident, you are always advised to write in pen rather than in pencil. Discuss as a group or with your tutor or adviser why this advice is given.

Monitoring accidents

In larger organisations it is normal practice for the safety committee to review regularly and monitor accidents which have occurred in the workplace (see page 54 for its other duties). What it will normally do is to:

- compare accident rates in the organisation with the national statistics
- identify areas of particular concern
- identify improvement or deterioration in standards
- identify any areas of change which may affect the statistics (e.g. the introduction of a new item of equipment or machinery)
- check that any recommended action has been taken.

Fire and evacuation

Another example of an emergency which can be foreseen and for which a company procedure is normally in place is that of a fire or bomb alert. Most companies will have formulated procedures to cover such an emergency and should have ensured that all employees are aware of them. When you first start work your attention should have been drawn to the code of practice in relation to fire precautions (look back to page 59 to remind yourself of one example) and you should also have been made aware of the evacuation procedure which should be followed in the event of a fire. Again, most companies ensure that fire notices are displayed in all areas. An example of a fire notice is given in Figure 2.1.6.

WAVERLEY ELECTRONICS LTD
EVACUATION PROCEDURE

INSTRUCTIONS TO ALL STAFF

Your assembly point is **DUKE STREET CAR PARK**

What you <u>must</u> do in the case of a fire or other emergency

When the fire alarm sounds

- Leave the building immediately by the nearest exit and report to the person in charge of the assembly point at the place indicated above. A roll call will then be taken.

- The senior person or authorised deputy on each floor of the building will take charge of any evacuation and ensure that no-one is left in the area.

Remember

- use the **nearest** available exit
- do **not** use the lift
- do **not** stop to collect personal belongings
- do **not** re-enter the buildings for any reason until the safety officer or his or her representative gives you permission

---

Figure 2.1.6 A fire notice

DID YOU KNOW?

Under the Fire Precautions Act 1971, now reinforced by the Fire Precautions (Places of Work) Regulations 1995, the fire authority has similar powers to the HSE in that it can issue Prohibition and Improvement notices and prosecute companies which ignore these. Designated premises, such as offices, shops and factories, each require a fire certificate which has to show a plan of the premises, with the position of all fire-resistant doors and also the fire extinguishers and break-glass alarms. There must be a proper fire alarm system and also a protected means of escape.

TEST YOURSELF

You have been appointed as the person responsible for evacuating the personnel on your floor of the building. Fortunately you have been given some training so that when the fire alarm sounds you start immediately to check that all staff are making their way to the Duke Street car park by means of the stairs. On this occasion it was a false alarm and the staff are back at their desks 20 minutes later. However, you have noted one or two matters of concern.

- When the fire alarm went off, a visitor to your company had just been directed back to reception and was found trying to use the lift. He had obviously no idea of what the company's procedure was in the case of a fire alert.
- One of your staff suffers from severe arthritis and had very great difficulty in walking down the three flights of stairs. He was at least five minutes behind everyone else and – apart from the obvious problem which would have been caused if there had been a fire – was very embarrassed when everyone gave a cheer when he eventually managed to reach the assembly point.
- One of the managers on your floor – who holds a more senior position than you do – refused to leave her desk. She told you that she would be prepared to take a chance and that she was too busy to be bothered with what was obviously a false alarm.

Prepare a memo for the company Health and Safety Officer outlining your concerns and suggesting possible solutions to each of the problems.

DID YOU KNOW?

Evacuations can occur not only because of a fire alert but also because of a bomb scare. The only difference in such an evacuation will be that employees will be told to take their belongings with them. This reduces the number of items which need to be searched.

Scope and limit of own authority to deal with emergencies

You cannot take chances with health and safety – particularly if an emergency occurs. The law states quite clearly what an organisation must do and places a specific responsibility on it to comply with all legal requirements. However, although everyone in the organisation has some part to play in the maintenance of high standards of health and safety, they should be aware of the extent of their authority in this respect – and be careful not to overstep it!

TEST YOURSELF

You work as PA to the Managing Director of a small engineering firm which manufactures a range of wrought iron appliances – gates, fences, etc. As it is quite a small firm, your boss is often away on selling trips and you are left to make a number of decisions on your own. Some decisions do not worry you – in fact, you rather enjoy the responsibility. However, you feel other decisions are outside the scope of your authority.

For instance, you are working in your office when you receive an unexpected visit from an HSE inspector who wants to look round the workplace and also to examine the documentation you have on accident investigation and monitoring. You are confident that he will find no fault with the paperwork because you keep a close eye on that. You are a bit worried, however, about certain 'working practices' you have observed on the shopfloor. You know that one of the supervisors tends to be a bit casual in his attitude towards tidiness. Consequently, when the HSE inspector starts questioning you about safe working practices you feel uneasy and, although you think you have done your best, you know that you were not sufficiently well briefed to answer some of his questions properly.

Two days later an accident does occur. One of the workers trips over a hammer which has been left lying on the shopfloor, hits his head against the edge of a work surface and knocks himself out. The one trained first aider you have is out at lunch and so is the supervisor. You ring for an ambulance and the injured worker is taken to hospital. You start to write out an accident report but then become anxious about possible legal repercussions.

You therefore decide that the time has come for you to have a talk with your boss about your level of responsibility. She is quite receptive to what you say but does point out that she cannot be tied to the office all day long – otherwise business will suffer. She asks you to prepare a short report indicating what you feel should be the division of responsibility in this area, i.e. what decisions *you* should be able to take and what must be *her* responsibility:

- when accidents or other emergencies occur
- when there is found to be an unsafe working practice
- when a visit from an HSE inspector takes place.

Types, purposes and usage of emergency equipment and consequences of inappropriate use

One of the most essential pieces of emergency equipment in an organisation is its fire fighting equipment. Since it is obviously a piece of equipment which will be used solely in emergencies it is important that everyone knows where it is and that *some specified people* know how to use it. Those people who are designated users must receive the appropriate training.

1 Either at your place of work or at your college check
   a the fire fighting equipment or protection systems in your building – extinguishers, hose reels, smoke detectors, sprinklers, etc.
   b where fire extinguishers are situated
   c how often and by whom checks on the equipment are carried out.
2 What type of training exists in your workplace to ensure that employees know how and when to use emergency equipment correctly?
3 As a group, brainstorm to compile a list of other types of emergency equipment.
4 List the consequences of inappropriate use of emergency equipment both from a *legal* and a *practical* point of view.

Types and positioning of safety signs, notices and equipment

Employers must make sure that they conform to the Safety Signs Regulations 1980 (now updated by the Health and Safety (Signs and Signals) Regulations 1996). These regulations state that certain signs must be displayed in certain shapes and colours.

1 Signs which prohibit dangerous behaviour, access to restricted areas, etc. must have a black pictogram on a white background, red edging and a diagonal line. The red area must cover at least 35 per cent of the sign.
2 Signs requiring a specific safety action, e.g. the wearing of personal protective equipment, must have a white pictogram on a round blue background. The blue area of the signs should account for at least 50 per cent of the whole sign.
3 Warning signs must be triangular in shape with a black pictogram on a yellow background with black edging. The yellow must account for 50 per cent of the sign.
4 Green signs should be posted to show no danger or the whereabouts of emergency escapes and first aid. They should be rectangular or square in shape with a white pictogram on a green background. The green should account for at least 50 per cent of the sign.
5 Red fire fighting equipment signs must be displayed to show the location and identification of fire fighting equipment. They

should be rectangular in shape with a white pictogram on a red background. The red area must account for at least 50 per cent of the sign.

TEST YOURSELF

You have to explain to a group of your junior staff the importance of checking that certain notices are displayed and that each of these notices must be in a certain style and colour. You know that if you hand them a summary of the information given above, they will not bother to read it. You decide, therefore, to make up a quiz which will consist of a number of headings, e.g. 'Wear dust mask', 'No entry', 'Caution – mind the step', 'Fire exit', 'Sprinkler control valve'. You intend to then ask them to match up the correct colours and shapes with the headings. For example:

'Wear dust mask' . . . .

should be completed as

'Wear dust mask' White pictogram, round blue background

Obtain a copy of an equipment catalogue containing examples of such signs and notices (either from work or through your tutor at college) and, from the information given, prepare a list of 20 signs for your juniors to match up.

Safety equipment

The most obvious example of an organisation's safety equipment is its fire fighting equipment (see page 67). However, there are also certain other items of equipment which can assist in providing a safer work environment. Depending upon your workplace, such items can include:

- safety lockouts on electrical items of equipment which prevents power from being restored until the worker has removed the lock
- plugouts which provide for the 'locking out' of any plug while performing maintenance on or servicing any equipment
- electrical safety matting
- fire retardant waste bins
- storage units and bins for flammable liquids
- fire extinguisher cabinets (to keep the extinguishers clean and to prevent them from knocks)
- fire-resistant filing cabinets and safes.

Personal protective equipment

Not all safety equipment relates purely to the work environment. The Personal Protective Equipment at Work Regulations require that 'every employer shall ensure that suitable personal protective equipment is provided to his employees who may be exposed to a risk to their health or safety while at work except where and to the extent that such risk has been adequately controlled by other means which are equally or more effective'.

The four main types of protective equipment are:

- **Head protection** – industrial safety helmets, scalp protectors, caps, hairnets, etc.
- **Eye protection** – safety spectacles, eyeshields, safety goggles, faceshields, etc.
- **Foot protection** – safety boots or shoes with reinforced toe caps, slip-resistant soles, foundry boots which are heat resistant, wellington boots for protection against water, anti-static footwear to prevent the build-up of static electricity and to give some protection against electric shock, etc.
- **Hand protection** – gloves designed to protect from cuts and abrasions, extremes of temperature, skin irritation and dermatitis, contact with toxic or corrosive liquids.

In some circumstances protective clothing for the body is also necessary, e.g. overalls and aprons to protect against chemicals and other hazardous substances, clothing to protect against cold, heat and bad weather, high visibility clothing, etc.

 DID YOU KNOW?

1 The Regulations place the self-employed worker under a similar duty to provide himself or herself with the necessary protection.

2 The employer must ensure that accommodation is provided for personal protective equipment so that it can be safely stored when not in use. It can be simple (e.g. pegs for weatherproof clothing or safety helmets) and it need not be fixed (e.g. safety spectacles can be kept by the user in a suitable carrying case). However, it should be adequate to protect the equipment from contamination, loss or damage from harmful substances, damp or sunlight. Training for the employees should include instructing them in where and how best to store such equipment.

 TEST YOURSELF

The Management of Health and Safety at Work Regulations 1992 require employers to identify and assess the risks to health and safety to enable action to be taken to reduce those risks. In such circumstances, personal protective equipment is regarded as a 'last resort'. Discuss as a group or with your tutor or adviser why you think that statement was made.

Organisations' security procedures and types of security risks

Although the two basic *types* of security risk common to all areas of work are:

a   risk to people, and

b   risk to property or equipment,

the *extent* of those risks can vary from organisation to organisation.

Much depends on factors such as the nature of the business, its situation, the type and design of the building, the number of staff employed, the number of visitors to it, the number and type of valuables kept on the premises and its hours of operation.

Large organisations employ security staff to monitor security arrangements and to deal initially with any breaches of them. Smaller companies have to rely more on the efforts of individuals. Again, however, the cooperation of all staff is required – particularly those in supervisory and managerial positions.

Risk to people
Violence

In recent years, companies have become more aware of the possibilities of attacks on staff, particularly where the general public have easy access to the place of work. Various measures have now been implemented to protect employees from the possibility of attack. Staff who work alone and those who handle money are particularly vulnerable not just because of possible personal injury but also because they may be accused of having provoked the attack – or of having fabricated the whole incident! Consequently some organisations have:

- improved communication systems by installing panic buttons
- installed protective glass screens (when you next visit your bank, building society, town hall, railway booking office, check to see whether or not such a device has been introduced)
- altered staff arrangements to make sure staff do not work alone in high risk areas (and/or have issued them with radio communications equipment)
- trained staff to recognise danger signals and the best way to deal with awkward or disturbed visitors.

Cash carrying

If you or your staff are involved in carrying cash from one place to another, you will pose an obvious security risk. Nowadays most organisations try to avoid asking staff to carry cash around simply because of that risk. However, if it is essential that cash is carried, there are certain steps which can be taken to minimise the risk. They include:

- sending the right people, e.g. *not* old, immature or recently recruited staff
- sending at least two people together
- varying the time and routes as much as possible
- using a vehicle whenever possible and varying it from time to time
- using special cash-carrying equipment such as a device that can raise the alarm or spoil the cash contents with a chemical marking agent should the carrier be attacked.

Risk to property

Large organisations tend to take a systematic approach towards the introduction of measures designed to protect their premises. They will arrange for a survey of the **external environment**, i.e. the external area surrounding the building, the **physical barrier**, i.e. the shell of the building – walls, roofs, doors, windows, etc. – and the **interior area**, i.e. the inside of the building. Having done that they can judge which areas are the most vulnerable. For example, there may be parts of the premises which are isolated and not overlooked by any members of staff; there may be a number of flat roofs; the ground floor windows may be extensive and easily accessible.

Once the survey has been carried out the organisation concerned can then estimate the level of risk involved and also the cost to be incurred in removing or reducing such a risk.

 ## DID YOU KNOW?

1 Some organisations are so concerned about security that they adopt a wide variety of devices to protect their premises. These can include earth banking around the building to prevent unauthorised vehicle access, the building of ditches, moats or crash barriers for the same purpose and the use of high levels of external lighting which are either permanently lit during the hours of darkness or are linked to Passive Infra Red Detectors (PIRs) or microwave detectors which will activate the lights should there be an intruder.

2 Large organisations employing security guards can now rely upon those guards having access to very sophisticated equipment. One security firm, for instance, can now create 256 guard patrol sequences with up to 12 patrols active concurrently. At each access control unit *en route*, the security guard inserts an ID card into a reader or trips a designated alarm point. If the guard does not arrive when and where expected, the system goes into alarm mode to alert the security office. Another firm follows the same principle with all guard movements being reported in colour graphics on a screen in the control office.

CCTV is also widely used but nowadays security personnel are no longer expected to watch screens for hours on end. One system allows them to be sent video stills at intervals of between half a second and five seconds from a camera triggered by an incident.

Access to buildings

Obviously, smaller organisations cannot afford such measures and have to modify their security arrangements. However, no matter what size an organisation may be it will almost certainly have imposed measures within its buildings to prevent access by unauthorised personnel.

These measures can include:

- keeping entrances and exits to a minimum
- monitoring all visitors either by security personnel, closed circuit television or electronic detectors
- restricting the number of people who have keys to the building
- issuing identification badges to all staff and visitors – many organisations now operate a computerised access control system by which all staff and authorised visitors are given a 'swipe card' which must be swiped through the entry point. The entry point is linked to a control unit able to recognise whether the card being used is an authorised one. In some cases the card has a built-in 'expiry' date so that it cannot be used again
- checking all rooms carefully at the end of each working day
- having clear signs which show which areas are restricted to visitors or staff.

TEST YOURSELF

What colour and design of sign would you use to indicate the restricted areas? (Look back to page 68 if you need to remind yourself.)

CHECK IT YOURSELF

Check what, if any, system of identification badges and/or access control systems are in operation in your own organisation or college. Discuss your findings with the rest of your group and prepare a brief summary of the different systems in use.

DID YOU KNOW?

Because of the increasing threat of arson to both staff and property, an Arson Prevention Bureau has been set up by the Home Office and the Association of British Insurers to advise organisations on how best to protect their premises.

TEST YOURSELF

Read the extract (Figure 2.1.7) from an advice leaflet prepared by the Arson Prevention Bureau.

Figure 2.1.7

Discuss as a group or with your tutor or adviser:

1   what difficulties this advice might cause to small firms
2   how such difficulties could at least be partially overcome
3   how staff could be made to take the threat of arson seriously (particularly if they have no experience of such an occurrence).

Risk to equipment

Valuable equipment is a very attractive commodity to thieves – whether it belongs to you or to the organisation. Obviously the measures used to prevent unauthorised personnel from entering the buildings is one form of protection. However, a good PA will also make sure that his or her equipment is not a potential target for anyone who does manage to circumvent the security measures. Steps he or she can take include:

● storing equipment in a safe place when it is not in use – the greater the risk the more secure the storage should be
● making a member of staff responsible for regular inspections of the equipment, which should be recorded on an inventory list containing details of its make, serial number and model number where relevant
● security marking of valuable equipment, e.g. by ultraviolet pen.

 DID YOU KNOW?

Business documents are often a target for thieves and it is therefore important that important documents are kept in a safe place. These documents include:

● cheque books
● bank statements
● plastic cards
● bank details (including copy correspondence)
● blank invoices
● company stamps and seal

- letterheads
- order forms.

TEST YOURSELF

It is obvious why thieves would want to steal some of the documents mentioned above – but why do you think they would steal bank statements? Discuss with either your group or your tutor.

Security of computer-based information

An administrator or PA must always be aware that not only can 'physical' property be stolen but so can what is known as 'intellectual' property. The theft of a blank computer disk is not too important – it can be replaced quite easily. The theft of a computer disk which contains some vital information (or information which has taken some time to collect together) is an entirely different matter. Consequently most organisations, particularly those with extensive computer networks, take specific measures to prevent such thefts.

Many, for instance, provide their staff with a security action list as an aide memoire. Items generally included are:

- the name of a member of staff with overall responsibility for the development and implementation of security procedures
- a list of security procedures to be followed, e.g.
  - siting all equipment in a secure location which is not vulnerable to vandalism or theft and where access can be restricted to authorised personnel
  - positioning VDU screens and printers so that they cannot be seen by members of the public or making sure that the equipment allows for the screens to be blanked out by the operator should someone walk by. One firm has even developed a new notebook computer with a privacy filter to allow the user to work on it when travelling by plane or train without worrying that other passengers may see what is on the screen
  - storing all disks etc. in secure lockable storage when not in use
  - restricting access to computer files by the use of privilege levels and passwords
  - enforcing regular password changes and limiting the number of access attempts
  - introducing audit trails to monitor access to sensitive information
  - establishing 'back-up' procedures to ensure that data can be recovered in the event of accidental loss or damage – and keeping back-up copies in secure storage if loss of data would have serious consequences
  - establishing strict procedures for the distribution, storage and disposal of printed output.

Find out what measures (if any) are in operation in your own organisation to make secure any computer-based information. Discuss these with either your group or your tutor or adviser.

Scope and limit of own authority for dealing with breaches of security

As with dealing with emergencies, it is important that everyone in an organisation recognises that they have a role to play in matters of security. However, it is management's role to determine the extent of that role and, again, the more senior you are in an organisation, the more involvement you are likely to have.

Most importantly, you must avoid placing either yourself or your staff in danger. The 'have a go' policy advocated by some is not one advocated by the police! They would prefer you to seek assistance rather than to risk injury.

As an administrator or PA, therefore, you should make sure that you and your staff know what the company rules are in respect of security and you should take personal responsibility for seeing that those rules are followed. You can also remind your staff to report anything suspicious to you so that you in turn can report it to your superior. Other than that, breaches of security are best dealt with by a security guard if your organisation employs one or otherwise by the person nominated by the organisation to deal with such matters.

TEST YOURSELF

The British Security Industry Association, in conjunction with Lancashire Constabulary, have produced a leaflet giving the key points to be considered in relation to office security. Contact them for a copy at Security House, Barbourne Road, Worcester WR1 1RS.

Organisations' procedures for recommending improvements to the working environment conditions

The workplace will obviously be a safer, healthier and more risk-free place if staff cooperate with management not only in following all safety and security procedures but also in identifying any opportunities there may be for improving those procedures. What can be frustrating, however, is for a member of staff to think of a way in which safety can be improved but to be unable to have that idea implemented.

Obviously a major role for the Safety Committee and safety representatives will be that of identifying any opportunities for improving the health, safety and security of the workplace and their job in this respect will be made much easier if they are assisted by suggestions from members of staff. However, not all staff want to take this route and prefer instead to talk to their immediate supervisor or manager. Much then depends on what action the manager takes. Some are more diligent than others!

ACTIVITY SECTION

1 You have just been promoted to the job of administrator in the Accounts Department. One day you overhear the following conversation between two of your junior staff.

Femi: If I've tripped over those boxes once I must have tripped over them a dozen times today.

Louise: What's happened to the caretaker – I thought he was coming back to move them?

Femi: Oh, he's never around when he's wanted. Do you think we could push them all into the other corner?

Louise: Dunno. I'm a bit busy at the moment.

Femi: I've a good mind to report them to the safety rep – someone is going to be hurt before long – and I don't want it to be me.

Louise: Who is our safety rep?

Femi: I'm not sure now – it used to be Jack but he gave it up when he got promoted. He said he'd got better things to do! I suppose I could tell the manager again but I got nowhere when I suggested that we should replace those old blinds with glare-free ones.

Louise: That reminds me. When I was coming out late last night, I'm sure I saw someone hanging about in the car park. He disappeared when he saw me but I was glad to get to the car. Do you think I should tell someone?

Femi: You can if you like – but if he ran away when he saw you, he's not likely to come back in a hurry.

Louise: Well, it's certainly no use telling the manager – the last time Eileen, the receptionist, reported someone acting suspiciously in the foyer, he picked up his coat and positively dashed for safety. I don't know what he'll do the next time the fire alarm sounds.

Femi: We'll have to leave him hiding under the desk – at least he'll be less bother there than he was last time. Can you remember him losing his temper with everyone when he found out he couldn't use the lift!

You realise that both members of staff have a somewhat negative approach to safety and security – and, from what you have heard, so has your manager! You decide to raise the matter separately with him and also with the staff at the next meeting you have with them.

Prepare some notes of what you will say:

a   (tactfully) to the manager, and
b   to the staff,

to try to persuade all of them to take a more proactive role in promoting health, safety and security.

2   You have been elected to be your department's safety representative. During the past three months you have been faced with the following issues.

● Susie is pregnant and is concerned that her job as a VDU operator may cause harm to her unborn child. She asks you for advice.

● A risk assessment has shown that the filing clerks are not handling heavy files in the correct manner and that, consequently, they risk injuring themselves. It has been recommended that they attend a course on manual handling but their supervisor is insisting that there is nothing to worry about.

● The Safety Committee has asked that all safety representatives should come up with at least six suggestions for the ways in which health and safety awareness could be improved in the organisation.

● You have a new manager who is not particularly safety conscious and who resents you spending time attending meetings and in talking to the staff about health and safety matters. You feel that the only solution is for you to resign but the rest of your colleagues are anxious that you should continue with the role.

● It has been agreed that all safety representatives take it in turn to write up the minutes of the safety committee meetings. You are quite used to taking notes at meetings but up until now you have always been involved in meetings in which the subjects discussed have been familiar. This is not the case with the safety committee and you are dreading having to make sense of what to you is sometimes quite incomprehensible information.

a   State in each case what action you would take.
b   Give your reasons for suggesting that course of action.

3   Look at the extract from an HSC Annual Report (Figure 2.1.8) and discuss as a group or with your tutor or adviser the answers to the questions below.

a   Why are the numbers of workplace accidents falling?

Accident rates stay on plateau

Numbers of workplace accidents reduced slightly over the last year, but rates remained virtually unchanged according to figures given in the HSC Annual Report. Even this slight reduction was due to shifting employment and industrial activity, particularly in high risk industries.

The final fatal accident rate for employees for the year is estimated to be 1.5 per 100000, down from 1.6 the previous year. The estimated final rate for injuries which caused absence from work for more than three days is 795 per 100000 compared with 816.4 the previous year. This represents 23.3 million lost working days.

The HSC chairman commented that the slight improvements could be explained by changes in the level and composition of employment and by the reduction in the level of industrial activities. There had been a shift away from the higher risk industries towards the generally lower risk service sector. Although some of the more traditional hazards and sources of accidents had been declining for some time there remained a large mass of injuries due to a variety of common causes, such as slipping, straining and falling. A new approach was therefore being adopted based on assessment of risk and improved safety management and training.

Figure 2.1.8

> **b** Why does the HSC feel that this reduction is not particularly satisfying?
>
> **c** Despite all the recent legislation and increased emphasis on health and safety, injuries caused by slipping, straining and falling are still occurring. In your opinion, is that the fault of the employer or employee – or both?

4 Read the extract of a report of an occupational health project undertaken by a local authority Prevention of Hazards Centre (Figure 2.1.9) and answer the questions below.

> **a** What kind of objections do you think there may be in trying to extend this type of project:
> **i** from doctors
> **ii** from patients,
> in respect of follow-up at the workplace?
>
> **b** What other ways can you suggest of influencing employer attitudes towards occupational illness?

5 You work as administrator for the Health and Safety Officer of a large organisation and you are asked to assist her in preparing and delivering a session on company fire precaution procedures for new members of the organisation. However, the very day on which you have planned to work together on the preparations, you receive a telephone call from your boss's husband who tells you she has been in a car crash and is

EXTRACT FROM OCCUPATIONAL HEALTH PROJECT

While deaths and injuries are the visible tip of the iceberg of damage work causes, it is ill health and disease caused by work which affect a far larger number of people: an estimated 20000 people die of occupational diseases and there are 70000 new cases of work-related illnesses every year.

To try to tackle this problem, the Centre has instigated some occupational health projects through which occupational health workers are seconded to health practices and act as part of the primary health care team. The workers sit in the surgeries and talk to the patients waiting to see the doctors – they take detailed occupational histories and advise on workplace hazards. The occupational history forms part of the patients' notes and is intended to help the doctor in diagnosing illness and treating it correctly. The occupational health workers can then follow up any specific problems in the workplace, often through trade union structures, so that something is done about the sick workplace rather than just looking at the sick workers.

Figure 2.1.9

in hospital with a broken leg. As the date of the training session has already been fixed (and is difficult to alter as it is merely one part of an overall induction training programme) you decide to go ahead and plan the session on your own.

Assuming that the session is to be held in ten days' time and that it is scheduled for a one-hour period:

a   prepare a list of the items you intend to include in the training session

b   allocate a time to each one, e.g. introduction five minutes (remember to leave at least five minutes at the end for questions)

c   include at least one practical activity – such as the completion of a quiz, handout or questionnaire about fire hazards

d   draw up a programme including all the above items to be given to staff at the beginning of the session

e   prepare a copy of a practical activity to be given to staff during the training session

f   prepare any handouts or overhead transparencies etc. you may wish to use

g   if possible, make a short ten minute presentation either to the other members of your group or to your tutor of one part of the training session

h   prepare a brief report of the feedback you receive from the group or your tutor after the presentation.

Element 2.2

Maintain effective working conditions

Legal and regulatory requirements relating to the working environment and work practices

Before 1963, most legislation relating to the working environment concentrated on factories and manufacturing establishments. It was not considered necessary to introduce legislation in respect of work in offices.

Nowadays, however, health and safety legislation tends to cover all working environments. The recent Regulations also cover working practices in all areas (refer back to pages 55–8 if you wish to remind yourself of some of them).

Although the HSWA and the ensuing Workplace (Health, Safety and Welfare) Regulations 1992 apply in general terms to the work environment and facilities, of particular importance to the administrator or PA are:

- Health and Safety (Display Screen Equipment) Regulations (1992) (which cover the use of VDU equipment)
- The Electricity at Work Regulations (1989) (which cover the safety of electrical appliances)
- The Provision and Use of Work Equipment Regulations (1992) (which cover, amongst other items, the maintenance of equipment).

These will be dealt with in more detail on pages 96–100.

Ways of organising workplace to suit workflows

As a good administrator or PA you will obviously always attempt to organise your workplace to achieve agreed work objectives – one of which should be health and safety. However, in order to be able to achieve any other objectives, you must first of all know what these objectives are. Even though your organisation may have a strategic development plan which contains details of its aims and objectives it is unlikely that those aims and objectives will specifically mention the organisation of the workplace. However, they may *indirectly* refer to it by, for instance, including an objective relating to increasing the productivity of the workforce or improving its efficiency or quality standards. One way of doing this is by making sure that all workers are working in an environment which helps them to achieve those objectives.

As an administrator or PA, therefore, one of your objectives should be:

- to organise your own work area and that of your manager to maximise your efficiency
- to ensure that your staff's working area is organised to achieve a similar result.

In order to do this you should:

- appreciate the importance of office layout – and the different types of layout which can be use
- be able to organise the workplace so that it suits work flows.

Office layout

As already mentioned on page 50, the amount of influence you have over the way in which your work area is organised depends to a certain extent on the type of layout adopted by the organisation. If, for instance, you are responsible for three distinct areas – your office, your manager's office and your staff's working area – you will have much more control over the layout of those areas than you would probably have if the entire work area was open plan or landscaped.

TEST YOURSELF

Two friends, who are administrators in different organisations, meet for lunch one day. Read the following extract from their conversation.

Pat: How are you enjoying your new job?

Ramona: Fine – everyone is friendly and, so far, my boss and I are getting on very well. My biggest difficulty is getting used to the office. I've never worked in an open plan area before.

Pat: Neither have I – what's the difference?

Ramona: I feel a bit on show all the time. The whole department is situated on one floor and we have one section of it. My boss has her own little office which is partitioned off – but the rest of us work together. It's nice and informal and I've got to know the rest of the staff much more quickly than I would otherwise have done – and I can keep an eye on my own staff much more easily – but it is a bit distracting. We're very near the door and when people wander past they tend to stop and have a chat.

Pat: What do you do if you want to talk to someone in private?

Ramona: There are some partitioned offices at one end of the floor which we can use – but the problem is that if two people suddenly disappear into one of them, the rest of the staff start getting curious. Sue, who's one of my staff, was very upset the other day because her husband had been rushed into hospital. I took her into one of the offices to have a chat but she was very embarrassed when she came out because she thought everyone was staring at her. I don't really know how to solve that problem. Mind you – I shouldn't really complain – the company has spent a lot of money on landscaping the office and it is certainly a lot warmer and better furnished than the office I worked in before. The centralised reprographic section, which is situated on every floor, is also wonderful – all the equipment is up to date, and it's replaced regularly. In my last place all the managers were constantly competing with each other to have their equipment updated and it was generally a case of who shouted the loudest.

Anyway – enough about me. How are you getting on with John lately? The last time we met you were wondering about getting engaged . . .

1 From what you have just read, list the advantages and disadvantages of an open plan or landscaped office.
2 Add to that list any other advantages or disadvantages which have occurred to you or which you have noted from personal experience or through your research in the library. Think, for instance, about possible problems of morale or ill health. Think too about better use of space, lower maintenance costs and possible savings in supervisory staff.
3 The problem of confidentiality was mentioned during the conversation between the administrators. Write a short paragraph on how you would try to solve the problem.

Workflow

One big advantage of the open plan or landscaped office is that workflow can be planned more easily. If the whole department is on one floor, the time taken to process a document from section to section is normally much less than it would be if different sections of the department were in different areas. It is also easier to have informal meetings between members of staff in different sections. Suppose, for instance, that you are an administrator in the Human Resources Manager and that you and your staff are involved in preparing an annual leave chart for each member of staff in the department. You have to:

● obtain the information from each member of staff
● have it verified and approved by the appropriate supervisor
● compile the information into a master chart
● check for any discrepancies and refer back to the appropriate member of staff
● check that there is a suitable balance of cover throughout the peak holiday periods and check back if there are any problems.

In an open plan office you or a member of your staff can obtain and check the information in a matter of minutes – or you can see at a glance if someone is not available to talk to you. In a more traditional office you will have to make more use of the telephone, memo or E-mail facilities.

DID YOU KNOW?

Some organisations are taking a very different view of the way in which their staff should be accommodated.

● When IBM executives in New Jersey arrive for work they are assigned a numbered cubicle in which there is a desk, a telephone, a computer jack and a black plastic in-tray. Nothing is allowed to be left overnight because every day somebody new is assigned to each desk. In order to 'encourage' staff to go on the road to meet new clients and find new business there are only 350 desks to accommodate 800 people!

● Nearer to home, a pilot trial of a 'non territorial' system of accommodation (or 'hot desking') is being run by a firm of city accountants under which consultants have to book a desk from a small pool. The idea here is to save space (and therefore money).

TEST YOURSELF

As a group or with your tutor or adviser discuss the advantages and disadvantages of the introduction of such measures.

Positioning furniture, fittings and equipment to promote effective working

No matter in what type of office layout you may work, you will be able to improve workflow by the correct positioning of furniture, fittings and equipment. There are certain general principles which you should bear in mind when planning or attempting to replan the office area for which you are responsible. Your objectives should be to ensure that:

● all legal requirements are fulfilled (see page 55–7)
● space is used to the best possible advantage
● there are appropriate 'services', e.g. telephones, lighting, heating, power, etc.
● movement between areas is easy
● noise is kept to a minimum and noisy machinery or equipment is in some way isolated
● the final result looks attractive and welcoming.

Space

In large organisations the correct use of space may have been determined by research and development or work study experts and you will probably have to do no more than make any minor adjustments you feel necessary. In smaller organisations, however, or in organisations where space is at a premium because it is so expensive, you may have to undertake a more direct role in using the space to the best advantage.

Whatever the situation, however, you should obviously try to make the best possible use of the space you have. Normally space is required for

a work in progress and the number of people employed to carry out that work
b the equipment necessary to assist that work
c adequate storage space, i.e. the space in which incoming work, completed work and supporting material is stored.

TEST YOURSELF

Can you remember what the Workplace (Health, Safety and Welfare) Regulations 1992 say about adequate space for staff? If not, check back to page 55–7.

Positioning of furniture, fittings and equipment

One of the major ways in which you can ensure that the best possible use is made of space is by selecting furniture and other equipment which is suitable for the space allocated – and preferably which is sufficiently flexible to allow you to make any alterations to the office layout to meet changing requirements. When purchasing and/or positioning equipment or furniture therefore you should always bear in mind:

● the size of the working area – however impressive a desk may look and no matter how many additional features it may have, it is useless recommending that it be purchased if the space in which it is to be put is so small that you can't open the drawers, or you have to crawl over it to open the window!
● the question of noise – if a piece of equipment is absolutely essential and yet you know it to be noisy, remember to enquire about any acoustic devices which may lessen the problem
● the problem of confidentiality – if a word processor operator is expected to work on confidential material there is little point in positioning him or her in the middle of a busy office
● the need for cleanliness and tidiness – both from a legal and an aesthetic point of view. If you know an area is likely to get

untidy because, for instance, there is a lot of highly pressured work going on there (think of the pictures you have seen of the Stock Exchange or a newspaper office at its busiest – the waste paper lying around is phenomenal!) or because of the equipment which is being used, it is not a good idea to make it the focal point of the department. It is better to situate that work or to position that equipment in a less public area.

TEST YOURSELF

When you start a new job as administrator/PA to the Office Manager of a road haulage company you are concerned to find that, although your work area and that of your manager are next to one another and are well planned, your staff are working in an area which you do not think is adequately laid out for their needs.

- The receptionist sits at a desk near the door so that she can receive visitors as soon as they arrive. However, she is also required to do all the office filing and the bank of filing cabinets is situated at the other end of the room.
- The two accounts clerks who are jointly responsible for preparing, sending out and checking accounts sit on opposite sides of the office and are constantly crossing the room to speak to each other.
- The clerk who is responsible for orders and invoices has to share a desk with the word processor operator and there is obviously not enough space for the two of them – plus the word processing equipment – to work comfortably. Their workspace faces the window and the word processing operator often complains that the light is shining directly in her eyes and she cannot see what she is doing.
- The remaining two word processing operators have a workstation in the middle of the room so that everyone has to be careful about the flexes from the word processors which stretch across the floor from desk to socket.
- The receptionist has a telephone on her desk and there are extensions on your desk, your manager's desk and also one on one of the accounts clerks' desks. The manager gets annoyed at constantly having to take messages or come out of his room to relay them to someone else; the receptionist doesn't like people using her telephone to make outgoing calls because then she has to deal with irate incoming callers who complain that the line is always engaged.
- The photocopying machine – which everyone uses – is situated immediately next to the reception area and the receptionist is always complaining that the area looks untidy and that it doesn't create a good impression for clients.
- Noise is a problem – from the telephone, the word processors, the staff themselves. You have noted a tendency for them to shout over the desks to one another.

- The whole area looks bleak – no plants, posters, screens, blinds at the window. In fact the only decorations are ancient postcards stuck up with Sellotape on the wall at the side of the receptionist's desk. The overhead lighting is adequate but cheerless.

One night, after the staff have gone you sketch out a plan of the office layout (see Figure 2.2.1).

To assist you to clarify your thoughts you decide first of all to:

- list where you think problems are occurring with the layout
- redraw the sketch outlining suggested improvements
- check various office equipment catalogues for additional items of equipment and/or furniture you feel may be necessary.

You then decide to incorporate these suggestions into a report to your manager recommending the changes and giving your reasons for these recommendations (but remember that he may not be over-enthusiastic if *all* your suggestions are going to cost him money!).

The office desk (or workspace)

A good administrator or PA pays attention to detail. It is no use establishing a well-planned office layout if, within that layout, staff are sitting at desks or workstations which are piled high with papers and other oddments and trying to use filing cabinets whose drawers are so full that they are difficult to close. Desks should be a workbench – not a store!

It is never a good idea, however, to antagonise staff by constantly nagging at them to tidy up their desks or working areas. It is important to lead by example and to make sure that you are always working in an immaculate area – and that your boss, with your assistance, is doing the same.

Bear in mind certain key points:

- Have as a large a desk or working area as space will permit (provided everything placed on it is within easy reach).
- Make sure your filing system (unless centralised) is near to hand. Try not to have too many files on your desk at one time – only those concerned with the job upon which you are working at that particular time.
- See that your telephone is positioned properly (depending on whether you are left or right handed) and that your keyboard is a help and not a hindrance to the rest of your work. An L-shaped desk is particularly useful as the keyboard can be positioned on the side attachment leaving the rest of the working space free.
- Pay attention to details such as desk accessories – pen holders, filing trays, etc. – but do not clutter your desk with non-essential items, however stylish. Once you have positioned all the items, keep to that arrangement so that even when in a hurry you will automatically find what you want.

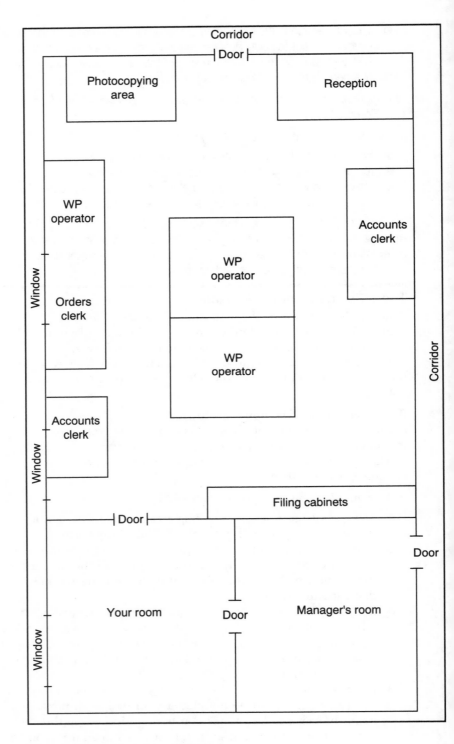

Figure 2.2.1 Sketch plan of office layout

- Check your own chair – if you feel at all uncomfortable it could be that your chair is too low, too high, the back is not positioned correctly or the arms impede your work.
- Remember that a notice board is useful provided you keep a check on it to see that the material is not overcrowded, untidy or out of date.
- Unless there is a separate reception area, make sure that there is a suitable arrangement of furniture to allow visitors to sit in comfort when waiting for your boss.

TEST YOURSELF

1   One management consultant, who runs a series of seminars on office management, always begins the session by asking delegates what *they* think should be on a desk. The answer he is looking for is 'nothing'. He believes that an uncluttered desk is the perfect sign of an uncluttered mind! Discuss as a group or with your tutor how far (if at all) you agree with him.

2   Look at the list of standard items of office furniture, fittings and equipment given on the next page. Assume you are in a 'green field' situation and are setting up a new office. Put an A against the items you would need on the first day, a B against all the items you would require within the first month and a C against those which you could obtain as and when required.

Desk layout

Some executives do not like using a desk. Instead they use a large square table on which all their work can be laid out. In theory they should have no need for a more traditional desk with drawers – you are paid to organise all their paperwork for them. You can similarly use a table rather than a desk if you wish, but remember that you may have more need of a standard desk with drawers in which you can keep a number of frequently used items.

Office equipment suppliers have catalogues which illustrate a wide variety of desks. Most of them, however, have standard drawer layouts comprising a left-hand set of three or four drawers of the same size and a right-hand set of two drawers, the bottom one being large enough to be fitted with lateral files if desired. Various locking systems are available.

Address book
Adhesive tape dispenser
Air cleaner and ioniser
Anti-static and other
    products for keyboards
Ashtrays
Badges (for visitors)
Batteries
Binders/binding systems
Bins
Blotters/deskpads
Book/magazine racks
Calendar
Calculator
Cash and security boxes
Coffee percolator (plus
    crockery/fridge etc.)
Clipboards
Clock
Coat racks/stands
Computer (plus
    accessories)
Desk top accessories
Diary
Dictionary
Duplicator/photocopier
Fax machine
Filing equipment/card
    index

First aid kit
Furniture
Guillotines/trimmers
Indexing equipment
Key cabinets
Labels/label makers
Laminating machine
Noticeboards
Paper clips and pins
Planners
Pencils/pens
Perforators/punches
Post-it notes
Postroom accessories
Safe
Scissors
Screen dividers
Shredder
Stamps
Staplers
Stationery
Steps
Telephone
    answering machine
Trays (filing etc.)
Trolleys
Typewriter/WP

TEST YOURSELF

1		4
2		
3		5

Figure 2.2.2

1   Your desk contains the set of drawers shown in Figure 2.2.2. You wish to keep the following items off the top of your working surface. Assume that only drawer 3 locks.

Put the number of the appropriate desk drawer against each of the following items to indicate where it will be stored: e.g. office stationery 4

paper clips	drawing pins
bottle opener	pens/pencils
computer labels	confidential documents
scissors	adhesive tape
stamps	stapler
staple remover	aspirins
petty cash	needle and thread
treasury tags	telephone directories
safety pins	screwdriver (a must!)

2   Discuss as a group or with your tutor the personal items you would want to keep in your drawer in case of emergencies.

DID YOU KNOW?

The personal items you keep may not just be for yourself. You may decide to have an 'emergency' drawer to assist your boss in times of crisis. Typical items can include: a spare set of car keys, the highly unattractive desk calendar given by an important customer last year (to be taken out and put on display when he next visits), the key code number to the changing room at the golf/squash/any other club, breath freshener and a packet of mints, plasters, a spare toothbrush and tube of toothpaste, emergency telephone numbers and a list of the birthdays of family and close friends.

Consequences of poor layout/furniture on productivity

It is important to remember in any attempt you make to improve a poor office layout or replace uncomfortable and inappropriate furniture that in doing so you are not merely improving the appearance of the area. You are also likely to improve productivity. From the example upon which you have already worked (see page 86) you will have realised that it is highly probable that both productivity and quality will suffer if you:

- work in an area which is completely isolated from the rest of your staff so that (a) they have to make an effort to come and see you and (b) you can't see what is going on!
- are separated by some distance from your boss and have to spend a lot of time walking up and down to his or her office

- fail to position staff who are working on the same project in the same area
- expect a member of staff to concentrate on a very important – or very detailed – piece of work in the centre of a crowded and noisy office
- make two people share a desk which is really only sufficient to accommodate one
- let your accounts staff work on a set of complicated figures where the light is poor
- let your word processor operator work in an area where light is shining directly on the screen.

What might have an even greater effect on productivity, however, is the problems which could occur through staff absence because of illness caused by having to work under unsatisfactory conditions. You are already aware of the health and safety legislation which must be adhered to (look back to pages 55–8 if you wish to remind yourself of the major statutory and regulatory provisions). What you should also remember is that some people may suffer an 'occupational' illness which is not covered by a statute or regulation but which nevertheless still causes the organisation to lose money because of their absence from work and which does nothing to improve staff morale. The consequent effects on productivity are obvious.

Sick building syndrome

Sick building syndrome is the term used to describe buildings which are considered to cause illness in staff, e.g. skin ailments, headaches, dizziness, nausea, fatigue, respiratory problems and eye irritation. Contributory factors include:

- faulty or poorly maintained air conditioning
- inadequate ventilation
- chemical emissions from photocopiers and laser printers
- office chemicals, e.g. correction fluids
- dust build-up in carpets and soft furnishings (often made from manmade fibres)
- fluorescent lighting
- chemicals in cleaning products.

The problem is supposedly more noticeable in buildings where ceilings have been lowered, windows made airtight and ventilation restricted. The air becomes stale and the emissions from synthetic materials and office machines increase the level of pollution.

Practical steps which can be taken include:

- repositioning office equipment
- reappraising ventilation and air conditioning systems
- installing filters to control dust and smoke
- using humidifiers and ionisers to purify the atmosphere.

DID YOU KNOW?

1 The sick building syndrome has been so marked in one multi-storey block housing an Inland Revenue Department that plans are being made to move all its staff from it to nearby offices or a newly constructed smaller building.

2 There is now a growing trend amongst architects to design buildings where workers can enjoy natural light and can also have some control over the air they breathe. Surveys have shown that employees are easily frustrated by minute changes in air conditioning temperature because they are unable to do anything to change it. However, where they have the power to open a window or turn up a radiator they are prepared to tolerate considerable fluctuations.

Stress

One leading psychologist has suggested that millions of UK workers are suffering from work–related stress as a result of the 'competitive eighties' and the 'recession hit nineties' – and his views are supported to some extent by a recent study in the USA in which, out of a random sample of 600 workers, 72 per cent said that they suffered from three or more stress–related symptoms.

Although pressure of work was seen to be the main cause of stress-related illness, the survey also found that workers who performed repetitive and monotonous tasks in isolation from the rest of the workforce were also at risk. VDU operators who work long hours at the keyboard may find themselves in this category, particularly if they face the additional difficulty of working under pressure and of dealing with any machine breakdown problems.

Whatever the reason, the number of days of lost productivity because of staff absence through stress is significant.

TEST YOURSELF

1 Answer the questions in Figure 2.2.3 with a 'yes' or 'no' to see whether or not you could be working in a stressful situation.

2 Discuss as a group or with your tutor which of those factors you feel would be the most stressful and give reasons.

3 Discuss what remedies there may be (think, for instance, of staff counselling or stress reduction classes, relationships between management and workforce, the provision of employee benefits such as crèches, flexitime, relaxing work surroundings, etc.).

Figure 2.2.3 Stress test

DID YOU KNOW?

You can read more about managing stress in the specialist section on this topic on page 105.

Ergonomics relating to office furniture and equipment

Ergonomics can be defined as the study of the working environment to ascertain how best to minimise discomfort to the workforce – and thereby increase their productivity.

Obviously the type of office layout used has some effect on the well-being of the staff. So too has the heating (or lack of it), the lighting and the ventilation.

What you should also realise, however, is the effect a poorly designed chair, desk or piece of equipment has on the people who have to use it constantly.

Ideally, the workspace should be large enough to allow for a flexible arrangement of any equipment required. There should be adequate leg space. The chair should be stable but allow easy freedom of movement with an adjustable seat and backrest. A footrest should be available if required.

All equipment used should conform to the appropriate health and safety standards in relation to ease of use, manual handling regulations and COSHH standards (look back to page 57 if you need to remind yourself of what these are).

DID YOU KNOW?

1   A recent survey claims that in the UK 60 million working days are lost each year through back problems alone – some of these thought to be caused by poorly designed office furniture!

2   Directory inquiries staff in Sweden often choose to stand up while operating their computer terminals. When they want to sit down, they can do so at the touch of a button or press of a lever, thanks to their height adjustable desks and chairs.

3   Although COSHH regulations tend to be ignored to some extent by office workers they do have some significance where, for instance, an office is being painted or a carpet laid, particularly if certain adhesives are being used.

Ergonomics and information technology

The huge increase in the use of VDU equipment coupled with recent EU legislation has made it an area of particular importance. Indeed, it has been strongly suggested that VDU operators can suffer a number of problems in relation to their health, such as:

●   stress (see page 93)
●   eye strain
●   tenosynovitis and repetitive strain injury (RSI), also known as work-related upper limb disorder (WRULD).

Eye strain

VDU operators can suffer eye strain either directly from

●   the screen (because the contrast is too high or low, there is a reflection on it from the window or lighting, the characters are too small or indistinct, the characters flicker)
●   the keyboard (because there are glossy keys or bright indicator lights in the field of vision)
●   the copy (if it is on glossy or very white paper)
●   the windows themselves,

or from reflected glare coming from the walls or ceiling.

Tenosynovitis and RSI

Repetitive strain injury relates to an injury caused by constantly making repetitive or awkward movements. Although recently a High Court Judge dashed compensation hopes for thousands of computer keyboard workers when he ruled RSI had 'no place in the medical books', a report of the Health and Safety Commission noted a rise in reported cases of such disorders.

Tenosynovitis refers to the inflammation of the tendon sheaths in the hand, wrist and arms and is an officially recognised industrial disease which allows sufferers to claim DSS benefits if they have medical support for their case. They can also claim negligence against their employer, especially if no improvements have been made after their complaint.

Fortunately some of these problems have been addressed through the Health and Safety (Display Screen Equipment) Regulations 1992 (see page 58) which imposes a duty on the employer to:

- plan the activities of the users to ensure that work is interrupted by breaks or changes in activity that reduce their workload at the equipment
- ensure that regular users are provided, on request, with an appropriate eyesight test
- ensure that they are provided with adequate health and safety training.

In addition, the employer is required to analyse all workstations to assess risks to health and safety and ensure that they meet minimum requirements.

The minimum requirements of the workstation which are in line with basic ergonomic principles are shown in Figure 2.2.4.

Pregnancy

There has been considerable public concern about reports of higher levels of miscarriage and birth defects among some groups of VDU workers. Although the Health and Safety (Display Screen Equipment) Regulations 1992 state specifically that in the light of the scientific evidence pregnant women need not stop work with VDUs, they also suggest that to avoid problems caused by stress and anxiety, women who are pregnant or planning children should be given the opportunity to discuss their concerns with someone adequately informed about current scientific thinking.

Workstation minimum requirements

Display screen – well defined characters of adequate size: stable image: easily adjustable brightness and contrast: easily tilting and swivelling screen: no reflective glare

Keyboard – tiltable and separate from the screen: sufficient space in front of keyboard: matt surface: easy to use: adequately and contrasted symbols on keys

Work surface – sufficiently large and low reflecting surface: flexible arrangement of equipment: adequate space

Work chair – stable, allowing user easy movement and comfortable position: adjustable height (seat): adjustable height and tilt (seat back): foot rests available on request

Space – sufficient to allow operator to change positions

Lighting – satisfactory lighting conditions: appropriate contrast between screen and background: prevention of glare through positioning of artificial lighting

Reflections – positioning to prevent sources of light such as windows, from causing distracting reflections on the screen

Noise – must not cause distraction of attention or disturbance of speech

Heat – must not produce excess heat causing discomfort

Radiation – reduced to negligible levels in respect of user's safety

Humidity – establishment and maintenance of an adequate level

Software and systems – software must be suitable for the task, easy to use and adaptable to the level of user's knowledge: principles of software ergonomics must be applied

Figure 2.2.4 Minimum requirements of a workstation

TEST YOURSELF

You are the supervisor of a group of word processor operators who are required to spend between four and six hours a day using VDU equipment. Your manager knows that *you* know what the regulations are but is a bit doubtful that your staff are in the same position – particularly the new ones. He is worried that an unexpected visit from the TU Safety representative may cause him some problems. To reassure him, you decide to prepare for him a list of what actions you *regularly* take to ensure that the Health and Safety (Display Screen Equipment) Regulations are being followed.

Operating manuals for equipment

Welcome though it is to receive a new piece of equipment, it is not a good idea to lift it out of its wrappings and then to consign those wrappings to the dustbin without first checking to see whether or not the equipment is accompanied by an operating manual!

Nor is it a good idea simply to keep the operating manual in a file. It is there to be used (in some cases quite frequently) and you should therefore make sure that it is:

a immediately accessible, i.e. positioned next to or near the relevant item of equipment – or alternatively that some indication is given on the piece of equipment as to the whereabouts of the manual

b durable (apart from looking awful, a well thumbed and dog-eared manual with some of the pages torn, written on or missing is of no use to anyone). If a new manual does look as if it will be prone to damage, make sure that you have it appropriately backed or bound before putting it on display for general use.

Make sure too that you have back-up copies and that you discourage staff from 'borrowing' a manual only to have it disappear completely.

Remember also to check each manual for any health and safety guidance it may contain. Some manuals have a special section of 'do's' and 'don'ts' which are included not only to help you to operate the equipment effectively but also to warn you of any possible hazards there may be and how to prevent them.

Staff training

As an administrator or PA, you may face a further problem when using a manual to train other staff. In some cases the manual might be totally 'user friendly' so that all you have to do is to run through the instructions it contains, watch inexperienced staff carry them out, and then do some follow-up training if necessary. On other occasions, however, you may be faced with a manual which is quite incomprehensible. It is your job then to make it easier for your colleagues by summarising it and highlighting the key instructions. If this sounds a bit daunting, it is sometimes a good idea to find a manual which is easy to follow and to adapt that style to the manual you are rewriting.

Key points to remember include:

● Do not give too much information at any one time.
● Break down the instructions into a series of small activities. If, for example, you want to describe how to carry out a complicated procedure on a photocopier you *could* include all the information in a continuous paragraph. However, by the end of

the paragraph, you've lost all but your most technically minded staff. It would be better for you to describe each process in turn using numbered points.

- Remember to use simple language, e.g. 'you should then make certain that...' rather than 'the procedure to be followed is to ensure that...'
- Display is important. Too much closely printed text on one page is off-putting. Diagrams and other illustrations are very useful and if you are artistic you can introduce some of your own. The occasional use of humour can also tempt the reader to persevere!

Organisations' procedures for maintaining equipment

Although most manuals include a section on care and upkeep of equipment, unfortunately it is a section which tends to be one that not too many people worry about! However, poorly maintained equipment obviously results in less effective results and also in increased costs to the organisation. Even more importantly, it can also pose a health and safety risk and it is to everyone's advantage therefore to see that adequate procedures exist for proper maintenance.

Indeed, for employers, the proper maintenance and upkeep of equipment is no longer a matter of choice. The Provision and Use of Work Equipment Regulations 1992 requires them to ensure not only that work equipment is constructed or adapted to be suitable for the purpose for which it is used but also that it is maintained in an efficient state. Note that the Regulations are concerned with safety, *not* productivity!

DID YOU KNOW?

The booklet *Work Equipment: Guidance on Regulations* recognises that the complexity and frequency of the maintenance of equipment will vary from simple checks on handheld tools to a substantial integrated programme for a complex process plant. It points out that maintenance should be carried out by those who have received adequate information, instructions and training related to the work.

It also suggests that routine maintenance should involve periodic lubrication, inspection and testing, based on the manufacturer's recommendations and any specific legal requirements. In addition, a formal system of planned maintenance may be necessary if inadequate maintenance could lead to equipment becoming dangerous.

Maintenance log

Although the Provision and Use of Work Equipment Regulations state that if a maintenance log is used it must be kept constantly up to date, how that is done depends on the organisation for which you work. In larger organisations a permanent staff is employed to check on equipment and the procedures for doing so are laid down centrally. In smaller organisations, however, more responsibility is placed on individuals. Whichever system is used the maintenance log (or equipment inventory as it is sometimes called) should include:

- a brief description of the equipment (including the make and the name of the supplier)
- where each item of equipment is situated – usually broken down into departments or sections
- its purpose
- whether or not it is deemed to be a hazard should it break down
- the date it was purchased and its cost
- any maintenance agreement in existence (and the length of that agreement)
- the projected date of replacement of the equipment (if the organisation operates a rolling replacement policy)
- when it was last checked (and by whom)
- how often it has broken down, the type of fault and how often repaired
- the cost of the repair and how long the equipment was out of operation.

DID YOU KNOW?

1 A copy of this inventory (plus updates at regular intervals) should be given to the Health and Safety Officer and/or the Health and Safety Committee so that they are able to make regular safety checks on relevant equipment.

2 A special set of rules, the Electricity at Work Regulations 1989, have been implemented in respect of all electrical equipment at work. They cover not only safe working practices but also the employer's duty as regards record keeping.
One organisation has realised that such duties can be onerous, particularly on smaller employers, and has developed its own computer software package for checking all portable electrical equipment. A bar code is fixed to each item of a client's electrical equipment through which details, including the nature of the equipment, its location and its history, are fed on to a floppy disk. The equipment is then passed as safe or the system explains where the trouble lies.

Monitoring of maintenance

There is little point in establishing a procedure and then forgetting about it. Since it is likely that it will be your job to make sure that any central procedures are followed, you should establish your own reminder system to assist you. In addition, you will have to assist your staff in remembering what action to take when:

a a machine is due for a maintenance check and/or
b it breaks down and repairs are required.

Find out what systems are in operation in your workplace (including, if possible, examples of checklists used, etc.). Compare your results with those of the rest of the group or discuss them with your tutor or adviser.

Good housekeeping

Remember that not all maintenance needs to be formal. In many cases, if a few simple procedures are followed in relation to the upkeep of equipment, both money and time can be saved. If, for instance, your staff are trained to treat a piece of equipment properly – to switch it off when not in use, to keep it clean, to avoid spilling liquids over it, etc. – this will probably prolong its useful working life and again will both cut costs and meet safety requirements. It is not always easy to convince a busy staff, however, that time taken in doing this is not time wasted!

 TEST YOURSELF

Discuss as a group or with your tutor how you would make sure that your staff realise the importance of good housekeeping in the upkeep of equipment.

Organisations' procedures for recommending improvements to working conditions

Obviously, if you are experienced in running a well-organised office, it will be automatic for you to identify any improvements which you think can be made and to take appropriate action. It is somewhat more difficult if you are new to the job, particularly if you have not yet found your way around all the central systems and procedures and have still to work out the appropriate channels of communication.

What you should find, however, is that opportunities for such improvements can be identified in a number of ways.

● From the evidence of your own eyes. Unless you are completely immersed in your work – or never in the office – you will not be able to help noticing that the VDU screen is flickering, that the electric kettle has a frayed flex or that the photocopier takes 45 minutes to warm up. You will also soon become aware if the office is organised in such a way that you have to take a roundabout route every time you want to speak to someone who is only a few feet away.
● From reports from other people. Even if you do not notice the faulty electric kettle, your junior may – and he or she is likely to let you know about it the next time you ask for a cup of tea. If staff are too hot or too cold, again they will almost certainly speak to you about it!

- From attendance at meetings. If you attend a safety committee meeting you will obviously be given up-to-date information about potential hazards and also about ways to avoid those hazards.
- From what you read. If you ever find time to read the latest editions of office equipment journals or articles about improvements to office efficiency, it is surprising how many new ideas you may discover.

Remember too that conversations with people outside your workplace can help – such as your administrator friends who work in other organisations.

As is the case when recommending improvements to the working environment (see page 76), the more difficult part of the exercise is to make sure that effective action is taken. However, any health or safety concerns which you may have are more likely to be remedied since in most organisations there will be a set of procedures laid down centrally for you to follow (see page 53 for information on the role of the Safety Representative and Safety Committee).

What in reality may be more difficult is to get some action on smaller issues (like the electric kettle) or on non-safety issues (such as the updating of a filing system). As always in cases such as this you have to determine what decisions you can make and what decisions you have to refer to other people – normally your immediate boss. Once having determined that the decision has to be taken by someone else, your next step should be to make sure that you present your case as persuasively as possible.

- Collect together all the facts you need. Don't just make a vague statement to the effect that the office filing system is overloaded – say instead that the volume of paperwork has increased because of the recent reorganisation resulting in an additional workload being taken on by the department.
- Include some costs – do not be tempted to minimise the amount needed in the hope you will be able to sneak through the invoice at a later date! You may get away with it once but your credibility will have been affected for ever. What you can do, however, is to justify the cost by pointing out the benefits to be gained from making the improvement.
- Present the information clearly and attractively. Remember, no matter how obvious or necessary an improvement you are recommending, you are still 'selling' it and your chances of success will be improved if your boss is presented with a clear, legible, well set out document. It also helps if he or she is presenting it further up the ladder to his or her immediate boss.

1   You take up a new appointment and arrive on the first day only to find that your office looks as if it has just been vandalised. It is dirty, the floor is uncarpeted and the vinyl cover is torn and stained. All the working surfaces are dusty. There is an old kettle and some unwashed crockery on a table in the corner of the room and the nearest washing up facilities are at the end of the corridor. The gas fired central heating seems adequate and there is some central fluorescent lighting which is bright but rather harsh. The windows look out on to a busy street. There is no space for visitors to sit. There is only one vertical filing cabinet which is so full that the drawers are half open. Its key is nowhere to be found. The only photocopier you can find is one which is situated a floor down from your office and is used by so many other clerical staff that there is always a long queue. Your desk is small and its desktop is virtually taken up by a typewriter, some filing trays and a few unmatched containers full of office sundries such as pencils, rubber bands and paper clips. Your chair is a standard upright model. You have one office junior whose desk is even smaller than yours. You have one telephone between you. Some out-of-date planners are stuck on to the wall.

Discuss as a group or with your tutor the steps you would take to effect improvements (and the order in which you would take them).

2   Select at least three pieces of equipment at present in use in your own organisation (word processor, fax machine, photocopier, telephone answering machine, etc.) and check
    a   to see if there is a manual in existence
    b   where it is
    c   how user-friendly it is.

Write a short report on your findings and compare your answers with the rest of the group. Include in your report any remedial action you would take in cases where you think the manual is hard to follow or is not readily available.

3   You work for a major distribution company situated close to a local airport and motorway junction. The company bought an old warehouse, had this converted to open plan offices and installed double glazing throughout to reduce the noise from aircraft. Air conditioning was installed and blinds fitted at all the windows. All the offices are carpeted and a considerable amount of money has been spent on greenery and acoustic screens.

The company is thriving at present and the offices are a hive of activity with fax machines, computer printers and telephones constantly in use. The pressure is considerable as the organisation operates in a very competitive environment and needs a high level of output to remain profitable. Despite the increase in business, profit margins have been cut and six office staff left last autumn and have not been replaced. The management insist that, so far as possible, staff cuts will be by natural wastage rather than compulsory redundancies.

You are worried about the increase in absence in your section. You are responsible for six members of staff all of whom have been absent for at least a few days over the past month. All have completed self-certification forms or obtained doctor's notes in accordance with company procedures. All their health problems relate to headaches, migraines, upset stomach problems and skin rashes. Your own manager considers these are minor ailments and has little patience with them. He has warned you that the company cannot afford temporary staff and disciplinary procedures will have to be taken against staff who are frequently absent.

You decide to hold a meeting of your staff to discuss the problem.

a One member of the staff alleges that all the problems are caused because of 'sick building syndrome'.
   i To what extent do you think this may be true?
   ii What action could you take to find out the validity of her claim?
   iii What recommendations could you make if the claim appears to be correct?
b What other reasons do you think there may be for the increase in staff absence and what suggestions could you make to improve the situation?

4 Select one alteration you would like to make to your own office which you think will improve your own personal effectiveness. Prepare a memo to your boss outlining what you want to do, how much it will cost and the reasons for the request.

Managing stress

If anything else goes wrong I will s-c-r-e-a-m !

Have you ever noticed that:

- things never go wrong singly
- some days you wish you had never bothered getting out of bed
- when you are in a hurry, or doing something very important, Murphy's Law always prevails, i.e. if anything can go wrong, it will?

Many factors in our lives lead to stress, such as:

- **people** – who can put us under pressure by their demands, their moods, their actions or even just by being talkative and delaying us
- **change** – whether good or bad, in our personal life or at work, puts us under strain
- **time** – when there never seems to be enough of it.

Work scheduling and time management is dealt with on pages 131 and 177. This chapter aims to help you to cope when all seems to be going wrong in your world and you begin to feel it's all getting too much for you.

> **RULE 1**
> Ironically we all need some stress in our lives to help us to function. Imagine a life with no challenges, nothing to achieve or complete – we would feel worthless. Many people take up hobbies and interests to provide the interest and focus lacking in their lives.
>
> It is therefore an excess of stress which leads to problems – not stress itself.

Type A or type B?

The American team of Friedman and Rosenman undertook research and isolated two main types of personality which they categorised as type A and type B. To find out which you are, do the following short quiz.

Answer Always, Sometimes or Never to each of the following:

1 I am never late.
2 I live for my job.
3 I eat quickly.
4 I am impatient.
5 I play to win.
6 I am ambitious.
7 I rarely show my feelings.

8 I talk rapidly.
9 I am usually in a hurry.
10 I feel guilty when I am not working.

Give yourself two points for each Always, one point for each Sometimes and no points for Never, then add up your score.

A high score indicates a Type A personality – who will experience considerable stress. A low score means you are a Type B personality – easy-going, patient, casual and unlikely to suffer from very much stress. The irony is that whilst type As are usually more successful on the climb to the top in an organisation (though not necessarily at the top) they are also more prone to heart disease and heart attacks.

RULE 2

Stress is the result of you upsetting yourself! Whilst other people and factors outside your control may contribute to a situation in the first place, it is your reaction to that situation which creates undue stress.

What can stress do?

In addition to leading to heart attacks, stress can also cause a whole range of physical illnesses – high blood pressure, skin rashes, bodily aches and pains, migraine, ulcers and arthritis – as well as tiredness, exhaustion and depression.

The initial symptoms of stress are even more diverse and often very personal – the effects that stress triggers in me will be different from those it triggers in you. These can range from sleeplessness to forgetfulness, a 'tic' developing on your eye or mouth to irritability, biting your nails to over-eating/over-drinking.

You need to learn to observe yourself and to identify those symptoms which require you to take action to prevent the problem becoming any worse.

Many working days are lost each year because of employees reporting sick with stress-related symptoms – and even if you manage to carry on working you are unlikely to be effective or efficient and may upset others by losing your temper or just being snappy or unreasonable.

RULE 3

Bear in mind that we all differ in our tolerance of stress. Even a small amount can be too much for some people, whilst others can cope with much more. Learn your own tolerance levels – and try to be aware of those of any staff for whom you are responsible.

How to cope

There is a variety of coping strategies recommended for when we feel things are all getting too much. The best idea is to try different ones out and find out which works best for you.

1   Identify the cause

If you feel stressed and wound up it is important to recognise why – and not 'pin the blame' on the first thing that comes to mind.

Areas to think around include:

- **Work overload**
  Probably the most obvious cause is too much to do and not enough time to do it – but also work which is too difficult or too demanding or even actually unpleasant.
- **Role conflict**
  This includes not being sure what people expect of you, with different people making different demands – often the case if you work for more than one boss – and/or finding junior staff difficult to control or cope with and not having the power to do much about it. (See also Unit 4.)
- **Change**
  Another American team, Ruch and Holmes, discovered that all changes in our life create stress – even 'pleasant' changes such as getting married, Christmas and holidays. Unpleasant changes, e.g. death of a close relative, being made redundant or getting divorced, score very highly indeed. Ruch and Holmes came to the conclusion that we can all stand a certain number of life or career changes but they have a very stressful impact on us if too many changes happen too quickly.
- **People, politics and personalities**
  Whilst this covers areas such as a personality clash with someone with whom you work, it also relates to your own personality – whether, for instance, you often take things personally (such as your boss being in a bad mood) and become upset about them where another person might just shrug them off.

  Office politics can also create stress – for example keeping on the right side of the group or doing what they expect you to do (or else risking being ostracised and isolated), or two people you know trying to get the better of one another with you acting as a reluctant referee or a 'sympathetic ear'.
- **Work/home conflict**
  This covers everything from conflicting demands in both places at once, to an uncooperative partner, to having to take work home on a regular basis and feeling that you are neglecting the family.

RULE 4

Always bear in mind that what seems catastrophic today is usually more tolerable in a week, a vague memory in six months and relegated to history in two years!

2 Face up to the problem

Having identified the problem, you need to analyse:

- what aspects of it you find stressful, and why
- who or what is involved
- what you can (or can't) do about it
- what you actually want to do about it (and be honest with yourself!).

RULE 5

Clarify your thoughts by

- making a list of what's bothering you (even if you tear it up later)
- talking to a friend – but choose your friend carefully!

At this stage you should have reached one of two conclusions:

a You can do something about the problem (e.g. reschedule your work, talk to the person who is causing you problems).

b You can do nothing about the problem – either because

- it is unchangeable (bereavement obviously comes into this category)
- the solution is out of your hands or not feasible (e.g. giving in your notice at work if you need the money and there aren't any alternative jobs available).
- the other person(s) involved are just not approachable.

RULE 6

Can't sleep?

- Physically tire yourself out – spring clean a room or dig the garden or go for a long walk. Then have a pleasantly hot bath, a warm milky drink and get into a warm bed with a good (but not too exciting) book. Turn the lights down low and read until your eyes start to close...
- Still no good? Then get up and walk about a bit, read the paper – DON'T lie there worrying about it. Have you ever read how many hours sleep hospital doctors get – and they still manage!

3a   Something can be done

This may mean tackling somebody senior to you to talk to them about the problem. Learning assertiveness can be helpful here (see page 510). Putting your problem as objectively and as unemotionally as possible is important – often the other person might be quite stunned to realise how you feel.

Be positive! If you think that change is needed, e.g. in work practices, then come up with some suggested solutions – not just a list of problems!

3b   Nothing can be done

This is the conclusion that can lead to a continuation of stress unless you take some positive action for yourself. However, before you give up hope of changing the situation there is one final thing you should check – your way of defining and thinking about the problem.

Ways of thinking

It is often the case that we get trapped into ways of thinking. For instance, we feel happier thinking about small adjustments to an existing situation rather than redefining it from scratch – yet this can often give us a new perspective on the problem.

As an example, think about the adult returner who has started work after five years of being at home with the children. She finds the conflicting demands of home and work too much – even though her husband helps her in the house. No matter how much they talk over the problem at home it seems that the only solution will be for her to give up work until the children are older.

Whilst there are no easy solutions to this problem, the couple should avoid the temptation of simply making small changes to the way they operated when the wife was at home all the time. It is significant that her husband refers to 'helping' her around the home – not taking a positive role in doing jobs because they need doing. The couple may gain a fresh insight into the problem if they forget how they have coped over the last five years and rethink their problem from scratch. For instance:

● list what needs doing (and what can be left or ignored!)
● consider how many people (e.g. teenagers) can be involved, when and how
● work out whether time schedules can be changed around
● calculate whether they can afford to 'buy in' some help.

If this still does not help then you will need to develop a method of taking your mind off the problem or making yourself feel better.

RULE 7

People under stress lose their sense of humour. One way to reduce stress is to try to see the funny side of something. A good laugh – especially with someone else – can make you feel better physically and help you to put a situation more into perspective.

Options to try

- Take up a hobby – anything which will distract you. Options include anything from going to the cinema to playing tennis or learning a musical instrument.
- Get the *angst* out of your system – write a hate note and then tear it up, have a good cry, scream and shout and thump the pillow, swear loudly.
- Give yourself a treat – have a day (or evening) off. Go shopping (window shopping if you have no money), go to a sauna or for a swim, buy and read a good book, have a long lazy bath, have your hair done.
- Plan something special for the future – a weekend away, a holiday abroad, a day out with a really good friend. Get lots of brochures and daydream.
- Cuddle and/or stroke something or someone – partner, cat, dog, rabbit or even an old moth-eared teddy-bear.
- Learn to relax – go to classes if necessary or buy yourself a relaxation tape or a soothing record and curl up by the fire.
- Give yourself a lecture – tell yourself how good you are, argue with yourself if you start to become negative, list all your strengths and ignore your weaknesses, tell yourself how lucky people are to have you as a colleague/friend.

RULE 8

DON'T take to drink or chain smoking to cure your problems – you'll only add to them! Reducing alcohol and cigarettes and improving your diet (e.g. by reducing the fat content) will also help you to cope better both physically and mentally.

4 Practise what you preach

Remember – you are not the only person who has to cope with stress! As an administrator you should be alert to any of your colleagues who may have problems.

- Be a good listener – don't just brush off their problems because you are having a bad day.
- Make sure people who are responsible to you know exactly what job they have to do and what is expected of them.

- Be supportive – stick up for your staff, colleagues and boss.
- Reduce conflict – never add to it.
- Recognise type A behaviour and don't encourage it.

RULE 9

Always be alert to signs of stress – in other people as well as yourself.

---

3 Contribute to the planning, organising and monitoring of work

Element 3.1

Plan and agree work

Part of your role as an administrator or PA is to identify and prioritise tasks to meet the requirements of the organisation. Before you can do that, however, you have to make sure that you know:

- the nature of your own role
- the responsibilities which are attached to it.

Work role and responsibilities

What should be of major assistance to you in establishing your role in the organisation is your job description. A good job description should outline:

- basic details such as your job title and the department or section in which you are to work
- a description of your duties
- (in more modern job descriptions) some stated objectives. In some cases these are categorised into major and minor duties.

In addition it should state:

- the person or persons to whom you are accountable
- the person or persons who are accountable to you.

Figure 3.1.1 gives an example of a job description.

TEST YOURSELF

1 Discuss as a group or with your tutor or adviser whether you would recommend any changes or additions to the job description in Figure 3.1.1. If so, what?
2 In many cases a final inclusion in a list of such responsibilities is often 'such other duties as may be required from time to time'. Discuss the advantages and disadvantages of such an inclusion – for the employer and for the employee.

Organisation charts

Another useful document for you to have is the company's organisation chart. That should tell you not only where your job role fits into the organisation but also that of your immediate boss and the people who will be working for you.

JOB DESCRIPTION

Job Title: Office Administrator

Department: Human Resources Department

Accountable to: Human Resources Manager

Accountable for: Two word processor operators

One receptionist/filing clerk

Two junior clerks

Objectives: To assist the human resource function within the organisation by providing an efficient and effective office administration service

Responsibilities: 1 To supervise the office staff to ensure that
- all correspondence is dealt with to a required standard and within a required time
- there is an effective
  - reprographic service
  - storage and retrieval system
  - computer database
  - petty cash system
  - stock control procedure
- there is an efficient and welcoming reception area
- meetings are organised and the relevant documentation prepared

2 To be involved in the training, discipline and welfare of such staff

Figure 3.1.1 A job description

In some cases, however, you may find that your position – and that of your staff – is not quite as clear as you may wish.

TEST YOURSELF

1 Look at the organisation charts shown in Figure 3.1.2. Each chart shows a slightly different structure.

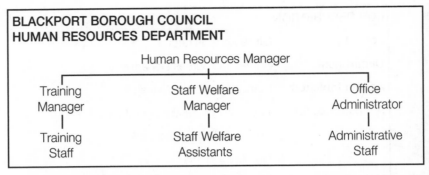

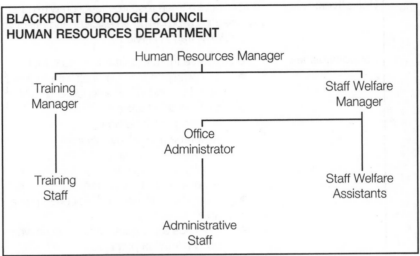

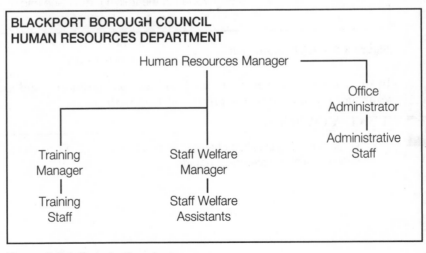

Figure 3.1.2 Organisation charts

In the first chart, the Office Administrator is on a level with the Training and Staff Welfare Managers and his or her staff are on a level with the staff in the other two sections.

In the second chart the Office Administrator is at a lower level than that of the two other managers and is responsible to one of them – although he or she has an overall responsibility for all administrative staff in the department.

In the third chart the Office Administrator is responsible directly to the Human Resources Manager but is not included in the vertical structure.

Discuss as a group or with your tutor or adviser the possible disadvantages the Office Administrator would face if he or she worked in an organisation in which the second or third structures were in operation.

2   In some organisations there is a definite distinction made between the job of an administrator and that of a manager – the job of a manager being regarded as a higher level job. Do you think there could be any dangers in taking that approach? If so, what?

3   According to the Managing Director of one employment agency, office administrators and PAs are increasingly being asked to work for more than one person. The difficulties that can be encountered in such a situation include the relationship between your two bosses, the possibility of your being accused of 'favouring' one boss over another and the dilemma you would face by being asked to do two things at once by two different people or even conflicting instructions. Discuss how you would try to overcome these difficulties.

Work roles and responsibilities of colleagues

Your next step, if you work in a team – and particularly if you are responsible for that team – is to be aware of what duties your colleagues are expected to undertake and how your role complements theirs. The job descriptions of existing staff should furnish you with some initial information and usually you would expect to have some say in the drawing up of any job descriptions for new members of staff who join your team.

However, particularly in small organisations, you may find that your colleagues do not have a formal job description – or, if they do, it is either out of date or not followed. As a newcomer to the organisation you may therefore find it difficult to:

● decide who is responsible for which job
● make any necessary changes.

1   Try to obtain examples of job descriptions of at least four different clerical jobs in your organisation. Compare your examples with those of the rest of the group.

2   If you work in an organisation which does not use formal job descriptions, write a short report about what procedures, if any, are in operation to ensure that staff know what their job responsibilities are.

TEST YOURSELF

One difficulty facing newcomers to an organisation is trying to make any changes without upsetting too many people. Suppose you find yourself in a situation in which you feel that the job descriptions of your staff should be altered in line with any changes you want to make in working arrangements but your staff are reluctant to agree any change in or reallocation of their duties. Discuss as a group or with your tutor or adviser what you would do. Include your suggestions in a short report.

Delegation

Whatever the work roles of your staff, you are responsible for developing their skills in a number of ways both for their benefit and for the benefit of the organisation as a whole. One way of doing this is by ensuring that they receive the appropriate training (see Element 1.2). Another is by means of **delegating** – which involves not only delegation of work but also delegation of responsibility.

However, many supervisors are reluctant to delegate. Among the many reasons given are:

● 'the only one who can do a good job around here is me'
● 'it's quicker to do it myself'
● 'I haven't time to show her'
● 'he may make a better job of it than I could – and where does that leave me?'

So why does anyone delegate? Basically because the pluses are greater than the minuses. If you do it properly then your staff will be well motivated and more productive, the working atmosphere and relationships in the office will improve, your section will be seen to shine and you will get the accolades – from your staff and your boss.

How to delegate

The golden rules of delegation include:

● explaining clearly and simply what is required and the standard of work expected at the start
● allowing your staff the freedom to decide how to carry out the task (though you could ask them to clarify this for you in the early stages)

- checking your instructions are understood by encouraging discussion about the task and how to do it
- being realistic about what you expect them to do and by what time
- being alert for signs that there are problems, but only intervening if absolutely necessary
- making certain that your staff know they can always come to you for help, advice and encouragement
- giving praise where it is due and constructive criticism only if necessary.

And don't give out just the boring jobs you hate doing yourself! Identify the tasks which could be delegated by asking yourself: 'If I were on holiday for the next three weeks, what tasks would really have to wait until my return?' Those are the only jobs you should keep!

DID YOU KNOW?

A modern term which has a similar meaning to delegation is **empowerment**. This refers to pushing responsibility 'down the line' to the employee. Some employees may consider that they are not paid enough to take full responsibility for all their actions, so for empowerment to work properly there must be a full understanding of the amount of responsibility and accountability at each level. In addition, the employee may need help and guidance in the early stages as well as assistance by management to take a broader-based and more strategic view of their function in the organisation.

The positive view of empowerment is that this gives the employee the freedom and scope to manage his or her job in the best possible way – given that only the job holder knows exactly what is required to gain maximum results.

CHECK IT YOURSELF

How do you feel about empowerment? Would you consider it a bonus or a nuisance? What would you consider to be essential pre-requisites for you to enter fully into the spirit of the idea? Discuss your thoughts with the rest of your group.

Work planning

As an administrator or PA it is your responsibility to plan your work and that of your staff efficiently and effectively. Even if you think your office is running smoothly, it is often a good idea to take some time to stand back from the everyday routine (however frenetic) and to analyse your workload and that of your staff to see whether or not any improvements can be made. (See page 146 for details of how to plan your work around objectives designed to assist you to meet specified targets.)

It may be, however, that you do not always receive total cooperation in your attempts to organise or reorganise work.

TEST YOURSELF

Imagine that the following remarks have been made to you by your office staff when you are trying to introduce a new system of work or to reorganise an existing one.

- 'We know what we're doing – don't try to alter things for the sake of altering them.'
- 'I'm untidy by nature – I can't change now.'
- 'Planning in too much detail leads to over-regimentation – it's going to destroy any initiative.'
- 'If it ain't broke, why mend it – it's working OK now.'

Obviously there is some truth in these comments. Change for change's sake or because you want to be *seen* to be making some alterations is not advisable: neither is it advisable if it leads to lack of flexibility and possible demotivation of staff. Again, you have to deal with different personalities – some people are organised: others are less so.

Discuss with your group or your tutor or adviser what answer you would give to the above comments.

Allocation of work
Staffing

Remember that your staff are your biggest and most important resource. In planning any work activity, you should therefore make sure that, as far as possible, the most suitable and the most qualified member of staff is allocated to it. In most cases, depending on the job description, this will be relatively simple. Someone employed as a filing clerk will expect and be expected to maintain the filing systems. Someone appointed as a word processor operator will obviously undertake word processing duties.

What may cause you difficulties, however, is where you have a mismatch of the work to be done and the staff available to do it. If, for instance, you have one word processing operator and two filing clerks, you may find that you have one person working at top speed all day long to produce all the documentation required and two people working at half speed to store it. You then have to make a decision whether to:

- put in a request for additional word processing staff
- arrange for some retraining of the existing staff
- analyse the work of the existing word processor operator to see what if any of the tasks he or she carries out can be transferred to the filing clerks.

At best any solution tends to be somewhat of a compromise – but a good administrator should be skilled at that particular art! The basic point to remember is that you should be constantly aware of possible imbalances in workloads and of the need to make changes where necessary to try to correct those imbalances.

Resources

In addition to planning the work of your staff you must also plan what physical resources you will require to complete the allocated jobs. Asking your reprographics assistant to do a large photocopying job without first having checked that there is sufficient paper in stock is unwise. So, too, is expecting one of your staff to produce high quality text if the word processor or printer he or she is using is incapable of performing that function.

Ways of target setting, and prioritising and organising work

Once having established your role and that of your staff you should then be ready to organise both your work and theirs to maximum efficiency.

Prioritising work

It is normally your responsibility to set individual targets for your staff (see page 149). It is equally your responsibility to establish priorities so that urgent work is completed before non-urgent work, important work before routine work and so on.

When you are new to the job it is a good idea consciously to make a list each week of:

- work which *must* be done – this is normally ongoing and sometimes increases as the week progresses
- work which *should* be done – eventually, of course, this turns into work which must be done
- work which *could* be done – although this is normally wishful thinking rather than a genuine expectation!
- work which *could* be delegated to others.

Remember, however, that one of your problems may be that you are often expected to work at the pace of your boss rather than at your own, and to complement his/her method of operation. This can make forward planning problematic and a good working relationship with your boss is therefore of the utmost importance.

Try to establish your boss's preferences as to working arrangements and the general pattern of the day and week. Persuade him/her to cooperate by pointing out that the time taken in such a discussion will be more than offset by the time saved later on. If your boss is still unwilling to give you any clear guidelines, try to find another experienced administrator who may be able to give you some advice.

Your boss's previous administrator, if available, is an ideal source – unless he or she gave up completely.

Organising work
Personal organisation

If you do not look organised, your boss and your staff will soon notice – and may follow suit. If, however, your method of working looks polished and efficient and your office systems immaculate, then everyone else is more likely to adopt a similar organised approach.

You may already congratulate yourself on this aspect of your work. Even so, you might like to consider the possible introduction of the following procedures – all of which are designed to help your personal efficiency.

1   Make out a file folder for each main area of work for which you regularly have 'work in progress' (WIP).
2   Make out a pocket or envelope wallet (in a bright colour) labelled 'miscellaneous two-minute jobs'.
3   Have a set of trays – In, Out, In Progress, Pending and Filing.

As you receive work put it in either the correct folder or the correct tray (or the wastepaper bin). Don't leave single papers lying around.

4   Keep your WIP file folders in priority order.
5   Given time to concentrate on a current job, start with the top folder. If you are interrupted, put the papers back again and return the folder to its tray.
6   If you only have five minutes, take out two jobs from your pocket wallet and get them out of the way.

It is important for you to remember also that there are certain crucial parts of the day to which you should pay specific attention and in which you should show specific organisational skills.

Arrival at the workplace

●   Forget about the lark/owl syndrome (unless your boss is of exactly the same mind as you); even if you are by nature an owl and want to work late at night rather than early in the morning you should still try to arrive at the office before your boss. Otherwise chaos could reign. Remember, too, that your staff will be watching you. If you arrive five minutes past starting time, they will probably want to do the same (or at the very least get to work at one minute past).

●   If you do arrive before your boss, remember there is nothing wrong with having a slow start and relaxing for a few moments with a cup of coffee. Treat this as your 'thinking time' and if it puts you in the right frame of mind to greet your boss, junior staff and any early morning visitors, so much the better.

- Carry out certain routine tasks (unless you have delegated them to a junior), e.g. check the fax machine and the telephone answering service.
- Make a physical check to see that all areas are clean, tidy and at the right temperature (if they are not, make a note to speak to the cleaner or to whoever else is responsible for office maintenance). Check also for any potential health and safety hazards or security risks – rooms left unlocked by the cleaners, etc.
- Check the diaries – remind reception of the arrival of any visitors.
- Either open or supervise the opening, sorting and date stamping of the incoming mail. Decide what you can do and what needs your boss's attention. Find and attach any relevant papers.
- Draw up or check the list of jobs for your junior staff.
- See your boss as soon as possible (or as soon as he/she allows) to discuss the day's programme.

During the day

- Much depends on the day. During the periods when your boss is away from the office, or involved in a meeting or other appointments, you can deal with the lists of jobs which must be done. If your boss is away all day, you may even be able to do some work from the list of jobs which could be done.
- Remember, however, to keep a general check on the work going on in the office and, in particular, the work of your junior staff. Much depends on how experienced your staff are – if they are, don't irritate them by constant checks; if they are not, keep a closer (but not too close) eye on what they are doing.

At the end of the day

- Check the outgoing mail and deal with any last-minute requests.
- Check on the work of your juniors to see whether they have left anything important outstanding.
- Check the diary for the following day and highlight the priorities. Sort out any documents which may be required for early morning appointments. Remember to check with your boss whether he/she is coming into the office or going straight to his/her first external appointment.
- Make end of day checks on security; see that equipment is switched off, that confidential papers are locked away, that filing cabinets are made secure. Check that the fax machine and telephone answering machines are left switched on.
- Check your list of jobs for the week to see whether any on the 'could be done' list have now to be moved to the 'must be done' list and adjust the following day's work accordingly.
- If your boss is staying on to work late, check that all the

documents he/she needs are available, and – if you really want your boss to think well of you – offer to make a cup of coffee before you go!

TEST YOURSELF

Various pitfalls can occur throughout the day. Look at those listed below. Put a tick against the one listed in each category which you would find the more difficult to avoid. Then discuss with your group or your tutor or adviser the best ways of overcoming them.

1 Acting without a plan
  Adhering too strictly to the day's plan

2 Being too optimistic about what you can achieve during the day
  Being too pessimistic about what you can achieve during the day

3 Being so engrossed in your work that you resent any interruptions from your boss, your juniors or visitors
  Having an 'open door' policy so that you make time to listen to everybody but have no time to do your own work

4 Spending too much time chatting
  Never having any time to chat

5 Doing everything yourself
  Delegating everything to your juniors

6 Constantly proof-reading and making other checks on the work of your juniors
  Leaving your juniors to it

7 Being indecisive
  Letting no-one else but you make a decision

8 Working in chaos
  Constantly tidying up

9 Making too many draft outlines of tasks to be carried out during the day
  'Dashing something off' within minutes

10 Not having the appropriate materials available – reference books, stationery, computer disks, etc.
  Being unable to start a job unless all the materials are to hand

11 Spending a long time each day doing the filing no matter what else happens
  Letting the filing accumulate

Office organisation

Your next job is to introduce a system into the office to enable your staff to carry out their tasks to the required level of efficiency.

One way is to classify these tasks into:

a those which are infrequent and which can be anticipated and planned well in advance, e.g. an annual general meeting

b those which occur more frequently but which can also be anticipated, e.g. monthly updating of price lists

c those which occur regularly but which cannot be identified precisely, e.g. word processing, dealing with visitors, taking dictation.

Then introduce a time element, i.e. what you can plan on a yearly, monthly, weekly and daily basis. Planning on a yearly or monthly basis is generally straightforward provided you use the most appropriate planning aids.

Planning aids

Some planning aids make it easier for you to plan ahead. Others make it less easy for you – and your staff – to forget to take certain important actions!

The list

Don't despise the making of lists! They can be the key to much of what happens in an office. After all, your filing system is no more than an elaborate list; so, too, is your database.

It takes only a few moments to make out a list of jobs to be done at the beginning of each day (or at the end of the previous day) but such a list can be invaluable. Don't overlook the psychological effect of being able to tick off or draw a line through certain jobs as they are completed, even if they are as simple as ordering coffee and sandwiches for a meeting. Most administrators learn this stratagem early and a 'sure-fire' method of picking them out from the rest of the office workforce is the notebook they carry with them constantly. If you want to be considered part of the electronic age then you may like to consider the use of a personal organiser (see page 171).

DID YOU KNOW?

It is no use carrying a notebook around unless you have a pen or pencil constantly on your person. Choose a pen which writes horizontally – many an administrator has been given important instructions when walking down the corridor and the only suitable surface to rest on is the nearest wall!

Permanent and temporary lists

Distinguish between lists which are temporary 'one-offs' and those which are permanent and act as constant reminders. Temporary lists are those which are changing all the time as you carry out urgent jobs and cross them off, and add new ones. Danger areas to watch for are:

- constantly avoiding doing jobs you don't like. (You can spot this if you find yourself making out new lists and regularly transferring one or two particular items!)
- doing the jobs in the order in which you write them down, rather than prioritising them into the order in which they should be done
- forgetting to add new jobs – especially when you receive the information from an unusual source or in an unusual place
- not crossing jobs off as you go, so that by the end of the day you don't know where you are.

Make yourself feel better by starting the day by doing one or two jobs you really hate. Having got these out of the way you can now work through the rest of the day with a clear conscience!

In contrast, because permanent lists are reminders, if you are going to cross off items as you go, then take a photocopy first. Examples of permanent lists include:

- arrangements for meetings (actions to be taken before/during/after the event etc.)
- arrangements for regular visits abroad
- Post Office services (which delivery services are faster, which are more expensive/economical, etc.)
- holiday arrangements for staff.

TEST YOURSELF

1 Discuss what other types of 'permanent' check lists you could use in an office.
2 Once having prepared these checklists, what factors would you have to bear in mind to ensure that they are always helpful?

The card index

You may find a card index system helpful as a reminder which you can check each day as part of your daily routine. Use one guide card for each day of the month (or month of the year) and place any reminders to yourself behind the appropriate number. If, for instance, you want to remind yourself that your boss's car tax expires in August, place a reminder to that effect behind the August guide card. If you know that your boss is attending an important meeting on 23 March, you could place a note behind, say, card 16 to remind you to collect together all the relevant papers he will need.

This system can be more useful than writing reminders in a diary which is already full of appointments, meetings and travel details. Equally, if you are suddenly given a letter during dictation with the instruction 'put that on ice for a couple of weeks and remind me to write to them again then' you can not only jot down the details on the relevant card, but also attach a photocopy of the letter to the index card so that you have all the details to hand when the couple of weeks has elapsed.

The strip index

A more complex, commercially produced system is the 'strip' or 'busy person' index by which reminders are entered on to individual strips which are then fixed into position in a strip index container for your boss's personal use. The information is seen at a glance and can be put in a container small enough to be carried in a briefcase. You would be wise, however, to have your own copy and to make frequent cross-checks (in the same way that you cross-check diaries).

Pre-printed forms

Don't assume that you are being extravagant if you decide to buy your requirements from outside suppliers. Make use of those organisations which specialise in preparing business forms which not only save your time (and therefore the company's money) but also act as built-in reminders. Bought-in forms also have the advantage that they are frequently printed on NCR (no carbon required) paper, so that copies can be taken easily and quickly.

Examples of frequently used pre-printed forms include:

● lateness records
● sickness and absence records
● holiday report forms
● holiday rota schedules
● suggestions forms
● message forms
● routing slips
● petty cash vouchers
● purchase requisition forms.

CHECK IT YOURSELF

A number of office supplies companies specialise in producing such forms. Contact at least one of them to obtain an up-to-date catalogue of what they have to offer.

Planners

Planners can be extremely useful, particularly if you use them in conjunction with your diary (see page 167).

The standard time span in most organisations is one year (which normally runs from January to December), so if you want to take a systematic approach to the planning of the work of your office you should take the annual cycle as your starting point. Even if your organisation works to a three- or five-year plan, you will still be able to incorporate the information into your annual planner by means of a carry-forward system each year.

Scheduling tasks

Once the yearly cycle has been established, you can then subdivide it into monthly, weekly and daily cycles to meet your own requirements.

Tasks which can be planned on a yearly basis include:

● the annual general meeting
● the annual sales conference
● dates of sales trips
● dates of quarterly reports
● directors'/governors'/councillors' meetings
● financial activities relating to the year end
● Health and Safety Committee (and other regular) meetings
● publicity campaigns.

Those which can be planned on a monthly basis include:

● a transfer of the relevant items from the yearly planner, e.g. an annual general meeting entered on the yearly planner for August would have to be included in the monthly planner
● meetings with Trades Union representatives
● monthly reports from departmental managers
● training courses
● interview arrangements
● production scheduling meetings.

Figure 3.1.3 shows a year planner, a monthly planner and a weekly planner.

Year planner 19--/19--

JAN	FEB	MAR	APR
MAY	JUN	JUL	AUG
SEPT	OCT	NOV	DEC

Monthly planner 19--

Week beginning 21/12	
7/1	
14/1	
21/1	
28/1	

Weekly planner

Week beginning......................

MONDAY	
TUESDAY	
WEDNESDAY	
THURSDAY	
FRIDAY	

Figure 3.1.3 Examples of planners

1   Using your own workplace as an example, add to the list of tasks which you think could be included in a yearly or monthly planner.
2   Given that the diary is the obvious alternative to the use of the weekly planner in particular, when might you find it more convenient to use the planner? Factors to consider include:
   a   the need to keep the information in the diary brief and uncluttered
   b   the fact that more than one person may want to have access to the diary at any one time during the day
   c   the advantages of seeing the week's events at a glance.

Devising your own planners

You have the option of creating your own planners (particularly if you have access to a desktop publishing system).

If, however, you feel that the planner system is likely to be a major factor in your overall strategy of monitoring targets you should consider using one of the many commercially prepared visual planning charts. Some of these are designed to fit your general requirements. Others are more specific: for example, if you work in a school or college you may require a timetabling planning chart; if you work in a production unit a production scheduling chart is useful; and many sales departments use a 'perpetual' or 'rolling' planner so that the next 12 months is constantly on view.

The advantages of such charts include:

● their appearance – if displayed on a wall or screen they look effective both to members of the organisation and also to visitors, particularly if use is made of accessories such as labels/coloured flashes
● their flexibility – many of them are re-usable.

They do have some disadvantages, however:

● They can become over-complicated (too many different coloured labels and signals can be confusing).
● They can be time-consuming to set up (although you should beware the false economy of neglecting to spend a couple of hours sorting out a system which is 'user-friendly' in favour of a system which can be set up within a few minutes but which nobody can understand or operate).
● If you use sticky labels they are usually there for good, whether you like it or not. Magnetic rubberised strips which can be cut to shape are better, but make sure they are large enough to hold on to the board – if they fall on to the floor it is doubtful if you will have much idea where they should go! (And beware the 'helpful' member of staff who, seeing them on the floor, adds them to the chart wherever they would appear to look best!)

Remember, however, that just because you organise a system, this does not mean that it will always be followed faithfully by all members of your staff. You have to be prepared to do some monitoring and follow-up of their work to ensure that it is being done and that you are satisfied with the quality as well as the quantity of the output. (See page 152 for information about monitoring and controlling the achievement of agreed targets.)

TEST YOURSELF

It is not always possible nowadays to assume that you will be working exactly the same hours as your boss or your staff. Some organisations operate a flexitime system so that staff may work certain 'core hours', e.g. from 10 am to 4 pm, but outside those hours can choose whether to come in earlier or leave later. Discuss as a group or with your tutor or adviser how that system may affect the ways in which you organise your work and that of your staff.

Ways of dealing with changed priorities and unforeseen situations

Nothing ever goes to plan – or at least nothing ever goes to plan 100% of the time. As doubtless you are already aware, no matter how carefully you may have organised your work, there will be occasions where a sudden emergency occurs and you will have to react to it no matter what other work you have planned or priorities you have established.

Much then depends on your approach to the emergency. Even if you are not by nature calm, cool and collected you will have to train yourself to at least give the appearance of being so. And there are some actions which you can take to minimise the effect of an emergency – and consequently to preserve your sanity!

- When planning your daily or weekly work schedule try, where possible, not to commit yourself to too tight a time schedule. Allow for some slippage so that if your plans are disrupted during the course of the day or week, you will still be able to complete what you want to do within the allotted period of time.
- Know how your staff will react to an emergency – who is likely to go to pieces, who is likely to disappear somewhere until it is all over, and who will keep calm along with you and actually try to do something to help.
- Know how your boss will react. Is he or she going to take charge or delegate the solving of the problem to you – or is it more likely that he or she will make matters worse by stampeding about the office in a mad panic!
- Try to think of what types of emergency could occur (remember that certain emergencies such as fire should already be covered centrally), such as:

- unexpected absence of an important member of staff
- breakdown of a vital piece of equipment
- last minute loss of computer- or paper-based data which is required urgently
- sudden unexpected demand for information/action by a senior member of staff.

You should then be able to draw up a contingency plan for dealing with each of them, listing:

- the type of emergency envisaged
- the action which should be taken
- the person(s) involved in taking that action.

Suppose, for instance, you know that each year you and your staff will be responsible for preparing all the paperwork for the Annual Conference and that you will be working to a very short timescale and an immovable deadline. You have one person who is responsible for inputting all the information and another who is skilled at preparing the necessary spreadsheets and computer graphics. The sudden absence of either of them will cause you great problems. Consequently, in your contingency plan, you would:

- outline the nature of the problem
- decide on what preventative action you could take, e.g. have a trained 'back up' either within your office or at least on hand within the organisation who could be available immediately during that period
- make certain that everyone concerned knows what the procedure is to be in the event of the emergency arising.
- If the emergency is such that it has not been – or could not have been – foreseen, you have no option but to deal with it as best you can. What is important to remember in this instance, however, is not to be too depressed if there has been chaos and you have not dealt with the situation as efficiently as you think, in retrospect, you should have done. Treat it as experience and in this case *do* have a post mortem. What exactly did go wrong? Was it you, was it your staff, was it lack of procedures or forethought, etc? Then prepare a contingency plan just in case the same emergency recurs. You will feel better and so will your boss and your staff.

CHECK IT YOURSELF

Try to find out if any contingency plans exist in your own organisation – other than those established for health and safety purposes. Discuss your findings with your group or your tutor or adviser and write a short report about the approaches taken in different organisations.

Methods of time management

You have probably heard the phrase 'time management' many times. Although it is currently quite fashionable to talk about it as if it is a new concept, good administrators and PAs have been practising it for years. They have improved their use of time by:

- personal planning (see page 120)
- target setting (see page 145)
- delegation (see page 116).

They have also developed appropriate technical skills, such as faster reading/writing and word processing skills, and personal skills such as assertiveness and negotiation.

However, when you first start a new job – or if you are not sure that you are using your time to the best advantage in your current position – it is a good idea to analyse:

a your personal characteristics
b the job context
c the people with whom you work,

and use this information as a basis upon which to begin to improve your time management.

Personal characteristics

As already mentioned (see page 119), you may not be able to act entirely independently. Your boss may have a different approach to time, and although you may be able to influence him or her to a certain extent, you will probably not be able to completely change an established system of working. However, you should still be able to take into account your own personality when dealing with time-related issues – provided you recognise certain of your personal characteristics.

TEST YOURSELF

1 Put a tick against the statements which you think most aptly apply to you and the way in which you work.
   a I prefer to work early in the morning
      I work best late in the day
   b I like to pace out my work over a period of time
      I prefer to work in short intensive bursts of activity
   c I like to concentrate on one issue at a time
      I like to have several jobs on the go at once
   d I want to be left alone to complete a job
      I like working with a group of people, each of whom contribute to the job in hand
   e I like to delegate
      I find delegating difficult – I like to get on with the job myself

f　I am naturally tidy and methodical
　　　　　Being tidy doesn't come easily to me.
　2　In the light of those answers discuss with your group or your tutor or adviser how easy (or difficult) it would be for you to deal with the following situations.
　　　a　Your boss insists on coming in quite late in the morning and working on well into the evening.
　　　b　You work in a busy office in which there are constant demands made on your time. You are never certain that you will be allowed the time to concentrate solely on one job.
　　　c　Your work consists of peaks and troughs. For long periods of time it is regularly spaced out and then – at specific times of the year – it becomes necessary for you to work at high speed for long hours at a time over a short period.
　3　If you do think that – given your personal characteristics and preferences – you would find difficulty in one or more of those situations, discuss what you could do to overcome those difficulties.

DID YOU KNOW?

Being always approachable is not necessarily a virtue in this context. One of the personal skills mentioned above as being necessary to promote good time management is that of assertiveness (*not* aggression!) – it is thought that a naturally assertive person is better equipped to deal with those who try to 'trespass' on his or her time!

Self discipline

Hopefully, one of the solutions you may have suggested to the above 'Test Yourself' will have been to exercise some self discipline. It is difficult to change the way you operate, and success is not always immediate, but it will help in the long run if you do try to eliminate time-wasting methods of working.

The job context

You may not always be helped, however, by the place in which you work.

　1　If, for instance, you work in an open plan office, you cannot shut your door on noise or other distractions. You are also more visible – although in other respects this is not necessarily a disadvantage, in the case of time management it can prove to be so. In such circumstances, some administrators resort to relocating furniture to create a 'thinking' space for themselves.
　2　Remember, too, that poor office layout can hinder time management simply because staff have to spend time unnecessarily moving about the area.
　3　What is also important to note, particularly if you are new to an organisation, is its culture. Some organisations do not encourage informal contacts: others do. Although there are many

advantages to the first approach, the saving of time is not one of them. Similarly, some organisations require great accuracy and precision from their workforce. This in itself is time-consuming.

In some organisations decisions can be made at a relatively low level: in others all decisions are made at the top and time has therefore to be spent in processing anything upon which a decision has to be made through the various layers of management.

In some cases you can work around the system; in others you have no option but to accept it and organise your work to encompass a longer time scale.

DID YOU KNOW?

If you want to manage your time better you have to bear in mind not only your personal characteristics but also those of your boss and of your staff. (See also 'Managing time', page 177.)

Methods of coordinating resources and tasks

You may have heard someone say that a certain person is 'always getting on to a horse and riding off in all directions'! It is very easy for an administrator to fall into that trap, particularly if he or she is responsible for both an area of work and a group of staff. Planning the work is only the first stage. Coordinating it is the second – and ongoing – stage. If, for instance, you have to complete a job which involves a number of people and the use of a variety of resources it is unwise just to dash into the office, hand out a few jobs and then hope for the best. You should be prepared to:

- look at the job as a whole and then divide it into a number of discrete tasks
- decide approximately how much time is needed for the completion of those tasks (counting back from the deadline of the completion of the job)
- decide the order, if any, in which the tasks are going to be completed
- decide who is going to complete each task and whether they are working alone, in pairs or in a group
- estimate what resources are required and whether they are readily available
- brief the staff accordingly.

It sounds easier than it actually is!

TEST YOURSELF

You work in the Administration Department as the Office Administrator of a group of administrative staff, part of whose responsibility it is to make all the necessary arrangements and prepare all the relevant documentation for the monthly Departmental Managers' meeting. Your immediate boss is the Manager of the Administration Department. Working for you are:

- your assistant administrator
- three word processing operators
- a receptionist/telephonist
- a filing clerk
- a reprographics technician.

You analyse the tasks to be performed as:

a preparing the monthly agenda
b word processing it
c collecting together all relevant information relating to agenda items and reproducing it for each member of the meeting
d checking to see who can and who cannot attend
e arranging for the meetings room to be booked and for tea and biscuits to be served
f arranging for car parking spaces to be available for those managers who work in branch offices
g taking notes at the meeting
h preparing and circulating those notes
i filing and indexing the notes.

Discuss as a group or with your tutor or adviser:

1 to whom you will allocate each separate task
2 what resources you will need to check before the work begins
3 in what order you will allocate the work and
   how you will make sure that each part of the work is completed on time
4 what procedures you will put into operation to prevent having to repeat the same instructions to the same staff each month.

Ways of informing and consulting with others about work methods

Informing your boss or a colleague about what is going on, and telling your staff what you want them to do in the office, are a normal part of your everyday life as an administrator. What is equally important, however, is *how* you inform them.

Look at the following scenarios, all of which involve conversations between an office administrator and his or her staff.

- David goes into the office mid-morning when the staff are busy and tells them about some changes that are going to be made in the way in which travel expenses must be claimed. At the end of the day, just as they are starting to tidy up before leaving, he decides to talk to them about some changes he wants to make in job roles.

- Farzana is called into her boss's office one afternoon and is told to find out urgently (a) the name and address of the local MEP and (b) some background information about him. She is under pressure with other work and therefore passes on the job to her assistant. She forgets to give her assistant the second part of the instruction so that the information handed over is incomplete.
- Bridget is rather shy and has difficulty in speaking to groups of people. It is company policy that supervisors should hold weekly team briefings with their staff and Bridget dreads them. She always reads straight from a piece of paper and is so thankful that it is over that she doesn't encourage any questions or feedback.
- Gary is very uncommunicative. He gives all his instructions in writing either direct to his staff or through daily bulletins pinned on the staff noticeboard.

TEST YOURSELF

In all four cases there has been an attempt to convey information but on each occasion – although for different reasons – the attempt has not been altogether successful.

As a group or with your tutor or adviser discuss why the four administrators may not have conveyed the information effectively. (Check your answers with the information given later in this element.)

DID YOU KNOW?

One experiment involved testing how much information was conveyed to workers through a notice pinned on the staff notice board. It was found that:

- 10 per cent did not read it
- 10 per cent did not understand it
- 10 per cent misunderstood it
- 10 per cent did not believe it
- 10 per cent criticised the spelling and grammar

Presumably the remaining 50 per cent were happy with it!

Preparation of information

There is an old saying that 'to fail to prepare is to prepare to fail'. If you want to make sure that the information you are giving is going to be understood and acted upon you should:

a define your objective, i.e. what you want to achieve
b think about your audience, e.g. are you talking to experienced or new staff, one of your colleagues, your boss or his/her boss
c determine where and when you are going to present the information
d decide on exactly what the nature of that information is going to be.

Keeping and holding attention

If no-one listens to what you are saying or reads what you have written you are obviously wasting your time! Points to remember include:

- be as brief as possible – or divide long and complicated pieces of information into smaller, more easily digestible sections
- use different methods of communication – you could prepare a list of written instructions for your staff but supplement that information with a brief verbal explanation
- encourage interaction – the more people are involved, the more likely it is that their interest will be maintained.

Making sure that the information is understood

- Avoid using too many technical terms or jargon – unless you are sure that your audience are as well aware of them as you are.
- Do not assume a knowledge that may not exist. Your junior staff may not like to tell you that they don't understand what you have said or that they don't have the same background knowledge as you.
- Avoid vagueness – again, a colleague or your boss (and certainly his/her boss!) may question you about anything they don't understand but junior staff may be less willing to do so.

Consulting

If you consult staff about their work rather than telling them what they should do, you are likely to achieve a more positive response. Most people prefer to have a say in what they are expected to do, and in many cases you are able to use their knowledge and experience to decide how best a job should be done. Consultation with a group of staff also has advantages in that their ideas can be pooled and their individual expertise used to the best effect. However, there can be some drawbacks.

 TEST YOURSELF

Jonathan and Derek are both office supervisors. They meet one lunchtime to compare notes and – as always – get round to the difficulties of dealing with staff!

Jonathan favours a very direct approach with his staff. He argues that he is paid to organise them and that they will lose confidence in him and in his ability to manage if he is always asking them what they think or how a job should be done. He also argues that if he has to consult staff on their likes and dislikes, it will be impossible to get anyone to agree to do the boring or difficult jobs.

Derek is much more democratic. He consults his staff on all issues but finds that some of them are more responsive than others and that consequently the strongest willed members of the group tend to have the greatest say. He also has difficulty in meeting targets, especially those with a deadline, as the consultation process tends to take some time. However, he is convinced that staff react better to being asked rather than being told how and in what time limit a job should be done.

Discuss as a group or with your tutor or adviser:

a   whether and for what reasons you think Jonathan may have some justification for his approach
b   how a compromise could be reached which would minimise the disadvantages and maximise the advantages of consulting rather than merely instructing staff.

Summarise your conclusions in a short report.

Ways of negotiating the assistance of others

The simplest way to get assistance is to ask for it. However, as you have probably already experienced, there are different ways of asking – some of which are more likely to be successful than others.

You first of all have to be clear about *what* it is you are asking. If, for instance, you are involved in preparing the departmental strategic development plan and need some information about what staff development has taken place over the past two years and what has been planned for the forthcoming year, you may need to ask for assistance from someone in the Human Resources Department. If so, you are more likely to be successful if you can tell him or her clearly and concisely exactly what information you need. Otherwise you may find that you have to ask for additional information on a number of occasions and you may find that the assistance given becomes more and more grudging.

Possibly even more important is the way in which you ask for assistance. It is obviously inadvisable to demand rather than ask for assistance from a colleague or boss but it is equally unwise to take that approach with your staff. There are many ways in which a resentful member of your staff can *appear* to be doing what you ask but, for various reasons, you fail to get what you want – as the following examples indicate.

● 'I'm doing my best but I've had so many interruptions that I've just not managed to finish it.'
● 'I'm sorry, I must have misunderstood – I thought you said you wanted me to sort out the filing before I did anything else.'
● 'I got to the mail room just too late for that letter to be sent – you know what the staff there are like about deadlines.'
● 'I feel ill – I think I'll have to go home!'

Points to remember include:

- consulting rather than demanding (see page 136)
- choosing the right person, e.g. trying not to ask someone to fit in an urgent job when they are obviously overloaded with work already
- not always choosing the 'willing horse' – you may ask once too often!
- giving as much warning as possible about when and for how long you want the assistance
- accepting that sometimes assistance just cannot be given – because of lack of knowledge, lack of time, etc. – and finding ways to deal with that.

TEST YOURSELF

Discuss as a group or with your tutor or adviser whether you agree or disagree with each of the following statements designed to test your skills of negotiation.

1 I never negotiate under pressure.
2 I find deadlines unhelpful.
3 I aim to win.
4 There is no point negotiating if the other side is being totally unreasonable.
5 If the other side says that a certain point is non-negotiable there is no point in going any further.
6 There is nothing I can do about a deadlock situation.
7 If I prepare myself properly I won't get any surprises.
8 I'll get the best deal if the person with whom I'm negotiating likes me.
9 I always offer something in return.
10 I am always logical rather than emotional when negotiating.

Check on page 143 for suggested answers.

Assertiveness

What you must avoid doing, however, is confusing pleasantness with weakness. You are entitled to ask for assistance from your staff and are equally entitled to expect them to cooperate with you where possible. Even if you are not naturally assertive you should try to adopt at least some of the following stratagems when making what you think is a reasonable request for assistance.

- Be direct – don't be over–apologetic.
- Give a reason for your request but don't feel that you have to justify yourself.
- Do not resort to unnecessary flattery – you should not need to coax your staff into doing something.
- Allow some debate to take place but remember, unless the reason for the unwillingness to give assistance is obviously justifiable, you can insist on receiving it.

Legal and regulatory requirements relating to work practices and work methods

Part of your role is to take responsibility for all aspects of the work of your staff – and that includes being aware of any legal or regulatory requirements which may affect them. (See Element 2.1 for details of all the relevant health and safety legislation about which a supervisor should be aware.)

Equal opportunities and working practices

However, another area of legislation about which a supervisor should be informed is that of **equal opportunities**. You will be dealing with all types of people including both male and female, people from diverse ethnic backgrounds and the disabled or disadvantaged. You should therefore know how far the law protects them from any form of discrimination.

 DID YOU KNOW?

A special body known as the Equal Opportunities Commission (EOC) has been set up to monitor the effectiveness of equal pay and sex discrimination legislation. The Commission for Racial Equality (CRE) does the same in respect of racial equality.

Equal pay

Under EU law, 'men and women should receive equal pay for work of equal value'. The Equal Pay Act 1970 (amended by the Equal Pay (Amendment) Regulations 1983) also provides for equal pay for men and women and states that a woman must get the same pay as a man (or vice versa):

1 if she is employed on the same work as a man
2 if her job is rated the same as that of a man's under a job grading scheme
3 if it is regarded as being of 'equal value'. For example, in one case a woman who worked as a cook in a shipyard canteen claimed that her work was of the same value to the organisation as that of a man who was a shipyard worker.

 DID YOU KNOW?

The last provision is particularly important in cases where women are segregated into women-only jobs – known as 'occupational segregation'. If, for instance, a group of female secretaries are working in an office and there is no male worker doing the same work, the women have no-one with whom to compare themselves. Their only solution therefore is to take the same route as the shipyard cook and to try to compare themselves with a man doing a different job but one which the women can claim is of no greater value than theirs.

Employer defences

However, an employer may be able to use one of two defences:

1. that there is an important difference between the two jobs. If, for instance, a male office administrator can prove that in addition to his other administrative duties, he has to operate a computerised accounts system, then he will be entitled to receive more pay than the female office administrator.

2. that there is an important difference between the man and the woman (e.g. the man is better qualified, older, more experienced, takes more responsibility, etc.). Again this must be a real difference. If, for instance, the man has only had a couple more years' experience than the woman he would not be entitled to be paid very much more than her.

 DID YOU KNOW?

At one stage some employers tried to maintain the pay differentials between male and female administrators by calling the men 'office managers' and the women 'office supervisors'. However, the courts have now held that different job titles do not necessarily prove that two jobs are different and they will look at the *actual* work carried out to see whether or not the duties are sufficiently different to justify the difference in pay.

Sex discrimination

Both men and women can be discriminated against in more ways than just the payment of money. They can find it hard to get a job in the first place; they can be passed over for promotion; they can be excluded from training opportunities or other fringe benefits. They may also find that they are the first to be made redundant. The law – by means of the Sex Discrimination Act 1975 (as amended by the Sex Discrimination Act 1980) – attempts to prevent this from happening by forbidding any discrimination on the grounds of sex. It does so in two ways:

- **direct discrimination**, where an employer refuses to employ a woman or a male administrator
- **indirect discrimination**, where an employer tries to circumvent the law by asking for a particular requirement designed indirectly to favour one sex over the other. If, for instance, an employer asked for a building worker who was over 6 feet tall and had a beard it is hardly difficult to guess which sex has the best opportunity for meeting that requirement!

 DID YOU KNOW?

Men are increasingly facing sex discrimination over jobs. EOC figures, published in 1994, show the highest recorded level of complaints of discrimination from men – much of it centred round employer preference for women part-time workers.

Employer defences

1 An employer *may* be allowed to employ one sex rather than another if he can justify it on grounds other than sex, for example:
   - if it is too expensive to do otherwise (although this defence is becoming more and more unpopular with the courts)
   - if there is a 'genuine occupational qualification' (GOQ) where the nature of the job requires a man or woman, e.g. modelling or acting
   - where the work is to be carried out in a private home or requires the employee to 'live in'
   - where the job is outside the UK in a country whose laws and customs prevent the work being undertaken by a woman
   - where the job is one of two to be held by a married couple
   - where personal services are required which are most effectively provided by a man, e.g. work in a boys' hostel.

2 An employer is allowed to take **affirmative action** (in some cases known as **positive discrimination**) so that, for instance, an advertisement can invite women applicants to apply for a job which traditionally has always been done by a man.

TEST YOURSELF

There have been a number of different views expressed about the advantages and disadvantages of 'affirmative action', one of them being that it perpetuates the idea of the 'token woman', i.e. one appointed to a particular job because of her gender rather than her ability. Discuss as a group or with your tutor or adviser whether you think the advantages outweigh the disadvantages and, if so, how this particular difficulty could be overcome.

Racial discrimination

The law protects people from different ethnic backgrounds in the same way as people of different sexes. The Race Relations Act 1976 (as amended by the Race Relations (Remedies) Act 1994) forbids discrimination on grounds of 'colour, race, nationality or ethnic or racial origin'. It contains much the same provision as the Sex Discrimination Act and forbids both direct and indirect discrimination unless there is a need for a GOQ or if the employer can justify it on grounds other than race.

CHECK IT YOURSELF

Today most organisations operate equal opportunities policies and include in job advertisements, job descriptions and other documents statements such as:

'This organisation will not discriminate against anyone on the grounds of race, sex, age, creed, colour, religion, nationality or disability.'

In some cases reference is also made to sexual orientation.

Check to see whether your organisation operates a stated equal opportunities policy and, if so, compare it with those policies operating in organisations in which the other members of your group work. Summarise your findings in a short report.

DID YOU KNOW?

Complaints about sexual or racial discrimination are made to an Industrial Tribunal. This comprises a legally qualified chairperson appointed by the Lord Chancellor and two people representing both sides of industry who are selected from a panel consisting of nominations from the Trades Union Congress and management organisations. An appeal against an Industrial Tribunal decision can be made to the Employment Appeal Tribunal.

Victimisation

In both the Sex Discrimination and the Race Relations Act there is a provision forbidding victimisation of people who have claimed racial or sexual discrimination. Examples of discrimination include:

- isolating the worker from the rest of the workforce
- checking his or her work much more rigorously than that of anyone else
- finding ways to discipline him or her for the slightest mistake
- transferring him or her to a less pleasant job
- finding a way to make him or her redundant.

If victimisation can be proved the worker can return to the Industrial Tribunal to complain.

TEST YOURSELF

Sometimes, discrimination occurs not at management level but on the shopfloor. There have been several cases where, for instance, a woman has been subjected to sexual harassment or someone from an ethnic minority group to racial abuse by members of the team in which they work.

Recent cases have included:

- the display of photographs of nude or partially clothed women in the inspection department of a factory where women worked
- sexually explicit remarks made to a woman police officer by her male colleagues
- offensive remarks to an Indian worker about his religious beliefs.

As a supervisor your duty is clear – if you discover this is happening you must report or discipline the offenders. However, you are also responsible for ensuring that the group of people concerned work together to meet the targets you have set. Discuss as a group or with your tutor or adviser the actions you might take to try to promote cooperation between different members of your group – particularly if you suspect that there is some unrest amongst them because of sexual or racial differences.

DID YOU KNOW?

Beware of the office party! Apparently the amount of alcohol consumed there can lower inhibitions and there tends to be a spate of claims – particularly about sexual harassment – brought before the industrial tribunals immediately after Christmas each year.

The disabled or disadvantaged

The law relating to the employment of the disabled or disadvantaged is far less specific than the law relating to women or ethnic minorities. The Disabled Persons (Employment) Acts 1944/58 place a statutory duty on all employers with 20 or more full-time workers to employ a quota of registered disabled people based on a percentage of the total workforce. In addition the Companies (Directors' Report) Employment of Disabled Persons Regulations 1980 requires that every annual company report to which the regulations apply should contain a statement outlining what the company has done to give fair consideration to applications for employment by disabled persons and to arrange for appropriate training for them. However, at present the law does not specifically protect the disabled from discrimination.

DID YOU KNOW?

A Disability Discrimination Bill has been drawn up which aims to do away with the existing requirement for employers to have at least 3 per cent of disabled workers on their staff and to introduce instead a statutory right not to be discriminated against in employment on the grounds of disability. The right will apply at every stage from recruitment to the terms and conditions of employment, promotion, training and dismissal. As yet, however, it has not been successful.

ANSWERS TO 'TEST YOURSELF' EXERCISE ON PAGE 138

None of the statements is correct!

1 *I never negotiate under pressure.*
   Being under pressure is a regular experience for a negotiator – the pressure of time, of breaking a deadlock, of coming to a decision
2 *I find deadlines unhelpful.*
   The whole point of negotiation is to reach a decision within a specified deadline – otherwise the decision may never be reached!
3 *I aim to win.*
   This shouldn't be your sole aim. Winning at someone else's expense is rather short-sighted. What happens when you try to negotiate with the same person again?

4   *There is no point negotiating if the other side is being totally unreasonable.*
    What you think of as unreasonable is merely your opinion. The other side may think that it is you who is being unreasonable.

5   *If the other side says that a certain point is non-negotiable there is no point in going any further.*
    If you always accept that something is non-negotiable you may find that everything you want to discuss is put into that category.

6   *There is nothing I can do about a deadlock situation.*
    If you negotiate with skill there is nearly always something that you can do about a deadlock situation

7   *If I prepare myself properly I won't get any surprises.*
    No matter how well prepared you think you are there is always room for surprises. Remember you are not the only person wanting to achieve a result!

8   *I'll get the best deal if the person with whom I'm negotiating likes me.*
    Being liked is not essential. What you should aim for is to conclude a reasonable deal first and hope that being liked follows – not the reverse.

9   *I always offer something in return.*
    Why? It's not always essential.

10 *I am always logical rather than emotional when negotiating.*
    Again, why? Sometimes emotion plays a part in the negotiation process. Enthusiasm, commitment or even persistence are all emotions which can help rather than hinder.

 ## ACTIVITY SECTION

Ann works as an Office Administrator to three partners in a firm of management consultants. She is also in charge of a small office staff comprising a receptionist, a word processor operator and an accounts clerk.

One of her bosses is young and ambitious and is something of a workaholic. He comes in early and stays late. However, he is rather inexperienced and tends to ignore any systems. Ann is never quite sure what he is planning – basically because neither is he! He tends to act on impulse and to work on what he wants to do at that particular moment.

Ann's second boss is older and more organised. However, he is rather dictatorial and does expect Ann and her staff to give his work priority. This can sometimes cause friction if one of the other bosses also has some urgent work to be done.

Ann's third boss is a member of a number of charitable and professional bodies and although he brings in a lot of business through the contacts he makes in those arenas, he is very rarely in the office. He tends to give Ann instructions over the telephone which are brief and sometimes a bit confused. Matters are not helped if he doesn't speak to Ann direct and his messages are relayed to her by the receptionist.

Ann is somewhat of a perfectionist and starts working longer and longer hours to try to cope with all three men. Her staff try to help out but she sometimes get irritated because they make mistakes – particularly under pressure – and she doesn't feel that she has any time spare to talk to them, let alone train them. Their job descriptions are incomplete and in some cases out of date.

Ann takes on more and more duties herself and often a situation arises when she is working to full capacity and her staff are trying to find something to occupy their time.

As she becomes more involved with her work, they become less involved and any initial enthusiasm they may have had seems to be disappearing.

One day Ann feels at screaming point. In fact, she is just about to go into see one of the bosses to hand in her resignation, when one of her friends – also an office administrator – telephones her and asks her to come round to her house that evening. For once, Ann decides to leave work early and to go and see her friend. During the course of the evening she starts discussing work and finds herself telling her friend all her problems. She talks through one or two ideas with her and leaves for home feeling a lot better and determined to put into effect some of the changes her friend has suggested.

1 Draw up a list of the problems hindering Ann from organising the work of the office in an effective manner.
2 List the improvements you think her friend may have suggested that she make.
3 Prepare two aide memoires containing points/arguments etc. for Ann to use when:
   a she speaks to her bosses and tries to persuade them to agree to her ideas and
   b she talks to her staff to tell them what changes she is going to implement and why.
4 Draw up a checklist for Ann to use to monitor the progress of any improvements she eventually introduces.

Element 3.2

Monitor and control the achievement of agreed targets

Own work and responsibilities

Nowadays the setting of targets is an essential feature of many business organisations. If targets are not set the organisation may have little idea of whether or not it is achieving sufficient success to keep it viable. These targets are monitored at regular intervals so that any deviations can be corrected before it is too late.

Some targets are imposed by the organisation. For example:

- a manufacturing organisation may impose specific targets relating to the number of goods produced over a set period of time and the number of sales made during that period
- a chain of restaurants may set targets relating to the number of meals to be sold each week
- a job centre may have targets for the number of people interviewed and counselled, the number of people undertaking retraining and the number of people finding employment
- a museum or art gallery may have targets for the number of people visiting it each year.

CHECK IT YOURSELF

Find out what, if any, targets are set by the organisation in which you work. Discuss these with the rest of your group or your tutor or adviser and prepare a short report outlining your findings.

Departmental targets

Within the organisation, different targets are assigned to different departments or areas depending on their specific function. A production department will obviously have to try to produce a pre-determined number of goods; a sales department will have to try to make the required number of sales and so on. As an administrator or PA you will be probably be part of the team and will therefore have to take joint responsibility for the achievement of the targets set for your own particular area.

However, the more senior you become in any organisation the more likely it is that you will be responsible for setting at least some of your own targets. Although you might feel that imposed targets are somewhat annoying, at least you know what they are. Establishing your own targets can be quite difficult, particularly when you first start.

Defining work objectives

What you must do is to establish your **objectives**. You are then much more likely to be in a position to start setting suitable targets to achieve those objectives.

Some organisations use the acronym SMART to define a good objective:

S = stretching
M = measurable
A = agreed
R = realistic
T = time related.

DID YOU KNOW?

Management by objectives was an idea introduced in the 1950s. It is based on the assumption that managers will be more effective and will be more committed to objectives if they are themselves involved in establishing them. It also pre-supposes that they work in an organisation which permits them to do so.

Work analysis

If you have the time – and it may be worth making the time (see page 177 for details about time management) – you can carry out a **work analysis** which technically involves an assessment of:

- the **job**, i.e. the work assigned to a particular person
- the **task**, i.e. the part of a job which has a distinct beginning and end and which makes a substantial contribution to the job. One obvious example might be the word processing of a particular document. You may need to consider, for instance,
  - the degree of difficulty
  - whether or not it can be carried out without supervision
  - how much training is necessary
  - what equipment is needed
  - what techniques have to be used
  - whether speed of operation is vital.

In addition you may also want to give some thought to user satisfaction – is the job so boring or so pressurised that to allocate one person to it will cause him or her to collapse under stress?

DID YOU KNOW?

A more detailed approach to work analysis also involves

- the **operation**, i.e. the part of a task which requires a particular set of movements – such as inserting a disk into a word processor
- the **element**, i.e. a small part of the operation – such as picking up the disk from the desk.

However, you will not be expected (nor probably will you have the expertise) to analyse your work in such detail. What you should concentrate on primarily is the job and – where relevant – the task.

Setting targets

Once having identified job roles and tasks, you can then identify the key result areas and set some appropriate targets.

Some targets are quantifiable and time based and can be expressed:

- in monetary terms – what profits are to be made, what income should be generated, what budget limits have to be kept, etc.
- in numerical terms – the number of products to be produced, the number of clients or customers to be contacted, etc.

Non-quantifiable targets

However, as an administrator responsible for setting targets for your staff or yourself, you may not be able to attach that type of target for *all* the activities carried out in your area. Although you may be able to set quantifiable targets for an orders clerk, i.e. that he or she must:

- process 100 orders a week
- at ten minutes a form
- with no more than 3 per cent error,

you may have difficulty in setting such exact targets for reception or customer care staff. In such cases you have to adopt a more **qualitative** approach – although, even so, you should still try to set a target which is **measurable**. You may, for instance, establish the following qualitative targets:

- dealing courteously with all customers at all times even if they are proving difficult
- making sure that the development of a new product is fully supported by the correct paperwork
- working productively and cooperatively with fellow team members.

The difficulty here, of course, is how to measure these targets. What you need to establish – whether or not your targets are quantifiable – is a set of **performance indicators** to assist you to measure them.

Types of performance indicator

Examples of quantifiable performance indicators include:

- to increase sales turnover for the year by 5 per cent
- to reduce the cost per unit of output by 4 per cent by the end of the year
- to reduce the error rate by 1 per cent by 31st December
- to achieve a 5 per cent improvement in customer ratings by the end of the year.

Examples of qualitative performance indicators would be:

- proportion of take-up of a service or facility
- the reaction of clients, internal and external customers and outside bodies to the service provided
- speed of activity or response to requests
- ability to meet deadlines
- existence of backlogs
- meeting defined standards of accuracy.

One County Council has identified four distinct types of performance measurement:

- *money measures*, e.g. maximising income, minimising expenditure, improving rates of return
- *time measures*, e.g. performance against a timetable, the amount of backlog and speed of activity or response
- *measures of effect*, e.g. attainment of a standard, changes in behaviour, the level of take-up of a service
- *reaction*, e.g. how others judge the job holder – measured by peer assessments, performance ratings by internal or external clients, analysis of complaints, etc.

TEST YOURSELF

1 Even supposing that all office work can be quantified in the same way as that of the example of the orders clerk given above, discuss as a group or with your tutor or adviser the possible disadvantages of imposing such specific targets.
2 Draw up what you think would be suitable targets for:
  a your filing clerk
  b your assistant administrator
  c your part-time typist.

Setting targets for your team

If you have the responsibility for the work of a particular group you may decide (or be asked) to establish targets for your team either instead of – or as well as – individual targets.

TEST YOURSELF

One management writer, Douglas McGregor, described an effective team as one in which:

- the atmosphere is informal, comfortable and relaxed
- there is a lot of discussion in which everyone participates but which remains relevant to the task
- there is full understanding and acceptance of the task
- disagreement is allowed and decisions are reached by consensus
- criticism is open but constructive
- when action is taken, everyone is clear as to their own role
- the leader of the team does not dominate the team.

Discuss as a group or with your tutor or adviser what targets you could set in order for you and your team to achieve the above objectives. Think, for instance, about the need:

- for everyone to contribute and cooperate
- for decisions to be made and adhered to
- for new ideas to be implemented

- for there to be achievement of the overall departmental or company targets etc.

Think also about the need to avoid time-wasting and unnecessary conflict. Try to distinguish between those targets which you think are quantitative and those which are qualitative.

Agreeing targets

It is generally accepted that an *agreed* target is better than an *imposed* one. However, getting someone to agree to a target is sometimes quite difficult.

Ideally what you should do is to discuss with each member of your staff:

- what company or departmental objectives need to be taken into account when setting individual objectives
- the overall purpose of the job
- the principal accountabilities or main tasks which have to be carried out to achieve that purpose
- what exactly is expected to be achieved in respect of each of these tasks, e.g. what standard of performance is required
- which of these objectives are specific, measurable, agreed, realistic and time-related (i.e. SMART)
- what the performance indicators are going to be (see page 148).

You should realise, however, that there are certain dangers in such discussions!

 TEST YOURSELF

You are in the process of trying to negotiate agreed targets with a number of your staff. Discuss as a group or with your tutor or adviser what you would do in the following instances.

- Alison refuses to agree with the targets you suggest.
- Dominic agrees immediately to the targets – but you know that he always agrees to everything anyway, and sometimes doesn't do what he promises.
- Part of Joanne's duties is to take visitors on guided tours of the company – and neither you nor she has much idea of what target should be established for that task.

Scope and limit of own authority for taking corrective actions

If targets are achieved, everyone is pleased – and many organisations award bonuses to those employees who have been involved in the process. If they are not achieved, the reverse is the case. What you, as an administrator or PA (and normally therefore a member of the first-level management team), have to determine is the extent to which you are responsible for taking action if you perceive that targets are not being achieved. As in many other areas there is a thin line between avoiding your responsibility altogether and overstepping your authority.

TEST YOURSELF

June works as a Telesales Administrator in the Sales department and is responsible for a group of telesales staff whose targets include:

- making a specified number of calls each day
- achieving a certain number of sales each week.

Her immediate boss is the Assistant Sales Manager and her fellow administrator is the Office Administrator in charge of all the clerical staff in the department. The computer staff, although situated within the Sales department, are the responsibility of the Computer Manager, who is also responsible for the computer staff in all the other departments.

June notes that one of the salesmen is disappearing early each afternoon and is certainly not spending the prescribed period of time making telephone contact with customers. She calls him into her office and tells him that she expects him to be at his desk during office hours.

Another of the sales staff is obviously struggling to cope. Her sales technique is not very polished and she often loses sales because she isn't sufficiently confident to 'push' the product. June therefore contacts the Training Manager and asks for her to be given further training. The Training Manager tells her that there is insufficient funding to do so and June therefore arranges for her to attend an external training course and to pay for it out of her own budget.

The database used by June's staff is getting more and more out of date and she is concerned that her targets will be affected if she does not have access to more current information. She tackles the computer staff and insists that they give priority to updating the database. When they protest that they are too busy she threatens to report them to the Sales Manager.

One of June's staff protests that he has great difficulty in getting the word processing staff in the department to prepare the necessary information to send out to customers once a sale has been agreed over the telephone and that he is frightened that the delay may cause them to change their minds. June speaks to the Office Administrator who says that he will do his best to help but that he is very short-staffed at the moment and the other sales staff are also pressurising him to get their paperwork done. June then takes the matter direct to the Sales Manager.

Discuss as a group or with your tutor or adviser:

   a where you think June has acted within the scope of her authority
   b where she may have overstepped it
   c what other action she could have taken in the circumstances.

Methods of monitoring achievement of targets

June was obviously worried about not achieving her targets. She was probably quite fortunate, however, that by the nature of the job she could monitor almost minute by minute what progress was being made towards achieving those targets. Other administrators or PAs may have more difficulty in keeping such informal checks.

What they must do, therefore, as part of their overall quality assurance system, is to develop a suitable system by which both the quality and quantity of the work they and their staff produce is to the required standard.

Checking

One simple method is to introduce a process of work checks. If you are organising the work of a number of staff you could introduce, for instance:

- the independent check, by which the work of one member of staff is checked by another
- the 'blind' check, whereby two members of staff perform the same task and then check that they have achieved the same results
- a double check, carried out by you
- a random sample check, carried out by you on some but not all of the activities.

TEST YOURSELF

Discuss as a group or with your tutor or adviser the possible advantages and disadvantages of each method of checking. Discuss also the types of office activity which could not easily be monitored in this way.

DID YOU KNOW?

One specific form of checking nowadays is the computer control check by which the computer is programmed to carry out automatic checking by data validation. It allows figures and text input into a computer to be checked for completeness, authorisation and reasonableness.

The Gantt chart

Checking ensures that a uniform approach is taken to the accuracy of the work carried out. It does not, however, entirely solve the problem of monitoring. As already discussed, most targets involve both quality and quantity and it may be that one of your staff carries out his or her duties meticulously but very, very slowly. Obviously you have to encourage both speed and efficiency. You also have to make sure that *all* members of staff are contributing properly and that the overall target is met – not just the targets allocated to individuals.

What you might consider in such circumstances is the introduction of the **Gantt chart**, which allows you to plan and control output. Suppose, for instance, that one of your responsibilities was that of the preparation of the payroll in which time and accuracy are of the essence – as those of you who have ever faced an angry workforce which has either (a) not been paid on time or (b) been paid the wrong amount, will know only too well! The use of a Gantt chart enables you to monitor daily or weekly exactly what progress has been made so that any slippage can be spotted almost immediately and corrective action taken (Figure 3.2.1).

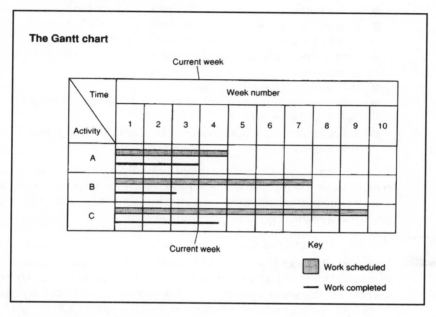

Figure 3.2.1 The Gantt chart

ℹ️ DID YOU KNOW?

Some organisations encourage the use of **individual output control** whereby, because the volume of work fluctuates from day to day, the work done by the staff is recorded and their actual times compared with the targets. Daily time sheets are made out by the supervisor showing:

- the work to be accomplished
- the standard time allowed
- the *actual* time, e.g. the starting and stopping times for the working day; the time spent in meal breaks and any time lost through factors such as machine breakdown or illness; the time spent on unmeasured work.

At the end of the day the total time at work, less any lost time and time on unmeasured work, is compared with the standard time for the work accomplished and the reason for any significant differences ascertained.

TEST YOURSELF

The internal management audit

Another form of monitoring can be by means of the internal management audit. As an administrator you may be involved periodically in such audits, which are generally organised centrally and can cover:

- various aspects of the personnel policies or systems
- communication systems – how well staff are able to communicate with each other and with customers
- equipment – whether the best use is being made of copying facilities etc.
- storage and retrieval systems
- staff training – are staff sufficiently qualified/skilled to carry out their particular tasks
- office layout – including cleanliness, furnishings, lighting, heating, etc.

Even if such audits are not organised centrally, you may want to carry out the same exercise on a more limited basis for your own particular area – perhaps concentrating on a **methods** audit, i.e. looking at a particular system.

TEST YOURSELF

You realise that your filing clerks are not meeting their targets of quick and accurate storage and retrieval of information. When you discuss it with them they tell you that the equipment is out of date and unsuitable for the purpose. Before you ask your boss for money to replace the system with a more modern one, you decide to audit the existing system (a) to see whether or not that is the problem (and not merely the inefficiency of the clerks) and (b) for evidence to support your request for a replacement system.

As a group or with your tutor or adviser draw up a list of questions you should ask either the staff (or yourself) to provide you with sufficient information to make a decision.

Ways of dealing with deviations from planned targets

It is always easier to see what is going wrong than to actually correct it. If targets are not being met because of lack of organisation or because of machine breakdown, it is up to you either to organise more effectively or put pressure on senior management to give you better resources. If, however, targets are not being met because of the *people* involved, life gets much more difficult.

Consider the following scenario.

Gwyneth works as Office Manager of a small carpet manufacturing company and looks after a group of office staff. The carpet manufacturing industry is highly competitive and pressure is put on Gwyneth to produce high quality work very quickly. As she used to work in a similar environment, Gwyneth is able to cope with the pressure. Some of her staff are not quite as experienced – or as capable.

Jamie is new to the organisation. He left college six months ago and is now employed to look after the computerised accounts system. He is technically well qualified but is a bit overawed by some of the more senior staff (including Gwyneth) and doesn't like to ask for help. Consequently when he comes across a problem, he tries to struggle on by himself and his output falls.

Maria has had a number of domestic and personal problems and, when pressure builds up, she tends to get a migraine and has to go home. As Gwyneth is so short of staff, she finds it difficult to find someone to stand in for her.

Len, one of the older members of staff, is nearing retirement – and he has lost interest in the job. His work rate is poor and so is the quality of his work.

Mike and Marilyn are supposed to work together on the payroll and to check each other's work. They do not like one another and therefore do not cooperate. There are constant complaints by the workers about mistakes in their pay.

The computer system is outdated and tends to break down quite frequently. Gwyneth is putting pressure on her boss to get the system updated, and she tries to persuade the two members of staff who are most affected by the machine breakdown to carry out other duties during the breakdown period so that overall targets can be met. They refuse to do so, saying that they are employed as computer operators and not general clerks.

The Sales department is rather disorganised and Gwyneth's staff are always complaining that they cannot prepare the necessary paperwork on time because the salesforce do not give them the information they need.

TEST YOURSELF

Discuss as a group or with your tutor or adviser the actions you would take in each case to try to overcome the difficulties and to see that the targets are met.

Points you may want to bear in mind include:

- your own negotiation and counselling skills

- peer pressure
- pressure from above
- reorganisation of duties and/or staff.

Ways of establishing and implementing control mechanisms

If targets are not being met, the sooner you realise this the better. It is of little use your finding out on the last day of the month that your monthly number of sales is 25 per cent below the agreed target as you will be in no position to do anything about it. What you need is ongoing control of the situation. The Gantt chart and other planning aids mentioned on page 153 should give you that day-to-day control, but it is quite easy to establish a system and then to forget to use it or to keep it up to date – particularly if you are working in a pressurised situation. What you must also realise is that although you may have established certain control mechanisms, you cannot achieve the targets all on your own. You have to be able to persuade your colleagues to cooperate.

You have two methods of doing this. You can use your authority and insist that staff cooperate. That might work to a certain extent, but you run the risk of always having to be on the spot personally to organise the work and of never knowing what is likely to happen if you are absent from the office for some reason. A preferable alternative would be to implement control systems which are welcomed by the staff, who appreciate the need to keep a personal check on progress. This is particularly the case if they realise that meeting targets results in their being paid a commission or bonus. Even if no payment is involved, most staff get some form of satisfaction from achieving what they have set out to do.

Consequently one important method of control is to keep staff informed of both their own personal progress and also the progress of the group as a whole. The approaches used might be:

- weekly team briefings to update staff about progress made
- eye-catching charts to indicate how close the targets are to being met
- meeting staff separately at least once a week or month to discuss individual progress.

In many organisations the annual staff appraisal is an official forum for discussion about targets set and targets achieved. Not only are staff thus kept informed, they are also constantly reminded of the importance placed on targets – and can never say that they didn't *know* what was expected of them.

Try to find out what mechanisms are used in your organisation to keep staff informed about what is expected of them in the achievement of any targets. Discuss your findings with the rest of the group or your tutor or adviser and summarise them in a short report.

Ways of reviewing and evaluating work outcomes against targets

The biggest difficulty, of course, in the setting and monitoring of targets occurs when they are not achieved. If, despite all your monitoring, the eventual target has not been met, you will have to carry out a detailed evaluation of what has gone wrong. However, you should also carry out a similar evaluation if you *over-achieve* your targets, i.e. produce more than you had targeted for – as in both cases some adjustments may have to be made.

Steps you should take include:

1   gathering together all the necessary information
    - the targets
    - when they were set and by whom
    - whether or not they were agreed or imposed
    - what staff and resources were involved
    - when the slippage was first noticed
    - what steps were then taken
    - when it was finally realised that the targets would not be met
2   discussing your findings with your staff and asking for their contributions
3   suggesting reasons for the under- or over-achievement
4   suggesting any improvements which need to be made in the case of under-achievement.

The under-achiever

If you have identified that it is a member of your staff (or yourself!) who is not achieving his or her targets (which is consequently affecting the targets set for the whole group) it is your responsibility to try to effect a change. It is not always easy! What you should try to do is establish:

- what was actually achieved
- where there are any shortfalls
- the reasons for those shortfalls
- any changes to the targets
- any actions required by either you or the member of staff.

Remember that it is important to *resource* any action you agree – by means of additional training or guidance, the provision of additional equipment or facilities, etc.

If you are inexperienced in dealing with staff – particularly when you have to discuss their shortcomings with them – you may find it easier to use a checklist as the basis of the discussion. It tends to calm the situation and to remove the emphasis from you as a person to you as the administrator of a system (Figure 3.2.2). You can also use the list as a check for yourself, if necessary.

Target achievement

Checklist

- To what extent have the objectives not been achieved?
- What specific instances have there been of that non-achievement?
- Did the individual fully understand what he or she was expected to do?
- Were these expectations reasonable in the light of the individual's experience and qualifications?
- Did the way in which the job was structured contribute to the failure?
- Did the individual get the required support from his or her colleagues and/or manager?
- Did the individual know that his or her work was not up to standard?
- To what extent, if any, was the failure to achieve targets the result of lack of effort or interest?

Figure 3.2.2 Checklist of target achievement

TEST YOURSELF

1   Discuss as a group or with your tutor or adviser which items on the checklist you feel would be most difficult to discuss with one of your staff – and what steps you would take to deal with the possibility of his or her negative or aggressive reaction.

2   One difficulty which *always* occurs in these circumstances is that staff will protest that the targets set were too high or too demanding. If you are their supervisor you are in a difficult position. It is unlikely that you can, even if you wanted to, just agree to the setting of a lower target for the next period. However, if you insist that the target remains unadjusted, it becomes an imposed rather than agreed target and you may have to face dealing with a disgruntled staff. Discuss as a group or with your tutor or adviser what you would do in such circumstances.

Procedures for reporting issues and recommendations

Even though, if you are a supervisor it is obviously not a good idea to shelter behind your boss whenever an unpleasant or difficult decision has to be made, there are occasions when you may have no alternative – and the failure to achieve targets is one of them.

What you can do, however, to avoid totally alienating your staff is to agree with them what you are going to say to your boss. You can also avoid totally alienating your boss by putting those suggestions in as tactful and constructive a manner as possible! For example, 'We'll never meet those targets no matter how loudly he shouts' can be translated into 'Staff expressed some anxiety about having to meet what they considered to be too high a target.'

ACTIVITY SECTION

You work in the careers office and you and your staff are responsible for:

a arranging interviews for all unemployed youngsters

b preparing the necessary paperwork including follow-up interviews for those failing to attend a first interview

c compiling and updating a database of information about universities and colleges of further and higher education

d making regular contact with local employers

e replying to all general correspondence.

Your agreed targets for the previous year include:

- arranging an average of 50 interviews a week depending on the time of year – e.g. fewer interviews to be arranged over the Christmas period or during the town's annual summer holiday period; a greater number to be arranged during the autumn and spring terms

- carrying out follow-up action no later than seven days after any failure to attend

- updating the databases at least once a month

- sending out a newsletter to employers at least once a month

- being no more than three days behind in replying to any correspondence.

Despite your best efforts you have not achieved any of these targets. Some of your staff have left during the course of the year and their replacements are not yet sufficiently trained or experienced to cope with the workload as quickly and efficiently as perhaps they should. In addition you have had some time off through illness and, because of staff shortages, no-one was able to stand in for you. Consequently you have not been able to monitor the situation as well as you would otherwise have done.

You are determined that the same situation should not occur again. You therefore hold a meeting with staff to discuss what action you should take. It is generally agreed that most of the targets are reasonable – other than the requirement to send a monthly newsletter to employers, which is thought to be an impossible target to meet given the level of staffing and the amount of work involved. It is also agreed that there has been an almost complete lack of monitoring of the targets by anyone throughout the course of the year.

Assume that you are the supervisor concerned.

1 Prepare a list of actions you would take to ensure that the targets are

monitored throughout the year and any deviations noted and dealt with immediately.

2 Write a short paragraph stating what measures you would take to deal with the difficulties caused by:
   a shortage of staff
   b untrained and inexperienced staff
   c any unexpected absence you may have.

3 Prepare a short report to your immediate boss, the Principal Careers Adviser, outlining why you have failed to meet the targets and also what improvements you hope to make to ensure that the same thing does not happen again. Include a request that the target in relation to the monthly newsletter be altered and give your reasons for making that request.

Element 3.3

Manage appointments

Own work and responsibilities

'Managing appointments! I've got past that – I leave that to my juniors.' An understandable remark for an administrator or PA to make – but also an unwise one. If you are ever tempted to say that, you are ignoring the importance of the word 'manage'. If your appointment system is inefficient, the effects on productivity and customer satisfaction may be difficult to quantify but they will still exist. So too will the effect it has on your relationship with your boss. You cannot blame anyone else if he or she misses an important meeting or there are two irate clients sitting in the office, both having been given the same appointment times. You are paid to manage the situation and if one of your junior staff makes a mistake, you have to bear that responsibility.

Therefore, the diary should be your primary aid in planning and organising your work, that of your boss and also that of your staff. It is not only a means of recording appointments but also the basis of your office planning system.

You should take particular care to train your junior staff to schedule appointments in the most effective manner and to link the information in the diary with that contained in other planning systems (see page 125 for information on planners etc.). Bear in mind, too, that other people may wish to have access to the information in the diary.

Methods of prioritising and organising appointments

One of your most important first steps is to talk to your boss about personal preferences in relation to the planning of appointments. The more experienced an administrator you become and the more long-standing the relationship between you and your boss, the easier it will be for you to 'second guess' him/her. In the early stages, however (or if – regrettably – your boss tends to be somewhat of a law unto him/herself), try to make time (or to make your boss have the time) to discuss certain general principles such as:

- the general pattern of the day's work – does your boss like a 'quiet hour' either at the beginning or the end of a day? Does he/she like a regular lunch break? Is he/she prepared to have a working lunch (or dinner or breakfast)?
- the general timing of appointments. Does your boss like to get through appointments in one block, e.g. every morning between 9.30 am and 12 noon? Or does he/she prefer to have them spread out to provide some breathing space?
- is your boss very anxious that appointments should not overrun? (If so, you must get some specific guidelines – what if the client is important or the member of staff is particularly worried or upset – do the same rules still apply?)
- does your boss want you to use one of several methods to 'speed up' visitors who outstay their welcome? If so, are you to use the tactic of the telephone call, the note placed on the desk or the verbal reminder of the next appointment? Some executives have a concealed buzzer or other signal which indicates to anyone in the outer office that they need rescuing – and quickly!
- In some offices you may find that you have one diary and your boss has another. In addition he/she may keep a personal diary. In such circumstances you must accept that it is your responsibility to update and coordinate all three diaries – otherwise you run the constant risk of double bookings or missed appointments. With some bosses you may find that the personal diary becomes the bane of your life – he/she may put in appointments without telling you about them. Try to make an agreement that the diary is handed over to you at least every two days so that you can make sure your version is up to date.

If possible, therefore, consider using one diary only, with all appointments made by you. It is also good practice to try to persuade your boss that if he/she is asked to agree to an appointment while out of the office, then you and your opposite number administrator should liaise over appropriate dates and times. You can then remain in control of the situation. Note also that you can photocopy a page of the diary each day so that your boss can use it as an aide memoire when travelling.

TEST YOURSELF

The advantages of recording all the information in one diary are outlined above. In some circumstances, however, there are corresponding disadvantages:

- lack of immediate availability to anyone who may need access (e.g. your office receptionist)
- difficulties in keeping certain items of information confidential
- problems of theft or loss.

Discuss as a group or with your tutor or adviser what steps could be taken to overcome these problems.

Scheduling difficulties

Some aspects of scheduling can cause problems which you should try to anticipate and prevent.

- The timing of appointments is all–important. Try to calculate how long each appointment will take. You may be helped by a boss who tells you that he/she will be back at a certain time or that an appointment in his/her office is scheduled for a certain period, but even this may be an optimistic rather than a realistic assessment. In the early stages, in particular, do over-estimate – too much time between appointments is better than too little.
- Do not overbook unless absolutely unavoidable. Try to maintain some 'blocked out' time to enable both you and your boss to get on with your own work. This is particularly important if he/she has just returned from or is about to go on a business trip or undertake some other work outside the office. It allows for both thinking time and time for reflection!
- If your boss has his/her own diary make certain that entries in both diaries coincide. Methods you can use to remind you to move appointments you have already entered include placing an asterisk by the entry, using a different colour of pen or writing any which have not been double-checked in pencil. Remember, however, to use this stratagem sparingly – a diary or other appointments system which is full of too many abbreviations or signals can become very confusing!

DID YOU KNOW?

You will find that executives vary considerably in their ability to calculate travelling time to and from appointments accurately. Some consider that it enhances their image if you think they can travel from London to Manchester in well under three hours. The opposite is the executive who plays safe and allows for three punctures and a two-hour traffic jam in every journey. Only experience will tell you how much time realistically to allow and this can depend on time of day, road conditions and weather. You will do both of you a favour if you read the road works reports in one of the national newspapers each morning and notify your boss of any adverse conditions on the route he/she may be using.

Organising the needs of others

Remember that it is not only your boss's schedule which you have to consider when arranging appointments. Other people will also have commitments which have to be taken into consideration. If the personnel involved are all members of the same organisation there are fewer problems – particularly if your boss is the senior person. Even then it can take some time to coordinate your diary with those of the other administrators. If you need to schedule an important or urgent meeting you may find that it is almost impossible to allocate sufficient time within the standard working hours of 9 am to 5 pm. In this case you have a choice between:

- holding the meeting out of hours
- trying to persuade one member to change an appointment
- holding the meeting without some members (particularly if these are not key people at the meeting).

More problems can arise if the appointment to be arranged is with someone outside the organisation and there are other people involved too. If you find that such an appointment clashes with another, then after discussions with your boss you will have to decide which takes priority. (See page 168 for details of how an electronic diary can take care of some of these problems.)

TEST YOURSELF

1 Your boss, the Managing Director of a department store, would like you to make the following appointments during the course of today. How long would you estimate each appointment should take and what additional factors, if any, should you take into account?

   a Your boss has a dental appointment at 3 pm (for an inspection only).

   b The Marketing Manager wants to discuss the cost of advertising the store's pre-autumn sale.

   c The weekly meeting of the Departmental Managers has to be fitted in some time during the day (it has been moved from its regular spot which was originally at 11 am yesterday).

   d Both the Human Resources Manager and the Company Accountant want to see your boss but both are available only between 11 am and 2 pm.

   e The Managing Director of a company which supplies the store with a lot of discount price furniture is calling for a 'flying visit' before catching the 10.30 am train.

2 You have been asked by your boss to arrange a meeting for him today

with the Human Resource and Assistant Human Resource Managers, the Training Officer, the Chief Administrative Officer and the Head of Computer Services. He wants to discuss the computerisation of the personnel records system and thinks the meeting should last about an hour.

You contact all the people concerned to find out the best time for the meeting and collect the following items of information:

- your boss is booked up between 11 am and 1 pm
- the Assistant HR Manager is away all afternoon on a training course
- the Training Officer has a lunchtime appointment and another at 5 pm
- the Chief Administration Office has an appointment from 1.30 pm to 3 pm
- the Head of Computer Services is not free until 3 pm.

Decide the most suitable time for the meeting. Justify your decision by stating the factors which made you come to this conclusion. Note down any additional action you now need to take.

Ways of monitoring and updating systems

Remember the old saying that 'what can go wrong *will* go wrong'. A good administrator or PA does not just wait until something goes wrong but tries to anticipate what is likely to go wrong – and to circumvent it wherever possible.

One of the methods which can be used is that of careful monitoring of the appointments system. Although you should be wary of constantly looking over someone's shoulder, you must check that the person responsible for making and entering appointments is competent – and trustworthy. A few minutes spent each day talking to those involved about the appointments for that day is time well spent. So too is the right attitude. You should try to encourage staff to ask you for advice if they are not sure whether or not to make an appointment and, equally, try not to show your annoyance if they admit they have made a mistake. Otherwise you may find that they make matters worse by trying to conceal any errors from you.

Some administrators and PAs make it their business to do 'spot checks' – normally on an informal basis. Others schedule a couple of hours a month to sit with the receptionist or junior responsible for inputting the appointments to see whether the system is working and where, if at all, any problems are likely to arise.

The monitoring of new staff is particularly important. In this case, although formal training sessions can be helpful, they need to be supplemented by 'shadowing' of experienced staff. You should know who to trust and who will set a good example. Sitting the newcomer next to the most slapdash member of staff is *not* a good idea! An informal word with the experienced member of staff – or a more formal report back as part of the induction training process – should either assure you that all is well or let you know that some further training is needed.

In the course of monitoring the work of other staff you may also discover that there are some obvious defects in the system. It is then up to you either to (a) decide unilaterally to make an alteration (if, for instance, you see that the communal office diary is insufficient and that another appointments system should be used) or (b) discuss the problem with your boss (if, for instance, the problem is lack of staff to keep the systems working efficiently).

Regular monitoring of an appointments system also assists you in determining whether or not it needs to be updated. If you never check what is going on, you might never realise that some changes need to be made. You may also be more receptive to articles you read in business journals about modern appointments systems such as the electronic diary (see page 168) or to visits from salesmen who want to demonstrate their firm's latest office aids.

Whether or not you perceive any problems, it is always a good idea to review all your office systems on a yearly basis (see page 154 if you need to remind yourself of the use of a methods audit). It is then up to you and your team to analyse how efficient your appointments system is and to agree and implement any possible improvements.

TEST YOURSELF

You work as an administrator in the Sales department. Your annual review meeting has gone quite smoothly until you reach the item on the agenda relating to the appointments system. Then tempers start running high. You operate a system whereby your boss has her own diary but there is also an office diary which is kept on the receptionist's desk. The receptionist is responsible for coordinating the diary entries (including transferring over the entries from the boss's diary). She also coordinates the appointments for the sales staff – both in and out of the office. When she is on her lunch hour or a break, the newest member of staff normally stands in for her as the rest of the staff always say they have too much else to do.

Normally this works quite well but in the past few weeks the receptionist has had some time off – for a training course and a holiday – and the junior has on occasions made some quite important mistakes. Several members of the salesforce are now arguing that they should be allowed to keep their own diaries because they can no longer trust the office system. Your boss is also getting irritable because on occasions her appointments have been muddled. The problem here is that she is a bit intimidating and when she has spoken to the junior direct, she has frightened her so much that the junior hasn't dared to tell the truth – which has made matters worse. The receptionist is indignant and asks why there is always mass hysteria every time she leaves her desk for a few minutes.

You realise that part of the problem has been lack of supervision. There has been a reorganisation at work and you have been so involved with that that you have left the office to run itself and have ignored the odd muttered remark about customers turning up and not finding anyone to speak to them or salesmen travelling miles to keep appointments which had been cancelled the day before.

Discuss as a group or with your tutor or adviser:

a   how you would calm the tempers of your staff during the course of the meeting so that they leave it feeling that something is going to be done

b   what follow-up action you would take to reorganise the system and institute monitoring and updating procedures to prevent a recurrence of these problems.

Ways of dealing with non-routine and emergency situations

Even the best planned system cannot possibly account for every eventuality. There will be times when an unexpected visitor arrives or your boss is faced with the dilemma of having to attend an emergency board meeting or meet an important client. There will also be occasions when someone fails to turn up for an important meeting or where a sudden crisis leaves you on your own in the office trying to coordinate a number of activities. As always, you can have a contingency plan to cover foreseen emergencies such as the absence of a key salesman (check back to page 129) but it is difficult to plan for something which is quite unforeseen. Much depends on your administrative skills – and your personality!

TEST YOURSELF

1   If you can honestly say that *none* of the statements given below apply to you in a crisis you don't need to read any further. If, however, you feel that one or two *might*, read on.

   –   I speak before I think.
   –   When I get excited, everyone gets roused.
   –   The more tense a situation, the more I talk.
   –   When I'm worried, I fall out with anyone who happens to be around.
   –   In an emergency I don't consult, I give orders – and woe betide anyone who doesn't obey them!
   –   When something unforeseen happens, it's always someone else's fault – never mine.

2   It is difficult to change yourself – but there are some strategies you can take to modify your behaviour in a crisis. Discuss as a group or with your tutor or adviser what you can do if you feel you ever react in any of the above ways whenever an emergency situation arises.

Types and uses of appointment management systems

The diary

As already indicated, the most frequently used 'appointment management system' is the diary.

There are very many commercially produced diaries from which you can choose, according to your own particular needs. Alternatively you may find that your organisation uses a standard diary bearing the company's logo and that these are issued to both staff and clients. Outside organisations may also supply your company with complimentary copies of their diaries. If, on the other hand, you work in a specialist area you may find that the appropriate professional institute (e.g. the Chartered Institute of Marketing) supplies its members with diaries designed around particular needs. These are likely to contain useful additional pages of information, e.g. on business travel or public holidays overseas, which you may find helpful.

If you cannot find a diary which meets your specific needs you may be able to create one for yourself. One approach is to use a ring binder in which you can insert customised diary pages designed specifically to meet your own requirements. Remember, however, to avoid a 'home made' appearance and to maintain your professional image; if you want to take this approach make sure that the binder is top quality and the sheets are produced on a desktop publishing system.

Whatever diary you use, you should check on the presence of certain essential features:

- it should be of adequate size (though not so large that it is difficult to carry)
- there should be at least one page for each day
- in normal circumstances it should run from January to December
- there should be an appropriate number of time indicators. This can vary from a page divided into 15 minute intervals to one which is divided into morning, afternoon and evening. (Note that unless you are working in a specialist area such as a dentist's or a doctor's surgery, it is normally advisable to have as few sections as possible to allow you more flexibility when making appointments. See below for details of an electronic diary.)

The electronic diary

Many offices today pride themselves on being 'electronic offices' and operate integrated computer networks with shared access to information (see Unit 6). If your company operates such a system then you should either make use of or investigate the possibility of obtaining an electronic diary facility. One example of such a system is shown in Figure 3.3.1.

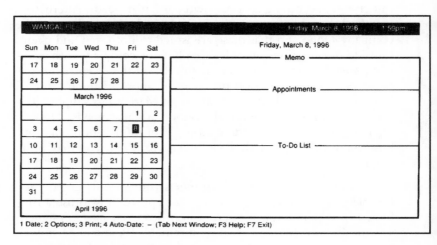

Figure 3.3.1 An electronic diary

The illustration shows the basic calendar screen. Note its four main features:

● **The calendar**
   You can select the date you require by moving your cursor key to the appropriate point.
● **The memo section**
   Use this section for reminder notes – the section will expand to incorporate all the notes you want to make.
● **The appointments section**
   Appointment times can be entered in this section – a 'window' will open for you to fill in the start time, the end time and the purpose of the meeting (see Figure 3.3.2).

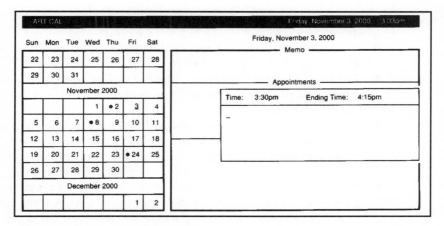

Figure 3.3.2 The appointments section

There is a 'zoom' option which allows you to see all the appointments for the day at a glance. Note that you will find it difficult to double-book appointments because the system will indicate to you where there is any overlap.

- **The 'to-do' list** You can list a number of actions you wish to take and, if necessary, have these prioritised. If, for instance, you enter two items and then decide that a third item takes precedence, the system will re-sort the list into priority order (see Figure 3.3.3).

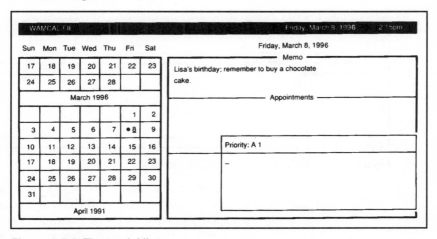

Figure 3.3.3 The 'to-do' list

Other facilities

- A recurring appointment need be entered once only. If, for example, you have a staff meeting at 10 every Monday morning, you need enter the appointment once only and it will appear on your calendar during the entire time period you specify.

- You can be reminded of appointments as they are about to occur by the sound of an alarm buzzer.
- The memos, appointments or 'to-do' lists can be merged into your word processing system if you require the information for, say, an invitation or an itinerary.
- The diary can also be combined with a small database containing names, addresses and telephone numbers of clients etc. You could therefore call up on your 'to-do' list the name of a person to telephone along with his or her telephone number.
- You may be given the responsibility for arranging a meeting for your boss which involves a number of people. A great deal of time can be spent telephoning round and making provisional bookings before a universally agreed time and date are fixed. The scheduling feature of your electronic diary system removes much of this work from your shoulders.

Figure 3.3.4 shows a computer screen on which is displayed a 'request' box and an 'organised' box. The request box lists the events your boss should attend. The organised box lists the events you have organised for him/her.

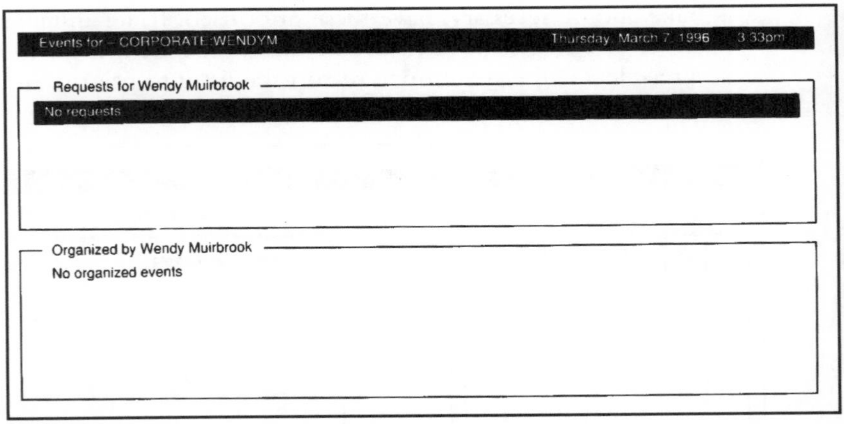

| Events for - CORPORATE WENDYM | Thursday, March 7, 1996   3.33pm |

Requests for Wendy Muirbrook
No requests

Organized by Wendy Muirbrook
No organized events

Figure 3.3.4 'Request' box and 'organised' box

If you move to the 'month' screen (see Figure 3.3.5) you will see that the calendar window on the left-hand side has a bullet (•) on every day for which you have an event scheduled. The window on the right shows the events for the day against which the cursor is positioned.

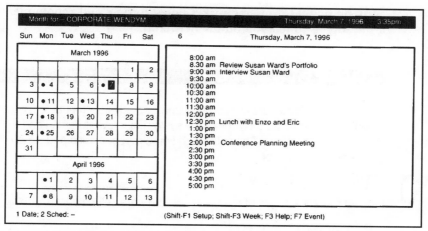

Figure 3.3.5 The 'month' screen

If you want to arrange a meeting for your boss with a number of people, you would key in the information relating to the event, the people involved, the place, the date and the length of the meeting. The information can then be transmitted to all the people on the list.

If someone is unable to keep that appointment because of another engagement, a bullet will appear to indicate a 'busy' time. You can then, if you wish, use the computer to search for an alternative available time.

Personal organisers

Your boss may wish to make use of a portable electronic diary rather than a Filofax. These are often known as electronic personal organisers with features which include:

- word processing facilities
- a database including diary and calendar facilities.

Info Bank, for instance, works as an address/phone book and a diary with a clock and basic calculator. When information is keyed in, the Info Bank itself sorts addresses alphabetically and puts diary dates in chronological order. It allows 'sensitive' data to be protected by a password. Another alternative is the AgendA, which contains a diary, calculator and file spaces for addresses. It also functions as a database and has a search facility which will find a file from any word entered into it.

You should note that unless your boss's personal organiser is compatible with your computer system in the office, and information can automatically be relayed and sorted between the two, a personal organiser can present the same sort of problems (and in some cases worse ones!) than the personal diary – especially if your boss takes it

Planning, organising and monitoring of work

away on business trips and makes notes, jottings and appointments in it but forgets to tell you on his/her return!

The *Business Equipment Digest* often contains advertisements for personal organisers and has an easy reference system of relevant names and addresses of suppliers. Check through some recent copies and send off for any relevant information.

 DID YOU KNOW?

Most of the advantages of the electronic diary are self-evident:

● reduction of paperwork
● reduction of time spent in contacting people
● reduction in the number of excuses about being 'engaged' at certain periods and unable to attend meetings!
● ability to combine a number of functions, e.g. appointments/database
● greater confidentiality (compared with the diary left on the top of a desk)
● on a networked system the receptionist can have automatic access to a chronological list of expected visitors.

There are, however, certain disadvantages:

● possible equipment breakdown or malfunction
● less room for manoeuvre if your boss wants an excuse for not attending a meeting!
● less persuasive than a telephone call.

Procedures and formats for recording appointments

Having agreed the ground rules, you can then turn your attention to the *ways* in which appointments should be recorded – no matter what system is used.

You must therefore establish certain basic rules for both you and your colleagues to follow to ensure that:

● Handwriting is clear and the names of non–regular visitors are printed. (You would also remind junior staff to obtain a first name and telephone number in case arrangements have to be changed.)
● Where necessary, the visitor's status or title is indicated (e.g. Councillor, Managing Director)
● Where relevant, an appointment made over the telephone is confirmed in writing
● A brief note is made of the business of a meeting (bearing in mind that some matters are confidential)

- All appointments are entered into the system as soon as possible. (If, on the first of the month, your boss mentions that he/she will be away on the 28th, don't wait until the 27th to enter the information!)
- There is some forward planning – regular meetings or appointments can be entered in the system weeks in advance or even for the full yearly cycle
- Provisional appointments are pencilled in so that they can be altered more easily (or erased altogether) should this be necessary. (Alternatively you may want to use certain abbreviations or signals [e.g. square brackets] to indicate that an appointment is provisional. Whichever method you use, make sure that everyone knows what it is and what it means.)
- If the system is to be used as an aide memoire or reminder system, those using it all follow the same approach. (For instance, everyone should be aware that it is office policy that reminders about collating papers for a meeting should be made a week in advance. See page 123 for further information about reminder/planning systems.)
- The procedure is adopted of crossing out entries immediately after the appointment has taken place. You can then tell at a glance what remains to be monitored, what has to be rearranged and what has to be checked up on (if, for instance, an important client has not appeared).

ACTIVITY SECTION

1   You work as administrator/PA to the Managing Director of an organisation which is at present experiencing some industrial relations problems. Several official meetings have taken place between the Board of Directors and Trade Union officials but no agreement has yet been reached. One afternoon you are attending an in-house training course on the new E-mail system which is being installed when you receive an urgent telephone call to return to your office. On your return you find your junior assistant in tears and your boss purple with rage. The 'behind the scenes' unofficial meeting he had asked you to arrange between him and the major trades union representative that evening is now common knowledge – there has even been a phone call from the local newspaper. You are amazed since you knew very well that the meeting was confidential and had not therefore entered it into the diary. However, you remember that you had asked your junior to get out some files for the meeting and also to arrange for some coffee to be available. She has tried to use her initiative and has entered the appointment in the diary which is available for anyone to consult. More worrying, however, is the fact that someone has apparently 'leaked' the information to the press – your junior totally denies having done this but it appears highly likely that the information must have been given to the press by someone working in your office.

Discuss as a group or with your tutor or adviser:

a what you would do to resolve the current crisis

b what measures you would take in future to prevent confidential information from being included in the diary

c what steps you would take to deal with a possible 'informer'
   i if you think you know who it might be
   ii if you have no idea at all who is responsible.

2 a You have been away on a week's training course on time management. You return to find that a series of notes has been left on your desk by a not-very-efficient stand-in administrator. You have to sort out your boss's diary for the following week (bearing in mind that you also have several regular appointments already scheduled).

State how you would deal with any obvious overlaps.

Regular appointments

Weekly Heads of Department meeting – Monday 9 am

Research and Development meeting – Friday 3 pm

Notes from temporary administrator

Norma Fairhurst coming at 9.30am on Monday to discuss final details of contract (must be away by 10.30am)

Don't forget – 21st Birthday Party – Sat 7.30pm for 8.

Fri to foll. Tues – International Energy Conservation Conference, Brussels. Leave office no later than 10.30am for airport!

Asif Patel rang – OK for lunch at 1pm Thurs – Providential Hotel.

(Golf lesson – Thurs 2.30pm!)

Jacques Lafitte – Paris Office – urgent tel. call – needs advice asap. Can be contacted in office between 9am & 11 Monday.

Figure 3.3.6

b Complete a standard page of a diary dated Monday, 19 August with the following entries and add any supporting information you think is relevant.
   – Your boss has to go to London on 20 August to attend a meeting at the London Chamber of Commerce and

Industry. Normally he travels on the 8.30 am train from Manchester Piccadilly to London Euston.

- Denise James, a chief reporter with an important technical journal, is coming from Glasgow by train to interview your boss at 10.30 am on 19 August.
- There is a monthly meeting of Departmental Heads next week and you will have to contact them to see if they have any items to put on the Agenda.
- This evening your boss will attend a Rotary Club dinner. Evening dress is required. Guests are requested to be there at 7.30 pm for 8 pm.
- A member of the Computer Services Department is coming to check your computer terminal at 9.30 am.
- Your boss has a lunch appointment at the Berlioz Hotel at 1 pm and wants to go straight from there to a building site in Didsbury to check over the findings of the surveyor with the Site Manager.
- Jim Robinson has an appointment to see your boss at 4 pm to discuss a building contract about which there has been substantial correspondence.

3 You work for Terry Gregory, Sales Director of a large company which exports textile machinery all over the world. The Sales department comprises a Sales Office Manager and ten Area Sales Managers, each responsible for a different territory – UK, Europe etc. In addition your company has agents and/or small branch offices both in the USA and most capitals in Europe. Mr Gregory is frequently away for several days at a time, during which period you liaise with the Sales Office Manager about any queries which may arise.

Mr Gregory is away at present at an exhibition in London. One of the Area Sales Managers, who was with him yesterday, has brought back a series of notes for you.

I appear to have some problems looming up for Tuesday, the 24th. Whilst I'm down here can you please try to sort out my diary for that day?

- You know that I want to travel to Paris that day but with all the other commitments it'll have to be an evening flight. Can you check what is available from Manchester?
- I know I'm due at the monthly Managers' meeting on Tuesday, but before that I must visit Production to see the new machine trials (for only about 20 minutes). I've also got to see the Area Sales Managers for about half an hour to discuss current sales positions.
- I need to have a separate word with Robert Evans and Barry Duerden. Bob sets off for Sydney on the Thursday and I think Barry leaves for Los Angeles on the Wednesday. Fifteen minutes with each will be enough.

- Fix up a meeting with Eileen Briggs in Personnel about the vacancy for Sales Coordinator – either in my office or hers.
- Can you confirm with Liam Neill of Dewey and Main that I can see him for about half an hour mid-afternoon to discuss the Canadian agency?
- If Farouk Aziz telephones, let him know the best time for him to drop in with some samples he wants testing – he'll only take a few minutes.
- Don Edwards wants to have a word with me about that computer program he's organising on sales statistics. He wants to demonstrate one or two things and is free either between 10 am and 11 am or after 3 pm. He says he'll need half an hour but you know him – try and make it longer.
- I'll need a breather – could you possibly schedule me to be in my own office between 2 pm and 3 pm – preferably seeing only internal people. If you arrange a snack for me at tea time we can go over the Paris stuff then – I'll go straight to the airport from the office. I won't be taking my own car so arrange a driver, will you?

After having read the instructions:

a   Draw up the draft diary Mr Gregory requires.

b   At the right-hand side of the page note down all the jobs you would have to do that day to make sure everything runs smoothly.

Managing time

Give me just a little more time. . .

If you think about it, the English language is full of phrases to do with time – and most of them are inaccurate! We talk about 'finding' time or 'making' time when we obviously can't do either! And we certainly can't 'manage' time in the literal sense, as this would imply being able to alter the clock whenever we felt like it.

Yet there are dozens of books written and management courses held about time management – so what is their aim? Quite simply, it is to enable you to identify how you spend your time so that you can control its usage more effectively. Good time management does not only relate to your work life, but also enables you to protect what the Americans call 'quality time'. This is the time you need for yourself – no matter how busy you are. Time to spend with your family, or your friends, to pursue a hobby or merely to relax – in order to recharge your batteries for the following day.

RULE 1

Learn to value your time – it is your most precious resource. It is the only one which is completely irreplaceable.

Time wasting

If time is so valuable, then wasting it must be a crime! If you waste an hour – and have to work late to catch up – you have eaten into your 'quality time' which you could have spent doing other things. So the pay-off for reducing time-wasting activities is tremendous!

Which of the following apply to you?

- Making unnecessary journeys (e.g. twice to the photocopier in ten minutes)
- Spending ten minutes looking for a document you should have filed last week
- Gossiping to colleagues (who call into your office, you meet on a corridor, etc.)
- Chatting on the telephone
- Shuffling papers – because you can't decide which job to start next
- Daydreaming – because you just aren't in the mood for work that day.

Most of us – especially on bad days – are guilty of some of the above. Problems occur when we regularly waste time in these activities.

> **RULE 2**
> You won't stop all your time-wasting activities overnight. Step one is to be aware of when you are wasting time; step two is to change your working habits.

The role of the boss

The problem for an administrator or PA is that even if he or she is organised, the schedule cannot be kept to if the boss wants to talk about recent happenings, the wording of a new report and so on! At the very least he/she will usually expect the administrator to be at his/her beck and call and to drop whatever is currently being done when an emergency occurs.

> **RULE 3**
> Standard time management rules cannot be applied to an administrator or PA as his/her boss is often the key controlling factor on time.

If you are very busy, and your boss constantly interrupts you or distracts you then you have to make a decision, is this because he/she doesn't know how busy you are – or doesn't care? If it is the former, then you need to be able to point this out, firmly yet politely (see *Managing communications*, page 506.) An executive normally wants his/her administrator to do a good job – after all, this is in the executive's own interests as well. You should therefore find that your boss will do everything possible to help you if there is an urgent job to be done, and you need a quiet hour to complete it – providing that you tell him/her.

If you have the type of boss who seems impervious to reason then you have a greater problem. One possibility might be to list all the jobs you have to do and ask your boss to prioritise them for you – he/she would then take responsibility for anything not completed. However, this is fairly drastic action and there is usually a better, more tactful method.

Other time stealers

How many of these are familiar to you?

- Procrastinating – i.e. putting off jobs which are boring or you don't want to do. Then getting irritable as the deadline gets closer . . .
- Flapping about – piling all your work in the in-tray and then dithering over what to do first
- Darting about – trying to do three jobs at once and not doing anything properly

- Taking on too much, from too many people, in an effort to please everyone – and ending up totally overloaded
- Having a schedule that goes to pieces the minute an emergency occurs
- Realising with a sinking feeling that the piece of paper you now have in your hand should have been posted two days ago!

RULE 4

Bad planning yesterday leads not only to wasted time but also to crisis points. These cause problems and take time to solve, thereby disrupting today's schedule – ad infinitum!

Techniques for time management

Learning to control and manage your time is a skill, and like all skills it has to be practised. Therefore do not expect to be an expert in five minutes. You will slip back into your old ways now and then – but remember, you have nothing to lose and much to gain from taking yourself in hand and trying again.

The areas to concentrate on are:

- office organisation and systems of work
- planning
- prioritising
- people
- self-discipline.

Because systems of work and planning are dealt with elsewhere, this short section concentrates on the people who may disrupt you – and how to deal with them – and the techniques you need to manage your time effectively.

People

There are three categories of people on which you should concentrate if you want to manage your time better:

- your junior staff – to whom you can delegate work (see Element 3.1)
- time-wasters – who may or may not be deliberate in their intentions!
- the 'do me a favour' sort.

Time-wasters

Be ruthless with the time wasters in your life (unless it's your boss!). This does *not* mean being rude to anyone!

Most time-wasters are colleagues who 'drop by' your office for some reason or another.

- Try to train them to phone you rather than visit.
- As an excuse to ring off, if necessary, say your boss is buzzing you on your other line . . .
- If the caller arrives in person, politely explain that you can't stop as you'll be in trouble if you don't finish the job you're doing in the next five minutes . . . or
- Keep a calculator on hand and a set of figures. When the caller arrives, frown and mutter to yourself. Say you can't talk or you'll forget where you are . . .
- Work out an emergency routine with your boss for real problem characters who can't take a hint. Arrange to be able to rush into his office with an 'urgently wanted file' so you can escape if necessary. (A variation on this routine also works well in reverse when your boss needs rescuing.)

The 'do me a favour' sort

Another type of problem person you will meet is the one who will ask you to do jobs 'as a favour'. Because most of us like others to think well of us we tend to say 'yes' in situations like this. Don't – unless there's a very good reason why you should (e.g. you're up for promotion and this person would be your next boss!).

Learning to say 'no' is very hard to do – but often essential. If you are asked to do something then ask yourself two questions.

1 Have I the time to do a good job, without jeopardising anything urgent or important?
2 Could it do me any good in the long run?

If the answer to both is yes, then go ahead. Otherwise say 'no' (see *Managing communications*, page 506).

RULE 5

It is not heartless to work out 'what's in it for me?' – simply cold business logic. However, don't think in terms of money. Building up favours can be far more useful – as you can call these in when you need help yourself!

Self-discipline

Probably the hardest part of all! We are all creatures of habit and it is therefore extremely difficult for us to change the way we operate. This is why you must work at time management if you want to see results – and not give up the first time something goes wrong.

- Eliminate time-wasting methods of working.
  - Reduce the time you spend walking around the building. Group jobs which have to be done or delivered elsewhere and do them in one journey.

- Don't put on the coffee machine and sit and watch the coffee filter through. You could do about three small tasks in that time.
- File whenever you have a spare few minutes. Don't wait for a chunk of time before you start it.

- Don't put off jobs which you don't like doing. Do them first – then give yourself a treat (a cup of coffee?) as a reward.
- Don't throw out your systems because you had a bad day. We all have occasional days where we seem to go backwards.
- Don't allow yourself to be lazy or idle! Set your own deadlines and challenge yourself to achieve them!
- Remember that a job well done doesn't come back to be redone tomorrow! Carelessness ruins both your image and your time schedules.

RULE 6

Don't expect miracles. Time management is a bit like going on a diet – you may slide back from time to time but if you keep at it you see the benefits later.

A final word of warning – and advice

Many people are hesitant about practising time management because they are frightened that if it works too well then they will have nothing to do. The extreme of this, of course, is that your job is seen as superfluous.

It is true, and rather sad, that if someone walks into your office while you are sitting staring into space, they are unlikely to believe your explanation that you were deep in thought about the best way to present the next monthly sales report. Instead they are likely to hurry away, comment to your boss that you have nothing to do, and he/she will feel honour bound to find you something.

Experienced administrators never quite operate time management to this extent but always keep one or two non-urgent tasks to do at quiet times. This prevents a disaster occurring as the MD decides to visit your particular patch on the very first day in the year that you have had very little to do. Remember your pending file? In moments of extreme crisis retrieve it and shuffle the papers, frowning at those you are holding. If you decide to wander around the office to see what is going on, carry a file or two with you. Remember that work in an office is always one of extremes and enjoy the reprieve – tomorrow will probably be hectic!

4 Create, develop and maintain effective working relationships

---

Element 4.1

Create, develop and maintain effective working relationships with colleagues

Few people work completely on their own, with no contact with other people. Even a teleworker will communicate with base or head office. The self-employed consultant will relate to clients, the self-employed shop–keeper will deal with customers and possibly a few members of staff. The fact that you are taking an NVQ3 award in Administration means that you are even less likely to be working alone.

Whether you are employed by a small or large organisation it is probable that you are working with a number of people every day. Some of these will be senior to you – from the managing director or chief executive to your own line manager. Others will work on the same level as yourself, though they may be employed in different sections or department. Yet others may be your juniors or subordinates – whether or not you have any direct control over them or their work. They are subordinate to you because they are lower than you in the hierarchy.

A further group comprises those with whom you have a working relationship but the scope of their job gives them a professional power over you, although they may be paid less or have only worked for the organisation for a short space of time. A typical example is a security guard or a canteen supervisor – both of whom have authority in their own areas. The security guard, for instance, has the authority to ask the Chairman of the Board to move his car if it is a security hazard.

Your relationships with all the people you work with are extremely important for a number of reasons. Firstly, because how you act and react to people will affect your own effectiveness and performance in the organisation. Secondly, how you relate to people will affect their behaviour and what they are willing to do for you and what they are not. This goes far beyond any official 'power' or 'authority' you may have. Official power may give people the power to instruct and coerce – it doesn't give them the ability to get instant and willing cooperation whenever it is needed! Certainly, you will never lead a team of people if you do not treat their personal needs as critically important – at least as important as your own.

A hierarchical organisation is one where there are several levels of authority. Often its shape is likened to a pyramid – because the higher you go in the organisation the fewer people you find at the same level. Today, flatter organisation structures are becoming more popular. The move towards this is often referred to as 'delayering' or 'downsizing' (Figure 4.1.1).

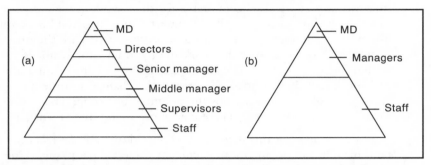

Figure 4.1.1 (a) A traditional pyramid structure (six levels); (b) a delayered structure (three levels)

Today you may also hear the term 're-engineering'. This refers to a complete restructuring of the organisation away from the traditional functional areas of Sales, Purchasing, Finance and so on towards a structure linked to the product range or other key aspects of the organisation.

Constructive relationships

What are 'constructive relationships'? Basically they can be defined as relationships where the parties involved:

● recognise each other's needs
● work productively together
● pull together and support each other when the going gets rough.

You will never have a constructive relationship with anyone all the time. However, the ability to be sensitive to someone else and do your best to work at and build on the relationship is a valuable asset – and not just in your working life. How to do this is the main focus of this element.

Your own work role and responsibilities

In many organisations your own work role and responsibilities will be documented in your job description. Your place in the hierarchy may be shown on an organisation chart. If you work for a small organisation it should be possible for you to draw an organisation chart yourself to show where you are – and to position yourself *vis-à-vis* the other people you work with. If you have no formal job description then it is fairly easy to make out a statement which shows:

- your main duties
- your responsibilities
- those people to whom you are responsible
- those people for whom you are responsible.

(See also Element 3.1, page 113.)

You should bear in mind that if you have authority over people then this means you are also accountable for their work as well as your own. Your line manager will not expect you to pass the blame on to them for incomplete or unsatisfactory work – if you are the one who is in charge of organising the work then you take the blame if something goes wrong. The higher people rise in an organisation, and the more staff they control, the greater the chance of something going wrong – and the more serious the potential outcome. This is one reason why senior managers are paid more than junior managers!

It is a good idea, at this stage, to also note down any *lateral* contacts you have in the organisation – whether these are people working in a similar or complementary work role in another section or people who provide a service you use, such as computer services staff, company drivers or the section head of the printing unit.

Use this information to list the people with whom you are in contact on a regular or infrequent basis. It is useful to highlight regular contacts in one colour and infrequent contacts in another.

Now think about the *importance* of each contact – regardless of their status or potential power position. Think more about:

- the people whose cooperation you need in order to function effectively
- the people you can bypass or ignore if absolutely necessary
- those who have the most influence over other people
- those who are the 'front runners' in the organisation and are admired by senior staff
- those people you find it easy to relate with and those who you find more difficult – and why
- the degree of importance you attach to
  - other people respecting you
  - other people admiring you
  - other people liking you.

CHECK IT YOURSELF

Discuss your answers to some of these questions with the rest of your group or with your tutor or adviser. Try to identify what your answers may be telling you about yourself – as well as about other people.

Colleagues' work roles and responsibilities

You can divide the people you work with broadly into three groups (Figure 4.1.2).

- Your inner circle comprises those whose cooperation is essential for the work that you do. They are people you interact with on a daily or very regular basis. These people are likely to include your own line manager, any staff for whom you are responsible, your immediate colleagues and lateral contacts who provide you with information or a service which is critical to your job role. These people comprise your immediate **role set** – i.e. the people who have expectations of you in relation to your own work and behaviour.

- The middle group is those people whose cooperation is extremely beneficial because it means you will be able to be both more efficient and more effective at your job. It should also include those who you would need to impress to gain future promotions – your boss's own boss, for instance. Don't forget that in this group will be some who can have negative power over you, e.g. by blocking what you want to do, refusing to help, giving your requests low priority or spreading disenchantment about you around the department.

- The third group comprises those whose cooperation you rarely need and who are normally outside your range of regular contacts. This includes people who have little, if any, contact with your boss.

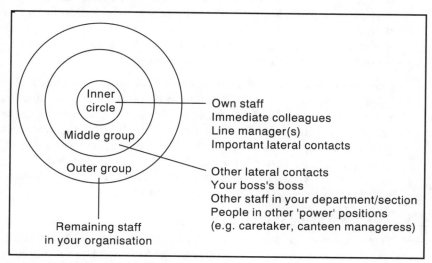

Figure 4.1.2 Groupings of colleagues

Your next job is to make sure that you know the work roles and responsibilities of all those in your 'inner circle'. This information will enable you to go to the right person with the right query or information and also to empathise more with the problems that person may face in coping with his or her own job. Knowing the work roles of these colleagues will on occasions also provide you with the ability to be one step ahead and to use your own initiative to provide information they may need or find useful – *without having to be asked*!

In relation to your own staff, it is absolutely essential that you are aware of the official work roles and responsibilities of all of them. You can hardly allocate work correctly, fairly or sensibly if you do not know who is supposed to do what.

The information is also important if there is an overlap between work roles which is causing problems. Often a section or department can grow rapidly and changing needs and requirements mean that work roles becoming out-of-date or blurred. Identifying a problem does not give you the authority to simply rewrite the job description of each of your staff, however! If a minor restructure could help the working of your section then a talk with your own boss, followed by discussions with your staff, is a far safer route to follow!

There is an old saying that 'information is power' and it certainly helps in relation to your circles of contacts. You know yourself that the longer you work for an organisation and the better you know who does what and who has the power to change schedules or procedures the more easily you can get jobs done. No longer do you have to spend ten minutes on the telephone trying to find out who deals with stationery orders or who keeps the software manual you need. If you have direct access to the people who make the decisions then this gives other staff less opportunity to be awkward or difficult to deal with – or to refuse, for instance, to book out a manual to you without written authority from your manager.

The outer group of people are not those for whom you need detailed information. However, it is sensible to be polite and courteous to everyone you meet or have dealings with – if your own work role changes then the people in your circles will change and someone with whom you had few dealings in the past may start to loom large in your life. It is far better if they react to the knowledge that they will be relating to you more often with pleasure rather than with irritation based on past mishaps or misunderstandings!

DID YOU KNOW?

Teams are more productive than groups. Whereas a group of people can have a common purpose and a common leader, a team has a balance of roles so that the weaknesses of one member are counterbalanced by the strengths of another. Further information on the difference between groups and teams and how to manage a team is given in the section on *Managing other people*, page 251.

Figure 4.1.3 shows the role set of Paul Watson, an office administrator. The importance of each person he deals with is indicated by the different sized circles. The closeness with which they work together is indicated by the length of the lines.

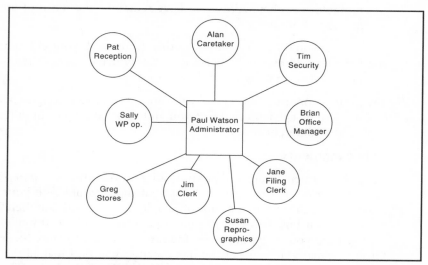

Figure 4.1.3 Role set diagram

Draw an internal role set diagram for yourself using the same techniques.

Roles and their implications

All employees have a formal role which determines the jobs and functions they are expected to perform. This is usually documented in a written contract of employment or a job description. The written role will determine the expectations of their colleagues. For instance, the switchboard operator is expected to answer incoming calls, the caretaker to keep the building secure and clean and so on.

However, there will also be informal expectations in relation to areas such as behaviour, appearance, communications and attitudes. It is likely, for instance, that your staff will expect you to be loyal to them and to defend them if they are criticised. In return, you may expect that they will be loyal to you and will not go over your head, e.g. by reporting a problem direct to your own line manager.

These expectations form a **psychological contract** between you and any group of people or individuals that you work with – in other words, an unwritten agreement between you. If this is breached, on either side, then relationships between you can deteriorate rapidly.

For instance, suppose you have always had an unspoken agreement with your boss that, in return for helping out during busy times, you can have personal time off by agreement. Then if you suddenly found your plans for a last-minute shopping trip were blocked after working unpaid overtime for two weeks you would probably want to renegotiate this 'contract'. Because it is unwritten, you are unlikely to burst into his or her office and demand an explanation. Instead, you would probably withdraw your own cooperation next time extra help was required. In other words, you have redefined the terms of the psychological contract.

Just as you would be tempted to do this, so too will your colleagues and your staff if you suddenly act in a way which breaches their psychological contract with you!

Two other important aspects of 'role' are those of role congruence and role conflict. Each can affect you and your colleagues in different ways and at different times.

Role congruence

Role incongruence means that your different roles do not agree with one another or are dissimilar. A typical example would be if your standing is high with one group of people but low with another. For instance, your boss sees you as a good performer and worthy of representing your department on the newly-formed Quality Steering Group. When you arrive at the first meeting you find that all the other members are fairly senior managers in the organisation. This would obviously present problems if, for instance, you disagreed with some of their suggestions or felt they were inappropriate for your own section.

Role conflict

This is a broad term which includes several problems where expectations about role are dissimilar between groups of people or individuals. It includes

- **role ambiguity** – when you are not sure what you are supposed to do or why. This could be because your boss is a poor communicator or manager and doesn't make clear his or her expectations in areas such as your behaviour, range of responsibilities or degree of initiative required.
- **role incompatibility** – where you have to cope with situations which include simultaneous different or contradictory requests or expectations. Administrators or PAs who work for two bosses may find they suffer this regularly. A less obvious example is being given express instructions from your boss which you know will be considered unpopular or unfair by your own staff. In other words, when there is a conflict between your loyalty to your boss and your loyalty to your staff.
- **role overload** – when you have so many people to keep happy and in so many different ways that you cannot hope to win. For

instance, if you run a large office and have to deal with a multitude of requests from staff you will always have to neglect some people in order to please others. Note that this is different from work overload when you simply have too many jobs to do at once.

- **role underload** – possibly the most unsatisfactory of all – is where you feel undervalued and dissatisfied because your perception of your role is greater than that of your boss. This may mean that you are not allowed to take on tasks which stretch your abilities. This can occur after you have been in the same job for some time and can do the routine parts easily. The problem is exacerbated if you work for someone who is a poor delegator or who feels threatened by the progress of others.

CHECK IT YOURSELF

1 Refer back to the role set diagram you created showing the people with whom you regularly interact in your workplace. Try to define the psychological contracts that exist between:
   - you and your own line manager
   - you and your colleagues
   - you and your staff.

   Think about the attitudes, beliefs and expectations that each of you has and the 'unspoken agreements' which exist in each arena.

2 Identify occasions when you have suffered from:
   a role incongruence
   b role conflict.

   Discuss what you have done or can do to prevent or solve problems in this area.

3 Identify occasions where your behaviour can cause role conflict for your colleagues or staff. What do you consider is the effect on them personally? Try to think of at least five ways to reduce or avoid role conflict for them.

DID YOU KNOW?

Role conflict is a key factor in determining stress at work. It can result in minor ailments, various illnesses and days lost through absenteeism.

CHECK IT YOURSELF

The best methods to use to reduce role conflict depend upon you, your boss and the people for whom you are responsible. Although guidance can be given, the degree to which it is applicable will vary from one organisation to another. Figure 4.1.4 gives some useful tips to help you wherever you work.

WAYS TO REDUCE ROLE CONFLICT

1 Where possible, try to define job roles precisely but still give scope for personal development and independent action.

2 Don't just issue written job descriptions – discuss how you interpret these and your own expectations of your staff with each person individually.

3 Don't deliberately ask people to do a job for which they will be unsuited and then watch on the sidelines as they make a mess of it. Match tasks to people's individual strengths and abilities to get the best out of them.

4 Offer immediate help and support to those who are struggling to cope with something new or a difficult member of staff.

5 Intervene if someone is making life difficult for your own staff. If necessary ask your own boss for help if a greater level of seniority is required or if the structure of the section is causing problems.

6 If a person is continually under-performing in a particular job or area then find out why. If necessary, be prepared to look at reallocating tasks or restructuring the section to change the person's job role.

7 Do not change a person's job role without consulting him or her first. Be sensitive to any implication that he or she will feel downgraded.

8 Arrange for training and retraining to take place in line with people's personal development and career plans.

9 Do not underestimate the abilities of your staff – and then grumble that you have all the work to do! But warn them when you want to do something extra or new, make sure they clearly understand what you expect and remove any barriers or obstacles to the task being completed successfully.

10 Learn how to:
   – motivate your staff
   – build a successful team
   – handle conflict situations.

Figure 4.1.4 Ways to reduce role conflict

The organisation chart and working relationships

The job titles of all of the people may be shown on the company organisation – together with their official links. However, do bear in mind that this chart only shows the **formal relationships** which exist. Informal relationships are not shown – and these can completely change your perspective of who has power and who has influence in your own organisation.

The type of **informal links** you may find include:

- **historical links** – the Human Resources Manager and the Production Manager went to school together; the Sales Office Manager and your own boss started work in the organisation on the same day 10 years ago
- **social links** – the Managing Director and the Finance Director play golf together every other Sunday; the brother of the Administration Clerk in Finance is married to the Sales Director's younger sister
- **employer/employee links** – the Managing Director was the Sales Manager until two years ago and is still good friends with the (now) Sales Manager; the new Marketing Assistant used to work with the Marketing Director at his previous company and has now been hired by him for his skills and ability
- **current links** – the company is currently concerned with installing a new computer system: a new computer expert has been poached from a neighbouring company because of his expertise and is at present very highly regarded by the Managing Director.

DID YOU KNOW?

There is a critical difference between power and influence. Power is the ability to make decisions about work and people – and some people are better at making good decisions than others. Power is linked to expertise, control, charisma, position or authority – from the army general or football manager who can give orders because of his position, to your doctor or solicitor to whom you defer because of his or her professional expertise, to the 'cult' leader or pop star who controls people through his or her powerful personality or charismatic qualities.

Influence, however, is the ability to change events – usually by persuading those who are in power to act in a certain way. As a specific example, the Managing Director's PA usually has little power but may have tremendous influence. Making an enemy of or ignoring a PA because he or she is not highly placed in the organisation could be one of the biggest mistakes you ever made!

TEST YOURSELF

Look back at all the executives and other personnel mentioned above. Identify:

a who has power
b who has influence

and how you would use this information to influence your own behaviour in relation to all these members of staff.

Discuss your ideas and views with your tutor and the rest of your group or with your adviser.

Establishing constructive relationships

Believe it or not, constructive relationships are formed more by the way you think than the way you act. The reason for this is that the way you think about other people influences:

a your behaviour towards them, and
b their behaviour towards you!

The whole thing becomes a spiral which can work evenly and constructively or can – all too easily – spin out of control for a number of reasons.

We all have our own perceptions of other people. These perceptions are based on:

● our own history and personal experience
● our beliefs, values and attitudes
● the amount of confidence (or insecurity) we have
● our personal history of that particular person.

Unfortunately, whether our perceptions are valid or accurate is something we rarely question. Instead, we are likely to act in accordance with our beliefs and then find evidence to substantiate our previous views (and ignore evidence which doesn't!). This is often known as **self-fulfilling prophecy**.

CHECK IT YOURSELF

To help you understand this concept more clearly, read the case study below and answer the questions which follow.

Sarah is in charge of four staff in the admin office. She had a bad experience with one, Mark, shortly after he started. Although Mark was basically insecure he covered this with a mask of bravado and irritated Sarah with his 'couldn't-care-less' attitude. Joanne is the newest member of the group. She is shy and timid and needs coaxing along.

Sarah is frantically busy at present and urgently needs two routine jobs doing very quickly. She rushes into the office and quickly gives Mark his instructions. She is quite short with him, so that he won't have any opportunity to be cheeky or answer her back. She takes her time explaining the job carefully to Joanne, knowing that the girl is unlikely to ask for help, even if she doesn't understand what to do.

One hour later Sarah returns to collect the work. Mark has completed his job but made two or three errors. Joanne is only half-way through her task. Sarah goes mad when she sees Mark's work and shouts at him in front of the others. She is more understanding with Joanne and tells her to continue as she is doing a good job.

When she leaves she confides in a colleague, 'That boy will drive me mad – he'll have to go. He can't seem to do anything right. Joanne is different altogether – I mustn't do anything to destroy her confidence.'

1 Can you identify both the differences *and the similarities* between Mark and Joanne?
2 In what way is Sarah's behaviour contributing towards *both* their problems?
3 How can you explain Sarah's apparently contradictory behaviour towards each member of staff?
4 In what way is each member of staff's behaviour reinforcing Sarah's perception of them?
5 What could you suggest to 'break the circle'?

TEST YOURSELF

Identify **one** person in your own workplace with whom you have difficulty. Try to identify and state your perception of that person and state *why* you hold those views. Now identify how those views affect your own attitude and behaviour towards him or her.

As an experiment, change your behaviour the next time you have some dealing with that person. Don't expect a miracle to happen immediately – or you may be very disappointed. Just remember, if you expect the worst you're likely to get it! Try to keep a note over a period of about a month to see if there are any changes in his or her behaviour in response to your own.

Forming constructive relationships

The basis of a relationship is often formed *before* you meet someone for the first time! This is because your reputation – and theirs – usually precedes the first meeting. As an example, before an interview you will be influenced by the written letter of application and the CV, and during the interview a person's manner and appearance will affect your perception of them. After making the appointment you may discuss the new member of staff with your staff and your colleagues. In this way you will influence their perceptions of that person – even before they have met each other! In a similar way, if you have recently been promoted to your job, you can be sure that rumours will already have been circulating and your new staff will be interested in finding out if what they have been told is true!

The difficulty for most new administrators is that they may have been promoted because of their *task* skills rather than their *people* skills. You may have got the job because of your ability to type the perfect report or deal with people expertly on the telephone. Now you need to acquire a new set of skills altogether – all connected to getting the work done *through other people*. This involves not only managing the tasks but also motivating, guiding, communicating, leading and developing your staff – and, possibly, relating to a new set of colleagues.

There is a danger in over-reacting at this stage of your career. You can either 'go in hard' in some mistaken belief that you should 'start as you mean to go on' and 'show them who's boss'. This approach is likely to lead to serious problems – particularly if your predecessor allowed the group considerably more autonomy!

At the opposite extreme, you may be tempted to be 'one of the gang' and to think that, although your job title has changed, you will get on better with everyone if you work alongside them and show them that you believe in equality for all. This, also, is usually unsuccessful. Your staff want to see you as a leader – someone upon whom they can depend for support, help and guidance. You can only provide this if you can stand back from the day-to-day situation and take a more objective and pragmatic approach.

A good starting point is to think carefully about your own expectations of other people and the style of leaders you admire. You can then come up with a list of 'golden rules'. For example, you may admire someone who:

- shows a genuine interest and always makes time to listen
- knows when to give support and when to stand back
- is always fair, consistent and doesn't play favourites
- trusts, respects and is loyal to his/her own staff
- has clear standards, sets measurable and achievable goals and gives praise where it is due
- is 'open' about feelings and beliefs
- doesn't insult staff – either intentionally or unintentionally
- helps people to believe in themselves
- fosters initiative in others
- is sensitive to the needs of others
- never makes promises and fails to keep them.

Working to this remit is not easy. It would be easier if people were all the same and could be treated as one. However, each individual you deal with has his or her own principles, beliefs and expectations – some of which will be consciously held and some of which will be unconscious. Therefore, even if you match up to the expectations of one person, you may disappoint someone else. Don't let this worry you. Part of being a supervisor is learning to live with temporary unpopularity! You will never please all your staff or all your colleagues (or your boss) all the time – and the quicker you come to terms with this fact the better!

 ### DID YOU KNOW?

Chris Argyris, a sociologist, identified a major weakness in many leaders. He considered that many people have one belief which actually influences their behaviour (their 'theory-in-use') and another which they say they believe in (their 'espoused theory'). Unfortunately, although the two may not be the same the individual concerned is usually in blissful ignorance of this fact. Therefore although your boss may say it doesn't matter if a particular job isn't finished on time because the deadline is unrealistic, you may also know that he or she expects everyone to work overtime to complete it. If you follow the 'espoused theory' you may wonder why you are less popular than the person who took the work home to complete it!

Maintaining constructive relationships

The golden rules given above for forming constructive relationships from the outset may seem overwhelming in themselves. However, to sustain constructive relationships you need to have additional skills or abilities. For instance, over any period of time there will be occasions when:

- you will have to give information or instructions which your staff or your colleagues do not like
- there may be disagreements or conflict which you have to try to resolve
- you may have situations to cope with which will stretch your loyalty, discretion or tact to the limit
- personal or work-related problems may arise
- you may have to discipline a member of staff
- the output or quality of work from either one individual, or the group as a whole, may diminish.

Each of these areas is dealt with separately below with suggestions to help you to cope. However, do remember that you can learn much from other people – from their experiences and how they have coped. Therefore, at the end of each short section which follows you will find points for discussion with either the rest of your group or with your tutor or adviser. You can benefit most by listening to the views of others (thereby testing your listening skills!) and exploring your own feelings and experiences in this respect. 'People-skills' is an area where you can benefit far more from exchanging views with other people than you can by reading books!

Seeking and exchanging information

In your job there will be times when you need to find out information, times when you need to impart information and other occasions where you need to exchange information. This can be done verbally or in writing, formally or informally, directly or indirectly, privately or publicly. The method to use will depend upon the type of information, its sensitivity and the person or people involved.

Seeking information

You should note that 'seeking information' in this context does not refer to researching external or internal data (see Unit 5). The type of information you require is much more likely to be concerned with:

- current work-in-progress and future tasks
- timescales allowed
- people's abilities to meet deadlines
- changes which are required
- problems and emergencies
- other facts which influence your own job.

Task-based information

The system you set up for ensuring that you know the amount of work being dealt with by your section at any point in time is up to you – and will vary depending upon your particular job and responsibilities. However, to be able to organise anything efficiently you need to know what is going on. You can usually find this out through:

- written documents, e.g. work plans, job schedules
- visual aids, e.g. planners and schedulers
- regularly talking to your staff
- regularly talking to your boss
- observing the amount of work in your staff's in-trays.

You may need to be particularly vigilant on this issue with some members of staff. Whereas some people may complain loudly the minute they feel over-burdened with work (or even *before* they do!), others will bear the brunt more stoically, may get snowed under with a multitude of jobs to do and say nothing. If you are insensitive to this, the first hint of a problem you may have is when that particular person goes off sick through stress! There is also a danger that you always give the work to the 'willing workhorse' – especially if he or she always goes a good job – thereby exacerbating the problem.

You can prevent this problem occurring by:

- good planning in relation to the delegation and allocation of work to your staff
- a good knowledge of their individual personalities, attitudes, strengths and weaknesses, skills and abilities
- having regular discussions about the amount of work which is outstanding and progress of existing jobs
- knowing the 'pattern of work' in your section – e.g. are you always busier at certain times of the year or on certain days? Is the morning always hectic and the afternoon less so?
- stepping in with support if problems occur which staff cannot be expected to handle on their own. For instance, if the workload increases dramatically or staffing levels are low because of a 'flu epidemic then hiring a temp for a week or so may be the answer. As another example, if one person in the office consistently gives out 'emergency' jobs which need doing immediately, so throwing out all the work schedules, then you may need to have a quiet word with this person.

DID YOU KNOW?

If you are in charge of a group of people it is likely that, although you know what *they* do, if you work in a separate office it is highly unlikely that they know what *you* do! This may lead to some unfounded rumours that you simply hand over all the work and sit around all day reading the paper! Part of your communication system with staff should be to make it clear just how busy you are as well. If you are not, and they are run off their feet or trying to complete an emergency job quickly, you would naturally pitch in to help ... wouldn't you?

People-based information

Information about tasks is far less sensitive than information about people. If one of your staff, a colleague or your boss looks particularly upset or distracted then you might want to find out why – but writing a memo to ask would not be the brightest idea you ever had! You may want to make some quiet enquiries through another member of staff who works closely with that person. If you are unsure as to the accuracy of the information you are given then the 'triangulation' technique (i.e. cross-checking with someone else) will usually give a better indication of whether it is true or not.

What you then do about the problem will depend upon the person involved and the information you have been given. Problem-solving is dealt with in more detail on page 209.

Your own work activities and patterns

In addition to having discussions with your own staff, you will also seek information from other people in your role set or inner circle on a regular basis. Your boss will expect to have some idea of what you are doing and when – and frequently administrators undertaking a PA role will have a 'diary check' with their boss at regular intervals to ensure each knows what the other is doing. These sessions are useful not just for logging new appointments, but also for giving a quick run-down on work-in-progress and obtaining an update from your boss on new developments, expected work, new orders and so on. You can then agree the action which has to be taken in each case. It is then up to you to communicate this information to everyone else who needs to know.

Making commitments
Task-based commitments

No matter what type of job you have to do, it is unlikely that you can have a totally flexible deadline for anything! Even if the only job outstanding in the office is a backlog of filing, it will get on everyone's nerves – and waste a lot of time – if all the papers have to be sorted through every time someone wants a document! You are likely, therefore, to be asked to agree a deadline when the filing will be up-to-date. Remember that the commitment will stand in relation to both yourself and any staff for whom you are responsible – as you will be making the commitment on their behalf (which is another good reason why you need to know what is going on in your section).

Task-based commitments may range from finding a piece of paper or researching some information to producing a 100-page report or undertaking a cost/benefit analysis on a new photocopying system. You have already seen how to plan and agree targets in Element 3.1. Any commitments you make must be honoured within the agreed timescale otherwise, at best, many people may be inconvenienced and, at worst, your company could lose an important customer or order. For that reason, you must ensure that:

- any deadlines or later changes to schedules or working instructions are communicated immediately to staff
- staff have the resources they need (including time!) to complete the work properly. This should include time for checking and revision, if this is likely to be required
- your own staff tell you if they are having problems meeting a deadline in good time for you to take remedial action
- prompt action is taken to rectify the situation. Whether this action involves renegotiating the deadline, helping out yourself, reallocating routine jobs or getting in extra staff will depend on the importance of the job and current work-in-progress.

People-based commitments

In terms of your personal working relationships, people-based commitments may be accorded even greater importance than task-based commitments by your colleagues and staff – if not by your boss! By doing things for other people – however small or insignificant these things may seem at the time – you will not only get a reputation for helping people and keeping your word, but will find that other people will help *you* when they can. This does not mean that you should either become the office 'general mug' or that you should carefully list every favour you do and then call in all your markers at the first opportunity! It simply means that by extending your commitment to people above and beyond that specified by your actual job, you will find that, generally, other people will want to do the same in return.

CHECK IT YOURSELF

Refer to the role set you produced for your own job (page 187). Discuss with your group or adviser:

- the type of information you would seek from each person listed and the type of discussions you would have on work activities
- the type of commitments you make to colleagues (and they to you) and the culture or 'ethos' in your organisation for doing this.

Imparting information

At times you have to provide information to other people. Good communication skills are a key aspect of your job. Neither you nor anyone else can operate effectively if you do not tell each other anything! However, there are right and wrong ways in which you can give information.

Don't

- make it a guessing game
- imply there are certain things you know but other people should not – either because they are not important enough or for any other reason. If the information is confidential then do not say anything!
- dissociate yourself from unpleasant news you are having to give to your colleagues, e.g. 'the boss has decreed, but I don't agree with him, that we should...' At this level you are paid to toe the party line in public
- pick a time or place to impart important, complicated information where people do not have the time or inclination to listen or where you may be frequently interrupted
- gossip, spread rumours or speculate, be two-faced, claim the credit for something which you haven't done, tell lies or exaggerate problems.

Do

- think about what you are going to say in advance to make sure you cover the key points in a logical way
- consider how the recipient(s) are likely to react to the information – and what you are going to do about this
- make it clear, if you are talking to a group, when people can ask questions to clarify what you are saying – i.e. do you want them to interrupt as you go or wait until the end?
- give basic facts as accurately as you can, without embellishment, using simple, straightforward terms. Don't give your opinions unless asked to do so and then be careful – these may be repeated in a way you had never intended!

DID YOU KNOW?

Many managers and supervisors devise a system of team briefings to impart important information to staff quickly. This ensures that all staff are kept well informed on all the issues which affect them and also know the reason why things are being done. Because all staff are 'briefed' at the same time they all receive the same message. There is therefore less opportunity for rumours to circulate or for misunderstandings to arise. Team briefings also give managers the opportunity to highlight achievements and success and this can boost everyone's morale. Even if you are not at management level, there is nothing to stop you implementing your own system of regular team briefings to keep your staff well informed.

Exchanging information

There is a vast difference between telling people something and exchanging information. In the first case you are stating a fact which is true or making a request which must be carried out. In the second you are asking for someone else's views and comments or asking your team for their contributions. Therefore, whereas a team briefing would be a suitable format for giving information, a meeting (or telephone call) is a more suitable arrangement for exchanging information.

Whenever you are in a situation where information is being exchanged there are various points you should bear in mind.

From your side

- the amount of information you wish to (or should) give
- the specific points you wish to stress
- the amount of 'negotiation' which is possible (see page 137)
- your personal view of the situation.

From the other person's side

- the individual personality traits, strengths and weaknesses of the person or people involved
- their relationships with you and other people
- their individual skills and areas of expertise
- their personal view of the situation.

There will always be members of staff who will listen, say little and just appear to 'go along' with anything which is discussed at a group meeting. This does not necessarily mean that they agree with everything which has been said. They may lack the verbal skills or confidence to participate or may have 'opted out' of the whole process. It is important that you identify which of these reasons is affecting their behaviour.

Equally, there will be others who are forthright – they will hold strong views and may put these forward quite forcefully! If these are the opposite views to your own then you may feel you are being overpowered or are losing control of the situation.

Talking to someone about a contentious issue may be very difficult, particularly if that person is senior to you. However, talking to a group of staff about an issue with which they disagree is not easy either! You will be helped if

- you normally have a good working relationship with those involved
- both you and they have an 'open relationship'. This means that fears, worries and concerns (including yours) can be openly discussed without recrimination. This reduces the amount of 'defensiveness' required and enables you to have a more full and frank discussion
- you are able to put your points in an assertive, rather than an aggressive, way (see *Managing communications*, page 506)
- you are able to 'pull it together' at the end by summarising the points raised and then agree on a way forward which recognises everyone's perception of the situation.

DID YOU KNOW?

The term **hidden agenda** is used to describe the hidden motives behind the actions or words of many people. For instance, during a meeting one person may raise an issue deliberately to embarrass or impress someone else. Alternatively, a member of staff (including your boss) may decline to do something but refuse to say why. This results in unequal knowledge within the group – one person knows something that the others do not.

Equally, individuals – or even the group itself – may have **blind spots** about which they are unaware. An individual blind spot may be known to the rest of the group, who all react with laughter at one person's offer to do a task because they do not think he is capable of seeing it through – although the person concerned is bewildered by their reaction. Similarly, the group as a whole may have a blind spot which they all cannot see – such as their difficulty in adapting to new procedures – but which may be very apparent to you and your boss.

Both hidden agendas and blind spots prevent a group from performing effectively. The more open you can be with one another, the better (see also the Johari Window, Element 1.1, page 9).

TEST YOURSELF

Discuss your answers to the following questions with the rest of your group or your adviser.

1. One member of your group is consistently under-performing at present. You want to find out the reasons for this but have a feeling the group as a whole will try to protect him.
   a. What methods would you use to find out the possible causes of the problem and why?
   b. What reasons can you suggest for the other members of the group wanting to protect this person?
   c. How would this affect your judgement about the information you receive?

2. In your workplace, what systems are used to ensure you are kept well

briefed in relation to information which concerns you? What systems do you use with your own staff? Do you feel these are adequate or could be improved – and in what ways?

3   Think of a meeting you have organised or attended at which information was exchanged (or make notes at a meeting you are about to attend). Identify the degree to which:
    –   the meeting was well-organised and well-run
    –   any member had a hidden agenda
    –   any member had a particular blind spot
    –   the meeting was controlled
    –   people's views were heard and considered.

What improvements could you suggest?

4   Count all the times in which you interrupt someone during the course of a week or fail to concentrate or show interest in something they are saying. Watch how often other people do this and note the effect on the other person. What are your findings?

Giving advice and support

If listening skills are important in relation to information in general they become *doubly* important in relation to counselling staff – whether your boss, colleague or junior. Indeed, all professional counsellors receive training in how to listen to the stated message and also recognise the underlying message – often shown by tone of voice, manner and body language. Frequently, people feel better just for being able to tell someone about a problem – whether or not that person can offer any specific help or assistance. If you are a particularly astute or sensitive person then you may even be able to identify when a person needs advice or support before they have asked you – though you will have to be careful not to rush in and offer it when it isn't needed!

The worst thing you can do, during such a conversation, is to leap to conclusions, give your own view of the situation, state how you would solve it and then expect the other person to do the same! Everyone is different and the solution which may be right for you may be an anathema to someone else. Equally you will probably need to have a different approach depending upon whether you are talking to your boss, a colleague or a member of your staff. Seniority, age, personality, work history and personal circumstances are all factors which influence the type of advice and support someone may expect. For instance

● your boss may simply want to 'let off steam' to you without expecting you to be able to do anything practical to help
● your colleague may simply want to chat and feel better afterwards – just because there has been a sympathetic person to talk to

- your staff may expect rather more practical advice and guidance in what they should do – particularly over work-related matters.

DID YOU KNOW?

When you listen is as important as *how* you listen! People who want your advice or support may come to you at the worst possible moment – yet if you send them away they may never come back again. If someone is worried or distressed it is important that you make time for them *now* – no matter how busy you are. However, there is no point doing this if you continue to fiddle with papers, try to read your mail and take two telephone calls at the same time! Neither will you get anywhere if you keep glancing at your watch or use any other form of body language which indicates to the other person that time is scarce or you have little sympathy for what he or she is saying. Listening means paying attention and not jumping to conclusions or making rash statements!

CHECK IT YOURSELF

Without giving away any confidences, identify occasions when your boss, colleagues or staff have needed advice and guidance. Think about how you felt, how you reacted and whether you think you gave positive assistance and support or not. Are there any ways in which you could have done better?

Discuss your ideas with the rest of your group and with your tutor or adviser.

Dealing with disagreements and conflicts

No relationships run smoothly all the time. Within any group of people there will always be occasions when people disagree. This may be a relatively mild incident and over in a few moments. On other occasions it may be quite serious and can even escalate into a mini 'war' between two people with the rest of the staff involved in taking sides. In this case the productivity of all staff is threatened as more energy will be expended on the conflict itself than on the work to be done.

Many writers consider that it is impossible for any organisation to operate without some conflict, mainly because of the different roles people have to undertake and the fact that each is competing for both resources and rewards. Two colleagues vying for the same promotion, two sales reps chasing high targets, two managers wanting an increase to their budget are all examples of people brought into conflict by the organisation itself and the way in which it operates. However, this type of conflict can be seen as **constructive** if it is controlled through a process of discussion and negotiation – so that, for instance, each manager sees the viewpoint of the other more clearly.

Conflict can, however, also be **destructive** when both sides become warring factions trying to destroy each other – and this is more likely to occur in some organisations than others. The culture of the organisation will, to a large extent, determine the type and degree of conflict that is and is not acceptable.

If you work for an organisation where everyone speaks to one another politely, where there is deference to those in authority and where few views are challenged, then this does not mean that everyone is happy and contented – it simply means that there is less open conflict. You will then get a shock if you change job and work somewhere else where people say exactly what they think, sometimes at the top of their voice, and think nothing of swearing at someone with whom they are annoyed!

In some organisations managers actually encourage conflict in the mistaken belief that this will increase performance as each person tries to outdo everyone else.

You can identify unhealthy and destructive conflict when you see:

- people becoming angry, hurt, upset or frustrated – and not doing their job properly
- more time spent discussing the conflict than doing any work
- people bearing grudges against others – and looking for opportunities to retaliate
- the person involved looking for other people to take his/her side
- a feud developing between different groups of people.

The difficulty with disagreements and conflicts is that people get themselves into a position where one of them has to back down. Both refuse to do so – and so the pattern is set. Ideally you should step in before the situation gets to this stage, otherwise the job is much harder – though not, usually, impossible.

Coping with conflict

Most disagreements and conflicts occur because of **blame allocation** – I blame you for something and you blame me. This may relate to an actual event where something went wrong – or because we hold different points of view. I say that you cannot see what I mean and you say the same about me. At that point there is stalemate. Each of us will concentrate on getting our version accepted but will not try to understand or acknowledge the other. The next time we have to interact we will be even more strongly fixed in our attitudes – and may have long since forgotten the original source of the problem. Such a feud can go on for years if nothing is done about it, and may turn into a vendetta where each of us resorts to 'dirty tricks' such as backbiting, lying or making life deliberately difficult for the other.

The only way to break the deadlock is for each of us to start to recognise that the other person has every right to have a different view of reality. This does not mean that there is agreement. It simply means that the other person's version of reality is acknowledged and given some validity. If you deny me my right to a point of view I will become very frustrated. If you acknowledge my point of view – even though you don't agree with it – then together we can work towards establishing a joint reality which contains a mixture of both views. There should be enough components from each viewpoint for each person to feel that his or her feelings have been recognised.

People who are aware of this can stop conflicts almost before they begin. You may hear someone saying, 'I hear what you say, and agree with your point about . . . However, I also think that . . .' This is much more productive than saying, 'Good heavens, where did you get that stupid idea from?' – a statement which immediately puts the other person on the defensive. For the same reason, you should also guard against accusing or attacking other people or coming out with any remarks which will invoke immediate hostility or irritation.

DID YOU KNOW?

One unfortunate side-effect of the modern way of working with its emphasis on high productivity, downsizing, delayering and increased workload has been the growth of the blame culture. You can see this in operation every day by just reading a newspaper or listening to the news. When something goes wrong it is easier to find a scapegoat to blame rather than to try to put the problem right. Preferably a 'faceless body' is named as the cause – such as an organisation, the economy, the government or a group of people, e.g. parents, young people, workers or management.

When blame is allocated in this way it does not solve the fundamental problem – it only avoids the issue and creates conflict between those who apportion the blame and those who receive it. The latter then defend themselves by blaming those who blamed them – and so it goes on.

The 'I win, you win' idea of conflict

Obviously it would be marvellous if every time there was a conflict or argument both people could come out of it feeling as if they had won! According to many writers this is quite possible.

Figure 4.1.5 shows the different results if either you or your 'opponent' are uncooperative/cooperative or unassertive/assertive. In the middle is the compromise situation. However, a compromise is usually a 'middle road' which neither of us are particularly happy about! How do you move towards the win/win situation in the top right hand corner?

Suppose that I want to go France on holiday and you want to go to Spain. A compromise may be to go to Switzerland, though this does not really please either of us. There are two ways in which we could move to the win/win situation. Either

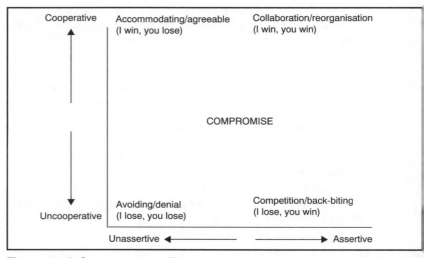

Figure 4.1.5 Outcomes to conflict

- we find another location which *does* suit us both equally, or
- I convince you (or you convince me), quite genuinely, that France or Spain would be the best for both of us.

Remember that win/win is a state of mind. If we are both really pleased to be going to the same place then that is the ideal outcome.

CHECK IT YOURSELF

How do you react when you are faced with conflict yourself or have to try to mediate between two other people embroiled in a battle? Do you join in the fight, try to help or run away? Try to find out by doing the questions below – and then discuss your answers, either as a group or with your tutor or adviser.

1   How much organisational conflict exists where you work? Is this encouraged or discouraged by management? Can you cope with the culture in respect to conflict or do you find yourself in situations where you are continually frustrated, upset or annoyed?

2   You have a distinct personality clash with a woman in your office which has been going on for some time. You know that she talks to your colleagues about you when your back is turned and can't believe she is saying anything positive. She withholds information she knows you need but afterwards denies having done this and says that she forgot. If she can show you up in front of other people – preferably with your boss present – then she does so. What is your response to this and how do you think you could break the pattern?

3   a   Everyone's response to conflict is based on how assertive they are

and how cooperative they are prepared to be. Check with your tutor or adviser that you understand how to 'read' Figure 4.1.5 and how the different win/lose, lose/win situations are reached.

b Map on Figure 4.1.5 your natural response to the last five conflict situations you have been in (either in your personal life or at work) and think about what this tells you about yourself.

c Look back at the scenario given in question 2. Given that the person described appears to be both assertive and uncooperative, what would need to happen to move towards a 'win/win' situation?

DID YOU KNOW?

You can use the 'win/win' logic to help you in many dealings with other people – not just conflicts. If you have a suggestion to put to someone, or want to persuade someone to do something, then thinking of how to state this so the other person comes out of it as a winner will help. In other words, what is the benefit to the other person of doing what you say? If you make this clear in your discussion then you will be more than half way to achieving what you want.

Dealing with confidential information

At this stage of your career, confidential information goes some way beyond knowing what your boss wrote to the MD last week or the sales figures for last month. As an administrator or PA you are paid to keep confidential any information which you have to handle in the course of your job – and this can now include confidential information about other people.

You may, for instance:

- regularly handle staff personnel records which gives information about their date of birth, last appraisal and salary
- type memos relating to disciplinary procedures being taken against a member of staff or grievance procedures being instigated by a member of staff
- be privy to your boss's views on members of staff and his or her perception of their performance
- be told, by your boss, of the latest discussions at Board level or about gossip concerning senior staff
- be told, in confidence by your colleagues, of personal problems they are experiencing
- hear, on the grapevine, about the escapades of junior staff or the high jinks of some others!

Generally, to be liked, respected and trusted, you have to learn to keep your mouth shut. People will only confide in you if they know you can keep a secret. If you once break a confidence and word gets out then no-one will trust you again – particularly your boss!

However, problems can occur when you receive or hear about information which could be detrimental to your boss, or the organisation, and which then causes a conflict of loyalty. At what point should you break a confidence and tell your boss – and, even more difficult, at what point would you or should you go over your boss's head?

TEST YOURSELF

Mary is the Administrator in charge of a large sales office. There are six members of staff in the office – mostly female – and the office is regularly visited by the sales reps. Mary's boss is the Sales Manager who is frequently away on business. He reports to the Sales Director of the company who operates at Board level.

Four weeks ago a member of Mary's staff, Julie, was absent with 'flu. During the same week, one of the reps also took two days off. Last week the sales rep had rung in sick with a migraine. This coincided with a day Julie had booked for some personal leave. The office is now buzzing with the gossip that the two of them are having an affair.

Mary's boss is away at present and she is in the process of completing his expense claims for last month. She notes that he has scribbled a figure for travel which she cannot read. When she checks this against her records she finds that the two do not agree – her boss's claim is considerably higher than the amount she has recorded. When she looks down at some other figures, she finds the same trend. Overall, his claim is £500 more than the actual figure.

Discuss the following questions as a group and with your tutor or adviser.

1   a   What action should Mary take about the gossip in the sales office:
      i   now
      ii if Julie and the rep are off together again?
    b   What could be the consequences of each course of action you have suggested? Try to think of best-case and worst-case scenarios and also possible consequences in between the two extremes.
2   What action should Mary take about her boss's expense claim – if any? Decide the advantages and disadvantages of:
    i   doing nothing
    ii   confronting him
    iii reporting him.

    Do you think it would make a difference if, on checking the records, Mary finds that his previous expense claims have been equally inaccurate?

Conflicts of loyalty

Thinking through the consequences of different courses of action is essential when you are dealing with sensitive issues or conflicts of loyalty. What you must *not* do is to act in haste or to react to rumours or unsubstantiated gossip. One way round this is to warn people about the gossip without saying that you agree with it or acting as if you do! Often a 'tip-off' is all that is needed.

Basically, if people are acting in such as way as to damage the reputation or standing of either your boss or your organisation then this must influence your decision. Your first loyalty, after all, is to those who pay your salary. If you are seriously worried about the actions of a senior member of staff then one way to solve your own dilemma may be to talk to another senior person in confidence – preferably someone who is not involved with and does not have line responsibility for the person concerned. Having passed on your worries in confidence you have then absolved yourself if something goes seriously wrong in the near future.

Problems and proposals

In the same way that information can concern tasks or people, so can problems. Again you are likely to find that the problems concerning tasks are far more straightforward. This is basically because you can identify what is wrong and then do something about it. The issue is likely to be fairly clear-cut – if the computer breaks down you need to get it repaired, if there is a backlog of work then you need to investigate why and suggest appropriate action, and so on. However, problems concerning people are usually much more difficult to solve – because often you are not sure about their possible reactions or what might happen next.

TEST YOURSELF

You have two problems to address as a matter of urgency.

- The photocopier has broken down for the fifth time this week and the repair person will not arrive until 3 pm. There is an urgent 45-page report to send out to 20 customers tonight.
- Your boss has informed you that on three occasions this week customers have complained about the attitude of one of the junior staff on the telephone. He tells you to sort this out quickly and to keep her off the telephone until she learns to use it properly. At present she is scheduled to relieve the receptionist at lunchtime and there is no-one else available to take over this duty. It is impossible to do this job and not answer the telephone. The time now is 11.30 am.

1 Which problem would you find the easiest to solve?
2 Which problem would take the least time to solve?
3 How would you solve the easy problem? Identify the steps you would take.
4 What are the difficulties you might encounter in solving the harder problem?
  i Start by listing *all* the people involved.

ii   Now identify possible courses of action you could take.

iii What are the range of possible reactions you might meet in each case?

iv   How would the personality traits of each person affect your decision about which course of action would be best?

Discuss your answers with the rest of your group or your tutor or adviser.

Problem-solving techniques

You learned about one problem-solving technique when you undertook the exercise above. This is based on the fact that people often go wrong by not thinking around a problem and by not thinking through the range of possible outcomes. There is a tendency to over-simplify problems – particularly those concerning other people. Other dangers include:

- acting first and thinking later – because you feel you are expected to do something quickly. You must make time to think things through first and analyse what is involved

- assuming you know the answer because it has happened before. It is very rare that one problem has identical components to another. Even if the problem is *similar*, the timescale and the people involved may be different – which makes it a completely different problem

- assuming you need to know everything there is to know before you can do anything. If you wait for this to happen then, nine times out of ten, you will not be able to do anything until it is too late

- thinking you can do it all on your own without help. A problem shared is almost always a problem halved – but do make sure you brief the person who is helping you properly by giving him or her the full picture. Two heads are invariably better than one – often you can encourage the whole team to help (see below)

- thinking you must solve every problem that crosses your desk. This is not the case. Firstly, some problems improve (or even go away) if you do nothing – or they may change or even solve themselves! Secondly, the more you involve your staff in solving their own problems – or making suggestions or ideas for solutions – the more committed they will be to making the solution work.

Golden rules to follow *always* include:

- defining the problem – is it likely to be
  - a temporary difficulty
  - a serious, ongoing problem
  - something between the two?
- defining where the problem starts and ends. Can you, in effect, draw a boundary around it or could it have repercussions in all sorts of directions?

- deciding if there an obvious solution or someone who could solve it easily for you
- deciding whether it is task-based (and therefore could be solved by changing working habits or routines) or people-based (and therefore likely to be more complex)
- considering the various approaches possible and then choosing one
- consulting your staff over their views
- deciding on or negotiating a solution.

(Note: see also the section on *Managing problems*, page 334.)

CHECK IT YOURSELF

Figure 4.1.6 gives some of the main theories on how people make decisions and is closely related to problem-solving. The aim is not to select one theory and decide to follow it. Instead, use the information to help you analyse how you think when you are faced with a problem – and the different ways in which it is possible to approach it. Used properly, the figure can give you some insights into alternative courses of action which you could follow – and their possible effects.

TEST YOURSELF

1   Identify at least one occasion when you had a problem, couldn't get round to doing anything about it and by the time you did, one of the following had happened:
  a   the problem had changed completely
  b   someone else had solved it
  c   it had gone away on its own.

2   Read the case study below and answer the questions which follow. Then compare your answers with those of other members of your group or discuss them with your adviser.

Mark was promoted to administrator two weeks ago and appeared to have inherited a series of problems from his predecessor. The staff for whom he was responsible couldn't wait for him to start in the job so that they could tell him all the difficulties they were experiencing. One which bothered them a lot was the fact that the computers and software they were using were out-of-date when compared with many of the other offices in the organisation. This restricted the type of jobs which could be done and the quality of work which could be produced. In particular, they had no access to a modern word processing or desktop publishing package and had been criticised on two occasions recently for producing sub-standard customer documentation.

  a   Using *each* of the decision-making theories given in Figure 4.1.6,

THEORIES ON DECISION-MAKING*

Theory	Method	Advantages	Disadvantages
The rational approach	Collect all information Analyse it Make rational decision based on data Evaluate possible outcomes Propose action	Easy to defend	Impossible to collect *all* relevant data Apt to favour data that proves own view!
Limited rationality	Collect as much information as possible Add to this with own opinions and views Obtain 'best possible' decision in time available	Allows for 'grey' areas Recognises personal input	Relatively inflexible method How good is 'best possible' decision?
Rules and precedents	Refer to similar past cases Look at precedents Find out organisational rules which apply Give ruling	Easy to justify People expect to follow rules Simplest method	Some cases have no precedent Few problems are exact repeat of others No staff input
Symbolic action	Obtain views of colleagues Interpret how they will react Take action which accords with popular view	Includes staff input/beliefs Usually popular choice	Often a compromise solution Time-consuming May not be best answer
Garbage can analysis	Only solve problems when need to (too busy to solve those which aren't urgent) Problems and information arrive in random order Match together in best way possible	Often accords with what really happens! Saves time working on problems which may solve themselves	Haphazard approach Some problems may be overlooked

Figure 4.1.6 Theories on decision-making

decide how Mark would handle the computer problem. Don't be surprised if you end up with five entirely different answers!

b   Analyse each answer and say which solution you think that you would favour – and why.

c   What limitations do you think there might be to Mark's possible plans for action and how could these affect the proposed outcome?

Informing versus consulting

The symbolic action method of solving problems involves the consultation of staff. However, this does not mean that with other methods you should not ask colleagues what they think! You would be very foolish to make any major decisions affecting other people without involving them at all. Everyone acts more negatively towards an imposed solution than a negotiated agreement. In addition, once you have people's approval of an idea you have also obtained a commitment towards making it a success.

The problem with consultation is that it is time-consuming and many administrators may be worried that staff views will be put forward which will be difficult to cope with. The advantage is that you can test people's reactions to any ideas you have had before you put them into practice and make sure you have backing – so that you cannot be accused of 'going it alone' and then failing if your idea doesn't work.

Consulting upwards

This means talking to your boss about your idea. It is a good idea to float the idea at an early stage with your boss, rather than to present a full plan. Otherwise you will look more as if you want a pat on the back than his/her views! However, you do need to have a fairly clear plan in mind, or you may look foolish if asked to explain it in more detail. If the plan is complicated then it is useful to have sent a draft outline of your suggestions to your boss earlier. This can then form the basis of the discussion.

If your boss is against the idea, try to find out why – it will improve your perception of the type of decisions he/she wants you to make and those which are outside your remit.

Consulting laterally

This means referring your idea to your colleagues for their views. One or two trusted mentors can be very valuable as sounding boards for your views and often give you useful guidance. The biggest danger in floating a good idea to the office at large is that someone tells your boss about it before you do – and gets all the credit!

Consulting downwards

This refers to asking your staff for their opinions. If your staff are unused to this approach they may be suspicious of your intentions or see it as a sign of weakness that you can't make any decisions on your own. They may also have little comprehension of the complexity of some of the problems and feel disheartened if they cannot contribute or all their suggestions are ignored. If you feel that they would have little to contribute then the answer is quite simple – don't consult them at all. Consultation must be genuine – not a stage in a process which everyone perceives as false.

DID YOU KNOW?

Almost the worst sin you can commit is taking an idea from your staff or one of your colleagues and presenting it as your own. Once word gets round, it is doubtful if anyone will ever suggest anything to you at all.

Varying your approach

It goes without saying, after all that you have read, that you should not expect to use the same approach for every situation that occurs.

Just as there are many ways in which you can look at problems, there are even more ways in which you can vary other aspects of your behaviour – how you communicate with people and how you act with them.

Sensitivity is a key issue in this; knowing where to draw the line is another. There is a huge difference between the approach you should use to help a member of staff who is encountering personal or work difficulties and that which would be appropriate if you are disciplining a member of staff who systematically turns in shoddy work or regularly arrives late. You need to use an approach which is suitable for the situation – plus a good sense of timing and a 'feel' for the possible reactions from other people.

There is a tendency to assume that everyone acts in the same way as yourself! If a quick reprimand from your boss would put you in agony for weeks then you may be more than a little surprised to find that the new junior seems impervious to the same treatment from you – and wonder where you have gone wrong! You must always remember that people differ in the way that they react to situations and allow for this where you can. This may mean acting in an unfamiliar way – e.g. by being tougher or softer than you normally would – in order to achieve the desired reaction.

Identify at least one person amongst your colleagues who would fit each of the following descriptions.

1　He's so thick-skinned that everything you say to him is like water off a duck's back!
2　He thinks he knows it all. I've never met anyone with such a good opinion of himself.
3　She's kind and understanding – always tries to help you if she can.
4　The most steady and dependable worker we've got – you can set your watch by him.
5　Up one minute and down the next. You never know where you are with her.
6　The dizziest person alive! If you don't spell out every instruction three times you might as well save your breath.

What approach would you use with *each* of them if:

a　you needed help with an urgent job
b　you were trying to point out that his/her current work was not up to standard
c　you wanted advice on a serious problem?

Discuss your answers with your group or adviser.

Methods of communication

There are a variety of ways in which you can communicate with people. You can:

● write to them or talk to them (or use E-mail)
● see them casually and informally, e.g. over a working lunch, or formally, at an interview or meeting
● see them in person or ring them up
● see them in private or discuss something in front of other people.

No matter which method of communication you choose, your aims should be the same:

1　to make sure people receive the information they need clearly, unambiguously and promptly
2　to maintain the constructive working relationships you have already established.

To achieve (1) you need to have good written and verbal communication skills. To achieve (2) you need to have additional skills in relation to 'tone', 'timing' and – in some cases – 'tenacity'.

Written communication skills are covered in Unit 7 of this book. Your verbal skills are something else – as, too, are your non-verbal skills. Verbally you should be able to:

- state your case simply and unemotionally
- use a range of vocabulary to express yourself clearly
- be tactful and diplomatic over sensitive issues
- listen carefully to answers you receive without interrupting
- generate enthusiasm and commitment
- emphasise key points
- refer back for clarification where necessary
- summarise a discussion easily.

However, no matter how fluent you are there is little chance that you will succeed if you:

- issue orders when you should be making requests
- forget the basics like 'please' and 'thank you'
- patronise people below you (by 'talking down' to them)
- spend twice as long as you need to telling people something
- interrupt people at their busiest times
- expect instant action to last-minute requests
- forget to follow things up later.

For that reason you should always make sure that your 'tone' is right in relation to the person to whom you are talking, you choose the right moment to approach someone and you make a note to follow up your request at a later date if nothing has been done. Reminding people tactfully is an even greater skill than asking them in the first place!

CHECK IT YOURSELF

As a group, or with your tutor or adviser, discuss the type of people who irritate and annoy you when they communicate with you. Then try to analyse *why*. Finally, try to identify any faults you may have which irritate other people – if you are brave enough you could ask a trusted colleague for his or her view!

 ### DID YOU KNOW?

Your style of communication is greatly influenced by your personality. A way of analysing this is through Transactional Analysis, which gives you a way of seeing how and why people say the things they do (including you!). It cannot guarantee to solve your problems in dealing with other people, but can give you useful insight into why you say the things you do! Transactional Analysis is dealt with in the *Managing communications* section on page 506.

Legal and regulatory requirements

The most obvious area where legal and regulatory requirements relate to working relationships is in equal opportunities legislation and policies. These were dealt with in detail in Element 1.2 and 3.1. Turn back to pages 40 and 139 now and refresh your memory if you need to.

Equal opportunities and working relationships

One of the most difficult problems you could encounter as an administrator/PA is a member of staff coming to see you because they feel they are being discriminated against or harassed – either sexually or racially. Harassment constitutes unwanted behaviour of a sexual or racial nature which adversely affects a person at work.

Sexual harassment

Both men and women can encounter sexual harassment. The degree of severity, however, can vary – there is a difference between complaining about hearing a sexist joke and a complaint by a junior that a senior director made a strong pass at her on the car park last night. A person has the right to complain about sexual harassment if he or she is:

- touched by a colleague either unnecessarily, repeatedly or intimately
- asked about his or her sex life
- the butt of sexual comments or innuendoes, lewd remarks or gestures
- the victim of an offensive joke or prank
- shown sexually offensive or explicit photographs or documents
- asked for sexual favours
- threatened for not complying
- sexually assaulted.

Complaints about sexual harassment in the workplace have increased enormously in the last few years. In 1993, the Equal Opportunities Commission received 793 complaints – an increase of 58% from 1992.

All organisations need a clear policy on sexual harassment which is communicated to staff. If no help is forthcoming from the organisation then the victim can seek help from the Equal Opportunities Commission.

A good sexual harassment policy will make sure that:

- sexual harassment is clearly defined and examples are given
- all staff are clearly aware that both sexual harassment and fake claims about sexual harassment are disciplinary offences
- a clear procedure is laid down for dealing with complaints
- the procedure gives the complainant the right to go over the head of his/her immediate manager if necessary
- an informal first step is available if this is appropriate
- both the complainant and alleged harasser are accompanied at any meetings held to investigate the complaint

- all complaints are handled discreetly, sensitively and confidentially.

Racial harassment

Although given less publicity than sexual harassment, racial harassment can be even more widespread and just as insidious. Originally harassment cases came under the 1976 Race Relations Act. Since July 1994, when the Race Relations (Remedies) Act came into force, there has been no ceiling on the compensation payable in race discrimination cases. In May 1995, a black salesman was awarded £34 000 in an out-of-court settlement by a car dealership in London. Do bear in mind that racial discrimination and harassment do not focus simply on black people. In June 1994, an Ulsterman received compensation after being sacked for objecting to a sustained campaign of jokes and taunts about being Irish.

An employee can complain about racial harassment if he or she is:

- subjected to taunts or racist jokes
- subjected to abusive language with a racial content
- called a racist name
- shown racially offensive material
- questioned persistently about his or her private life, culture, ethnic origin or religion
- given more work than other members of staff
- given more menial jobs that other members of staff
- unreasonably excluded from normal conversation or events.

 DID YOU KNOW?

- Although the term 'harassment' may seem to imply that several incidents must have taken place, this is not true. A person can successfully claim to be harassed if only one incident has occurred.
- Race for Opportunity, launched in autumn 1995, has been formed to help organisations to implement racial equality policies in the workplace.

Methods of motivating people

A good starting point for thinking about motivation is to think about what motivates you! However, it is worth noting that the factors which motivate you can change – from person to person and over a period of time. Therefore when you are young, a key motivator may be risk and excitement (which is why some people like working as tour operators or war correspondents!). When you are older, money may loom large in your life – especially if you have a family. From 40 onwards you may be more keen on security and stability. However, do bear in mind that these are very broad generalisations and will not be applicable to everyone!

Generally speaking, however, key motivating factors for everyone are factors such as:

- demanding, challenging and interesting work
- having a sense of achievement at the end of each day
- having achievable, clear standards to work to
- being rewarded for effort and results.

These factors are far more important than good food in the canteen and new paint on the walls – although a pleasant working environment is obviously a bonus.

Today, when organisations are often struggling to make sizeable pay awards or delayering has meant that promotion prospects are limited, some companies are coming up with more original and sophisticated ways of rewarding high flyers and good performance. These range from Marks and Spencer's gift vouchers to driving rally cars or taking holidays abroad for the fortunate few. One recent winner chose an audience with the Pope as the prize!

Incentive programmes or flexible benefits – which can include medical insurance, life assurance, policies for dental care, childcare and disability protection – are also becoming more popular and are slowly taking precedence over standard 'perks' such as a company car. There is a recognition by employers that staff welcome more varied ways of rewarding them.

Motivation, however, is not just about rewards. Motivation also includes staff involvement and participation in decisions which affect them. Many companies 'tap into' the wealth of staff experience and knowledge by having suggestion schemes.

Motivation guidelines

- Get to know your staff as individuals – if possible find out what 'makes them tick'.
- Keep staff up-to-date on information which affects them.
- Involve your staff in decision-making whenever you can.
- Encourage staff to bring their ideas to you – often they will know better how to do something than you will!
- Don't worry, frighten or threaten them – or use the grapevine for this purpose either.
- Support people with problems and advise or coach those who are making mistakes or having difficulty mastering a task.
- Keep them interested and challenged without being stretched too far or overloaded.
- Build on their strengths and help them to disguise their weaknesses.
- *Always* give immediate praise for a job well done.
- Help them to solve their own problems.
- Delegate work to them – not the bits you don't want to do or

can't be bothered to do, but work which they will find interesting (see Element 3.1, page 116).

- Make sure good performance is recognised through any company scheme.
- Protect them from attack and unfair judgements.

DID YOU KNOW?

Whereas many companies operate performance-related pay awards for individuals, a recent survey carried out by the Institute of Employment Studies found that only 10% operated these for teams and team achievements. If your company has a suggestion scheme in operation, perhaps you should suggest that it does this!

CHECK IT YOURSELF

There are many theories of motivation to which you can refer for guidance. Additional information is given in this book in the section on *Managing other people* on page 251.

In addition, you may like to look through some management or business textbooks for the theories of Herzberg and McGregor to broaden your understanding of this area.

Organisations' reporting procedures

All organisations have a range of reporting procedures to cover different events and contingencies. These can relate to issues as diverse as lost property to grievance procedures, work planning and appraisal interviews.

It is important that you are aware of any reporting procedures which you must follow in your dealings with staff at all levels. These can include:

- records of meetings and discussions
- minutes of meetings
- internal memos sent in relation to staff
- other forms and documentation.

If you do not follow the correct procedures then you may cause difficulties for other staff – particularly if a problem or complaint escalates. If disciplinary action is taken against a member of staff, for instance, it is very important that records have been kept on earlier discussions and copies of memos and letters regarding this person are on file.

Similarly, if you fail to keep any record of your response to serious problems you could find difficulty in defending your own position later. In the case of a complaint about harassment, for instance, you could even be accused of trying to do a 'cover up' campaign to protect the alleged harasser!

A good rule of thumb is to identify any issue which could become a major item and to make sure that you keep full records as evidence of the actions you took.

Finally, in any case where you are having a major difficulty with a colleague or a group of staff, do be prepared to refer the problem upwards for help, advice or guidance. This is far better than 'going it alone' and, eventually, handing over a massive problem which you have made even worse! You are also advised to exercise caution if you are not sure whether or not you have the authority to take a certain action. Again, it is better to refer the problem to your boss for clarification and agreement than to exceed your own remit.

Most line managers will respond positively to requests for assistance and would infinitely prefer this to sorting out a myriad of problems later – after all, when the day comes when you are sitting behind that desk, isn't that what you would want, too?

CHECK IT YOURSELF

1   Make a list of six issues in which you could be involved which involve other people in the organisation.
2   Check that you know the reporting procedures to follow in each case in your own organisation.

ACTIVITY SECTION

1   Your friend has recently moved from working in a solicitor's office to working as an administrative assistant on a local radio station. Claire was thrilled to get the job but is having difficulties adjusting to the change. She argues that it is not the content of the job which is causing her problems but the people.

   –   There appear to be frequent arguments and disagreements between staff. One producer hasn't spoken to another for over six months.
   –   Several production people have been made redundant in the past few months or have had their contracts renegotiated. This has created a feeling of insecurity amongst existing employees, some of whom seem to delight in boasting of their own success and belittling their colleagues.
   –   Claire has been promised day release next year and wants to take her NVQ3 in Administration. Her boss thinks a media course might be more suitable.
   a   If Claire has to deal with both the 'warring' producers, how could she cope with conflicting instructions from them both?
   b   Claire is involved in confidential meetings regarding the possibility of further redundancies – which the Station Manager is trying to avoid if possible. A female member of staff is becoming a pest trying to

find out what is happening at the meeting. She has told Claire that her husband is ill, she has four young children and must keep her job to survive. Claire knows that this woman is not on the possible list anyway. What should she do?

   c How can Claire move the disagreement about her future training to a 'win/win' situation?

2 Your boss is having an extremely fraught week. She has two complicated reports to produce for her own boss and an urgent statistical return to complete. To help her with the latter she enlisted the help of a member of your staff. On the morning the return is due, the junior concerned rings in with a migraine.

   a How would you break the news about your junior to your boss?
   b What difference would it make to your approach if your boss was:
     – usually laid-back and easy-going
     – highly strung?
   c If your boss then blames you for the problem, how would you react?
   d What practical help could you suggest?
   e What would you say to your junior, if anything, on his/her return?

3 Your boss has asked for some key points in relation to defining and implementing a company code of practice about racial harassment. He realises this is extremely prevalent and wants to improve practices and procedures in the organisation.

Using the guidelines on page 217 (under Sexual Harassment), make a list of the key points he should bear in mind.

4 Identify one problem you have had at work in the past few months. Outline the problem clearly, including what you did about it at the time.

Now analyse what you *could* have done had you followed each of the approaches outlined in Figure 4.1.6 – and the possible outcomes that might have occurred in each case.

Element 4.2

Create, develop and maintain effective working relationships with external contacts

An interesting – although brief – exercise on some management or supervisory courses is to try to identify a type of organisation which has no contact with the outside world. This organisation is 'closed' in that it is totally self-supporting and self-generating. Suggestions usually include prisons (not true – they need supplies) and eventually end up with enclosed orders such as Trappist monks or Carmelite nuns. In reality all enclosed orders have lay workers who communicate their requirements to the outside world – although this is probably about as close as you will ever get to a completely closed environment.

The conclusion from this is that in the modern world virtually all organisations interact with a variety of different external bodies and organisations every day. These include suppliers, customers, shareholders, public sector organisations (police, fire brigade, local authority, government departments and quangos, educational institutions), and other commercial organisations, such as banks, accountants, solicitors and architects. In addition there are a whole host of other 'support workers' – from cleaners to security staff, from the plumber to the electrician to the technician who checks the burglar alarm. This is especially true for organisations where the majority of this type of work is contracted out to outside suppliers.

Whilst the range and scope of external contacts will vary from one organisation to another, and from one job to another, their existence is a key aspect of most administrative jobs. All organisations will be more productive and more profitable if there is effective liaison with outside contacts.

 ## DID YOU KNOW?

A modern term for describing the range of people with an interest in an organisation is **stakeholders**. In other words, all the people who have a 'stake' in the organisation and its future. If the company 'goes under' then a host of people suffer – from the window cleaner to the stationery supplier. In addition, of course, staff would also suffer (probably the most) and the employees are therefore key stakeholders in the organisation.

CHECK IT YOURSELF

Start by listing all the external contacts you have in the course of your work. These are your **external role set** (as compared with your internal role set identified in the previous element).

Now design a chart showing yourself in the middle, important contacts close to you and less important contacts further away. Try to make sure that you have covered as many people as you can. (If you have forgotten how to do this, look back to page 187 for guidance.)

Note: if you deal with hundreds of customers as part as your job then obviously you don't have to try to list these as individuals!

Types of external contacts

Basically there are two types of external contacts:

- those who **supply** services – from the newsagent to the electrician

- those who **require** services – basically, the customers of the organisation. Do bear in mind, though, that the term 'customers' includes both private individuals and business organisations.

Methods of working with external contacts

Normally your relationships with external contacts are relatively pre-defined – unless you are the buyer of a large organisation or someone with a five- or six-figure budget to control! If you work for a large organisation then you may find that your suppliers are pre-selected and you can only use people who have already been identified as suitable. These are usually listed for reference. If you work for a small organisation then you may have more flexibility to pick and choose your suppliers. This will give you the opportunity to try out new people, take advantage of special offers and stop dealing with suppliers who give a poor service – without necessarily asking anyone else for permission first.

So far as customers are concerned, your dealings with them will depend upon your job role and the items or service sold by your organisation. Organisations which sell specialist products or services normally leave the selling of their goods to trained representatives. However, you may still be expected to deal with general enquiries and provide information when it is requested in a wider, more 'marketing-based' role. Smaller organisations – particularly those with a more general product line or service – will expect everyone on the staff to be able to undertake a much wider role in relation to customers. Think, for instance, of how your local library staff, superstore and hospital operate – and the range of enquiries they might receive from customers. Any organisation which deals predominantly with members of the public will offer a different type of customer service from a specialist manufacturer of industrial goods.

All organisations have standard policies and procedures for dealing with suppliers and customers. The degree to which these are specified and detailed will vary – but not the overall aim, which is to standardise and record the working methods of all members of staff. Supplier documentation will include contracts (for services), quotations, estimates, invoices and statements. Customer documentation will also include these documents as well as marketing literature and product information. In both cases there may be a range of internal forms used – for recording telephone messages, logging enquiries received, recording customer complaints and so on. It is your job to know the documentation and procedures which are used in your own organisation so that you always know that you are following standard procedures.

- Because of the danger of false claims or litigation, most companies insist that any dealings with suppliers or customers are documented. Even telephone conversations must be recorded on an internal memo. All documents are added to the appropriate file and kept on record in case there is any dispute about what actually happened.
- Companies working towards the quality award ISO 9000 (formerly BS 5750) have to demonstrate a standardised system of documentation and quality procedures in relation to both suppliers and customers.

Scope and limit of your own authority

Just because a system has been instigated this does not mean that all the staff can use it! Signing orders for goods, for instance, is normally limited to a few people in the organisation – particularly where a substantial contract is involved or where the order is worth a considerable sum of money. For instance, a contract for building repairs costing £250 000 may need signing by the Managing Director, whereas 50 reams of photocopying paper may be sanctioned by the Office Manager.

The ability to carry out negotiations with other commercial organisations and suppliers will also vary depending upon your level and status in the organisation. You are very likely to have the authority to contact British Rail for a train ticket but far less likely to be given permission to see your company's bank manager to discuss the possibility of an overdraft!

Similarly, in relation to customers, whereas the organisation would probably be happy if any member of staff made a large sale, negotiating discounts and delivery dates may have to be undertaken by specialist sales staff who have access to information on customer accounts (and bad debtors), production schedules, work-in-progress, stock levels and delivery procedures. This is especially true in relation to international sales where export documentation has to be prepared and goods specially prepared for shipment.

Customer complaints, on a basic level, may be recorded and discussed with any member of staff. However, decisions in relation to compensation or problems concerning threats of legal action are likely to be dealt with at a higher level.

Knowing the scope and limit of your own authority is vital at every stage of your career if you are not to make major mistakes. Always default *downwards*, i.e. if you are in doubt then check first. This is always the safest policy. When your boss confirms that you could have done this without permission then you have a precedent for next time. This is far better than having to apologise for taking a decision which was beyond your authority and then having to try to undo it afterwards – and far less embarrassing!

For each of the external contacts you identified on page 223, state:

a the procedures in operation in your organisation for working with that person (or group of people)

b the scope and limit of your own authority in each case.

TEST YOURSELF

Although your organisation has staggered holidays, the majority of people wish to take their annual main break in August. The company complies with this request whenever possible, which means that only a skeleton staff is in operation during this time.

After two weeks away in the sun you return to find that your junior has:

● called out the repairman to her computer, found out it is virtually irreparable and ordered a replacement

● sold goods to a customer who has an outstanding debt of over £10 000 and has been blacklisted by your Accounts department

● arranged to deliver a new item of stock to an important customer in three days' time whereas you know that the items are not due off the production line for at least another month

● been contacted by a company selling advertising space and has agreed to take an advertisement in an unknown magazine which will cost the company £600.

a What would you do to solve *each* of the above problems?

b What would you do about your junior who, at this moment, is congratulating herself about using her own initiative?

c What does this say about the systems and procedures in operation in your organisation?

Developing constructive relationships with external contacts

You have already learned much about establishing and maintaining constructive relationships in Element 4.1. In relation to external contacts most of these guidelines still apply. The main differences you have to note are that:

● the range of people you have to deal with will be much wider – suppliers can be small-business people or multi-million pound organisations; customers can include pensioners, young children or large-scale international companies

● the type of procedures you have to follow may influence

your relationship with your contact – you are unlikely to be as free to negotiate with your customers as you are with your colleagues

- making wrong decisions can cost money! A poor deal from a supplier or a poor choice of customer can be an expensive mistake
- the 'angles' people use (especially to sell you something!) are more varied and you are likely to be more susceptible to persuasion by external professionals than to internal colleagues whom you know very well
- external contacts will be less understanding than your colleagues. They are simply not interested in the fact that you are having a bad day or have other priorities when they call. Each has his or her own agenda – sales people have targets to meet, customers want information or to make a purchase
- external contacts have no reason to protect you personally if you upset them.

For all these reasons your relationships are more sensitive – you have less scope for manoeuvre and have to be more careful what you say and what you do. You will also be wise if you build up your relationship with each contact slowly and keep it impersonal but professional. That way, you are not compromised if there is a change of policy which prevents you from dealing with them in the way you would prefer or ends your relationship completely.

Given all this you are, of course, expected to fulfil your role as an important 'representative' of your organisation when you deal with them. To the external contact, you *are* the organisation – if you are inefficient, impolite or make promises that you fail to keep then not only will your own reputation be damaged but so will that of the company which employs you.

TEST YOURSELF

1 A junior member of staff has been given the job of contacting several customers for information. She has never had any dealings with outside contacts before. From what you have read above and in Element 4.1, prepare a list of about ten points giving her some 'golden rules' when dealing with them, so that she gives a good impression of both herself and your organisation.

2 What do you think are the key aspects of *maintaining* a constructive relationship with external contacts? Again, use your previous reading as a guide to help you. Discuss your answers with the rest of the group or your adviser.

Seeking/exchanging information, advice and support

You will receive requests for information from both customers and suppliers. Customers will usually be enquiring about your products or services – including details of prices, discounts and delivery times. They may also want to ask about the progress of an order they placed previously, to query details someone else gave them, to find out about the state of their account, to ask about your after-sales service or methods of finance.

To be able to help someone properly you may need to question them more closely to ascertain their exact needs. This may require a considerable amount of tact and diplomacy – particularly if you are having to ask for financial information or other personal details. It is this process which can be described as exchanging information. The more freely information is given and received, the more you will be able to provide the customer with exactly what he or she wants. It is at this point that your questioning skills become important. You should not fire questions at people as if they were taking an oral test – but neither should you forget to find out important facts which would influence your decision as to what to recommend. Usually, you will find that industrial customers are more specific about their needs than private individuals – but they will also expect a higher degree of expertise and product knowledge in return!

The key rule is not to give any information unless you know it is correct. When in doubt, check – and call back as soon as you can with the facts. Whatever you do, never promise to call someone and then forget – this is a cardinal sin and you will deserve to lose the customer forever if you do this. Today most organisations operate in a buyer's market – if you don't give good service then one of your competitors almost certainly will!

Suppliers can also ask for information – and often you may be less well prepared for their questions. There can literally be dozens of requests made by suppliers from 'We can't provide the disks you ordered until next week – do you want to accept a substitute or wait?' to 'I've come to measure up to give your boss an estimate for painting the place – how many rooms does he want doing?' or even 'There are no seats available on the 17.20 to Frankfurt on Tuesday – what do you want to do?' Unless you are a walking encyclopaedia it is doubtful you would have all these answers at your fingertips. Sometimes you will not know because you have not been told what is happening (e.g. the painter); at other times you would have to check before you made a response (e.g. the current stock of disks or your boss's preference for flights).

In some cases you would benefit from an exchange of information before you make a decision. For instance, the price of the substitute disks (and their reliability) may be a factor – after all, the alternative disks may be a better buy! Again don't be worried about questioning to ascertain what other choices you could make – the travel agent, for example, could give you a range of other options to choose from. By thinking ahead, finding out as much as you can, and noting this down you save everyone's time. You can then notify your boss of a suitable alternative flight without finding out later that this flight is also full!

It is also beneficial to ask for advice when you need it – never be too proud to do this. The painter, for instance, could be asked to walk around and give his recommendations. You will also find that people are likely to give you their support if you need it – both customers and suppliers. Asking the travel agent to search – *please* – to find some likely alternative because you are desperate is likely to be more productive than simply accepting the message at face value or even showing your annoyance or exasperation. Generally, people want to help other people – and this is particularly true if you have built up a constructive relationship with them in the past.

TEST YOURSELF

1   A customer makes an enquiry for a product your company manufactures. When you question her closely about her needs you realise a competitor's product would be more suitable for her. What would you do?

2   A customer calls when you are busy and your boss stops to chat to him for a few moments. You hear them discussing the possible sources of finance available and hear your boss giving totally incorrect information. What would you do?

3   What strategies would you use for questioning
    a   an elderly person
    b   a young child
    c   an over-confident salesman
    d   an important business customer

    to ascertain their exact needs?

4   Collect examples of the types of literature and product information produced by your organisation. Critically analyse this for its usefulness and impact. Can you make any suggestions for improvement? (*Note*: if you are working as a group you may like to exchange information so that it is evaluated by other people. They may see things you have been missing for years!)

Disagreements and conflict

This is a very contentious area in relation to external contacts. There is a very old saying that 'the customer is always right' but this is difficult to believe if someone is shouting at you or insulting you because of an error made by your company.

At this point it must be emphasised that whilst you should keep calm and deal with complaints in a professional manner, you should *not* be expected to put up with threats of violence or foul language. If this happens, get help immediately.

There are several golden rules to remember if you are dealing with an irate customer.

- Apologising does not mean you have to grovel personally for forgiveness. You are apologising on behalf of your company, not yourself.
- Do not admit liability or put the blame on anyone.
- Calm an irate customer by letting him or her talk without interruption. Only when he or she runs out of steam should you intervene.
- If you cannot help immediately then take copious notes. This helps the customer to believe you are taking the complaint seriously and also gives you a proper record to refer to later.
- Don't argue. Remain polite, patient and reasonable yourself.
- If the complaint is serious, the customer obdurate or you feel the situation is getting out of control then get help. Don't try to prove how good you are by handling it all on your own.

A disagreement with a supplier is likely to be taken out of your hands quite quickly – particularly if it is serious. This is because there is likely to be a question as to whether the account should be paid or not. This is probably enough to make your boss take an immediate interest in the problem! Quite obviously, however, there is a substantial difference between minor irritations, such as the electrician who promises to turn up and then forgets, and major disputes, such as the builder who quoted completion of a new warehouse in April and is still laying the foundations in July! In the first case your boss will probably expect you to sort it out on your own; in the second – where settlement may only be decided in the courts – the problem is likely to be outside your authority.

It is worth keeping a record of your suppliers – both in terms of standard of goods provided and reliability of service. If you are dissatisfied then you have every right to change to someone else – or persuade your boss to do so. It is also useful to have a good knowledge of your consumer rights in law. These are covered on page 235.

Confidential information

There are a variety of confidential matters you may have to talk about with customers including:

- financial discussions – on loans, income, expenditure, payment difficulties, etc.
- medical discussions – about personal health or the health of close family, serious illnesses, etc.
- personal discussions – about marital history or relations, criminal record, etc.

Quite obviously the nature of your organisation and your own job role will be the determining factor in the type of confidential information you discuss with customers. However, there are several basic rules which should always be followed.

- Don't conduct such discussions in a public area. Even if such questions are an everyday experience to you, they are unlikely to be regarded in the same way by the other person.
- Don't make notes and then leave them lying around for everyone to read.
- Keep the information to yourself. Someone else in your office may know this person in private life and be delighted to find out such intimate details.
- Quite simply, treat other people with the same respect you would like to be accorded yourself.

TEST YOURSELF

1   Can you think of two occasions when you have been embarrassed by being asked a personal question in public? If so, can you say when this was and what happened (or would you rather not?!).

2   You have recently obtained a job working in a doctor's surgery. Give three examples of occasions when you would need to either find out information or give information to a patient in private.

3   You have a good relationship with one of your customers and, over several months, have become quite friendly with Frank, the clerk who rings with their orders. Whilst on the telephone to him today he lets you know, in strict confidence, that their company is in serious financial difficulties. He then proceeds to give you an order worth over £10 000. What would you do?

Informing and consulting others – problems and proposals

In Element 4.1 you looked at several different ways of thinking about problems within an organisation which were probably new to you. These techniques can be applied in just the same way to solve problems outside the organisation. Again, in each case, you need to think through the problem and decide whether it is 'task-based' or 'people-based'.

External problems come in all shapes and sizes. Customers can have problems which range from changing a delivery date to wanting to defer paying off a loan to changing their minds about what they want to buy. They will bring these problems to you and expect you to solve them. In most cases there will be a standard procedure for dealing with problems. For instance, your company may have an official policy regarding returning goods, special forms may have to be completed if a loan is overdue and so on. It is likely to be the minor problems (to the company) which you can solve on your own. However, as these may be major problems for the customer it is usually very good practice to try to help where you can.

Suppliers may also encounter problems which they will then refer to you. Nearly always these will focus on their inability to supply goods according to the original agreement – and they will usually propose their own solution which may or may not be agreeable to you. This has already been covered on page 228.

These are all typical 'task-based problems'. 'People problems' can occur if a customer or supplier makes a complaint about one of your colleagues. The situation is even more difficult if the person they are complaining about is senior to you. The first thing to establish is the severity of the problem. It may be that your colleague has behaved perfectly properly but the customer does not understand this. A clear, reasoned explanation may then suffice. If the complaint is more serious and justified then you have three choices. You can:

- ignore the situation
- see the person yourself
- refer the matter to your own boss.

The correct action will depend on the situation – as a general rule you are better keeping the situation informal. If it involves staff at your own level or below you, then it is best to talk to them directly. Telling 'the boss' may be interpreted as disloyalty. If the person involved is more senior to you then *do* ask your boss for help. It would be inappropriate for you to confront that person directly.

You are unlikely to have to deal with the personal problems of your external contacts unless you specifically work in an organisation which deals with this type of work, e.g. the Citizens' Advice Bureau, a hospital, a counselling, voluntary or advisory service or a local authority/government office concerned with people. If you regularly deal with customers with serious personal problems then you should have received some training to cope with this. You should never give advice in any of these areas without knowing what you are doing. If the problem involves more than basic facts, obtain help from an expert.

Different styles of approach/methods of communication

Some organisations consider that all staff should be trained to be polite, courteous and helpful to external contacts all the time and actually teach them the correct response. In such organisations, everyone is trained to answer the telephone in the same way or to greet customers personally using an identical greeting. This is certainly the case in the United States where 'Have a nice day' is well-known as the standard farewell.

In Britain, people sometimes become annoyed by standard responses. The waiter who leaves you saying 'enjoy your meal' is regarded as courteous the first time, irritating on the sixth occasion and downright infuriating on the twentieth! This is because, by now, you have become a 'regular' and probably consider you deserve more personal service and attention.

Familiarity with customers is only one reason why you should vary your approach. It would be silly to use exactly the same approach regardless of whether you were dealing with an elderly person or slick business person, a young child or a teenager, a handicapped person or someone who didn't speak English very well. Common sense should tell you that you will need a different approach in each of these situations. If you are in any doubt, look at Figure 4.2.1 for help!

Suppliers will also expect you to have a different relationship with them after a period of time. Indeed, many organisations today work towards developing a good relationship with a few key suppliers rather than 'shopping around'. The benefits are that they can usually shorten their order times and the amount of stock they keep on the premises – because the supplier knows they are a valued contact. However, you are always wise to maintain an objective and professional relationship with suppliers in case there are problems or difficulties – and *never* accept money or gifts in agreement for giving an order! If there is a dispute in which you are involved it is easier to cope if you are not 'best chums' with the people in their sales section!

CHECK IT YOURSELF

1 Discuss with your tutor or adviser the range of customers/suppliers you deal with and the different approaches you need to use.
2 As a group, if possible, discuss how you would deal with:
   - the customer who 'knows it all'
   - the persistent sales person

DIFFERENT TYPES OF CUSTOMERS AND A SUGGESTED APPROACH

Children	The elderly	The handicapped	Foreigners with limited English
Use simple vocabulary	Don't rush them	*The deaf* Look at the person Speak relatively slowly Remember it's useless to shout!	Listen carefully
Help with money and change	Don't patronise or speak 'down' to them	*The blind/partially sighted* Speak as you approach Don't 'grab' them Don't use visual comparisons	Use simple English words and phrases – no slang expressions or colloquialisms
Use their names	Don't use jargon or technical words	*The disabled* Open doors for them Don't rush them	Don't shout or use long sentences
Stop misbehaviour by distraction rather than rebuke	Be prepared to repeat main points	Concentrate on the *person*	Repeat what they say to check you have understood their needs correctly
	Write information down if long or complex	*The mentally handicapped* Be patient Use straightforward vocabulary	Ask for help if necessary

Figure 4.2.1 Different approaches to customers

- a customer who becomes abusive
- a customer who is very shy or nervous.

Relevant legal and regulatory requirements

The major legislation you need to consider in relation to your external contacts is that concerning consumers – although, of course, Health and Safety legislation applies to people visiting your premises just as much as to employees (see Element 2.1).

If you are dealing with customers then they are obviously the consumers in the transaction. If you are dealing with suppliers then you are the consumer. All consumers are protected from inferior or dangerous products, poor or inadequate service and from being deliberately misled by those out to make a quick profit. The aim is that all consumers can turn to either the law or a specialist organisation for help if they have a problem.

Specialist organisations include 'watchdogs' such as Oftel, Ofgas and Ofwat, consumer bodies such as the Office of Fair Trading, the British Standards Institute, the Trading Standards Office, the Environmental Health Office and the Consumers Association, and trade associations such as the Association of British Travel Agents and the Building Employers Federation. If a dispute still cannot be resolved then, in some industries, it may be referred to the appropriate Ombudsman. However, you should note that the Ombudsman is the last resort in the process, not the first!

To understand how legislation operates to assist the consumer, first of all you need to understand what happens when you enter into a contract of sale – either as the buyer or the seller. The information you learn will be just as useful in your private life as it will in business!

DID YOU KNOW?

There are several Ombudsmen, all with the same type of role. They provide an independent and objective method of resolving problems and complaints that arise between an organisation and a customer. Today there are Ombudsmen covering:

- **local government** – to investigate complaints against local councils
- **insurance** – to investigate complaints about the small print of insurance documents, poor communication and inefficient service
- **legal services** – to investigate complaints against barristers and solicitors
- **health service** – to investigate complaints by both patients and staff
- **investment** – to investigate complaints in this area (see Financial Services Act, page 244)
- **estate agents** – to investigate complaints such as gazumping and misleading descriptions (see Property Misdescriptions Act, page 242)

- **banking** – to investigate complaints about bank charges, interest rates, poor service, etc.
- **building societies** – to investigate cases involving surveys or fraudulent withdrawal of funds
- **pensions** – to investigate complaints about personal, state or company pensions.

The contract of sale

When you buy goods or a service then you become a 'party to a contract'. A contract is a legal agreement between a seller and a buyer and has two elements:

1. the customer's offer to buy the goods at a given price
2. the supplier's acceptance of the order and/or agreement to sell the goods.

When both elements have been completed there is a **binding contract** and neither side can simply change their minds or alter the terms of the contract. Therefore the customer cannot suddenly return goods without good reason and expect a refund, and the supplier cannot raise the price or make other changes to the agreement. If you are involved in making a contract you are advised to read it carefully and also find out when and how you can cancel the contract, if necessary.

DID YOU KNOW?

A supplier has no legal obligation to accept an offer to buy from a customer, so long as the refusal is not on grounds of race or sex.

The parts to a contract

There are three parts to a contract:

- **the offer** – for example, you offer to buy a jacket in a shop
- **the acceptance** – the shop assistant accepts your offer
- **the consideration** – you pay the assistant. (The idea of the consideration does not apply in Scotland.)

Factors to remember

- To become a party to the contract you must intend to enter into the agreement. If you make an agreement with someone who is very young (or very drunk!) the court may hold that the agreement is invalid. This means it cannot be enforced. In the same way, if someone forced you to enter into an agreement (e.g. by threatening you) then legally you would not be held to it.
- The offer must be **certain** and **specific.** Saying 'I may be interested' is not a specific offer.
- The offer must be communicated to the person to whom the offer is intended to be made. Therefore, for instance, advertising

in a newspaper for a jacket is not an offer because no specific person is named. Neither is an offer specific if it is sent in writing and lost in the post – as it has not been received by the correct person.

- An acceptance can be verbal, written or by conduct. Taking money in response to an offer would be acceptance by conduct.
- The acceptance must be **unqualified**. This means it must correspond in every detail with the original terms. If the offer introduces new terms this is known as a counter offer and would have to be specifically accepted.
- The acceptance must be **certain**. If someone says she will think seriously about your offer then this is not a certain acceptance and you cannot hold her to it.
- A contract must involve some kind of payment or other consideration (except in Scotland). The courts, however, are not too interested in the adequacy of the consideration. If, therefore, you buy an article at a ludicrously cheap (or expensive) price, that is not a major factor. However, if the consideration is extremely inadequate the courts may look at the situation to see if there has been any undue pressure placed by one party to the contract upon the other.

DID YOU KNOW?

- An offer does not last indefinitely. It lapses if:
  - either the person making the offer or the person to whom it is made dies
  - it is not accepted within a specified or reasonable time
  - there is not a valid acceptance
  - it is subject to the fulfilment of a condition and that condition is not fulfilled.
- An offer can be revoked (i.e. withdrawn at any time) *before* it has been accepted.
- Certain people are restricted in their capacity to make a contract, such as people suffering from a mental disorder listed in the Mental Health Act 1983 and minors (i.e. those under 18 years of age).

Terms of the contract

Terms can be **express** or **implied**.

- **Express** Here the terms are specifically stated either orally or in writing. Note that in most cases a contract need not be in written form although, for obvious reasons, you would be strongly advised to have some written proof of any business contract you make with another party.
- **Implied** Here the agreement does not contain an express term but the courts are prepared to imply a term into it to give effect to the **clear** but **unexpressed** intentions of the parties to the contract. If therefore you agree to buy a jacket and no price at all

is mentioned the court may hold that there is an implied term in the contract that you pay a reasonable price for it. The court will, however, always look *first* at the express terms in the contract and will not generally imply a term which contradicts an express term. Consequently, if you have agreed a price, however unreasonable it might be, you will probably be held to it.

Contractual terms can also be divided into **conditions** and **warranties**. Not all terms in a contract are of equal importance. You may find, for instance, that you have bought a car which does not have a heated rear windscreen even though that was part of the contract. You may find, further, that the car has no engine! There has been a **breach** of contract on both occasions; but in the first instance the breach has been in respect of a less important term (known as a warranty) whereas in the second instance the breach has occurred in respect of a very important term (known as a condition).

DID YOU KNOW?

You can deliberately make a term of the contract an express condition. For instance, if you order a jacket in a particular size and need it by a particular date, you must state this clearly (and preferably put it in writing). The correct phrase to use is 'time is of the essence in this contract'.

The ending of the contract

There are three main methods by which a contract comes to an end:

- by **performance** – where you buy a jacket, pay for it and walk out of the shop with it
- by **agreement** between both parties – where you are employed under a contract of employment, you decide to resign and your employer accepts your resignation
- by **breach** – if the other party to a contract you have made is in breach, i.e. does not carry out his part of the agreement, you have certain remedies. If the breach is a breach of warranty, you may be able to claim damages but it is unlikely that you will be able to reject or **repudiate** it. If, on the other hand, the breach is of a condition, you may be able to choose either to claim damages or to repudiate it, in which case the contract ends.

DID YOU KNOW?

Some organisations try to evade their legal responsibilities by using exclusion clauses or disclaimers on their premises, tickets, contracts or booking forms.

Under the Unfair Contract Terms Act 1977 none of these disclaimers is valid unless the organisation can prove that their terms are fair and reasonable. Therefore if an article is lost or damaged through negligence then the owner is probably entitled to compensation. This will not be the case if the organisation can prove it took reasonable care of the goods and could not be held responsible for what occurred.

Notices and disclaimers can *never* absolve an organisation from its liability to either staff or customers if personal injury or death is caused through their negligence.

TEST YOURSELF

Obtain a copy of a travel brochure from major tour operator. Read the booking conditions carefully and use them to help you to answer the questions following the case study below.

You work as an Administrative Assistant for a large organisation where you are frequently responsible for making travel arrangements for your boss, the Sales Director, the Area Sales Managers, sales representatives and, when required, technicians who fly abroad to mend equipment your organisation has installed.

1   What do you think would be the situation if:
   a   your boss wanted to cancel a trip to South America 24 hours before he was due to leave because there was a dispute with the organisation he was going to visit
   b   the airline decided to cancel the flight because of terrorism in the area
   c   your boss couldn't go on the trip because of a personal crisis and wanted his deputy to go on his behalf.
2   Do you think you could take action for breach of contract if any of the following occurred?
   a   Three technicians are refused permission to board an aeroplane in Greece, after completing a contract there, because they had too much to drink in the airport bar. Two are needed urgently for another job.
   b   Your boss's plane is delayed for three hours because of a computer fault.

DID YOU KNOW?

In July 1995 a new law, Unfair Terms in Consumer Contract Regulations, was announced. This effectively gives the consumer the benefit of the doubt in most disputes over contracts and goes much further than the existing Unfair Contract Terms Act. Now consumers can contest any contract they think is unfair through the courts or the Office of Fair Trading.

The new law demands that not only must contracts be fair but that plain English must be used. Any tiny, unreadable typeface or gobbledegook may be judged to be unfair. The law has meant the redrafting of contracts issued by insurance companies, banks, building societies, travel companies and estate agencies – to name but a few! The aim is to do away with small print, make contracts easily understandable and remove all conditions which may be considered unfair – such as withdrawing a service at a moment's notice or denying liability for a faulty or damaged product or service.

Consumer legislation

The relevant laws you need to understand are:

- The Sale of Goods Act 1979
- The Trade Descriptions Act 1968
- The Consumer Protection Act 1987
- The Supply of Goods and Services Act 1982
- The Consumer Credit Act 1974.

These five Acts apply to all transactions involving goods and services. However, specialist legislation is in force to cover specific industries – such as the Financial Services Act (see page 244).

DID YOU KNOW?

The above Acts all apply to England and Wales – the situation in Scotland and Northern Ireland is broadly similar, though some Acts have different names and dates. The Office of Fair Trading issues special leaflets on consumer rights in Scotland and Northern Ireland and these can be obtained by writing to the OFT, Field House, Bream Building, London EC4A 1PR.

The Sale of Goods Act 1979

This is probably the most important piece of legislation as far as the customer and supplier are concerned. The main purpose of the Act is to prevent buyers from being deceived into buying goods which are not fit to be sold. Under this Act, goods for sale must be:

- as described
- of merchantable quality
- fit for the purpose for which they are intended.

As described

Where there is a contract for the sale of goods there is an implied condition that the goods will correspond with the description. If you bought some scissors labelled 'stainless steel' and then found out they weren't, you could claim your money back. The Trade Descriptions Act deals even more fully with the question of description (see page 242).

Of merchantable quality

This means that the goods must work and includes goods sold at sale prices. However, various points should be noted.

- If a defect is specifically drawn to the buyer's attention before the sale is completed then this is acceptable.
- If the buyer examines the goods before the sale and should have been able to see the defect easily (e.g. a scratch on the paintwork of a car) this is also acceptable.
- The seller must be a business seller – private sales are exempt.
- The seller can be a manufacturer, wholesaler or retailer.
- A person cannot reasonably expect the same standard of quality

and durability from cheap goods as expensive goods, although if the goods were bought in a sale the price would probably not be relevant.

- Goods described as 'shop soiled', 'seconds' and 'manufacturers' rejects' cannot be expected to be of the same quality as a new or perfect product.

Fit for the purpose for which they are intended

Most goods have an implicit purpose for which they are intended, e.g. a hole punch should punch holes in paper. If it will not, then the seller is contravening the Sale of Goods Act.

Consumers often place considerable reliance on the advice and experience of the seller or sales representative. If he or she indicates that the goods will do a particular task and they fail to fulfil that purpose then the seller will be liable.

If the goods do not conform with any one of these three criteria then the buyer is entitled to a **refund**.

- If the buyer *prefers*, he or she can accept a replacement or repair but the seller is not obliged to offer anything except cash compensation.
- The buyer does *not* have to accept a credit note – if he or she does then there may be difficulty in getting a refund if no other goods are suitable.
- Notices such as 'No money refunded' are illegal and should be reported to the local Trading Standards Officer.
- Second-hand goods are also covered by the Act, but the buyer's right to compensation will depend on many factors – price paid, age of the article, how it was described, etc.
- Sale items are also covered by the Act but if the price is reduced *because* the item is damaged the buyer cannot complain later about that particular fault.
- There is no legal obligation on the buyer to produce a receipt and signs such as 'No refunds without a receipt' have no legal standing. However, the buyer can be asked for proof of purchase, e.g. cheque counterfoil, credit card copy sales voucher.

DID YOU KNOW?

The buyer is *not* entitled to anything if he or she:

- has a change of mind
- decides that something does not fit
- damages the item
- was aware of the fault or should have seen it
- did not purchase the item personally (e.g. received it as a gift).

Trade Descriptions Act 1968

The main purpose of this Act is to prevent the **false description of goods**. Any seller who gives a false trade description of goods or supplies or offers to supply goods which are falsely described is guilty of an offence. This includes

- selling goods which are wrongly described by the manufacturer, e.g. 'made of real leather' when they are not
- implied descriptions, e.g. a picture or illustration giving a false impression
- false descriptions of other aspects of the goods, including quantity, size, composition, method of manufacture, etc.

Usually the spoken word of the seller overrides the written description of the goods as the buyer can rely on the expertise of the salesman.

Complaints under this Act are investigated by local Trading Standards Officers. In one case, Boots were fined £250 for selling a diet chocolate bar, called Shaper, which actually contained as many calories as ordinary brands of chocolate.

 DID YOU KNOW?

The Property Misdescriptions Act now makes it an offence for estate agents to give misleading or dishonest descriptions of properties. No longer can they write:

- interesting town view (when it is really over the gasworks)
- small compact garden (for a one-metre-square plot of land)
- interesting original features (when it means nothing has been done to the house for 50 years!).

Even casual remarks by junior members of staff can mean the agent is liable under the Act. In future, estate agents may have to be rather more careful with adjectives such as 'quiet', 'pleasant' and 'rural' – and stick to the facts!

Consumer Protection Act 1987

This Act introduced two new areas to consumer protection in general.

- A person is guilty of an offence if he or she gives consumers a misleading indication of the price at which any goods, services, accommodation or facilities are available, e.g.
  - false comparisons with recommended prices (e.g. saying the goods are £20 less than the recommended price when they are not)
  - indications that the price is less than the real price (e.g. where hidden extras are added to the advertised price, or VAT has been deliberately omitted)

- false comparisons with a previous price (e.g. a false statement that the goods were £50 and are now £25)
- where the stated method of determining the price is different to the method actually used.

- The Act also states that it is an offence to supply consumer goods which are not reasonably safe. An offence is also committed by offering or agreeing to supply unsafe goods or possessing them for supply.

The Supply of Goods and Services Act 1982

This Act is in two parts, the first broadly concerned with goods and the second with services.

Part 1 – Goods

This extends the protection for consumers provided by the Sale of Goods Act to include goods supplied as part of a service, on hire or in part exchange. These, too, must be as described, of merchantable quality and fit for the purpose made known to the supplier. Therefore if a garage fits rear seat belts to a car, a woman hires a carpet cleaning machine (and specially asks if it can cope with long-pile rugs) and a couple trade in their old gas fire for a new one at the gas showroom, these 'goods' are all covered under the Act.

Part 2 – Services

This part deals with the standard of services such as those provided by builders, plumbers, TV repairers, hairdressers, garages, etc. It protects the buyer against shoddy workmanship, delays and exorbitant charges. The Act states that all services should be carried out:

- for a reasonable charge
- within a reasonable time
- with reasonable care and skill.

The Consumer Credit Act 1974

This Act applies to a wide range of types of credit agreement and places strict controls upon organisations which provide credit facilities in the course of their business.

The Act also lays down strict rules governing the form and content of agreements. The object of the rules is to protect the borrower by providing the fullest possible information about his or her legal rights and obligations.

The three major provisions are as follows.

- A credit agreement must be issued to the buyer in a form which complies with regulations made under the Act. It must contain details such as:
  - the names and addresses of the parties concerned

- the APR (Annual Percentage Rate of charge)
- the cash price, deposit, total amount of credit
- the total amount payable
- the repayment dates and amount of each payment
- sums payable on default
- other rights and protections under the Act.

● Customers who buy goods on credit may have the right to cancel the agreement if they change their minds, provided:
  - they have signed the agreement at home or anywhere else *except* on the trader's business premises
  - they have bought the goods 'face-to-face' with the dealer. As yet, goods bought over the telephone are not covered.

● If a person signs a credit agreement at home he or she must receive a copy immediately. Every copy of a cancellable agreement must contain a box labelled 'Your right to cancel' which tells the buyer what to do. About a week later a further copy or separate notice of the cancellation rights must be sent to the buyer by post. Starting from the day after this second copy is received the buyer has 5 days in which to give the trader *written* notice of cancellation.

 ## DID YOU KNOW?

The APR – annual percentage rate of charge – must be calculated by all credit companies in a standard way set down by law. Basically all the interest and administrative charges are added together and the total expressed as an annual percentage rate. The APR should always be obtainable on request and clearly stated in all written quotations and credit agreements.

The Financial Services Act 1986

This Act will apply to you and your company if you are involved in the investment business – whether dealing in stocks and shares, life assurance or pension plans. The Act does *not* cover ordinary banking and building society deposits or other types of insurance.

The rules are complex but basically all investment businesses are answerable to the Securities and Investments Board (SIB) and must be officially authorised to carry out their business by one of the five Self-Regulatory Organisations (SROs) set up for this purpose. Any investor losing money in one of the authorised businesses can claim full compensation from SIB.

Both SIB and the SROs have detailed rules about the conduct of the business.

● Investment advisers must state whether they are giving independent advice or working as the agent or representative for one particular company.
● Advisers must find out enough information from the investor to give the best personal advice to the client – not try to make the best deal for their company.

- Advertisements must not mislead by, for example, exaggerating expected financial returns or missing out relevant information.
- Independent advisers must be prepared to reveal to the client the amount of commission they will be receiving.
- Any client who signs a contract in his or her own home has 14 days in which to cancel (28 days in some cases).
- High pressure selling is banned.

Anyone who has a complaint about an organisation should complain first to the company itself, then to the relevant SRO and then to SIB.

TEST YOURSELF

1   A customer left his personal computer with you for repair. Last night, despite the fact that the premises have a burglar alarm fitted and security locks on the windows, your company had a break-in. The computer was one of the items stolen.

   The customer has read the report of the burglary in the press and is now insisting that you have to reimburse him.

   a   Do you have to do this?
   b   Would the situation be different if you had a prominent notice saying that all the articles are left at the owner's own risk?

2   A customer and his wife call in to see you. They bought goods from your organisation on credit two weeks ago and are now demanding their deposit back. They claim that the sales person said that the credit agreement with your company would be at a reasonable interest rate and the repayments only small. The customer has now calculated that the interest payable per annum is 25 per cent and has discovered he could borrow the money cheaper from his bank. He says that had he known this he would never have entered into the agreement.

   a   Can he insist on his deposit back?
   b   Would the situation be any different if the interest rate had been lower?

Discuss your answers as a group and with your tutor or adviser. (*Note*: the answers are given on page 248.)

External contacts and health and safety

Any organisation which deals with or admits members of the public on to its premises can find it is liable to claims in law, for example if:

- a customer (or workman) is injured through negligence on the part of an employee, unsafe premises or fittings, etc.
- a customer is injured because a product is faulty
- a customer suffers personal financial loss or distress through professional negligence, faulty workmanship, etc.

For this reason most firms take out insurance to cover themselves against such claims. Typical policies include:

- **public liability insurance**. This is a legal requirement for some businesses such as builders and hairdressers. It covers the business against claims because of personal injury caused by negligence, defects on the premises, etc.
- **product liability insurance**. This covers claims for injury caused by faulty goods.
- **professional indemnity**. This covers claims for damages caused by professional negligence. This type of policy is usually taken out by architects, accountants, solicitors, etc.

Most **trade associations** offer policies for their members. Trade associations are bodies associated with specific trades, e.g. the Building Employers Federation and the Association of British Travel Agents. They provide advice, assistance and information to their members and frequently have a voluntary code of practice to which their members subscribe. A code of practice is a guide to all members on how customers should be treated and complaints should be handled. Trading associations will also deal with complaints from members of the public about companies in their industry, though they obviously have more influence over companies who are members, rather than those who are not.

DID YOU KNOW?

- Many insurance policies have a condition attached that the insurance company will defend any claim on behalf of the insured. They also insist that the company shall not make any admission of liability to the person who has been injured.
- All companies must *by law* insure their employees against accidents at work. This type of insurance is called Employer's Liability insurance and it covers employees against bodily injury or diseases contracted as a result of their work.

TEST YOURSELF

1 A considerable amount of legislation has been introduced to prevent 'high pressure' sales people talking customers into buying goods they do not want. Discuss as a group what you would do if you constantly received complaints from members of the public that a member of your sales staff is using this approach.

2 Discuss as a group the different types of public liability claims which might be received by:
a a dentist
b a hotel
c a builder.

3 How do you think staff in an organisation will be affected in their dealings with a customer who has been injured on the premises,

bearing in mind the condition made by insurance companies that they must not make any admission of liability to the injured person? Discuss your answer with your tutor or adviser.

Methods of motivating people

Most of the studies carried out in relation to motivation have concentrated on employees – because it is in everyone's interest that those who are employed in an organisation are keen to perform well. This was covered in Element 4.1, page 218.

However, it is, of course, possible to apply some of the theories on motivation to those people who you deal with outside the company. Indeed, many sales teams are trained to recognise and appeal to people's needs – and many advertisements are designed with the same purpose in mind.

The main studies about people's needs were conducted by Abraham Maslow, who devised a hierarchy of human needs. The reason for the 'hierarchy' was that Maslow considered some needs to be more fundamental and basic than others. These, therefore, had to be satisfied before people concentrated on their higher level needs. Maslow's hierarchy of needs is shown in Figure 4.2.2. It implies that customers will buy a loaf of bread before they will take a course in yoga, that burglar alarm salesmen will be more successful than those selling the *Encyclopaedia Britannica*. It also suggests that the way in which staff approach customers – and respond to suppliers – will be affected by their own needs in this respect. Therefore, the salesman who is paid on a commission-only basis and has three hungry mouths to feed at

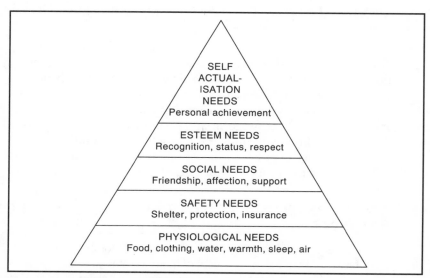

Figure 4.2.2 Maslow's hierarchy of needs

home will be more desperate to make a sale – any sale – than the one who earns a good basic rate – whether he works for your company or is trying to sell you something.

Organisations' reporting procedures

All organisations have specific reporting procedures and documentation concerned with both customers and suppliers. This includes:

- issuing or requesting estimates or quotations
- receiving or placing orders
- payments for goods
- agreeing terms and signing contracts
- dealing with bad debtors
- dealing with complaints
- making complaints.

You must be absolutely clear about the procedures in force in your organisation and understand the precise extent of your own authority. For instance, it is likely that you can enter into agreements for small orders for consumable items but would not be involved in negotiating for expensive capital equipment, such as a new photocopier or switchboard system.

In addition, you also need to know how to expedite these procedures in the case of an emergency or stop everyone in their tracks if there is a sudden problem.

Large organisations which deal regularly with members of the public are likely to have a clearly stated 'returns policy' or 'refunds policy'. They may also have a specific customer complaints procedure which must be followed by all staff.

An organisation specialising mainly in providing a service or only dealing with industrial buyers is likely to operate in a different way. For instance, complaints about a solicitor would not be handled by administrative staff, neither would an administrator be expected to respond definitively to a complaint that equipment costing £2 million and installed two weeks ago in Stockholm has suddenly developed a fault! It is vital that you understand exactly what you should do if you are the recipient of either of these complaints to ensure that you follow procedures properly – or refer the matter to your boss for clarification.

ANSWERS TO 'TEST YOURSELF' EXERCISE ON PAGE 245

1   You are only liable to reimburse the customer for the stolen goods if you had not taken reasonable care of them whilst they were in your possession. The fact that the company had an alarm fitted and security

locks on the windows would make it seem likely it had done all it reasonably could to take care of the goods.

If the company has goods insured against theft it may be prepared to reimburse the customer from this money, but is not legally required to do so if it has not been negligent. The customer should be covered under his or her own insurance policy and can claim on this. Having a notice disclaiming responsibility is irrelevant.

2   Under the terms of the Consumer Credit Act the customer should have been issued with a credit agreement detailing all the terms of the sale, including the APR. As your company has not done this you have contravened the Consumer Credit Act 1974.

A customer cannot insist on cancelling a credit agreement just because he or she finds that the money could have been borrowed more cheaply elsewhere unless the amount of interest is exorbitant. The term 'exorbitant' would certainly not cover an APR of 25 per cent (credit card companies charge between 15 per cent and 25 per cent APR!). Exorbitant would be more likely to apply if the APR were in the region of 200 per cent!

ACTIVITY SECTION

1   Obtain a copy of (or clearly state) the policy and procedures used in your organisation for:

   a   dealing with customer complaints
   b   purchasing office consumables
   c   passing accounts for payment.

2   Identify six advertisements in the press which are targeted at fulfilling the needs of a customer. In each case identify the need to which the advertisement appeals and, in a few words, give your opinion of the advert.

3   A customer has just taken delivery of a new photocopier from your company which you are advertising at £2700 + VAT. He has now contacted you to point out that his invoice is for £3655 and he has no intention of paying any more than the advertised price.

When you investigate you find that the additional charges are for a variety of extras, including service, maintenance, paper not yet supplied by your company and so on. The customer says that had he known of these he wouldn't have bought the copier.

   a   Can the customer insist on a refund?
   b   Would your position be any different if a sales representative had clearly explained the situation on a visit to his premises?
   c   What would you do if the sales rep alleges he *did* point this out to the customer at the time the agreement was signed?

4   Your company has a specified list of suppliers. Photocopying paper is

always purchased from a particular organisation in a nearby town. It is part of your job to order this paper whenever it is needed.

When you ring this organisation one person always takes your orders but has started making progressively more personal remarks. Two weeks ago there was a distinct suggestion that you should meet for an evening out. You are now finding it very difficult to contact this company and are dreading having to ring again.

What should you do?

5   Some organisations order goods from suppliers by using EDI – electronic data interchange. Although this is covered briefly in Unit 6, see how much you can find out about EDI on your own and, above all, whether it is used by your organisation.

Managing other people

I am reasonable – it's other people who aren't . . .

As you move up the hierarchy, there will be more and more occasions when you have to lead other people – either individually or in a team – and try to get them to do what you want them to do. At this point it is worth noting two basic facts.

1   Anyone can get someone else to do what they want to do – it is much harder to get them to do something they are not so keen on!

2   If you persuade someone to do something they didn't want to do originally, it is harder still to make them feel happy about it!

Managing other people is a complex business and involves enough to fill several books on its own. This brief section therefore only gives you pointers and ideas on which to work – if we whet your appetite then it is a good idea to study some other books which deal with this topic specifically.

RULE 1
Whilst other people's behaviour may seem illogical and irrational to you, it will always seem perfectly reasonable to them.

Motivation

Any management book will contain much information on the topic of motivation, i.e. what makes people go to work and – even more important – what makes them work hard when they get there.

There have been many theories about this, and the main ones are given in the table below. The important point is that we often think that other people are motivated by different things from those which motivate us. For example, we may consider we are motivated by achievement, an interesting job and being made to feel important while others are motivated by money, status and security. Why?

RULE 2
The key aspects of your job that make you feel good make other people feel good, too!

Theories of motivation

Our style of leadership is strongly influenced by our assumptions about motivation. Research has shown that there are four main groupings, each defined by different factors. Frederick Taylor, sometimes termed the 'Father of Management', was successful in increasing productivity by offering payment incentives and accentuating the division of labour in organisations in the 1920s. He believed that people were motivated mainly by money and self-interest. About ten years later, research by Elton Mayo and his colleagues in the famous Hawthorne study showed that people are influenced by the social aspects of their job. Other findings by such writers as Maslow, McGregor and Herzberg all focused on the individual and his/her needs. A further viewpoint is that put forward by Schein, who argued that the reasons for motivation change and can be different from one situation to another.

Rational/ economic man	Social man	Self-actualising man	Complex man
Factors: Money Self-interest	Groups Working with others	Self-esteem Achievement Self-fulfilment	Depends on situation and experience, therefore can change
Therefore: Provide controls and monetary incentives	Help satisfy social needs – link these to company goals	People naturally behave responsibly and enjoy achallenge. Encouragement vital	Respond to people individually, bearing in mind the circumstances

CHECK IT YOURSELF

1 From the following list of motivating factors, write down (in descending order) those which you consider most important to you, then to your boss and then to a junior employee in your organisation. Then compare your lists!

Achievement	Salary
Advancement	Recognition
Job growth	Job interest
Status	Power
Responsibility	Social contacts

If your lists don't match, consider whether you are correct or whether your assumptions about other people perhaps need re-evaluating!

2   As a group, hold a brainstorming session to discover as many additional factors as you can.

3   Read more about the work of the writers mentioned by visiting your local or college library.

Leadership

There have been many theories about leadership – but the general findings are that a good leader is not some special creature, born with special attributes not given to the rest of us. You can learn to be a good leader by watching those people who you consider to be effective at leading others – and noting how they do this. You can judge a good leader by his or her ability to increase work output and keep subordinates happy at the same time! The situational theory suggests that in different situations we would choose a different leader: the person best suited to help you to set up a new computer system may not be the one who would make the best leader on a camping weekend in the Lake District!

RULE 3

Good leaders are made, not born. The most general theory is that we choose as a leader someone who, in a given situation, will help us to achieve our objective.

CHECK IT YOURSELF

Think of a good leader you know and note down all the factors you think contribute to this. Now think of someone you know who is not a good leader and list down the important factors here. What can you learn from the exercise about your own style of leadership?

The key aspects of leadership

Whilst there are no all-encompassing qualities which make a good leader, some key aspects are given below. Check how many appear on your list – though you may have thought of several other good qualities not shown here:

● an interest in people at least equal to a desire to get the job done
● a good listener who takes note of another individual's view and, wherever possible, utilises it
● decisive but makes decisions on sound reasoning, not impulse
● owns his or her own problems – never places the burden of these on subordinates

- sets high standards but also sets a good example to be followed
- is sensitive to the needs and expectations of others
- is a good communicator
- knows what motivates each individual and uses this to gain cooperation and interest in a job
- gives praise and recognition for a job well done. Offers help, rather than criticism, if the job is not well done.

Assumptions, theories and actions

Start by reading the following situation.

Karen, Fatima and Steven met the new girl for the first time over coffee on Tuesday morning. They talked with her for 15 minutes. Later, back in the office, they talked about the impression they had gained of her.

Karen: 'I think she's really nice. She was really friendly and obviously interested in what we do'.

Fatima: 'Interested? She never stopped asking questions. You want to be careful what you tell people you hardly know.'

Steven: 'Anyone who wants to know so much must have a reason. I'm not struck on her – I think she's very ambitious myself.'

The important question here is not who is right – because we don't know – but why they all have a different version of the same conversation and a different impression of the same person!

Our assumptions about people and events are coloured by our own views on the world which, in turn, are affected by our experiences, attitudes, values and expectations. It is therefore hardly surprising that we view the same events in completely different ways.

The problem is that we all think that our own view of reality is correct – and, indeed, is the only one possible. In truth, we may often be wrong and can learn much by comparing our own view of a situation with someone else's view.

For the same reason that we are not aware of alternative versions of an event, unless we really sit down and think about it, we are also not aware that the assumptions we make about a situation affect the way we act. Chris Argyris, a well-known management writer, called this our theory of action, but pointed out that it often differs from what he called our espoused theory (see also Element 4.1).

RULE 4

What we say we believe in and therefore do, and what we actually believe in and therefore do, are often completely different – and are noticed by others far more than by ourselves!

In a leadership situation, you may have an espoused theory which allows for delegation, praise of subordinates, helping them if they are in difficulty, etc. However, your theory of action may be completely different – or at least be perceived by your staff to be different. They may see you as autocratic, bossy and only concerned that a task is done – not with how they feel about it.

CHECK IT YOURSELF

A way of finding out about this, if you can bear to do it, is to write down all the attributes of a good leader that you noted before – plus the ones we gave – and score yourself on each one as very good, good or poor.

Now give the same list (without your scores) to two friends and ask them to score you in the same way. Be prepared for some shocks! But note – if you thought you were good at something and both of them did not, who is right?

Groups and teams

In addition to managing other people on an individual basis you may also be involved in managing or working with a group of people. The behaviour of groups or teams is determined by:

- who is the informal leader
- standards of behaviour in the group
- group cohesiveness or loyalty
- the nature and motivation of the members
- the similarity (or otherwise) of the tasks in which they are involved
- the size of the group.

RULE 5

The *difference* between a group and a team is that whilst both may have a common purpose, a common leader and a common identity, the team will also work together to accomplish a communal goal, utilising the strengths of each person to the best effect.

The *similarity* between a group and a team is that both can be evaluated in two ways:

- their effectiveness in accomplishing tasks
- the satisfaction of the members.

Some general principles are:

- groups become more effective the longer they are together
- groups are more cohesive if they are small and/or if the members are involved in similar work
- a group is easier to control if the informal leader has the same aims and goals as the formal leader
- groups can impose their own rules and norms – which can include sanctions against members who do not conform to the ideas of the rest.

Tips for successful management of a team include:

- finding out the informal leader and, if possible, getting him/her on your side
- being alert for signs of trouble
- fostering team morale, rather than individual morale
- making their work as interesting, challenging and demanding as you can
- concentrating on managing the team, not the individual tasks
- being prepared to intercede on behalf of your team
- helping individual members to achieve their personal aims.

RULE 6

The natural instinct of a team is to protect itself. If there is a problem then the formal leader may be the last to know. The first inclination of all members will be to solve the problem themselves – and not involve 'outsiders'. Be aware of this and keep your eye open for any danger signs that all is not well. Try to identify one person in the team who may be prepared to tell you what is going on.

Team danger signs

These include:

- poor performance – missed deadlines, shoddy work
- bickering and arguments amongst members
- the team breaking up into different factions
- lack of interest in the well-being of the team as a whole
- taking no interest in solving problems, effects of actions or team activities.

If the problems stem from the behaviour of one person – who seems impervious to your attempts to help – then you must seek help yourself. There are times when all theories of motivation can appear to fail and the only solution is to move someone out of the team. For this, you need to have explored all other possible alternatives and have the support and backing of your own boss.

5 Research, prepare and supply information

Element 5.1

Research, locate and select information to meet specified needs

You work in the Human Resources department of a large organisation – and you are about to have a busy day!

Your new receptionist greets you with the news that she has just taken a telephone call from 'someone' who wants to have an urgent meeting with you immediately. She *thinks* his name was something like 'Naylor' or possibly 'Taylor' but isn't quite sure. You restrain yourself from strangling her – after all she is new – and set about trying to find out who the caller is and whether it is someone from inside or outside the organisation. You check the internal telephone directory for anyone of the same or a similar name and, after a few discreet enquiries, you discover that the caller was Mr Tyler, the Finance Director.

Your manager has asked you to write a section on the recruitment of physically disabled staff for inclusion in the department's strategic development plan. You have most of the factual information on the department's computer database, which makes life easier. However, you contact the Disabled Resettlement Officer at the local Employment Service office to check that the legal information you are going to include is up-to-date.

You draft out some advertisements for staff vacancies based on information sent to you by the relevant departmental managers. In one case, the information is incomplete and you therefore telephone the manager concerned to get further information. He is slightly offended that you cannot read his handwriting – he has apparently never heard of a typewriter, let alone a word processor – but you manage to find out what you want to know.

You send letters to three different conference centres asking for their tariffs and for details of any discount they may be prepared to offer for bulk bookings.

In the afternoon, you attend a training session on new training awards – and come away with a mass of documentation. You are quite pleased, however, because not only will it be useful in your job, it will also help you in the course you are undertaking on a part-time basis at the local college.

In the interval between your finishing work and attending college that evening, you call into the library to check the library catalogue for any relevant journals you can use to complete your next assignment.

Although your day has been varied in many respects, there is a common theme running throughout – that of locating and using information. In the above example you used paper-based and computerised sources of information. You also made good use of people. You acquired information both to satisfy your own needs and also those of others.

An administrator or a PA cannot operate effectively without having a trusted and extensive database of information – whether it is in written or computerised form. Equally he or she should have ready access to a network of people who can supply information when needed.

The key word here is 'trusted'. Out-of-date, incomplete or inaccurate information is at best irritating and at worst dangerous. If you have an inaccurate telephone list it is time-consuming and therefore costly to make unnecessary telephone calls or to track down the correct number. If you know only half of a story then you could make totally wrong decisions based on that information which you will regret long into the future. If you have an out-of-date set of safety procedures, you may be standing next to your boss in court if the HSE Inspector turns up unexpectedly!

Ways of determining information needs

Before you can set about finding a relevant source of information you have first of all to determine what you want to know. In some cases this is straightforward; in others, it is less so.

Read the following script of a conversation between Julia, an administrator, and her boss, Andre, who is the manager of a family-owned seaside hotel. His boss is the Managing Director.

Andre: The printers have sent through the first draft of the new brochure but there are still some gaps in it. Can you let them have the up-to-date tariff – including the discounts we give for off-season bookings?

Julia: What are the discounts?

Andre: I don't know exactly – I'll have to talk it over with the boss but I don't think there's going to be too much change on last year. You could do a bit of phoning round the other hotels to see what deals they are offering – don't say who you are of course.

Julia: I'll do my best.

Andre: Good – now the next thing is the businesswoman's lunch organised for the 27th. Their secretary nabbed me in the bar last night and in a weak moment I agreed to find two suitable speakers. She was a bit vague about who she wanted – she just said that they must be female and successful. Can you do something about it? She frightens the wits out of me.

Julia: I'll try.

Andre: Fine – now what's next – oh yes – I was at the Grand Hotel last night and noticed some really nice sketches in their restaurant. I think they are by a local artist. Can you find out who did them and see if we can commission whoever it is to do some drawings for us? Oh, and one more thing, early warning about the series of wine tasting evenings we are holding next month. We're having a French evening, a German evening, a Californian evening and – as a change – an Australian evening. Can you get together some information about those countries for me – interesting facts and figures, national characteristics and so on? It might also be a good idea to find out if any of the hotel staff speaks French or German or is from the USA or Australia – they can be on duty that night to add a bit of local colour. Just see what you can do, will you?

Julia: OK.

Obviously Julia is either very new or a bit frightened of her boss! She has been asked to find out a lot of information and in some cases the instructions have been less than precise.

TEST YOURSELF

Even given that an administrator has to use his or her own initiative, Julia should have asked for more clarification on certain points. Alternatively she could have made some initial investigations and then reported back to her boss to check whether or not she was on the right lines.

1 Discuss as a group:
   a which information Julia could obtain without further assistance
   b which she could prepare in draft form prior to checking back with Andre for further instructions
   c which of the information she has been asked to find involves primary research and which involves secondary research.

2 Write a short report on the sources of reference you would use to find out the information required. Check your answers with those of the rest of the group. (See page 261 if you require any assistance.)

DID YOU KNOW?

Sources of information can be classified as primary or secondary.

Primary research is original research – where you have to find out and collate information which does not yet exist in that particular form. Methods include interviews, surveys and questionnaires. This is sometimes known as 'field' research.

Secondary research relates to accessing information which already exists – either inside or outside the organisation. Sources include computer databases, CD-ROMs, office files, reference books, journals and newspapers. This is sometimes known as 'desk' research.

As an administrator or PA you are more likely to be involved in secondary research.

Identification of own needs

Difficult though the situation was for Julia, at least Andre was giving her some guidance. She was not acting purely independently. In some cases, however, that is exactly what an administrator or PA must do. This will therefore mean:

- setting a specific objective, e.g. 'to obtain information about local employment agencies to include in a report to the Board of Directors'
- placing limits on that objective, e.g. 'within a 10 mile radius', 'for secretarial staff only', 'by the end of this month', etc.
- checking back to the original objective at intervals to see whether it is in the process of being achieved or whether it needs adaptation
- asking advice – even though an administrator or PA may be acting independently there is rarely a need to operate in complete isolation. There may, for instance, be another administrator in the organisation who has carried out a similar job and who is prepared to pass on his or her experience.

Identification of departmental needs

Most administrators work in a specific area of an organisation and will therefore need to be aware of the information needs of that particular area. If you work in the Human Resources department, for instance, you or your boss may want to know:

- the wage rates locally for staff employed in similar organisations
- any changes in employment or health and safety legislation
- the age, experience and qualifications of all staff aged under 25 in the organisation.

On the other hand, if you work in the Marketing Department you may be more interested in finding out about:

- results of surveys relating to customer preferences, product test marketing, consumer buying trends, etc.
- information about competitors
- the financial status or credit rating of foreign organisations interested in buying from you for the first time.

Select *either* the department or area in which you are at present working *or* one of the areas listed below and discuss as a group or with your tutor the types of information which would be of most interest to each one:

● Research and Development
● Production
● Finance and Accounts
● Sales
● Computer Services.

Sources of information

Once you have identified what information is required, the next step is obviously to start acquiring it. Sources of information are numerous – computer databases, books, journals, professional experts, etc. – but it is *your* knowledge and your experience which can prove of most help initially.

Personal and office files

Do not be tempted into thinking that time spent organising the office filing system, computer database or internal telephone directory is time which could be spent on more important work. If your personal and office files are not comprehensive, up-to-date and tailor-made for your own particular needs, they are of little use. In general terms you should have readily available information on:

● names, addresses and telephone/fax numbers of clients (plus, where relevant, the name of their administrator or PA)
● internal telephone users
  – names, titles and extension numbers of everyone in the organisation
● agencies
  – travel
  – employment
● sources of supply
  – office stationery and equipment
● maintenance services (either within or outside the organisation)
  – electrical
  – plumbing
  – heating
● local restaurants/hotels/caterers
● local garages.

Your office files, too, should supply you with most of the information you need about both your own organisation and your outside business contacts.

Your computer system

Most organisations today keep a wide range of information on computer. This is particularly the case if a computerised Management Information System (MIS) is in operation. This can provide you with reports on sales, purchasing, recruitment and profitability as well as lists of customers and suppliers. Technically an organisation's MIS system should be organised to meet the needs of the users – if you have a definite need which is not met then it is well worth talking to Computer Services about it (or asking your boss to do it for you). Do bear in mind, however, that you may not have automatic access to all the information you want – some may be for executive eyes only! One way round this is either to ask your boss to obtain it for you or ask for his or her written authorisation to the computer services department to issue you with the most up-to-date printout.

If your organisation runs a networked system then you may find additional information available – you may also have access to Internet or to computer databanks. These are covered on page 266.

Outside sources of reference

Julia may have found difficulty in obtaining some of the information Andre requested because, in order to do so, she had to go outside her own organisation to find it. Even Andre suspected that the other hotels might not be too interested in supplying her with the information she wanted! Although in most cases you do not have to resort to giving a false name, it is wise to remember that many outside organisations are not normally paid to help you and that therefore you have to be polite rather than demanding when asking for information. However, it pays to be persistent – whilst always remaining tactful. Remember that contacting the right person is the key to success, and it is an old sales trick to telephone the switchboard first to try to ascertain the name of the person you want – rather than just 'cold calling' and asking to be put through to a particular department. Remember, too, that if you are completely at a loss about whom you should contact, ask for the Public Relations department, if you think there is one, or throw yourself on the receptionist's mercy. Even if he or she cannot help, don't sound exasperated – you may need assistance on another occasion.

Outside organisations

Much depends on the nature of your query. However, examples of **general** sources include:

- local government and town hall departments
- the Post Office
- newspaper information services, e.g. *The Times*, the *Daily Telegraph*
- consumers' associations and consumer watchdogs, e.g. OFTEL

- individual advisers, e.g. solicitors, accountants.

Outside organisations which may be able to help you with a **travel** query are:

- embassies and national tourist offices
- local tourist information centres
- travel agencies
- AA/RAC/National Breakdown
- airline offices/shipping offices
- British Rail
- local car hire firms
- passport offices
- local Customs and Excise Departments
- hotel booking services.

Business queries tend to be more specialised, but useful sources include:

- the public relations departments of large firms
- local Chambers of Commerce and Industry
- London Chamber of Commerce and Industry
- the Institute of Management – its information centre in London houses one of the world's largest management libraries
- professional bodies (a full list is given in *Whitaker's Almanack* – see page 326 for further details)
- trade associations
- HMSO (see page 332 for details of its publications)
- British Standards Institute (for approved standards of production, etc.)
- Advisory, Conciliation and Arbitration Service (ACAS) – its Work Research Unit provides details of published articles on all aspects of employment
- the Department of Trade and Industry (particularly for information about registered companies)
- the Commission of the European Union (background report sheets are available on a wide range of topics of interest concerning the EU).

You may also have **staff welfare** queries to answer. In most organisations people are the major and most expensive resource. If, for some personal or domestic reason, they become demotivated or less effective than usual, the whole productivity of the organisation will suffer and as their supervisor it may be your job to try to help them with their problems. Remember, however, that no matter how sympathetic and empathetic you may be, you are probably not qualified to give expert advice on dealing with awkward neighbours or bad-tempered husbands or to sort out someone's love life or financial problems! What might be useful to you on such occasions is to know what professional help there is available.

Below is given a list of organisations (or people) who could assist you with staff welfare problems. Find out the addresses and telephone numbers of each one and use these as a start to your own personal staff welfare file:

- the local Department of Social Security
- the local Department of Inland Revenue
- the local Employment Service office
- the local Citizens Advice Bureau
- local councillors
- the local MP
- the local authority Trading Standards Inspector/Public Health Inspector
- Race Relations Commission
- Equal Opportunities Commission
- the appropriate Ombudsman (see also page 235).

DID YOU KNOW?

Some attempts are now being made to charge enquirers for the provision of statistical information. The head of the government's statistical service, the Central Statistical Office, is keen on doing just that. He argues that the provision of information should be paid for in the same way as the provision of any other service.

The reference library

The local library is an obvious source of reference for you not only because of the books and journals it contains but also because of the specialised knowledge of the library staff. Part of their role nowadays is to deal with a wide and varying number of information queries. If you are a regular user then it is useful to get to know the staff – then, if you are lucky, not only will they be more willing to help you but they may be quite happy to answer a simple query over the telephone. (See also page 268.)

DID YOU KNOW?

The *Guide to Government Departments and other Libraries*, published bi-annually by the British Library, lists a large number of specialist libraries, as does *Libraries in the UK and Republic of Ireland*. In addition, you might want or need to make use of books such as the *Guide to Libraries and Information Units (in Government Departments and other organisations)* and the *Guide to Libraries in Western Europe*.

Reference books

A single list of reference books is often meaningless, unless the index of the entire contents of the British Library is reproduced! However, it is possible to classify the major reference materials into the following sections:

- Books about books
- General reference
- People
- English usage
- Travel
- Business – at home
- Business – overseas
- Government publications
- Statistics.

CHECK IT YOURSELF

Rather than just reading through the list in the Appendix at the end of this Unit (pages 325–333), take it to your college or nearest town library and check to see how many are on the shelves or in stock. (Remember that some libraries keep certain reference books in reserve storage to be handed over only on request.) Remember also to use the library index! (See page 277 for ways of locating and selecting information.)

If you are working in a group it might be a good idea to impose a time limit of, say, 20 minutes for each member to locate at least five titles in a particular section and to compare notes afterwards.

DID YOU KNOW?

Although in most cases you can make use of the reference material in your nearest reference library, you may also need to buy some books. If possible, choose those which are in loose leaf form in a binder so that they can be updated. In such cases the publishers will provide a regular updating service in return for an annual subscription. A further option is to subscribe to a weekly or monthly journal on the topic.

Business periodicals/journals

The choice of journals depends very much on the specialised area in which you work. However, certain journals are of interest to almost anyone working in the business sphere. Examples are:

- *Accountancy*
- *Business Equipment Digest*
- *Computer Bulletin/Computer Weekly*
- *European Management Journal*
- *Financial Management* (US)
- *Human Resource Management*
- *Industrial Relations Journal*
- *Journal of General Management*
- *Journal of Marketing*
- *Management Accounting*
- *Management Today*

- *Modern Management*
- *New Statesman and Society*
- *New Scientist*
- *Spectator*
- *Office Equipment News*
- *Training*

Journals can often be more useful than books because they are more up-to-date. For instance, if you wanted to find out details of the latest types of fax machines on the market, you would be well advised to look in the latest edition of *Office Equipment News* for information on different models and the names and addresses of suppliers – rather than relying on a textbook which may be out of date.

Computer databanks

An increasing amount of information is now held in computer databanks – the name given to a database which contains a large quantity of reference material. Some information is stored on library databanks: other information can be accessed through public computer databanks and private viewdata to which you pay a subscription.

Public computer databanks

In the case of a public computer databank, the information can be recalled in the usual way on to a computer VDU or an adapted television set. Such databanks include the following.

- **Teletext**
  This is a one-way communication system by which the user can request information but cannot transmit any. In the UK, Teletext is known as Ceefax (available on BBC) and Oracle (available on ITV). It is essentially a free service although the user must purchase a television with Teletext included or an add-on Teletext facility for an existing television. When Teletext is accessed an index is displayed on the screen and, with the aid of a hand-held digital unit, the user is then able to request the pages (or frames) of information required. Information available includes subjects of general interest.

- **Videotext (or viewdata)**
  This is an interactive system through which users can both request and transmit information. A keyboard and a modem are required to enable the user to communicate with viewdata and the viewdata equipment is connected to a telephone line.

  One form of viewdata is a public system known in the UK as New Prestel. To access this service the user dials a given number and then enters his/her identity and personal password. An index is displayed on the screen and there is also a directory which can be consulted. Users pay a quarterly charge for the service, the charge of a local telephone call to access the system and a charge for computer time during business hours. Most of the information is available to all users but some is restricted to closed groups, i.e. specified users.

Information provided includes both general and specialist topics. The following services are also available:

- an electronic mail service (see page 479)
- a telex link.

What you may also find, however, is that you have access to a private viewdata system.

● **Private viewdata**
A complete private viewdata package usually includes a computer, a number of viewdata terminals and the viewdata software. The normal procedure is for an organisation to create and maintain a private database for certain specific applications, access being available to both staff and clients. Tour operators, for instance, often allow travel agents to access their system. In addition, travel agents can participate in the Galileo system which enables them to access a wide range of travel information and produce their own tickets.

It is also possible for the Prestel and the private viewdata system to be interlinked by means of the Gateway system so that you can make use of both systems.

● **Internet**
Today the most rapidly growing method of accessing information and transmitting messages (and even research papers) is through the Internet system. This was established in America in the early 1970s when the American government set up a communications system designed to survive an all-out nuclear attack. In 1990 the system was opened up to universities, colleges and private institutions. The number of users has grown from about 5000 in 1985 to over 30 million today.

Internet contains a huge variety of information – from news and travel to the complete works of Shakespeare. With an additional piece of software you can access the World Wide Web. This is a network which includes multimedia libraries, newspapers, magazine publishers and many others. The pages also offer graphics and sound as well as basic text. To access Internet you need to be connected to a service provider. A Bulletin Board service provider such as CIX or CompuServe is usually best as they also have their own services and help you if you have any queries. They will charge you a registration fee and monthly fees plus a charge for the time you spend linked to their computer.

The advantage of Internet is the huge amount of information it contains and the fact that it is interactive – you can exchange information with someone else or even order goods and services via the Net. The disadvantage is the fact that the information is stored randomly so it can be difficult to find what you need. In addition – as you have probably read in the press – there are as yet no controls on what is put on Internet so you may find some of the material unsuitable or even offensive.

Internet is dealt with again in Unit 6 – but this time more in terms of the hardware and software you will need to use the service.

DID YOU KNOW?

1 A pilot project is currently under way – authorised by the Cabinet Office – to distribute government information through the Internet system. (See page 344.)

2 One of the most useful functions of Internet is E-mail. This is dealt with in Unit 7.

3 If your organisation does not want to set up a system for its own use but wants to access other subject-specific systems, there are now a number of such services available. If, for instance, you work in exporting, you might want to make use of an organisation such as Export Network, an information system for exporters which covers areas such as marketing, business contacts, local agents and distributors, finance and insurance regulations, documentation, freight, transport and communications. The information is accessed via a computer terminal and modem through a telephone line.

CHECK IT YOURSELF

If you want to try out Internet for yourself then there are cafés and pubs in Belfast, Brighton, Cambridge, Edinburgh, London, Manchester and Nottingham which offer you the opportunity for about £2.50 for 30 minutes! Alternatively, find a friend who has a link and ask him or her to let you try it.

You can also find out information on service providers by ringing CIX on 0181 296 9666 or CompuServe on 0800 289378 and asking for further details.

Library databanks

Other useful sources worth noting are the databanks now used by many libraries. These contain a wide variety of information on any number of topics and are normally designed to list the titles of any publications relating to your specific inquiry. In addition, some databanks will provide you with summaries of book contents or journal articles. Examples include:

- MARC (Machine Readable Cataloguing) – details of books and journals published worldwide
- DIALOG – details of publications from a wide variety of general sources
- IRS (Information Retrieval Service) – general information on a variety of topics
- TOXLINE/MEDLINE – specific information on medical matters
- LEXIS – legal information.

Note that although you may be able to gain direct access to a library databank, it is also possible to ask the library to institute a search for you (normally for a fee).

DID YOU KNOW?

BLAISE (British Library Automated Information Service) provides computer access to a database held at the British Library which tries to keep a copy of every book published in this country.

Ways of researching information

The way in which you should set about researching the information you want depends very much on:

- the problem you have been given
- whether you are expected to find out and present objective facts or your own opinion
- whether your research is primary (i.e. original) or secondary
- your possible sources of information.

Some problems are very specific and you have fairly obvious 'known' sources you can turn to. Others are more 'woolly' – as shown in the case study at the beginning of this Element. Often when you start exploring the problem other ideas will come to light. This is frequently the case if the need for research is not clearly specified by someone else but is identified by yourself.

The first stage is to gather preliminary information to help you to understand the problem in more detail – and then to list possible methods of investigation. This will usually give you a clue as to how to start.

As an example, imagine that your boss arrives in a state one morning. Yesterday he bought a new tax disc for his car but, search though he might, he cannot find it. He leaves the office in a rush for an urgent appointment and asks you to solve the problem while he is away. You are a non-driver and have no idea how to help him. Where do you start?

Questions to ask

1 Where did he buy his new tax disc and what paperwork was involved? Who could give you this information in his absence?
2 What could be the consequences of the loss?

Method of investigation

You ask another driver in the office who tells you that he always goes to the Post Office to renew his tax disc. He also tells you that tax discs are handled by the Vehicle Licensing Office in Wales (somewhere) and that your boss will be in trouble with the police if he doesn't display a current tax disc on his vehicle.

At this point you ring the police and ask for advice. They tell you to telephone the Post Office, they also ask you for the registration number of your boss's car and his name. Luckily you have the number of his car in your personal file. The police give you a reference number and tell you to inform him to put a note in the windscreen where the new tax disc should be, quoting this number.

You then look up the central number of Post Office enquiries in your Phone Book, contact them and are informed you will need to collect form V20 for your boss to complete. He will need to send off his car registration document as well and enclose a small fee for a replacement licence. You collect the form during your lunch hour.

Presenting the information

Because you will have left the office by the time your boss returns you type a short memo giving him the facts, attaching the note for his windscreen and the form for the Post Office. You keep a copy on file – just in case your boss loses the memo in the same way he lost his tax disc!

Reviewing the procedures

From the above example, you will see that you can combine several sources of information to satisfy your specific need. For instance, you can:

- ask someone for the information – either personally or over the telephone
- look in your office files (see page 279)
- search for it in a book, journal or newspaper
- consult a computer database.

Sometimes, however, it is difficult to determine which is the best source to use. Suppose, for instance, your boss wants to know about the latest EU legislation on health and safety. You could:

- look in a reference book such as *Croner's A–Z of Business Information Sources*, a copy of which you may have in your organisation

- visit the reference library to see if it has any relevant information
- speak to your own Health and Safety Officer
- telephone the HSE.

Any one of these approaches is likely to provide you with the information you require. What you must decide is which is:

a quickest
b most convenient
c most accurate
d most complete.

Again you may decide to use more than one source. You may, for instance, decide to consult your reference library *and* speak to the HSE. However, in this case you are using this method to check the **validity** of the information you have been given by one source. Indeed, the more important it is that the information should be accurate, the more vital it is that you should cross–check it somewhere else.

TEST YOURSELF

You have been asked to find out the following information.

a Suggest at least two sources from which it might be obtained.
b List which items of information you would cross-check from more than one source.

1 Your firm has just won a lucrative contract to supply goods to a firm in Spain and there is likely to be a considerable amount of correspondence between the two firms. You have been asked to find out the name and address of a Spanish/English translator.

2 Your boss is going on a business trip to Brussels next month. He wants to know the name of a good 4-star hotel and the times of flights from the nearest airport (he wants to fly direct if possible). He will be travelling outwards on a Tuesday and returning on Friday of the same week.

3 Your department is updating its reprographic facilities and your boss asks you to write a short report giving details of what you think are the two leading makes of photocopying equipment – together with your reasons.

4 You work as an administrator at the local radio station and you are asked to find out about two guests who are to appear on one of the programmes. One is the local MP and the other a well known local businessman. The radio show presenter likes his show to be contentious and often tries to provoke his guests by asking them an unexpected question about themselves.

Legal and regulatory requirements

Copyright

There is only so much that you can remember – or so much that you want to write or type out when you are gathering together information for a particular job. In such circumstances your photocopier becomes one of your most valuable pieces of equipment!

However, you are not allowed to copy anything you want. You must be aware of the provisions of the Copyright, Designs and Patents Act 1988 and make sure that you do not break copyright law by either carrying out or allowing unrestricted photocopying of certain documents.

The Copyright, Designs and Patents Act 1988

Works protected by copyright

- literary, dramatic, musical and artistic works
- sound recordings, films, broadcasts and cable programmes
- the typographical arrangements of published editions
  (i.e. the whole layout of the printed pages of a published edition of a work)

Length of copyright period

Literary, dramatic musical and artistic works	copyright expires at the end of the 50th year after the year in which the author died
Sound recordings and films	copyright expires at the end of 50 years from the end of the year in which the work was made or released
Typographical arrangements	copyright expires at the end of the 25th year after the year in which the edition incorporating the arrangement was first published.

Rights of the copyright owner

The owner has the exclusive right to

- copy the work
- issue copies of it to the public
- perform, show or play the work in public
- broadcast it or include it in a cable programme service
- adapt it

Copyright will not be infringed if the work is used for certain specific purposes such as

- research or private study
- criticism or review of a work provided the identity of the author and the title of the work are acknowledged
- the reporting of current events provided the identity of the author is acknowledged
- incidental inclusion of any work in an artistic work, sound recording, broadcast or cable programme, e.g. a shot in a film showing a book lying on a table with its title visible
- educational use

Note: If a licence has been negotiated, such exceptions do not apply.

- libraries and archives – specific regulations are contained in the Copyright (Libraries and Archivists) (Copying of Copyright Material) Regulations 1989
- the reporting of Parliamentary or judicial proceedings, the proceedings of a Royal Commission or statutory enquiry
- abstracts – the copying of an abstract (summary) or an article on a scientific or technical subject published in a periodical containing both the abstract or article

Other exceptions relate mainly to the use of sound recordings and artistic designs.

Figure 5.1.1 The Copyright, Designs and Patents Act 1988

If someone writes a book, composes a song, makes a film or creates any other type of artistic work, the law treats that work as his or her property (or copyright). Anyone else who wishes to make use of it (by, for instance, taking a photocopy of it) must get permission to do so and – on occasions – must be prepared to pay a fee.

One difficulty for authors and composers in the past has been how to collect the fees owing to them. Today, however, there are a number of collecting agencies which have been established to ensure that such payments are made:

- the Copyright Licensing Agency (CLA)
- the Performing Rights Society (PRS)
- the Mechanical Copyright Protection Society (MCPS)
- the Phonographic Performance Ltd (PPL)
- the Video Performance Ltd (CPL)
- the Design and Artists Copyright Society (DADS)
- the Educational Recording Agency Ltd (ERA).

In most cases, therefore, authors or composers will entrust the administration of their copyright to these societies in return for a percentage of the fees collected. What the societies will also do is to grant a blanket licence to both public and private individuals to give them the right to photocopy certain publications on the payment of a fee. Such licences now cover most educational institutions and negotiations are currently taking place with government establishments, industry and commerce.

The most important thing to remember, of course, is that these societies act as watchdogs and protect the interests of their members by checking on both libraries and other organisations to see that no unauthorised photocopying is being carried out!

CHECK IT YOURSELF

Most libraries display notices giving details of

a   what you are or are not allowed to photocopy, and
b   the penalties for breaking these regulations.

Most organisations have similar notices displayed in their reprographics sections. Try to obtain a copy from your place of work and compare its contents with those obtained by the rest of the group.

 ## TEST YOURSELF

You have made yourself aware of the provisions of the Copyright, Designs and Patents Act. You want to make sure that your junior staff also know about them.

1   Prepare a brief summary of the relevant provisions of the Act for them.

2   Discuss with your tutor what procedures you could institute to ensure that your junior staff do not breach copyright by accident. Consider points such as:
   –   a check on what (if any) licensing arrangements are in existence and what paperwork needs to be carried out
   –   an audit of the types of document normally photocopied (and the quantity)
   –   the classification of documents into high/medium/no risk areas
   –   the use of forms to be completed and signed by individual users stating the purpose of the photocopying
   –   the use of training sessions to raise the awareness of your junior staff
   –   your role as administrator and your responsibility for any decision taken in this area.

Defamation

Breach of copyright is not the only legal concern you may have when carrying out any research. You may, for instance, discover some information which you should not pass on to anyone! Look at the following example.

Your company is preparing a very important tender for a building contract with the local authority. Your boss knows that two other local firms are preparing tenders and is worried that one of them at least might submit a lower tender. He suspects that the Managing Director of that firm might have some 'insider knowledge' as his daughter is going out with one of the senior members of staff in the Housing Department. He asks you to find out as much information as possible about both the firm and the personal relationship between the individuals concerned. You happen to know the daughter slightly and have seen her with the housing official on more than one occasion. Indeed, when you last met her in a wine bar she intimated to you that your firm had no chance of winning the contract as she was going to use her 'influence' to make sure her father was the lowest bidder. You tell your boss about this and also include what you have been told in a short report.

You have been rather unwise! Almost certainly you will have been guilty of defamation – what you said about the daughter may be slanderous: what you have written about her may be libellous. Your defence may be that you are justified in making that statement – but to be successful you must *prove* that you are telling the truth and in this situation, unless you have a witness to support you, you have little chance in doing so. Unless, therefore, the injured party, i.e. the daughter, is prepared to accept your apology, you may find that you have to pay her some compensation in the form of damages.

The moral – be *very* careful about what you say or write – even if, as a loyal administrator or PA, you have discovered some information which you think is of vital importance to the organisation.

Data protection

The law not only protects people from having their work copied without their **consent** or their reputation from being harmed, it also protects them from having information stored about them without their **knowledge**. The Data Protection Act 1984 places restrictions on the information which can be stored on a computerised data system. This Act is covered in more detail in Unit 6, page 368.

TEST YOURSELF

You have just started a new job as the office administrator in the Human Resources department of a large organisation and have been asked to oversee the installation of a new electronic filing system. You have made yourself aware of the provisions of the Data Protection Act but when you have a chat with your senior filing clerk you begin to be concerned about his apparent lack of knowledge of the Act.

Read the comments he has made and discuss with the rest of the group or your tutor whether or not you have reason to worry! (You might find it useful to look ahead to page 368 before you answer this question.)

'Can you let me know as soon as possible when this new system will be up and running? I need to let all my staff have access to it. Alison was speaking to me the other day and said that you intended to give free access to everyone in the organisation but I reassured her and said that confidentiality was still our main priority. She was also worried about getting rid of any records – we've always had a policy of keeping *all* records in case references are required – no matter how old or out-of-date they are. Surely we're still going to stick to that. Incidentally, I need your advice – the senior managers always put comments into the personnel files of their staff about whether or not they are suitable for future promotion. Do we transfer over that information along with everything else?'

Ways of preserving the confidentiality and security of information

Even if the information you supply to your boss is not defamatory or in breach of a statutory requirement, it may be sufficiently confidential for him or her not to want it on view to all members of the staff. As an administrator, however, you may find some difficulty in keeping information confidential and secure, particularly if you are also responsible for coordinating the work of a number of staff. Avoid the temptation of merely having a filing cabinet marked 'Confidential – keep out.' You can virtually guarantee that the office snoop will spend hours trying to work out how to find the key to it. Avoid also trying to find a totally secure 'hiding place' – you won't be able to!

Much depends on your relationship with your staff. Most staff know that there is information to which they will either have no access or only restricted access and, in most cases, provided you make the reason clear to them, they will cooperate with you. Any rules about the locking of filing cabinets or the storage of particularly vital documents in safes or vaults are then likely to be accepted as part of normal office procedure.

What you may also want to establish – either independently or after consultation with your boss – are **levels** of confidentiality. It might be that your boss does not want even you to see some information, in which case he or she has to make that clear. The same procedure can be repeated down the structure to the newest junior although, if you do decide to take this route, you will have to be prepared to spend a long time deciding what type of information is confidential and who is to have access to it.

If the information is in disk form or stored electronically, you have additional options open to you. You can, for instance, make use of a password to which only authorised users have access. In some cases there may be several levels of user, some being allowed access via a password to some levels of information; others being allowed access to all levels. As an extra precaution, passwords can be changed at regular intervals. Even so, confidentiality can never be assured – especially given the expertise many computer users now possess which they can use to 'hack' into a system. (*Note*: confidentiality and security in relation to computers is dealt with in more detail in Unit 6, page 361.)

DID YOU KNOW?

Some organisations are so worried about the possibility of their computer-based confidential information being accessed by unauthorised members of staff that they are now including in their disciplinary procedures a rule stating that any such unauthorised access will result in summary dismissal – and the industrial tribunals have supported them.

Ways of locating and selecting information

In the 'Test Yourself' exercise on page 271 you were asked to name two sources to which you would make reference in order to obtain certain items of information.

However, identifying the sources you are going to use is only the first step. What you then have to do is to find out where they are and how they can be accessed. The next step is to select the information which is most appropriate for your use – particularly if you are drowning under a plethora of paper and reference books!

People

You should already know that one of your major sources of reference is people. Quite often, they are your best source of reference in that, unlike books or computer databases, they can be asked questions or can provide you with additional information about which you were unaware at the beginning of the conversation. However, because they are human, they might need to be dealt with more tactfully and persuasively than a book or machine.

Trained personnel such as library staff or information officers of large organisations will normally be able to assist you with your request even if you are able to give them only a broad outline of what you want – or even if you are not sure whether or not they are the right person to ask. Consequently they are often the best initial source of reference if you are not sure where to start.

As you saw in the example about the lost tax disc, other people can be very useful sources of information provided you make it clear exactly what you want to know. If, therefore, you want to include some statistics about rates of unemployment in a report you are preparing for your manager and decide to contact someone in the Employment Service office, it is a good idea for you to clarify your own thoughts about what questions you are going to ask before making any contact. Otherwise you may find that you have only half the information you want and you risk irritating your source by repeatedly returning to him or her for additional information.

If the information you want is not likely to be readily available, it may be preferable to put your request in writing (possibly with the inclusion of a SAE). The recipient of your letter will then have the time and the opportunity to gather together the required information – and may also be saved from the embarrassment of admitting over the telephone that he or she doesn't know the answer to your questions right away. Remember, in many cases you are asking a very busy person to do you a favour and you do not want to run the risk of a curt refusal.

Asking for information from people who work in your organisation has both advantages and disadvantages. If they are junior to you they will obviously have to try to comply with your request (provided they are sufficiently well trained to do so); if they are colleagues of yours, they will probably be willing to assist you as a matter of professional courtesy. However, if they are senior to you in the organisation you may face some difficulty if they cannot be bothered to help you or have some other reason for not wanting to give you the information.

Ideally you want to talk to someone who is:

a knowledgeable
b articulate
c approachable

– a rare combination!

TEST YOURSELF

Discuss as a group or with your tutor or adviser what you would do if you wanted some information from:

a a clerk in the Accounts department who is junior to you but who is known to be awkward and whose boss is too laid back to do anything about it

b a colleague who is quite willing to assist you but who is rather scatterbrained and you are therefore doubtful about the accuracy of the information she gives you

c a member of the Computer department who will let you have any information you ask for but who gives it to you in an incomprehensible form and full of jargon and terms you've never heard of

d a senior manager who is becoming irritated at your repeated requests for some statistical information

e a manager who responds to your request for information but never gives it in the correct form or amount

f your boss, who sometimes takes the easy way out and tells you what he hopes is the right information – but very often it isn't!

What action would you take in each case? Bear in mind factors such as:

- alternative sources of information
- appeals to other people (either lower or higher in the organisation) – but be careful here!

Office filing systems

The amount of information you will find either in your own office files or in those of other members of staff in your organisation can be quite considerable – and should be easily accessible to you. This pre-supposes, of course, that not only is your filing system immaculate (as, of course, it will be!) but also that other filing systems are equally well kept – which may be a bit more problematic!

It is important to make sure that your staff know how to operate the system as skilfully and accurately as you can.

If you are new to an organisation – or if you feel that the time is appropriate to review your filing system, it is a good idea to check that the information you need is:

- stored in the most appropriate manner
- classified and indexed properly
- accessed quickly and correctly.

CHECK IT YOURSELF

There are several ways in which documents can be stored within a filing cabinet or storage unit. Look through some business supplies catalogues and discuss with your group or your tutor or adviser which type of folder you would use for the following. Note that there may be more than one which is suitable in each case.

- Booklets and catalogues.
- Copies of invoices received.
- Minutes of meetings.
- Day-to-day reminders.

Methods of classification

There is little point in buying expensive storage equipment if no thought is given to the order in which the documents should be stored. Depending on the type of documents with which you are dealing, you can choose from a number of systems, normally known as methods of classification.

1   Check in your own organisation whether the system of classification you use is

- alphabetical
- numerical
- by subject
- geographical
- terminal digit
- chronological
- a combination of systems.

Write a short report describing the system and outlining what you think are its advantages and disadvantages.

2   Obtain some information from the library about each of the other systems mentioned above and add a brief paragraph about them to your report

Methods of indexing

Although many filing classification systems depend on an index, an index can also be useful in its own right to record information such as telephone numbers and addresses. In addition, other facts may be included, e.g. the name of the representative responsible for that account or the credit limit. Often the same index system can be used for both purposes, particularly when a numerical system of classification is used.

Note also that it can be an invaluable tool when you are researching for a large or ongoing project (see page 286).

You can choose from:

- **vertical card index** – the most widely used system whereby cards are stored one behind the other in a box or cabinet
- **strip index** – where the information (normally no more than one or two lines) is stored on one narrow strip of card and housed generally in book form, on a rotary stand or on a frame fixed to a wall
- **visible edge card index** – a series of index cards arranged to overlap, leaving a strip of each card exposed. They can be contained in cabinet or book form.

 ## DID YOU KNOW?

You can locate files stored in an electronic filing system by means of the database menu. No other indexing system is required unless you are storing the disks yourself, in which case you would have to index the disks, normally numerically.

Reference books and journals

If you cannot find what you want from talking to people or looking at your internal reference systems, you will obviously then have to turn your attention to external sources. You are at a slight disadvantage here in that when talking to people you can find out almost immediately whether they have the information you want – and even if they can't help you they may be able to direct you to someone who can. Similarly, you should have a fairly good idea whether you have the information you require in your office files – even if you can't immediately lay your hands on it. Trying to obtain information from a library may, at first sight, feel more daunting. It needn't be!

DID YOU KNOW?

Your organisation may choose to pay a subscription to obtain the services of ASLIB (Association of Special Libraries and Information Bureaux) which will:

- undertake searches for specialist technical and commercial information
- locate reports and articles
- trace references and search for other bibliographic information.

It also maintains an index of English translations of articles originally in foreign languages and a register of translators with an indication of their qualifications and specialised subjects.

Finding the material

If you want to find a specific book or journal and are not immediately sure of the section in which it is located, you should first of all consult the **library catalogue** to see whether or not it is actually part of the library stock. The catalogue may be:

- in a card index – with the information normally filed under subject headings in alphabetical order. In some larger libraries an additional method of classification is by number to correspond with the Dewey Decimal classification system which is the system of classification most generally used in libraries. This system operates by dividing works into ten main classes each denoted by three digits:

  000 General Works
  100 Philosophy
  200 Religion
  300 Social Sciences
  400 Language
  500 Natural Science
  600 Applied Science or Useful Arts
  700 Fine Arts and Recreation
  800 Literature
  900 History, Biography and Travel

Each of the main classes is divided in turn into ten sections which can be further subdivided as required. If therefore you want to check on a number of books in, say, Social Sciences, you can consult the library catalogue under '300' which will give you the initial information you require. The information is then further subdivided numerically into a number of more specific topics – and so on.

- on microfiche (although this method seems to be losing its popularity).
- accessed via a computer terminal (look back to page 268 to remind yourself of library databanks if necessary).

You may find that you can access one or both of two types of database – the online database or the CD–ROM. The former refers to databases that are stored in the mainframe computer with which your own or the library computer can link. The latter refers to disks which look something like audio CDs but which can be inserted into a computer like any other floppy disk.

Normally you will be able either to find out how to access the information by means of the 'help' facility on the computer database or by referring to the list of instructions which are located near to the computer system itself.

If the book or journal you want is not in stock, remember to check either in the catalogue or with the reference librarian to see whether or not an alternative is available. Check also to see if the catalogue makes reference to 'reserve' stock which indicates that not all books are on display but are stored in the library archives. Some libraries – particularly the very large reference libraries – still make use of this system.

 ## DID YOU KNOW?

In many cases you may need to refer to journals or magazines rather than books for copies of articles on various subjects. Manually searching through these journals can be laborious and time-consuming and, where possible, you should therefore make use of an **abstract** journal – which gives a concise version of an original document together with details of where the full version is located.

Alternatively, you may be able to make use of an **index** journal or database which is similar to an abstract journal but normally contains only references. Frequency of publication varies from quarterly to monthly or even fortnightly and most abstracts and indexes are housed both in paper form and on database.

Conducting a search

If you think that the information you want is somewhere in the library but you are not quite sure where, you should:

- take time to familiarise yourself with the layout of the library – no-one is likely to stop you!
- look at the general reference sources – encyclopaedias, handbooks of professional organisations, reference books containing statistical information, etc.
- look through the library database catalogue if one is available – or through the subject index – to see if you can find any broad areas which may contain the information you want
- ask someone directly! Apparently many library staff are plagued by library users being unwilling for some reason or other to tell them why they need the information. It is normally a good idea to take the librarian into your confidence and to say that you want the latest unemployment statistics for the region because your boss wants to refer to them in his Annual Report to the Board of Directors rather than merely to say that you are 'doing some research into employment in the area'. You are likely to get much more helpful directions if you do.

Even if you *are* sure about what you want to know, you might still find difficulty in locating the information under the subject heading allocated to it by the library.

Suppose, for instance, that you want to know about how to start your own business and you decide to consult both the library catalogue and computer database. What you should do is to start to look up or insert different words and phrases to see what you can find, e.g. small business, self employment, freelance work.

The more often you experiment, the easier it becomes.

TEST YOURSELF

1 You want to find some information about:
   - customer care
   - decision-making
   - marketing
   - office management
   - staff development
   - stress management.

   Check in your nearest library to see which 'subject number' is allocated to each of these areas.

2 You work in the Finance and Accounts department. Your assistant has been trying to help you to gather some information for the new Departmental Manager about new methods of cost accounting, budgetary control and auditing. The only problem is that she has

returned from the library with some rather confused information:

Cost Accounting   658.154
Auditing   657.4
Budgetary Control   657.64

Your boss asks you to sort it out.

3   Your boss asks you to try to find some information about establishing trading links with France and Germany.
   a   Prepare a list of key words or phrases which you want to use when consulting your nearest library catalogue or database.
   b   Experiment with them at your nearest library and write a short report listing what information you were able to obtain by using this method.

DID YOU KNOW?

In some libraries, additional prefixes have been added to the subject numbers in the catalogue if the items are anything other than lending books. One example would be

Audio tapes	A
CD-ROMS	C
Computer disks	D
Educational material	E
Project files	F
Local information	L
Interactive videos	N
Reference-only books	R
Slides	S
Slide/tape sets	T
Videos	V

Obviously this system is designed to help you not to waste time looking for a book when in fact you should be looking for a video or computer disk!

Selecting information

As you have just seen, there are literally dozens of ways in which you can locate information. The problem is then likely to be one of having too much. If you conduct a massive search on a particular topic you will probably find that you have some information which:

● is partially helpful but contains insufficient detail
● appears to be 'spot on'
● is too complex and lengthy
● is dubious in terms of whether it is still current or rather out-of-date
● contradicts something else you have read
● you cannot understand.

At this point you may wonder where to start! A piece of good advice is to slim down the information if you have too much of it. A second is to re-read your brief – what *exactly* are you trying to find out? There is a temptation when you have lots of information to try to include all of it – whether or not it is relevant!

Start by getting out of the way anything which is too high level or low level and anything you can't understand at all no matter how hard you try. If you are confused then you will confuse everyone else! Then get rid of anything which is out-of-date. This is usually why you find one piece of information appearing to contradict something else. Find the update and throw the old version away. Try to end up with three or four items which are *really* useful.

Now go through making a note of the main points – or highlighting these if you are working from photocopies. Then, if the information is complex, think of categories into which you can subdivide your information. Don't spend too long reading – start to key in the main points under each heading on your word processor, so that you can jump to a suitable heading as you read something else. Be methodical and move away material as you finish with it.

Print out your draft document. This is your 'plan' containing the key facts you have found out so far. Additional help on this area and on presenting the information you have is given in Element 5.2.

Ways of planning and organising research

You may be asked by your boss to find some information about a country which he is to visit shortly. You have not only to establish what he wants to know (see page 258 about ways of determining information needs) but also how you are going to set about obtaining it. As in all other aspects of your work as an administrator your planning and organisational skills are useful here.

If the information you are asked for is relatively straightforward then your plan of action can be equally straightforward. You should:

- decide on the various sources of information you will use, e.g. the embassy of the country concerned, the local Chamber of Commerce and Industry, background information from the local library, a discussion with a member of staff you know has visited that country
- allocate yourself sufficient time to carry out the research (preferably with a deadline)
- book in the necessary space in your diary – look back to Element 3.3 to remind yourself about how best to organise your working day and week!
- decide which source to access first – if you find what you are looking for from your first source it is time-wasting to continue

searching (although remember the need for cross-checking in certain circumstances – see page 271)

- determine whether or not you need help from your staff. Remember that if the research required is extensive you may want to delegate some of it to others – provided, of course, that you (a) can trust them and (b) have trained them in research techniques.

You face a more difficult problem if you are not sure where to begin. Even experienced researchers can be uncertain of how to start work sometimes, particularly if it has to be carried out on a relatively short timescale. Experiment with the following strategies.

- 'Brainstorm' with your colleagues – where do they think the information might most easily be obtained? (Remember that someone's personal knowledge can help.) If you need some government statistics in a hurry and you are not sure where to start, it could be that a member of staff has a friend or relative working in that particular area who could provide the information – or at least tell you where to locate it).
- Do *something* – even if you find eventually that you are on completely the wrong track. Wandering into the library or picking up the telephone to talk to a colleague may not give you the answers you need, but at least you will feel better.

Ways of recording information searches

If your boss wants you to find out the time of the next train to London or the address of the local TEC, you can give him that information directly – either verbally or in written or word processed form. Where, however, you are asked to find out some information which is rather more complicated – and which is obtained from a number of sources – you need to have in place some system of recording all the material so that it can easily be accessed at a later date.

You may, for instance, have been asked to write a short report about quality assurance systems operating in other similar sized organisations. The information you gather together will probably be taken from a number of sources to which you may want

a   to make reference in your report
b   to refer back to at a later date.

What is essential for you to remember is that *accuracy* is of the utmost importance – and so is attention to detail. What you write down for future reference must be precise, clear and complete. Finding a relevant article in a journal in your library but forgetting to write down the name of the journal or the date it was published might result in your having to revisit the library to retrace the reference. Failing to write down some information given to you over the telephone – possibly somewhat reluctantly – by an official in a government department may cause you even greater problems.

Remember, therefore, to always state the source of your reference – the name, address and telephone number of the person you have contacted; the title, author, date and page number of the journal or the book; the title of the file folder, etc.

It is a good idea to remind any junior staff – and yourself, if necessary – of the rules for accurate notetaking.

- Make sure the information is complete, i.e. that a note has been made of *all* the research.
- Do not use an already overfull notepad in which the information required has to be fitted on to the last few pages.
- Use as big a notepad as possible – A4 size at least – so that the information can be arranged in clear, easily definable sections.
- Use either a pen or a pencil – but remember that both have advantages and disadvantages. Pen notes are clearer: pencil notes can be altered more easily.
- If more than one topic is being researched, adopt the obvious strategy of using a different page for each topic.
- Number the pages and cross-reference where necessary (if, for instance, one source of reference covers two or more topics).
- Use short sentences and preferably listed points – do not write an essay!
- Use abbreviations if necessary – but make sure that they can be translated back – does TUC stand for Trade Union Committee, Trades Union Congress, etc.?
- Make sure that any handwritten material is legible.
- Make use of the photocopier wherever possible – writing out notes is time-consuming and may therefore cost more in the long run than the price of the photocopies (remember, however, to check that there is no breach of copyright).
- If at all possible use a laptop computer – much of the required information can then be input, edited and indexed much more easily.

DID YOU KNOW?

1 Remember always to:
   - look at the date of the book (old editions can confuse or – even worse – give false information)
   - check on the country of origin (if, for instance, you are looking at an American reference book you may find that the information given relates solely to that country). CD-ROMs should be used with similar care. One popular CD-ROM is slanted towards the US market and, for instance, although its information about Alabama includes photographs of the state flower, its car number plate and seal, its interactive climate chart that compares its population and weather

with that of any other US State and a huge collection of cross-referenced articles, its information about Kent is rather more limited! That entry comprises a single paragraph with a photograph of the centre of Canterbury and a small number of cross-references!

2   If you are engaged in a relatively long-term project – or one which occurs at regular intervals and needs updating – you may find it useful to abandon your notebook in favour of a card index system. You would need a guide card for each letter of the alphabet behind which you could store information on separate cards. Each time the information had to be updated you would therefore have the advantage of being able to destroy unwanted cards and insert new ones in their place. Such a system, however, can only cope with a small amount of material, e.g. a reference to a book, journal or document in a filing cabinet.

3   If you have a sufficiently high-powered computer you might be able to use its computerised indexing capability to record details of your sources of reference. This has the advantage that not only can it be updated easily, but also it will classify each reference as it is received in the correct order.

TEST YOURSELF

You are involved in the production of the Staff Handbook which your Managing Director regards as extremely high profile not only because of the information it contains but also as a promotional exercise – mention is always made, for instance, of the donations to various charities made by the company. The Board of Directors receive copies and so do all the important clients and contacts. Given the pressure you are under you are therefore very pleased that you have been allocated an assistant to help you to gather together some of the material. Unfortunately, however, you do not realise just how inexperienced he is in researching information. You give him several jobs to do:

● to ask Mr Johnson, the Human Resources Manager, about an update on the company procedures relating to absence through sickness (you have last year's version)
● to find out what the latest legal position is relating to the employment of part-time workers
● to research the names and addresses of all the charities concerned with child welfare
● to find out what use is made of the Job Centre when recruiting staff compared with the use made by other firms in the area.

The week before the handbook is due to go to print your junior comes to you in a bit of a panic. You ask him for details of what he has done – and you aren't very pleased with his reply.

'When I rang Mr. Johnson, he was a bit irritated and wouldn't slow down even though I asked him to – so I have only got a few notes. I can't really understand them. I did ring him back the next day but one of his staff said that he and his deputy were both off on holiday and couldn't be contacted. He also said no-one else could help me.'

Hopefully, you ask him about what progress he has made in finding out the rest of the information.

'I didn't dare ask Mr Johnson about the part-time staff so I went to the library to get the information. I was in such a rush that I had to borrow some scrap paper from someone in the library – and I didn't have any money for the photocopier. I'm sorry, but I forgot all about the list of charities you wanted me to get.'

The notes on the scrap of paper are about as helpful as the notes from his telephone call with Mr Johnson. Ever the optimist, however, you ask him if he has made any contact with the Job Centre.

'I did try – I went up there myself but it was lunchtime and everyone was busy. The receptionist said that she had no idea where to look for the information I needed. She did let me look through some of their folders on statistics but they were so large and complicated I didn't know where to start. I did remember money for the photocopier, however, and the girl let me use hers.'

At this stage he produces a sheaf of at least 40 pages of photocopied documents!

Discuss the following with your group or tutor or adviser.

1 Given the time available, what sources of reference you would access in order to try to:

   a complete the gaps in the sickness absence document, and
   b obtain the information relating to part time staff, relevant charities, and the Job Centre information.

2 What suggestions you would make to your assistant about improving both his research skills and the way in which he recorded his findings (or lack of them).

3 What measures you would take to ensure that, in future, not only you but also any staff who are nominated to work with you are trained to record accurately any information they research.

Summarise your answers in a short report.

ACTIVITY SECTION

1 You are undertaking a course of study leading to a first line management qualification. As is the case with all higher level qualifications you are expected to do some research on your own. You are also expected to demonstrate verbal as well as written communication skills. As part of your course of study each member of the group has to give a short presentation each week of about 10

minutes' duration on a topic which has previously been agreed with your tutor. You know you will be assessed on:

- the content of your presentation
- the way in which you present it
- the quality of any visual aids, e.g. handouts, OHTs
- the number of references you have used.

You are given the following list of topics from which to choose:

- A short history and description of one company in the local area
- The employment/unemployment situation within the area
- Ways in which companies can obtain information about trading within the EU
- Setting up a small business
- The work of voluntary agencies – both locally and nationally
- A topic of your choice – provided it is agreed with your tutor.

a Research one of these topics and prepare a short talk on it.
b Prepare any relevant visual aids.
c Give the talk to either your group or your tutor or adviser.
d Provide one copy of:
  - the talk
  - the visual aids
  - a list of references used – including any information obtained from talking to people or from consulting a database.

2 Discuss with the rest of your group or your tutor or adviser the sources of reference (not just the books) you would find most useful if you were an administrator working for each of the following people:

a the Public Relations Officer of a cosmetics company who is involved in setting up exhibitions both in the UK and abroad. He needs frequent updating on rival companies' products and the progress they are making
b the Director of an animal welfare charity who is responsible for mounting fund-raising campaigns and increasing public awareness of the charity. She is also much in demand as an after-dinner speaker
c a university professor whose particular field of research is Industrial Relations. He has frequent contacts with Trade Union officials, Personnel Directors and ACAS. In his spare time he 'dabbles' on the Stock Exchange.

3 Your boss arrives at the office in a temper. His car window has been smashed and he wants a replacement urgently. It's over to you to find someone who will come and do it.

In the morning post he receives an acceptance of his invitation to the local MP to open the company's new annexe. He wants you to find out the MP's biographical details so that they can be included in the company publicity for the event.

The MP will require overnight accommodation at a local hotel and would like to stay somewhere which has a health and fitness club.

Some disciplinary problems have arisen in one department and your boss wants an up-to-date copy of the ACAS Code of Conduct on Disciplinary Procedures. He thinks that staff shortages may be at the root of the problem and asks you for a list of local agencies supplying temporary workers, particularly in the clerical area.

He remembers that he has promised to contribute an article on staff appraisal systems to a management journal and asks you to find some abstracts on the topic from various books and journals (plus any information that may already exist in the company).

His parting shot as he leaves the office at the end of the day is that his grand-daughter is coming for the weekend and he wants you to find out what films (with a PG classification) are showing at the local cinemas and the times of the performances.

Provide the necessary information for him.

Element 5.2

Prepare and supply information to meet specified needs

You should now have a very good idea about how to research and select appropriate information for your own needs and those of other people who may ask you to find out about something. However, the job does not end with having the information to hand – unless it is merely a telephone number or a letter retrieved from a filing cabinet! In most research tasks you then have the job of arranging the information and preparing it so that it is presented in an appropriate form. This is necessary for several reasons. People using your information need to find it easy to read and understand – you don't want to type a 30-page report when a short table is all that was required, and you *always* need to prepare material which gives a good impression of both you and your organisation.

Ways of interpreting, organising and referencing information

There are normally three stages in the processing of information:

- finding it
- storing it in such a way that it is easy to relocate
- using it.

It sounds self-evident to say that in order to be able to use any information, you must be able to understand it. However, in some cases, you may find that you are struggling to make sense of what you are reading – particularly if the material is on a topic about which you have little background knowledge or is in a format which does not make it immediately readable. Alternatively, you may find that if you read an article and your colleague also reads it then you do not immediately agree about the point the writer was making or his or her justification for making it in the first place! In other words, you have both interpreted the information differently.

Interpreting information

How can you cope with this additional complication when you are deciding how to prepare and arrange information? There are usually two reasons for different interpretations of the same information:

- some people do not understand it properly
- each person who reads it 'interprets' it from his or her own point of view.

Each of these aspects is dealt with separately below.

Understanding information

You are more likely to understand information which relates to a previous experience or common knowledge. For example, if you work for the Purchasing Manager you may find little difficulty understanding a report about the latest developments in Just-in-Time systems because you already have a working knowledge of what it means. A similar report from the Financial Manager about a change in budgeting procedures may cause you more problems. Similarly, if the information is presented in a narrative form – such as a summary, article or report – you may find it initially more understandable than if the same information is presented in statistical form, particularly if you don't understand the headings that are used or how columns of figures are supposed to relate to one another.

Unfortunately, however, despite the fact that you are having difficulty understanding some complicated information you are still expected to *do* something with it – for instance include it in a report or presentation or summarise it for your boss. Fortunately, there are certain strategies which you can use to help you.

- Take your time – accept the fact that you may not understand everything you read first time through. Very few people can!
- Skim through the full document/set of figures quickly – don't try to understand any of the details. What you are doing here is to try and get a general idea of the theme so that at least you know what the writer is trying to tell you.
- Then try to digest it in small sections. If you can understand the first paragraph, look on that as a small triumph – and carry on from there.
- Write down your interpretation of each section – even if you

end every sentence with a question mark because you are not sure whether or not it is correct. You are giving yourself the chance to translate something which is not immediately understandable into something which is.

- Don't ever be too nervous or too proud to ask someone for help. Most people are flattered if you do – and it is silly for you to struggle for hours over some complicated financial information when the accountant sitting at the next desk to you can understand it and interpret it at a glance. If the author of the document is one of your colleagues, or even your boss, he or she will be your obvious first contact.
- Accept the fact that there may be some part of the information which you just cannot understand. It is likely that it will not affect your overall understanding of the topic.
- Use a dictionary to look up words you don't understand – that is its reason for existing!

Eliminating bias

There is a tendency for people to think that because some information is in print (or has been given out on television or radio) that it must be correct. This isn't true, for various reasons:

- Everyone can make a mistake! An error in this book could result from incorrect information being included, confusion as to what is meant by the scheme, a keying-in error or a dispute between an editor and an author and the wrong one winning!
- Everyone has their own point of view and this affects what they write. This is most noticeable in newspapers. If you read the same story in a left-wing newspaper and a right-wing newspaper you will probably get a totally different picture. Therefore each journalist is writing from a different angle.
- The facts given to journalists in the first place may be incorrect or slanted. Is the government really going to tell the complete truth when it is under attack about rising unemployment or inflation?

Interpreting information means that you do not just accept what has been said. You must try to distinguish fact from opinion – and that is not always easy! Reading widely and comparing accounts can help; so too can being aware of your own views and trying to allow for these. Bear in mind also that bias can start much closer to home – if one of your colleagues very much dislikes another member of staff, for instance, you will be lucky to get an objective opinion from either of them about the other!

DID YOU KNOW?

- Everyone has heard the expression, 'lies, damned lies and statistics.' Try this as an example. When the government and trade unions are arguing about the average pay in Britain each will be correct – but both

obtain their figures in different ways! The government will use the mean (or average) figure. This will be fairly high because it will include all the high earners in the country. The unions, on the other hand, will use the mode. This is the most common wage to be found and will give a lower figure because it is closer to what most people earn.

TEST YOURSELF

1   a   Read the following paragraph. If you understand it immediately – fine. If you don't, follow the steps given above to see whether after the end of a specified period – say 15 minutes – you feel you have a greater understanding of it.

'The Factory Acts continued to be the primary source of industrial safety standards until the passing of the Health and Safety at Work Act 1974 although they were supplemented by the specialised provisions of a number of Acts relating to particular sections of industry or industrial processes. This pattern of legislation laid down no general standard of care but dealt with particular abuses piecemeal. The fragmentation produced by the specialised legislation simply enhanced this effect and even the area of the operation of the legislation was diverse. None applied to all working environments but each statute defined its own area. Duties were imposed on "occupiers" and "contractors" but rarely on "employers". Systems of enforcement varied most notably with the establishment of separate inspectorates (sometimes not even having informal links with each other) under the supervision of different government departments. Worst of all, the piecemeal applications of standards of care were nonetheless defined with relatively precise detail. Not only was it possible to argue on a strict application of its language that a section governing the fencing of machinery did not apply to something that might be described as a vehicle or to a machine produced, as distinct from in use, in the factory but it was also common to find a different standard of duty applying according to whether what was in question was the provision of a fence or the maintenance of a stairway. When this inconsistent mass was used as a standard for the assessment of liability to pay damages the proliferation of fine judicial distinctions meant inevitably that everyone was more concerned with the application of words than the attainment of reasonable safety. The Health and Safety at Work Act changed this by establishing a set of basic outline duties which were far more difficult for the employer to circumvent.'

    b   Check to see how successful you were by outlining verbally to your tutor the information given in the extract.

2   Your boss has asked you to obtain information on training needs for your staff. You have listed these in order of importance. When you present them your boss returns your sheet with a line through two names and 'waste of time' written alongside. You do not agree with her

judgement and feel that she is prejudiced against both these members of staff. What would you do?

Organising the information

Once you have interpreted the information you will then have to adapt it for your own specific purposes. Unless you are acting completely independently, however, it is at this point that you need further liaison with your boss. You should:

- check with your boss as to the format required (is it a summary, a report, a set of statistics, etc.?)
- assess what time you have – is the information required for the next day or have you a couple of weeks before it is needed? In the latter case you have much greater room for manoeuvre (although a better finished result may be expected!)
- list the sources from which you are going to obtain your material; from that list you can then ascertain how long it is likely to be before you can start work. If, for instance, you are able to obtain all the information from a library you can estimate fairly accurately the length of time you will need. If, however, you are relying on other members of staff or outside organisations to supply you with some information you may encounter problems – you have to work to their time schedule, not yours!
- remember the old trick of setting a deadline for the return of the information you need a few days before you actually need it (but don't overdo it – otherwise everyone will realise what you are doing!)
- once you have collected the information, recheck your terms of reference with your boss. (If you are in any doubt you should make a rough draft of what you think is wanted and show it to him or her.)
- make some 'quiet' time for yourself. Make sure also that you have all the material to hand before you start your first draft
- sort through your information to select that which is the most up-to-date and relevant for your purpose
- make certain that the required reprographic/desktop publishing facilities will be available when you need them. A one-page document for limited circulation is normally no problem; a detailed high-profile report to the company shareholders will require more attention both in relation to the numbers produced and also the standard of presentation.

Referencing information

If you have recorded the information searches you have carried out accurately (see page 286) you should have little difficulty in including references to them in any material you prepare. Much, of course, depends on the source.

Paper-based information

If you are making reference to any paper- or computer-based information you should always include:

- the name of the journal, book, newspaper or other publication
- the name of the article plus the name of the author if available
- the date of the publication
- the page number (and sometimes, if the document is very long and complicated, the paragraph number).

See page 307 for further details of how to **display** references in reports and other narrative material – and also ways of displaying appendices containing relevant information and bibliographies containing lists of books, journals, etc.

Charts, graphs, tabular or statistical information

If you are expected to make reference to pictorial information the same rules apply. However, in this case, it is more likely that you may wish to include a complete reproduction of the information – a set of government statistics, a table setting out certain information, etc. – and you may therefore have to seek permission to include the material. (Look back to page 272 for details of the Copyright, Designs and Patents Act 1988 if necessary.) In some cases a mere acknowledgement of the source is sufficient; in other cases a fee will have to be paid to the copyright owner. You (or your boss) then has to make the decision whether or not the information is sufficiently vital to warrant the payment of the fee.

Methods of integrating and arranging information

Preparation is all-important. Do not fall into the trap of thinking you will save time if, the minute after you have obtained your information, you sit down at your word processor and start hammering away at the keyboard. Even given that you will be able to arrange and rearrange the material as you wish, you may still end up with a disorganised document.

- Draft out the document. At this stage do not be over-concerned about detail but concentrate instead on the correct framework and a logical sequence. Make a note at the appropriate place of any charts, tables or diagrams which may be required. Note that if the information is to be displayed in a relatively complicated format, e.g. a report incorporating graphics/illustrations, it is likely that you will need to prepare a number of drafts before the final document is produced. In such cases remember to number each draft.
- Use short rather than long sentences and a simple rather than complicated sentence and paragraph structure.

- Remember your 'audience' – is the report for the Board of Directors, for customers or for your junior staff? Pitch it accordingly.
- Check the draft to see whether:
  - the facts are accurate and complete
  - it is properly punctuated and grammatically correct
  - the vocabulary is clear and easy to understand. (Any technical terms or initials should be explained where necessary – for example, not everyone will be aware that APL stands for Accreditation of Prior Learning.)
  - it is not too long
  - the charts/graphs/illustrations are appropriate.
- Check that the numbering system is appropriate (see below for further details).
- Remember that another opinion can be valuable, particularly if you are anxious about the style, spelling, grammar, etc. Unless the material is confidential ask another colleague to read through and comment on your draft.
- Correct the draft and check with your boss; ask for constructive comments.
- Prepare the final document and make certain at this stage that your proofreading is really thorough. If you can, make use of someone else to proofread a second time. If using a word processor, remember to use your spellcheck!

DID YOU KNOW?

Many of the latest software packages are integrated. This means that you have a database, spreadsheet, word processing program and – often – additional software such as a presentation or slide creation package – all of which link together. These types of packages are ideal for integrating information as you can switch from one program to another to access existing charts and tables, create your own, import text and tables into different documents, create a slide show and many other things besides! Full details of integrated packages are given in Element 6.2.

Presentational styles and formats

You may have to follow house style. If not, adopt your own (and persuade your junior staff to follow suit). Bear in mind the following.

The numbering system

There are two standard systems from which you can choose. One is to use a combination series of figures and letters, e.g.

1 ....   A ....
  a ....   1 ....
    i .....   a ..... etc.

Another approach is to use the decimal system of numbering, e.g.

1.0 ....

    1.1 ....

    1.2 ....

2.0 ....

    2.1 ....

    2.2 ....

        2.2.1 ....

        2.2.2 .... etc.

General layout

Remember to check what reprographic or computerised equipment is available to you in respect of the following:

- varied typeface or fonts (italic, bold, Courier, etc.)
- change of pitch (elite, pica, micro, etc.)
- emboldening
- line spacing
- graphic symbols (bullets, asterisks, leader dots, etc.)
- use of capitals/underscore/boxes, etc.

Remember, too, to make use of any additional equipment available for binding, stapling and laminating.

Application of specific formats

Your boss will normally have in mind the format in which the material is to be presented. In general you will be required to:

- summarise the information as one continuous narrative, or
- display it as a report, or
- put it into statistical form
- display it as a table or as a graphic
- use a combination of formats.

Narrative
Summarising

Unless you are naturally gifted in this area your heart will probably sink at the sight of this heading. Don't despair – summarising information for business purposes is not as difficult as you may think, particularly if you follow certain basic procedures. Suppose, for instance, you have been asked to summarise an article for inclusion in a sales report. What you should do is to break down the task into several stages.

Stage 1

- 'Skim' read the document – don't try to take in every detail the first time through.
- List the main points in note form – don't bother to rearrange any material at this stage.
- Check your list against the original document to see that you have included all the main points.
- If your list indicates that the original document has made several 'scattered' references to one item of information, link them together.
- Check that the names (and titles) of people are included if their identity is relevant.
- Draft out a heading for the beginning of the summary and an indication of its source – the name of the author, the title of the book or journal title, the publisher and the year of publication (if relevant) and the page number(s) of the original document.
- Draft out your summary from your notes – not from the original document. Try to keep your sentences short but not too disjointed. Remember to use 'joining' words where relevant.

Stage 2

- Check that the summary is factual and does not include your opinions. You don't have to agree or disagree with what is written – merely to record it accurately.
- Check your draft against the original and add or delete information as necessary.
- If you know you have a particular weakness in an area such as spelling, try to keep to the vocabulary of the original document as far as possible – and check the rest.
- Check the tense. Use either the past or the present throughout the summary – not a mixture of both.
- Learn to recognise the difference between sentence form and note form, e.g.
  - *Sentence form*: The company's sales figures for the past five years showed a steady increase.
  - *Note form*: Steady increase in company's sales figures over past 5 years.

TEST YOURSELF

Change the following notes into sentence form.

1 Few department stores opened on Sundays last December. Large increase in the number now doing so.
2 Monopolies and Mergers Commission report – British motorists pay too much for cars – should be a radical change in pricing policies.
3 Pensions – divorced women likely to be in poorer position than married women or widows.

DID YOU KNOW?

In an office it is unlikely that you will be asked to summarise information in a stated number of words. It is more usual for you to be asked to 'cut it down to a couple of paragraphs' or to 'list the main points'. If, however, your boss asks you to make your original summary shorter or longer try to resist the temptation of cutting out or adding odd words. It is far better to rewrite a complete paragraph in order either to shorten or lengthen it.

For instance, if your original paragraph reads:

> Two distinguished legal writers have compiled a practical guide to quick and effective Court procedures for recovering debts in each EU Member State including procedures to obtain interim and final judgements.

you could abbreviate it to read:

> A practical guide has been compiled which outlines the Court procedures involved in recovering debts in each EU Member State.

TEST YOURSELF

1   Your boss is a marketing consultant and has been commissioned by a major chain of garages to get as many articles as possible into the local press about their latest bargains. She is desperately seeking a different angle when she finds a long article in a motoring magazine about the benefits of cars equipped with airbags. She tears it out of the magazine and hands it to you with the instruction that you should cut it down to about half its size.

ARE AIRBAGS AS GOOD AS THEY SOUND?

How did we ever manage without airbags – they're the latest thing in road safety – and no car should be without one. In case you don't know what one is – it's a cloth cushion that inflates rapidly in an accident to help prevent the head from striking hard parts of the car's interior. The most common and useful airbag is one in the centre of the steering wheel to save the driver's head from being thrown into the wheel. The passenger's airbag, on the other hand, is normally mounted in the dashboard. When sensors in the car body detect an impact in the relevant direction, the airbag is inflated – it takes about *25 thousandths* of a second for a driver's airbag – and his or her head will strike the bag as it starts to inflate.

Just how big a safety aid is it? Motoring experts agree that it can prevent injuries but say that it should be used in conjunction with other aids such as a correctly adjusted seatbelt and head rest, seatbelt pretensioners and anti-submarining seats. It should never be seen as an alternative to a seatbelt.

Again, although current statistics indicate that a driver's airbag reduces the risk of death in a frontal accident by about 10 per cent, this does not mean

---

that it makes the car 10 per cent safer. It means that if drivers all wore seatbelts and continued to drive as safely as before – and if all cars were fitted with airbags, the number of driver deaths in Britain might fall by about 75 each year.

It should also be remembered that the airbag, even though giving some protection, can also cause some damage. Although the gases that inflate the airbag are non-toxic and so is the lubricating dust that is produced on inflation (often mistaken for smoke), the loud bang it makes on impact can cause ear problems (although permanent hearing damage is extremely unlikely) and there may also be friction burns to the skin or eyes. However, these are minor injuries compared with what might have happened if the airbag were not there at all.

In some cases manufacturers offer 'retrofit' airbag equipped steering wheels where the sensor is incorporated into the wheel. However, some specialists are concerned about this development in that they feel sensors are very reliant on the characteristics of the individual car and a universal sensor might go off too soon or too late. They recommend that only 'manufacturer approved' systems should be considered as they will have been designed to suit the characteristics of the relevant models.

Prepare a draft summary of the article for your boss. Remember:

- she will want the advantages rather than the disadvantages highlighted – she wants to promote her client's interests!
- to check on any vocabulary which may be unfamiliar to you (some of the words in the article may not be in the dictionary and you may have to ask a motoring 'expert').

2 Look in a newspaper or business journal to find an article which is of interest to you and/or has a bearing on your place of employment (preferably both!). Summarise it to approximately one-half of its length. Remember in this case to include a heading and also a note of your source of reference.

DID YOU KNOW?

On occasion you may be required to summarise a set of correspondence between your executive and one of his business contacts. The same rules as above apply, but in addition you should remember to:

- include the exact dates of all items of correspondence and summarise them in chronological order
- provide a comprehensive title, e.g.

> Summary of correspondence between Arthur Jensen, Managing Director of Longman Cybernetics Ltd and Diana Maddox, Sales Director of Maddox Computer Services on the subject of the late delivery of the networked computer system.

TEST YOURSELF

Discuss with the rest of your group or your tutor the circumstances in which you may need to summarise correspondence.

Report writing

Most reports fall into one of the following categories:

Research reports where the writer has collected together some information and has presented his or her findings together with some possible conclusions and recommendations; for example, a report by you as administrator on the staffing levels in your department.

Work reports where an account is given of work which has been accomplished during a given period together with an indication of future plans; for example, a report written by a sales representative to his or her head office on the calls made during the period covered by the report, potential new customers, increases or decreases in sales, number of new orders, quality issues, etc.

Eye-witness reports where a brief account of an accident or other incident is required.

Work reports and eye-witness reports are normally no more than summaries and are often set out on pre-printed forms. Research reports, on the other hand, require a different format:

- **The long formal report**

  A long formal report is normally laid out in several well defined sections:
  - the front page – containing the title, the author, the date (and possibly the circulation list)
  - table of contents – listing the headings section by section
  - the body of the report – including appendices and sources of reference.

- **The short formal report**

  The short formal report is similar in layout but is normally displayed in a somewhat abbreviated form and often omits the front page and table of contents.

- **The brief informal report**

  This type of report may be little more than a summary in three sections:
  - an introduction to the problem
  - an analysis of the problem
  - a proposed solution.

DID YOU KNOW?

A factsheet may be used as an alternative to the summary or report. Note that:

- it is brief
- it is written in the form of a number of short points rather than a continuous narrative
- it is intended as an 'aide memoire' for the reader.

For example:

PROPOSED INTRODUCTION OF TRAINING MODULE 'INTRODUCTION TO OFFICE TECHNOLOGY'

1   Existing training
    1.1   General unit in all induction training programmes
    1.2   In-house one-day course for junior clerical staff
    1.3   In-house two-day courses for administrators
    1.4   External short courses on specific IT areas

2   Proposed additional training in the form of a supported open learning unit in office technology
    2.1   Microcomputers
        2.1.1   How to set up a microcomputer and run programs
        2.1.2   Essential terms and concepts
        2.1.3   Computers in the office – what they can do and how they can be used etc.

TEST YOURSELF

You have been asked to provide some information for the following occasions. For which topic(s) do you think a fact sheet would be the most appropriate form of communication? (Aim for communications where a short list of key points only would be required.)

1   A brief summary of the possible effects of wages increases on profits – intended as a working document for a meeting of the Joint Consultative Committee of management and trade union representatives.
2   An investigative report on possible replacement of stand-alone computer equipment with a networked system for the Board of Directors.
3   An in-depth article for a journal on recent European legislation relating to occupational pension schemes.
4   Background information to be used as the basis for a handout to visitors attending a launch of the latest model of a car.

Check at your place of work to see if there is a standard approach to the presentation of reports (either across the organisation as a whole or in the department or area in which you work).

Standard report layout

Many companies have their own house style for reports and during your induction programme you may be given an outline of how reports should be presented. Whatever the layout required, however, it is likely that there will be certain similarities, as follows.

1 Terms of reference

Sometimes a heading will suffice:	**Report on the proposed reorganisation and refurbishment of the reception area.**
On other occasions you might have to give more details (*Note*: you may also be expected to give the name of the person who has requested the report):	**As requested by the Managing Director I give below a report on the proposal that the reception area be reorganised and refurbished.**

Note that at this stage you should check on the confidentiality of the document; this will affect both your subsequent investigations and your circulation list.

2 Procedure

In most cases you have to state from which sources you have obtained your information. There are normally three approaches:

Direct – e.g. watching the demonstration of a piece of equipment, checking personally on a situation:	**On Tuesday, 4th May, I visited the reception area to check on the facilities and decor.**
Personal – e.g. what you know already or the information you have obtained from talking to someone else:	**I spoke to the receptionist on duty and the commissionaire.**
	I also talked to the visitors in the waiting area.
Written – e.g. what you have obtained from a	**I wrote to four firms of office furniture suppliers and asked**

previous report or other information on file, what you may have obtained from outside sources:

for details of their up-to-date provision. I also contacted a firm of office consultants who specialise in advising on office decor and furnishings and asked them to visit the reception area and give their views.

3 Findings

Summarise the information you have obtained (see page 298 for details of how to summarise).

3.1 During the course of my visit I formed the impression that the reception area was unwelcoming. It was cold and rather drab and the receptionist on duty was obviously very busy and had difficulty in coping with the constant flow of visitors.

3.2 The receptionist confirmed that she was under pressure given the emphasis there was on security and the need for her to issue security passes to all visitors in addition to her normal reception duties.

3.3 The commissionaire was concerned that his desk was not situated near enough to the door for him to spot any potentially difficult visitors *before* they actually entered the reception area.

3.4 All the visitors I spoke to felt that the reception area was uninviting. They also criticised the lack of privacy — the windows looked straight out on to the street so that passers-by had a clear view of everyone who was in the waiting area.

3.5 All four office furniture companies contacted sent me their up-to-date price lists and catalogues. The representative from the firm of office consultants, who visited the area, supplied me with three specifications of the way in which the reception area could be reorganised and furnished — together with costings (see Appendix 1).

At this stage you may have completed the work asked of you, in which case you sign and date the report and hand it to your boss. However, your opinion may also be needed, particularly if the report has some relevance to your work, the work of your staff or the organisation of the office. In such circumstances you may be asked to add your conclusions and/or recommendations.

It is quite common to read a report in which a conclusion is followed by a recommendation which contains almost the same information. Try to distinguish between the two by keeping your conclusion short and your recommendations more detailed.

4 Conclusion

One or two sentences should be sufficient:

4.1 The existing reception area does seem to require refurnishing.

4.2 The area also appears to be understaffed.

5 Recommendations

The recommendations should be more detailed and, where relevant, should follow the same order as the findings:

I therefore recommend that

5.1 one of the suggested specifications submitted by the firm of office con-sultants be considered or that quotations are invited from a number of office consultants and a decision made at Board of Director level as to the action then to be taken

5.2 consideration be given by the Board of Directors to the possibility of having two receptionists on duty, particularly during peak periods.

6 Signature and date

It is usual to sign and date any report.

Note that in most reports you are able to use relatively informal language, i.e. 'I recommend that . . .' rather than 'it is recommended . . .' Make sure, however, that you have established which approach is required before you begin the report.

7 References

If you want to make a general reference to some more detailed information in another source, remember to make use of the footnote. If, for example, you refer to the Health and Safety at Work Act in your main text, you may want to put a more detailed reference either at the foot of the page or at the end of the report. For example, the main text could read: 'Attention should be paid to the relevant provisions of the Health and Safety at Work Act 1974.[1]' The corresponding footnote would be displayed as shown at the bottom of this page.

8 Appendices

If the information to which you want to refer is extensive, a footnote would not be sufficient. In such cases you would make use of an appendix attached to the report. For example: 'A list of names and addresses of potential clients is contained in Appendix 1.'

9 Bibliography

In some cases, details of books, journals, magazine articles, etc. for which some material has been obtained for use in the report are normally listed at the end. The information given usually includes the title of the publication, surname and initials of author, the name of the publisher and year of publication.

10 Circulation list

If required, put the circulation list at the end of the report, either by individual name, e.g. R. James, Technical Director, or by group, e.g. Members of the Staff Welfare Committee.

DID YOU KNOW?

You could be asked to present the same information in a memorandum. If so, use the normal layout (see Unit 7) and then follow the report format with or without the headings.

Review your work

After you have completed a draft report – particularly if you are new to the job – it is sometimes helpful to cast your eyes down a checklist to see that you have covered the main points. Questions you should ask yourself are given below.

- Why have I been asked to write this report?
- Are the terms of reference clear?

---

[1]ss 3–5.

- Do I have to give my findings only, or have I to state an opinion, i.e. come to a conclusion and make a recommendation?
- For whom am I writing the report? Do they have any prior knowledge of the topic or is it new to them?
- Have I checked all the relevant sources of information?
- Have I considered the possible repercussions – financial/legal etc.?
- Do I know whether or not it is confidential?
- Is my report arranged logically, do the conclusions follow on naturally from the findings, etc.?
- Is the style acceptable, is it too informal/too formal/too full of jargon? Are the spelling, punctuation and grammar all correct?
- Could I have presented any of the information in a different form, e.g. in a diagram/table? (See below for details of different methods of presentation.)
- Have I included all the necessary footnotes/references?
- Have I included any relevant appendices, bibliographies, circulation lists?

Statistical information

Although statistical information may sometimes be more difficult to **interpret** than narrative information, problems of **presentation** tend to be fewer. The information is presented as columns of figures either in tabular or graphical form and you therefore have fewer decisions to make than when you prepare a document in narrative form. However, if you are preparing any statistical information there are certain points you should bear in mind.

- Because, by its very nature, statistical information is numerical, it is very much more difficult to check than narrative information – your trusty spellcheck is useless in such circumstances! You have therefore to build in a much longer period of checking time than you might otherwise have allowed yourself. Indeed, if the accuracy of the information is crucial – end-of-year accounts etc. – you might have to resort to the very traditional method of proofreading whereby one member of staff reads aloud to another. It is boring and time-consuming but at least there is less danger of vital errors being missed. Remember – a computer spreadsheet may add up figures accurately but it will not be any help if the input figures are inaccurate.
- Sets of statistics are very rarely included in a document without a commentary – and it is the commentary which is normally studied with the most interest. If you are working on a document which your boss is preparing, you could expect him or her to provide you with the commentary. If, however, you are preparing a document independently and wish to include a set of figures to substantiate an argument, you will need to provide your own commentary.

TEST YOURSELF

You work for the Training Manager and have been asked by him to prepare a report to be submitted to the Board of Directors. The report is to support the argument that all managers of a certain seniority should be allowed the opportunity to attend a university or college of higher education to obtain higher level qualifications – either on a part-time basis or through secondment. You discover the statistics shown in Figure 5.2.1 relating to 16 well-known universities and hand them to your boss. He does not have time to read them in detail and asks you to give him some information so that he can reply to the following queries he has been receiving.

- The Managing Director is very 'league table' conscious and has asked which is the best university overall in the north of England.
- One of the young managers wants to live away from home and would like details of those universities which would be most likely to offer him accommodation.
- The Research and Development Director is an academic and she wants to know which universities have the best research records.

Your boss also wants you to highlight the particular strengths and weaknesses of the universities on the list.

	Entry grades	Student/staff ratio	Library spending	Accommodation	Post graduates	Completion rates	Firsts	Employment	Research	Value added	Total
	100	100	100	100	100	100	100	100	100	100	1000
Oxford	94	84	99	89	84	99	73	79	97	56	854
Imperial	85	96	37	47	95	94	88	63	96	50	749
UCL	78	88	31	50	83	95	59	62	97	60	703
Edinburgh	84	77	31	60	73	95	54	66	93	59	693
Warwick	80	80	26	84	91	90	34	62	93	51	693
Durham	81	71	39	82	72	97	38	73	83	57	693
Nottingham	86	79	31	61	79	98	40	67	86	65	691
York	79	78	29	78	76	97	46	65	86	57	691
LSE	83	59	54	32	96	97	30	61	99	50	663
Birmingham	80	91	27	39	83	95	44	59	79	67	663
Bristol	87	77	31	53	70	98	48	65	79	55	663
Bath	77	76	29	39	75	94	56	68	89	56	658
Manchester	80	77	34	51	66	98	46	61	91	54	658
Sheffield	75	75	27	95	68	90	33	61	79	53	655
St Andrews	80	77	32	74	40	99	54	64	81	54	655
Surrey	63	71	24	89	95	87	42	66	74	52	655

Figure 5.2.1 University comparison table

Discuss your answers with your group or your tutor or adviser and include them in a short report.

Graphical information

Another method of presenting information is in pictorial or graph form. This can be very effective in illustrating certain points in a report or summary.

DID YOU KNOW?

Charts and graphs are used in many departments of a company, to show for example:

- sales comparisons of sales in various areas, at various times, of various products, etc.
- marketing analysis of results of research, e.g. share of market compared with that of competitors, consumer demand, publicity material, etc.
- accounts analysis of profits, breakdown of costs, salary increases, etc.
- rates of production (including actual as against anticipated targets), operating costs, etc.

Examples include pie charts, line graphs, bar charts and pictograms.

Pie charts

A circle is divided into proportional segments (usually expressed in percentage terms). The circle can also be shaded in different colours or otherwise distinguished to represent different areas (Figure 5.2.2).

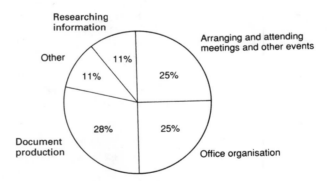

Analysis of work carried out by an
administrator during the course of a week

Figure 5.2.2 A pie chart

Line graphs

Line graphs may be single-line or multi-line and are normally used either to show comparisons or to indicate a trend (Figure 5.2.3).

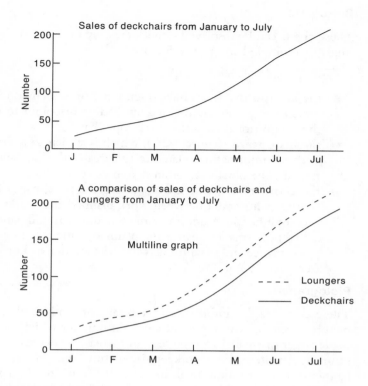

Figure 5.2.3 Line graphs

DID YOU KNOW?

A Z chart is a form of line graph so called because its shape resembles a Z. It is used in areas such as sales or production to indicate individual figures, cumulative figures for the whole period and a moving total (Figure 5.2.4).

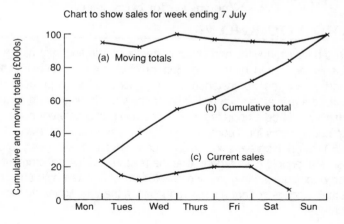

Figure 5.2.4 A Z chart

Bar charts

These charts can be displayed either vertically or horizontally and with single or multiple bars (Figure 5.2.5).

Other types of bar chart include:

- the **compound bar chart** (Figure 5.2.6), which consists of bars which are themselves divided by shading or colour to illustrate the proportional parts that make up a bar
- the **histogram** (Figure 5.2.7), which is similar to a bar chart but with the information related to the area of the bar, not just its height. The blocks are often drawn close together
- the **Gantt chart**, which is a specialised type of bar chart used to show a comparison between work planned and work accomplished in relation to time schedules. It compares the actual performance against the planned, anticipated or target performance. In a Gantt chart the bars are drawn horizontally (see page 153).

Pictograms

These charts display information pictorially or symbolically. One picture or symbol can represent a certain number which can then be made larger or smaller to represent an increase or decrease in that number. An alternative is to keep the pictures the same size but to add to their number to indicate an increase. It is usual to choose a picture or symbol which is relevant to the information being displayed (Figure 5.2.8).

More specialised pictorial representations include:
- the **flow chart**, which portrays a series of steps either in a course of action or in the progress of a document. It breaks down an otherwise complicated operation into a series of simple actions
- the **algorithm**, which is similar to the flow chart but which requires a yes/no answer for every stage.

DID YOU KNOW?

You have already learned about correctly interpreting information and identifying biased information. Bear in mind that you can detect bias in charts and graphs too! For instance, the designer of a line graph does not have to start the axis at zero. In fact, if he or she was dealing in very large quantities there would be a good argument for starting at a different point – for instance to show profits for a company which always ranged between £30 million and £50 million. However, be careful in case anyone challenges you on this. Several people have argued that the reason that the government often produces graphs (e.g. on unemployment) which start high and show a small range is so that a small reduction in the total figure will look much greater!

Sales of agricultural machinery

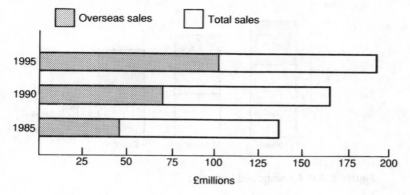

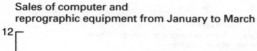

Sales of computer and
reprographic equipment from January to March

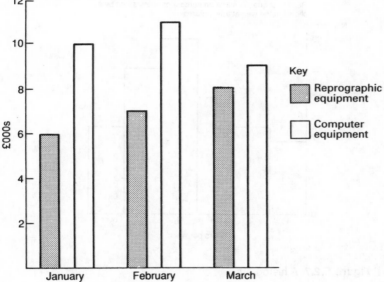

Figure 5.2.5 (a) A horizontal bar chart; (b) a vertical bar chart

TEST YOURSELF

1   As a group or with your tutor or adviser decide which set of advantages
    and disadvantages applies to the pie chart, the line graph, the bar chart
    and the pictogram mentioned above.

    A   **Advantages**
        – simple
        – eye-catching.

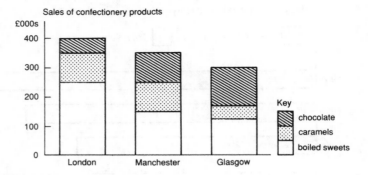

Figure 5.2.6 A compound bar chart

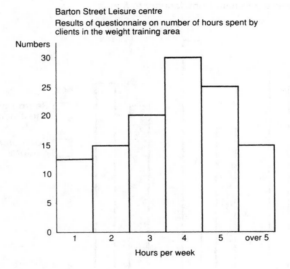

Figure 5.2.7 A histogram

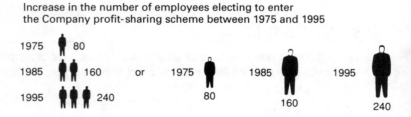

Figure 5.2.8 A pictogram

Disadvantages
- unsuitable for presentation of detailed information.

B **Advantages**
- eye-catching
- effective in indicating comparisons
- more detailed than a pie chart.

Disadvantages
- sometimes a more cumbersome method of presenting information than a line graph.

C **Advantages**
- a very individual form of presentation
- eye-catching.

Disadvantages
- unsuitable for detailed information.

D **Advantages**
- detailed comparisons can be made
- detailed information can be displayed.

Disadvantages
- can be time-consuming to compile
- can be over-complicated for some purposes.

2 Discuss as a group the sort of information which could be displayed pictorially or graphically if you were working in:
- a marketing department
- a library
- the office of a large garage.

Computer graphics

In many cases any graphical information required is either contracted out to a freelance graphic designer or is prepared by specialists within the organisation. However, given the growth in desktop publishing techniques and integrated packages, you and your staff may now be expected to have some expertise in this area.

In such a case, you should first of all find out what your computer can do. Apart from anything else you will probably need to advise your boss as to which type of graphics are possible and which are not. In most offices you will probably be expected to prepare only relatively simple charts such as basic line graphs or bar charts. If you have access to a modern integrated package then your options are more extensive.

More complicated diagrams or illustrations are normally prepared by more technically qualified personnel. If, however, you have access to a graphics application software package and a laser printer, you may have a much greater opportunity to display the information you collect in a variety of ways.

Most graphics packages allow you to create line graphs, bar charts, pie charts or even pictograms. You will normally be able to use a range of colours together with a variety of fonts and images accessed from scanners. (Remember that you would need a colour printer to be able to generate a coloured chart or graph.)

In addition you will be able to:

- 'explode' pie charts, i.e. separate certain wedges from the whole (Figure 5.2.9)

Exploded pie chart of a young woman's spending, emphasising 'Travel to work' and 'Leisure'

Travel to work

Food

Leisure

Housing

Figure 5.2.9 An exploded pie chart

- create a 3D effect on a bar chart or pie chart (Figure 5.2.10)
- incorporate copyright-free published drawings (called clipart), e.g. houses, cars, into pictograms (Figure 5.2.11).

Constructing charts and graphs

It is possible that you may have to construct a chart or graph without the aid of a computer, although in such circumstances it is likely that you will only have to do a rough sketch to hand over to the designer or artist. Even so, it is wise to be aware of what the basic rules of construction are – and to be able to relay this information to your juniors.

TEST YOURSELF

1   You work as an administrator in a University Faculty and you and your staff are being asked more and more frequently to prepare charts and graphs for eventual inclusion in student handbooks and other information packs. Although the computer staff will 'translate' the graphical information, they need an initial draft before they start. You therefore decide to hold a short training session for your staff on how to prepare and construct a pie chart, line graph, bar chart and pictogram.

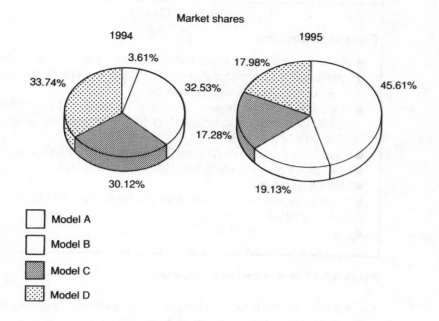

Figure 5.2.10 A 3D effect on a pie chart

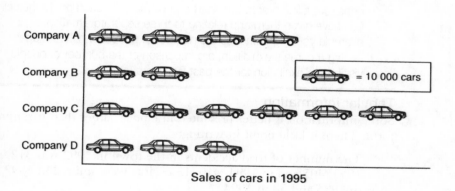

Figure 5.2.11 Use of clipart in a pictogram

Your predecessor was in the process of preparing a series of briefing sheets for the staff before she left. You decide to use the sheet she prepared on how to construct a pie chart as a model upon which to base the sheets for the remaining charts and graphs (Figure 5.2.12).

THE PIE CHART

Rules of construction

- Draw the circle. (Easier said than done! Use a pair of compasses.)
- Work out the percentage that each subdivision will represent. (Remember they will total 100 per cent.)
- Calculate the angle for each subdivision by multiplying the percentage by 360°. (A subdivision representing 30 per cent will need an angle of 30/100 x 360° = 108°.)
- Subdivide the circle as necessary, using a protractor for the angles.
- Decide on what colours/shading you are going to use.
- Shade as required.
- Add a key if necessary (sometimes the information can be written on the chart itself).
- Add an explanatory title.

Figure 5.2.12 How to construct a pie chart

a   Obtain from the library (or your place of employment if possible) some information on how to construct a line graph, bar chart and pictogram.
b   Summarise each section of information on separate briefing sheets.
c   Prepare an instruction sheet for your staff in which you ask them to construct a line graph, bar chart and pictogram based on the guideline you have given them and relating to three separate situations. For example you might choose the number of people of different ages visiting a careers exhibition, a comparison of the number of people visiting the exhibition for the past five years, etc.

Tabular information

Some information is better presented in tabular rather than narrative form. There is little point in writing:

> The number of road accidents in the town in 1992 was 312, in 1993, 405 and in 1994, 410. 15 cyclists were injured in 1992, 2 in 1993 and 30 in 1994.

The information could be more clearly displayed as a table (Figure 5.2.13).

As with other statistical information, in many cases you will be required simply to reproduce tables from other sources such as technical journals or official reports. Other than making sure you have obtained the necessary copyright permission, your job will end there.

In some cases, however, you may want to put the information you have obtained from various sources into one tabular statement.

Year	Number of road accidents	Number involving cyclists
1992	312	15
1993	405	23
1994	410	30

Figure 5.2.13 Example of a table

TEST YOURSELF

After several complaints from staff, your executive has asked you to prepare a brief report for him on the number of non-employees using the company's car park. The caretakers have reported that during the previous week they found that on Monday 15 out of the 60 available spaces were being used by 'unofficial' parkers, on Tuesday 12, on Wednesday 17, on Thursday 15 and on Friday 25. They have also discovered that many of the unofficial parkers are employees at the nearby entertainment centre and it is their vans and cars (clearly marked with the centre's logo) which are causing most of the problem. Twelve were identified on Monday, 10 on Tuesday, 13 on Wednesday, 12 on Thursday and 15 on Friday.

Write the report and include, where relevant, a tabular presentation of some of the information. If possible, try to do this on an integrated computer package.

Legal and regulatory requirements relating to the supply of information

Unless you work for the Civil Service or a government contractor it is unlikely that you will be constrained by the requirements of the Official Secrets Act. However, you should remember that the area of 'official secrets' is not just related to espionage activities! An administrator working in the tax office would equally be in breach of the law if he or she chose to discuss the tax affairs of different citizens and organisations with personal friends and relatives – let alone the local newspaper!

Normally your contract of employment will contain any particular stipulations in relation to secrecy of information. If, for instance, you worked in a research and development office where the information was highly secret or for a organisation working in a 'sensitive' area – such as nuclear fuel or drug production – you may find that there are a variety of regulations with which you have to comply. Failure to do so may result in summary dismissal.

It is important that you are clear about the type of information you can disclose to other people and that which you cannot. It is no good claiming that you never read the conditions under which you were employed or didn't notice that you would be in clear breach of contract and subject to formal disciplinary procedures if you gave information freely to others! Do be aware that if you deal with financial, medical or personal information of customers and clients then you should be very aware of its 'sensitivity' if you are questioned. Two golden rules:

- Never be pressurised into giving out information just because you are in a hurry or distracted without checking the authority of the recipient.
- If ever you are in the slightest doubt, *check first*. If you have to get rid of a persistent enquirer the simplest way is to say that you do not have access to the information at present but will check with the person who has, and get back to them.

DID YOU KNOW?

- You have the right, under the law, to withhold certain personal information about yourself from your employer. The Rehabilitation of Offenders Act 1974 allows you to 'forget' about certain criminal convictions after a certain period of time even if you are asked to give details at an interview.
- Industrial espionage does not just mean microfilming the contents of the filing cabinet and passing it on to a rival! You could unwittingly give someone vital information even without thinking – for instance, by telling them about the layout of your buildings. Bear in mind that all 'restricted areas' are kept that way purely to prevent such information becoming public knowledge!

Ways of preserving the confidentiality and security of information

Confidentiality and security in relation to the storage of information has already been discussed in Element 5.1. However, if you have been researching and preparing information it is possible that you have obtained information which is confidential or needs special care in relation to its distribution. The main points you should bear in mind are that:

- any sensitive documents you have used should be returned to their source and *never* left lying around on your desk (even overnight!)
- draft documents – even your handwritten notes – should be shredded when you have finished with them
- your completed report or document should be put into a file
- each report or document issued should be numbered and the number issued should correspond to the number of files

- there should be a limited distribution list
- files should be distributed in sealed envelopes – preferably by hand with a trusted courier
- in some organisations, 'top secret' or 'limited distribution' stamps or stickers are put on the top of all such documents and files. Often their very use means that a special procedure has to be followed in relation to the supply of such information
- such files should never be used or carried into public areas.

CHECK IT YOURSELF

Discuss as a group the restrictions in place in your own organisation on the supply of confidential information and security procedures in relation to this.

If you work in an organisation which deals with sensitive issues – or for the Civil Service – and are subject to any special terms in your contract of employment, it would be useful to mention this to the group and discuss how it affects your work.

However, in both cases remember to be careful what you tell the rest of the group!

ACTIVITY SECTION

1   Your partner has recently started studying for a Business Studies degree at the local university and has been given one day off a week in order to do so. Although, overall, the course is enjoyable, one cloud on the horizon is the 2000 word dissertation which has to be prepared on 'The management structure in the organisation in which you work – its strengths and weaknesses'. Nevertheless, your partner has made a start. After a short time, however, life at home seems to be ever more chaotic as certain problems start to emerge.

   a   Although your partner has made reference to a number of leading management writers, a large proportion of the information required is information relating to the internal workings of the organisation. Your partner is worried that there may be a breach of confidentiality – *everything* known about the structure is included – particularly since the dissertation requires a comment on its weaknesses.

   b   Your partner has found several sets of statistics in various business journals which are very relevant and which should be included but is worried about possible breach of copyright in using this material.

   c   A colleague in the same organisation is undertaking the same course and has been asked to write the same dissertation. He is not particularly hard-working and is always trying to persuade other people to share information with him. Your partner doesn't want to offend him – after all, he is a colleague – but doesn't see why he cannot do the work on his own. There is also the worry that the

tutor might accuse both of them of copying – because it would ther
be hard to prove who had done the actual work.

d Your partner is getting distinctly more bad-tempered as time goes
on. When you walk into the area designated as your joint 'study'
you are horrified. Books, files, leaflets and pamphlets are scattered
all over, together with dozens of rough notes. There appears to be
no order and no cataloguing has been done at all, so far, to list the
information which will be used.

In a weak moment – and for the sake of harmony – you agree to
help. You look through your partner's notes and find all sorts of
interesting and apparently confidential information about the
organisation – sales figures, budget forecasts, potential new
markets, etc. – which would be of great interest and assistance to
your own Board of Directors.

As a group or with your tutor or adviser discuss what you should dc
in each of the above cases. Include your answers in a short report.

2 You work for the Sales Director of a company which manufactures
office planners. The three major lines are:

● year planners
● job progress planners
● holiday planners.

You have branches in Glasgow, Newcastle, Liverpool, Sheffield and
London.

Your executive has been asked to prepare a six-monthly sales report for
the Board of Directors. You have obtained for him in tabular form the
number of sales of each planner in each area over the past six months
(see Figure 5.2.14) but he is now wondering whether certain information
would look better in graph form.

He asks you to draft out:

a a line graph to show total home sales for each of the three planners
b a bar chart to show the total sales of each appliance
c a compound bar chart showing the proportion of total sales of each
planner to the overall sales for each of the five areas.

(Note: you do not need to draft to scale.)

3 You work for the Director of a charity involved in raising money for
impoverished Third World countries. You are asked to prepare a
publicity leaflet in which brief biographies are to be given of a number o
influential sponsors, including Richard Branson.

From the bibliographic information contained in a suitable reference
book, prepare a one-paragraph summary of his biographical
details.

Planner	Area	Period			Total
		Jan – Feb	Mar – Apr	May – Jun	

NUMBER OF SALES
JANUARY – JUNE

Planner	Area	Jan – Feb	Mar – Apr	May – Jun	Total
Year	Glasgow	169	130	119	418
	Newcastle	166	136	126	428
	Liverpool	155	130	118	403
	Sheffield	148	126	136	410
	London	203	145	192	540
		841	**667**	**691**	**2199**
Job Progress	Glasgow	134	126	140	400
	Newcastle	138	119	127	384
	Liverpool	150	115	129	394
	Sheffield	121	112	118	351
	London	188	148	172	508
		731	**620**	**686**	**2037**
Holiday	Glasgow	117	114	116	347
	Newcastle	121	119	123	363
	Liverpool	135	120	139	394
	Sheffield	116	111	114	341
	London	166	126	129	421
		655	**590**	**621**	**1866**

Figure 5.2.14 Sales for each planner in each area over a six-month period

4   Your executive is responsible for financing and running the company crèche. She wants you to put a summary in the Staff Handbook of the extent to which its use has increased over the past few years, i.e. 20 children in 1986, 30 in 1988, 50 in 1990, 70 in 1992 and 80 in 1994. The crèche is open from 8 am to 5.15 pm. There is a staff of 15 (not including cleaning and clerical staff). It was visited by Prince Charles in 1992. It has also won several awards.

Prepare the summary for her and illustrate as a pictogram the increase in the number of children being cared for at the crèche from 1986 to 1994.

5   You work for the Chief Librarian of a large public library which is situated in a busy town centre. Over the past six months there has been an increasing number of thefts and incidents of vandalism and the librarian is therefore anxious to introduce certain security measures. She feels

that closed circuit television may be one possibility. An alternative would be the employment of part-time security guards.

She wants to put a case for extra funding to the Library Committee which meets every quarter and, in order to make the strongest possible case, she has asked library staff to make a note of every incident which they have observed during the course of one week.

She has received the following replies.

Reply 1

Monday, 2 March – 10 am

Saw two young boys throwing magazines around. They ran off when I went over to stop them.

Wednesday, 4 March – 2.15 pm

Middle-aged man spotted putting copies of today's *Daily Mail* and *Daily Mirror* into his bag. He gave them back when requested to do so but was rather abusive.

Thursday, 5 March – 11 am

Group of children constantly running in and out of the main doors. They went away when I told them to do so but kept returning.

Richard Presco
Assistant Librarian

Reply 2

Monday, 2 March – 10 am

Old lady nearly knocked over by group of youths running about the reference area.

Monday, 2 March – 7 pm

Man (very much worse the wear from drink!) fell asleep at one of the tables. When woken up and asked to leave he refused to do so (even when threatened with the police). Remained in library until closing time.

Thursday, 5 March – 7.15 pm

Four books found torn up in the non-fiction area. Estimated total replacement value £75.

Carolyn Le
Assistant Librarian

Reply 3

Wednesday, 4 March – 6.30 pm

Fight in the foyer between a group of youths. Police called but did not appear until 20 minutes later, by which time the youths had gone.

Friday, 6 March – 6 pm

Check on magazine racks revealed that current copies of six of the most popular magazines were missing.

Mohammed Hanif
Library Assistant

You are asked to draft out a brief report of the incidents for your librarian to present to the Library Committee. Remember, where possible present the information in tabular form for easy reading.

6   You work for Patsy Alexander, Sales Director of a large distribution company. Ms Alexander has asked you to investigate the possibility of turning the department into a 'no-smoking' zone. Accordingly you have:

–   gathered together some statistics relating to the dangers of passive smoking; recent figures indicate that people with respiratory and bronchial illnesses are particularly affected. One survey compared absences of staff with such illnesses in two departments of similar size over a three-month period. One was a smoking and one a no-smoking department. In the 'smoking' department there were 15 absences in January, 10 in February and 5 in March. In the 'no smoking' department the figures were 6, 2 and 1 respectively

–   prepared and circulated a questionnaire to all members of staff asking whether or not they preferred to work in a no-smoking zone. Out of 30, 5 objected strongly, 10 had no strong views and the rest favoured the proposal

–   checked in a number of personnel journals for articles describing ways in which other companies have overcome the problem: some have used union influence; some, peer pressure; others have set aside a small room for smokers to use at specific times.

You are now in a position to prepare a report for your executive giving him your findings and recommendations. Use a line graph to indicate the correlation between an increase in the respiratory related infections and the presence of smoking in the office.

Appendix

Major sources of reference material

1   How to find out about books

British National Bibliography
Whitaker's Cumulative Book List
The Bookseller (published weekly and brought together quarterly in *Whitaker's Cumulative Book Lists*)
Management Bibliographies and Reviews
Current British Directories
Directory of Information Sources in the UK

2 How to find out about periodicals and newspapers

British Humanities Index
Guide to Reference Material (Library Association)
British Sources of Information (Jackson P)
Facts in Focus (Central Statistical Office)
ANBAR Abstracts (various)

3 Books about newspapers

Willing's Press Guide
UK Press Gazette (Trade Press – mainly for journalists)
Ulrich's International Periodical Directory

General reference

Telephone Directories

- Main telephone directories
- Classified business (Yellow Page) directories
- Local alphabetical directories
- Business to business directories listing businesses in classified order which are of predominant interest to the business community

The information contained includes:

- names, addresses, businesses, telephone numbers
- details of services such as conference calls, freephone, star service

Royal Mail Guide

- information on all Royal Mail departments
- principal services and regulations

British Telecom Guide

- Telecom services and facilities

UK Telex/Fax Directories

- names, addresses and numbers of subscribers
- (telex only) – details of answerback codes, charges and services

Whitaker's Almanack

- world organisations and events
- areas and populations of the world
- lists of MPs/peers
- lists of government offices/professional bodies/embassies/legations/trade unions/insurance companies/building societies
- forms of address

Keesing's Record of World Events

- reports and statistics summarised from newspapers/periodicals/official publications

Encyclopaedia Britannica

- a standard work of general knowledge

People

Who's Who

- short biographies of living contemporaries in all walks of life

Specialised versions include:

Who's Who in Art
Who's Who in Education
The International Who's Who
Who's Who in the Theatre
The World of Learning
The Academic Who's Who
Who's Who in the World of Oil and Gas
Who's Who in the City
Note also *Who Was Who* – prominent people who have died

Debrett's Peerage, Baronetage, Knightage and Companionage/Burke's Landed Gentry/Kelly's Handbook

- biographical and genealogical information on the peerage
- correct forms of address

Dictionary of National Biography (up to 1985)/Chambers Biographical Dictionary

- biographies of prominent people past and present

Civil Service Year Book

- members of royal households, public departments, Commonwealth representatives and others

Diplomatic Service List

- British representatives overseas and civil servants connected with diplomacy

Vacher's Parliamentary Companion

- members of the Houses of Commons and Lords, government ministers, staff of government and public offices

The Times Guide to the House of Commons

- biographical details and photographs of present MPs
- texts of party manifestos
- unsuccessful candidates of the corresponding general election

Dod's Parliamentary Companion

- biographies of peers/MPs
- forms of address
- constituencies
- parliamentary terms

Specialised reference books relating to particular professions, e.g.

The Army List/Navy List/Air Force List
The Medical Register
The Dentists' Register
The Law List/Scottish Law Directory
Kemp's International Music and Recording Industry Yearbook
Retail Directory
Insurance Directory and Year Book
Education Authorities Directory and Annual

English usage

Dictionary

- spellings, pronunciations, parts of speech, meanings, derivation, cross-reference to related words, plurals

Note the use of specialised dictionaries such as;

- *Chambers Dictionary of Science and Technology; Dictionary of Economics and Commerce; Black's Medical Dictionary; Dictionary of Architecture; Dictionary of Music; Authors' and Printers' Dictionary; Dictionary of Legal Terms*

Roget's Thesaurus/Webster's New Dictionary of Synonyms

- synonyms

Modern English Usage (Fowler)/*Usage and Abusage* (Partridge)/ *The Hamlyn Guide to English Usage/An ABC of English Usage* (Treble & Vallins)

- points of grammar, style and accepted usage

The Complete Plain Words (Gower)

- the way to communicate in unambiguous language

The Spoken Word – a BBC Guide

- pronunciation, vocabulary, grammar

Dictionary of Acronyms and Abbreviations/British Initials and Abbreviations/World Guide to Abbreviations of Organisations

- acronyms, abbreviations

Oxford Dictionary of Quotations/Oxford Companion to English Literature

- quotations, sources

Pears Cyclopaedia

- dictionary/gazetteer/ready reckoner
- synonyms/antonyms

British Qualifications

- degrees granted by British universities
- professional qualifications and what they mean

Travel

Atlas

- maps of various continents/countries

Gazetteer

- geographical dictionary of countries/towns/
- populations/chief products/national incomes

AA Members' Handbook/RAC Guide and Handbook/Michelin Guides

- maps/gazetteer section
- hotels
- garage facilities

The AA and RAC also produce their own Guides for Motoring in Europe.

AA Guide to Hotels and Restaurants in GB and Ireland/Hotels and Restaurants in GB

- hotels and conference facilities

National Express Service Guide/ABC Railway Guide/ABC World Airways Guide/ABC Shipping Guide/Worldwide Guide to Passenger Shipping/ABC Air/Rail Europe/ABC Guide to International Travel/Cook's International Timetable

- timetable services both in the UK and abroad

Travel Trade Directory

- forms of travel
- details of various travel operators/specialist travel services
- addresses of passport and visa offices

World Calendar of Holidays

- chronological and alphabetical details of public holidays of each country

Travel Information Manual (information accessible by airline computer terminals)

- data for all countries on requirements in respect of passport, visas, health regulations, airport taxes, customs and currency

Executive Travel/Business Traveller (published monthly)

- items and articles of general interest for regular travellers

Business at home

Directory of Directors

- directors of all the principal companies of the UK and of a large number of private companies

Stock Exchange Official Yearbook

- details of organisations and membership
- lists of groups of securities and companies
- short history and description of each company

Federation of British Industries Register of British Manufacturers

- addresses of companies, firms and trade associations
- description of products and services
- branch and trade names
- trade marks

Kelly's Business Directory

- alphabetical list of manufacturers
- classification of all companies into trade sections

British Rate and Data (BRAD) (published monthly)

- data and information of rates for all British media trade journals and magazines

Guide to Key British Enterprises (Dun and Bradstreet)

- factual information about prominent British companies

Who Owns Whom

- information on British companies owned by American firms and information on the American firms owning them

UK Trade Names/Patents, Designs and Trade Marks/The Trade Marks Journal

- trade marks

Kompass UK

- lists of products and services
- company information listed geographically and alphabetically

Croner's A–Z of Business Information Sources/Croner's European Business Information Source

- major sources of business information

Advertiser's Annual

- companies and their advertising or public relations agencies

Investor's Chronicle (published weekly)

- prices of stocks and shares
- news about investment

The Financial Times

- share prices and rates of exchange

BSI Standards Catalogue

- details of the British Standards Institution

Note: Extel Statistical Services Ltd produce annual Extel cards stocked by many public libraries which contain details of a large number of quoted British companies including the directors, capitalisation, activities, subsidiaries, profit and loss accounts and balance sheets. A similar service exists for European and North American companies. Note also Macarthy Cards which contain details of newspaper articles about major companies.

Business overseas

Statesman's Yearbook

- current information on each country of the world
- information on international organisations

Jane's Major Companies of Europe

- information on major European companies

Kelly's Business Directory

- information relating to products, subdivided by countries within continents

Yearbook of International Organisations

- information on international organisations

A Yearbook of the Commonwealth

- production and trade statistics for Commonwealth countries

Europa Yearbook: A World Survey

- international organisations in Europe
- as above in Africa, America, Asia and Australasia

Croner's Reference Book for Exporters/Croner's Reference Book for Importers/Exporters' Yearbook/Exporters' Encyclopaedia

- information on exports/imports

British Exports

- products
- technical data
- British exporters

Trade Directories of the World/Anglo-American Trade Directory

- general trades information

Government publications

(published mainly through the HMSO and available from Government bookshops in London and other large centres, official agents throughout the UK or major booksellers)

Parliamentary papers

- individual reports of Royal Commissions and other inquiries and statements of Government policy, e.g. Report of the Committee on Data Protection, CMND 7341
- votes and proceedings of the House of Commons and Minutes of Proceedings of the House of Lords, i.e. concise records of the business transacted each day
- daily or weekly editions of the verbatim reports of debates in both Houses published in Hansard
- House of Commons papers, e.g. annual reports from Government Departments and reports from Government Committees
- reports from House of Lords Committees
- Acts of Parliament, e.g. Health and Safety at Work Act 1974

Non-parliamentary papers

- *Civil Service Year Book* – a summary of the functions of Government Departments
- *Britain: An Official Handbook* (annual) – details of legal institutions and financial structures
- individual Government Departmental publications
- publications by international organisations such as UNO
- various catalogues of Government publications published monthly, annually and every five years.

The Central Office of Information (COI) prepares and supplies publicity material on behalf of the other Government departments.

Statistics

Government Statistics – A Brief Guide to Resources

- guide to statistics available from all official and important non-official publications

Annual Abstract of Statistics

- statistical surveys of the social and economic life of Britain in all aspects (supplemented by the *Monthly Digest of Statistics*)

Business Monitors

- business trends
- progress of a particular product
- rating of companies' performance against the industry as a whole

Employment Gazette (published monthly)

- statistics on manpower, wages, hours of work, index of retail prices

Statistical Yearbook

- international statistical data collected by the UN Economic and Social Affairs Statistical Office

The HMSO also publishes a variety of specialised statistical booklets, for example:

National Income and Expenditure
Family Expenditure Survey
Monthly Digest of Statistics
Financial Statistics
Overseas Trade Statistics of the UK
Statistical News
International Financial Statistics Yearbook (up to 1987)
Economic Trends
Social Trends
Sources of Unofficial UK Statistics (University of Warwick Business Information Service)

Managing problems

The only reason a lobster is stuck in a trap is because it never looks up . . .

There are always some days when you will feel beset with problems – nothing seems to go right. True problems – as opposed to minor difficulties – are often caused by people. This is not usually deliberate, but is because they have a different way of seeing the world than you do and therefore operate in what might appear to you to be unexpected or illogical ways.

RULE 1

All problems have two aspects.

- technical
- social.

You must think about both to find a solution.

You will encounter a variety of different types of problems at work, including:

- conflict between people with whom you work (or between yourself and another person)
- crises and emergencies
- problems created by conflicting objectives within the organisation
- problems you have created for yourself!

Each of these can be a real problem which needs to be coped with by developing a deliberate strategy or technique.

RULE 2

Never act in haste to solve a problem without first identifying all the key aspects.

Rational thinking

Many books on problem-solving will give you a simple four-step approach to finding the answer.

1 Define a problem.
2 Choose a solution.
3 Implement the solution.
4 Check it has worked.

This is perfectly acceptable if the problem is localised, i.e. you are trying to find a difficult piece of information, sort out when everyone can attend a meeting or work out a difficult travel itinerary. It will not work if the problem is widespread, involves several people or is very complicated. Instead you may be simplifying it to an extent where you just make matters worse.

In many cases, doing the first thing that comes into your head has the same effect. Consider the following scenario. A junior colleague of yours is making life difficult for you by not giving you the information you need when you ask for it. You complain to your boss who promptly hauls her over the coals. Now she gives you the information on time, but not in sufficient detail for it to be of any use . . .

Did you solve the problem? No. Did you make it worse? Yes. Because you can hardly go running back to your boss again (without appearing to be unable to cope yourself), you still have not achieved what you want and there is now open antagonism between your colleague and yourself.

The irony is that you may have used this approach before quite successfully, with a similar problem, and this led you into the dangerous belief that it would work in this case.

> **RULE 3**
> Never assume that a problem is similar to a previous one. Each is usually unique in relation to the people, the timing and the context. Each therefore needs a different solution.

A different approach

A more successful way of problem-solving is usually to change your own way of thinking. We all get trapped into our own ways of viewing a situation which blinds us to other ways.

 TEST YOURSELF

Go back to the scenario above and write down the action you would take to solve the problem. Do not spend more than five minutes searching for an answer.

Changing your thinking

There are several ways in which you can approach this. One is to develop a form of lateral thinking when you reject the obvious solutions and search around for alternatives before you act. You can only attempt this if you start by redefining the problem itself.

1 Find the key factors

Start by writing down every key factor associated with the problem. A list of those for the scenario above could be:

- you
- your boss
- the type of information required
- the atmosphere at the office
- the relationship between your colleague and yourself
- the historical perspective (e.g. your predecessor was unreasonable, or never asked for this type of information)
- the time span between request and delivery
  and several others!

2 Look for related areas

Now try to find 'sub-areas' which fit with the factors you have listed. If you think of other areas then don't discard them. Simply make a note of them elsewhere – they may come in useful later. Examples under 'you' could be:

- the way you ask her
- your job description does not give you the right to ask her for this information
- you never show appreciation
- you ask for too much, too often
- you have never shown her what you really want
  and again several others could apply too!

3 Analyse your notes

Go through your notes methodically and honestly, checking which factors are likely or unlikely. Do not strike out anything which could be even marginally possible.

4 Group the factors you find

Try to link the factors you highlight under certain headings. In this case you may end up with three headings, e.g. Training, Timescale and (even) Miscellaneous.

5 Find another perspective

If possible, at this stage talk through your ideas, preferably with a true and trusted friend. The chances are that yet more possible or relevant factors will come to light.

6 Find some common ground

With every problem concerning another person there is always some common ground – even though it may not be very large! This is your basis for negotiation and moving forward. It is a good idea to define

a what is the best possible solution, and
b what is the least you can live with.

Whilst you might start off aiming for (a), you may find the realistic solution is to settle for (b)!

7 Open communications

Now is the time to start to talk to the other person involved. Your style of communication is very important. Whilst you must be assertive so that your colleagues know your feelings, you must be prepared to acknowledge their perspective of the situation – and not simply dismiss their views as irrelevant.

RULE 4

Don't expect to get all your own way – a common approach which goes half-way towards a solution has a much better chance of success than one which appears to solve it outright but involves the total capitulation of one party.

---

8 Move forward slowly

Don't expect miracle results. So long as the general trend is forward you are making progress. Remember that the solution may lie in other areas – such as your own time management, people or communication skills – and everyone (including you) will need time to adapt.

TEST YOURSELF

Go back to the previous scenario and work through this from steps 1 to 8. At stage 5 pool all your ideas and information with the rest of your group and discuss it between you. You will be surprised at some of the different ways of thinking this highlights! Then decide on a joint approach to taking action.

Now compare this with the quick answer you thought of when you did the first exercise on page 335. How does it compare? Hopefully this exercise should have opened your eyes to how easy it is to over-simplify a problem.

Doing nothing

Another approach to problem-solving is, believe it or not, to do nothing! This makes sense once you realise that acting in haste can make problems worse. Doing nothing at least stops you from doing that. Will it solve anything? Possibly. Some problems – especially those which are loose and woolly – change and take shape as time goes on. Others solve themselves. Much will depend on the other problems you have to deal with at the time. If you are too busy to get around to it at once, then by the time you do it may have simply gone away.

RULE 5

In certain circumstances procrastination can both solve and improve problems. Always consider whether a problem can be kept 'on ice' for a while until more information comes to hand.

 TEST YOURSELF

Again go back to our original scenario. Try to write down at least five events which could occur which would simply solve the problem without your doing anything. Now compare your ideas with the rest of the group. How many suggestions have you listed altogether?

Owning your own problems

Finally, if you want to be considered a good colleague, do not offload your problems onto someone else and expect them to be solved for you. Equally do not try to act as the office 'agony aunt' and solve other people's problems for them. Yes, you can act as a 'help-mate' and listen to their ideas and comment on them. No, you can't offer a solution because what would suit you won't necessarily work for them.

RULE 6

A problem shared is a problem halved only when the one who does the sharing is the one who eventually takes action.

Once you have taken action, and consider the problem solved, don't forget what you have learned – or throw your notes away. There are often connections and interrelationships between different problems, and a fresh insight into one area can lead you on to revolutionary ideas in another.

Enter and integrate data, and present information using a computer system

6

Element 6.1

Enter data into a computer

Today the use of computers is widespread in all commercial and industrial organisations. They are used to assist with communications, production processes, ordering procedures, financial and production planning, monitoring, stock control and security – to name but a few of their many applications! Technological developments have revolutionised the way in which businesses function – and these changes are by no means at an end. Innovations are reaching the market all the time.

As an administrator you have several responsibilities in this area. Not least is the requirement to keep yourself up-to-date with new developments which could affect or improve your own area of work. You need to know how current systems can be used so that you, your manager and your staff can gain maximum benefit from its installation. You need an excellent working knowledge of the systems and packages yourself – firstly so that nobody can deceive you into thinking something isn't possible when it is, and secondly so that you can provide a role model to other staff in what to do and how to do it. It goes without saying that you, of all people, should be following the correct procedures and consistently using your own computer system to the best possible advantage.

The degree to which you can do this already will depend upon the amount of specialist IT training you have received, the computer system in your workplace and your specific job role. You will be disadvantaged if you work in a small firm with one personal computer and three electronic typewriters and may need to consult your tutor or adviser about the need for top-up training or additional experience.

Special note

Because the number of jargon words and terms used is increasing all the time, an IT reference section has been compiled and included at the end of this unit (page 392). You should find that this gives a short definition for most of the terms you know already – and includes others which you don't!

Use and operation of hardware and software

Most people today are quite clear about the difference between hardware and software. The hardware consists of the computer equipment and the software relates to the computer programs or packages which can be bought.

Hardware

Computer hardware will vary depending upon the systems in use in an organisation. These may be:

- **Stand–alone systems** – where each person has an individual personal computer (PC) with a monitor, CPU (processor) and keyboard (Figure 6.1.1). Today, this configuration is usually known as a **workstation**. Printers may be provided for each workstation or they may be a shared resource controlled by a printer server or switching system.

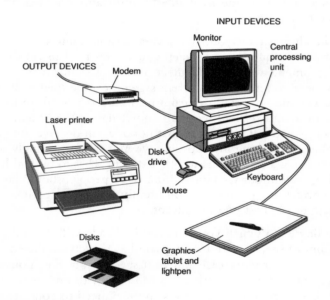

Figure 6.1.1 A stand-alone system

- **Networked systems** – where all the PCs in the organisation are linked together either over a **local area network (LAN)** (Figure 6.1.2) or a **wide area network (WAN)** (Figure 6.1.3). The latter is used when the computers are geographically separated. Using a network means that users have shared access to software programs and company information (e.g. through bulletin boards). On a network it is not only computers which can be linked. Fax machines, 'intelligent' (digital) photocopiers and telex machines can also be integrated as part of the system.

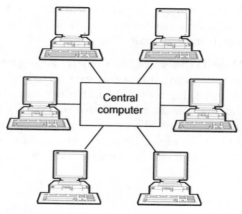

Figure 6.1.2 A local area network

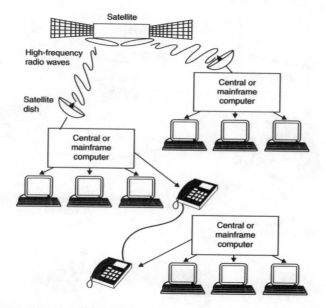

Figure 6.1.3 A wide area network

Users on a network usually log on by using their own user ID and a personal password, although the level of access to data can be restricted by the network administrator (see Security and confidentiality routines, page 361).

Networks are growing rapidly in popularity – not only because of the advantages of shared corporate data, but also because of the ease with which they can be linked to global communication systems, such as Internet (see below).

A wide range of jargon has already developed around networks. The main terms used are included in the IT reference section which starts on page 392.

- **Mainframe systems** – where the organisation has installed a large capacity, high-processing-speed computer as a central resource (Figure 6.1.4). Individual users will operate a terminal (i.e. a keyboard and monitor or a workstation) which is linked to the mainframe. The mainframe will be used centrally, often during the night, for batch processing of company documentation, e.g. orders, invoices and payroll.

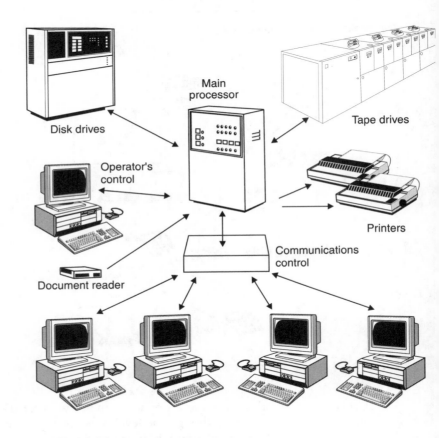

Figure 6.1.4 A mainframe computer system

- **Portable systems** – today these range from laptop and notebook computers, to palmtop or pen computers, some no larger than credit cards! The advantage of the miniature versions is that they can be taken anywhere very easily; the main disadvantage is the size of the keyboard – which can make them very difficult to use. The processing speed and memory capacity of portable computers is increasing all the time – and prices are falling. Most portable computers have a built-in modem so that communications with the office system are easy – both in terms of downloading and receiving information.

In addition, all companies can today take advantage of **communications** systems by linking their own computer system to the outside world. This can be achieved by the use of modems, ISDN and broadband cabling – depending upon the frequency of use and capacity required and links to Internet or satellite transmission systems. (See IT reference section, page 392.)

Computer hardware not only includes your monitor, processor, keyboard and printer: it also includes any other type of input or output device which you can connect to your system (Figure 6.1.5).

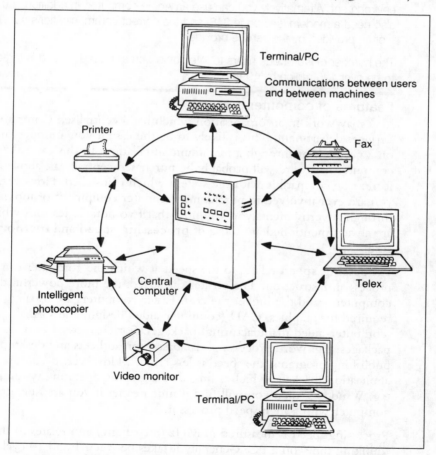

Figure 6.1.5 An ideal set-up, where everything is interconnected and compatible

DID YOU KNOW?

You will have probably already heard the term Internet or the Information Superhighway. Internet is the International Network of Computers, over which computer users can communicate in 'cyberspace'. This was also referred to in Unit 5.

Internet originated in the United States in the 1970s – today any computer user with a modem, telephone line and relevant software can gain access.

Any organisation can register as a **site** with its own address, though a charge is made for access to the system. It is popular with users for sending E-mail and accessing several databases through a service provider (see Unit 5, page 267).

To use Internet you need a PC with a minimum 386 processor (see page 345). If you are using an IBM-compatible computer you will need a Windows environment. Alternatively you can use an Apple computer. In addition you will also need a modem (see page 348) and the correct communications software – often provided by the service provider.

The number of worldwide users to Internet is increasing rapidly and is forecast to be over 125 million by 1998/9.

Features of computer systems

You may work in an organisation which has a centralised Computer Services department. This is likely to be the case if you are operating on a network or through a mainframe installation. In this case, all computer hardware will probably be purchased centrally as, above all, it must be compatible with the system which is installed. However, if you are ever involved in purchasing computer equipment or looking through advertisements you will note that two notable features which are always mentioned are those of **processing speed** and **memory size**.

Processing speed relates to the speed at which the computer can process an instruction. The greater the speed, the more powerful the computer – and the higher the cost. Faster computers are usually required for graphics, CAD (computer–aided design) and CAM (computer–aided manufacturing) packages. For character–based packages, e.g. word processing, databases, spreadsheets and desktop publishing programs, the speed is less critical. However, if you use an applications package which is linked to a graphic operating system, e.g. Windows, then you will find it much easier if you are operating a computer with a high speed processor.

Processing speed is measured in MHz (megahertz) and relates to the 'thinking time' on a PC. Generally it takes between 1 and 10 cycles for a PC to process one instruction. MHz means millions of cycles per second. Therefore a PC which is advertised as having a speed of 75

MHz operates at 75 million cycles per second and could therefore process between 7.5 million and 75 million instructions per second!

DID YOU KNOW?

- You will read about computers described as 386 and 486. This, again, refers to the speed of the processor. The 'new' 586 chip has been issued by Intel under the name of Pentium (for copyright reasons). For the technically minded, the P75 chip is a 75 MHz machine; the sizes currently go up to 175 and Intel are now working on a 600 version!
- On a mainframe the speed is easier to understand because it is given as mips – which stands for 'millions of instructions per second'. Most mainframes operate at between 30 and 40 mips although the highest available is approximately 450!
- Be careful not to confuse 'thinking time' of the processor with 'transfer time' of data. The speed of transfer of information from one device to another – say disk drive to processor – is measured in bps – 'bits per second'. (See also page 348.)
- To make things easier, quite simply the higher the number the faster everything operates!

Memory size relates to the amount of data which can be processed by a computer at any one time. The memory size is measured by the number of characters or **bytes** which the computer can store at any one time. (Note – a byte of information equals 8 bits.)

The memory capacity of PCs is measured in kilobytes, abbreviated to Kb, or megabytes, abbreviated to Mb (kilo = 1000, mega = 1 000 000.) Most business microcomputers have a base memory size of 640K with optional extended memory of usually 4 or 8 Mb. You will find computers on the market which, with the addition of extra memory cards, can have a capacity of up to 64 Mb. This would be unnecessary additional expense if the computer is just being used to run business packages. Additional memory is more likely to be required for sophisticated graphics packages or multimedia applications (see page 399).

The memory capacity of mainframe computers is measured in Megabytes or Gigabytes (Gb – giga = 1000 million). However, the memory of the latest machines being developed is now measured in Terabytes (1000 Gb)!

The proper term for a computer's 'working' memory is **RAM – random access memory**. You can access any part of this data as you are working and replace it with something new if you want to. RAM only operates on a temporary basis – when the computer is switched off any data held in RAM is lost. For this reason you need a **backing store** – usually a disk drive – so that data can be saved until it is next required.

Computers also have a **ROM** – a **read only memory**. In this part of the memory you can read the information but cannot change it.

When you switch on the computer it already knows how to operate because a systems programme is already stored in ROM. You can therefore use this information – but cannot change or delete it. This basic program is different from the operating system (such as DOS or Windows) which is loaded into RAM every time the machine is started, usually from the hard disk.

DID YOU KNOW?

Your computer screen can be known by several different terms! The original term was VDU – visual display unit – although this is now less popular. In health and safety legislation you will see the term DSE – display screen equipment. In this unit we have referred to 'monitor' – the most recent term and the one you are most likely to read about in the future.

Two terms you will see in relation to monitors are resolution and colours. Resolution is determined by the number of pixels on the screen (the more the better). A pixel is a small square dot on a computer screen and good graphics requires lots of them! Colour and shades are useful and easier to look at on-screen, but remember that you cannot print them out without a colour printer!

Storage devices
Hard disks

A hard disk is an unremovable disk positioned inside the computer which can hold a large number of programs and a large amount of data.

Before a hard-disk computer can be moved, special 'heads' must be parked to secure the disk to avoid damage. This is usually either an option on the menu when you are exiting the system or else it occurs automatically.

The size of the hard disk relates to the amount of memory in your backing store (don't confuse this with RAM!). To give you some idea of computer development, in 1990 hard disks regularly had 40 Mb capacity. Today 500 Mb is common and 1 Gb hard disks are on the market.

Floppy disks

These are available in two sizes, 5¼" and 3½", although the former is now becoming obsolete. Storage space available depends on the size of the disk; however, all but double-sided, high density disks are becoming obsolete and will only be encountered on older systems.

The type of disk you use will depend on the type of data you need to store. For instance, graphics take up much more space than text – therefore double-sided, high density disks should be used for this purpose.

The 5¼" disks have a vinyl jacket and a dust sleeve. The 3½" disks have a hard plastic case with a metal cover which slides back when the disk is placed into the disk drive.

All floppy disks have the ability to be read/write protected so that no further information can be added to or deleted from the disk. This can protect your work and prevent anyone else from overwriting something important by accident. On a 5¼" disk you must cover the read/write protect notch with a small piece of paper (provided with the disk). On a 3½" disk there is a small plastic clip which can be slid into position.

Some floppy disks are preformatted by the manufacturer, while others must be formatted so that they are configured for use on your particular computer system. Remember that a disk formatted for one system will not work on another – unless you reformat it, in which case you will lose all the documents you have saved (see page 359).

 DID YOU KNOW?

Floppy disks are often used as back-up disks. In this case, work stored on floppy disks or on the hard disk is transferred, for safety, to back-up disks, in case anything goes wrong with the original (see page 363.)

Optical disks

These are said to be the floppy disks of the future – although erasable optical disks (see below) are still very expensive. Optical disks can store a vast amount of information, are less prone to damage and data can be retrieved from them very quickly. There are three types of optical disks.

- **CD-ROM** disks are used for large databases. The user can access the information but cannot erase or replace it.
- **CD-WORM** disks enable the user to write information to the disks but again it cannot be erased. They are mainly used with electronic filing systems. (Note – WORM stands for Write Once, Read Many times).
- **Erasable optical** disks can be used as ordinary disks, i.e. the user can store and erase data as often as wished. The data on some disks is guaranteed for 40 years in addition to offering virtually limitless storage. The amount of text held on one disk can range from 128 Mb to 1.3 Gb – which takes quite a lot of filling! These are the disks which are likely to become the 'floppy disk' of the future.

DID YOU KNOW?

A wide range of encyclopaedias and dictionaries are available on CD-ROM; it is also possible to obtain CD-ROMs containing newspaper articles. Through Internet you can even call up references to CD-ROMs held far away – such as the Folger Shakespeare Library in Washington.

The ability of CD-ROMs to store large quantities of information is having several effects. Some universities are putting their prospectuses on CD-ROM, publishers are setting up electronic publishing divisions and even the National Gallery is not immune. In June 1995 it launched a portable audio CD-ROM guide – as you stand in front of a picture you can punch in a number to hear a detailed commentary on the work. Unlike a standard cassette guide, the CD-ROM gives visitors the ability to wander around the paintings in any order they choose. The Gallery is now investigating producing different guides for students, young children and experts.

Peripherals

A peripheral is any item of equipment which is attached to or controlled by the computer, such as a modem. Generally the term is used to describe a wide range of input, output and communications devices. The word modem stands for **mo**dulator **dem**odulator. This converts an analogue signal (e.g. that received over a telephone line) to a digital signal (i.e. that required by a computer) and vice versa. The speed of data transfer via a modem will depend on the power of the modem – and the more powerful the higher the cost. If you want to receive graphics you will also need a fast modem, otherwise your telephone bill will be astronomical as you sit and wait for your picture to arrive down the line – say from Internet. Modem speeds are always given in bits per second and the most common one now – and the minimum really required for Internet – is 14 400 bps.

 ## DID YOU KNOW?

Data transfer between geographically separate locations can be undertaken in more technologically advanced ways than by using a modem and a basic telephone line – although this is obviously still the main choice for executives travelling abroad. A company can subscribe to ISDN or use optical fibre (such as that installed by cable television companies). ISDN stands for Integrated Digital Services Network. Data can be transmitted at about 64 Kbps by this system. Using optical fibre this rate can be increased considerably. Indeed, it was the discovery and widespread installation of optical fibre which generated the phrase 'Information Superhighway'. Both systems have the advantage of transmitting voice, data and images as well as text. Therefore a company using either system can take advantage of the potential for video conferencing, voice messaging, data or image transfer as well as standard text transmission, such as E-mail or fax messages.

CHECK IT YOURSELF

Contact British Telecom (ask Directory Enquiries for their 0800 number) and ask them for a copy of their current ISDN booklet.

Output devices

These include your monitor, plotters (used to produce graphs and charts – usually in colour), computer output to microfilm (COM) and computer output to laser disk (COLD). However, the most common output device of all is the ubiquitous printer.

The type of printer you have installed will depend upon the output you produce and the amount of money you have to spend. There are three main types in operation – **dot matrix**, **ink** (or **bubble**) **jet** and **laser printers**. A variant is the GDI – for Graphics Device Interface – which is only compatible with Windows-based software. Full details of printers are given in Element 6.3, page 383.

Types and application of software

There are a vast range of software packages on the market today. However, all can be divided into two types:

Systems programs	which tell the computer how to function, e.g. DOS, OS/2 or Windows. OS/2 is an IBM operating system which can replace DOS and uses a GUI (graphical user interface) like Windows. Its main claim to fame is its ability to run multiple applications simultaneously. Figure 6.1.6 should make the different operating systems rather clearer!
Applications programs	programs which are used for specific purposes, such as business applications programs – e.g. word processing packages, databases, spreadsheets, desktop publishing packages, payroll and accounts. Today many packages are sold as 'integrated'. This means that you can transfer text or data easily between two compatible packages (see Element 6.2, page 378).

DID YOU KNOW?

● It is normally the case that the higher the number after the package, the later the issue – therefore WordPerfect 6.0 is an improved and later version than WordPerfect 5.0. However, the latest version of Windows is Windows 95 – in this case the year of issue has been used rather than an ordinary number.

COMPUTER		
DOS (or OS/2) must be present in all cases		
DOS or OS/2 **applications** **packages** (require DOS or OS/2 only)	**WINDOWS** (requires DOS or OS/2)	
	DOS or OS/2 **applications** (can run under Windows)	**WINDOWS** **applications** (require Windows)

Notes

1 OS/2 can run both DOS and OS/2 application packages.
2 DOS cannot run OS/2 applications.
3 Both OS/2 and Windows applications use Graphical User Interface (GUI). DOS applications use textual interface.

Figure 6.1.6 Systems programs

- The term 'package' rather than 'program' is used because you don't just buy the program – you also buy the manuals and other documentation – all of which equal a 'package'!
- Specialist software is purchased for communications purposes – and would be required, for instance, if you were using a modem. Software is also available for use with fax machines – to control the sending and distribution of faxes from computer to machine and to select automatically the cheapest routes for transmission.

Business application packages

Today there are many types of software packages on the market. These can either be purchased to run on their own or as part of an integrated set of packages, e.g. Microsoft Office or PerfectOffice or SmartSuite. The main types of packages and their features are summarised in Figure 6.1.7.

It is often the case that Murphy's Law prevails in that the system and software installed in your organisation (or when you apply for a new job) is different to that which you learned at college or in your last job. Hopefully this problem will reduce if the current trend towards integrated packages and Windows operating systems continues.

Hints and tips you may find useful to learn a new software package are given below. However, we are assuming that you know the basics – such as how to log on or log off, use a mouse, load a program etc.!

BUSINESS APPLICATION PACKAGES		
Type of software	**Main features**	**Examples**
Word processing	Used to produce letters, memos and reports. Enables the user to insert, delete and amend text easily. Text can be moved from one part of a document to another or from one document to another. Personalised mailshots can be produced using mail merge. Documents can contain enhancements, such as bold or underline, different styles of text can be produced and documents can be formatted according to the user's specifications. Additional features include pagination, spell checking, access to an electronic Thesaurus, footnote insertion and the creation of headers and footers. The customised design of any document can be stored using the macro facility and recalled at the press of a key.	Word Word for Windows WordPerfect
Database	An electronic filing system to store records which can be sorted to find specific information. Information can be printed out in the form of reports. Each record is designed on a database 'form' containing a number of fields in which data is entered. Data can be entered and updated – often automatically. Records can be searched and retrieved by means of 'key fields'.	Access Paradox Oracle
Spreadsheet	Used for financial analysis and the production of charts and graphs based on financial information. Each worksheet consists of a matrix of cells placed in columns (down) and rows (across) the spreadsheet. Figures are entered into the cells and the results calculated or recalculated according to the inserted formula.	Excel Quattro Pro Supercalc Lotus 1-2-3

Type of software	Main features	Examples
Graphics and presentation packages	Enables graphics and text to be imported and combined in a document and printed on paper, overhead transparencies of slides. Additional images can be bought as 'clipart' packages and most presentation packages contain guidance to the user on creating charts, expanding outline thoughts into finished documents and creating special effects.	PowerPoint Presentations
Desktop publishing	Enables text and graphics to be combined in a poster, notice, report, newspaper or other type of 'publication'. Different styles of text fonts, lines, boxes, shadings and designs can be used to obtain a variety of effects.	PageMaker Ventura
Accounting/ Payroll/ Stock control	Accounting packages enable records of all cash and credit sales and purchases to be entered in relevant accounts and for invoices and statements to be produced automatically together with other accounts such as VAT returns, bank analysis, trial balance, profit and loss account and balance sheet. Some are integrated with **payroll** packages which calculate and produce wages documentation and **stock control** packages which can be used to monitor stock usage.	Instant Accounting Sterling Sovereign

Figure 6.1.7 Business application packages

- Don't be put off by the number of manuals included in some 'suites' of software. Often there are some quick reference manuals which lead you in gently!
- Comfort yourself by the fact that no software user ever learns or, indeed, *needs* to learn all the possible functions on the package. Work on the 80–20 rule – for 80 per cent of the time you will use 20 per cent of the functions. Learn the basics first and learn them well.
- Learn how to find the 'help' screen!

- Make a note of commands or 'steps' you need to go through for something – particularly if you find the 'help' screen doesn't live up to its name too often.
- Find out whether your package includes the ability to ask for a short demonstration on something new you want to do.
- If there isn't a 'hints and tips' section in your manuals then devise your own.
- Invest in a *short*, simple, purpose-written book which tells you how to use your software quickly. It will usually be easier to understand than the manual. Make sure it has a good index.
- Ignore any 'tutorial' manuals which insist you produce a dozen practice documents to master one simple facility.
- If the package is complicated, try to enrol on a good short course which will teach you the basics quickly.
- Never forget to read your screen – especially if a normal command is being ignored. Most software packages either include prompts to help you when you get stuck or give you visual information on your status at the moment.
- Don't become complacent once you know the basics. A quick browse through the manual – or referring to it when you want to do something – will enhance your capabilities.
- Don't be frightened to experiment – but not on an important report you must get right in the next 20 minutes! If you are trying something new then **save** the document before you play – so that you are covered if something goes wrong. Don't forget you have an Esc key plus an Undo or Undelete function to get you out of trouble on virtually all packages!
- Consult other users – a quick chat with them often works wonders and makes an instruction understandable.
- If you are completely on your own and find an instruction in the manual totally unintelligible then ring up the software company for advice.

CHECK IT YOURSELF

1   List all the packages used in your workplace and say why they are used. Discuss your findings with those of your fellow students.
2   Check through Figure 6.1.7 and check with your tutor or adviser any types of software or any terms used which you do not understand. Bear in mind that you will have to prove your competency in using textual, graphical and numerical pages to gain this award. If you do not normally use a particular type of package at work, discuss with your line manager, tutor or adviser how you can gain the experience you need.
3   Prepare a table headed as below. Enter the information from both your own workplace *and* the named packages given in Figure 6.1.7 into the correct column.

TYPE OF APPLICATION		
Textual	Graphical	Numerical

DID YOU KNOW?

Hypermedia packages are now available which will store, retrieve and manipulate information in the form of text, graphics and **sound**. These packages are commonplace in recording studios to produce electronic music – which is often indistinguishable from the 'real thing'.

Methods of inputting information

You can input information using any of the following devices – a keyboard, bar-code reader, touch-sensitive screen, mouse, light pen, graphics tablet, digitiser, document reader or magnetic ink character reader. The device used will be that which most effectively serves the needs of the organisation or department. Bar-code readers are a common feature in superstores; touch-sensitive screens are available in banks and hospitals where staff are not trained to key in data. Document readers are used with some DTP packages and all electronic filing systems. Magnetic ink character readers are used for reading cheques and for quickly computing the results of customer surveys.

Technology has developed to such an extent that there is usually little reason to input a document which someone else has already keyed in! If you find yourself retyping something then you are usually going wrong somewhere! Word-processed documents can be transmitted as E-mail, document scanners can be used to 'scan in' typed documents – although you should bear in mind that you may have to clean up any dirty marks which may otherwise be read as text! At the most basic, you can borrow someone's floppy disk to download the information onto your computer.

DID YOU KNOW?

Digitisers convert drawings, photographs and video stills to digital impulses which are displayed on a monitor. The quality of the image will depend upon the number of pixels on your screen. Each pixel is a small square – high resolution monitors have a greater number of pixels so you are less likely to look as if you have a slightly 'square' face or nose! Their applications range from 'fun' T-shirts to serious security. ID cards can easily be created with a photograph of the person and act as a further check to ensure that the carrier of the ID is the authorised user.

- Find out about electronic filing and document management systems by reading a modern business equipment magazine and sending for information. If you cannot easily find a provider yourself, telephone Canofile on 01293 561180 or fax them on 01293 533558.
- If your organisation has issued you with an ID card find out if computers were used, at any stage, in their processing.
- List the input devices used in your workplace *in addition* to keyboards. In each case state why they are used.

Ways of referencing information

Imagine a filing cabinet into which you throw all the papers each day. Now try to think how you would find something! This is the equivalent to having an 'unmanaged' hard disk on which you simply save everything at random. Basically, within a week you have a mess, in a month you have a tip and in a year the equivalent of a junk yard! Now think what fun you could have with an optical disk with its potential capacity for storing thousands of documents! Indeed, the more disks are manufactured with high-capacity storage space the greater the necessity to save documents in an ordered and rational manner.

To do this you need to understand how to reference information so that you can obtain maximum benefit from the system.

Directories and subdirectories

All operating systems give you the ability to set up a series of main directories and subdirectories from the main – or 'root' – directory. Your subdirectories can then be further subdivided as required.

This is known as **tree and branch filing**, where the root directory is the tree and the subdirectories are branches of the tree. You may find it easier if you equate your directories to a hard copy filing system. The root directory is your filing cabinet. The subdirectories are the files inside the cabinet and the titles you then give your documents are the equivalent of being able to label each individual paper within the file (Figure 6.1.8).

It is important that you think carefully before creating your directories. A useful way is to analyse your job and the tasks you carry out on computer – and group these into various headings. If you are not sure how to do this, imagine you have a series of huge box files and are labelling them to contain all the paper you produce in a sensible way. As an example, Phil, a busy sales office administrator, has a job description which shows that he:

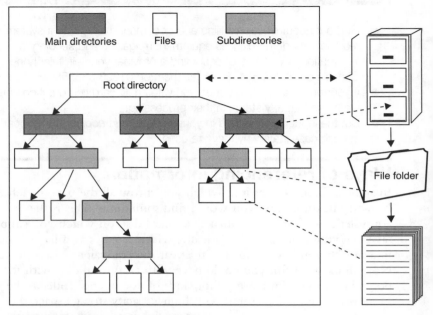

Figure 6.1.8 Tree and branch filing

- co-ordinates the monthly **sales report**
- is responsible for placing **advertisements** in the paper and monitoring response rates
- organises **travel** for sales reps
- takes the minutes at the monthly **sales meetings**
- communicates with **customers**.

He uses a word-processing package for all these documents and his directories and subdirectories have been set up accordingly. In addition, he also backs-up his work regularly on floppy disk – and has allocated separate floppy disks to match each directory.

Phil always makes sure that he is operating in the correct directory and gives a clear title to each document he produces. His word-processing package gives the facility to search for documents on different criteria – such as date created or revised, key words, author's name, etc. – and he uses this to his advantage to find an individual document quickly. He is also aware that he can print out a list of file names in a directory if he wants a hard copy for reference.

TEST YOURSELF

1   If you were Phil, how would you name your directories and sub-directories? Discuss your ideas with the rest of the group or your adviser.
2   Identify the jobs you do at work which would necessitate using a word-processing package. Then decide on the directories and subdirectories

you need. Finally, consider the individual titles you could give to documents within a directory to make sure you can find them quickly and easily. Check your ideas with your tutor or adviser.

File referencing and databases

A different method of referencing is used in relation to databases. The terminology used is the same as that used by computer personnel who design programs or maintain files on a network. Therefore, although we are talking about databases here, the application of this system of file referencing is far more widespread.

In a database system each file is made up of a number of **records** of related data. Each record is then divided into a number of **fields**, each of which contains specific items of data (Figure 6.1.9).

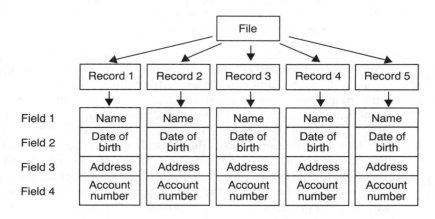

Figure 6.1.9 Database records and fields

The files can be organised in several different ways and this determines the ways in which the records can be retrieved.

Serial file
This contains records in random order. A specific record can only be accessed by reading through them all. This method is obviously the most time-consuming.

Sequential file
This contains records in which a key field has been identified – for instance customer name. The records can then be sorted using this heading – for instance, into alphabetical order. In some cases the sequential file can be indexed. This speeds up retrieval time

as the computer looks to the index to find the 'address' or position of the required block of records and just searches this area, rather than the whole file.

Random access file

This contains records that can be accessed direct by the computer.

All files must be updated regularly. Random access files are easy to update because records can be accessed individually and changed at any time. This is the type of updating which takes place when you visit the travel agent to book a package holiday. As the travel agent confirms your booking on the computer the database containing the 'holiday availability' information immediately notes your request and recalculates the total number of holidays still available.

In contrast, commercial databases holding, for instance, customer accounts records or staff payroll records may be ordered sequentially. The records are contained in a **master file** which contains the **constant information** (e.g. name, address, bank account number or payroll number). When the records are updated (e.g. when invoices are being sent out or wages paid) the master file interacts with a specially prepared **transaction file**. This file contains all the **variable information** required to add, delete or amend information on the master file. The transaction file is prepared so that the information is sorted into the same order as the master files. The computer reads both files and produces a new **generation** of the file which is stored until the next updating occurs (Figure 6.1.10). However, you should note that this applies predominantly to older systems and is becoming increasingly rare.

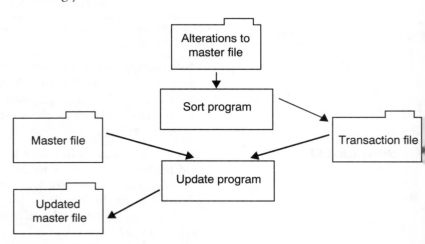

Figure 6.1.10 Altering sequentially ordered records

Ways of formatting

Disk formatting

Disks are formatted when the operating system of a computer inserts control information on the disk which enables the stored data to be retrieved correctly by the disk drive. Disks are divided by the operating system into tracks and sectors. A sector is a small area on the disk on which an item of data is recorded. Today some disks are sold already formatted for use on popular makes of computers, such as those which are IBM compatible. A disk formatted for use on one system cannot usually be used on another unless it is reformatted, in which case any existing data is destroyed. If a disk fault occurs, this is usually because a sector or track has become damaged – this then means that data in this area is lost. However, some organisations exist which will try to retrieve important information from damaged disks – at a fee. Disk damage is one reason why back-up disks are essential for keeping a copy of important files.

Hard disks, too, have sectors and tracks. Over a period of time – as information is added and deleted – the data can be spread all over the disk with blank sectors in odd places. Special programs exist which can reorganise the existing files and maximise the amount of available space left on the disk. This form of disk 'house-keeping' also increases retrieval speed because the files are stored in a more organised way.

Data formatting

The format of data relates to the way in which data is displayed. In all related documents it is important that the format is the same – despite the number of people accessing the system or inputting information. This is particularly important where reports will be generated based on the contents of different records – for instance in a database, or an accounting or payroll package.

The main considerations to be borne in mind are:

- the design of the form or record
- the type of data which must be entered
- the style in which the data should be entered
- the type of reports which will be required
- the ways in which users will wish to search for individual records.

For instance, a college may set up a complex student database. Not only will each record card contain basic information such as name, address, age and course attended, it will also contain information such as qualifications upon entry, achievements during and at the end of the course, attendance pattern, disciplinary record and so on. If some courses are fee-paying then the record may also include a field which shows tuition or examination fees.

Different users may wish to print out reports to reflect their own area of interest:

- the course tutor may wish to monitor patterns of attendance
- the programme leader may wish to check on student achievements
- the finance section will want to know which students have not paid their fees
- the marketing section may wish to mailshot all students about next year's courses.

The person who designs the record card has to take all these different needs into account and use as many techniques as possible to ensure that:

- only accurate information is keyed in
- only sensible information is keyed in
- the information is keyed in under the correct field names
- the information looks the same when it is printed out on a report.

For that reason, he or she will – at the design stage – have the ability to:

- change the maximum size of the field
- enter a specific field name
- assign a 'default value' to a field. This is the value stored if a specific value is not allocated to a field
- apply 'validation rules' to certain fields, e.g. M or F are the only two possibilities for entry under 'gender', while in a field for 'months' acceptable values must be between 1 and 12!
- control the style of data entry – for instance for dates (so that you do not get a mixture of 14 May 199_ and 16-03-9_ on the same report)
- control the style of data display, e.g. whether in whole numbers, percentages, to two decimal places, etc.
- specify 'mandatory fields' where data *must* be entered for the form to be valid. For instance, if no name is entered the record is useless. However, telephone numbers are not essential – and must not be – otherwise no record could be created for someone not on the telephone. The opposite of a mandatory field is an 'optional field'

- set 'key fields' – these fields have a unique value and are used as the main index to access the data.

Data is entered into three types of fields:

- **alphabetic** – where the data is entered and stored alphabetically. An obvious example is student names
- **numeric** – where the data is entered as a numeric value which may, if required, be sorted into ascending or descending order. On some databases a formula can be entered to undertake calculations on these fields
- **alphanumeric** – for a mixture of letters and numbers (e.g. a postcode) or a field which contains numeric information which will not need to be sorted, e.g. telephone numbers.

If a field is indexed, a record can be directly located based on the value of the field. However, the format of the data and the type of field nominated for each speeds up searching and retrieval and the acquisition of information in report format.

(*Note*: document formatting is dealt with in Element 6.3, page 386.)

DID YOU KNOW?

Bear in mind that in any computer package the usefulness of the reports generated is determined by the accuracy of the information entered and the way in which this information is used. If you don't think things through properly you can end up with some very odd results!

For instance, in one hotel a room utilisation survey was carried out and put onto computer. Each room was assessed for its capacity and this data was included on the database. An extract was then taken to check on utilisation. However, the way in which this was done meant that a public room which was unpopular but held 12 people, and was used once a week but by 16 people, had a reported usage of 133 per cent whereas a large popular seminar room, which held a maximum of 100 people and was used frequently by groups of about 70 people, only had a usage of 70 per cent. The booking clerk was then reprimanded for not utilising the rooms as effectively as he might!

TEST YOURSELF

What was wrong with the reports generated in the case above? What should be done to obtain a more accurate reading?

Security and confidentiality routines

Security of data is a major headache to many network administrators and a large number of computer users. This is particularly the case with very sensitive information. It is notable, for instance, that the British Medical Association, in looking for a way in which patient's computerised clinical records can be transferred from one consultant to another, have rejected Internet completely because hackers (see below) could gain access to them and tamper with important data such as drug dosages or recommended treatment.

There are two major ways in which data must be protected:

- from theft, fraud, interference or unauthorised access. This is often termed **access security**
- from accidental loss – this is often termed **back-up security**.

Access security

Access can be in relation to the equipment or system as a whole or in relation to the data held on the system. Large mainframe installations usually have sophisticated entry requirements which may include hand or voice prints to prevent unauthorised people entering the building.

In a network system, this type of security is pointless because there is often a PC on virtually every desk. Access security has therefore to be focused on the data which is held on the system. As a basic precaution, all users of a network have to **log on** to gain entry to the system, by keying in their user ID and their password. When they have finished working on the machine they must **log off** so that access has been officially ended. The network administrator can keep a record of system usage to identify the main users and the amount of usage – for instance, to monitor whether or not the system is becoming overloaded and how frequently this happens.

The level of access of individual users can be determined by assigning their ID to different categories of files. The computer system will hold a set of authorities against each ID which can only be changed by the system administrator. Therefore, for instance, a clerical employee may have access to part of a corporate database on a 'read only' basis but access to another part on a 'read and amend' basis. A further category of confidential files on the database may be inaccessible to that particular employee. An additional, specific password may be required for access to higher level information or for those employed in computer maintenance who may need to be able to access system or operating files not available to other employees.

Another method of protecting confidential information is by coding or encrypting data. One method is to assign a meaningless code which needs a key for interpretation. For instance, the result of a disciplinary interview may be listed on a personnel record in code form as

120 = verbal warning
128 = first written warning
130 = second written warning
140 = final warning
150 = dismissal
160 = summary dismissal

Each figure may have a suffix added which indicates the type of offence committed. Only personnel staff who have access to the key know what actually happened.

Quite obviously, data security needs cooperation from individual employees. This goes beyond not telling anyone your password, using a word anybody could easily guess or writing it down! Network users who remain logged on but leave their workstation unattended risk allowing any stranger who visits the office access to the data. It also gives people the opportunity to send unauthorised E-mail messages under someone else's name!

Data security has also to be addressed if employees are allowed dial-up access into the system, e.g. reps travelling abroad or staff working from home. Most systems today are programmed so that the staff member dials up the system, logs in and records the fact that he or she requires access and then logs out. The computer then automatically calls that particular user back at the **prearranged** telephone number. Even, therefore, if someone is impersonating a member of staff and has acquired his or her ID and password, access to the system is impossible unless the correct telephone is used.

Back-up security

It is estimated that more than a third of the companies which suffer a computer disaster take over a day to recover and 10 per cent of companies take longer than a week. Computer disasters can be caused by fire, flood, theft and other events which are classified by insurers as Acts of God, such as earthquakes. In the event of such a disaster the biggest risk is that of data loss. It is therefore essential that back-up copies are regularly made and securely stored – preferably at a remote location.

The final way in which data can be lost accidentally is through a break in the power supply which wipes the computer's memory – possibly destroying hours of work. A device called a UPS (uninterruptible power supply) can be installed which not only protects the system from fluctuations in the electricity supply but also provides back-up if there is a power cut. The latest devices link with a software package which informs the computer that the mains supply has failed and shuts down the system cleanly. This can be vital if a power failure happens at night when the computer is involved in back-up routines. (See page 366 for further information about backing-up data.)

 ## DID YOU KNOW?

A **hacker** is a person who illegally gains entry into a computer system by working out or bypassing the password. Six minutes after the government joined Internet, a man from Edinburgh University hacked into the system used by the Office of Public Service and Science and redesigned some of the pages of information. The spokesman was grateful – he felt the new pages were an improvement!

Ways of developing and maintaining storage systems

When you use a computer system, you have two types of material to store:

a source data, i.e. the material from which you are obtaining the data for inputting

b the electronic file you produce.

Your source data should be returned to the originator or filed according to a recognised 'paper' filing system. Do bear in mind that if your source data is confidential then not only must you be careful where you store it but you must also take care not to leave it lying around during inputting – or to leave your screen on for everyone to see!

Storage of electronic material should be undertaken by means of the procedures given under file referencing (page 355). You should note that it is important not to try to overload your subdirectories on your hard disk (as this makes it harder to find individual documents and search routines take longer), nor to store so many documents on a floppy disk that nothing can be updated or amended without receiving a 'disk full' message. Do bear in mind that when you store a document on a floppy disk it needs the same number of bytes available *again* to cope with updating – as, in effect, the system rewrites the whole document before deleting the original.

You should regularly maintain your storage systems by undertaking 'good housekeeping' tasks such as

- going through files on directories and subdirectories and deleting those which are out-of-date or no longer used
- deleting subdirectories and directories which are no longer needed
- clearing out outdated files stored on floppy disks
- wiping floppy disks containing confidential information if they are to be thrown away.

Ways of protecting equipment and data

Equipment

Equipment can be protected from damage by:

- siting it on specially designed workstations or in a sensible layout on a desktop
- proper wire management – preferably built into the workstation or desk itself
- keeping movement of computer equipment to a minimum
- always closing down a system properly, for example
  - logging out of a network

- waiting until a disk has finished spinning (and the light has gone out) before removing it from a drive
- making sure all staff do not put food, drinks or other liquids near a computer (especially the keyboard!)
- not leaving a computer switched on when you are not using it – particularly for long periods or if your screen does not automatically 'blank out' after a few seconds or display a 'screen saver'. This is a screen with constantly moving images – which can range from simple letters to fish swimming in front of your eyes! Otherwise you are risking screen burn where the images are burnt onto the screen and cannot be removed.
- reading the 'trouble-shooting' guide in your computer and printer manual before trying to rectify faults yourself
- keeping the equipment and keyboard clean – but only by using the right products for the job.

Equipment can be protected from theft by:

- fixing alarms which sound if the equipment is moved any distance
- siting valuable or desirable equipment, where possible, away from public areas
- marking all equipment with a special security tag or ultraviolet pen to show the rightful owner.

Data

Data can be protected by:

- storing floppy disks in a proper disk box – and allowing sufficient space for each
- using proper disk holders for carrying disks or sending them through the post
- writing the label for the disk before attaching it to the disk
- keeping disks away from magnetic sources (such as magnetic catches on office cabinet doors!) and direct heat (such as radiators)
- never using disks in faulty equipment or storing data on a disk you have had lying in your desk drawer for the past seven years
- never touching the recording surface.

Data can be protected from accidental damage by:

- **priority one** – taking regular back-ups of your work
- ensuring the read/write protect notch is in position on floppy disks
- identifying the 'protection' elements inherent in many software programs – for instance, formula entered into a spreadsheet can be protected, as can the field titles in databases
- thinking very carefully and clearly before you embark on a programme of deleting files and documents. If you are careless you may easily delete the wrong one in error
- never using anyone else's disk from outside your system or a disk from an unknown source – either of which may contain a virus.

A virus is a rogue program which, when introduced into a computer system, can create untold damage. This may include blanking screens, wiping hard disks or even making the whole system inoperable. Floppy disks can 'carry' the virus and pass it on to every computer in which it is used. Some viruses can even infect a whole network.

DID YOU KNOW?

- If you accidentally delete a file from a hard disk then you may be able to 'undelete' your action through your operating system. Of course, if you already have a back-up file (see below) then total panic will be avoided!
- Disk manufacturers will only guarantee information on disks up to 52 degrees Celsius. Beyond this it is probable that all information will be lost. If such disks contained all the company's records and there were no back-ups stored in a separate place, it could be weeks if not months before the organisation is operational again.

CHECK IT YOURSELF

Obtain information on the security procedures in force in your organisation to protect both equipment and data. Compare your findings with other members of your group.

Back-up/safety routines

The main safety routine in relation to computer viruses is the 'sweeping' of all floppy disks to check if a virus is present. Sweeping gets rid of the virus and any other information stored on the disk. Most networks have a virus detection program installed which checks, the minute you switch on, whether any virus is present. Only if the system gets the 'all clear' are you allowed to log on. In this way, any virus is contained within one machine and cannot spread through the network. However, a virus checker can only detect 99 per cent of all known viruses (a bit like Domestos!), therefore it is still essential not to use disks of unknown or dubious origin even if a virus checker is used.

Because disks may need to be swept, may be damaged accidentally or lost, it is important that all staff are aware of the importance of taking back-up copies. The worst scenario of all is your computer failing and, as part of the repair, the computer engineers having to wipe all the information from your hard disk!

Bear in mind that the data contained on your hard disk will vary depending upon whether you operate a stand-alone PC or a networked PC. In the first case your PC will hold both software and data. In the second case it is more likely to just hold data – software programs being accessed from the network.

If you are only involved in saving data then the normal method is to have *two* disks – one as your working disk (which may be a hard or a floppy disk) and the second (a floppy disk) containing exactly the same information, as a back-up for the first disk. This can also help if you accidentally delete any information or files from your working disk – you can restore them again from your back-up.

If, however, you need to back-up the entire contents of your hard disk – including software programs – then floppy disks are highly unlikely to be suitable. For example, a machine with a 500 Mb hard disk would need no less than 400 diskettes to back up the work – and several hours of inserting/removing disks from the floppy drive! Today, therefore, many computer users back up their hard disk by using **tape streamers**. These fit in a 'letter box' in the front of the computer and are like a small cassette (Figure 6.1.11). They automatically compress (or reduce) the data by half during the back-up process so that the total amount of data on the hard disk can be saved on two tapes. The whole process takes about 3.5 hours.

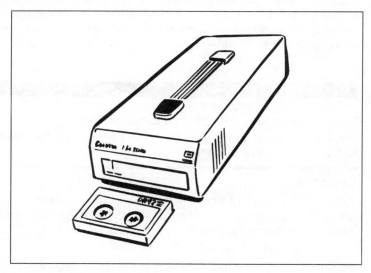

Figure 6.1.11 A tape streamer

Always bear in mind when considering security in an organisation that some of the most valuable items in an organisation are not the most expensive! Whilst floppy disks are very cheap to buy, the information they contain may cost a considerable amount of time and money to replace.

For that reason, back-up disks or tapes need to be stored in special boxes inside heat resistant safes so that, in the case of fire, the contents will not be damaged.

Legal and regulatory requirements relating to the use of equipment and data

Use of equipment

The use of computer equipment is featured prominently in Health and Safety legislation – primarily in the Display Screen Equipment regulations. It is important that you are aware of the requirements under these regulations and that you ensure that they are complied with by all computer users – including yourself. You may find that you need to keep a watchful eye on the actions of others – for instance moving a monitor to an area where there is reflected sunlight on the screen, not sitting properly or working long hours to finish an urgent job.

Use of data

The confidentiality of personal data held on computers is covered by law under the Data Protection Act. So if you leave disks with confidential documents on them lying around, and they fall into the wrong hands, you could be liable under the Act.

The main requirements of the Act are given in Figure 6.1.12.

In addition to the Data Protection Act, software users must also bear in mind that Copyright Law also affects their actions. It is an offence, for instance, to copy software held on another machine and use it on your own. All software today is sold with a Licence Agreement – which is proof that the person using the software is the accredited purchaser. Any user who could not produce a Licence Agreement when asked could be liable to prosecution.

On a network, the software is usually held on a file server and is available to all users. To do this legally the organisation has to purchase a site licence from the software house which covers the maximum number of users for a specified fee.

The Data Protection Act 1984

The Act requires employers using a computerised data system to register as data users. They must state

- what information is being stored on computer
- why it is stored in such a way
- how and from where they have obtained it
- to whom it will be disclosed.

The Data Protection Registrar must then try to ensure that personal data

- is obtained and processed fairly and lawfully
- is held only for one or more specified and lawful purposes
- is adequate, relevant and not excessive
- is not kept for longer than necessary
- is stored in a way which prevents unauthorised access of accidental loss or destruction.

Additional safeguards are required in respect of personnel data covering

- racial origin
- political opinions or religious or other beliefs
- physical or mental health or sexual life
- criminal convictions.

Note: Employees have a **right of access** to all computerised information held about them and may claim compensation for damage and distress if the information is inaccurate.

Exemptions

The provisions of the Act do not apply to data held for

- the purposes of national security
- the detection or prevention of crime
- calculating payroll or for keeping accounts
- household affairs or recreational purposes
- the subsequent preparation of text (such as documents held in a word processor)
- the purposes of recording the 'intention' of the data user.

Figure 6.1.12 The Data Protection Act 1984

DID YOU KNOW?

Many organisations publish their own systems or protocols for using computer systems. This is, in effect, a code of conduct which must be followed by all computer users in the organisation. You are likely to find this if your organisation has achieved BS 5750 or ISO 9000, which are only awarded if the company has set up clear systems and procedures for its operations.

Organisations' procedures for retaining source material

We have already covered the importance of good housekeeping in relation to your hard disk directories and floppy disks. However, if you regularly input information from source documents into a computer system and then save your source documents carefully, you may find that after a while you are submerged underneath a great mound of files. So much for the paperless office!

It is important that you are aware of any specific requirements in your organisation for retaining or storing source data. Some may have to be kept in a central file, while other types of data may be allowed to be destroyed after a certain time. Some documents may be subject to legal restrictions in terms of retention. This is likely to be the case if you are inputting information on payroll, tax or company accounts – where the legal retention time is six years – sales orders or quotations (12 years) or accident reports (30 years).

ACTIVITY SECTION

1   You have recently moved to a new job where each member of staff has his or her own workstation and a computer linked to the organisation's network. You are appalled, however, at the casual attitude of staff in relation to the care and maintenance of their own equipment. All the computers are filthy, the keyboards are full of fluff and dust and yesterday you saw a junior member of staff perching a cup of coffee at the edge of her keyboard and then tossing two floppy disks casually into her desk drawer. You have been given the authority to 'sort things out' in the office and decide that you need to improve the resources for cleaning the equipment and also change staff attitudes.

   a   Obtain a computer supplies catalogue which gives details of cleaning materials. List those you think you will need. Prepare a brief memo to your boss requesting permission to purchase these items and justifying the expenditure.

   b   Discuss as a group (or look up in relevant manuals) how to care for both computer hardware and floppy disks. Draw up an instruction list for your staff which gives the key points in each area.

   c   Before you have had a chance to have a word with the staff you receive an irate memo from the network administrator. On three occasions in the last fortnight his service staff were called to repair machines in the office without good cause. In one case the member of staff had not even bothered checking whether the cable links were still connected. Prepare a sheet which tells staff the basic checks which should be made before either telling you *or* telephoning for a technician.

   d   Set out the key points you would bear in mind in relation to changing staff attitudes in this area. You may wish to refer back to Unit 4 for tips or look at the Managing Other People or Managing Change sections in this book to help you.

2   You are the newly appointed administrator in the Purchasing department of an organisation. Until recently, purchasing of goods was undertaken by administrators in each department – Sales and Marketing, Production, Human Resources, Finance and Administration. It has now been decided to centralise this function to save duplication of resources and to build up a network of reliable suppliers. The Purchasing Manager is your immediate boss and has asked you to decide which systems you think should be computerised in the section and which you think should remain paper-based for the time being.

   a   Draw up a list of the type of data you would wish to store on a computer system and the best type of software package to use in each case.

   b   Identify where you would locate this data and how you would store it after entry.

   c   Decide the types of output you think would be most useful for the Purchasing Manager and yourself in relation to the ordering of goods and the monitoring of expenditure.

   d   Your boss has been reading about EDI in a magazine called *Electronic Trader*. He tells you that EDI is a system by which all orders and invoices are communicated by computer. He understands that some organisations, such as Tesco, order over 95% of their goods by this system. He has asked you to find out more. The magazine shows an Editorial Office address at Suite 10, Fourways House, Canning Road, Croydon, CR0 6QB. Alternatively you could visit your local or college library or write to the EDI Association at 148 Buckingham Palace Road, London SW1W 9TR (tel. 0171 824 8848). Your boss has also suggested you find out about the EDIPOST service offered by Royal Mail.

   When you have researched the information, prepare a memo giving the main facts about EDI.

3   You work for an employment agency which has, to date, only used computers for word processing activities. Your boss now wants to introduce a database both of organisations which employ temporary staff and people who have registered with the organisation for temporary work. He is aware that this information will be held subject to the terms of the Data Protection Act.

   So far the agency has been quite lax in its security procedures. Computer screens are quite visible to clients, disks are kept in unlocked drawers, passwords are not necessary to access the system. Both you and your boss appreciate that measures must be taken to train staff properly and to hold the data in a lawful manner.

a Contact the Office of the Data Protection Registrar, Springfield House, Water Lane, Wilmslow, Chester, SK9 5AX (tel. 01625 535777) and obtain a set of Guideline Booklets. From this information prepare a short report for your boss stating the action the organisation must take both to register as a user and to hold the data legally.

b Draw up a list of security measures which you think should be taken to reduce the possibility of unlawful access to data.

Element 6.2
Integrate different types of data

Integration refers to the moving, copying, linking or embedding of data from one document to another or from one file to another. This has long been possible in relation to two documents produced in the same application but it is only recently that software manufacturers have acknowledged the need of users to move or copy documents – or extracts from them – from one application to another. It is very frustrating for a computer user to have to create a document twice.

For instance, if you prepared a chart showing monthly sales figures on a word-processing package it would be infuriating if you wanted to E-mail this to sales reps but could not simply recall your document within your E-mail message. Similarly, it is a waste of time and effort to have a database containing customer names and addresses and then have to replicate these within your word processing package to send out a mail shot.

The new generation of software has addressed – and solved – all these problems, as well as a few others which you might not yet have thought about.

Use and operation of hardware and software

The hardware installed can limit your choice in relation to integrated packages. Basically, you should be operating on at least a 486 computer. A 386 computer will run some packages, but only slowly – which can be very frustrating. Graphics-based operating systems need more memory than DOS – so if you intend to run a Windows integrated suite of packages then you may need to upgrade your computer system.

The software can be installed either on a stand-alone basis or on a network. If shared access of documents is to be a feature then obviously a network is essential.

Most integrated packages give stand-alone users the ability to select those applications (or parts of applications) they wish to load onto the hard drive to reduce the disk space used for items which are only used infrequently (e.g. clipart). You decide which items you want when the applications are being installed on your computer. On a network, the network administrator will make this decision and may take advantage of the facility to customise the package for the organisation's own use. The opinions of users should be sought before major decisions are taken – though it is usually possible to change or recustomise the facilities available if demand increases or decreases for a particular facility.

Types and application of software

Early Apple Macintosh software was notable for its compatibility. In other words, the screens for each package were similar, the commands were usually given in the same way and, in some cases, documents produced in one package could be transferred to another. By contrast, many software products produced for use on IBM and IBM-compatible equipment were less so. Some could not be linked at all, while in other cases a conversion program had to be run before data in one application could be used in another. Even then there could be problems with formatting and other commands which were either ignored or changed when the document was transferred.

However, software developers were quick to spot the potential for true integration – where a spreadsheet table or graphic could be imported to a word-processed document, or a mail merge facility on a word processor could utilise customer names and addresses stored on a database (Figure 6.2.1). This is a feature of integrated packages such as Ability and Microsoft Works which contain 3-in-one or 4-in-one

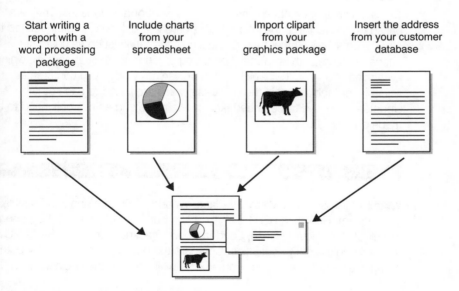

Figure 6.2.1 Using a software suite

facilities. However, the latest generation of integrated packages – often referred to as 'suites of software' – such as Microsoft Office, Lotus SmartSuite and PerfectOffice have improved on these ideas still further by designing integrated packages where every program operates in the same way by using the same system of operation and the same type of commands. For instance, in Windows, where menus, commands, toolbars and dialogue boxes are used, these are designed to be almost the same in each program in the suite. The idea is obvious – instead of learning a set of different programs the user only needs to learn one to have a broad understanding of all the others. In addition, the programs may all access the same type of speller, thesaurus, help guides and so on (Figure 6.2.2).

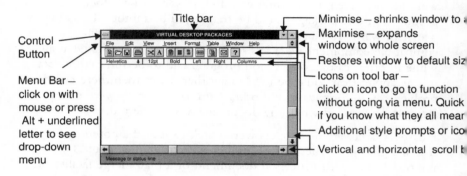

Figure 6.2.2 Each program in a software suite has similar commands

 DID YOU KNOW?

The latest type of databases are known as **relational** databases. They are based on the fact that the information stored in a database is often related to other information. Rather than duplicating information (such as customer phone numbers in three places!) or having an enormous database containing everything you need (but which would be very unwieldy), you can create several small tables within the database which are linked to each other. Updates only need to be undertaken in one place and entries only need to be made once (Figure 6.2.3).

CHECK IT YOURSELF

Write to Microsoft Ltd, Microsoft Place, Wharfdale Road, Winnersh Triangle, Wokingham, Berkshire RG11 5TP to obtain details of Microsoft Office; and to Novell UK Ltd, Novell House, London Road, Bracknell, Berkshire RG12 2UY to obtain details of PerfectOffice. Compare the packages produced by both companies and decide which you would buy if you had the choice.

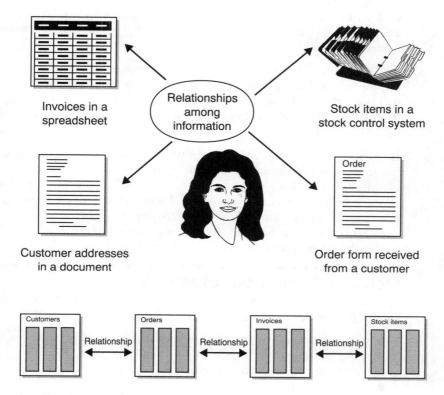

Figure 6.2.3 Relationships among information

Computer conventions

A convention is an accepted term or way of doing something. When software packages – and computers – were in their infancy there was a certain amount of confusion and conflict brought about because of the different terms used by different software manufacturers. Anyone who has ever transferred from an early word-processing package to a much later version will tell you that they had to relearn virtually all the skills they had ever possessed! The situation was even worse for those transferring from, say, an Apple Mac to an IBM system or vice versa. Today there is much more commonality in this area, with standard terms being used and accepted and some others dropped. Software producers do not want to make things difficult for users who have to convert to their package – otherwise it is unlikely to sell very well. For that reason, there is sense in having a standard set of conventions which everyone knows and understands.

In the case of integrated packages – especially those with shared access – standard conventions are essential. Without them you would not be able to talk the same language – let alone carry out the same operation! For that reason, you are likely to see similar wording used to describe standard computer operations in all manuals today – although you still have to be careful of minor idiosyncrasies by some software houses!

You have already met dozens of standard terms in this chapter – log on, file access, file transfer and so on. Throughout this element you will meet those which relate to integrated packages and transferring data. In the IT reference section at the end of this unit most are listed for convenience. Check that you understand what is meant by each.

In addition to the terminology, you will find that each organisation has its own conventions in certain areas. These may relate to naming files and directories so that they are easily understandable by all staff, following security routines and standardising other working practices. It is important that you understand and adhere to these conventions not just because someone says so but because you clearly realise the dangers inherent in 'doing your own thing'!

Use of information reference codes

A code is a shortened version of a piece of information which can be used for identification. The reason why a code is used is usually:

- because the information is too long to be remembered (or input) in its full form
- for rapid identification of information
- for security reasons.

You have already met an example of a code used for security in Element 6.1, page 362. Many computer systems also use codes as a shortcut and to save memory. The same codes can be used to search for or retrieve data. An obvious example is that of staff IDs. If each member of staff is allocated a code then the same code can be entered to retrieve the personnel record or the payroll record or to send E-mail messages to them.

Staff ID codes are usually *meaningful* codes in that they are often devised from a combination of letters and numbers based on the name or date of birth (similar to, but shorter than, the code on a driving licence). A *meaningless* code is one which has no obvious relation to the original source of information. These are more suitable for security purposes as they can be less easily guessed (see page 362).

There are many applications for codes, including:

- customer or supplier names and addresses
- purchased items held in stock
- goods sold by the company
- accident categories
- standard paragraphs (see below).

Codes are useful in helping you to identify information. A basic example is inserting a header or footer on documents as standard, and in this area placing a code which is comprised of the date, author and, perhaps, some key words. The code you devise should be:

- logical and meaningful – so other people can follow it
- short enough so that it can be input as the document reference on the disk
- clear enough so that you can identify what the information was concerned with when you read the code.

It is even better if your paper filing system also reflects the code system as this way you link everything together.

The system comes into its own when you are linking together or embedding (see page 379) extracts from a variety of documents into other documents – or using a variety of small documents to compile into a master document.

A typical example would be legal documents such as contracts or sales presentations which regularly feature the same information but are often customised for a specific occasion. It would be most annoying to know that you had a good paragraph on the structure and organisation of the company or the distribution network in another sales report but not be able to find it! If you have an integrated package which gives you the ability to produce tables, charts, lists, reports or even presentation slides then you need a clear referencing system so that you can easily find earlier documents which can be updated and used again.

DID YOU KNOW?

Inserting a date in a code helps you to identify the most recent copy of a document – especially if you have three print-outs and aren't sure which is the right version to use!

TEST YOURSELF

Your organisation has decided to customise all its forms on computer – including templates for letters, memos and fax messages. Your new package allows the insertion of all information on standard templates set up and stored in the network. You want to devise a system of codes so that when each form is created and stored in the system it is readily retrieved by keying in a meaningful code. You also want to take account of the fact that some forms are updated on a regular basis.

Either using examples from your own workplace *or* by assuming you work in the Sales office, list the forms you would need and devise a meaningful coding system which all staff could understand.

Check your answer with your tutor or adviser.

Methods of retrieving, transferring, integrating and editing data

Retrieving data

As you have just seen, use of a sensible system of referencing means that data can easily be identified for retrieval. You also saw in Element 6.1 the importance of naming files correctly and clearly and learned the basic principles of directory management.

If you adhere to these ideals then it should not be difficult to find the information you need. On most packages it is useful to retrieve data by accessing the same application again on your computer and calling up the document. If you want to find a particular piece of information in a document then there are usually commands which will enable you to find it quickly rather than scroll through the document. If you are completely stuck on a word-processing package then try to think of a few key words and use your search facility to help you. Some integrated packages have the ability to help you search quickly through filenames or directories relating to all applications – in case the document is lurking where you least expected it!

Transferring and integrating information

Data can be transferred and integrated in one of three ways:

across applications	when you transfer it from one software package to another, e.g. inserting a table produced in a spreadsheet package in a word-processed report
across computer files	when you transfer data from one document to another, e.g. by copying information found in one database into another or duplicating a paragraph in one letter in another
using functions across applications	by using basic commands and functions which are common to more than one application (see below).

Depending upon the type of application package(s) installed, it is usual to transfer information by using one or more of the following functions:

move block	where you define the start and end of the data to be moved, put your cursor to the position you want the data to appear and then place the block in that position

copy block	where you define your block but then replicate the identical information somewhere else – usually in another document or file.
drag and drop	the same as 'move block'. If you want to drag and drop data from one file or application to another then both must already be open
cut and paste	when you want to identify a block of information to move into another application or file which has not yet been opened.

Bear in mind that **moving** information means that it is deleted in its first location. **Copying** information means that the data is now saved in more than one location.

In addition, if you use a fully integrated package then you will also have the choice whether to **link** or **embed** information.

Linking information

You can choose this option to save data which is used in different documents or applications and which is regularly updated. An example would be financial information or sales figures which may be created as an individual table but also form part of a monthly report. You should bear in mind that you edit a linked document by referring to your original, or source document. As you change the data in the source document then the data in your destination document is updated automatically (Figure 6.2.4).

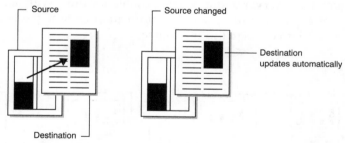

Figure 6.2.4 Linking data

You do not have to restrict yourself to one location when you link documents – data can be linked to several locations (Figure 6.2.5). In addition you also have the option to break a link or to lock a link – to prevent other people updating the information.

Linking is the ideal choice if you regularly need to incorporate up-to-

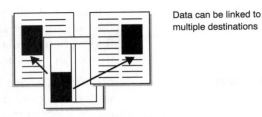

Data can be linked to multiple destinations

Figure 6.2.5 Linking data to multiple destinations

date information from other sources in a document you produce or if you are expected to create a summary document regularly from larger, more complex documents. You should also choose linking for information which changes regularly, e.g. customer addresses. As you update your database the address carried forward to your word processed document automatically changes too.

DID YOU KNOW?

Data from one application which is transferred to another is always called an **object**. The object does not have to be text – it can be graphics, a table of figures or even a voice recording!

Embedding information

Embedding is a more suitable option if you want to save data created in several applications in one master document – particularly if this information does not have to be updated frequently (Figure 6.2.6). An example would be when a graphic, table and report have been created using different applications and then you want to bring the three together. The original application in which each object was created is known as a **server** and it is only possible for those with access to the server application to update the information because the embedded copy is not connected to the source.

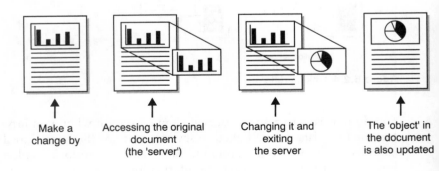

Make a change by | Accessing the original document (the 'server') | Changing it and exiting the server | The 'object' in the document is also updated

Figure 6.2.6 Embedding objects

In any information on integrated packages you may see the letters OLE. This abbreviation stands for Object Linking and Embedding. It enables you to move or copy data easily from one application to another and then edit it or update it in either the source or final document.

Editing information

A good integrated package will move or copy information from one application to another in the same format. This means that you can edit the information easily in its new position. If you do not have this facility then you have to go back to the application in which it was created, do your changes there and then insert your updated version in place of the original in your second document.

Don't forget that if you link or embed information, even in one of the latest packages, you will have to go back to the source document or server to change information – in the new document you may just have a static set of text or picture which cannot be changed.

CHECK IT YOURSELF

You have already learned about protecting equipment and data, back-up/safety procedures and legal and regulatory requirements in Element 6.1. Discuss with your tutor or adviser, or as a group, the additional precautions which may have to be taken to maintain security and confidentiality of information in an organisation which installs an integrated suite of packages.

ACTIVITY SECTION

1   Either using your own job role as a guide or by brainstorming as a group, identify as many occasions as you can when it would be useful to be able to integrate data between files or applications.

2   You have recently seen the new junior trying to edit a document on her word processor. You were horrified to see her deleting large chunks of text and then typing in an update. It then took her another 10 minutes to find a sentence she had to change. Using a package with which you are familiar, prepare a 'short cuts to editing' instruction sheet which you could give to her for reference.

3   You are about to set up three databases for your boss. One will contain all your customer files, the second will include details of all your products, and the third will divide up the customers geographically to match the areas covered by each representative.

  a   State the information you think is likely to be included in each database.
  b   Identify the information which is common to more than one database.
  c   State clearly the way in which linking information could save time in keeping the databases up-to-date.

Element 6.3

Present information in various formats

The effectiveness of being able to enter or integrate data is reduced if you do not present that data properly. As every first-class administrator or PA knows, you are judged on the quality of your output. Today, more than ever, people expect to see professionally designed and high quality documents as standard. The additional facilities on many of the latest packages mean that a host of special effects can often be accessed at the touch of a key or two. If you want other staff to be able to use these properly then the best way is to lead by example – and use them effectively yourself first. They will then want to copy you – and you will be in a position to show them what to do!

Use and operation of software

As you should already know, different types of software are used to produce different types of documents. Basically, a spreadsheet is used to prepare a financial worksheet, a chart or a graph; a database produces a record or a listing; and a word-processing package is used to create text-based documents, such as letters, memos or reports. However, today many word-processing documents will produce charts or tables and you may even be able to import clipart of objects or outline diagrams. If you have a presentation package then you may have access to an even greater array of features.

Start by checking that you know how to use the software you already have to its fullest extent. For instance:

- On a **word-processing** package – can you embolden, underscore and centre text without difficulty? Do you know how to reformat a document (see page 386)? Can you type in a range of fonts, i.e. different typefaces, styles and sizes? What other character sets can you access to print unusual characters? (See also page 388.)
- On a **spreadsheet** package – can you design a worksheet so it has clear headings and totals? Can you print out showing either figures or formulae? Can you change the format of cells easily or align data to right or left? Can you compress the information to print out a large spreadsheet on a small sheet of paper? Can you produce graphics with clear labels and a readable key?
- On a **database** package – can you design a clear form with sensible field lengths? Can you design or redesign a report so that it is user-friendly? Do you know how to change the style of a form or report to suit your needs? Can you take advantage of all the visual styles available, such as italics, bold or alignment of text?
- On a **desktop publishing** package – can you design a page in

different column widths and draw a thin line between each column? Can you use different fonts and types of shadings? Can you reflow text around an imported graphic for effect? Can you rotate images to give a different look to a graphic?

Usually all these facilities are clearly stated in the manual and all are familiar to professional users. If you want to be considered a professional yourself, now is the time to get to grips with them.

Use and operation of printers

It is useless designing a chart in four colours if you are using a printer which only prints in black and white! It is also pointless trying to design a huge heading on a desktop–published document if all you possess is a basic ink-jet printer. You must remember that on many software packages you will not be limited by the options available but by the ability of your printer to support them.

The type of printer you have is likely to fall into one of the following categories.

Dot matrix

Used for payroll or other listings. Depressing NLQ (near-letter quality) means that the printer goes over each character twice to improve the density. These printers are unsuitable for external documents and are also the slowest and the noisiest in operation.

Ink jet or bubble jet

Ink-jet printers can produce both text and graphics. They work by means of tiny droplets of ink from a cartridge being sprayed onto the surface of the document. Colour printers are now available quite cheaply (at less than £300) but different colour cartridges are required. The cartridges are quite expensive but a new service initiative is the refilling of used cartridges. This saves money and is also environmentally friendly. (Do not be confused by the term 'bubble jet' – it is just a trade name, used by one company, for a similar type of printer.)

Laser

Laser printers work by using laser beams to transfer the original image onto a drum, which then transfers it onto paper. Desktop models are becoming more and more common in offices, even though they are quite expensive. The copy quality is excellent both for text and graphics. A Postscript laser printer is one that can produce very sophisticated text and graphics using a special built-in processor. Such a machine is ideal for desktop publishing work, although it may be expensive. Laser printers also use cartridges – this time containing toner – and these are far more expensive than those for ink jet printers. It is estimated that printing costs average about £6000 per laser printer installed – but this can be reduced by over £1000 a year if refillable cartridges are used. Laser printers are often 'paper-sensitive' – therefore the latest discount offer from your local stationery store may be unsuitable for use as a means of saving money!

GDI printers

These are the latest printers coming on to the market at half the price of standard laser printers but with the same facilities. How? GDI stands for Graphics Device Interface. These printers have been designed to use Microsoft Windows printer drive software and are therefore only usable with applications formulated under Windows. In addition, the printer uses the PC to obtain the processing power to construct its pages and does not have its own power. You therefore need a fairly powerful PC with at least 8 Mb of RAM to use one. Finally, the printers do not work well in a network. However, if you have Windows, a powerful computer and a printer of your own they can be a very useful, cheap alternative!

House style

Many organisations have a specific house style which they insist upon for business documents. This gives a uniform look to all the documents which are produced. House style may refer to the layout of the document or may go further and include the style of headings, typeface and the fact that a logo must always be included at the top right-hand side! Modern computer packages give people the ability to incorporate any of these features in a standard way – usually by setting them up as a template or master document on the system. This way the user simply recalls the template and adds his or her own text.

Document layouts can vary enormously – you only have to compare three letters in your incoming mail in a week to see this for yourself. The basic rule to remember in an organisation is that 'he who pays the piper calls the tune'. So no matter what your personal view of the house style you are usually well advised to keep your opinions to yourself – at least until you feel very secure in your job! You may also like to bear in mind that if you work for a small organisation or for a new business then your suggestion to introduce a corporate style may be more appreciated and easier to introduce.

The golden rules for coping with different house styles include:

- looking in the files upon your arrival at a new company to see how documents are set out
- knowing the alternatives available, e.g.
  - full punctuation (and all its variations)
  - semi-blocked style where the date is typed alongside the reference and ends at the right-hand margin, indented paragraphs are used and the complimentary close is centred on the page
  - blocked style which is like the above except that the paragraphs are blocked
  - fully blocked style where *everything* starts at the left-hand side.
- knowing what the existing hardware and software can do – both its possibilities and its limitations.

It is useful to design a house style manual containing examples of all the documents and the required formats. Then no-one has any excuse for not keeping to them.

Types and application of software

Software has been covered several times in this unit and on page 382 in this element. Basically you need to choose the type of software which is most suitable given the intended use of the information you are about to produce and the way in which you want to present it. You also need to consider ease of use and your own familiarity with a package.

If your word-processing package supports two- or three-column documents or boxed tables then you may decide to use this option rather than start up another application with which you are less familiar. This would also be the case if you were designing a report which incorporated tables and you did not have access to an integrated package.

Types of format

The format refers to the way in which you decide to display your information. You normally have a choice between text, graphics and tables. The option may be chosen for you if your boss decides he or she wants a pie chart on page 2 and a table on page 4. In other cases you may be left to decide yourself.

As you have already learned in Element 5.2, you must consider the amount of information, its complexity and its intended audience. A presentation to the Board of Directors is likely to need a more serious image than handouts for a talk to a party of visiting schoolchildren! The main thing to guard against is the urge to simply write masses of text when a graphic or table would not only reduce the amount of input for the reader but also make things clearer for everyone!

If you have forgotten what was said in Element 5.2, or are not reading this textbook through from the beginning, turn to page 310 for the main points to remember.

CHECK IT YOURSELF

If you are hopeless at thinking how graphics could be used then it is useful to look at a book which gives you some hints and tips! Either by looking at a beginner's book on graphic design in your library or by looking at some of the sample illustrations in a desktop publishing software manual, try to improve your appreciation about how graphics, tables and 'white space' can be used effectively.

Types of presentation

The presentation of your document should be such that the information is digested easily – with the most important information given the most prominence. The modern approach is to keep things simple yet follow standard conventions. This means:

- highlighting headings and important words in **bold** (rather than underlining them)
- leaving a clear space after a heading and between paragraphs
- making sure headings in a long document relate to each other (i.e. all your main headings are in one style, your subheadings in another, etc.) and are consistent throughout
- leaving two spaces after the punctuation mark at the end of a sentence and one space in other cases
- using block paragraphs (unless the house style is different!)
- using a consistent form of numbered or decimal numbered paragraphs and insetting.

In addition to setting out the text correctly, you also need to choose:

- the most appropriate paper size and decide whether this should be used portrait or landscape
- the size of all margins – left, right, top and bottom (the default is equal horizontally and then equal vertically for good effect!)
- the line spacing
- whether or not text should be justified (usually yes!)
- whether or not the document should be paginated
- whether or not headers and footers are required
- the type and size of characters to use
- how to display the information on the page.

Do bear in mind that there is a world of difference between displaying text in a straightforward report and producing a newsletter which needs an eye for design and the judicious use of space.

Choice of presentation

Again you are likely to be limited by your hardware and software. Here are some potential options and hints and tips to help you.

1 Don't plan on outputting documents on a page size which is incompatible with your printer! Few will produce documents larger than A4. Before you decide to make a larger version on your photocopier remember that solid black text turns grey and loses its definition when it is enlarged.

2 If you do not have a colour printer then your local print shop may have one. Investigate. Then find out if they have a computer system compatible with yours so that, on special occasions, you could obtain colour printouts simply by giving them a disk containing your document.

3 Avoid orphans and widows where single lines of text are left at the bottom of a page or taken over to the top of the next page. Some software packages will adjust these for you automatically. On others you can simply define the number of pages to use and the package will condense/expand the text for you!

4 Learn how to paginate. If you are producing a long report then put your page numbers bottom centre and include page 1. Alternatively, some organisations like pages paginated at the top − on opposite sides for facing pages.

5 If you display text in columns, do not use more than three or, at most, four columns. Use equal columns and equal spacings. Draw a thin vertical line between for a professional look.

6 Do not mix typestyles and character sizes too much or use too much colour. Using too wide a variety simply looks amateurish.

7 Use bullet points rather than numbered points if you do not want to denote an order to the subsections.

8 Make sure tables and diagrams are well-balanced, easy to read, clearly labelled, positioned centrally on the text or the page and pleasing to the eye.

9 Use boxes to display important text or to indicate a graphic which is to be inserted later.

10 Investigate the capacity of your software to produce different character sets, typefaces and character sizes − and the capacity of your printer to output these!

All computers operate using one character set − usually ASCII codes. You often have the opportunity to use other sets which include mathematical and scientific signs, typographical symbols and foreign characters, e.g. Greek, Hebrew and Cyrillic letters.

The term 'font' refers to the style of typeface being used. Typeface comes in two styles − serif and sans serif. Serif has 'curly bits' whereas sans serif is 'without curly bits'! As an example our typesetter has given you an example of some typefaces in Figure 6.3.1 – both serif and sans serif.

This is an example of a serif typeface

This is an example of a sans serif typeface

Figure 6.3.1 Serif and sans serif typefaces

In addition, on most printers today, you can purchase additional typefaces to add to the ones which are standard when you buy the equipment (Figure 6.3.2).

This is an example of Times typeface

This is an example of Courier typeface

This is an example of Helvetica typeface

This is an example of Palatino typeface

Figure 6.3.2 Further examples of typefaces

The term 'point' relates to the size of the text. The larger the number the larger the text, so it is quite easy to remember (Figure 6.3.3).

This is 8 point

This is 12 point

This is 24 point

This is 36 point

Figure 6.3.3 Examples of different point sizes

11 Find out about additional enhancement features on your packages, e.g. shading, three-dimensional imaging and unusual alignments.
12 Read your printer manual and find out what additional facilities you could 'buy in' if you need them to extend your current options.

Security and confidentiality of information

You already know the most important aspects of document and disk security. However, you must remember that when you are producing hard copies – particularly of confidential information – then these need the same care and attention as your disks. Do not leave hard copies lying around on your desk, or take them into public areas. If a document is particularly sensitive then do not throw all your trial copies in the wastebin and then carefully insert the final version in a sealed envelope! Shred all the evidence of your mishaps carefully – that way even your boss can't tell how many times you printed it out before you got it right!

DID YOU KNOW?

A final – but essential – word! It is absolutely useless spending hours upon the presentation of a document if it contains basic typographical errors for all the world to see! Proofreading is a skill you must learn (see Element 7.1, page 473). If you are hopeless at checking a document on screen (and some people are) then recognise this fact and take a hard copy to check – before you give the command to print out 25 copies! In addition, recognise the limitations of your spellchecker – it cannot pick up errors which are input as 'meaningful words'. Finally, did you know that some word-processing packages also contain a facility to check your grammar? So you can even obtain help if your sentence construction is a bit wobbly – or, of course, you could turn to page 486 in this book instead!

ACTIVITY SECTION

1   Obtain a selection of 10 documents – either received by you personally or in the course of doing your job. Evaluate each of these in relation to format, presentation and content. Compare your findings with those of the rest of your group. (*Note*: do not include any documents which could, even loosely, be described as confidential or containing sensitive information.)

2   Your boss is preparing notes for a presentation to sales staff at the annual conference. He wants to prepare slides as well as hard copies to give to the reps. His aim is to give an overview of sales to date, forecasts for the future, the key points in relation to a new product and a summary of the terms in the new sales agreements. He has asked you to help him to prepare and compile his information.

   a   In which application are you most likely to find
      i   current sales figures
      ii   a list of customers
      iii a copy of the new sales agreement?
   b   Your boss has prepared his sales forecast using a spreadsheet. What graphics would you recommend to display these figures and what factors would influence your choice?
   c   The only graphic you can find on the new product is an illustration in a booklet. How could you input this into your computer? State clearly the equipment you would need.
   d   Given an unlimited choice of software products(!) what type of package(s) would you use to produce the slides and documentation required and why?

3   You have been asked to prepare a newsletter for staff on one double-sided sheet of A4 paper. It will contain two illustrations and one photograph – and you have the final say on the size of each of these. You also have an introductory statement by the MD to include and six separate articles. Two of the articles are very short, three are medium-length and one is quite long. Finally there is a brief quiz for staff.

On two sheets of paper give an indication of a suitable design which will clearly show the positioning of all the text and graphics. Indicate, too, the size of heading you would use in each case.

IT reference section

The following are all IT terms which you should know. Read them once through and then check that you could write a definition for each one which closely resembles that given.

Note that words and phrases which are highlighted in **bold** are those for which a separate definition is to be found elsewhere in the section.

Applications package	A package containing a program designed to carry out a specific task for the benefit of the user, e.g. an accounts package or a word processing package, plus all the instructions and manuals for the program.
Backing store	A device for storing programs and data other than in the computer's RAM memory, e.g. a disk drive.
Back-up copies	Copying data on to floppy disks or a tape streamer for use if the first disk or hard disk fails to work.
Bar code	A pattern of bars and spaces which can be read by a computer scanner. Examples can be found on virtually all supermarket products.
Baseband cabling	May be used over short distances to transmit data over a network from one computer to another. Because it is a single-channel system, usually only one device can transmit data at a time.
Broadband cabling	Used in larger organisations to transmit data quickly. Can be used over long distances. Because this is multi-channel, different communications can be transmitted simultaneously on different frequencies, e.g. data, voice and video.
Bubble-jet printer	*See* **Ink-jet** printer.

Buffer	The part of memory which stores data temporarily. For example, a printer buffer will hold documents until the printer is free to print them.
Bug	An error in a program which causes it to fail or not to operate properly.
Byte	The amount of computer memory required to store one character of data. A byte contains 8 bits. Computer memory is measured in bytes, e.g. **kilobytes** and **megabytes**.
CAD (Computer-aided design)	Using computers to create drawings and designs which may be 2-dimensional, 3-dimensional or even animated.
CAM (Computer-aided manufacture)	Using computers to help in the production of goods, e.g. by controlling robots or machines.
CD-ROM	A compact disk with a **read only memory**. The disk is manufactured with the data in place and this cannot be changed by the user.
Ceefax	The BBC teletext service – a form of 'online' database.
CPU (Central processing unit)	The 'brains' of the computer which processes information, carries out instructions and controls the **peripherals**.
Character set	A set of symbols which can be recognised and used by the computer.
COLD (Computer output to laser disk)	Downloading computer output to optical disk.
COM (Computer output to microfilm)	Producing microfilm on a mainframe computer.
Compatibility	The ability of one terminal or computer system to understand and 'talk' to another.
Computer graphics	Pictures, photos, drawings and scanned images stored digitally on computer or created by means of a **graphics package**.

Computer support	Usually a centralised unit of computer support staff whose function is to assist network users, resolve difficulties, monitor usage and instigate network development.
Cursor	The symbol which shows the position where the next character will appear. It is usually a small flashing block which may appear in reverse mode.
Database	A program which enables the user to reorganise and re-sort data to give particular types of information; *or* a collection of related data which is stored and accessed by a database program.
Data communications	The use of communications equipment to transfer data from one computer terminal to another.
Data encryption	The assigning of codes to blocks of data which make it unreadable to anyone without access to the key.
Data protection	Safeguards for individuals to ensure that information about them which is held on computer is only used for specified purposes.
Data security	Measures which are taken to prevent data being lost or misused; for example, user IDs, passwords and write-protect mechanisms on floppy disks.
Desktop	Virtual desktops are a feature of Windows and other graphical systems. They aim to make the system more user-friendly by replicating an ordinary 'desktop' on screen.
Desktop publishing	Packages which bring together text and graphics to produce newsletters, posters and other types of advertising material.
Digitiser	A device which enables a video image to be captured by computer. (*See also* **scanner.**)

Directory	A list of file names under specific headings.
Disk	A backing store for data.
Document reader	An input device which recognises characters on pre-printed documents by the use of Optical Character Recognition software.
DOS (Disk operating system)	The most common type of operating system for micro-computers – must always be present on a computer unless OS/2 is installed (see Figure 6.1.6, page 350).
Dot matrix printer	A printer which produces characters by making a pattern of small dots. The final result is not of a high quality but is suitable for internal documents, e.g. payroll and accounts listings.
EDI (Electronic data interchange)	Often called 'electronic trading' – this system is concerned with the electronic transmission of documents and payments. All orders and invoices are communicated by computer to companies worldwide. Order processing is rapid, thus reducing stock levels and storage costs. Invoices can be sent by the purchaser and payments can be made by using a smart card in a specific computer terminal.
E-mail	Electronic mail – messages are sent from one user to another over a network and stored in the user's personal mailbox.
File	A collection of data in a computer's memory.
File access	The way in which the records in a file are stored, retrieved or updated by computer, i.e. either serially, sequentially or by random-access.
File generation	A specific version of a file. When updating takes place, a new file is generated. Generally the old file is

	stored as a security measure in case the latest generation is lost or damaged.
File server	The hard disk micro, mini or mainframe computer which coordinates and controls the storage of shared data for a network. It carries out the dual functions of organising and prioritising all file-related tasks received by the network at tremendous speed.
File transfer	The transmission of a file from one machine to another through a physical link between the two machines, e.g. a telephone line and modem.
Floppy disk	A flexible and removable disk on which data is stored.
Font	The printing design of a set of characters.
Format	The layout and design of a document.
GDI printer (Graphics Device Interface)	A printer suitable only for use with Windows-based software.
GNS (Global Network Service)	A networking service, managed by BT, which interconnects IPSS and other international networks.
(GUI) Graphical user interface	A way in which a user can communicate with the computer by means of a mouse, keyboard and screen which provides a graphical portrayal of a virtual desktop.
Gateway	A device to enable users to pass from one network to another, e.g. from UK to international data transmission services.
Gigabyte	Generally used to represent 1000 **megabytes**. More precisely it is equal to 1024 megabytes.
Graphics packages	Programs which enable the creation of drawings and paintings on a computer.

Graphics tablet	A device which enables drawings to be input into a computer by moving a stylus over a special pad.
Hacking	Illegal access to a computer.
Hard disk	An unremovable disk which can contain large amounts of data.
Hardware	The physical components of a computer system.
Hypermedia	Software in which text, pictures and music may be linked to create a presentation.
Icon	A small picture which represents the function a user may wish to use.
Impact printer	A printer which creates characters by hitting an inked ribbon which transfers the image to the paper beneath.
Importing	The practice of inserting text or graphics created in one package to a document created using another.
Ink–jet printer	A printer which creates graphics and text by spraying fine jets of ink onto paper.
Information referencing	The generation of references – often as headers or footers – on a document, e.g. date, page, title.
Information superhighway	A term used to describe the potential for the rapid transfer of information via fibre optic cable by telephone, computer and through cable television transmissions.
Input device	A device for entering data into a computer.
Integration of data	The merging or linking of data created in one application with that created in another.
Internet	A worldwide public computer network.
Joystick	A vertical control stick which operates as an input device for computer games.

Justification	The alignment of text to the left or right of a page.
Kilobyte	A unit of computer memory which equals 1024 bytes.
Laptop computer	A portable micro-computer.
Laser printer	A printer in which a high-quality image is formed by laser beams.
Light pen	An input device which can indicate certain locations on a computer screen.
LAN (Local area network)	A system which links computers over a small geographical area, e.g. between certain rooms or buildings.
Log off	The process by which a computer user exits the system.
Log on	The process by which a computer user identifies himself or herself to the system.
Mainframe computer	A powerful computer with a large memory capacity.
Megabyte	Memory equal to 1024 kilobytes (approximately 1 million bytes).
Memory	The storage of data or programs on a temporary or permanent basis.
Menu	A list of options from which the user can choose.
MIDI (Musical instrument digital interface)	An interface which enables electronic musical instruments to be linked to a computer.
Modem	A communications device which enables computer data to be transmitted over a standard telephone line by converting computer digital language into analogue signals which can be transmitted via the telephone system. A modem is required at each end of a remote system.
Monitor	The screen on which computer data is displayed.
Mouse	An input device which is used to

	manipulate objects and select options on a computer screen.
Multimedia	A combination system which offers video/TV, sound systems, telephone, computer programs, etc.
Network	A series of connected computers which share the same data and programs.
Network configuration	The way in which the devices on a network are connected.
Network domain (or network segment)	The subdivisions of a large network. Each domain is part of the total network and may represent, say, one department or floor in a large building. Each domain has its own file server(s) and manager station.
Notebook computer	A small, portable computer.
Object	The term used for any type of data which is moved from one application and inserted into another, e.g. text, graphics, figures, voice recordings and animation graphics.
OCR (Optical character recognition)	The means by which text can be identified from a graphical image which has been input into a computer via a scanner.
OLE (Object linking and embedding)	A support function in integrated packages which enables text or graphics to be moved easily from one application to another and edited.
Online help	Help given on-screen by pressing a designated 'help' key.
Optical disks	Laser disks which can store vast amounts of information.
Optical fibre	Transparent, hairsbreadth fibres with virtually limitless bandwidth. They are the fastest means of transmitting information.
Oracle	The viewdata service provided by independent television. Also a database package!

Output device	A device for displaying computer data and information.
Packet switching	A technique for delivering messages by means of small units of information (packets) which are relayed through stations in a computer network along the best route available at that time.
Palmtop computer	A tiny computer which can be held in the palm of the hand.
Password	A secret word which confirms the authenticity of the user.
Peripheral	A device which is linked to or controlled by a computer.
Pixel	A single dot on a computer screen.
Plotter	An output device which draws pictures or diagrams, often in colour.
Prestel	The viewdata service provided by British Telecom.
Printer driver	The software which controls a printer and enables it to interpret print commands correctly.
Printer server	A device which controls a group of shared resource printers on the network. In some networks this function is carried out by the file server.
Processor speed	The 'chip speed' which determines the 'thinking time' of a computer. Measured in megahertz.
Publication	A document produced on a desktop publishing system.
RAM (Random access memory)	Memory which can be read and changed by the computer but which is lost when the computer is switched off.
RDBMS (Relational database management system)	A database system which enables data to be organised and analysed in tables which are part of a larger database
Reformatting	Changing the design or format of a

	document, e.g. paragraph layout or column size.
Restructuring	Radically changing the sequence of text in a document.
ROM (Read only memory)	Memory which can only be read but cannot be changed, e.g. the operating system of the computer.
Root directory	The top directory in a 'tree and branch' filing system.
Scanner	A device which produces a digital image of a document for inputting and storing in a computer. (*See also* **digitiser**.)
Scrolling	Moving the screen image upwards, downwards, left or right to view data not currently displayed.
Search	A specific request for information by the user of a database or directory.
Search criteria	Specific details which are given to be searched for, e.g. gender and age details.
Server	*See* **file server** and **printer server**.
Smart card	A plastic card which stores data which can be updated.
Software	Computer programs.
Source information	The origin of the data being input. This ranges from an original document to an idea in the mind of the operator.
Speech recognition	The ability of a computer to respond to spoken commands.
Speech synthesis	Computer-generated speech (e.g. Directory Enquiries).
Spooling	The system whereby data is stored on disk until the printer is free to process it. Applies to all workstations using Windows or OS/2.
Spreadsheet	A program which enables calculations to be input and analysed.

Systems program	The operating system which enables the computer to function.
Tape streamer	A device which automatically compresses, transfers and stores a large amount of information onto tape. Used to back up high-capacity hard disks.
Touch screen	A screen which enables the user to input data by touching certain parts of the screen.
Tree and branch filing	A system where files are stored in directories. Main directories may be subdivided into smaller directories and so on.
Uninterruptible power supply (UPS)	A device which provides back-up to a computer system in the case of power fluctuations or power failure.
User documentation	Instructions and manuals provided with a computer program.
User ID	The special name input to identify a certain user.
VAN (Value added network)	A network which offers additional services besides communications connections and data transmission, e.g. message routing, resource management and conversion facilities to link incompatible computers.
Virtual reality	Computer simulation where the participant perceives himself or herself as part of a simulated environment.
Virus	Software which can transfer itself from one computer to another via floppy disk and which can damage or destroy data.
Voice output	*See* **speech synthesis**.
WAN (Wide area network)	A network which connects computers over a wide geographical area.
Windows	An operating system which uses a **GUI** and is controlled by pull-down

	menus and toolbars. Windows 95 is the latest version.
Word processor	A program which allows for the manipulation, storage and retrieval of text.
Worksheet	A spreadsheet currently being worked on.
Workstation	The configuration of computer hardware on (usually) a specially designed desk.
WORM (Write once read only)	Similar to a CD-ROM – once the disk contains data it cannot be erased or replaced.
WYSIWYG (What you see is what you get)	A program which prints documents in the same format as that shown on screen.

Managing the job

IF – you can keep your head when all about you are losing theirs and blaming it on you . . .

(Rudyard Kipling, *If*)

The term 'competence' is difficult to describe, especially when related to a specific job. What is it that makes some people extremely capable at doing their job and others merely mediocre?

Many training courses for administrators, PAs and secretaries start by listing the skills required for proficiency, and continue by identifying a list of traits which have more in common with an archangel than any normal human being. Whilst technical skills are undoubtedly important, we all know people who are excellent at their jobs but may not live up to 'textbook' descriptions in terms of abilities and attributes. So what have they got which others have not? What is that indefinable 'something' which they bring to their job and yet cannot describe to anyone else?

RULE 1

All jobs have two aspects.

- technical knowledge and skills
- personal skills, abilities and experience which lead to operational competence.

The first can be learned by training. The second is more intangible as it involves judgement and techniques for coping when things go wrong.

To be able to 'manage your job' you first need to be able to analyse it in terms of its components. Then you need to identify the intangible aspects which go towards making all the difference.

Technical knowledge and skills

The duties and responsibilities of an administrator or PA vary tremendously from one job to another. Much depends on the organisation or department, the way it functions, the nature of the job itself and the status and attitude of the boss(es). There are, however, certain key skills which are always required.

 TEST YOURSELF

List the skills you consider are essential for a professional administrator or PA and the minimum level of competence you think is acceptable.

Essential abilities

Although your list may be slightly different from ours, you should have included the following:

- good command of the English language – both when writing and speaking
- thorough knowledge of standard office procedures and clerical duties
- the ability to deal with a wide range of people at all levels
- management skills – to plan and organise the work and motivate any staff for whom he or she is responsible
- keyboarding/proofreading to ensure the rapid production of accurate and well-presented documents
- good computer skills with a good knowledge of relevant and modern software packages
- efficient operation of all types of office equipment
- good numeracy skills.

How would you score yourself on each of the above, on a rating of one to ten? If you are low on some areas you have a choice – either improve them or choose a job where they don't matter.

> **RULE 2**
> No-one is competent or incompetent as such – only in relation to particular activities. Make sure you choose a job which requires your particular strengths, not your weaknesses.

Administrative attributes

You can roughly divide these into two types: those required for specific jobs and those required for all administrative or secretarial work. In addition, the more you climb the ladder the more important some become, e.g. diplomacy, tact and discretion.

It is possible to get too carried away when considering this aspect. If you consider that all good administrators are patient, loyal, adaptable, reliable, tolerant, have a good memory, an eye for detail and a sense of humour 100 per cent of the time – then you begin to get the idea that they are born, not made! Such a paragon of virtue can also become extremely irritating for other people to have to deal with. Therefore whilst some qualities are obviously useful and should be cultivated, remember to play to your strengths, not your weaknesses.

> **RULE 3**
> No-one functions more effectively by trying to be something they are not.

The intangibles

Even if you are now certain that you understand what a top administrative or PA job entails in terms of content and attributes required, does that mean you will be super-efficient? In a word, no. Just as reading about woodwork cannot make you a master craftsman, neither can reading about – or training for – a top office job. Why? Quite simply because the intangible aspects are missing and it is these which really determine whether you can manage your job.

The best way to identify these intangibles is to isolate some of the characteristics of the really competent administrator or PA, i.e. one who:

- can handle change positively
- can move to a different organisation and work out quickly how to make the best of the new circumstances
- can tackle the work in a variety of different ways
- knows when to stand up for himself or herself and when to keep quiet
- knows when to take risks and when to play safe
- copes and deals with the problems of the job smoothly and efficiently
- has an excellent memory
- can keep several balls in the air at once
- can prioritise and delegate quickly and effectively in a crisis
- always gets the best out of people.

RULE 4

Those with operational competence always find it difficult to put what they know into words, mainly because operational competence usually relies on awareness and judgement.

Learning operational competence

So how do you learn awareness and judgement? Undoubtedly much of this is learned by experience, but some aspects can be identified, for example:

- **knowing your organisation** – its rules (both written and unwritten), its methods of operating and its style, image and culture
- **knowing the people** – who has power and must be kept happy, the background behind relationships, the idiosyncrasies and temperaments of those involved
- **knowing the climate** – expanding or contracting, reactive or proactive, defensive or open
- **knowing the issues** – what is top priority at present, what can

be ignored, who is involved and why, who is in favour and who is not, the political aspects of a situation.

All these factors may alter the way in which you do your job and the way in which you approach different tasks. Prioritising tasks takes on a whole new meaning when you consider some of the factors given above, and so does 'dealing with others'. If you find out that Keith, a rather cantankerous colleague in a nearby office, is the MD's golf partner every Sunday morning, this fact will probably influence what you tell him and how you deal with him!

RULE 5

In any new job find a mentor – someone who will quickly put you wise to the aspects of the organisation you won't find in any written handbook!

Problems and conflict

Probably the key area which distinguishes the super administrator or PA from the average is the handling of difficulties, crises, disturbances and dilemmas. Good administrators cope when all goes smoothly. The super versions come into their own when things get rough, and because of this people rely on them to solve their problems – quietly, efficiently and effectively. Some of these may be everyday routine difficulties, e.g. finding out obscure information or contacting someone urgently. In other cases there may be more serious implications and skilled judgement may be required to decide on priorities and action. In this case the average administrator may rush in where angels fear to tread – and actually make things worse!

RULE 6

Develop an empathy with your boss's style, preferences and modes of operation. The more you can identify with this the more likely you are to 'second-guess' what he or she would want you to do in any given situation.

Developing your skills

If you are working, start by trying to analyse your current role. It is likely that this will include:

- operating as a member of a team in your section or department
- managing your own and your boss's time
- acting as a communications link between your boss and other staff/outside organisations
- planning and organising
- making decisions
- supervising others – either formally or informally.

This book, and the course you have undertaken, will help you to understand the skills required in many of these areas. Developing these can only be done through practice and by trying to do your best – even if this occasionally means making mistakes.

RULE 7
A mistake is only a disaster if you fail to learn anything from it. Reflect on what happened without blaming anyone else or the situation in general.

Finally, learn to acknowledge your own potential and your own abilities. Have as your top priority the development of the technical skills you need in order to do your job efficiently and then think positively about how you can best contribute to the future development and growth of your organisation. Be aware of the intangible aspects inherent in the job and develop a sixth sense for the hidden factors which the less experienced may miss. In this way not only will your own organisation be strengthened by your foresight but so will your own ability to 'manage the job'.

Draft and prepare documents

7

Element 7.1

Draft documents to meet specified requirements

One common feature of the job of all office administrators and PAs is the handling of a large number of documents in the course of the average day. Letters, memos, reports, faxes, messages, minutes of meetings, listings and notices are only a few of the many items which may flow through the office. These will have been received from other organisations and other departments and will all need a response – sometimes urgently and always in a form which combines accurate information with good presentation and excellent writing skills.

A key requirement, therefore, for operating at this level is not just the ability to communicate with people verbally and to work with them to achieve the desired objectives of the organisation (see Unit 4) but also the ability to demonstrate fluency and persuasion in written communications. Indeed, it could be said that your skills in this area will mark you out, quite distinctively, as either an excellent administrator or one who, at best, is only about average.

Special note

If you are worried about your skills in this area, then you will find a section at the end of this element to help you, entitled Tools of the Trade. This gives you guidelines on written English conventions and then includes questions for you to test your own ability. You can check your answers with the key at the end of the section. Make sure that you talk to your tutor or adviser about anything you still do not understand after completing it.

Ways of establishing purpose of documentation

A major part of your role as an administrator or PA is to prepare a large number of documents. At your level, however, you are not merely following instructions – in most cases you are using your own judgement and initiative in relation to:

- what you prepare
- in what format
- for what purpose.

Whenever you need to prepare documents, you are not doing so aimlessly. You have a particular purpose in preparing them, and until you determine exactly what that purpose is you may have difficulty in choosing the most appropriate format, vocabulary, tone and style for any response.

TEST YOURSELF

Read the case study below and answer the questions which follow.

You work in the Accounts and Finance department of a large firm and decide to spend a morning sorting through your in-tray.

Your first job is quite easy. You have received confirmation of a place on a first-line management training course and have to complete and return the tear-off slip to confirm that you will attend.

Your next job is more complicated. The department has changed the system of claiming expenses and you have to prepare a memorandum to all staff informing them of those changes.

One of the accountants has just had a baby. You send her a congratulations card signed by all the staff.

The newest member of your staff is proving a bit difficult. His timekeeping is poor and he is generally lazy and uncooperative. You have already had to give him an oral warning which has had no effect. After consulting your own manager and also the Human Resources Manager, you then decide to take the next step of giving him a written warning.

The department has recently purchased some new computers, several of which have proved faulty. You have had no success in solving the problem over the phone so you draft out a strong letter of complaint to the firm of computer suppliers to be signed by the Finance Manager.

At the last meeting of your quality steering group it was agreed that the work of the group needed to be outlined in more detail to the rest of the staff, most of whom had little or no idea of what it did. You therefore prepare a fact-sheet to be included in the monthly newsletter circulated to all staff.

You send a memorandum to the Computer Services Manager, thanking him for his involvement in training the staff in the use of the new computers and passing on all the favourable comments made by the staff about the way he helped them.

You have been asking your manager for some time for another word processor operator. He tells you to put your request in writing, stating why you need an additional member of staff, so that he can make a case out to the Managing Director.

You reply to an irate memo from the Sales Manager who is complaining that there are mistakes in last month's budgetary figures.

You send a memo to one of the filing clerks reminding her that, yet again, she has left the filing cabinets unlocked overnight.

You feel that you have earned your lunch!

1   Your purposes in preparing the above documents were to
    –   inform
    –   complain
    –   acknowledge
    –   praise
    –   reprimand
    –   congratulate
    –   warn
    –   persuade
    –   explain
    –   apologise.

    Refer back to each of those documents and discuss as a group or with
    your tutor or adviser which of the above purpose (or purposes) applies
    to them.
2   You produce documents for two managers in your office. Both often
    leave a note on your desk if you are not there. Today you find two notes
    – one from each of them – both attached to work you did for them
    yesterday. The notes read as follows:
    A   'Please have a word with me about this'
    B   'When you have a minute, can you see me about a change to
        section 6? Thanks'
    a   Do you consider that the same purpose is implied by each note?
        Give a reason for your answer.
    b   If both writers did mean the same thing, what other factors do you
        suggest contribute towards the difference in tone?
    c   What effect would the difference in tone of both notes have upon
        you as the recipient?

Assistance in establishing purposes

In most cases you will have little difficulty in establishing the purpose
of the document – particularly if you are originating it. In some cases,
however, you may be asked to prepare a document but are not quite
sure *why* you have been asked to do so. You may be able to work it
out for yourself – if your boss asks you to send a memo to the
Purchasing department to find out what has happened to the goods he
has requested, you can be pretty sure that the purpose of that
document is (a) to inform (i.e. the goods have not arrived), (b) to
persuade (i.e. can you hurry them up) or even (c) to complain (i.e.
where are they!). In other cases it may be less easy.

TEST YOURSELF

Your boss appears in the office one morning and issues you with a hurried set
of instructions before dashing off to catch a train. He asks you to:

●   summarise an article in a business journal about performance-related
    pay

- draft out a report to the Managing Director about the number of staff who are computer literate
- prepare a memo to be sent to a member of staff outlining the possibilities of early retirement.

In all three cases you realise that *one* of the purposes is to explain. However, there may be other – equally important but not so obvious – purposes for preparing and sending those documents. Discuss with your group or your tutor or adviser what these could be.

Different methods to use

In the above case, even if you could not ask your boss immediately why he or she wanted those documents to be prepared, if you were in any real doubt you would wait for his or her return to check that you both had a common understanding of the real purpose behind them. Indeed, if you have worked with someone for some time you will have a good knowledge of most of the issues addressed in the relevant documents and will therefore know their purpose without having to ask for further clarification. It is obviously more difficult if you are new or are standing in for someone – in such a case you will need more direct guidance.

Another useful way of determining why a document is being sent is to look at any previous documentation in that area. If, for instance, the memo to the Purchasing Manager had been one of a series, you could tell by looking at the previous memos between the correspondents whether the initial purpose of a request for information had been replaced and that the present purpose was now to complain. Similarly, a glance through the past minutes of a meeting will give you an idea of the purpose behind repeatedly raising a particular topic. Is it to keep reminding someone that the action he or she promised has not yet been taken? Is it meant to be a form of pressure on senior management? Or is it simply such an important and on-going topic that it needs to be discussed at every meeting?

If all else fails, you can often ascertain the purpose of sending a particular document by considering at the person to whom it is being sent.

TEST YOURSELF

You are asked to send:

- a memo to the trade union representative outlining details of the new disciplinary and grievance procedures
- a report to the Managing Director explaining why the departmental targets have not been met
- a letter to the editor of the local newspaper about the opening of a new crèche for children of your firm's employees.

Discuss as a group or with your tutor or adviser why you think those documents are being prepared.

Written documents

The word 'document' pre-supposes that it is in written, typewritten or word-processed form. Some of the disadvantages of using a written form of communication include:

- expense – the time taken preparing a written document is normally much greater than that needed for any form of oral communication
- the lack of any personal face-to-face contact which may result in misunderstandings which cannot immediately be recognised or corrected.

Despite these disadvantages, however, one of the main **advantages** and **purposes** of producing a written document is that it provides a record of a communicated message. It also allows the preparer of that document to take his or her time in considering what should be said and in consulting other people for their advice – both of which are less easy to do when the communication is verbal.

DID YOU KNOW?

A very basic, although in some cases all-important, purpose for preparing a written or word-processed document (as distinct from a verbal communication) is that it acts as **proof** or **evidence** of an agreement.

Sources and uses of information

Once you have established your terms of reference, which means that you

- know exactly what you have been asked to do by someone else *or* what you plan to do yourself
- know why you are doing it – i.e. the purpose of the documentation

then you are in a position to begin consulting relevant sources of reference. The sources you use, of course, will depend on the nature and the purpose of the document.

TEST YOURSELF

You work for the head of a large secondary school and are in the process of preparing a set of documents for the annual speech day. You are responsible for producing:

- a programme for the evening
- a list of the prize winners
- a letter of invitation to parents and other guests
- a guest list
- a seating plan
- notes about the guest speaker

- a letter to the civic hall booking appropriate accommodation and making the necessary catering arrangements
- a press release
- a letter to a local bookstore arranging for book tokens for the prize winners
- a memo to all staff outlining their role in the proceedings.

Discuss as a group or with your tutor or adviser *who* and *what* you will have to use as a source of reference in the course of preparing each document (refer back to Unit 5 on sources of reference if you need to remind yourself of them).

Uses of information

Documents themselves are used for various purposes – and so is the information they contain. When you state information, then you are doing this either:

- to inform someone of the facts, or
- to present an argument or make a case for a certain course of action – in some cases this may be a defensive reaction if you have received a letter of complaint or a memo criticising you or your section for some reason.

In the majority of cases you are either attempting to **activate** a situation by producing a document or responding to someone else's attempts to do the same thing.

TEST YOURSELF

The different types of commonly prepared documents in business are shown in Figure 7.1.1.

Identify which are likely to contain:

a largely factual information
b opinions or arguments to set out a particular case.

CHECK IT YOURSELF

Try to run a mini audit of the written forms of communication used in the organisation in which you work (or department if you feel that is a large enough area) to see:

a which of the documents in Figure 7.1.1 are in general use and
b what – if any – additional forms of written communication you use.

Discuss your findings as a group or with your tutor or adviser and write a short report on any additional written forms of communication used – giving an indication of the purpose(s) for which they are used.

```
┌─────────────────────────────────────────────────────────────┐
│                TYPES OF WRITTEN COMMUNICATION                 │
│  Internal                                                     │
│                                                               │
│     ● Memoranda                                               │
│     ● Reports                                                 │
│     ● Notices                                                 │
│     ● Agendas                                                 │
│     ● Minutes                                                 │
│     ● Staff handbooks                                         │
│     ● Information manuals – equipment, health and safety, organisational │
│       policy, etc.                                            │
│     ● Personnel information – application forms, job descriptions, │
│       specifications, appraisal records                       │
│     ● Budgetary information                                   │
│                                                               │
│  External                                                     │
│                                                               │
│     ● Letters                                                 │
│     ● Invitations                                             │
│     ● Publicity and marketing material – advertisements, features, circulars, │
│       press releases, publicity and promotional leaflets      │
│     ● Commercial material – estimates, quotations, order forms, debit and │
│       credit notes, statements                                │
│     ● Export documentation                                    │
│     ● Financial information submitted to IR and other external bodies │
└─────────────────────────────────────────────────────────────┘
```

Figure 7.1.1 Types of written communication

Ways of verifying information

One objective of communicating in written rather than in verbal form is to substantiate what has been agreed or said. An acknowledgement of a letter or a receipt for goods received, for instance, both fulfil that objective. So too does a set of minutes or a copy of a memo or letter. However, a written form of communication also provides the opportunity for verifying (i.e. establishing the correctness of) such information. Verifying information (as distinct from proving that it merely *exists*) can sometimes be quite difficult. Just because something is written down does not necessarily mean that it is either accurate or valid.

There is a difference between accuracy and validity.

Accuracy applies to facts – are they true or not true? Are they up-to-date? Can you cross-check your information to make certain that you are right?

When preparing any document, particularly one which may have important repercussions if the information it contains is incorrect, it is absolutely essential that it is checked for accuracy – and it should possibly be cross-checked, i.e. verified from more than one source. You can do this by:

- asking an expert (or preferably more than one if the information is of particular significance)
- checking in one or more sources of reference – either paper-based or computer-based
- using your own expertise (although you have to be very confident to make that your *sole* source of reference).

Validity applies to assumptions – an 'invalid' statement is easy to identify if you think of the writer having made 2 + 2 = 5! This normally occurs when the writer links two (or more) separate facts and then uses these to draw a conclusion!

Try this:

> Preparing budgets helps people to control their spending. I prepare a budget each month. I therefore control my spending.

How valid is this? What assumptions have I made from the statement and, if the final sentence is incorrect, where have I gone wrong?

The answer, as you may have guessed, is that the third sentence may be complete rubbish! I may be the world's expert on budgets but still be a spendthrift. Let us analyse these statements in more detail.

- The first sentence is a very sweeping statement (often called a **generalisation**) and basically inaccurate. A more precise definition is that a budget helps people to analyse their income and expenditure. It may, *or may not*, help them to control their spending.
- The second sentence may be true or false. For our purposes we will assume I am a truthful person and do, in fact, prepare a budget each month.
- The third sentence is an invalid assumption drawn from the first two. Ability to control spending depends on other things – none of which is mentioned in this argument.

Therefore the argument is invalid.

Arguments can also be shown to be invalid if they are built on irrelevant statements. If the above argument had included the sentence 'I write very neatly' then this could have been discounted because it contains irrelevant information.

Identifying whether the information you are dealing with is accurate, relevant and valid is important. By verifying information in this way you will build sounder arguments in support of a case than you would otherwise.

DID YOU KNOW?

It is important to distinguish between facts and opinions. Bear in mind that you may be able to give the facts and to use these to present a case – what may not be required is your own opinion of the situation. If you do not have expert knowledge of a situation then your opinion may be discounted – unless it has been specifically requested.

TEST YOURSELF

1   Discuss as a group or with your tutor or adviser how you would verify the following information (preferably involving cross-checking from more than one source):

   a   the latest developments in health and safety legislation
   b   a letter from a member of the public claiming that a bus driver – she doesn't know who – has used racist language to another passenger
   c   a report from the maintenance manager claiming that he is too short staffed to offer a full maintenance service to the Production department
   d   a newspaper article claiming that unemployment has fallen by 5 per cent in the past 12 months.

2   Examine each of the arguments below and say whether they are valid or invalid, and why.

   a   Some men are liars. Some liars can't be trusted. Therefore some men can't be trusted.
   b   Some birds talk. Some pets are birds. Therefore some pets can talk.
   c   Some trains are late. We despatch goods by train. Therefore some of our goods arrive late.

3   Read the following paragraph.

   'It's a well known fact that, unlike women, men are born leaders. Look at all the great heroes of the past – all of them are men. It's also evident that women have little musical or artistic ability. You've probably heard of Mozart, Beethoven, Bach and Brahms and dozens more – including Andrew Lloyd Webber. They're all men! What about Rembrandt, Picasso, Degas, Turner – they're all men too! I prove my point! That's not to say that women don't have *some* good qualities. They're very reliable and loyal. They pay attention to detail. They are born homemakers.'

   a   Distinguish between the facts, opinions and assumptions in the paragraph.
   b   You tell your friend you consider the argument is invalid. Present a valid case to prove this to her.

4   Look at the following situations and discuss as a group or with your tutor or adviser whether a communication containing the following is likely to contain
    i   facts only
    ii a combination of facts and arguments.

    a   A memo to staff to inform them that one of the members of your staff is leaving.
    b   A press release for the local paper to say your organisation has just won a national training award.
    c   A letter to customers which says that the price of one of your main products is going to increase by 2 per cent at the end of the year
    d   A memo to your boss in response to a report that there has been an increase in the number of complaints from members of the public about the way in which their telephone queries are handled.

Conventions in drafting documentation

Giving people what they expect to see or read is quite a good maxim to follow, particularly in business when first impressions are all-important. Consequently, although you may think you have a brilliant new way of communicating some information, you will not necessarily impress some of your long established customers. Remember, for instance, that although open punctuation has been accepted as the norm by examination boards and many organisations, there are still some people who regard it as a new-fangled invention and who struggle to come to terms with it.

It is important, therefore, that you both know and follow the accepted conventions when drafting out documents. In general, business conventions demand that a document:

- is typewritten or word processed
- has numbered pages
- is laid out in paragraphs or as a series of numbered points
- has suitable headings
- is written in sentence rather than note form (unless the document is very informal, such as a reminder note to a colleague)
- has grammar, spelling and punctuation of a high standard (see page 486) – and is free from slang, meaningless abbreviations, and jargon
- follows the usual conventions for document presentation (see page 449)
- is written in a style which suits the content – a formal document must be drafted in formal terms; an informal document can be more relaxed
- follows house style (see Unit 6 page 385 and this unit page 442)
- is dated and – where relevant – signed
- where appropriate, is displayed in pre-printed format.

THE ALTERNATIVE DOCUMENT PRODUCTION GLOSSARY

(Especially useful for those without an 'all-singing and all-dancing' computer package!)

Abbreviations *Standard abbreviations* are those you will find at the end of a good dictionary, for example VAT, UK, ie, nb. Easier and quicker to type using open punctuation (as shown above with no full stops).

Bear in mind that some abbreviations should only be used in certain circumstances:

- only with figures – am and pm, abbreviations for measurements and weights (kg, mm, ft, etc) and %
- in specific cases – &, Ltd, plc, @.

Longhand abbreviations are shortened versions of ordinary words, for example th = that, sep = separate, wl = will, etc.

Don't expect your boss to know or use any of the official versions except for basic ones such as Thurs, Feb, etc. More likely are written notes such as 'aka' (also known as) and 'wef' (with effect from) and a few more invented on the spot! Note these down and *always* expand them in formal communications.

Accents Those signs in foreign language words you always mean to write in afterwards and keep forgetting. Many wp programs have these as optional extras but even on a typewriter there are some shortcuts you can use. Type a comma under a c for a cedilla (eg garçon) and quotation marks (") for an umlaut, eg Zoë. Other accents you need to insert in black ink afterwards. To stop yourself forgetting, at the point you see where the first accent should be inserted get out your black pen and either put it behind your ear or between your teeth. Leave it there until you've finished the document, then you can't possibly forget.

Boxes and spaces A typical example of this type of document is an estate agent's sheet where spaces have to be allowed for photographs of the property to be inserted later. Read your instructions on photograph size carefully! The greatest calamity is to leave too small a space (for obvious reasons). In addition you will have to allow for a margin around the photograph.

Life is easier if you draw a box in the position you want to place the photograph. You can then type merrily around it. If you can't do this officially then you certainly can in pencil – and then rub it out later.

Cards and labels It is always difficult to use small pieces of paper and card in ordinary electronic typewriters and computer printers. However, you should certainly be able to print on labels from your computer these days.

If you are stuck, then forget any automatic procedures available to you and do everything manually – there is less likelihood of anything slipping (this is one occasion when old-fashioned manual typewriters had the edge!). If you are dealing with perforated labels or cards don't separate them until after typing. Check that lines low down on the card or label are aligned with your alignment scale and adjust as necessary. Go slowly – the moral of the tortoise and the hare story applies here.

Charts The main types you will be asked to type are flow charts and/or organisation charts. If you haven't a computer package to cope with these then try the following.

Practise typing rectangles so that you can always place the text exactly in the middle. (Remember to turn down twice as many spaces after the top line as you do before the final line.) Work out what your widest rectangle will be and, if you are creating a vertical chart, type them all this size for simplicity (ie start at the same left-hand margin point).

If you have any other shapes to create (eg diamonds, triangles, etc) then type the rectangles first then draw in the other shapes and type the text in last.

Don't forget to finish off your chart by drawing in the connecting lines at the end!

Circular letters (and tear-off forms) Note whether an external address is required so that you know how much space to leave.

Standard date lines are – 'month and year' or 'date as postmark'.

Note your salutation – whether a generic name is required (eg clients, customers, parents, etc) or a blank space must be left.

The ending may or may not require a signature. If none is required it is usual to type the name of the signatory midway between the complimentary close and the name/designation.

A tear-off slip requires an edge-to-edge row of hyphens (not dots!). The form should be in double-line spacing and rows of dots should be typed for completion. Any white space should be immediately above the tear-off slip – not below it! You can count the lines required for the tear-off slip then add the space at the foot of the page and the cut-off line by remembering that 6 lines = 1 inch if you have to. On a word processing package simply move the text around until your 'white space' is in the right place!

Column displays Easy on a desktop publishing package and some wp packages, a nightmare on some others and very difficult on a typewriter. Do a rough first to give you an idea of column widths possible given the text you have to include. Adjust by varying pitch of type and/or spaces between paragraphs or articles.

Consistency Essential throughout any one document. Pitfalls include

Time – either use the 24 hour clock throughout (1700 hours – note there are no full stops) or the 12 hour clock (5 pm). Don't type useless zeros, eg 5.00 pm.

Words and figures – eg the figure 2 on one page and the word two on another (unless the latter starts a sentence). Apart from starting sentences you are better to stick to one in words and everything else in figures – always.

Names – don't refer to someone as Tom Smith on one page and Mr Smith on another.

Dates – don't date a letter as '14 June' and refer to next Tuesday as 25th June in the text.

Format – don't change the margins from one page to another – try to aim for equal top/bottom and left/right margins throughout (unless you are insetting text for some reason).

Continuation sheets It is doubtful whether any company in existence has ever used the time-honoured practice of typing the name of the recipient, the page number and the date on continuation pages of business letters. Make life simple for yourself and simply type the figure at the top left margin, then leave two or three spaces and continue typing. Don't forget to use plain paper!

With formal reports and anything where lists of numbered points are involved, a figure at the top of the page can be confusing. It is then better to opt for bottom of the page, centre position. This way you can number page 1 as well.

A point to remember in multi-page documents are what are known as **orphans** and **widows**. These are single lines of text at the end of one page and/or the start of the next where the rest of the paragraph is on the other page. They look sad and lonely and need joining up – so do so.

Combination characters Few are used in business today as most electronic typewriters and word processors incorporate the main options (degree signs, equals. etc). They can be fun to practise but in reality, if you regularly need to type a square root sign, buy a system which incorporates it.

Copies The distribution of letters is rarely shown on top copies unless you want to make a point to the recipient! It is more usual to type a circulation list (initials only) just on the copies. Memos are different. If you have more people to write to than you can fit in the space allocated simply type the words 'see below' after the heading 'TO' and type the circulation list at the bottom. If you circulate a memo to someone but don't signal this to the recipient this is known as a blind copy. Don't forget to tick off the copies or you won't know who has one and who hasn't.

Correction signs Unless you work for a publisher it is doubtful if you will ever meet these at work – apart from obvious ones such as NP.

Decimals Must be aligned throughout – learn how to use any decimal command facility you have to save messing about.

Degree sign For some exams you may be taught to type this with a space between the figure and the degree sign, eg 20 °C. Now look at the weather forecast in your local paper. You will probably see either 20C or 20°C! The latter version is the more common in the business world – correct or not.

Diagrams – see under **Charts** Just make sure any shapes are large enough to contain the information they need.

Division of words at line ends Quite simply, don't! It looks old-fashioned and isn't needed with a justified right margin.

Draft copies Should be clearly marked 'draft' so nobody posts them by mistake.

Display Rarely done at work unless you type the canteen menu every day. Vary the weighting of lines with underscore, capitalisation, emboldening, etc. Don't go overboard on centring, and forget fancy edges and borders. Modern displays are plain and easy to read.

Ellipsis Used to signify missing words. Quite simple . . . just use three spaced dots.

Enclosures Although it is essential these are signified in memos and letters in most exams, at work no-one is likely to notice providing that you remember to actually include them! In minutes or reports type a list at the bottom for ease – and to help you check everything off.

Enumeration In other words, numbered points. Line these up properly and use a consistently inset left-hand margin for clarity. If you need to use decimal points

1   The first main point goes at the left-hand margin.
    1.1 Line up a decimal at a new inset point.
    1.2 Make sure your spacing is even
        1.2.1 both within each point
        1.2.2 and between points.

Envelopes and postcards Always start half-way down and a third the way across so the address is roughly in the middle. Don't measure or calculate it! Put a small pencil dot at the right place to start until it becomes second nature. Better still, use window envelopes.

Financial statements Nothing like as hard as they seem *provided* you understand what they are saying! Keep columns and tens and units aligned and type your total lines accurately so that the figure is in the middle. Learn to understand why a figure is carried to the next column so that you type it correctly, for example

	£	£
Income		3000
Expenditure		
Rates	500	
Rent	500	
Food	800	
Clothes	400	
Misc	<u>350</u>	
		<u>2550</u>
Savings		<u>450</u>

Practise typing the double underscore at the end by means of your variable line spacer or interliner to get the gap right – or use a word processing package that will do this automatically!

So far as commas or spaces are concerned, commas are generally old-fashioned but still preferred by some companies. They are usually inserted only in 5 digit numbers and over, eg 10,000 or 10 000 (though some organisations prefer 4 digits and over). Internationally, the modern convention is to use neither space nor commas up to 9999, then group in threes, leaving spaces from the right. Don't forget, always align all tens and units!

Footnotes If several are required forget the asterisk and use figures. On a typewriter these should be raised half a line space in the text with no space between the word and the footnote, eg today[1]. On a computer these can usually be done automatically. The footnote itself should appear at the bottom of the page to which it relates – see below. (If you put it at the end of the document it is technically called an 'end note'.) The figure now goes on the line and there is one space between this and the explanation. It is usual to have a solid line, margin to margin between the text and the footnotes so that you don't thoroughly confuse the reader.

Forms See **tear-off forms** under **Circular letters** above. *Always* use double spacing and leave a long enough line or no-one will be able to complete it. Use equal margins and aim for a balanced appearance.

Fractions You can mix and match between those which are on your keyboard, eg 4½, and those which aren't, eg 5 3/16.

Headings After a main heading text still looks better with two clear spaces between (ie turn down three on a typewriter). If you have a subheading then

---

[1] As shown above.

leave one blank line after your main heading, then (again) two before starting the main text.

On a typewriter use shoulder headings rather than side headings – they're quicker and you won't forget to inset your text and return to the left margin by mistake. On a word processor learn the difference between the indent and the tab function!

Horizontal centring Only centre anything if absolutely necessary – block everything you can at the left-hand margin.

Inset material Use the automatic inset function on an electronic typewriter or use the indent facility on your wp. The cardinal sin is to drift back to the left-hand margin in error. Learn the difference between a left-hand margin inset and an inset which is

> equally inset from both the left-hand and the right-hand margins.

Invitations Buy them and write in the gaps, create them on a dtp package or have them professionally printed.

Justification Always looks better than a ragged right-hand margin. You'll also need to use a flush right-hand margin for the internal address of personal letters (see below).

Leader dots Forget the fancy versions, just use continuous dots for ease. Always remember to leave a clear space before they start and after they finish.

Letters If you can't type a standard business letter you shouldn't be reading this book! You should know by heart the main components and where these are typed. Most textbooks today will tell you to turn down a standard two spaces between each component, apart from where the document must be signed. Many bosses hate this layout and insist on a variety of styles and formats (see house style – Unit 6 and Unit 7). In addition the printed design of your letter-headed paper may make the 'recommended' layout an impractical option.

If you have to sign letters in your boss's absence find out how you should end the letter as there are a variety of ways of doing this:

a   Write the letter on his/her behalf (eg Mr Bloggs has asked me to write and thank you for your letter . . . etc). In this case you would use your own name and designation at the bottom of the letter.

b   Write the letter from him/her. In this case you can

   i   sign it as below

     Yours sincerely
     T L PETTIGREW LTD

     L. Cappitello

     pp John Bloggs
     Sales Manager

or

ii opt for this version

Yours sincerely
T L PETTIGREW LTD

L. Cappitello

Dictated by John Bloggs and signed in his absence

If you are expected to type personal letters for a boss who does not have printed headed paper, type them with the address at the top, with a flush right-hand margin. Leave 2 spaces, type the date at the left margin and then continue as usual.

Memos The standard headings can vary greatly from one company to another. Be consistent in style – don't write to Bill Rogers from J P Jenkins. Either include titles for both sender and recipient or miss them out completely.

If you are composing memos stick to one topic for each memo and keep them short. People lose interest after the first paragraph.

Numbers Ordinal denote order, ie first, second, third – stick to words in continuous text as they're easier to understand than 1st, 2nd, 3rd.

Roman numerals are rarely used these days and can now be aligned from the left or the right, eg

iii	or	iii
iv		iv
v		v

The latter is more up-to-date and easier. It helps if you know which number you are typing. The greatest danger is not leaving enough space for the longest, eg viii.

Cardinal are standard figures. Clearer and easier to use a figure for everything except the number one.

Paper Comes in different sizes, types and weights. You should know the difference between the various sizes and why they are used – ie A3, A4, A5 and A6 – and the difference between portrait and landscape.

You should be typing top copies on bond paper and carbon copies on bank paper. Good quality bond paper is watermarked and has a right side and a wrong side (the latter is slightly fluffy). You will know when you are looking at the right side because you can read the watermark. Insert the paper into your typewriter or printer with this side on the top, or else you defeat the object of using top quality paper!

Paragraphing Usually block style, though if your boss wants 10 space indented paragraphs in every letter, and he is paying your salary, who are you to argue?

Rearrangements Be methodical. No matter how easy your list may seem to start with, always mark it up first and tick off as you go. Otherwise at the first interruption you will have to start all over again.

Reports Simple provided you know the basic rules of paragraphing, headings, pagination and enumeration and are consistent throughout.

Tabulations Think of these as a large-scale, divided rectangle, which you want to appear roughly in the middle of the page. At work, if you are working from previous typescript on a typewriter then you can easily cheat by drawing the box the same size as it was before and then inserting the information! Most modern wp packages will do these for you automatically.

If you are typing from manuscript and only have an electronic typewriter then work out the width carefully and then guestimate the length for vertical centring. If you get this wrong keep going and then photocopy your tabulation onto another sheet of paper. Reposition it (centrally) on the glass just before you take the copy.

Don't forget to draw in all the vertical lines!

Vertical headings Again rarely used. If essential use the modern version:

T
O
D
A
Y

No other version is possible on a wp!

Figure 7.1.2 The alternative document production glossary

TEST YOURSELF

You have written a small handbook (see Figure 7.1.2) for your staff containing a glossary of hints and tips for document production. You feel this may help to 'speed up' staff who have several word processing or typing qualifications but very little experience of producing documents in a stressful environment or of working on anything but the latest word-processing package!

You realise, however, that whilst some explanations are straightforward, some would be easier to understand if there was an example attached. You decide therefore to select at least five of the most difficult areas and to type or word process a short example of each one for the staff to copy.

Produce the five documents together with a brief paragraph on your reasons for regarding the examples chosen as the most difficult.

Different types of documents

The letter and the memorandum are still the most commonly used business document and therefore particular attention will be paid to them and to other forms of correspondence such as invitations in the next element (see page 446). However, other documents also require attention. You already know what conventions are involved in the construction and writing of a report (see Unit 5, page 302), and the conventions relating to the preparation of a set of notices, agendas and minutes is covered in (option) Unit 10. You also need to know the conventions relating to other documents such as:

- handbooks and manuals
- personnel information
- publicity and marketing material
- financial material – estimates, quotations, order forms, debit and credit notes, statements, export documentation, etc.

Handbooks/manuals

The contents of a handbook depend very much on whether it is intended to inform or train staff. However, in both cases its layout is quite similar. You would normally expect to find:

- a title page
- a list or table of contents
- a layout which follows most of the conventions listed on page 418
- an index
- in some instances (particularly in the case of a training manual) a bibliography.

In addition you could expect the handbook to contain illustrations, diagrams or sketches, each numbered and with subheadings.

Personnel documentation

Because of the importance now placed on staff as a resource, the need for detailed documentation of all aspects of their working lives is considered of great importance and there are well established conventions as to how to do this. The major documents are:

- the job advertisement
- the application form
- the job description and/or job specification
- the interview form
- the personnel record
- the staff appraisal form.

The **job advertisement** normally has two sets of conventions to follow – those laid down by the organisation and those by the publication in which it is to be placed. Remember, however, that in this case, cost is the major influence and that normally you would be expected to do the following.

- Check on a number of possible outlets – obtain details of costs, types of layout, distribution area, numbers of entries, etc. Consider specialist journals – for example, if you are advertising for a PA to the Manager of a Leisure Centre an obvious outlet would be the *Leisure Management Journal*. Consider also the use of Job Centres.

- Check with your boss where the advertisement should be placed (although if you have carried out sufficient research you should be able to give some advice in this respect). Check on the amount he/she wishes to spend.
- Check whether your boss wishes the name of the organisation to be included in the advertisement or whether he or she prefers a box number.
- If required, draft out the advertisement. It should be:
  - factual
  - informative but brief
  - eye-catching but in line with your company image. A traditional organisation may want to 'play it straight'; a modern one might prefer a 'Hey, are you just what we're looking for?' approach.
- If the advertisement is to be inserted in several different outlets, make certain that you ask applicants to state where they read the advertisement. You can then assess which outlets are the most useful.

CHECK IT YOURSELF

1 Look in both local and national newspapers for examples of both 'traditional' and 'trendy' advertisements. In each case, discuss as a group why you think that approach has been taken.
2 Try to find at least one advertisement which quotes a box number. Why do you think some organisations prefer to use a box number? Why do others see it as an advantage to have their name included in the advertisement? To which type of advertisement would you prefer to respond, and why?

Other personnel documents

Personnel documents for internal use nearly always follow the convention of displaying the information on a pre-printed form.

Forms are, of course, an essential part of business documentation and, again, tend to follow a set pattern. A well designed form should:

- include a prominent heading for identification
- state its purpose – who is to complete it, where it should be sent, etc.
- have an appropriate amount of space for the recording of entries
- contain complete and unambiguous instructions
- list the information required in a clear and logical order
- include a space for date/signature.

In addition, however, a good administrator or PA will try to ensure that, when completed, the form:

- looks professional and the actual layout creates a good impression
- makes sense – and does not just contain a scribbled set of notes
- contains only relevant material
- is concise.

CHECK IT YOURSELF

Figure 7.1.3 gives some standard examples of the forms containing information about staff.

Check in your own place of employment:

a whether such forms are in use, and
b what differences, if any, there are between the two sets of forms.

Discuss as a group or with your tutor or adviser the results of your findings.

APPLICATION FOR EMPLOYMENT
Job title

....

| Surname | Forenames |

| Address |
| Tel. No. |

| Date of birth | Nationality |

State if registered
under Disabled Persons
(Employment) Act

Education
Schools attended
(from age 11)

Examinations passed – subject, board, level and grade

Colleges/universities attended

Qualifications attained

Details of previous employment
Employer   From   To   Job title

Membership of professional or other associations

Leisure interests/voluntary work

Name and address of 2 referees (please state below if you do not want your current employer to be contacted prior to interview)

Additional information in support of your application. You may continue on another sheet if necessary.

Signature   Date

JOB DESCRIPTION
Job Title:

Department:

Accountable to:

Accountable for:

Objectives:

Responsibilities:

JOB SPECIFICATION

Title

1 Physical

Essential:

Desirable:

2 Attainments

Essential:

Desirable:

3 Abilities

Essential:

Desirable:

4 Personality

Essential:

Desirable:

5 Circumstances

Essential:

Desirable

INTERVIEW ASSESSMENT SHEET

Post:

Department:

Name of applicant:

Name of interviewer: Date:

Details	Remarks	Grading
Age		
Education		
Training		
Skill qualifications		
Communication skills		
Present post (if any)		
Present job experience		
Special experience		
Present salary		

Suitability for the department

Appearance
Personality
Self-confidence
Courtesy
Voice
Facial expressions
Image

Suitability for the job

Understanding
Speech
Fluency
Knowledge of the organisation
Relevance of the questions asked
Knowledge of current affairs
Reason for applying for the post

Special requirements

Unsocial hours
Overtime
Need for travel
Domestic commitments
Availability of transport

Other information

Key for grading

A	Excellent	D	Fair
B	Very good	E	Poor
C	Good	F	Very poor

PERSONNEL RECORD FORM

Surname   Forenames

Date of birth   Nationality

Name change   Sex

Address   Tel. No.

Change of address

Education   Qualifications

NI No.   Bank account no.

Disablement reg. no.   Union membership

Date interviewed   Job offered

Department/Section

Occupation

Record of illness

Training details

Appraisal record

Transfer of employment

Date   Reason

Termination of employment

Staff appraisal (1)

Name:

Job title:

Department:

To whom responsible:

Date appointed:

Job skills

	1	2	3	4	5	6
Knowledge						
Skills						
Problem solving						
Decision making						
Delegation						
Output						
Quality						
Administration						
Oral communication						
Written communication						
Creativity						

Personal characteristics

Initiative

Co-operation

Relations   – peers

             – manager

             – customers

Adaptability

Persuasiveness

Leadership

Confidence

Judgement

TOTAL PERFORMANCE RATING

Signature   Date

REVIEW PANEL – comments

Signature   Date

Employee comments

Signature   Date

Staff appraisal (2)

Name   Job Title

Grade   Manager

Date of appointment   Date of last appraisal

PERFORMANCE AGAINST KEY AREAS OF RESPONSIBILITY

Key areas   Results and comments

Personal effectiveness in the job

Customer satisfaction
Personal qualities
Personal productivity
Innovation and change
Teamwork
Leadership
People management

Performance against objectives for period under review

Objectives   Comments

New/changed objectives for next period

Overall view of performance

Trend: Declining   Stable   Improving

Training for improvement and career development

Employee's comments

Employee's signature   Date
Manager's signature   Date
Next level Manager's signature   Date

Figure 7.1.3 Staff information forms

TEST YOURSELF

Discuss the following issues with your group or your tutor or adviser.

1 **Job application form**

  a Why do you think most organisations include questions about voluntary activities or leisure interests? Surely all the interviewer should be interested in is the applicant's work record and his or her personal characteristics.

  b Why is the applicant normally asked whether he or she is registered as disabled?

2 **Job description/job specification**

  a It is normal practice for employees to be given a job description. The advantages are obvious but what disadvantages do you think there may be – both for the employee and employer?

  b It is less common for employees to be given a job specification. Why do you think that is the case?

3 **Interview assessment sheet**

  a Why should the interviewer be interested in the applicant's knowledge of the company?

  b The interviewer is asked to comment on the applicant's answer to the question about domestic commitments. Why, legally, could that be rather dangerous?

4 **Personnel record form**

  a Personnel records can be stored either in paper form or on a computer database. What are the advantages and disadvantages of each method?

  b The reason for recording most of the information contained in the example is self-evident, but why do you think it is necessary for the trade union number to be included?

5 **Staff appraisal record**

  a One appraisal record system allows the appraiser to grade the appraisee numerically. The other merely asks for comments. What are the advantages and disadvantages of both methods?

  b The idea of an appraisal is that it should be objective not subjective, i.e. based on facts not on someone's opinion. Which of the sections contained in both appraisal record schemes would you think would be the most difficult to answer objectively? How do you think this difficulty might have been overcome in at least one of the systems?

  c Everyone is interested in everyone else's appraisal results. How would you ensure that the confidentiality of this information is preserved?

Publicity and marketing documentation

One of the areas in which there are perhaps fewer conventions is that of promotional material. Posters, leaflets and other display material tend to be produced to meet individual requirements and it is therefore less easy to decide on a standard format for these than for other documents. Certain conventions, however, seem to have been established, for example

- the standardised use of colour and logos
- the relaxed use of language – paradoxically the convention here tends to be not to use conventional language
- the use of a distinctive house style designed to make the reader recognise immediately the organisation using it (see pages 385 and 442).

Moreover, one area in which certain conventions remain is that of the **press release**. Sometimes a press release forms part of an advertisement feature (in which case you pay for the insertion). In other cases it forms part of the general news section and is a channel of free publicity. In the latter case in particular therefore you should try to assist the sub-editor by setting out the information in a specific form.

- Use A4 paper and a clear and concise heading (but don't be upset if the sub-editor changes this!).
- Since the article may have to be cut, it should be written so that it can be 'pruned' from the last sentence upwards. Make sure, therefore, that you put the most important information first.
- Be factual rather than imaginative – the sub-editor can attach the appropriate captions and 'jazz up' the style if necessary. Be very careful to check and double-check the facts. Even the mildest person can become irritated if he sees his name mis-spelled or, having given you permission to say how old he is, finds that he has aged 10 years because you typed 70 in place of 60! If you have any doubts as to the technical accuracy of an item of information ask an expert to check it for you.
- If you are sending the article to several newspapers, alter each version slightly. Papers tend not to like copies of a release which has been sent to their competitors.
- If you include a photograph, make sure that the appropriate caption or information is written on a label which is then attached firmly to the reverse. Do not send colour photographs to newspapers and never write directly on to the reverse of a photograph – the pressure shows through and the photograph cannot be used for printing.
- Always include a name, telephone number and extension number of someone the press can contact for further information.

CHECK IT YOURSELF

Check in your own place of employment:

a if press releases are used as part of your organisation's promotional or marketing activity

    b if so, for what purposes, and

    c how far the format used corresponds to the norm as indicated above.

Discuss your findings with the rest of your group or your tutor or adviser.

Financial documentation

The documents needed to record financial information are possibly the most standardised documents in any organisation, given

- the nature of the information to be displayed
- the need for total accuracy in the face of possible legal and financial implications.

The principal documents include:

- the profit and loss account
- the balance sheet.

The profit and loss account is produced on a pro-forma normally designed to satisfy the requirements of the Companies Acts. Equally the balance sheet is normally designed to satisfy not only the requirements of the Board of Directors or its equivalent but also those of the shareholders and the company employees.

DID YOU KNOW?

From the management's point of view, the ability to interpret accounts and statements greatly assists their control and coordination and provides trends for forecasting and planning.

To assist them to do that, the Centre for Inter-Firm Comparisons, an independent body acting as a data collection point, compares the results of a number of firms indicating achievements and weaknesses. Standardised documentation assists it to make those comparisons.

CHECK IT YOURSELF

If you work for a public limited company or an organisation in the public sector then obtain a copy of last year's report and accounts as issued to shareholders. You may find this more difficult if you work for a private company or a small firm because there is no legal obligation for them to make this information public knowledge! In this case, find an example of the same information in a 'serious' newspaper or in the *Financial Times* or write to a large public company and ask for the information. Check the format used. Do not be too worried if you cannot understand every heading – but try to grasp the basics of the layout and content.

DID YOU KNOW?

No matter what type of document is required, it must be produced by the deadlines specified. If this is not possible, for any reason, the originator should be informed immediately a delay is suspected. This enables him or her to make a decision as to how best to rectify the situation. You should never tolerate a situation where work is not delivered in time without any explanation. It goes without saying, of course, that you would treat your own boss in the same way that you would expect to be treated!

Effective use of language and grammar

Look back to page 418 which outlines the conventions which generally apply to business documents. One of these related to the way in which the information was expressed and the expectation that it would be expressed clearly, concisely and grammatically. The section entitled Tools of the Trade, which follows Element 7.2 (page 485) gives the basic grammatical rules to be followed, but there are also certain other pitfalls to be avoided when preparing such documents.

Style and meaning

Look at the following extract from the Employment Protection (Consolidation) Act 1978.

> 'If provision is made by Northern Irish legislation (that is to say by or under a Measure of the Northern Ireland Assembly) for purposes corresponding to any of the purposes of this Act, except sections 1 to 7 and 49 to 51, the Secretary of State may, with the consent of the Treasury, make reciprocal arrangements with the appropriate Northern Irish authority for coordinating the relevant provisions of this Act with the corresponding provisions of the Northern Irish legislation, so as to secure that they operate, to such extent as may be provided by the arrangements, as a single system.'

All that information and only one full stop! In this case, of course, style is irrelevant, absolute precision being the only requirement. When preparing non-legal documents, however, you should bear in mind other factors.

Some people dress with style – it comes naturally to them. Others have to work at it. The same applies to writing style. If you are good at expressing yourself in writing you will probably find it difficult to understand why anyone has any problems in this respect. Good mathematicians have equal difficulty in understanding the problems of those who cannot add up.

Nevertheless, you should be try to bear in mind the following.

- The reader and the reason for sending the document.

    Note that an informal style has been used throughout this book. If it had been written as a PhD thesis to be submitted to a university its style would have been very different.

- The use of abbreviations.

  It is all right for you to use 'don't', 'I'll', etc. in an informal piece of correspondence – but not in more formal documents. Remember that 'all right' is acceptable – 'alright' is not.

- The use of clichés or stereotypes.

  Try not to use over-used or hackneyed expressions – 'time alone will tell'; 'least said, soonest mended'; 'my lips are sealed'; etc. If your boss likes them you can either try to limit the number which are contained in one document or use the old device of putting them in inverted commas (to indicate that they are used in a semi-humorous fashion) – I must remind you that 'silence is golden'.

- Business jargon.

  If you work in a specialised or highly technical area, some jargon is unavoidable. If, for instance, you work in a company specialising in the selling of computer software you would expect to use a somewhat esoteric vocabulary. Even so, you would have to distinguish between information which is to be sent to other computer experts and that which is to be sent to 'lay' personnel.

- The avoidance of tautology, i.e. using two words or phrases with the same meaning, for example
  - This is a once only, unrepeatable offer
  - Finally and in conclusion.

- The length.

  Although it is customary to say that business documents should be as short as possible, this does not necessarily mean that they will always be short. Some documents must, of necessity, be quite long because of the subject matter they contain. What is advisable, however, is to choose short words and phrases rather than a longer equivalent.

TEST YOURSELF

Rewrite the following sentences more simply.

a We shall endeavour strenuously to assist you.
b The Sales Manager was made the recipient of a gold watch.
c The new edifice is very imposing.
d Could you give me an inventory of the damage caused by the recent conflagration?

DID YOU KNOW?

Recognition that a good writing style is necessary is illustrated by the number of training courses which are now available not only for junior staff but also at senior management level. On one senior executive training programme, a three-hour session out of a two-week course on management skills is devoted to this topic.

Barriers to effective communication

However technically correct your documents are, they may still not convey the message you intend unless you recognise the fact that you may have to overcome certain barriers.

In any written document, therefore, you must try to avoid:

- vagueness or uncertainty
- negativity (unless you intend to be negative!)
- preconceptions
- stereotyping.

TEST YOURSELF

1   You work in a large city employment agency and are responsible for dealing with a large number of employees and employers. Part of your job is to prepare all the documentation each time an employer requests a member of staff and a potential employee registers for work. During the course of one day you interview a number of people and, on each occasion, make a brief summary of their qualifications, experience and requests to be circulated to possible employers.

At the end of the day you have completed a number of these summaries and you hand them over to your typist for word processing and circulation. However, despite your efforts, very few of your interviewees get the jobs they want. Look at the following extracts.

'Although Maria is only 5' 2" and not very well built, she is keen to get a horticultural job and does not seem to be concerned about having to work in all kinds of weather.'

'Jacques is now living permanently in this country and would like a job in computers. Although his degree is from a French university, his computing skills should be quite sufficient for your requirements.'

'Although Alex is 54 he should still have more than enough energy to cope with the pressures of the job.'

'Gemma's references show that she is hard working, reliable and punctual. She wants to be considered for a job in management.'

'Patrick is very interested in any part-time work which is available and is not concerned that he may be the only man in an otherwise all-female environment.'

Although your notes are well written and grammatically correct, you are conveying a negative message to the reader which in this case is not a message that you want to convey!

Discuss as a group or with your tutor or adviser why the wrong message is being conveyed in each of the above cases. Rewrite each to convey a positive message.

2 You spend the next day in the agency reading through requests for sta made by several different employers. In one case you have difficulty in determining what is required as the following extract from a request form for an office manager indicates.

'I require someone who is self-reliant and can follow orders. He must b bright. He must have some qualifications – but they must not be too high level. I'll need proof that he can work under pressure (but don't send me anyone who is too pushy!). I don't want anyone who is too ol – nor do I want a clock watcher.'

You know that you are going to have some difficulty finding a suitable applicant for the job if all you have to rely upon are the above notes. Discuss as a group or with your tutor or adviser:

a what further information you would need from the employer and what questions you would have to ask him or her to make sure tha you are both thinking on the same lines.

b the basic legal right the employer may have breached (or be about to breach).

House style

Many organisations are very concerned to convey the correct 'corporate image' to the outside world in every area of their operation. One basic method of doing this is to make sure that all their documentation conforms to certain standards. Consequently although many text books (including this one) outline the conventional ways in which business documents are normally prepared, you must always be aware that your own organisation may have its own 'house style'. Most organisations, for instance, have:

- a distinctive logo
- documents pre-printed with basic details such as the name of the organisation (including its legal status) and its address, telephone and fax number. Occasionally the names of the owners or directors are included together with their titles/qualifications. In addition, some indication is often given nowadays of a training award, the IIP (Investors in People) scheme or an initiative such as the MCI (Management Charter Initiative).

Some organisations also require their staff to follow certain standardised forms of presentation. There may be a house style, for instance, in the way in which documents:

- are compiled – in relation to layout, numbering systems, signatures, etc.
- are circulated – to whom, in what order and by what means.

Some golden rules for new administrators or PAs who may not be aware of the house style include:

- checking the office files to see how documents are laid out – including such basics as punctuation styles
- checking to see if there is a manual containing examples of standard layouts (normally available only in larger organisations).

(See also Unit 6, page 385.)

DID YOU KNOW?

Your organisation may be one in which, in order to prove that it is offering a high quality product or service, will have ensured that its procedures conform to the BS EN ISO 9000 standards. If this is the case, one area which will be completely standardised is the documentation used and you will be expected to adhere to that system.

CHECK IT YOURSELF

You have already checked on certain documents in your organisation (see page 414). Obtain at least four other examples of documents used and discuss with the rest of your group or your tutor or adviser the way in which they are laid out and how they conform to the organisation's house style. Compare any differences in approach. If you happen to work in an organisation in which no *formal* house style exists, give examples of the way in which you personally prepare four different documents.

Legal and regulatory requirements

A letter or other written document may look innocuous. In some cases, however, it can cause endless legal problems.

Note, for instance, the legal effect of a signature. It is binding! You and your boss should also be aware of the law relating to copyright (see page 272 for full details), defamation and negligence.

Defamation

(Look back to Unit 5, page 275 to remind yourself of the need to avoid an accusation of defamation when finding out and passing on information.)

It is defamatory to publish, i.e. to put in writing for someone else to read, anything about a person which could 'lower him or her in the eyes of right thinking people'. If, therefore, you write something defamatory you may be accused of libel (if you write it down) or slander (if you communicate it verbally). Before setting light to everything in your filing cabinet, however, remember that you have certain defences.

- You can claim 'justification', i.e. that the statement is true (bear in mind, however, that if you do use this defence and repeat what has been said, the damages awarded against you will be increased if you lose the case).
- A safer defence is that of 'qualified privilege' i.e. where individuals honestly believe that what they state is true *and* they are under some sort of legal, moral or social duty to provide that information. Provided the statement has not been made maliciously, the person making it is protected. *However*, one exception is letters of reference. In that case, if the statement has been made negligently – even though not maliciously – the employer can be sued. Remember, therefore, that a disclaimer can be very useful!

ACTIVITY SECTION

1   Nathan has taken over a position as office administrator at very short notice and has found himself in the middle of preparations for the organisation's annual conference, the date for which is only three weeks away. He soon realises that there are problems.

- He has only one word processing operator, who is overwhelmed with what she is expected to do. When Nathan asks his boss for some assistance, a temporary word processor operator is transferred from another department but it soon becomes apparent that although she is quite a fast keyboarder, her knowledge of grammar, punctuation and spelling is non-existent! Even with the aid of the spellcheck on the word processor she is still producing documents with 'bare' instead of 'bear', 'nut' instead of 'not' and 'stationary' instead of 'stationery'.

- He reads the draft information document for delegates and is not at all impressed with either the contents or the style. It is full of jargon, the style is very stilted and the presentation is not consistent. Unfortunately, however, it has been drafted by his boss who, he thinks, may be rather offended if he criticises it.

- The number of documents which have to be prepared is considerable and as the date of the conference draws nearer and nearer, Nathan realises that he has little chance of meeting the deadline set – and also, that, given the nature of the event, there is no chance of the deadline being altered.

- Nathan reads a draft summary of the opening speech to be given by the Managing Director which contains some rather critical remarks about a member of the government. He contacts his boss immediately who agrees that the remarks are unwise and tells him not to go ahead with the preparation of the document until she has had a word with the Managing Director. Unfortunately, that paper is one which the word processing operator *has* been able to complete and it has been sent direct to the Press Officer without Nathan's knowledge or approval. Nathan telephones the Press Officer who manages to prevent the paper from being sent to the local newspaper but Nathan is still concerned in case the information is 'leaked' – given that the paper has now passed through a number of hands.

Discuss as a group or with your tutor or adviser what action Nathan should take:

a in the short term, i.e. before the conference starts, and
b in the long term to prevent a recurrence of the same problems.

Summarise your answers in a short report.

2 One of the staff in your organisation, Martin Chadwick, has achieved an MBA at the age of 28 – through part-time study over the past twelve months – despite the fact that he works tirelessly for local charities and recently ran the London marathon! Your boss think this would be an ideal way of getting some local publicity – particularly as Martin is about to be promoted to Administration Manager.

Invent any further details you wish to include and write a suitable press release for your local paper in no more than 200 words.

3 A member of staff in your office consistently produces either sloppy work or nothing at all in response to deadlines. On the last occasion you insisted on a written explanation and received the memo shown in Figure 7.1.4.

a Examine the arguments given and identify those facts which you could check as being correct and those which you could not.
b Examine each argument given and state which you think are valid and which are not valid – and why.
c Bearing in mind the correct action you think Sandra should have taken, and your answers to (a) and (b) above, draft a memo to her in response.

```
MEMO

TO          (you)

FROM        Sandra Difford

DATE        (today)

DELAYED SALES REPORT

I regret that I could not complete the sales report for you by the deadline.
I know it was required by 3 pm yesterday but several things went wrong.

  ●  I didn't receive the final piece of information from the sales reps until
     the day before.
  ●  My computer wasn't working properly last Thursday and it took until
     Friday for the computer services engineer to arrive.
  ●  I had to cover reception on Friday lunchtime.
  ●  Mr Robbins had already told me that I could have Monday morning
     off because I worked overtime one evening the week before.
  ●  I had trouble reading Greg Thompson's writing and couldn't get hold
     of him until Tuesday to clarify the problems with him.
  ●  On Tuesday afternoon the receptionist was away and I had to cover
     for her.

If you can arrange for me to have more time to do it in future then I will
complete it in time.
```

Figure 7.1.4

Element 7.2

Initiate and respond to correspondence

Scope and limit of own authority relating to correspondence

Throughout this book, emphasis has been placed on the difference
between someone who carries out basic clerical duties in an office and
an administrator or PA. One of the most important differences you
will note (or have already noted) is the way in which you are asked to
deal with correspondence.

As a junior you are normally expected to carry out instructions from
other people, perhaps by transcribing accurately the notes left on an
audio tape or dictated to you or, more usually, given in manuscript
form. You are expected to display them in the required format. As an
administrator or PA you may be the one who is doing the dictating!
Even if you are not, there will certainly be occasions where you have
to prepare the correspondence either on your own initiative or – at
best – from brief written or verbal instructions.

To undertake this task you need a mixture of skills. You must be capable of making a range of decisions in relation to the type of document, the priority level and even the legal implications of your actions. You must be able to differentiate between types of correspondence and be capable of composing documents which are effective in a wide range of situations. Not least, you need the 'tools of the trade' – the ability to produce documents which are not only grammatically correct, but which are accurate in terms of punctuation and spelling. If you are in any way worried about your abilities in this area, then you are advised to turn to page 485 and work on the final part of this unit first. If you are more confident of your skills then you can use it as a reference section at any time in your career.

At this stage in your career or training you should be familiar with the standard layouts for all types of correspondence. You should also be capable of dealing with your boss's mail and of making decisions as to what is:

- to be dealt with by him or her
- to be handled by someone else
- your responsibility.

Some bosses are more than willing to let you make such decisions; others are more cautious. Normally the longer your working relationship with your boss and the greater the trust shown in your judgement, the greater will be your responsibility in this area.

If you are given this responsibility, you should be able to rely upon your boss to help you in the early stages by checking with you some of the decisions you have made. After that initial stage you need refer back only matters about which you are uncertain.

 ## TEST YOURSELF

You work for the Managing Director of a company which manufactures garden furniture. The following items of correspondence have appeared in his in-tray. Classify them into:

a those items with which your boss should deal directly
b those with which you can deal independently
c those with which you can deal initially but which then require reference back to your boss
d those which you can hand over to others.

1 A letter from a shareholder asking whether the annual company report will make any reference to company policy on the employment of disabled workers.
2 A note from the Office Manager asking for a copy of the departmental staff holiday list.
3 A memorandum from the Catering Manager asking for details of the catering arrangements required for the next lunchtime meeting of the Board of Directors.

4   A letter from a large supplier apologising for a delay in supplying some raw materials and asking if a further two-week delay is acceptable.

5   A letter from a company offering a reduced rate telephone cleaning service on a monthly basis.

6   A letter from an irate customer complaining that one of your company's chairs she had bought from a large department store has become rusted and unusable after only a month's use.

7   A letter from the owner of a chain of small furniture stores asking for an up-to-date catalogue and price list.

8   A letter from an unemployed labourer asking if there are any vacancies.

Establishing priorities

You must be able to prioritise the order in which you deal with and reply to correspondence in exactly the same way as you prioritise your other work (see Unit 3).

Working in chronological order through your boss's in and out trays, through your shorthand notebook or through an audio–dictation tape is not a good idea. You should sort out the correspondence in the mail trays into urgent and less urgent items both for your attention and that of your boss. As you were being given dictation you should have been annotating items to indicate their importance or the need for an urgent response.

Dictation on an audio–cassette is less easy to re-sort. In this case try to impress upon your boss the need to:

● dictate the items in order of importance (which may be rather a forlorn hope!), or
● leave a space at the beginning of each cassette so that at the end of the dictation he or she can use it to give some indication of urgent items, or
● attach a note to the cassette with similar indications.

 DID YOU KNOW?

Digital message storing is now possible. This type of equipment enables messages to be added anywhere in the sequence of already stored messages and also enables you to 'step through' the messages either forwards or backwards. This makes it far easier to prioritise work – both for you and for your boss.

 TEST YOURSELF

In your boss's out-tray are the following pieces of correspondence:

1   a reminder that a notice should be sent to all sales representatives giving them details of the price increases on the new summer range of products

2   a note asking you to refuse on his behalf an invitation to an official banquet at the Town Hall next week

3 notes for a letter to accompany an article for a business magazine – the deadline for receipt of which is this coming Friday.

The items on the audio machine are:

4 a letter to a customer demanding full payment of an outstanding account

5 a memorandum to the Managing Director giving him details of the press release which is to be sent to the major newspapers in the next few days

6 a reply to the Health and Safety representative who has queried the way in which some dangerous substances are being stored in apparent contravention of the COSHH regulations.

Your notebook contains the following items:

7 a letter replying to a request for a donation from a charity
8 an 'in sympathy' letter to the wife of a retired employee following his recent death.

List the order in which you will deal with each item (from 1–8) and give reasons for your decision.

Conventions in drafting correspondence

One of your first tasks may be to decide what type of document is required. In some cases you may have no choice – your boss asks you to write a letter of reply to a complaint he has received. In other cases, however, you may have to decide whether a memo, a notice or a letter is the most appropriate form of communication. Indeed, you may decide that a written form of communication is inappropriate and that a telephone call will suffice.

Whatever form of communication you do choose, however, you will again have to determine its purpose – is it to inform, request, advise, explain? (Look back to page 409 to remind yourself of other purposes.)

Types of correspondence

The standard list from which you would normally choose includes:

- a letter
- a memo
- a notice
- a bulletin/newsletter/house journal
- an invitation.

(Note that production of reports or summaries is dealt with in Unit 5.)

Letters

Given that by now you are likely to have typed a large number of letters, you will probably already have realised that the most acceptable structure for most letters comprises:

- an introduction or opening paragraph which should state the reason for writing
- the 'body' of the correspondence. Remember that it is usual to:
  - use a number of short paragraphs rather than one long one
  - give the most important information first, the least important last
  - move from the 'known' (i.e. information both parties already have) to the 'unknown'
  - list advantages and disadvantages separately where relevant
  - list information in chronological order
- the closing paragraph which should
  - state the desired outcome
  - if relevant, give an indication of the time at which this action should take place.

DID YOU KNOW?

It may be company policy that:

- your boss signs all correspondence
- you sign some items on your boss's behalf, e.g. Susan Carpenter, Administrator/PA to Mr F Charteris, Managing Director
- you sign your boss's name but add your initials.

Main purposes of letters

The major types of business letter can be classified into those which:

- make or answer an enquiry
- give or request details of goods, products or services
- issue an order/statement/tender
- make or answer a complaint
- seek settlement of a debt or payment of an account
- check financial status or creditworthiness
- authorise credit advances
- outline interview arrangements
- offer or refuse employment
- outline conditions of employment
- give references.

Less frequently required letters include those which:

- give thanks
- give sympathy
- offer congratulations
- issue or reply to invitations
- reply to charitable appeals.

Given the relevant information, you should be able to compose a suitable letter for most occasions. Certain types of letters, however, need particular attention, for example:

- because they are 'selling' your company and you want therefore to present the best possible impression
- because they are dealing with a topic whose potential repercussions could be either very beneficial or very harmful to your company
- because you need some urgent action to be taken.

In such cases it may be helpful for you to have available a skeleton outline of the way in which such information should be presented (or requested).

Sales letters

There are several formats recommended for sales letters. One approach is known by the acronym AIDA:

A every sales letter should gain readers' **attention**
I their **interest** should be aroused and held
D their **desire** should be kindled
A they should be persuaded into taking some **action**.

An alternative American method is divided into four similar stages:

- 'Ho hum!' – the opening gambit designed to attract attention
- 'Why bring that up?' – answers designed to point out the benefits of the proposition
- 'For instance?' – claims are supported with examples
- 'So what?' – the request for an order, a signature, etc.

Another approach is to remember the three Ps:

- Picture – what the thing you are selling is like
- Promise – what it will do for the buyer
- Push – now buy it!

Examples

Opening paragraphs	How to be safe rather than sorry!
	How many work hours did you lose last year because of injury-related illness?
Body of letter	Let our company solve all your problems by advising you on the correct safety equipment for your particular organisation – and all the up-to-date UK and EU legislation.
	The benefits to you:

  – fewer accidents
  – increased production
  – higher morale
  – NO legal repercussions.

Closing paragraphs	Why not telephone us on . . . and ask for Peter Clark. He will be happy to give you more details, without any obligation whatsoever on your part.
	Hadn't you better get in touch with us right away?
	Our representative will be in your area next month and will phone you before then to arrange a mutually convenient appointment.
	Complete the enclosed pre-paid reply card if you want further details of our service.
	May I come along and tell you more about this service?

TEST YOURSELF

Many organisations prefer to end their sales letters by retaining the initiative – this means that they do not give the customer control over the next move to be made in the selling game. Can you identify which of the above closing paragraphs loses the initiative and which retains it?

Acknowledging orders

It is relatively simple to acknowledge an order when you are able to supply the goods. It is a different matter if, for some reason, the goods cannot be supplied. To help you, examples are given below which cover both alternatives.

Do remember not to promise anything you cannot fulfil. If you know there is no hope of supplying the goods within a certain period, don't let the customer think there is. In the long run it will do more harm than good to customer relationships.

Opening paragraphs	Many thanks for your first order. We look forward to being of service to you and appreciate your interest in our products.
	Thank you for your first order which we received today. It is a pleasure to welcome you as a new customer and we look forward to doing business with you.
	Thank you for your order no . . . dated 16 October 199_

Body of the letter

a *if the goods*
can be supplied

The order will go out by parcel post next week and should reach you well before the date you specify.

We are putting your order into production immediately and shall let you know its date of despatch as soon as possible.

The goods ordered can be supplied from stock and will be sent to you on . . .

The goods will be sent within . . . days/weeks.

b *if the goods*
cannot be supplied

Every item on your order except . . . will be sent to you from stock within the next few days. The rest of the order will be sent as soon as possible, and certainly within 14 days.

Unfortunately we are unable to meet your requested delivery date. The response to the advertisement has been so overwhelming that we are having difficulty in keeping up with demand. However, we hope to be able to supply you with the goods by the end of the month.

Unfortunately the item you have ordered is no longer in stock. Could we suggest that an alternative might be . . .

Closing paragraphs

We look forward to hearing from you.

Thank you again.

If we can be of assistance to you in the future please do not hesitate to contact us.

DID YOU KNOW?

You may not be expected actually to prepare statements, invoices or accounts. Nor are you likely to have to draw up tenders. What you may have to do is to check that:

● they have been sent out
● they have resulted in a response.

Check in your own organisation that you know the steps to be taken in the ordering and invoicing of goods and the way in which a statement of account is drawn up. Check also that you understand clearly the difference between a quotation, an estimate and a tender.

TEST YOURSELF

You work for the Managing Director of a company which manufactures fireplaces. One customer is always submitting incomplete orders and tends to describe what he wants in imprecise terms. For example, he will say that wants 'one of those Victorian style fireplaces' rather than indicating the order number specified in the catalogue. As a result he tends to argue about what has actually been supplied and takes little notice of the invoice. He often disputes the statement of account and delays payment for as long as possible. Draft a letter for your boss to sign which:

- emphasises the necessity for a correct order (and for payment on time)
- outlines the company's invoicing procedure.

Credit checks

Although payment on credit is a common business transaction, it is open to abuse and it may be that you are asked to refuse credit terms to a particular customer. Be careful! Although the decision to refuse credit is not likely to be yours, the way in which you write the letter can either calm or exacerbate the situation!

Opening paragraph	Thank you for your letter in which you ask for credit facilities.
Body of letter	While we are not at the moment in a position to comply with your request, we hope it will be possible for us to do so at a later date.
	Unfortunately, as you have in the past tended to be rather slow in paying invoices we feel that at the moment it would be wiser to continue our dealings on a cash-only basis.
	(*Note*: remember defamation – be very careful!)
Closing paragraphs	We are sorry to have to refuse you credit but feel that, as a business person yourself, you will appreciate our position.

Outstanding payments

If you are asked to remind someone of an outstanding payment, be prepared to write a series of letters at intervals of 10 to 15 days. Remember always to bear in mind the desired result. However tempted you may be to send off a series of increasingly abusive letters you may find this counterproductive – at least at first when persuasion rather than threat is to be advised. Even a final demand in which you state that legal action will be taken need not necessarily be rude. Persistence is the key!

Recommended stages

First reminder

May we remind you that there is a balance due on your account.

Note: in the USA it is common to use a 'humorous' tone on a first reminder – often in the form of a printed reminder card, e.g.:

> *Your bill's overdue*
> *I'm surprised at you!*
> *Please pay at once*
> *We know you're no dunce*

It's supposed to work, anyway!

Follow-up(s)

Do you recall our sending you a reminder about your overdue account?

Possibly our reminder about your overdue account has escaped your attention. If it did, may we remind you again to send you the payment within the next few days.

We are disappointed to note that despite several reminders you have still not settled your outstanding account.

Your account has now been outstanding for a considerable period. We must therefore insist that we receive full payment from you within the next seven days.

Final reminder

Unfortunately, you leave us no choice but to withhold further deliveries until this amount is paid (*if you are able to do that*).

We regret that we have no option but to hand the matter over to our legal advisers.

DID YOU KNOW?

Bear in mind that at any stage of the correspondence it is possible that your letter and their payment may cross in the post. For this reason it is wise to include a proviso in case payment has just been sent, e.g.:

If you have already sent the payment please accept our thanks.

Remember, however, that a claim that 'the cheque is in the post' is a very common delaying tactic! Remember also that some payments arrive in instalments. Keep going, but acknowledge the part-payment.

Finally, don't forget to distinguish between a letter of reminder to an individual asking him or her to fulfil an obligation and one in which you are reminding him or her to do you a favour, e.g. supply some information. Again persistence is the key. Consider such phrases as 'At the risk of being a bore, may I ask you to . . .' or 'I know how busy you are but dare I remind you . . .'

TEST YOURSELF

As light relief, prepare an American-style reminder card for your own organisation. Use verse and an appropriate illustration or logo.

Making complaints

Be specific – give facts rather than vague generalisations. Make reference to back-up information. Remain polite even though you may feel you have been driven beyond endurance. Start gently – do not use up all your ammunition at the first stage. Decide on the best person to whom to address your complaint – the easy answer is to say that it should be addressed to the Managing Director or the Chief Executive. It might be a good idea, however, for you to keep this as your last resort. Otherwise you risk antagonising more junior personnel with whom you may have later dealings.

Opening paragraphs

I do not often have cause to complain about your organisation but for the second time in three weeks an order has been delivered in which several of the items were missing.

I must complain about the unsatisfactory way in which my enquiry about possible job vacancies was dealt with by your reception staff.

Since you installed my central heating

	system last May, it has broken down on three occasions.
Body of the letter	I give below a detailed list of the shortages in the order . . .
	When I arrived at the reception desk I was asked to wait. This I did for 20 minutes but eventually asked the receptionist if she could help. She told me she could not and that if I did not wish to wait any longer I could always leave.
	Your maintenance engineer has been called out on each occasion but has been able to effect only temporary repairs.
Closing paragraph	I should be grateful if you would look into this matter.
	I must insist on some further action being taken without delay.
	Unless I hear from you within the next few days I shall take the matter further.
	I have complained many times. This is the last.

Responding to complaints

Check and double-check the facts. Answer all the complaint, not just one part (although concentrate on the stronger part of your response). Say sorry – you'd be surprised how often this disarms even the most irate customer.

Opening paragraph	I was concerned to hear that you had not received the goods you ordered.
	We do apologise for the apparently offhand treatment you received when you called in to our office last week.
	I am concerned to hear that you are so dissatisfied with our after–sales service.
Body of the letter	I shall make sure that the goods are delivered to you without delay and that no further mistakes are made.

I have investigated the matter and find that during the period in question the senior receptionist was off duty.

I have discussed the problem with my senior engineer who assures me that the system is now in full working order.

Closing paragraph

I apologise again.

I hope that the matter is now resolved.

Please let me know if you have any further problems/require any further information.

DID YOU KNOW?

Even if you are 100 per cent sure that you or your organisation are at fault, it might still be a good idea for you not to admit complete liability because of possible legal repercussions. Words and phrases such as 'apparently', 'it may have appeared', 'a misunderstanding', etc. are useful.

Note also that if you feel the complaint is unjustified (or that the writer is a regular or 'professional' complainer) you can take a slightly different approach. Remain polite – you have nothing to lose – but do not put yourself in a false position. Use sentences such as 'while we are very sorry that you are upset about . . . we must point out that . . .' or 'I am sorry but rather surprised that you were annoyed by my letter' etc.

TEST YOURSELF

You are an administrator working for the Managing Director of a chain of bookshops. You receive a letter from a customer who complains that he has tried unsuccessfully to order several books over the past few months. On the first occasion he was told that an ordering service was not available. On the second occasion he was asked to complete a form with the details of the book he wanted. Although he was told that it would be in stock within three weeks, two months later it has still not arrived. Last week he tried to order another book but was told that it was pointless because 'the ordering system is in chaos' and he would be better writing to the publisher direct or going to another bookshop.

You make enquiries and find that on the first occasion it was a new Saturday-only assistant who dealt with the matter. The book the customer ordered on the second occasion is a best seller, is being reprinted and the publishers have promised to send a new supply by the end of next week. No-one admits to having been involved on the third occasion!

Write a letter of reply for your boss to sign.

The circular letter

You may be asked to prepare a circular letter to be sent to a large number of people who are from different backgrounds and are also unknown to you. In such circumstances the way in which the letter is written has to differ from a letter from one correspondent to another.

- There must be a more general salutation, e.g. Dear colleague, friend, subscriber.
- As this communication is normally unsolicited, it should be brief and eye-catching as well as informative.
- The tone should be friendly and informal.

TEST YOURSELF

In many cases, circular letters are sales promotion letters. However, they can also be used on other occasions. Suggest some.

Alternatives to the standard letter

Cost is always a factor which has to be taken into account. There is little point, therefore, in composing a full reply to a letter when a cheaper written alternative may suffice.

A 'blitz' reply

Where a letter requires either a 'yes', 'no' or 'noted' answer you may wish to use the option of writing this reply on the original letter, taking a photocopy of it and sending back the original. This method can also be used to 'buy time', e.g. by writing a note such as 'will reply in full in the next two weeks' or 'information to be sent out within 10 days'. Organisations which receive a large number of requests for information use this method – many of them have special rubber stamps specially printed for this purpose.

TEST YOURSELF

Even in cases where a very brief answer is possible, in what circumstances would it not be advisable to use the 'blitz' method of replying?

Quick reply forms

Another cost-saving device is the use of a quick reply form which is normally printed in triplicate, in three different colours on NCR (no carbon required) paper. It is divided into a left-hand and right-hand section. If used as a letter it is printed in the same way as a letterhead.

The sender of the letter writes the message on the top copy and sends it together with the second copy to the recipient, and keeps the third copy for temporary reference. The recipient writes the reply on the top copy, keeps it for reference and sends back the second copy. The temporary file copy can then be destroyed.

The advantages are considerable:

- replies are normally short
- certain information need not be repeated
- an immediate check can be made that all points have been answered.

You should note, however, that because of the increased use of fax this method of communication seems to be decreasing in importance.

CHECK IT YOURSELF

Check in your own organisation to see if any department or section operates a quick reply system and, if so, for what purposes.

Form letter

More frequently used are form letters which come in a variety of designs. They are normally pre-printed to give the recipient a number of options of replying. The advantages include:

- a number of specific options can be outlined, thus making any subsequent action needed easier to identify
- the fact that the sender or recipient need only tick a box or circle an entry rather than make a written response may encourage a response.

Examples include:

- letters which highlight discrepancies in invoices, e.g.:
  'You have not
  sent the required number of copies ☐
  signed the copies ☐
  given the current discount' ☐
  etc.

- letters pointing out mistakes made in the writing of cheques, e.g.:
  'You have
  failed to sign the cheque ☐
  failed to date the cheque ☐
  filled in the incorrect amount ☐
  mismatched the written amount
  with the amount given in figures' ☐
  etc.

Overseas correspondence

If you work in a company which has a number of overseas clients, you should be aware of company policy on the way in which correspondence should be handled. In large multinational organisations there will be a team of translators to deal with the correspondence. Smaller organisations may call upon the services of translators provided through various agencies. Alternatively, the organisation may employ bilingual administrators or PAs.

In such circumstances you will have to do little more than give details of exactly what is required. When any replies are received you return to the same sources for translation.

If, however, you want to send a letter overseas which is written in English (in the expectation – or hope – that your correspondent can read it or will be prepared to have it translated) you should remember to:

- write in short sentences
- use simple language
- avoid colloquialisms or jargon
- give the meaning of any abbreviations
- avoid any over-long introductory or closing paragraphs.

You should also be careful to avoid the use of words which have different meanings in other countries – even if you are sending correspondence to someone in a country such as the USA, where English is the national language.

Memoranda

The memorandum – or memo as it is more usually known – is a document for internal use and can therefore normally be couched in more informal terms than correspondence which is intended for external use. It is a useful way in which to remind staff of certain jobs or to keep them in touch with current developments.

Points to note are given below.

- Apart from the usual memo heading – To/From/Date/Subject – no salutation is necessary. Neither is a complimentary close. It is usual for a memo to be initialled rather than signed.
- Although most memos are likely to be brief and their subject matter contained in a couple of short paragraphs, this is not always the case. Some memos can be quite long, particularly if they are explanatory (e.g. outlining new security procedures) and in such circumstances can become akin to a report (see page 307).
- Memos are usually sent through the internal mail or – if urgent – delivered by hand. Most memos from Head Office to branch offices are normally treated as letters, although if the company has an electronic mail network then they will be sent by this method for speed and economy (see page 479).
- Multiple circulation of a memo can cause problems. Assuming there is no electronic mail network then you have the choice of either sending a separate copy to each individual concerned (with all names being typed on the top copy and ticked off individually) or circulating one copy with an attached circulation slip.
- You can distinguish between those recipients by whom some

action must be taken and those who have received the memo for information purposes only by putting FIO (for information only) or FYI (for your information) after the appropriate name.

- Be careful to use both name and job title if there is even the slightest possibility of confusion. In a large organisation there may be a number of J Smiths. Where necessary, include room location.
- One problem of protocol which can arise is the order in which names should be listed. You have the choice of typing them
  - alphabetically
  - by location
  - according to rank
  - according to job priority.
- Be careful when dealing with confidential memos. Most memos are not in envelopes – confidential memos must be. You should be particularly careful about transmitting confidential information over an electronic mail system unless there is an effective password system. Remember to store mail you wish to keep – or take a hard copy – if your particular system purges mail automatically after a certain period. You must also remember that if you or your boss has prepared a hasty or ill-thought-out memo it can be recalled easily from an out-tray. On some electronic mail systems you can retrieve it only if the recipient has still to read it – on others you cannot recall it at all!

TEST YOURSELF

1 Look back at the different methods of listing names. Discuss as a group the advantages and disadvantages of each one. What method would you recommend?

2 You work for the Head of a Business Studies department in a college. It is departmental policy that all full-time students should undertake at least two weeks' work experience each year. Because of the large number of students in the department, however, there have been certain problems in finding suitable placements for them all. It has been suggested that a part-time clerical officer be appointed to undertake this task. Another suggestion has been that work experience placements be spread out more evenly throughout the year, although tutors have made the point that to do so may involve clashes with examination schedules and final assessments of coursework.

One tutor has suggested that consideration be given to the idea of sending students out on a one-day-per-week basis (possibly to coincide with groups of part-time students attending college so that employers may be more willing to take student replacement on those days). Your Head decides to discuss the matter at the next meeting of her senior team of six Divisional Managers. She wants them to have this information before the meeting (to be held on Wednesday of next week) and asks you to prepare a memo outlining the main points for discussion.

DID YOU KNOW?

An even more common form of written communication within an organisation is a scribbled note. There is nothing inherently wrong with this method, but it has its drawbacks. It can get lost easily and its importance may be overlooked because of the way in which it is presented. In such circumstances you should consider the use of action slips which can be produced in small packs of brightly coloured paper with or without a printed heading. In some organisations each department has its own colour; in others, the executives use individually coloured slips so that messages from them can be identified at a glance.

You may also like to consider the use of pads, the sheets of which are held attached at the top by adhesive and which, when separated, retain some of that adhesive, e.g. Post-it notes. The messages are then easier to attach to desktops, computers, etc.

Notices

You may be asked to communicate the same information to a large number of people within the organisation. To communicate directly with everyone is both a lengthy and an expensive process and in some cases it may be better to display the information in notice form.

Points to note are given below.

- Check that the notice board(s) on which the notices are to be displayed are:
  - well sited (not at the end of a long, little-used corridor)
  - large enough to be noticed
  - attractive (clean, in bright colours, etc.).
- Organise the boards to accommodate various types of notices – permanent notices, notices about events held at regular intervals, 'one-off' notices, etc. Remember that permanent notices should be laminated (to prevent their becoming dirty and fingermarked) and displayed separately.
- Write the notice so that everyone can understand it. (If you write a letter or other document to a named individual, you normally have some idea of the type of person likely to read it. With a notice, you have not.)
- The language should be clear and simple. The style should normally be informal (unless it is a permanent notice outlining details of disciplinary procedures, etc.). Avoid saying 'May I draw your attention to the new opening hours of the canteen.' Say instead 'ATTENTION ALL CANTEEN USERS – Note the new opening hours!'
- Be brief. Few people read notices anyway – very few read long notices.
- Check whether or not it is company policy to have notices signed. Normally they are. Remember always to date a notice –

this will help juniors who are delegated to do the job of checking notice boards regularly to remove out-dated material.

TEST YOURSELF

1 Discuss with the rest of your group or with your tutor or adviser the circumstances in which a notice would not be a suitable form of communication.

2 The following information has been received. It is your job to write and prepare attractive and eye-catching notices. Group these appropriately either on an actual noticeboard or on a suitably sized piece of card.

 – The Staff Welfare Group want to know if anyone is interested in becoming a member of the local health and fitness club – reduced rates are being offered if a group of more than 20 people apply. Expressions of interest to Louise Inman (ext. 324).

 – Joseph Akinwumi in the Accounts department (ext. 532) has been given a set of garden gnomes as a birthday present. He doesn't want them and will accept offers from £15 onwards.

 – Up-to-date information about changes to the existing pension scheme is now available from Kathleen Lambert in the Personnel department (ext. 335).

 – Peter Ellington (Purchasing department) is now the proud father of a little girl (Mary Elizabeth).

3 You have asked one of the junior staff to draft out a notice for the noticeboard reminding staff that any requests for photocopying must be handed to the reprographics staff at least 24 hours before it is required other than in exceptional circumstances, in which case permission from the reprographics supervisor must be obtained. Both you and she know that there has been some friction lately between the office and the reprographics staff, the office staff complaining about what they consider to be excessive delays and the reprographics staff complaining about having to do everything at short notice. This is what the junior comes up with:

Notice to all staff – as from tomorrow photocopying to be handed in to reprographics staff a day ahead. Almost no exceptions. If in doubt see supervisor.

Discuss as a group or with your tutor or adviser which conventions she has ignored and redraft the notice where you think it necessary.

Bulletins and staff newsletters

There are certain jobs in an office which somehow always end up as part of an administrator's job description. The preparation of a bulletin or the staff newsletter tends to fall into this category. If it is intended to be an informal document containing short items of information and 'gossip' you should have little difficulty (other than making the time to collect, prepare and edit the material).

Points to note are given below.

- The frequency of production – if you have to prepare one each week you need some assistance, or at least relief from other duties.

- The format required. The normal procedure is to collate the information in numbered points under a heading such as 'Staff Bulletin w/e 25 March' etc. Note that some bulletins have an ongoing numbering system so that one copy of the issues for the entire year can be kept for reference purposes.

- The type of information. Examples include
  - information about certain company activities, e.g. the opening of a new branch office; promotions; transfers; new appointments; launch of new products; references in the press; extracts from AGM reports
  - general information, e.g. changes in car parking arrangements; new security arrangements
  - 'fun' items, e.g. who has become engaged/married, had a baby, achieved the Duke of Edinburgh's Award.

  Remember that it is always advisable to check that the personnel concerned in the last item will actually appreciate their names being mentioned – and to double-check that the facts are correct! Be wary also of mentioning someone's age – many people (of both sexes) are very sensitive to public announcements of this. You could make an enemy for life if you confirm what the office staff have suspected for ages – that Mr Parker, who prides himself on his youthful image, is really eight years older than he has always claimed to be!

Bear in mind that some organisations pride themselves on their good industrial relations and, to foster that image, spend time and money on the preparation of a house journal which is, in effect, an up-market version of the staff newsletter or bulletin. In such circumstances you may be asked to make a contribution but you are unlikely to be in charge of the entire production.

Invitations

The normal rule is that 'like must match like'. If you receive an invitation which is in letter form, you should reply in the same format. Similarly, a formal invitation should be given a formal response, e.g.:

> Oakworth House
> Saddleworth
> 4 October 199_
>
> Mr and Mrs R Samuels have pleasure in inviting you to the
> 21st birthday party of their daughter, Rebecca, to be held at
> their home on Saturday, 3 November 199_ at 8 pm.
> RSVP

Points to note are given below.

- It used to be customary to have invitations typed on plain cards
  of A5 size. Nowadays pre-printed cards are more popular.
- If the name of the recipient is to be included, it is normal to
  handwrite it rather than type it, e.g.:

> Mr and Mrs R Samuels have pleasure in inviting
>
> ....
>
> to the 21st birthday party of their daughter . . .

- The information should be complete, i.e.:
  - the date, day and time of the function
  - the venue
  - the purpose.

  The third person, i.e. 'Mr and Mrs R Samuels' should be used in
  preference to the first person, i.e. 'We'.

If, therefore, your boss asks you to reply to such an invitation, you
would use the following format.

> 24 Kenilworth Road
> Farnham
> 17 October 199_
>
> Mr T Raphael has much pleasure in accepting Mr and
> Mrs R Samuels' kind invitation to the 21st birthday party
> of their daughter, Rebecca, to be held at their home on
> Saturday, 3 November at 8 pm.

If your boss wanted to refuse the invitation, the refusal should be
couched in the same terms – although it is usual to give a reason for
the refusal:

> Mr T Raphael regrets that he cannot accept Mr and Mrs R
> Samuels' kind invitation . . . He will be out of the country on
> a business trip on that date.

Don't forget to distinguish between a personal and a business invitation. In the latter case the address given would be that of the organisation. Remember, too, to check if your boss's partner is included in the invitation. If so, you should reply for both of them.

Sources of information

Normally the sources of information required for the preparation of correspondence are closer to hand than those required for other documents. In many cases you will have a detailed knowledge of the subject matter and will be able to draw on that knowledge when preparing the relevant paperwork. If your memory fails you, your office filing system should not! In addition, of course, you can always draw upon the expertise of your colleagues.

An additional and all–important source of information is the information you get from your boss. The difficulty here, of course, is 'translating' that information into the appropriate format!

TEST YOURSELF

1 You are in the process of preparing the following correspondence. Discuss with the rest of your group or with your tutor or adviser the *internal* sources of reference you would use in the course of such preparation.

   a   a letter to your solicitors asking for clarification about an ex-member of staff who is claiming unfair dismissal

   b   a memo to all staff explaining the temporary measures to be put into place when the car park is closed for resurfacing

   c   a notice reminding staff to take particular care of their belongings given a recent spate of thefts

   d   a reply to an invitation on behalf of your boss

   e   an item in the staff newsletter about arrangements for the annual inter-departmental cricket match.

2 Discuss also the action you would take if your sources of reference do not match up, i.e. if you obtain conflicting replies from different sources.

Drafting correspondence from written sources

Once you have established the type of document you need, you then have to establish whether you are going to prepare it independently or whether you are working from material given to you by your boss. In the latter case there is a certain art to doing so! You must be able to prepare the correspondence required from his or her draft typescript, a scribbled manuscript or even a few notes jotted on the bottom of a letter or memo – from which, even though you have to compose a sensible, grammatical business communication, you will at least obtain some information. It is wise, however, to make life easier for yourself by remembering the following points.

Draft typescripts

These are the easiest to follow, provided they are in double-line spacing and your boss has good handwriting and has clearly indicated where he or she wants each alteration. Otherwise you may be struggling to make sense of some of the comments.

If you are having problems, then read the original text to see where alterations should logically be inserted. If you cannot check any dubious points immediately, type the text as you think it should be written, but mark problem areas clearly (with a light pencil cross in the margin) and resubmit the document for your boss's attention before taking a final printout.

Manuscript

If you regularly type up documents from manuscript (i.e. handwritten material) then you should get used to your boss's writing.
- Read through the document before you start in order to get the sense of it.
- Make sure you can differentiate any notes to you from text which must be typed.
- Underline any difficult-to-read words in pencil and read on for a few lines to try to get the meaning from the context. Look for similar letter patterns to give you a clue.
- Make a note of phrases, technical terms and abbreviations your boss uses regularly.
- If you are still having problems, and you are using a word processor, type the document and print it out in draft first. Again mark any doubtful passages or words for clarification.

Notes for expansion

The ability to write a good, well-constructed business letter or memo is an essential weapon in the armoury of any administrator or PA.

If you are given a list of notes in reply to a document remember that:
- the order of the notes may not be the best order for the finished document
- you are not expected merely to join together the notes with a few well-chosen conjunctions!
- the tone of the letter must be correct, bearing in mind the topic and the recipient.

It also helps if you are given the original document to which you are replying. Try to train your boss always to pass this to you – you then have the means of checking the recipient's correct name and title, the address and any other details you may require, such as reference numbers which must be quoted in reply.

Drafting correspondence from verbal sources

One variation on the theme of written notes is the verbal notes dictated to you. These may be even more random and sketchy than written notes, depending on how much of a hurry your boss was in when he or she gave you the information! They are also likely to contain several asides to you, and phrases about the recipient that your boss does not want to be incorporated into the document itself.

Make sure you write down everything you are told, and repeat the main points to make sure you have listed everything. The chances are that your boss will expand on some of the information during this 'repeat' session. Query anything you are not sure about – especially if your boss is on the way out of the office and wants you to send off the document in his or her absence. It is far better to check this now than risk the problems inherent in sending out a totally inappropriate document.

Audio dictation

If you transcribe audio dictation for your boss, you need to know how to make the most of the system. There is a wide variety of portable audio equipment – often known as 'pocket memos' – on the market. The aim of these machines is, in theory, to enable the high-flying and well-travelled executive to be able to dictate correspondence at virtually any hour of the day or night, no matter where he or she is at the time. The problem with this is that the tapes on which you learned and practised your audio skills in college can bear little resemblance to those you are expected to transcribe at work. The departure lounge at Heathrow airport or the M25 in the rush hour do not make for meaningful and literate dictation.

To get the best out of the system it is essential that both of you know the basic rules for audio dictation and transcription.

Make sure that your boss:

- starts by identifying himself or herself (especially if you regularly receive tapes from several people)
- indicates what is going to be dictated before starting on the text proper. At least you then know which type of paper to use. Some clue as to the likely length and any copies required is a bonus
- makes it clear whether the document is a draft or whether you are supposed to type it in its final format and, if your boss is away, send it out in his or her absence
- makes a clear distinction in his or her voice between instructions to you and the actual material you should type. Otherwise you can end up with totally unintelligible documents
- speaks clearly and at a steady pace and with a sense of rhythm so far as sentence construction is concerned

- holds the microphone relatively near his or her mouth all the time
- remembers not to move around, eat or drink whilst dictating, and reduces or eliminates background noises (this includes sneezing and coughing mid-way through a sentence)
- spells any unusual names or words, preferably at the point at which they are dictated
- states when new paragraphs are expected or required
- stops dictating if disturbed, e.g. someone knocks on the door or the telephone rings, and when the out-of-tape audible warning signal is heard
- avoids asides, e.g. 'ah, yes, where were we?' and other distractions you might find yourself typing in error
- clearly indicates when one document is finished and another begins.

For your part you should:

- be prepared to put up with the untrainable boss who ignores all your hints and advice on how to dictate properly (or practise your newly found assertiveness, see page 510)
- listen to each piece of dictation first – especially to pick up the key piece of information left until the end, e.g. 'forget that letter – I'll ring him tomorrow'
- use the best layout for the work required (don't expect or ask for advice from your boss on this – it is your job to be able to produce good business documents, not his or hers)
- have a good knowledge of his or her usual phrases and style so that you can substitute suitable words for mutterings and incoherent noises
- spell, punctuate and type the document so that it is 100 per cent accurate
- know how to get the best out of your transcribing machine by knowing all the functions it can carry out, e.g. automatic search control, variable automatic backspacing and last word repeat, tape speed control.

The advantages of using audio are considerable. You can listen to the tape over and over again if necessary, and are not reliant on your own scribbled and sometimes incomprehensible notes. In addition, if you both have access to dictating equipment then you can use the system for leaving recorded messages for one another. This is especially useful if your boss is only due in the office after office hours and will then be away for several days. Try to keep the tone of any verbal messages relatively formal and stick to the facts you wish to convey – in priority order.

The main disadvantage with audio is that it is difficult to type the documents in priority order, unless you are working on one of the new digital systems.

Effective use of language and grammar

The same criteria apply to correspondence as to all other documents.

- The language used must be suitable for (a) the purpose and (b) the recipient.
- It must be grammatically correct and the spelling and punctuation must be of a high standard.

Again the section headed Tools of the Trade should help you if you have any doubts about your ability *or* if you have doubts about the ability of one of your staff and you need some assistance in improving his or her performance in this area.

If you have not already done so, turn to page 485 and try the first set of questions. The results will give you some objective feedback on the amount of work you need to do in this area!

Context in which correspondence is prepared

When preparing correspondence it is your job as an administrator to be aware of the context in which it is being prepared. Quality is always important. Image is also important – but probably more important in the case of an external rather than an internal document. Accuracy again is always a high priority, but in some documents an error is merely irritating – in others it can be very dangerous. Some documents can be seen by everyone: others by only a selected few! The final important aspect is speed – some documents are far less urgent than others. If you are into a 'drop everything' situation then you will be expected to respond very rapidly indeed – whilst not forgoing quality, accuracy or any other basic requirement!

Consequently a good administrator always takes into account:

- quality control
- the need for accuracy
- the importance of 'image'
- the need for confidentiality
- the need for speed.

Quality control

Quality is an 'in' word. In this context all it means is that you should institute a system which prevents substandard correspondence leaving your office.

In some organisations a senior executive has the overall responsibility for all quality issues within that company. One of his or her duties is normally to keep a check on the standard of correspondence and in some cases he or she may ask for a number of 'sample' copies of correspondence which have been issued by each department each week. This can cause problems, however, and you may find that you are acting as a buffer between this executive, your boss and your staff.

A more usual method is for you either to set your own standards for layout and style or to ensure that the company 'house style' is followed. (See also pages 485 and 442.)

Questions you should ask are:

- Have all the original instructions been carried out?
- Have all the queries or objections been answered?
- Has the necessary information been requested or communicated?
- Has the most suitable form of communication been used? Have you, for instance, written a memorandum, which on reflection you feel should have been a report?
- Has the correct paper choice been made?
- Has the correct layout been chosen?
- Is it dated? (The date is almost always included on a letter or memo but quite often forgotten on a report or notice – where it should appear at the foot of the document.)
- Are the enclosures mentioned in the correspondence actually enclosed?
- Have the requisite number of copies been taken?
- Should it be marked 'Personal', 'Confidential', etc.?
- Have any specific mailing instructions been included?
- What is the overall impression? Can you see any errors in grammar, punctuation and spelling? (If you are not sure, turn to page 485!) Does it 'read' well?
- Have any 'follow up' reminders been placed in the appropriate system?
- Has it been signed or initialled?

Accuracy

Normally any communication containing statistical or financial information should be in writing – there are too many opportunities for error if this type of information is transmitted verbally.

Certain documents may have legal implications. If so, they should be in writing and couched in formal terms – a letter, a memorandum or a report rather than a brief note – and their accuracy should be checked and double-checked!

Everyone who keys in text makes mistakes. However, the difference between a good administrator and a bad one is that the first spots the errors and the second doesn't. Sending out documents which contain typing errors or – even worse – mistakes which keep the staff laughing for weeks can ruin your reputation completely. One harassed administrator sent out a memo to the MD which started 'We have just received your daft proposal for a new computer unit to be situated in this department . . .'

The second fact to remember is that nobody likes proofreading and no-one is born to the task. It takes time to learn how to do it properly, it is always tedious, and it is the first thing you are likely to skimp if you are under pressure or overworked.

If you are using a word processor then complete your document and run through a spellcheck as your first test. This will highlight the first type of error (you'll probably be surprised how many!), i.e. words which are completely mistyped and make no sense at all. Do remember that a spellcheck will not pick up many transpositions, e.g. 'form' not 'from', and 'stain' not 'satin', because the alternative is a valid word. Equally, homophones will also remain undetected ('check' not 'cheque', 'revue' not 'review', 'draught' not 'draft', etc.), as will words with the wrong ending ('cause' not 'caused', 'standing' not 'standard', etc.).

Give the document a second read, one word at a time (read it as if it is an instruction on how to tune your new video recorder). If the document is long then give yourself a break mid-way through, or enlist the help of a friend – you read and your friend checks, then swap over. Use a ruler whenever figures are involved to avoid jumping a line, and read digits in pairs. Remember to take more care over these as there is no 'meaning' to help you and a mistake in a critical figure could be disastrous.

For very important documents enlist the help of a colleague and ask him or her to check it for you with fresh eyes. A variation on this theme is to read through your documents once again later in the day before submitting them to your boss – when they are 'hot off the press' you are still apt to miss even obvious mistakes as you read what you think should be there, not what you have actually typed. When you can approach documents 'cold' you are more likely to notice any errors. Also, remember that it is easier to proofread a hard copy rather than a screen.

Danger areas include:

- word substitution (form/from, is/it, as/at, our/your/you, etc.)
- letter substitution/transposition (r/t, i/e, n/m, u/y, etc.)
- faulty spacing and inconsistency in presentation (e.g. 24 and 12 hour clock times, words and figures, capitalisation, etc.)
- forgetting to expand abbreviations (or expanding them wrongly)
- names, addresses and figures
- words transposed or omitted – or even lines of text missed out
- wrong endings to words – e.g. 's' omitted from plurals, 'ed' instead of 'ing', etc.

Mark each error boldly so you won't miss it when you correct the page.

Image

This factor is often linked with that of cost. A handwritten note to a colleague is cheap and effective – so is a brief telephone call. Sales literature intended for use in a high profile sales presentation requires a more sophisticated approach. So, too, does a communication to a valued customer who would expect a well-presented letter.

DID YOU KNOW?

On occasion you may want to write in by hand the salutation and subscription on a letter. This indicates to the customer that he or she is held in regard. A completely handwritten item of correspondence from a senior executive to a client or colleague is also regarded as a mark of esteem.

Confidentiality

A notice on the staff noticeboard is not a suitable method of informing members of staff that they are to be made redundant or that certain individuals are going to get a pay rise!

The higher you rise in the administrative world the more likely it is that the correspondence and other documents you type will be confidential. There is a whole range of procedures of which you need to be aware if this is the case.

- If you are in the process of typing a confidential document on your computer and someone enters the room, then turn the brightness control down immediately so that no-one can read it on screen.
- Better still, position your desk or angle your monitor so that your work cannot be read by visitors to your office.
- If you have to leave the room, either lock your door or close down the system and lock away the disk.
- Lock both the documents and any related computer disks away at the end of the day.
- Keep confidential documents in a folder on your desk and close the folder when someone enters the room (the office gossip is often adept at reading upside down!).
- Make a note of those people who have received confidential documents and always despatch the papers in sealed envelopes, clearly marked CONFIDENTIAL.
- Destroy any spoiled copies in the shredder.
- Do not discuss the content of the document with anyone. If pressed, deny having had anything to do with it and feign ignorance.
- Keep the keys to your office, desk and filing cabinet on your person at all times.
- If you are involved in highly confidential work and you find anyone snooping around your office or behaving suspiciously then inform your boss immediately.

- Take care if photocopying – at least 10 per cent of users regularly leave the original on the glass of the machine!

DID YOU KNOW?

Certain top administrators recently revealed their 'tips' for maintaining confidentiality at a board level. They included:

- a word processor with a password known only to the administrator and which is not networked to the system, to avoid the possibility of someone hacking into it
- locking the office door when taking dictation so that no-one can come in unexpectedly and overhear something confidential
- a filing cabinet kept locked all the time and only opened when a document is required.

Urgency

Very urgent documents can present problems, if only because emergencies always happen on the wrong day and usually come in twos and threes! The day two people are off with 'flu and the photocopier has just jammed for the fourth time is the very day your boss will need a very urgent and very long piece of work to be prepared and sent to the recipient. The nature of the work you do and the type of boss you work for will influence the frequency of these requests. If you work for someone who is frequently away from the office and who has a huge amount of work to cope with on the occasions when he or she is available, then you should learn to schedule 'gaps' in your week to cope with these times. If you normally work for a very well-organised boss and operate in a smoothly run office then, ironically, top priority jobs may create more problems for you because you are less used to them.

The first golden rule is not to panic! The second is to quickly go through everything else you have to do and *either* put it on hold, get someone else to deal with it or put it to one side to complete immediately you have finished this job.

Now tackle the emergency. Shut the door, divert your telephone and tell people not to disturb you (nicely!) If you can operate in 'tunnel-vision' mode so much the better because you will be able to concentrate solely on the task in hand. Remember to allow enough time for checking afterwards and work out how to transmit your document in the most effective way. This is dealt with below.

DID YOU KNOW?

You are obviously aware that today, if you are trying to get through to someone by telephone, you can often reach them on a mobile phone or leave a message on an answering machine. However, many organisations now operate a voice mail system through their switchboard so that you can automatically leave messages for a specific person in an organisation if he or she is out. An even more recent innovation is voice processing where computers can be used to deal with urgent calls, to route dictated materials and even, on the most sophisticated PC voice dictation systems, to prepare the document itself from verbal dictation!

Methods of transmitting correspondence

As you have just seen, an administrator's responsibility for correspondence does not begin and end with its preparation. He or she must take into account how quickly it needs to be prepared and sent to its destination – and also how much it will cost. Normally the more urgent and important the document, the more likely it is that you will sanction an expensive rather than cost-saving means of transmission!

You may, of course, wonder whether any written document is the correct form of communication in an emergency and choose instead to use the telephone. There are occasions, however, when an urgent written communication is required, particularly when the information it contains is too long or complicated to be transmitted verbally, for example:

- details of current price lists and product information to a sales representative who needs them to close a deal
- a last-minute request for information from a senior executive who needs it for a top-level board meeting or conference or to send to an important client.

In such cases the use of telecommunications systems, an express delivery postal service or even courier service is obviously advisable.

Cost

A ten-minute transatlantic telephone call or fax may be necessary on occasion (where urgency outweighs cost) – but only on occasion! Where possible use a cheaper method of communication such as a letter. You must remember, however, that there are 'hidden costs' in any written document, e.g.:

- preparation – gathering together the material and drafting out the reply (although even a telephone call requires some preparation)
- transcription
- proofreading
- preparation for mailing
- stationery – letterhead/envelope/photocopy, etc.
- postage.

Telecommunications systems

Most administrators can now choose to transmit correspondence:

- by post
- by means of a telecommunications system.

In most organisations this is likely to include:

- a fax machine
- possibly a telex machine – to reach those customers not yet on fax and to transmit 'special' documents – although now very little used
- electronic mail
- transferring computer files.

A company which needs to set up a permanent communications link with a branch office or distributor can arrange to have its own national or international private circuit over which to transmit either voice or data. In most cases, however, organisations use the standard public network. As an administrator it is your responsibility to make sure that both you and your staff know how the systems operate and in what circumstances they are best used.

Fax machines

Fax machines are the fastest growing sector of the telecommunications market – which is hardly surprising given the benefits they offer of being able to transmit text, graphics, photographs and anything else which can fit onto a sheet of paper quickly, easily and cheaply to almost anywhere in the world.

The price of faxes has fallen to bring them within the reach of even the smallest businesses. There are portable faxes (which can be used on a train or carried in the car and then carried in a purpose-built shoulder case), faxes and answering machines combined, coated paper and plain paper faxes and larger models which can call other faxes on their own without your help!

In addition, today most faxes can be interfaced with your PC. This allows you to transmit direct from your computer, receive faxes on disk and print them out on your own printer, scan in A4 documents, logos or photographs or even redirect an incoming fax to another number. You can even convert incoming faxes to text files to edit them.

What to buy and which features to select will depend very much on the requirements of an individual organisation.

Using a fax

The most difficult part of using a fax is setting it up when it is first purchased. If you are ever in a position where you order a new fax, make it a condition of purchase that the shop sets it up for you – unless you or your boss really enjoys staring at sometimes unintelligible manuals and playing with keys and codes for hours.

Your next step should be to 'translate' the manuals into a simple user instruction sheet for all staff. To ensure only good quality faxes are received it is important that you emphasise the type of documents which can be faxed well and those which can not – and what staff should do about it. If staff are well trained then you can pass on the transmission of a long, urgent message with confidence and not feel that you have to stand over them to check or to do it yourself!

Receiving faxes

Most fax machines are left on 24 hours a day, seven days a week to receive incoming messages. Identifying incoming messages very much depends on:

- where the fax machine is sited
- whether or not incoming messages are stored in a paper tray.

Everyone in the office should know that incoming faxes must be delivered quickly – the whole idea of using fax is to give instant information! You must devise a system for coping with incoming faxes for executives who are out of the building – if necessary insist that you scan all incoming faxes prior to delivery. Not only will this enable you to decide the best course of action to take if someone is absent or away, but it will also keep you extremely *au fait* with what is going on!

DID YOU KNOW?

In a 1994 survey of Financial Times 1000 companies carried out by Pitney Bowes, 68 per cent of daily fax users did not know how much it cost to send a fax! And less than 2 per cent took advantage of cheap rate times (the evening and overnight) or any other cost-saving method. If you are studying option Unit 9 then you will find this topic raised again in more detail.

If you are interested in the potential of linking your PC to the fax then you need to contact one of the companies which sells linking software and find out how it works. BT will willingly supply you with details of their OfficeLink system (call Freefone 0800 800 855 or Freefax them on 0800 800 955). Two other companies offering fax software are Delrina (Winfax Pro) (0181 207 3163) and Olympus Business Communications (0171 253 2772).

Telex machines

As fax machines have increased in popularity, the use of telex machines has declined. That does not mean to say that organisations no longer use telex – it is still useful in a some situations where fax facilities are either not suitable or not available.

The critical difference between fax and telex is that because the answerback code of both the sender and receiver is printed at the top of the telexed document and at the end, there is proof that transmission took place and was completed. A telex is therefore recognised as a legal document in most countries of the world – the position is less clear as regards fax messages. If, therefore, you are contacting a company to ask them to agree to accept new terms of delivery you would be well advised to send the communication over telex, rather than fax – and to ask them to reply in the same way.

It is also advisable to use telex in any situation where you want unqualified evidence that you were in touch, e.g. when booking your executive a hotel room halfway across the world (make sure he or she doesn't forget to take the copy telex!).

Today the need for special telex machines has declined because telex messages can be prepared on computers and downloaded to linked telex transmission equipment on a network – or the messages sent direct to the recipient's computer via ISDN or Internet.

Electronic mail

Electronic mail (or E-mail) is a messaging system whereby documents prepared on a PC are then transmitted to another PC via a 'mailbox' system. The mailbox stores messages until the user is ready to access them. The user can reply to, store or delete messages, print out, redistribute and even check if the messages he or she sent have been read by the recipient.

Electronic mail systems are becoming more and more common as in-house facilities for organisations which have networked their PCs (see Unit 6, page 340). The advent of Internet has meant that any organisation can subscribe to a worldwide E-mail network and send E-mail messages easily from one computer user to another (see Unit 6, page 344).

In addition, the company can subscribe to either Telecom Gold or New Prestel (or both) to send messages to customers and suppliers – but these systems are likely to decline in popularity as Internet becomes more widespread.

The advantages of any electronic mail system are that:

- all forms of data can be transmitted (graphics, text, spreadsheets, etc.)
- there is complete confidentiality as only the user can access his or her own mail by means of a password or ID
- a recipient who wishes to incorporate information received by electronic mail into another document stored on his or her computer does not need to key it in for a second time
- messages can be sent to several mailboxes simultaneously
- travelling executives can access their mailbox via a laptop computer from virtually anywhere in the world.

Internal electronic mail

This is usually installed via 'off-the-shelf' software which may also comprise additional facilities, such as electronic diaries and schedulers. To give additional security, users normally have to key in a second password to access their mail, in addition to the one used to log on to the network in the first place.

External electronic mail

The most common system today – and the most rapidly growing – is Internet. In this case you simply prepare the message as you would for your internal E-mail system but insert a different (and longer!) address line. If your organisation is linked to Internet you may find that your messages are transmitted once or twice a day in 'batches' – to save money. Bearing in mind that you may want to transmit a document very urgently indeed, you would have to check with your network administrator whether it could be sent immediately or, if not, what time it would go. You can then decide whether or not a fax is a better option in this case.

 ## DID YOU KNOW?

Many organisations are printing their Internet E-mail addresses together with their fax numbers and telephone numbers on adverts. You can even contact the BBC Points of View programme using that method. If you are into computers in a big way then you could E-mail the *Guardian*'s Computer Editor (Jack Schofield) by sending a message to jack@cix.compulink.co.uk or you could contact a company which teaches you how to use Internet for learning at salesdesk@rmplc.co.uk. The 'co' means that it is a commercial organisation – alternatives are 'gov' (guess!) and 'coll' (educational establishments). The final letters represent the country – the only exception being the USA. Because they invented the system they have the unique right of not having to have their country specified at the end of an address line!

Transferring computer files

Many organisations today use data transmission systems for sending or receiving computer files 'downline'. This method is used by teleworkers who work from home and are linked to their organisation by computer, banks, travel agents and newspapers (who can receive articles from journalists direct into their computer system). Supermarkets and motor vehicle companies order goods and supplies by computer using EDI (see Unit 6).

The size of a network or data link can range from the office next door to a company on the other side of the world. Many organisations with a constant need for the transmission of information at high speed use BT's Integrated Services Digital Network (ISDN) where data, computer files, video images, voice messages, faxes, E-mails and video conferencing can take place much more quickly. As a comparison, the equivalent of 60 sheets of A4 paper transmitted between computers linked through a modem and standard telephone line takes about 23 minutes – between computers linked by ISDN the transfer takes place in 25 seconds! Systems are available for small and large services.

CHECK IT YOURSELF

Find out more about ISDN by contacting BT on Freefone 0800 800 983 or contacting Ascom Telecommunications Ltd and asking for details of their Ascotel ISDN system – telephone 01276 418 000.

TEST YOURSELF

Throughout this section you have been given guidance on the different types of postal and telecommunications systems currently used by organisations and – in several cases – asked to find out more information yourself.

Use this to calculate for yourself the most cost-effective method(s) of sending each of the following urgent documents. Assume that you have the full range of equipment and services available.

1   A confidential message to a director in your organisation.
2   A package with accompanying documentation to a firm in Paris.
3   A set of presentation slides to a representative in Scotland.
4   A sales pack containing updated price list and two photographs to a firm in New York.
5   A signed contract to a company 12 miles away.
6   A letter of authorisation to your local bank.
7   An advert to a national newspaper.
8   An order to a large supplier.

9   A 10-page quotation to a company in Sydney.
10   A 50-page draft for the company glossy publicity book to a printer 150 miles away.

House style

Look back to page 385 in this unit and page 442 in Unit 6 which discuss the growing trend towards the use of a house style and, in particular, to the section outlining the details normally contained on company stationery.

TEST YOURSELF

1   A current joke is that soon there will be no room for anything on company-headed paper other than the logo and all the pre-printed information. Discuss as a group or with your tutor or adviser *all* the reasons an organisation may have for including such a large quantity of information.

2   You start work as an office administrator in a small office of a family-owned bakery. Apart from a very basic letter-head no attempt has been made to introduce any form of house style. Your boss has succeeded his father in running the business and he hopes his daughter will take over from him and does not really see the need for any change. The business is thriving and has recently undertaken several catering contracts to provide buffets for birthdays, weddings, retirement parties, etc. Write a memo to your boss explaining why you think there should be a move towards the adoption of a house style and listing the steps you would take (including the timescale) in order to achieve that change.

Legal and regulatory requirements relating to the use and provision of information

The same legal regulations apply to correspondence as to all other documents (see page 443). What you should remember, however, is that **internal** documents such as notices or memos can equally be the subject of a claim for breach of copyright or defamation as any **external** documents. It is also dangerous to take a too relaxed approach towards confidentiality just because you think you can completely trust all your colleagues. A throwaway remark on a scribbled note to a colleague could lead to your appearing in court! Look at every document you prepare – no matter how informal – to check that what you have written will have no adverse legal consequences!

ACTIVITY SECTION

1   On page 413 you were asked to consider the ways in which you would find out information to enable you to prepare the following documents for a school's annual speech day:

–   a programme for the evening
–   a list of the prize winners

- a letter of invitation to parents and other guests
- a guest list
- a seating plan
- notes about the guest speaker
- a letter to the civic hall booking appropriate accommodation and making the necessary catering arrangements
- a press release
- a letter to a local bookstore arranging for book tokens for the prize winners
- a memo to all staff outlining their role in the proceedings.

Assume that you have now obtained all the following information you require. See below for details. Incorporate that information into the documents required and make certain that they are:

- complete and factually correct
- written in an appropriate style
- grammatical and with correct spelling and punctuation
- consistently presented.

a The speech day is to be held in a month's time on the Tuesday evening. It is scheduled to start at 7 pm and end at 8.30 pm after which there will be a buffet for the invited guests. The Head will make a few opening remarks and will welcome the guest speaker who has been invited to speak for about 10 minutes. The prize winners will then be presented with their book tokens. The school choir will sing a selection of Lloyd Webber songs and the presentation will end with a vote of thanks from two of the senior pupils, Mario Florenzo and Gillian Thomason.

b The school is Ivy Bank Secondary School in your home or nearest town. The headmaster is Stephen Ball MA.

c The venue is your nearest Civic Hall of a size capable of accommodating 300 people.

d Your guest speaker is the present Secretary of State for Education and Employment.

e You are intending to invite the local mayor, a well-known local businessman or woman, the manager of the local Employment Service office, the principal Careers Officer, and the Principal of your nearest FE College as VIP guests and to form the platform party

f The bookstore you are using is your nearest or largest local store. Each prize-winner will receive a £10 book token and you are hoping for a discount for a bulk order!

g You are going to send the press release to your nearest local newspaper.

h The list of prize winners is:

Year 1
Danny Rivers: Elspeth Foreman: Sangeet Dal

Year 2
Joanna Luxor: Kevin Garrity: Rosie Deedes

Year 3
Yvonne Ramirez: Otis Holby: Tim Naughton

Year 4
Viv Meredith: Imtiaz Seedat: Patricia Blundell

Year 5
Hannah Frazer: Judy Montessori: Leni Robens

Year 6
Graham Jordan: Simon Dyer: Flavia Morris

Special prizes will be given to

- Davina Price for the most improved performance from Year 5 to 6
- Warren Leibovici for outstanding all round achievement
- Frances McEvoy for overcoming severe health problems to achieve examination success.

2   You have been engaged in correspondence with a customer with whom you have provided a delivery of knitting wool but who has settled only part of his account. Generally he is a good payer and has been a regular customer. His business tends to be seasonal and you feel that he may be able to pay his bills on time in the future. However, your boss is very worried about his cashflow and wants to have as many accounts as possible settled. Write the appropriate letter.

3   You work for the Managing Director of a company which specialises in making dried flower arrangements. A customer who is about to open a small chain of health food shops sends in the following order from your catalogue (which contains details of over 400 arrangements)

Order Number	Description	Quantity
342	'Heliotrope' arrangement	4
356	'Delphinium' arrangement	6
393	'Carnation' arrangement	3

She needs these arrangements within seven days (the week before the actual opening of the shops). You check with the Production Manager who tells you that Item 393 is out of stock (and is too complicated to be produced within the time period specified). There is a sufficient number of Item 342 but there are only two left of Item 356. It is probable, however, that there will be a sufficient number of Item 356 available by the end of the week. Write to the customer informing her of what you can do.

Note that she may turn out to be a regular customer if you treat her properly! Repeat business is a distinct possibility here.

4 A group of you have decided to get together to run a cleaning agency. You intend to offer a general cleaning service to both private households and offices. In addition you will offer an upholstery and carpet cleaning service. You will all be involved in the business side of the agency but intend to employ both full-time and part-time staff to carry out the cleaning duties. At one of your first meetings you decide:

a to draw up an advertisement for both the local evening paper and the Job Centre giving details of the cleaning staff required (including rates of pay). Note that one of you has volunteered to visit the Job Centre to look at the vacancies already on display and to check on current rates of pay for cleaners; another has volunteered to look through the evening paper for similar information
b to prepare a circular letter suitable for a mailshot to local businesses and small companies containing details of the services you intend to offer
c to draft out an invitation to the official opening of the agency in six weeks' time, which you intend to send to local dignitaries and business people
d to prepare a press release for the local paper, giving details of the services you intend to offer, the reasons for the setting up of the agency and also some background information about the personnel involved (i.e. you!).

Prepare the necessary documents ready for a second meeting in a week's time.

5 Your office staff have little idea of how to assess different forms of document transmission for urgency, suitable use and cost. Yesterday a new member of staff faxed a 60-page document abroad which was not even remotely urgent, whilst his colleague posted a vital letter using second-class mail.

Prepare a memo to your staff outlining the systems available in your own office for document transmissions and giving brief guidelines as to use and cost in each case.

Tools of the trade

When you accept a job as an administrator or PA you will be expected to have certain skills. One such skill is that of being able to put together a grammatically correct piece of work with no spelling or punctuation errors.

It may be difficult for you, however, to determine just how good you are. The following section is designed therefore to:

- act as a brief 'aide memoire'
- allow you to test your proficiency
- show you how to avoid certain difficulties
- offer you some assistance in training junior staff.

In order for you to test your proficiency and then work onwards without any difficulty, the answers to all the Test Yourself sections of this part of the Unit are given on page 503. For ease of reference, therefore, each of the Test Yourself sections is numbered.

Grammatical construction

There is not enough space in this book to detail all the rules of English grammar – nor do you really need them. What you should know is contained in the list below. If you want to read further on the topic look at standard reference texts such as *The Complete Plain Words* by Ernest Gowers or *Modern English Usage* by H W Fowler.

TEST YOURSELF 1

Spot the genuine mistake in each sentence! Award yourself two points for each correct answer.

1 I would be delighted to see you on 25 May.
2 Due to an unavoidable delay, they were late for the meeting.
3 Miss Lyons, my administrator, who you met yesterday, will take you round the showrooms.
4 I apologise for him not contacting you at the time you expected.
5 I think it is wise for you and I to meet next week.
6 Do you wish the colour scheme to be different to the one illustrated in the brochure?
7 The profits must be divided between the three departments.
8 Every one of the articles are of top quality.
9 Looking forward to hearing from you.
10 Please remember to carefully check the draft.

Now check your answers with the key on page 503. If you scored 20 out of 20 you can skip the rest of this section.

Rule 1 The difference between note and sentence form

The usual method of explaining the difference between a sentence and a phrase (or note) is to say that a sentence has to have a verb. If you went to a school where formal grammar was not taught, you may still have difficulty in deciding whether or not you have included a verb. Look at the following examples.

Note   Delay in sending the goods.

Sentence   There will be a delay in sending the goods.

Note   Looking forward to seeing you.

Sentence   I am looking forward to seeing you.

Alternative: If you are in any real doubt – copy. Look at a previous piece of correspondence on the topic which seems to read well and try to imitate its construction. If you do this often enough you will find that you are writing in sentence form almost without realising it.

TEST YOURSELF 2

Complete the following.

1 *Note*   Thanking you for your order.
   Sentence
2 *Note*   Apologies for the delay in replying.
   Sentence
3 *Note*   Have the goods in stock. Shall send them to you by the end of next week.
   Sentence

DID YOU KNOW?

A common mistake in sentence construction is to write:

Passing the shop, a large flower display was visible from the doorway.

The sentence does not say who was passing the shop. Say instead:

As I passed the shop, I noticed that a large flower display was visible from the doorway.

Rule 2 Matching up the verb with its subject

Again, if you do not know which word is a verb and which a subject, you may have difficulty in matching them up. Look at the following example of incorrect matching.

Details of the new car is to be found in the latest catalogue.

The subject of this sentence is 'details', which is a plural word. The verb therefore should also be plural, i.e. 'are' not 'is', and the sentence should read:

Details of the new car are to be found in the latest catalogue.

It may help if you cross out (either mentally or physically) the material between the subject and the verb. If, for instance, you read the word 'details' and then the word 'is' immediately afterwards you will realise that it sounds wrong.

TEST YOURSELF 3

Complete the following sentences with the correct verb. (Remember to ignore the words between the subject and verb.)

1 The girl, who was with some friends, . . . late. ('was' or 'were'?)

2 His knowledge of Accounts, Computer Services and Economics . . . good. ('was' or 'were'?)

3 Long and complex items of information . . . difficult to assimilate. ('is' or 'are'?)

DID YOU KNOW?

Examples of variations on this theme are given below.

- If you start a sentence with 'either', 'neither', 'each', 'every' or 'any' you should use a singular verb because you are talking about a single person or entity, not a group, e.g.:

  I think neither is suitable for the job.

  Everyone who applies has to be over 18.

  Each of them has the opportunity to do well.

  Although it has been held traditionally that 'none' should be followed by a singular verb, it is now more common to use the plural verb because it reads better, e.g.:

  None were aware that their overtime pay would be reduced.

  reads better than

  None was aware that his overtime pay would be reduced.

  Remember also that where a collective noun is used (such as 'committee' or 'jury') you can use either the singular or the plural verb – but not a mixture of both, e.g.:

  The committee is scheduled to report its findings to the Board at the next meeting.

  or

  The committee are scheduled to report their findings to the Board at the next meeting.

  but not

  The committee is scheduled to report their findings to the Board at the next meeting.

- The words 'either . . . or' and 'neither . . . nor' are word combinations which again require a singular verb, e.g.:

  Neither the Office Manager nor her secretary was aware that the telephone call had been made.

  Either the Personnel Manager or his assistant is required at the reception desk.

- If you want to use an opening such as 'This is one of the documents . . .' relate the verb to 'documents' not 'one', i.e.:

This is one of the documents that are to be circulated at the meeting.

- Remember to match up pronouns (e.g. we, I, you, our, one) as well as subjects and verbs. Do not say

> I feel that we shall be able to accept the offer.

but

> I feel that I shall be able to accept the offer.

or

> We feel that we shall be able to accept the offer.

Rule 3 The difference between 'who' and 'whom'

The rule is that 'who' is used as the subject and 'whom' the object, e.g.:

> This is the candidate who has been selected by the committee.

or

> This is the candidate whom the committee has selected.

Alternative: If you are in any doubt in this situation you can normally find another way of writing the sentence, e.g.:

> This candidate was selected by the committee.

Avoid also the common mistake of using 'him' for 'his' and 'you' for 'your', e.g.:

> I am disappointed at his refusing to see me.

not

> I am disappointed at him refusing to see me.

Alternative: If you are unsure, write instead:

> I am disappointed at his refusal to see me.

or

> I am disappointed that he refused to see me.

You should also note the difference between 'whose' and 'who's'. 'Who's' is merely an abbreviation for 'who is', e.g.:

> Who's coming to the party tonight?

'Whose' is used to indicate possession, e.g.:

> The young man, whose qualifications were very impressive, was disappointed at not being given the job.

> Whose bag is this?

Rule 4 The use of 'I' or 'me'; 'we' or 'us'

It is sometimes quite difficult to decide whether a phrase should read 'You and I' or 'you and me'. A simple way of resolving the problem is to translate it into 'we' or 'us' – that normally gives you an indication of which version is correct, e.g.:

> You and I (i.e. we) should make arrangements for the Paris trip as soon as possible.

> Mr Brown wants to see you and me (i.e. us) as soon as he arrives back from lunch.

Note that if you want to end a sentence with either 'I' or 'me' and are not sure what version to choose, again mentally add a verb at the end of it. If a verb reads correctly then 'I' should be used; if not, 'me', e.g.:

> He can deal with that question better than I (can).

Alternative: Avoid using 'I' or 'we' at the end of a sentence. Say instead:

> He is the better person to deal with that question.

Rule 5 The difference between 'should' and 'would'; 'shall' and 'will'

'I' and 'we' are followed by 'shall' or 'should', e.g.:

> I shall be pleased to see you.

> We shall be pleased to send you details of our current stock.

but

> You will hear from us next week.

This rule is followed unless you wish to indicate a definite intention or determination, e.g.:

> I will get away by 4 pm no matter what happens.

> What I would like to do is to go to Disneyland.

Use either 'shall' and 'will' or 'should' and 'would' in the same sentence, not a mixture of both, e.g.:

> I should be grateful if you would (not will) call in.

> If you will consider this matter as urgent, I shall (not should) be grateful.

Try to not confuse 'would' and 'could': 'would' = willing to; 'could' = able to. For example:

> Could you complete this job any earlier?

> Would you be prepared to work late tonight?

Rule 6 The 'split' infinitive

It is inadvisable to write a phrase in which the word 'to' and a connecting verb is split by an intervening word, e.g. 'to boldly go', 'to hurriedly decide'. This rule is not applied as strictly as it used to be but it may be as well not to include many split infinitives in a document – it is unlikely, but you may have a purist boss who picks up such errors.

TEST YOURSELF 4

Rewrite the following sentences to avoid splitting the infinitive.

1 The Managing Director decided to immediately call a meeting.
2 He promised to urgently deal with the matter.
3 We advise all our clients to carefully consider these new developments.

Rule 7 The use of prepositions

Again it is considered ungrammatical to end a sentence with a preposition (e.g. 'to', 'of', 'with', 'about').

Avoid therefore constructing sentences such as:

> I give below, details of a number of problems we are dealing with.

Say instead:

> I give below, details of a number of problems with which we are dealing.

Note that nowadays, however, there is a relaxation of the rule in cases where to avoid putting the preposition at the end of the sentence would result in a very awkward construction, e.g.:

> What do you want to see me about?

rather than

> About what do you want to see me?

Again, though, be careful if you have a boss who likes all the niceties to be observed!

TEST YOURSELF 5

Rewrite each sentence to avoid placing the preposition at the end.

1 She is a client I have always had difficulty with.
2 I can find no-one whom I can apply for information to.
3 What do you want this information for?

Rule 8 Prepositions at the end of phrases

Some phrases are always followed by a preposition, e.g.:

acquiesce in   relevant to

dependent on   compatible with

Remember in particular that 'similar' is followed by 'to' and 'different' is followed by 'from'.

Rule 9 The use of 'only'

Where possible place the word 'only' next to the word it modifies – otherwise the whole meaning of the sentence may be changed. Look at the following sentence.

> We offer an annual maintenance contract.

'Only' can be put in several different places, each conveying a different meaning, e.g.:

> Only we offer an annual maintenance contract (i.e. we, and no-one else, offer such a contract).

> We only offer an annual maintenance contract (i.e. you are not obliged to accept this offer or that's all we offer, so tough!).

> We offer only an annual maintenance contract (i.e. not a monthly or weekly one).

> We offer an annual, maintenance-only contract (i.e. we offer a maintenance service and no other).

TEST YOURSELF 6

Use the word 'only' in three different positions to give three different meanings to the following sentence.

I want a cup of coffee.

Rule 10 'Pairs' of words which are often mis-used

- *Not only/but also*

Make certain that the whole sentence links together, e.g.:

> I want to know the price of the car not only for this year but also in future years.

not

> I want to know not only the price of the car at present but in future.

- *Due to/owing to*

'Due to' is used after words such as 'to be' (is/are), 'seem' or 'appear'. Otherwise use 'owing to', e.g.:

> It is due to an operational failure.

Owing to an operational failure, the train was 30 minutes late.

Alternative: In most cases you can use the word 'because', e.g.:

Because of an operational failure, the train was 30 minutes late.

- *Alternative/option*

'Alternative' means a choice of two; 'option' means a choice of more than two.

You have the alternative of choosing either the black or the white model.

Of the three options, he preferred the first.

- *Between/among*

'Between' is used if only two people/items are concerned; 'among' if more than two, e.g.:

Divide the takings between the two of you.

Divide the takings among all three.

- *Less/fewer*

Use less for an uncountable amount; use fewer for countable numbers, e.g.:

There was less space in the reception area.

but

There are fewer examination successes than in previous years.

- *There/their*

'There' is used either to refer to a place or in conjunction with the verb 'to be', e.g.:

Put the parcel over there.

There is plenty of time to catch the train.

'Their' is a possessive pronoun such as 'you' or 'our', e.g.:

Their commitment to the cause was absolute.

Are you going to give them back their answers?

TEST YOURSELF 7

Retest yourself by rewriting the following sentences to see whether you have improved!

1   Neither of my colleagues were there.

2 You and me must fly to New York.
3 The foreman failed to fully read the instructions.
4 She is the supervisor who the office juniors dislike.
5 I was surprised at them leaving so early.
6 Less than a dozen requests have been received.
7 This is a meeting which he must come to.
8 I shall be pleased if you would provide the information I require by
Friday.
9 Who's errors are these?

Punctuation

The compilers of the rules for modern typewriting examinations may
have assisted you at the time you were taking your examinations by
allowing you to use 'open punctuation' (i.e. minimal punctuation) in
all the correspondence you produced.

However, even nowadays, by no means every company has a 'house
style' which obviates the need for the use of any punctuation (see page
442) and even when you use open punctuation for addresses,
salutations and complimentary closes, you still need to insert
punctuation in the body of the letter for it to make sense to the
reader. The basic rule here is to keep it simple. Master the use of the
full stop, the comma and the apostrophe. The question and
exclamation marks are unlikely to cause you much difficulty. The
colon and semi-colon can be effective but you can live without them.
Inverted commas (or quotation/speech marks) may be needed – but
normally only on infrequent occasions.

 TEST YOURSELF 8

Punctuate the following sentences.

1 The Chairman who had a particular interest in the issue agreed to raise
it at the shareholders meeting in a weeks time
2 At the meeting he observed I am pleased that the companys profits last
year were so high
3 He appreciated one shareholders concern at the increase in the cost of
goods labour and transport
4 What more could I have done to solve the problem he asked
5 The new product Fastflow had proved cheap to produce simple to
package and easy to sell
6 It should improve the organisations financial position in a few years time

Check your work with the key on page 504. If you experienced any difficulties,
read on!

Rule 1 The full stop
Use

● at the end of a sentence (although not at the end of a heading)

- traditionally after abbreviations (B.A., e.g., enc.).

However, you should note that it is more usual nowadays to omit full stops in such circumstances even in otherwise fully punctuated documents: eg, ITV, LLB, etc.

TEST YOURSELF 9

On what other occasions would you expect to use a full stop?

Rule 2 The comma
Use

- to separate words or phrases, e.g.:

    You will require a pen, a pencil and a notebook.

    Note that to be strictly accurate you should not use a comma before an 'and' in such a list.

- after introductory words or phrases, e.g.:

    Having discussed the matter with my colleagues, I am now able to give you a decision.

    to separate phrases mid-sentence, e.g.:

    Miss Matthews, the Senior Accountant, will give you the relevant information.

- to introduce a quotation, e.g.:

    As Tiny Tim observed, 'God bless us.'

- if required (i.e. company house style) to separate names, addresses and dates on a letter, e.g.:

    Mr. L. Brookes,
    32 Sunningdale Crescent,
    SHEFFIELD,
    S4 2YD

    24th January, 199_

    Dear Sir, ...

    Yours faithfully,

    Margaret Lammack,
    Purchasing Director

Note that you can alter the meaning of a sentence by the mis-placing of a comma. For example, compare

    Frank, Lenny and I who are good friends, went to the cinema (i.e. Lenny and I are the good friends).

with

Frank, Lenny and I, who are good friends, went to the cinema (i.e. Frank, Lenny and I are all good friends).

Rule 3 The apostrophe

Many people have a mental blank about apostrophes. In reality the rules are quite simple.

Use them

- in the place of a missing letter or letters, e.g.:

    You'll be sorry

means 'You will be sorry' (with the apostrophe taking the place of the first part of 'will').

Remember this rule when writing 'its' or 'it's'. Use the apostrophe only when you mean to say 'it is', e.g.:

    It's cold outside.

Otherwise use 'its', e.g.:

    Its major function is to keep out draughts.

- to indicate possession, e.g.:

the work of the organisation becomes

    the organisation's work ('s)

the work of the organisations becomes

    the organisations' work (s')

Alternative: If you are in doubt, you may be able to use the longer version. For example, if you are worried about where the apostrophe is to be placed in 'the organisations work' use instead 'the work of the organisation' or 'the work of the organisations'. Be careful, however, to check that the construction is not too awkward (the reason for having an apostrophe in the first place!).

A rule of thumb method is to put an apostrophe and add an 's'. However, if the word already ends in 's', you don't need another, e.g.:

    St Thomas' Church

In the case of plural words which do not end in 's', you have no option but to write the apostrophe and then the 's', e.g.:

    children's books, men's hairstyles

Remember that certain words change from singular to plural, which could affect the use of the apostrophe, e.g.:

    secretary's skills

becomes

secretaries' skills

The apostrophe is not used with words such as ours, yours, theirs, hers. The exception is 'one's', e.g.:

One must fulfil one's obligations.

Note also that it is a common error to forget to put apostrophes in phrases relating to time, e.g.:

two years' time, one week's time

Rule 4 Hyphens

Use them

- in what are known as 'compound' nouns and adjectives, e.g.:

  semi-detached house

  up-to-date information

- after certain prefixes, e.g.:

  pre-Christmas sales

  anti-war demonstrators

  vice-chairman

Rule 5 The dash

Use it

- to indicate a break or interruption or to precede a list, e.g.:

  English summers are renowned for the amount of rainfall – but this year has been an exception.

  She had all the qualities necessary for an administrator – intelligence, tact, charm, technical ability.

Note that in formal correspondence a dash should not be used. Use a colon instead.

Rule 6 The colon

Use it

- to introduce a list of items or a quotation, e.g.:

  Please check the items you require: computer disks, daisywheels, stationery.

  Hamlet said: 'To be or not to be, that is the question.'

Rule 7 The semi-colon
Use it

- to link two parts of a sentence where the intended pause is not as long as that indicated by a full stop or as short as that indicated by a comma, e.g.:

> The goods ordered are of two kinds; one suitable for outdoor use and the other for indoor use.

Alternative: When in doubt, use a full stop, e.g.:

> The goods ordered are of two kinds. One is suitable for outdoor use and the other for indoor use.

Rule 8 The question mark
Use it

- if there is a direct question e.g.:

> What time is it?

but not if the question is indirect, e.g.:

> He asked what time it was.

Rule 9 The exclamation mark
Use it

- In informal correspondence, sales or promotional literature, e.g.:

> Cheapest goods in town!

Rule 10 Quotation marks or inverted commas
Use in certain limited circumstances only. Where used, however, the rules are simple:

- to separate direct speech from the rest of the sentence, e.g.:

> The speaker observed, 'Our business is suffering because of the recession.'

Note that is now seems acceptable to put a full stop either before or after the final quotation mark (although the norm would be to put it before).

- to enclose direct quotations, e.g.:

> It may be said that 'there is no smoke without fire'.

- to indicate a trade name, a title of a book, film or play, etc., e.g.:

> 'Oliver Twist', 'Hoover'

Again the modern trend is to omit quotes in these cases.

- to indicate a colloquialism (slang term), e.g.:

  This colour scheme is 'in' this year.

- for a quotation within a quotation (in this case use double inverted commas), e.g.:

  The speaker told his audience, 'The most useful piece of advice I have ever been given is "Moderation in all things".'

Rule 11 The capital letter

Use it

- in the main at the beginning of a sentence
- for titles, e.g.:

  The Princess of Wales

- for proper names, e.g.:

  Take That

  Panorama

  Georgian architecture

- for headings, e.g.:

  Report into Crowd Violence at Football Matches

Note that although traditionally all words except prepositions (of, to, etc.) and conjunctions (but, and, etc.) require an initial capital, modern usage is to reduce the number of capitals in headings.

- at the beginning of direct speech (in the middle of a line), e.g.:

  He said, 'You must be congratulated on your efforts.'

Rule 12 Brackets (or parentheses)

Use instead of commas, e.g.:

  Popular items (such as the tie-necked blouse) are sold out.

  When I was young (many years ago) I went to seek my fortune.

TEST YOURSELF 10

Retest yourself by punctuating the following passage – correctly, we hope!

under a new law and order initiative young offenders will be sent to an adult prison for 24 hours the shock treatment never before tried in the uk is an attempt to halt the increase in the crime figures among young people ministers worried that offenders still regard probation and community service as a soft option hope that the short sharp shock of spending time in a prison cell will have a deterrent effect giving them a taste of prison life locking them up in a cell making them experience the smells the noise and the slopping out should have a dramatic effect one official said they are not likely to want to return prison reform groups have protested that it is a very short sighted approach they say that if the scheme is put into effect there would be a significant increase in the number of prison suicides in a years time

Spelling

The advent of the word processor has meant that most administrators and PAs can rely to a certain extent on the spellcheck facility it often contains. Remember, however, that although few people will notice if you use a comma instead of a semi-colon or if you split the occasional infinitive, they will notice if you mis-spell a word – and your image will be somewhat dented. More importantly, the document containing those spelling errors may not be taken as seriously as it might have been if its spelling was impeccable.

Note that even if you have little difficulty with spelling, the same may not be the case with your juniors. They are not likely to have to compose correspondence but they may be asked to type from a handwritten script in which certain words are either mis-spelled or illegible or from audio tapes where the ability to spell correctly is critical.

You should therefore make sure that your staff can spell – otherwise you will have to proofread every piece of correspondence they type.

The basic rule is that where in doubt (and in the absence of a spellcheck) you should refer to a dictionary. This is of little use if (as junior staff might easily say) you do not know that you are mis-spelling the word. There are certain rules for you to follow, e.g.:

> 'i' before 'e' except after 'c', e.g. piece, ceiling, or unless the word sounds like 'a', e.g. reign and weight

but there are so many exceptions to them that you may confuse yourself. It may be better, therefore, for you to familiarise yourself with some of the more commonly used words in business correspondence. We realise you've heard this many times before but it is true – the more you read, the better you will spell. You pick up the correct spellings automatically.

 TEST YOURSELF 11

Choose the correctly spelled word to complete the following sentences. Note that the number of dots is not significant.

1   .... makes the heart grow fonder. (absence/absense)
2   The two men are .... (aquainted/acquainted)
3   Make sure the .... for the job is put in tonight's paper. (advertisement/advertisment)

4   The sub-......... comprised a number of financial experts. (committee/commitee)

5   Could I have the .... on the Derbyshire file? (correspondance/correspondence)

6   He is very .... (conscientious/concientious)

7   I hope that the MD is not going to be too .... that his administrator is leaving. (dissapointed/disappointed)

8   How many HP .... are there left to pay on my car? (instalments/installments)

9   Do we have any details of the cost of ....? (maintainence/maintenance)

10 We met together .... to discuss matters of policy. (occasionally/occasionnally)

11 This is becoming a frequent .... (occurrence/occurence)

12 It is a great .... to be asked to speak at this conference. (priviledge/privilege)

13 I can .... the chocolate cake. It is delicious. (reccomend/recommend)

14 Pack each item .... (seperately/separately)

15 .... this is the action we should take (undoubtedly/undoubtedley)

TEST YOURSELF 12

Correct the spelling mistakes in the following passage. (Remember that typing it out and running it through your spellcheck is cheating and not always successful!)

The situation has become agravated by the number of adolesents who felt embarassed by the way in which they were treated. A conserted effort by a group of them, in liason with a number of wellfare societies, has resulted in some reforms. Psyschologically, they gained an advantage when they pursuaded a number of senior personel to support there cause.

Vocabulary

Knowing how to spell a word is one skill; knowing what it means and where best to use it is another. If, as is likely, you are expected to compose letters and other documents for your boss you should take care to choose the most appropriate vocabulary and should try to avoid making any obvious errors in that choice. Watch in particular that you do not 'mix up' the meanings of words which both look and sound similar, e.g.:

accept/	I accept the compliment.
except	I like all sweets except chocolate.
affect/	Too high a pollen count affects my hay fever.
effect	What effect has this price rise had on sales?
complement/	The flowers complement the colour
compliment	scheme. (Remember the word 'complete'.)
	May I compliment you on this excellent piece of work.

discreet/ discrete	A good administrator is discreet enough never to reveal any confidential information. Structure the report into five discrete units.
formally/ formerly	Interviews for senior posts are normally conducted more formally than those for junior posts. He was formerly in the army and now works for the local authority.
practice/ practise	It is now normal practice for a child to learn a foreign language. How much time should each child be given to practise that skill? Note that practice is a noun (e.g. choir practice) while practise is a verb (e.g. to practise playing the piano). Similar considerations apply to advice/advise and licence/license
passed/ past	He has passed all his examinations. In the past too much attention has been paid to learning by rote.
personal/ personnel	Personal skills are of the utmost importance for an administrator. Please make sure that all company personnel are aware of the provisions of the Act.
stationery/ stationary	Remember to order adequate supplies of stationery. (Note – stationery – think of 'e' for envelope.) Was the car stationary or moving at the time?

CHECK IT YOURSELF

Check the meaning of the following pairs of words:

1 alternate/alternative
2 comprehensive/comprehensible
3 respectfully/respectively
4 uninterested/disinterested
5 continuous/continually.

TEST YOURSELF 13

Complete each sentence with the correct word.

defer/differ

1 I shall have to .... that decision until I receive last month's sales
figures.

2   We shall have to agree to ....

eminent/imminent

3   The .... politician was invited to make the opening speech at the conference.
4   Rain looks ....

impressionable/impressive

5   It is surprising that at his age he is so ....
6   One cannot help but find the Taj Mahal ....

lose/loose

7   The tape around that parcel looks rather ....
8   Be careful that you do not .... the contents.

tolerant/tolerable

9   At school it is not always the .... teacher who gets the best results.
10 The headache became .... after she had taken an aspirin.

Key to 'Tools of the Trade'

Test yourself 1
1   I should be delighted to see you on 25 May.
2   Owing to an unavoidable delay, they were late for the meeting.
3   Miss Lyons, my administrator, whom you met yesterday, will take you round the showrooms.
4   I apologise for his not contacting you at the time you expected.
5   I think it is wise for you and me to meet next week.
6   Do you wish the colour scheme to be different from the one illustrated in the brochure?
7   The profits must be divided among the three departments.
8   Every one of the articles is of top quality.
9   I look forward to hearing from you.
10 Please remember to check carefully the draft *or* Please remember to check the draft carefully.

Test yourself 2
1   Thank you for your order.
2   I apologise for the delay in replying.
3   We have the goods in stock and shall send them to you by the end of next week.

Test yourself 3
1   was
2   was
3   are

Test yourself 4

1 The Managing Director decided to call a meeting immediately.
2 He promised to deal with the matter urgently.
3 We advise all our clients to consider carefully these new developments.

Test yourself 5

1 She is a client with whom I have always had difficulty.
2 I can find no-one to whom I can apply for information.
3 For what reason do you want this information? *or* Why do you want this information?

Test yourself 6

1 Only I want a cup of coffee (no-one else wants one).
2 I want only a cup of coffee (i.e. not a pot).
3 I want a cup of coffee only (i.e. not a cup of tea).

Test yourself 7

1 Neither of my colleagues was there.
2 You and I must fly to New York.
3 The foreman failed to read the instructions fully.
4 She is the supervisor whom the office juniors dislike.
5 I was surprised at their leaving so early.
6 Fewer than a dozen requests have been received.
7 This is a meeting to which he must come.
8 I should be pleased if you would provide the information I require by Friday. (*or* shall/will)
9 Whose errors are these?

Test yourself 8

1 The Chairman, who had a particular interest in the issue, agreed to raise it at the shareholders' meeting in a week's time.
2 At the meeting he observed, 'I am pleased that the company's profits last year were so high.'
3 He appreciated one shareholder's concern at the increase in the cost of goods, labour and transport.
4 'What more could I have done to solve the problem?' he asked.
5 The new product, 'Fastflow', had proved cheap to produce, simple to package and easy to sell.
6 It should improve the organisation's financial position in a few years' time.

Test yourself 9

1 After initials, e.g. Dr. L. Robinson, P. L. Harmsworth & Co. Ltd. (but *not* if open punctuation is used).
2 Between hours and minutes with the 12-hour clock, e.g. 10.30 am, 1.30 pm. With the 24-hour clock punctuation should never be used, e.g. 1030 hours or 1330 hours.

Test yourself 10

Under a new law and order initiative, young offenders will be sent to an adult prison for 24 hours. The shock treatment, never before tried in the UK, is an attempt to halt the increase in the crime figures among young people. Ministers, worried that offenders still regard probation and community service as a 'soft option', hope that the 'short, sharp shock' of spending time in a prison cell will have a deterrent effect. 'Giving them a taste of prison life, locking them up in a cell, making them experience the smells, the noise and the "slopping out", should have a dramatic effect,' one official said. 'They are not likely to want to return.' Prison reform groups have protested that it is a very short-sighted approach. They say that if the scheme is put into effect there would be a significant increase in the number of prison suicides in a year's time.

Test yourself 11

1	Absence	9	Maintenance
2	Acquainted	10	Occasionally
3	Advertisement	11	Occurrence
4	Committee	12	Privilege
5	Correspondence	13	Recommend
6	Conscientious	14	Separately
7	Disappointed	15	Undoubtedly
8	Instalments		

Test yourself 12

aggravated	welfare
adolescents	psychologically
embarrassed	persuaded
concerted	personnel
liaison	their

Test yourself 13

1	defer	6	impressive
2	differ	7	loose
3	eminent	8	lose
4	imminent	9	tolerant
5	impressionable	10	tolerable

Managing communications

How many times do I have to tell you? If you'd just listen for a minute you'd be able to see what I mean . . .

Communications are a vital part of all our relationships, yet they are also the cause of the majority of misunderstandings. Written communications in business are dealt with fully in Unit 7. This section deals in particular not only with verbal communications but with the difference between what we mean to say and what we are perceived as saying by our 'receiver'.

RULE 1

All communications involve at least two parties – the sender and the receiver. Only when your receiver receives the identical impression in his/her mind to the one in yours have you been successful in transmitting your communication.

If you think about it, it is amazing how many times we misinterpret communications we receive from very good friends and colleagues – or even our own family. And yet these are the people we know best! Misinterpretations can occur because of:

- the situation and the timing – people are too busy, too harassed or too stressed to listen to what we are really saying
- the mood we are in – we vent our feelings most on those we know best (who we know will forgive us later!)
- the words, phrases and gestures we choose – which are often ambiguous or inappropriate under the circumstances
- the tone we use – which may give a totally different impression from the one we meant to convey
- the fact we expect people to be semi–psychic and know what we really mean and how we really feel.

Transactional analysis

Transactional analysis (TA) is a technique you can use to analyse the way in which you speak to people (and the way in which they speak to you!). It has many applications – e.g. learning how to speak to a client when you are in a difficult situation, knowing how to address your boss to give the real impression you want to convey, and realising how you often speak to people and create problems by mistake!

RULE 2

Resist the temptation to speak on impulse about anything which may be in the least contentious. Putting your brain into gear before engaging your voice is a sensible lesson to learn! If the outcome could be really serious, sleep on it before taking any action.

Transactional analysis was developed by a man called Eric Berne[1] who considered that we all act and speak on three levels:

- as a child
- as a parent
- as an adult.

Within each of those main sections there are subsections which characterise our behaviour and our communications (both verbal and non-verbal). The table on the next page shows the sub-personalities Berne analysed.

The child

According to Berne, although we all start off as a Free Child, we progress to become the Adapted Child (to gain approval) and its opposite (when thwarted) – the Rebellious Child. Child-like behaviour is always characterised by being rather 'over the top' – either by being rather too goody-goody or by being silly to gain attention. At work, the Adapted Child is the 'yes-man' employee or the one who behaves in a deliberately avant garde manner to gain attention.

The parent

Many older people may react with you in Parent mode. On one hand they are seen to be helpful, giving you advice which they feel you should take to heart – and this is genuine and well-meant. However, should you choose to disregard this then the Critical Parent may surface; you will be told that it is all your own fault that things turned out the way they did, if only you had listened to them . . .

The adult

The Adult mode is not subdivided in every book on TA and can be examined in one category. Basically the adult is objective and analyses facts unemotionally before making a decision. The benefit of highlighting the Primitive Adult, however, is considerable. This is the behaviour which is characterised by an 'inner voice' which tells us – often – that 'something is wrong'. Some people never seem to hear (or heed) that inner voice. Others are so acutely aware of it that they feel powerless to act in many situations.

[1]Berne E (1963) *The structure and dynamics of organisations and groups*, Grove Press, New York.

Sub-personalities

MODE	SECTOR	CHARACTERISTICS
Adult	Rational	Making a decision, collecting information, assertive
	Primitive	Intuitive – sensitive to 'vibes' and sixth sense
Parent	Critical	Judging people, critical, domineering, paternalistic
	Nurturing	Protective, helpful, giver of advice (for your own benefit!)
Child	Free	Emotional, playful, curious, wanting own way, excitable
	Adapted	Wanting to please, clinging or attention seeking
	Rebellious	Devious, jealous, stores up 'slights' to get revenge later on.

How can TA help you?

Knowing about TA can help you analyse your own reactions to a situation (and other people's reactions to you). This is not to say you can alter other people's behaviour – you can't. That is conditioned by many factors, including their previous experiences of dealing with you. What TA can do is enable you to select, perhaps, the correct mode of communication for a particular person or situation – or at least help you to analyse where you went wrong in an encounter.

As an example, try the following.

TEST YOURSELF

Your boss returns from a meeting where everything has gone wrong. His proposal for a new computer system, on which he has been working solidly for the last two weeks, was rejected. His staff were criticised by two members of the committee for not passing on urgent information when it was needed. The MD informed everyone that budgets will be reduced – and targets increased – next year. Your boss comes into your office in a foul mood. Which statement are you most likely to greet him with?

a   Oh, dear, never mind – put your feet up and have a rest while I make you a nice cup of coffee. Then you can talk about it if you want.

b   I told you those proposals would never get through, not with the mood the Board are in at the moment.

c   Never mind – when you're on holiday in Hawaii next year none of this will matter.

d   Let's talk about it. I'm sure things can't be as bad as they seem.

e   I'm not staying here if you're going to be like this – I'm going home.

f   What can I do to help? Make a drink? Tidy up? What would you like me to do? Just say the word.

g   Say nothing immediately. Make a cup of coffee, give it to him and perhaps add 'Do you want to talk about it?'

Try to identify, for each of the statements above, the 'mode' the speaker is in. Discuss as a group the likely reaction you will get to each comment before you read on.

Crossed transactions

One of the reasons that we don't appear to 'see eye to eye' with people is that we often have a crossed transaction. That is, your 'modes' are non-complementary. If your boss wanted to be pampered after his meeting he would have appreciated reaction (a) as then you would be acting as Nurturing Parent to his Child. If he regularly likes to act as a Parent to your Child then he would have preferred reactions (c) or (f) (the Free Child or the Adapted Child). It is doubtful whether he would have appreciated reaction (b) (the Critical parent) or (e) (the Rebellious Child) – as neither mode is what most executives require from their administrative staff!

Adult modes really require and adult response. Statement (d) is the Rational Adult, whereas (g) is the Primitive Adult – more sensitive to mood swings. Your boss would only appreciate these if he felt like being rational himself – but with option (g) you give him the choice whether to discuss the matter or not. However, if he was not being rational he might perceive either of these responses as critical!

RULE 3

There is no straightforward answer to 'how to react'. This will depend on the circumstances, the person and your past relationship. It is far better to judge each situation on its own merits.

Ambiguous messages

You should be aware that you give away the 'mode' you are in not only by your verbal communications but also by your non-verbal signals!

As an example, imagine your boss sends for you about a problem which has occurred involving you and your staff. Although he sounds as if he believes your side of the story he is tapping his foot, stroking the side of his face and slightly grimacing. He is also leaning away from you as opposed to towards you. The signals he is giving are those of disbelief – and therefore you would return to your own office feeling uneasy.

What has happened is that he has reacted to you on the surface as an Adult, but subconsciously his gestures reveal a Parent to Child transaction. If you have only responded as an Adult (i.e. given him the facts of the situation) you have not reacted to the underlying transaction. Had you suddenly reverted to the Child mode yourself – or reacted to him on this level – you may have done better ('Oh, dear, what do you think we can do about it?' or 'I need your help to be able to cope with problems like this.').

RULE 4
Give out consistent messages yourself! Don't say one thing and let your non-verbal gestures tell a different story – you will only confuse, annoy or upset your listener.

Assertiveness

One of the 'buzz' words these days is assertiveness. This is the ability to say what you honestly feel without upsetting anyone around you – which is far from easy! Not only do your message and your non-verbal gestures have to be coordinated, but you will also need to choose your moment with care. Acting assertively is acting in Rational Adult mode – and will not go down well if your boss is in Parent or Child mode!

If something upsets or worries you then you have two basic options:

● do nothing – and hope it will go away
● say something.

If you choose the latter then you have to decide what to say. Let us assume a tricky situation.

Your boss is, by nature, disorganised and frequently asks you to stay on in the evening to help him get straight. Sometimes, after half an hour, he decides it's all a waste of time and abandons the effort anyway. On other occasions the odd fax or telex message does get sent after hours. You are fed up with this. Night after night he asks you to wait – sometimes for up to an hour – and yet criticises you if you are two minutes later than him in the morning. You feel it is unfair. Last week you decided to put an end to the matter and made a variety of excuses as to why you couldn't stop late. He sulked all week and is now muttering about finding a new administrator who is more committed to the job. What are you going to do?

Remember, this situation won't go away if you don't say anything. When your pool of excuses runs dry you are in a mess – and the requests to stay late will resume. You therefore need to talk to him.

TEST YOURSELF

From what you now know about TA, can you identify which 'mode' you are in if you start the conversation with each of the following statements?

1 I have a problem I'd like to talk to you about. Can you spare me a few minutes some time today?
2 I can't carry on like this any longer. Do you realise what an awful position you're putting me in? I'm not doing it any more.
3 You know I always like to help you when I can. I'm finding it difficult to cope with working late every night – but if you really want me to do so I can make suitable arrangements.
4 I'm fed up with staying late every night – and you making me feel guilty if I don't. If you were better organised this wouldn't happen.
5 Work, work, work – it's all you think about! I like to escape from this place and live it up after hours!

TA and assertiveness

Let us analyse the responses given above. There are three 'child' responses. Number 2 (the Rebellious Child – the ending 'so there' fits well after the statement given!), number 3 (the Adapted Child – will do anything to please), and number 5 (the Free Child – escapism is all!).

All these responses are likely to result in a (Critical) Parent reaction from your boss. You can imagine the kind of statements which could ensue!

The only way in which a 'child-like' opening could help is if he often operates in a 'Nurturing' Parent mode. Then you could open the conversation with: 'Please can you help me – I've a dreadful problem I really can't solve on my own.'

Response number 4 is putting yourself in Critical Parent mode! Unless he is prepared to act like a guilty little boy it is doubtful that this would succeed.

There is also another key problem with responses 2 and 4. Both put the onus on him as the guilty party (read them again!) – but he hasn't got the problem, you have. Only response number one shows you owning your own problem and approaching him as a Rational Adult. This should trigger a Rational Adult reaction – and in this mode he is more likely to see that his behaviour is unreasonable.

> **RULE 5**
> Own your own problems! Assertive statements contain the word 'I', rather than the word 'you' (which signifies aggression).

There is a very fine line between assertiveness and aggression. Aggressive statements are responses 2 and 4 where you have shifted the onus onto your boss – and attacked him for causing your problem! People who are attacked go into defence mode – or attack back!

The basis of assertiveness, therefore, is to be able to stand up for yourself by reacting as a rational adult, and staying in this mode despite the provocation to change. The urge to change – and revert back to Child mode – is very strong and often pre-conditioned from our childhood. As an example, think of the following situations.

● You order a meal in a restaurant which, when it arrives, is inedible. You pluck up the courage to complain. The waiter replies 'Oh, no, sir – you must be mistaken – our chef is one of the best in this area.'

● A friend asks if she can borrow your favourite dress one evening. You really don't want to lend it to her. She counters with 'Oh, please, you can't let me down now.'

● Your boss criticises the lack of detail in an investigation you carried out for him. You explain that this was because she asked for it in a hurry and you were very busy with other things at the time. She replies with 'Well, to top it all, there were two typing errors in it as well.'

In each one of the above cases you have initially tried to be assertive, and stated your case clearly and unemotionally. Each time the person you are talking to has countered your reply. How will you cope?

The temptation is to resort to child-like behaviour – i.e. either give in or become aggressive and lose your temper. Neither is suitable and in both cases you are likely to lose. What you must do is to press your case by sticking to Rational Adult behaviour.

TEST YOURSELF

1 Discuss as a group how you could reply in each of the scenarios given above so that you remain assertive.
2 Each person in the group should write down a similar scenario where it is difficult to be – or to remain – assertive. The group as a whole should discuss and decide the best reaction in each case.

RULE 6
Assertiveness takes patience, practice and courage! It also requires the ability to stand up for yourself and yet, at the same time, be sensitive to the reactions of others.

The benefits from being assertive are tremendous and will help you in many situations both at work and in your private life. If you are interested in the topic, then you are strongly recommended to read about it in greater depth.

Develop, implement and maintain procedures

Element 8.1

Develop procedures to meet specified needs

Before you start to study this unit it is useful to review what is meant by a procedure – and what is not meant. Only when you have some idea of the standard types of procedure in operation and their scope and limitations can you start designing procedures on your own.

We all follow a variety of procedures every day. Sometimes we are aware that we are conforming to a standard set of instructions or a method of doing something – but only occasionally do we realise that we are following a certain procedure.

You follow a procedure when you get up in the morning – although no-one has told you what to do – and the methods used by people to get themselves up, ready and out of the house in time on an average working day are many and various! You follow a procedure when you make a piece of toast. This time the procedure is rather more standardised, basically because there are few possible variations if you aim to achieve the desired result. You also follow a set of very specific procedures if you drive to work in the morning – coping with traffic lights, pelican crossings, roundabouts, turning right and even driving on the left-hand side of the road. If you fail to observe the prescribed procedures for driving in Britain – as specified in the Highway Code – you are likely to find yourself on the wrong side of the law very quickly indeed!

The benefits of having specific procedures should be fairly obvious. Imagine the chaos and the accidents which would occur on the roads if everyone could do his or her 'own thing'! Specifying what must be done, by whom and when means that you have some degree of control to ensure that:

- everyone does the same thing
- certain standards are achieved
- 'quality' is therefore higher.

When you learn to drive, as you know, you will have to pass a test to prove that you know and can follow the procedures which have been formulated. In business there are similar 'tests' of competence in operating equipment – even the fire drill can be viewed as a means of checking that everyone knows and can follow the correct procedures.

The benefits to the organisation of clear, accurate and specified procedures are those stated above. Indeed, if your company has achieved BS 5750 or ISO 9000 – or is working towards the latter award – you will find that a large number of procedures in your organisation are already clearly documented to ensure standardisation and high quality of service provision.

Types and applications of procedures

Procedures can be simple or complex; informal or formal; suggested, recommended or prescribed (Figure 8.1.1). On the other hand, of course, there may be no procedure at all for a certain operation, in which case you would be starting from scratch. Alternatively, although no procedure at all may be laid down, you may find that everyone follows one – simply from habit.

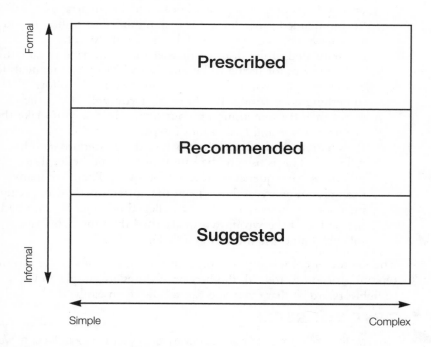

Figure 8.1.1 Types of procedure

As you can see from the figure, the more formal the procedure the more likely it is to be prescribed or compulsory. The different **types** or levels of procedures can be categorised into:

- **No procedure at all** In this case each person does his or her own thing – and there are no penalties for non-conformance.
- **Suggested procedures** This usually means that there are

several equally effective ways of doing something – which you choose is up to you, although you may take advice from others who have more experience. As an example, you may decide to read this book from start to finish, in the given order of the units. However, if you want to concentrate on specific units first then you may dip into the book in a different way – though you may ask your tutor's advice before doing this. Again there are no penalties for doing things differently and people usually follow the method which suits them best.

- **Recommended procedures** In this case there is often an example of a procedure to follow. This is usually a tried and tested procedure and it is usually safer, quicker and easier to follow this. Although you are unlikely to be penalised if you do not follow this procedure, people are likely to have little patience with you if you decide not to and something goes wrong. For instance, a recipe book contains an array of 'recommended procedures' for making different dishes. If you try an experiment and are successful you are likely to be congratulated; if the dish is a disaster then you have to take the consequences for trying to be innovative! Most user manuals for equipment give you recommended procedures to follow if something goes wrong. It is likely that you will follow these rather than try something on your own – in case you make the problem worse and have a lot of explaining to do!

- **Prescribed procedures** In this case the procedure *must* be followed. This is usually the case if there could be legal or disastrous consequences if it is *not* followed. There are many examples in everyday life – from the correct method of giving an injection to the way in which an alleged offender is cautioned by the police. If the wrong words are used then the defendant's solicitor could use this fact as a defence.

The degree of complexity of a procedure is not usually related to the type of procedure. Indeed, the best procedures are simple and straightforward so that everyone can follow them easily.

TEST YOURSELF

Can you think of a procedure you follow either in your personal life or at work which is an example of:

a a suggested procedure
b a recommended procedure
c a prescribed procedure?

What would be the possible consequences of non-compliance in the case of your answer to (c)?

Scope and limit of own authority in developing procedures

The key role of the administrator can be seen as setting up and maintaining procedures. In fact, you can think of this unit as bringing together all the knowledge you have already gained as part of your NVQ3 award. The type of procedures you have the authority to develop yourself will depend upon your job role and status in the organisation. Remember that without authority you will be wasting everyone's time (including your own) trying to design a new procedure and will have no right to insist that people follow it! Rather than adding to your status, you are more likely to lose face if you have to back down and continue to let people go their own way – or return to the previous procedure instead.

The need for a procedure is usually identified if you spot that the company as a whole, and those doing certain jobs in particular, would benefit if there was a standard way of doing something. At this stage you need to check if there is a procedure already in force which specifies what must be done. If there is not, or if it is out-of-date or ignored by the majority of staff, then you have a case for suggesting that a new procedure be designed and developed.

Normally you will have the authority to develop procedures which relate to your own area of work or those of your staff. As a brief guide, your own authority is likely to be limited when:

- your procedure would affect other people as well, e.g. those senior to yourself, those in other departments or contacts outside the company
- there would be legal or financial implications if it is introduced
- you are asking staff outside your own area of control to do something
- you are overriding the instructions of someone else – especially someone senior to yourself
- a procedure is already prescribed or recommended.

Whenever you are in doubt it is always safer to check with your line manager first. The setting up of procedures might be necessary in many different areas of your job. The following situations all make use of a formalised way of working:

- researching and supplying information
- drafting, preparing and delivering reports
- initiating and responding to correspondence
- planning and agreeing work tasks.

Your job as an administrator is to improve the way work is carried out, wherever possible. New procedures may be designed to:

- make jobs easier for staff

- make work more cost-effective for your organisation
- deliver a better service to customers and clients.

There is no point in introducing a new procedure if it does not bring at least one of these benefits – changes in procedures should not be introduced for their own sake.

The planning and setting up of new procedures will often involve you in staff training and in the evaluation of health and safety implications.

Ways of informing and consulting others about procedures

Once you have decided to introduce a procedure, your first step should be to consider the needs of those people who will have to follow it – i.e. the **users**. In addition, you need to think about anyone else who may be affected – and this may include your boss, other departments and even another organisation. You then have a choice to make – you can either go ahead and **inform** people of what you have done or you can **consult** them first.

The consultative approach is often recommended because:

- generally, several heads are better than one when it comes to new ideas or suggestions
- people have a different range of knowledge and experiences and it is useful to draw on this expertise as much as you can
- users are far more inclined to follow a procedure if they have been consulted beforehand and feel they have contributed to it being drawn up – they too will feel ownership of the procedure
- people may give you insight into the consequences of a particular course of action which you did not know about
- people who are involved in something every day have first-hand knowledge of what should be done. They resent someone else telling them how to do the job – particularly if that person has never had to do it himself or herself!
- your boss may feel somewhat aggrieved if you formulate plans for new procedures without involving him or her in the consultation stage. You may also find that less support for your ideas is forthcoming, though this will depend largely upon the type of boss for whom you work – some may want as little involvement as possible!
- staff in other departments or people you liaise with in other organisations may have useful contributions to make and are likely to see things from a different perspective.

However, there are also problems and dangers with consultation:

- some people do not like to be seen as 'knowing nothing' or to be known as 'non-contributors'. They may therefore make suggestions which are unhelpful, naive or even negative

- consultation is time-consuming – especially if you want to give everyone involved an equal say in the matter
- you may end up with a dozen conflicting suggestions
- people get annoyed when their own suggestion is discarded – and may be waiting to sabotage the new procedure which contains other people's ideas.

Do remember that there are occasions when it is more suitable to tell someone than to ask him or her! You wouldn't, for instance, ask for opinions on whether to use the lift in an emergency evacuation. If you know anything about the Health and Safety at Work Act you would know that this would go against standard procedures and would be positively dangerous. In this case, you can insist that the correct procedure is followed and there is no room for negotiation. Therefore, in all the following cases, it is usually more suitable to **inform** people than to consult them:

- when you are following specialist advice and no-one else has as much expertise on the matter
- when legal requirements are laid down
- when too many people would be involved to make consultation meaningful or appropriate
- when a procedure is imposed from above, i.e. from higher authority or an external organisation (e.g. the government)
- when there is nothing anyone can do about it! For example, if your department had to move offices because the building has just been condemned there is little point in consulting staff for their opinions!
- when the procedure is fairly routine and basic and the timescale extremely short.

You may find that the section on Managing Change, which follows this unit, is helpful for giving you guidelines in relation to the type of issues where staff will feel aggrieved if they have not been consulted and those which they will be less bothered about.

DID YOU KNOW?

There is nothing worse than 'meaningless' consultation. In other words, asking people for their opinion when it is either:

a already too late
b not wanted.

No matter how you try to justify your actions few people will be fooled and will be much less willing to help you next time.

Golden rules about informing people
- If necessary, make it clear why they are being informed and not consulted.
- Set out the information clearly and unambiguously – preferably in writing.

- Make it clear whether the procedure is suggested, recommended or prescribed.
- Make it clear what the consequences are if people do not follow the procedure.
- Be prepared to answer questions.

Golden rules about consulting people

- Make it clear that this is 'true' consultation and suggestions are genuinely welcomed.
- Decide who you are going to consult – if possible, limit the number of people to those who
  - have some expertise in the matter
  - will have to follow the new procedure
  - will be affected by its implementation.
- Have a broad plan in your own mind before consultation, but do not have a fixed view that cannot be changed.
- Fix a time limit to the consultation process.
- Try to get difficult individuals to work towards the 'common good' rather than their own self-aggrandisement.
- Try to include some (or at least one) of the suggestions in your specification.
- Be prepared to justify your choice – and give reasons for the rejection of other suggestions. Usually this is possible by weighing up the possible outcomes from different courses of action.
- If you are still undecided, implement the draft procedure for a 'trial period' and then obtain feedback on its success (see Element 8.2).

 DID YOU KNOW?

Consultation does not have to be with several people! You may decide simply to call upon the expertise of a particular person in a particular area. In addition, if you are the only expert in a particular area it may be far more appropriate for you to design the procedure yourself and tell other people what you have decided.

Sources of specialist advice relating to procedures

Before you even think of designing a procedure you need to obtain a range of information to make sure that the steps in your procedure are sensible, lawful and do not conflict with other procedures in operation within the organisation. Staff are hardly going to thank you if you tell them to do one thing whilst another procedure instructs them to do exactly the opposite!

Even different instructions can cause problems. A procedure for dealing with customer enquiries in Sales which states that a response must be made to all letters within three days should not conflict with a procedure for customers in another section, e.g. with one in Finance which says that interdepartmental queries in relation to invoices should be dealt with in seven days. If this was the case then a member of the Sales staff would be unable to obtain information quickly enough from Finance to be able to comply with the customer care procedure in force in the Sales section.

In cases like this it is sensible for the company to have a standard procedure which affects all departments and which has been drawn up by senior managers or directors at Board level.

Therefore you need to be aware of existing policies and procedures and the views and specialist knowledge of other people. You can obtain specialist advice both from within the organisation and from sources external to the organisation. Much will depend upon the procedure you are trying to design.

Internal sources

If you work for a large organisation the range of expertise is likely to be greater than in a small firm. For instance, you may have a Computer Services Manager, a Health and Safety Officer and a Personnel or Human Resources Manager – all of whom would give you valuable information in relation to their specialist areas. If you work for a small firm then you may have to go outside for assistance – particularly if you are involved with a procedure which may have legal consequences (unless, of course, you work for a solicitor!). Basically your internal sources are likely to relate to people – although you should also remember (from Unit 5) that there are additional sources of information:

● manuals and reference books
● company files
● literature from suppliers
● copies of past procedures which have been followed
● copies of existing procedures in force in other departments or for other areas.

We have already discussed consultation with other people. Do bear in mind that existing users of similar procedures or potential users of your proposed procedure may also be a useful source of specialist information and advice.

External sources

Sources external to the organisation are many and varied – depending upon the type of procedure you wish to implement. Computer software or hardware companies, the Health and Safety Executive and a solicitor specialising in employment law may be your choice if you are involved in suggesting procedures for computers, health and safety or human resources procedures and you have no internal specialists. Again, bear in mind that people may not be the only sources of specialist advice. You can also obtain advice from booklets, leaflets and your local library by researching the wealth of material on their shelves. CD-ROMs, too, may be a useful source of more up-to-date or current information.

It is possible that you will benefit by obtaining specialist advice from inside the organisation and supplementing this with additional information from outside the organisation. This gives you a wider view. For instance, you may ask your line manager for his or her suggestions for reorganising the filing system and setting up a procedure for issuing absent files, but gain a wider insight if you visit two or three organisations and see how they cope with similar problems. If you can lay your hands on a copy of their official procedure so much the better – provided you remember to 'customise' it for your own use.

TEST YOURSELF

Discuss with your tutor or adviser the sources of specialist advice you would contact before considering designing procedures covering each of the following areas. Then compare your answers with the rest of your group.

- A procedure for the issue and return of personal protective clothing.
- A procedure for clocking-in and out by all staff.
- A procedure for the issuing of rail warrants to staff.
- A procedure for rectifying a paper jam in the new photocopier.
- A procedure for collecting and storing used toner cartridges from your organisation's computer printers and sending them away for refilling.
- A procedure for dealing with bomb threats received by the switchboard.

Ways of designing, specifying and developing procedures

At this stage, probably the first thing you should establish is whether, within your own organisation, there is a procedure for designing procedures! As an example, see the instructions in Figure 8.1.2 for designing quality procedures in one organisation.

Normally a new procedure would go through a variety of stages before it is finally approved – as shown in Figure 8.1.3.

The design stage

The design stage of a new procedure can take anything from several hours to several months – depending upon the complexity of the procedure, the specialist advice you have to obtain and the amount of consultation involved. From the outset you must think carefully about several issues:

INSTRUCTIONS FOR DESIGNING QUALITY PROCEDURES

1 All procedures should be clearly documented.
2 Procedures must contain sufficient detail for all users to clearly follow the procedure.
3 Procedures must specify
   - what has to be done
   - by whom it must be done
   - how it will be done
   - where it will be done
   - when it will be done.
4 A procedure must be written by a member of staff responsible for the activity.
5 Each procedure must be numbered.
6 All procedures must follow the standard company format:
   - the first section must state the objective(s) of the procedure
   - the second section must identify the departments and personnel to whom the procedure applies
   - the third section must list other procedures which are linked to this procedure
   - the fourth section must clarify any terms which would not be immediately known by users
   - the fifth section should give details of the procedure itself.
7 All procedures must have a front sheet which identifies
   - the procedure involved
   - the originator of the procedure
   - the approver of the document
   - the date of implementation.
8 A copy of the procedure should be held by the departments and users concerned.
9 A full set of company quality procedures will be held by the head of quality assurance.

Figure 8.1.2 Designing quality procedures

STAGES IN DRAWING UP A PROCEDURE

The design stage
↓
The draft specification stage
↓
The developmental stage
↓
The implementation stage

Figure 8.1.3 Stages in drawing up a procedure

- What is the procedure designed to achieve, i.e. what are its objectives?
- How can its effectiveness be measured?
- What other effects might its implementation have – both good and bad?
- Who will be the users?
- What laid-down procedures must you follow in drawing it up?
- Will the procedure be suggested, recommended or prescribed?
- What format would be the most appropriate for users?
- Over what timescale should it be introduced?

Costs and benefits are covered on page 530 and timescales in Element 8.2. This section looks, in particular, at objectives, side-effects and formats for drawing up draft procedures.

Objectives and side-effects

The objectives of your procedure may be quantitative, qualitative or both. A procedure, for instance, for delivering mail quickly in the morning may have two objectives:

- to ensure that recipients receive their mail within 20 minutes of arriving at their desks
- to ensure that urgent mail is dealt with more promptly.

The first objective is quantitative – a time period is specified and success in achieving this objective can be measured easily. The second objective is qualitative and implies a change in behaviour by the recipients of the mail – something which may be outside your control.

In addition, your new procedure may have side-effects. For instance, it may mean that if the mail is delivered late by the post office it is impossible to sort the mail quickly in time to meet the objectives. If the post office deliver special items later in the morning it may mean these are missing from the first delivery. You may decide that mail room staff have to start earlier each day, which would have financial implications.

You can cope with all these side-effects if you have identified them beforehand. What you do not want to do is to draft out a procedure and then have other people point out all its flaws and possible other effects when you have not identified them!

 ## TEST YOURSELF

Bear in mind that a procedure may have multiple objectives and may also have side-effects you hadn't considered!

In the case of each procedure stated above (in the previous Test Yourself on page 522) state what, in your opinion,

a   should be the objective(s)
b   may be the possible side-effects.

Formats for procedures

There are several ways in which you can go about designing a procedure – much will depend upon the type of procedure you are trying to develop and its complexity.

You may find it helpful to bear in mind the following points.

1   It is usual for a procedure to be documented using a step-by-step approach, in the order that users should follow – rather like a checklist. If the procedure is simple then this can be designed simply by preparing a typed list which people keep for reference (Figure 8.1.4).

COMPANY PROCEDURE FOR GREETING VISITORS
(To be kept on reception at all times)

1   Greet visitor(s) courteously.
2   Find out if visitor has appointment and/or the person he/she is visiting.
3   Ask visitor to complete visitor book.
4   Notify member of staff by telephone of visitor's arrival.
5   Check all sections in visitor's log have been completed by visitor.
6   Tear off bottom section of visitor log (top copy only) and give to visitor. This is his/her official pass. Inform visitor that the pass must be handed in to reception upon departure.
7   Ask visitor to wait in reception until collected by member of staff.
8   Remind member of staff if visitor still in reception after 10 minutes.
9   When visitor leaves, collect pass.
10 At end of day check that number of passes handed in matches total number of visitors into building. Report any discrepancy to the office administrator.

Figure 8.1.4 A step-by-step procedure

2   If the procedure will have 'loop backs' at various points, or alternative actions to take, then it is more usual to summarise this in a flow chart. This helps people to see at a glance the alternative actions they can take. Figure 8.1.5 gives you an example which also summarises the actions you should have taken so far!

3   If the procedure relates to operating equipment then graphics and diagrams can help enormously. Look in any manual on how to operate a remote-controlled video, or open your photocopier doors and look at the pictures inside to see what is meant by this!

Start by dividing the proposed procedure into simple steps. Then decide if you can rely solely on text or if graphics are needed. Finally,

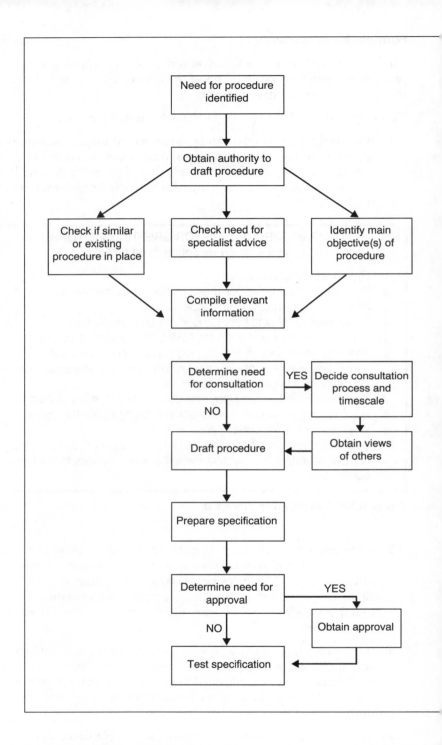

Figure 8.1.5 A flow chart for drafting, specifying and developing a procedure

think about whether you need 'loop backs' at any point and how to illustrate this.

Bear in mind that the instructions to staff need to be as simple and clear as possible. You can always attach explanatory notes for first-time users.

DID YOU KNOW?

If you are trying to draw a diagram for the first time, one method is to write all the stages on a piece of paper as they come into your head, draw boxes around them and then try to link them by drawing flow lines between them. You will probably have to redraft this several times before you have a working document where your lines link properly and in a logical order.

Some ordered minds try to start by thinking of the first stage and working this through; others start at the end and work backwards! The key point is not to miss out an essential stage in the procedure!

CHECK IT YOURSELF

It can be surprisingly difficult to draw a flow chart containing the sequence of events for even a simple procedure. Try it now by drawing one to show someone the recommended procedure for running a bath – from walking into the bathroom to stepping into a bath which neither scalds nor freezes! And don't forget your need for certain essentials to be close to hand once you have actually got into the bath! Compare your attempts with the other members of your group.

The specification stage

Whereas the design stage is the 'broad brush' stage, the specification stage puts in the details. In other words, it specifies what will be done, by whom and when, where and how. If all the stages in a procedure will be carried out by one person in one place then your job is much easier. If several people are involved then the task becomes more difficult. You also have to allow sufficient time for each person to carry out his or her part of the process properly and to bear in mind that some people may operate as bottlenecks for others at some stages in the procedure.

A specification can be set out as a checklist with several columns alongside – as in Figure 8.1.6, which shows a specification for a procedure for dealing with interview candidates.

The development stage

Once the procedure is specified it is sensible to obtain feedback from other people that it does, indeed, contain all the elements it is supposed to contain and would appear to be workable. This is the

Action	By whom	Location	Time
Greet candidates and direct to waiting room	Receptionist	Reception	Upon arrival
Notify administrator of number of arrivals	Receptionist	Administrator's office	At nominated time for start of interviews
Greet candidates and give brief introduction to company and interview procedure	Interviewer	Waiting room	As above
Escort first interviewee to interview area	Interviewer	Interview area	At appointed times
Candidates to be taken on tour of building	Admin staff	Waiting room	At pre-arranged times
Candidates to be served coffee	Canteen staff	Waiting room	At pre-arranged times
Candidates to be notified individually of result	Interviewer	Own office	At end of session

Figure 8.1.6 Specification for a procedure for dealing with interview candidates

secondary consultation stage when you perhaps go back to potential users or your specialist advisers and ask for their comments.

Be prepared to redraft your specifications to take account of their comments. Then it is useful to test it in practice to see if it works. At this stage you are checking to find out if:

a   people understand your instructions
b   the procedure works
c   the procedure achieves its desired objective(s)
d   there are no unexpected or problematic side-effects or consequences.

Test the procedure yourself *and* on other people. You are always more likely to understand your own instructions than anyone else! Ask people for honest, objective feedback. You might design a questionnaire so that you can analyse the responses more easily.

Do not forget to check the degree to which your procedure met its objective(s). Some procedures to be designed may need to meet 100 per cent of their objectives 100 per cent of the time. This would be the case in a fire drill. However, in other cases such a condition could not be achieved. For instance, you are unlikely to develop any procedure for dealing with customer enquiries which would result in zero complaints all the time!

Always be prepared to adjust your procedure in the light of any feedback you receive. If several adjustments have been required then test your redrafted specifications again. If you are new to designing procedures then you may need to make several adjustments before it is 'tight' enough to put into operation. Do remember, you will never make a fool of yourself by refining a procedure several times – but you *will* make yourself look silly if you try to implement a procedure which clearly doesn't work!

CHECK IT YOURSELF

1   Obtain five examples of procedures which give a range of different types of format, such as typed lists, flow charts or graphics. Compare your samples with those obtained by other members of your group.
2   Try to think of at least one occasion when you have changed your ideas about doing something because of information received from someone else. Also, if possible, think of an occasion when you have influenced an outcome yourself by your contribution at the design stage.

DID YOU KNOW?

People are more keen to follow a procedure if they can see the end result or the benefits of following it. They also find it easier to follow if any difficult steps are broken down into stages and illustrated clearly. Imagine trying to assemble a flat pack wardrobe or a do-it-yourself greenhouse without any illustrations!

Ways of obtaining approval for procedures

The procedure you have to follow to obtain approval will depend upon the size of your organisation and the degree of bureaucracy in operation! If you work for a small firm with only a handful of staff then the only approval you may need is your manager's agreement with your ideas. However, do be prepared to justify your specification – particularly if you have a 'hands-on' manager who likes to be very involved with what is going on. If you have a boss who has little or no interest so long as things work smoothly then you are likely to have fewer questions to answer.

If you work for a large organisation – and particularly if it is in the public sector, such as a hospital or local authority – then you may find that there are very formalised approval procedures which you have to go through. This may, for instance, mean the submission of your specification to a committee or, at least, to a senior member of staff for approval. There may be a time delay in this process which you have to take into consideration. You may also have to comply with requests for supplementary information regarding justification and methodology.

Do bear in mind that if you have formally received approval from the right person to draw up the procedure in the first place, then you have already paved the way for yourself. If, too, you have complied with all other requirements and done a thorough job of examining all the aspects – and have a good reputation in the organisation – the approval process will be much smoother.

DID YOU KNOW?

Organisations designing procedures to conform with ISO 9000 requirements normally draw up a front sheet which shows the name of the person who drafted the procedure and the name of the person who approves it (Figure 8.1.7). This is done to prevent unauthorised procedures being introduced and as a check to ensure that all procedures which are implemented have been rigorously checked beforehand.

Ways of formulating costs and benefits of procedures

Anyone giving approval or authorisation to a new or redesigned procedure will be very concerned with the possible costs and benefits of its implementation. Indeed, for a committee approval you may have to attach a paper giving a summary of the proposed costs and benefits.

J F BROWN PLC

OFFICIAL PROCEDURE TITLE: PURCHASING PROCEDURES NO: 234/A DATE: 24 February 199_

Designed by:	Approved by:	Implemented from:

Figure 8.1.7 Example of a front sheet used when designing a procedure

One way to do this is to undertake a cost/benefit analysis beforehand.

Identifying costs

The 'costs' of a proposal for a procedure are not just financial costs in relation to its implementation. You should remember that:

- a cost is always negative
- costs may be financial or social
- costs usually mean the increased use of materials, equipment, labour or capital
- a cost can usually be quantified.

It is easier to illustrate this point with a specific example. Let us assume that there have been several instances lately of people rushing out at night without logging off computers properly, turning off lights and closing windows. Your boss is worried about the safety and security implications of their actions and has asked you to devise a 'closing down' procedure which all staff *must* follow before leaving in the evening. What are the proposed costs of this procedure assuming that to follow the procedure properly will take all staff 10 minutes?

- Staff will either want payment for the additional 10 minutes or will want to stop their normal duties 10 minutes earlier, in which case slightly less work will be done each day.
- Staff trying to finish an urgent job may leave it until the following day to complete. If the job is important this could have serious consequences.
- Someone will need to have the responsibility for checking on their actions by going around the offices afterwards. This person will also require payment.

Now you need to consider these costs more carefully and, if possible, try to convert them to monetary terms.

- You may calculate that the cost of everyone being paid for an extra 10 minutes each day will amount to £600 per week given current wage rates. You may decide, however, that most staff are 'winding down' at the end of the day and the last 10 minutes is often spent chatting and tidying up. In this case your organisation would get better value for money by asking employees to stop work ten minutes earlier.
- If your office undertakes few important or urgent tasks you may decide to disregard the second point you thought of. However, if there are many such tasks you may decide that one person in each office should be responsible for ensuring the procedure is implemented but that person should not be the one most likely to be doing the most critical work.
- It is possible to cost out the additional wages which would have to be paid to a member of the security staff to do this check – or the fee which would be charged by a security firm. However, if the checks are carried out already, and staff following the procedures correctly would shorten this time, then you can reclassify this cost as a benefit instead (see below).

Identifying benefits

In the same way that you considered costs, you need to remember that:

- a benefit is always positive
- benefits may be either financial or social
- social benefits may be very difficult to quantify
- financial benefits usually imply the more effective use of materials, equipment, labour or capital.

In the example given above, what would be the benefits of the procedure being implemented?

- There would be less likelihood of a fire or similar emergency after hours.
- There would be less likelihood of a break-in as a result of the premises not being secured.

- Security checks would take less time.
- Equipment would last longer and need less servicing.

As you can see, it is harder to quantify some of these benefits in financial terms. A serious fire could cost the company millions of pounds in lost business and damage repair but an overheated machine may simply cost a few pounds to put right. The variations in the consequences of a burglary are equally broad.

The important thing is for you to have considered both aspects and to have rejected a procedure which will have horrendous costs and few benefits! To be worthwhile there should be a net gain to everyone involved, i.e. the benefits should clearly outweigh the costs.

TEST YOURSELF

Your office has no systematised procedures for stock control of stationery. This has resulted in many problems over the past few weeks. Your boss has asked you to institute a proper system which will mean keeping accurate stock records and following a standard procedure for ordering goods and checking them on delivery.

As a group, hold a brainstorming session to determine the costs and benefits of implementing this procedure both to the office staff and to users who require stationery supplies.

ACTIVITY SECTION

1   Draw up a simple procedure for new junior staff to ensure that they answer the telephone effectively and take sensible messages for staff. Design this in the form of a simple checklist which can be kept by all staff for reference.

2   Read the following case study and then answer the questions which follow.

A health centre owned a large piece of land adjacent to the centre upon which visitors to the centre would park their cars at random. This regularly resulted in some drivers being 'blocked in' by the inconsiderate parking of others and in several people failing to find places because the space was not used effectively.

In an effort to achieve some order out of chaos the practice manager at the centre arranged for the area to be resurfaced and for white lines to be painted to indicate where cars should park. Some people conformed with the markings and others did not. In addition there was no allowance made for disabled people parking their cars. The practice manager then arranged for 'DISABLED' signs to be painted in the three bays nearest the main door and for a clear notice to be erected saying 'PLEASE PARK IN MARKED BAYS ONLY'. This resulted in some improvement, but now local shoppers started to use the car park because it was free – it was well worth shoppers walking for an extra five minutes to save the cost of parking at the short-stay car park which was more centrally situated. Patients started to complain that there was no room to park when they visited the practice.

At a recent meeting the doctors and practice manager decided that the car park could be a useful, additional source of revenue for the health centre. They contacted a local company and arranged for a system of pay and display parking to be installed. Cars not showing a ticket would be clamped. The company they contacted warned them that ample signs must be erected giving instructions on how to use the machines and the consequences of not using them.

The health centre went ahead with this proposal and installed pay-and-display machines and charged 50p for 2 hours – the minimum length of parking time. The machines chosen did not give change as these would have been far more expensive to install. The health centre also agreed a contract for the clamping company to visit the car park, at random, at least 4 times a day to check unauthorised parking.

a Identify at which stage there was
   i   no procedure in operation
   ii a suggested procedure in operation
   iii a recommended procedure for car park users
   iv a prescribed procedure for car park users.
b i   Why do you think the company insisted that clear signs must be erected if a combination of pay-and-display and clamping was brought into operation?
   ii What do you think might be the legal consequences if the health centre disregard this advice?
c i   Imagine you are the practice manager. You are delighted to find that local shoppers now keep away but are disturbed by the number of complaints from patients receiving regular treatment at the centre about the cost of parking. Discuss as a group and with your tutor or adviser what could be done to solve this problem.
   ii Undertake a cost/benefit analysis to support your proposals.

3 You work as sales office administrator in a large reception area office with four staff. One member of staff processes sales enquiries on computer and keeps the customer database up-to-date, another deals with telephone calls and reception enquiries, and the third and fourth are mainly responsible for producing sales correspondence, contracts and reps reports on computer. Frequently the company wants to send out mail shots to customers to publicise new products and your boss is aware that by following certain procedures you can take advantage of Royal Mail savings for large batches of mail. In addition, he is also concerned that it is taking far too long for the mail shots to be despatched.

He plans to send out a printed leaflet to all customers next month and has asked you to devise a procedure whereby the mail shot can be ready for posting two days later. It is up to you to decide how to do this and which staff to use.

a   Decide what specialist advice or information you need to obtain before you draft the procedure and acquire this from the appropriate source(s).

b   Draw up a sheet which briefly gives the pros and cons of consulting the staff concerned or informing them once the procedure has been decided.

c   Draft a proposed procedure and draw up a specification which will show each person's responsibilities clearly.

d   Identify the costs and benefits of your proposal and state these clearly, together with a justification for your suggested procedure, for consideration by your manager before he approves your ideas.

Element 8.2
Implement and maintain procedures

There is very little point in spending a considerable amount of time carefully planning and drafting procedures, holding consultations with users, obtaining feedback on proposed specifications and gaining formal approval for a new procedure if you are not prepared to put the same amount of effort into implementing the procedure and monitoring it to check its effectiveness at regular intervals.

At least as much care and consideration must be given to the actual introduction and operation of the procedures as to their development. Your aim should always be to introduce a new procedure with the least amount of fuss and as few problems as possible. In this way staff will retain a positive approach and will be more willing to help you to iron out any minor teething problems – and to support you when you want to review the procedure or introduce yet another one!

Types and applications of procedures

You have already read much about the types of procedures and their applications in Element 8.1. However, the type of procedure you have designed, its degree of formality and complexity and its objectives will all affect the way in which you introduce it to staff.

● A **suggested procedure** is likely to be introduced in a fairly informal manner, perhaps only verbally. You may develop the theme of 'how to introduce it' in a general discussion with your staff.

● A **recommended procedure** will probably have gone through a more formal drafting and approval process. You will have to ensure that all users have accurate and clear guidance on how the procedure will work, their own contribution, and where to get help if it is needed.

- A **specified procedure** will definitely have gone through a formal drafting and approval process and all users will need comprehensive guidance which covers all aspects of its use. They may also need special training and support until the procedure is well established. This is particularly the case if the procedure is complex or very different from the existing routines undertaken by staff. Staff also need to be very clear about any penalties for non-compliance.

Ways of implementing procedures

A procedure can be implemented in stages over a period of time or very rapidly indeed. The shorter the timescale the greater the training and information needs of users beforehand. 'Practice runs' can also be useful to help people to get used to a new way of doing something and to answer queries.

As an example, when Britain converted to decimal currency in 1973 the changeover was publicised for weeks beforehand in newspapers, on television and on radio. Organisations held training sessions for staff – especially those concerned with cash handling. In a more recent example, think of the publicity which surrounded the change of telephone codes early in 1995 – and even then large numbers of users regularly heard the pre-recorded message telling them what to do as old habits refused to die for several months! Compare this with the lack of formal introduction of the metric system in Britain. Although the younger generations are now comfortable with the metric system the older generation is not – and there is a mixture of both systems to be seen everywhere. In Australia, by contrast, the changeover to metrication was far more formal – with regulations introduced forbidding garages and other organisations to quote the imperial system at all. This resulted in people having to get used to the new system far more quickly.

It is not usually a good idea, therefore, to run both the old and the new procedures in parallel for a while – although this is sometimes done with critical processes relating to key information. An example is a changeover from a manual payroll procedure to a computerised procedure. Wage earners are less interested in the company procedure for processing wages than they are in receiving an accurate pay packet at the end of the month! For that reason, as a safety precaution, both systems may be operated in tandem for a month or two. However, you should note that this is the exception, rather than the norm.

When you are deciding the best method of implementation and the timescale involved, make sure you do this in consultation with both the users of the new procedure and other people who may be involved – including your own line manager. Everyone affected should be consulted before you draw up your implementation plan.

This should clearly show the timescale by which you aim to achieve everything and the date on which the procedure will be fully operational.

Ways of supplying guidance to users

There are many ways in which you can supply guidance to users:

- through formal training sessions
- through guidelines set out in memos, leaflets and help sheets
- by issuing checklists
- by issuing policy documents and instruction sheets
- by demonstration
- by coaching
- by open discussion with small groups of staff.

Needless to say, you will have to draw up all the documentation to fit in with the requirements of your implementation plan. This means allowing time for anything which needs to be specially prepared – particularly if an outside printing firm is involved or staff training sessions have to be planned. If you are asking specialist advisers to contribution to these sessions then you will need to take their schedules into account as well.

CHECK IT YOURSELF

1 Try to think of one example when you have tried to follow a procedure but have been prevented from doing so – either because the instructions were unclear or they didn't seem to work. Compare your ideas with other members of your group.

2 Look at the procedure given in Figure 8.2.1 for setting up a gas appliance. How many criticisms can you make of this?

3 Obtain copies of any documentation with which you have been issued in the course of your job to help you to follow recommended or specified procedures in your workplace. Compare your examples with those of other members of your group.

Types of support systems related to procedures

A support system is a 'back-up' aid to users of a procedure. It should be put in place to help people to familiarise themselves with the new ways of working, clarify any queries and assist those who are having difficulties in any way. The British Telecom recorded message played to everyone who kept forgetting to insert a '1' in the dialling code was a type of support system – and was more helpful to people who forgot than an 'open' line would have been.

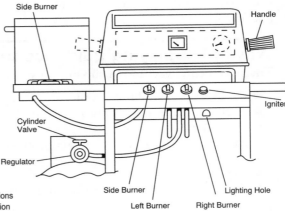

1 The appliance must be fully assembled as per the detailed assembly instructions.

2 Make sure your gas cylinder is filled with gas.

3 Check that there are no gas leaks in the gas supply system. See leak testing.

4 Check that the venturis are properly located over the gas valve outlets.

5 Read carefully all instructions contained on the information plate attached to the barbecue.

6 **WARNING: Raise lid before lighting.**

Figure 8.2.1 Procedure for setting up a gas appliance

New procedures involving the use of computers or other equipment can be supported by a 'help desk' to deal with queries – even if only for a short period after initial implementation. In the same way, users of a new procedure can provide a 'support network' for each other.

At the very least, even with the simplest procedure, there should be one expert on hand in the early days to answer queries.

TEST YOURSELF

You recently ordered a new fax machine which is considerably more complicated to operate than the old model you had installed.

1 Upon delivery, what guidance documents would you expect to receive?
2 What additional support would you expect to receive from
  a the person who installs the machine
  b the company itself, if you have a problem at a later date?
3 How would you 'translate' the instructions you have received into an effective procedure for staff to reduce the initial problems they may have?

Ways of monitoring effectiveness of procedures

Regular monitoring of any procedure is essential for several reasons.

● No matter how carefully you have drafted and planned the procedure, there may still be improvements which can be made at a later date.
● You need to measure whether the procedure is meeting the objectives you set – both quantitatively and qualitatively. If it is

not, then adjustments need to be made – either to the objectives themselves or to the procedure.

- Over a period of time your procedure may become out-of-date or be affected by another procedure introduced into the organisation.
- Over time your costings may change, affecting the whole justification for the procedure.
- New legislation may change the way in which the procedure should be carried out.

Procedures, however successful, should not be regared as rules carved in stone. Ways of doing things can and should evolve – situations change and new technologies are continually being developed, so new and better ways of going about tasks can always be found. Your staff should be encouraged to be flexible and creative, because that way they will contribute more *and* make your life easier

Monitoring procedures implies seeking and receiving information to enable you to make regular checks and, if necessary, periodic adjustments. You can obtain information either informally or formally.

Informal methods would include:

- chatting to users
- using the procedure yourself
- discussing outcomes, benefits and possible changes in informal meetings.

Formal methods would include:

- devising a questionnaire for users
- calculating accurately the cost of implementation and operation
- calculating accurately the benefits of implementation and operation
- formal discussions with users
- a formal review meeting at a pre-planned date.

In a large, bureaucratic organisation you may find that all procedures are subject to a formal review process. If you have to attend, then you will be expected to bring documentation concerned with its operation and how well (or badly) the procedure meets the objectives set. You will also be expected to have to hand any current information which may affect operations.

TEST YOURSELF

You implemented the customer complaints procedure shown in Figure 8.2.2 several weeks ago. You now wish to monitor its effectiveness.

1 What would have been the objectives of introducing such a procedure?
2 What information would you require to enable you to assess whether these objectives had been met?
3 How would you obtain this information?

4 a What account would you take of the personal views of users if they considered the procedure was too lengthy, whereas your data showed it to be effective in terms of meeting its objectives?

   b What could you do to take account of their views without changing the overall structure of the procedure?

Legal and regulatory requirements relating to the implementation of procedures

You have already learned much in previous units about legal and regulatory requirements – in relation to health and safety (Unit 2), employment law (Units 1 and 3) and consumer legislation (Unit 4). Quite obviously any procedures you introduce – either in their design or implementation – cannot contravene legal requirements. However, there are also other legal implications about which you should be aware.

Firstly, an organisation which fails to implement a procedure in line with legal requirements can be found guilty of negligence. This could be the case, for instance, if procedures for the disposal of hazardous waste contravened official laws, bye-laws or regulations issued by local authorities. An organisation would also be negligent if it failed to take account of the legal procedures and regulations in force in relation to consumer credit or the sale of goods.

Secondly, an organisation can expect little support in law if procedures are laid down but are not followed by staff. This is the case, for instance, in relation to disciplinary and grievance procedures. For example, if there was a clause in your organisation's grievance procedure which stated that until the matter is resolved the status quo would apply, and your manager insisted that you had to accept a change of job role despite the fact that you objected, this would prejudice the case in your favour and against the organisation because procedures had not been followed.

In some cases, the consequences of non-compliance may be even more serious. As an example, if the correct disciplinary procedures were not followed in an organisation and a member of staff was dealt with arbitrarily in relation to an alleged offence, rather than by recourse to the official procedure, this can result in a dismissal being found as 'unfair' by a tribunal even though the offence itself would have resulted in a fair dismissal if the correct procedures had been followed.

TEST YOURSELF

Your younger sister has just started work as a Saturday assistant at a local record shop. There is one other Saturday worker who has been there for two months, 2 part-time employees and 2 full-time employees. Last Saturday a sum of money was missing from the cash register. The manager is unsure

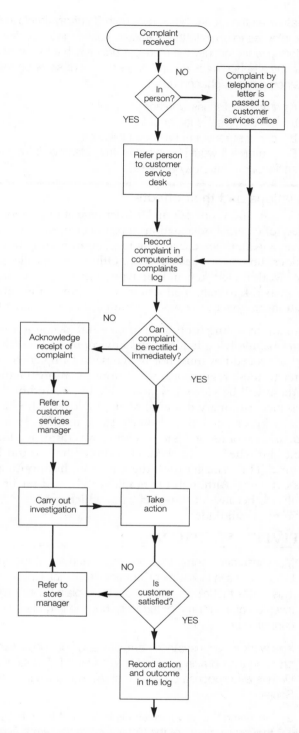

Figure 8.2.2 Example of a customer complaints procedure in a large retail store

who has taken the money but knows both Saturday employees have been the only employees to operate that particular cash register all day. Because she only started work recently the manager decides that the other Saturday worker has a better 'track record' and sacks your sister on the spot. She comes home distraught and upset.

1 As a group, discuss whether you think:
a the dismissal is fair or unfair
b correct procedure has been followed.
2 Do you think it would have made any difference if the manager had sacked both Saturday workers?

Regulations and their effects

Many organisations operate under strict regulations imposed on them by a variety of external organisations. For instance, some departments in some organisations are affected by regulations relating to the storage of hazardous substances – such as acids. Others are less affected because the type of work undertaken and the type of materials they handle means there is less risk to staff. You would hardly expect the same type of regulations to govern the work of both a scaffolder and a filing clerk!

Organisations selling food have to take into account a wide range of regulations involving hygiene and environmental health. In the same way that procedures must not be devised or implemented which run counter to these regulations, the actions of an organisation to comply with these will be viewed as favourable by the authorities. Therefore, for instance, summary dismissal of an employee who has endangered others by his or her actions is likely to be upheld. As an example, a supermarket worker at a Safeway store was dismissed for eating a currant bun where he worked. He claimed he was too hungry to pay for it first! The manager took the bun from his mouth and froze it to use as evidence. Although the employee claimed unfair dismissal he lost his case because of the strict rules which govern the handling of food in the retail trade.

ACTIVITY SECTION

1 Many insurance companies are concerned about the implications of the Unfair Terms in Consumer Contract Regulations introduced in 1995. This states that all contracts must be in plain English and forbids the insertion of small print or terms included in jargon which customers cannot understand.

You work for an insurance company and your boss wants a new procedure for drafting contracts to be introduced as quickly as possible. He has also suggested that you obtain guidance from the Plain English Society.

a Research the new regulations to find out how these have amended the requirements of the Unfair Contracts Terms Act of 1977.

b Find out the address of the Plain English Society and write to them for a copy of their current guidelines.

c Draft a procedure which would enable your organisation to comply with the requirements of the Act and the suggestions made by the Plain English Society.

d Attach an implementation plan which includes suggested guidance notes and indicates how the new procedure can be brought into operation as quickly as possible.

2 Obtain a copy of your organisation's grievance procedures and disciplinary procedures and compare these with examples provided by other members of your group. Discuss the type of actions which could be taken by management which would be prejudicial to the outcome of any tribunal hearing because they fail to comply with the specified procedures.

3 You work in a busy Human Resources office in a large organisation which has a frequent requirement for temporary office staff. Up to now individual departments have advertised for temporary staff in the local paper but there has been little consultation between departments with the result that sometimes conflicting advertisements have appeared. Response has been variable, as has the quality of the applicants, mainly because some of the advertisements have not been specific enough about the requirements. Your boss is also worried about the legal implications of employing temporary or casual staff.

He has decided that it would be better if the Human Resources office handled all requests for temporary staff and coordinated these properly. He wants you and your staff to refer the requests to a local employment agency if this would be a more cost-effective alternative. He then wants you to design a procedure for all departments to follow if temporary staff are required and for your staff to follow when handling these enquiries.

a Contact your local paper and a local employment agency to find out their rates so that you can make an accurate comparison of costs of recruitment.

b Decide which would be the most cost-effective method of recruitment and draft out a procedure which could easily be followed both by other departments and by your own staff.

c Draw up an implementation plan to show the timescale over which you plan to introduce the change. Show clearly
 i the documentation you intend to give users
 ii any additional support or training needs you have identified.

d State how you would monitor the effectiveness of your procedure and the information you would need to assess this properly.

e If, several weeks after implementation, you found that another department was continually ignoring the new procedures and placing advertisements directly, what would you do?

Managing change

God grant me the equanimity to accept the things I cannot change, the courage to change what I can – and the wisdom to know the difference.

The first thing to remember about change is that it can be very stressful. Even positive changes in our personal life, such as moving house, getting married or having a family can put us under stress. Negative changes – especially those which are imposed upon us – can create distress, confusion and worry.

The problems in a working situation can be summarised as follows.

- Organisations have to change to survive.
- Most changes are imposed upon an organisation by forces outside its control – new legislation, technology, actions by competitors, social changes, . . .
- People vary in their ability to welcome or cope with change.
- For many people change is threatening – in terms of their lifestyle, their status or even their job.
- Change can be managed so that people can cope more easily – but often this is mishandled or even ignored.

RULE 1
Learn to differentiate between basic change and fundamental change.

Basic change

This relates to changes to basic operating procedures which may create short-term inconvenience and annoyance but can be managed relatively easily. Such changes are task-centred.

Examples include changing the design of forms people complete, changing the rules for expense claims and changing a filing system.

Fundamental change

This relates to more far-reaching changes which can cause long-term anxiety, worry or distress and can only be managed with difficulty. Such changes are people-centred.

Examples include increasing the responsibilities of a job, changing the hours people work, changing their location and changing the structure of an organisation (i.e. how many departments, who should work where and for whom, etc.)

RULE 2
Treating a fundamental change in the same way as basic change usually makes the problem worse, not better.

Identifying fundamental change

Usually the change is fundamental if it involves any of the following:

- job security (e.g. redundancy, less money)
- status (e.g. loss of perks, 'distance' from the boss greater)
- prestige (e.g. loss of self-identity or self-worth – for instance if learned skills lose their value)
- social ties (e.g. social life disrupted because of shift changes, work group disrupted)
- personal anxiety (e.g. cannot cope with/dislike new job, natural fear of the unknown).

Our natural reaction when threatened is one of 'fight or flight'. Therefore if such changes are imminent the reaction of employees may range from outright aggression/militancy to absenteeism.

RULE 3

Good management of change will lessen problems, not create them.

TEST YOURSELF

Your company has recently reorganised its offices. Joanne, a typist who worked in the Sales office with three other girls, has been upgraded and given the job of coordinating the sales reports received every week from the sales representatives employed by your company. She has her own word processor and her own small office. To your surprise, after four weeks in the job, she comes to you to tell you that she is miserable in her new role and wants to go back to the Sales office.

a Think of as many reasons as you can why Joanne may be unhappy in her new job. (If possible do this as a group exercise.)

b For each reason listed, what advice would you give to Joanne?

c Assuming her main problems are loneliness and a fear of coping with the new job, what suggestions would you make to your boss to solve the problem?

d How do you think the problem could have been prevented in the first place?

Planning for change

The biggest problem when planning for change is that the planners concentrate on the tasks involved and not on the people. It is all very well to make suggestions about how you think a job should be done, but if you are not the person who will be doing it then the suggestion could well fail.

RULE 4

Whenever possible, consult the people who are doing/will be doing the job first – never automatically think that you know best!

Remember that the biggest demotivator for staff is the feeling that they have no control over what is happening to them. Listen to what they have to say even if you don't like what you are hearing! Staff may be genuinely unhappy if they feel they cannot cope with the work, or if they consider that suggestions are unworkable. This may mean implementing staff training sessions or redesigning the job specifications.

RULE 5

Introduce change gradually and be prepared to modify your original ideas if necessary.

Coping with change yourself

In the previous pages we have dealt with change as if you have the ability to affect some of the decisions which are being made. However, unless you hold a very senior position it is likely that the most fundamental and far-reaching changes will be decided above your head. You will then have the double problem of helping your staff to cope with change and coping with it yourself. Although you may be against some of the ideas, there may be little you can do to alter the situation.

RULE 6

No changes are all wrong! List all the benefits from the change that you can think of (ask your staff to join in) and remember that to ignore change means you won't survive (think of the dinosaur!).

Communications are vital at this point – both with anyone else affected and with your boss – to clarify worries, problems and even minor difficulties. If you honestly think someone (or yourself) will be adversely affected or won't be able to cope, or if you consider that the change could be introduced in a more beneficial way, then try appealing to your boss. If you have a constructive, open relationship then he or she may be glad of your contribution so long as it contains ideas and solutions and not just a list of problems and moans.

It may be the case that at the end of the day you – and your organisation – are considerably better off. Your working relationships and systems of work may be more streamlined and your organisation more profitable. If it results in your being beset with problems, or even losing your job, you could be fatalistic and consider that it was 'meant to happen' and something better is round the corner.

RULE 7

Learn to cultivate a positive attitude towards change – look upon it as a challenge with new opportunities around the corner, rather than as a threat.

If you approach change from this point of view then you will develop a good working relationship with both your superiors and those below you. You will also be more flexible and adaptable in your own ways of working and more creative in terms of making suggestions yourself.

From this point it is but a short step to learn to use change for your own benefit – to help you to improve your performance and your achievements and reap the benefits later when your talents are recognised.

TEST YOURSELF

Your boss wants to introduce a computerised stock-control system for all stationery supplies. The two stock control clerks are against the idea and consider that the existing record-card system works very well indeed.

1   What other reasons might the clerks have for resisting the change?
2   What benefits do you think there might be to your organisation in implementing a computerised system?
3   What measures would you take to reduce the clerks' anxiety/resistance and ensure their commitment to the change?

9 Obtain, organise and monitor the use of materials and equipment

Element 9.1

Obtain and organise materials and equipment

You should note that this unit is an **option** unit. The fact that you have chosen to study and prove your competence in this area should mean that as part of your job you undertake duties which involve acquiring, organising and monitoring materials and equipment in your workplace. If you do not, then you are advised not to select this option. If you only do part of the work outlined in the scheme then you will need to talk to your tutor or adviser about the best way to demonstrate competence in the remaining areas.

Scope and limit of own authority, including financial, for obtaining materials and equipment

All organisations need a wide range of materials and equipment to be able to operate. The exact type of materials and equipment and the quantity required will depend upon:

- whether the organisation produces goods or provides a service
- its size and scale of operation.

Items required can be divided into five categories:

- raw materials (manufacturing companies only) which are converted in production to finished items and then sold
- consumable items – from tools and overalls to office stationery and cleaning products
- capital items – which are expensive to buy or replace – from production equipment to computers and from vehicles to office furniture
- specialist services – from security to catering, from a cleaning company to an employment agency
- maintenance services – from the central heating contractor to the burglar alarm company to the photocopier supplier.

The scope and limit of your own authority, as an administrator, is *likely* to be restricted to

- obtaining consumable office items – possibly being able to order items up to a certain financial limit without seeking permission, thereafter obtaining approval for large or expensive purchases

- investigating sources of supply, obtaining quotations and making recommendations in relation to the purchase of office equipment and furniture
- organising specialist services in an emergency or arranging those which relate to your own area of work
- overseeing the fulfilment of maintenance contracts relating to your own area and, possibly, reviewing their costs and benefits.

However, this is only a broad outline – individual jobs and responsibilities can vary enormously. What is always true, however, is that the job holder should *clearly* understand the scope and limit of his or her role, particularly in relation to any financial constraints in operation. This is particularly the case if the job description is rather vague or the responsibility level has never been clarified. If this is the case where you work, it is essential that you sit down with your line manager and discuss these issues in detail – before you overstep your area of authority accidentally.

Ironically, your responsibilities may be greater in a small organisation than a large one, where the storage, maintenance and control of the majority of the materials and equipment is the responsibility of a centralised section. In this situation an administrator is likely to be responsible for maintaining departmental supplies by placing orders through a central system, rather than dealing with suppliers direct. In this case, therefore, you would be dealing with other employees in your organisation who deal with work related to your own.

In a small organisation, however, an office administrator may have to undertake the full range of responsibilities in relation to office supplies and to devise a system which incorporates not only ordering and storage procedures but also keeping comparative notes on suppliers and monitoring usage as well as costing and valuing stock for auditing purposes.

 ## DID YOU KNOW?

The extent to which budgets are devolved varies tremendously from one organisation to another. The more devolution there is in your organisation, the more likely you are to be working in a particular cost centre which is responsible for its own income and expenditure. This has advantages and disadvantages! You may be nearer the decision-makers in terms of obtaining permission for expenditure but you are also likely to have greater personal accountability. If you have your own budget to manage this is even more likely to be the case!

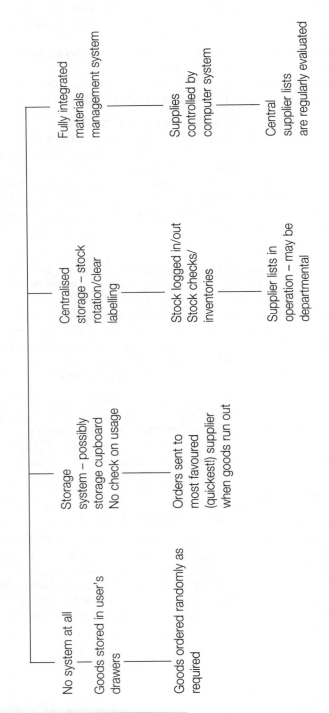

No system at all
Goods stored in user's drawers

Goods ordered randomly as required

Storage system – possibly storage cupboard
No check on usage

Orders sent to most favoured (quickest!) supplier when goods run out

Centralised storage – stock rotation/clear labelling

Stock logged in/out
Stock checks/inventories

Supplier lists in operation – may be departmental

Fully integrated materials management system

Supplies controlled by computer system

Central supplier lists are regularly evaluated

Figure 9.1.1 A spectrum of purchasing and stock control systems

Organisations' procedures for obtaining materials and equipment

As you will see from Figure 9.1.1, the range of procedures in a given organisation can vary from none at all to a formalised materials management system! However, it is true to say that the larger the organisation the more likely it is that standard systems and procedures will be in operation.

In contrast, especially in the early days, a small organisation may have no procedures at all. Consumable items and even office equipment may be ordered on a 'needs must' basis, when both the range of requirements and the quantities needed are only small. Stock may be stored randomly where there is some space, the area may be open access and items available to staff on a 'first come, first served' basis.

However, this situation is unlikely to be tolerated for long by either management or accountants (the financial implications of operating at the lower end of the continuum in Figure 9.1.1 are discussed in Element 9.2, page 573).

At the opposite end of the spectrum is the organisation which operates a fully integrated materials management system. There is a standard list of suppliers, all of whom are classified using the A, B, C categories shown in Figure 9.1.2.

CATEGORISATION OF SUPPLIERS	
A	Trusted – quality and delivery excellent. Competitive prices.
B	Usually good service. May be rather pricey.
C	Unreliable delivery, quality variable.

Figure 9.1.2 Categorisation of suppliers

B and C 'grade' suppliers are only contacted when 'A' suppliers cannot provide the goods. There are regular re-evaluations of suppliers and reclassification if required. The organisation may also operate an EDI (electronic data interchange) system where all goods are ordered and paid for via their computer network (see also Unit 6, page 371).

In most organisations you are likely to find you have some procedure to follow, even if it is not as formalised as this last example. In some cases you may find that a different procedure operates for each type of item purchased. As a guide, the difference is likely to be as follows.

- Raw materials for manufacturing organisations are usually bought by specialist buyers from established suppliers and not by administrators. This is usually a function of staff in a centralised purchasing section because their expertise means that due account can be taken of discounts, possible shortages, space for stock, turnover of stock, price variations and trends, delivery details, reliability of suppliers and so on. However, there is much you can learn from this approach to buying, as you will see later.

- Consumables may be purchased by a central department but may be ordered or purchased by individual administrators on behalf of their section. In a small firm, the administrator may have the remit to contact suppliers and place routine orders direct.

- Capital items are usually purchased from the organisation's reserve account. Requests or 'bids' may have to be submitted by each department at certain periods of the year and the reserve funds may be allocated according to need. Often a rationale for expenditure has to be appended and, unless you can present a good argument for what you need, you may find that you are often overlooked – unless your organisation divides up its reserve funds more equitably amongst departments. In this case you simply have to persuade your line manager of the worthiness of your cause – rather than the board of directors as well!

- Regular providers of services and maintenance personnel are usually under contract to the organisation. Today there has been a move in most organisations to 'contract out' a greater number of services rather than provide them 'in-house', because this is usually more cost-effective. Your canteen service may have ended and outside caterers may be hired for special events. The tea-person may have been replaced by a vending machine. The old reprographics section may have closed since a print shop opened on the corner and so on. Contracts are normally agreed centrally and reviewed regularly – both in terms of cost and quality of service. In today's competitive world, organisations can be quite ruthless in terminating a contract if they do not feel they are receiving value for money.

Determining suppliers and buying procedures

At the outset, the organisation should consider:

- the importance of quality versus costs for each particular item
- possible discounts available (which may affect the cost-effective operational levels of stock)
- which items can be supplied in-house (e.g. should the company undertake its own printing or buy in ready-printed forms, letterheads, etc.)
- whether to operate a policy of cultivating particular suppliers or shopping around to take advantage of competitive prices
- the degree to which re-ordering can be undertaken automatically, i.e. which items and/or level of expenditure are subject to management approval

- the procedure for checking orders prior to despatch and determining those staff who are to have official authorisation to order on behalf of the organisation
- the system for checking goods and invoices upon receipt and who should be authorised to pass these for payment
- the procedure for monitoring total expenditure in this area as an ongoing management information item.

You will obviously be expected to know and understand the procedures which relate to your own area and responsibilities.

A large organisation is likely to have a centralised Purchasing section through which all goods must be ordered. In this case you may find you have to operate to a recommended list of suppliers and/or leave the choice up to them. However, if you feel strongly that another supplier would give better value you can, of course, make the suggestion that they may be worth evaluating – though the eventual outcome will be up to your company buyer.

In a smaller organisation, or one without a centralised purchasing section, you may have full responsibility to select a supplier and buy the goods you need. You may also find it useful to start your own list of suppliers – and to categorise them as shown in Figure 9.1.2. Bear in mind that the aim of this is to always deal with category A suppliers unless they are unable to help you for a particular reason, in which case you move down to category B and so on.

When you are deciding upon a suitable supplier for a particular item of stock you have a variety of factors to take into consideration – and only one of these is the actual price of the goods. Other factors you need to think about include:

- **Delivery** How long will you have to wait for the goods? Does the company have its own door-to-door delivery service?
- **Reputation** How long has the company been established? How did you find out about them? Do you know anyone else who has used them? Are they known to be reliable and/or responsive in the event of an emergency?
- **Location** How far away are the suppliers? If they are very distant will you have to pay carriage charges and/or will there be difficulties in returning faulty or damaged goods? If equipment is involved, what arrangements would be made for servicing and/or maintenance?
- **Range of goods** Are standard, branded products available and if so what choice is there? Is the catalogue helpful or merely informative? Do you have an up-to-date price list?
- **Discounts** Does the company offer cash discount (for prompt payment) and/or trade discount (for bulk orders) and if so what are the conditions attached to these? Will your company require sufficient quantities to benefit from trade discounts? How do any

cash discount terms fit in with your company's policy for paying invoices?

- **Credit** Assuming no cash discount is offered, what credit terms are available (especially on large orders or for items of equipment)?

You need to be able to weigh up the advantages of cultivating a local supplier, who will then consider you a good customer and give you priority service, against those of shopping around. The danger of keeping all your eggs in one basket is, of course, that you may be inconvenienced if the company you always use is itself out of stock or if it becomes complacent in relation to the business you put its way. In theory, if you use a company regularly, you should be able to expect a more sympathetic ear from its staff if you need goods in an emergency or a junior member of staff ordered some goods by mistake and you want to send them back!

A sensible compromise may be to develop a good working relationship with one or two suppliers in your own area, but keep your eyes open for other sources, possibly further afield. Change your supplier only if you are actually unhappy with the service you receive or if there is a substantial price difference. Then try out the new company with one or two minor orders and evaluate the service you receive before giving them more custom.

DID YOU KNOW?

Specialist magazines and journals are on the market which give details of new equipment and their features. Equally you can read *What to Buy for Business* – a sort of business *Which?* magazine which assesses more objectively the features of different types of office equipment. Alternatively there is a series of buyer's guides produced on fax machines, copiers, laser printers, phone systems, electronic filing, mobile communications and notebook PCs. You can obtain a copy of any of these by phoning 01732 458 202 if you have any of these items on your shopping list.

CHECK IT YOURSELF

1   Find out what written procedures exist in your workplace in relation to obtaining materials and equipment. Obtain a copy of these. Alternatively, write a brief description of the procedure which you actually follow, the type of materials and equipment you order and give an indication of the limit of your authority – including any financial constraints.

2   Find out what suppliers' lists there are, where these are kept and whether the list operates as a formal requirement or an informal guide for staff purchasing goods or services.

Ways of estimating materials and equipment requirements

The type of materials and equipment for which you are responsible will depend upon the work carried out by the organisation. However, all organisations require standard items, such as paper, envelopes, pencils and pens, filing materials, printed materials and office sundries such as punches, paper clips, scissors, etc. Today a wide range of computerised items may also be held in stock, from disk boxes, printer leads and cartridges to computers themselves, if, for instance, laptop computers are held in stock for executives to take abroad or to use at home.

You should bear in mind that the quantity required will depend upon frequency of use and this is determined by current work loads. However, you must also consider anticipated work loads – not just for yourself but also for your section. If your staff are about to prepare a mailshot to 10 000 customers you need to ensure that they have enough envelopes to cover their special requirements whilst still retaining enough for general use.

Estimating the requirements of materials

You can estimate the requirements of materials by taking into account:

- the frequency of use of materials for routine work
- the type of materials which are required for specific tasks
- the frequency and timing of specific tasks.

However, in addition you also need to bear in mind:

- the available storage space
- any restrictions on expenditure you may have
- the cost of the items
- safety and security implications.

For that reason, even if six representatives will be in Europe at a major exhibition next week and all would like their own laptop to take with them complete with suitable software and a copy of all customer files stored on disk, you would be very unwise to agree to this without doing an awful lot of checking up beforehand!

It is useful to start by defining straightforward consumable items which require no special treatment. Then categorise these items into those relating to everyday needs, where a high level of turnover and demand is expected, and those which are required on a more infrequent basis. One technique for doing this is known as Pareto Analysis and is described in Figure 9.1.3.

If you have to rationalise stock requirements and movements and project usage, then your first step should be to itemise all items

---

PARETO ANALYSIS

The easy way to understand Pareto analysis is to relate it to yourself first. Unless you are very unusual you will find that

- you wear 20 per cent of the clothes in your wardrobe 80 per cent of the time
- 20 per cent of the tasks in your job description take up 80 per cent of your time
- you access 20 per cent of the files in your filing cabinet 80 per cent of the time.

The 80/20 rule (as it is known) can be applied to many areas; sociologists often say that 80 per cent of the world's wealth is held by 20 per cent of the population.

Items which are used most of the time are known as Pareto items. If the items which make up this 20 per cent can be identified, isolated and given special attention then it is logical that major benefits will flow automatically. The remaining 80 per cent can be virtually ignored. Or, in other words, concentrate on 20 per cent of the items 80 per cent of the time!

Figure 9.1.3 Pareto analysis

currently kept in stock and note alongside each item the usage to date. Now divide your stock into highly active (Pareto) items, less active and non-active items. Then note down any factors which could create variances from the situation you have at present, e.g. proposed projects and their effects, seasonal requirements and so on. This will show you whether the level of demand is likely to be static or fluctuating over a period of time and will help you to plan ahead.

For all non-active items examine the lead times from suppliers, i.e. the length of time it normally takes from order to delivery. Many companies now are changing to 'JIT' systems of working. The acronym JIT stands for 'just-in-time' and if your organisation subscribes to this philosophy it will prefer any item which is used infrequently and can be obtained quickly and easily to be purchased only as needed. This immediately reduces the amount of capital which must be tied up in stock and the amount of storage space required.

For all items the obvious basic rule is that you will need a higher level of buffer stock for goods which take a long time to deliver than for those which do not. Now prioritise your active list into essentials and those items of lesser importance. Letter headings, for example, are critical – and may take longer to print and deliver than, say, shorthand notebooks. The former should therefore be higher on your list.

Alongside each item enter two figures: your minimum stock (i.e. the lowest possible amount you will always need to keep in stock) and the maximum stock you consider you should hold, given the constraints of space and the budget you have been allocated. You should note that you will actually re-order goods before the minimum stock figure is reached, to allow for delays in the new stock reaching you and the fact that whilst the stock is still on its way people will continue to need supplies.

Once this exercise is completed, calculate the full value of all stock which would be held if all items were at maximum level. Work this out at cost price – you can ignore VAT as the company will claim this back on expense items. Your final total is the amount of capital you are asking the organisation to commit to stock. It is a good idea to be slightly below budget so that you have some flexibility in relation to emergency requests and changing needs over the next twelve months. It is now time to check this figure with your boss.

During the discussion session you should be prepared to negotiate and adjust your initial forecast. There may be additional items required which you have not included, or your boss's views on priority may differ slightly from yours and you will have to allow for this.

Estimating the requirements of equipment

The type of equipment in operation in your organisation will be determined by the type and volume of work carried out by your organisation. For instance, every organisation sends out items through the mail. However, postage requirements can vary from a packet of stamps to a franking machine linked to a computerised mailing system and capable of processing thousands of envelopes an hour! All manufacturers make a wide range of models of each type of equipment to cope with the requirements of different organisations. When you are estimating your requirements in this respect, you therefore have two factors to bear in mind:

- the type of equipment which is required
- the potential capacity of the equipment and the range of features which are available.

It is the latter which will influence the price you are asked to pay.

Do bear in mind that equipment requirements do not remain static. Several factors cause them to change, for example:

- an increase in workload
- a change in the type of work undertaken
- the introduction of new equipment or features
- changes in price (new models are often expensive initially and then the price falls – think of plain paper fax machines and computers as two obvious examples).

It may be the case that you identify that the needs of your section have changed long before your boss does so – particularly if you have been managing to cope so far!

Your first job may be to evaluate and specify exactly how your needs have changed and then to identify the type of equipment which would be best and to obtain further information on prices. When you do this, it is sensible to take note of the following.

- If you are thinking of spending a considerable sum on an item of capital equipment, e.g. a photocopier, fax machine or computer, it is usual to start by contacting various competing companies for quotations. Do not accept an estimate as this simply gives a total estimated price rather than an itemised list. You cannot therefore hold the company to its quoted figures to the same extent.
- If you wish to obtain comparative figures on buying, renting and leasing make sure you specify this clearly. You will also need details of the terms of the rental or leasing agreement.
- Be aware that in certain areas (photocopiers being one), once you start making general enquiries you may find that you are inundated with representatives calling to try to persuade you to buy their product! This can be counterproductive, confusing or time-wasting and, at worst, may tempt you to buy something you don't really want simply for the sake of peace. Because of this, some organisations operate a system whereby they will only see representatives by invitation and they specify this on their initial enquiry. If you are still pestered you could try the tactic of telling them that you routinely cross any suppliers off your list if they unduly harass you for business!
- Make sure that you obtain full information on:
  - warranty periods (for which servicing and repair is free)
  - maintenance agreements (under which the warranty period is extended) and the terms/cost of these
  - routine servicing – how often, what work is carried out, etc.
  - emergency call-out arrangements if the equipment breaks down (in particular find out what timescale is likely to be involved)
  - whether essential supplies for the equipment must be purchased from that particular company and, if so, the cost
  - what training is provided for staff in how to use the equipment – and who provides this.
- It is usual for most administrators to make an initial assessment of the available equipment, its features and cost and then report back to the boss who will make the final decision on which particular item or model should be purchased. If you need to produce such a report, then summarise the advantages and disadvantages objectively and attach relevant documents as your appendices (see Unit 5, page 302).

Ways of siting materials and equipment safely for access and work flows

You have already studied the main points which relate to this section in Element 2.2, where you learned about work flows and the positioning of furniture and equipment. Refresh your memory by turning back to pages 82–7 and noting the main points which were mentioned.

Siting equipment safely

Quite obviously no-one can work effectively in an area where equipment impedes access or progress through an area or where it is a major job to set something up before it can be used and then have to put it all away again afterwards – especially if usage is frequent. In addition, you obviously need to observe basic safety requirements and avoid trailing leads, restricted airflow around certain types of equipment (such as photocopiers) and siting smaller items where they could easily be knocked or damaged.

When you buy large items of equipment or those which have specific safety requirements then you can usually expect the seller to give you sound advice on positioning. When the equipment arrives, do supervise its installation – often the people installing it will not be those who sold it to you! Book a day when you know you will be available so that you can make sure it is placed where you want it and also that you receive all the necessary documentation – handbook, guarantee, etc. With many machines (e.g. photocopiers, faxes) the person who installs it will set it up and then explain its functions to the staff. Make sure you are the person who receives this initial instruction so that you can then train your own staff. Check the 'trouble-shooting' guide in the manual with the person who installs the machine to make sure you understand clearly how to rectify basic problems and for which faults you must call out an engineer.

DID YOU KNOW?

Always calculate the space required for a piece of equipment before you order it. Never forget to include:

- the space required for air flows
- the space required for the operator
- other relevant features in the area, e.g. pipes, window sills, skirting boards and opening doors in the vicinity
- the distance to the nearest power point, if applicable.

Ideally, you should also allow for the storage of basic materials which will be required in the immediate working area. This may mean purchasing a storage table on which to site desktop items so that the operator does not spend more time walking to cupboards and back again than actually doing the job!

Siting materials safely

You have three main considerations in relation to the siting of materials:

- where current materials are kept, i.e. those kept in the working area
- where stocks of materials are kept, i.e. the main bulk of the items
- who should have access to the stock.

Current materials

Again, much that you learned in Element 2.2 is relevant here. You need to decide which items are sensible to keep in people's desks, which ones are better in a large cupboard and which ones need to be in specific areas.

- Items used by everyone frequently are usually issued 'per person' and kept in desk drawers.
- Items used less frequently and needed on a 'communal' basis are better kept in a large cupboard. Otherwise one person will constantly be pestered by everyone else!
- Items used specifically in relation to one item of equipment should be stored nearby, e.g. photocopier paper near the photocopying machine, fax rolls/paper by the fax machine, printer cartridges near the printer and so on.

Stored materials

When you are determining storage and access to stock you must think first about:

- the space you have available
- the type and quantity of materials which are being stored
- the best layout in the storage area to prevent damage and to provide safe and easy access to items
- whether additional storage areas are required, e.g. for dangerous substances, confidential items or valuable goods and equipment
- who will be the key holders
- the requisition or order system to be instigated before stock can be obtained, and authorisation procedures
- the availability of stock for staff (e.g. constantly, daily, twice weekly, weekly)
- the method of retrieval and issue, i.e. FIFO (first in first out) or LIFO (last in first out).

CHECK IT YOURSELF

Check that you know the basics about the care and storage of stock and the safety procedures to be followed by looking at the storage and safety procedures relating to the stock rooms of one organisation (Figure 9.1.4). In each case identify the rationale behind the requirement.

 ## DID YOU KNOW?

You should always keep a list of any hazardous items you may need to store. Bear in mind that under COSHH (Control of Substances Hazardous to Health) regulations 1988 you will have to have these items assessed by a competent person to ascertain the level of risk involved (see also Element 2.1).
Dangerous chemicals must be kept in a separate area (e.g. a chemical safe or bonded store) with restricted access and all keyholders must be listed. Items which are hazardous, rather than dangerous, can usually be stored with other consumables but it is advisable to keep these on a separate shelf. Typical examples are chemicals related, say, to offset litho duplicating. Most items are flammable, e.g. blanket wash and etching fluid, and others are even more volatile, e.g. MEK (methyl ethyl ketone) which is a blanket conditioner.

All hazardous substances are marked with special hazard warning signs and a hazard data sheet can be obtained from the supplier. If the latter is difficult to understand then simplify it for any staff who may be handling the substance and check that your handling and storage arrangements do not contravene

---

CARE AND STORAGE OF STOCK
1 All stock must be kept in a dry, well-ventilated and lockable room.
2 Only designated keyholders should have access to the area.
3 The shelves must be of a slatted design and clearly labelled.
4 All paper products must be kept wrapped at all times.
5 All stock must be stored with descriptive labels facing outwards.
6 New stock must be placed under or behind old stock items.
7 Bulk items must be broken down before issue (e.g. paper-clips, elastic bands, envelopes).
8 Pens and pencils must be kept in boxes.
9 The door must be kept locked.

SAFETY REQUIREMENTS
1 Large and bulky items must be stored on low shelves.
2 Any hazardous substances must be clearly labelled and stored on the floor.
3 Hazardous substances must never be ordered or stored in bulk quantities.
4 Dangerous substances must not be stored in the area.
5 Packing cases or empty boxes must not be left in the area.
6 A safety stool must be provided in the area.
7 Pins, breakable items and those which could cause damage when handling must be clearly labelled and kept on low shelves.
8 Large 'no smoking' signs must be clearly visible.

Figure 9.1.4 Care and storage of stock, and safety procedures

the supplier's instructions in any way. As a final safety measure draw up a list of emergency procedures, e.g. what to do if the substance is spilled, inhaled or gets into someone's eyes.

Valuable stock and security

If part of your remit is also to store equipment then you may have to decide whether or not a special secure area needs to be provided. However, it is worth noting that whilst, say, a camcorder or laptop computer may cost a considerable sum to purchase, it is likely that such items will be covered by the company's insurance. They may also be quite difficult for anyone to steal as, unless someone has a lot of nerve, it is not easy to sneak around the corridors with a laptop computer under one arm. Conversely, many consumable items are quite expensive to buy, are very useful at home and can quickly be hidden in a bag or under a coat. As an example, a developer and toner cartridge for a laser printer can cost between £80 and £100 to buy; similarly, your company's stock of audio or video tapes may be extremely desirable items. It is sensible to check whether consumable items are also covered against theft under the company's existing insurance policy.

The most sensible arrangement is for all stock to be stored in locked cupboards and for a limited number of keyholders to be appointed, all of whom are responsible for undertaking the stock inventory at given periods and reporting on discrepancies. This does not mean expecting a ten–page explanation because three paper-clips have gone missing, but does mean invoking an atmosphere of collective responsibility and good communications so that you are informed at the outset if there are requests – by anyone – for deviations from the system.

Special items

Special items are those which are a specific requirement of your organisation or your boss and may not be available to every member of staff. These could be classified as 'confidential' – except that when any item is placed in a general stock cupboard it usually ceases to be confidential! As an example, consider the case where an MD obtains leather-bound desk diaries for senior staff but does not want these open to general use because of the cost – and may not want their existence to be discussed amongst the staff in case everyone thinks they deserve one! Even more 'confidential' may be gifts for clients at Christmas time, e.g. whisky or cigars, and special items stored for commemorative occasions, e.g. cut glass items produced for an anniversary. If you are involved in storing items such as these you are strongly advised to set up a separate system that only you and perhaps another administrator know about. Do train your boss to keep you informed if he or she takes items away so that you can keep a check on the contents.

Special items which are also valuable may require storage in a safe. If you stock sterling or dollar travellers' cheques, for instance, you would be extremely foolish to place these anywhere else. For that reason many executive offices contain a small safe which can be used to store confidential papers, cash and small but valuable items.

Access to stock

The frequency with which stock can be accessed will depend mainly on the scale of operation and your staffing in this area. If you have a full-time stock control clerk and your organisation is fairly large (or needs constant flexibility) then you can cope with stock being available on a constant basis. More usually, however, stock is issued at either specific times of the day or on specific days of the week. However, the more infrequently you issue stock the more likely you are to be faced with emergency requests – so you need to take this into consideration when devising your system. A sensible compromise may be to have stock available for collection either once or twice daily. The usual paperwork in relation to this type of operation is discussed on page 577.

Organisations' procedures for the maintenance of equipment

There are basically two avenues you can go down in relation to the maintenance of equipment:

- wait until it breaks down
- have it serviced and maintained regularly.

Whilst the second option may seem to be the obvious choice it is not always the best or most cost-effective one. You can usually calculate which is the one to choose by applying a concept known as 'total cost of ownership' – and measuring this against the possible 'worst case scenario' of a breakdown.

Total cost of ownership refers to the total amount spent in buying, running, repairing and selling something. A good example is a car. If you estimate the cost of having a car just by thinking about the purchase price you will be in for a shock when you see your bank balance some time later! In addition to buying it you have obvious running costs of tax, fuel, insurance and servicing and repair costs. Finally, when you sell it you will receive less than you paid for it because, during the time you have owned it, it has depreciated in value. Only when you do all the sums can you calculate your total cost of ownership.

Office equipment can be assessed in the same way. You already know the purchase price. You may have calculated the running costs. You may also be offered a service or maintenance contract which means that, for a set price per year, the equipment will be regularly maintained. You may also have a call-out facility in the case of a breakdown. In some cases you may find that the price of such a 'deal' is reasonable while in other cases it can be very expensive. In fact, a company selling office equipment may have costed its service such that it makes very little profit on the sale of the original item but 'loads' the maintenance contract to make high profits on it – year after year!

If the equipment is known to be unreliable or problematic and if there would be a catastrophe if it was out of action, then, despite the cost, it may be more cost-effective to pay the price asked for service. However, if the equipment is usually reliable and a breakdown would not matter too much then your organisation may prefer to call someone in only when needed.

A final point to bear in mind is that you can often obtain a better 'service deal' on certain items by shopping around locally. However, the important point to check if you are going down this route is whether spare parts can be obtained easily – some manufacturers make certain you are tied to them for service by restricting the availability o spare parts only to approved repairers.

CHECK IT YOURSELF

1 Find out the maintenance procedures and agreements which relate to photocopying equipment in your organisation.
2 How may the policy for maintenance of photocopiers vary between
   a an organisation with a large centralised print-room where all the photocopying takes place
   b an organisation with several small photocopiers sited around the building?

Organisations' procedures for recording the acquisition of materials and equipment

No matter where you work, you will be unlikely to have the option of simply picking up the telephone, ordering goods or services and then just sitting back and waiting for them to arrive! If you have a sensible storage system for stock, it is highly unlikely that you can simply go and help yourself to whatever you want, when you want. In both cases you will usually find that you have to follow standard procedures in relation to completing the relevant documentation.

Purchasing materials and equipment

The documents relating to the actual buying of goods are likely to include some or all of the following:

- a formal enquiry requesting prices, delivery details, etc.
- an order with an official and unique order number, signed by a member of staff allowed to authorise the purchase
- a goods received note – completed when the goods are delivered and checked against the delivery note.

Bear in mind that you may not be allowed to order items yourself if:

- you have not followed the correct procedure in obtaining quotations or estimates
- you do not intend to use a recommended supplier
- the item has not been approved by your line manager.

Do make sure that you keep copies of all documents, carefully filed, in case there are any queries between the initial enquiry and payment for the goods. This includes also keeping safely all documents you receive from the supplier, e.g. quotation or estimate, delivery note, invoice and statement.

You will need to train your staff in both identifying the items which need re-ordering (unless your computer gives you this information automatically) and following the ordering procedures of the organisation. Do bear in mind that 'exception management' applies – if your communication systems are good then you should be forewarned if anyone will be wanting large quantities of certain items in the near future for a special job. Such requests can mean that you increase the priority level of an item to ensure that stocks are adequate.

If a centralised purchasing system is in operation then it will be your task to complete a standard office order form, send it to the Purchasing section and keep a copy for your records. If you have full responsibility for ordering goods then your order must still be made out on an official order form. You should note that if you telephone an order to a company it is standard practice for them to ask you for your official order number. If you are not going to make out the order and send it off immediately, do make sure that you clip a note to it to remind you not to use it for anything else! In an emergency make out the order promptly and fax it through for confirmation. In normal circumstances, obviously, it would be sent by post.

Again it is useful if orders are pre-printed in NCR (no carbon required) pads, so that the copies remain in the pad for reference.

Authorisation procedures for signing orders vary considerably and you need to check the policy of your company. At administrative level you may have authority to make out orders for up to a specified level of expenditure or you may have to ensure that all orders are signed or countersigned by your boss. Check also whether it is company policy that the order form has to detail the exact amount of expenditure or whether an estimated amount is acceptable (provided this is within certain parameters, e.g. 5 per cent of the eventual invoice.)

DID YOU KNOW?

Many organisations log all orders placed on computer and match these against goods received. The items ordered are usually categorised for costing purposes.

Companies using EDI to order goods often do not wait for invoices to arrive. They issue their own by computer and send them electronically – with the payment – to the supplier. They consider this to be more efficient because it reduces errors. It is then up to the supplier – rather than the buyer – to prove that the calculations are wrong!

Obtaining materials from stock

In most organisations stock is only issued against authorised requisitions and you need to decide your turn-around time between receipt of requisitions and stock availability. Stock is usually ordered on an internal stationery requisition form, the design of which will vary from one organisation to another. These forms are usually printed in pads of NCR paper. Three copies are usually required: the top copy and second copy of the order are sent to the stationery section and the third copy is retained for departmental records. When the requisition is received and the order completed, the top copy is returned with the goods (and any items to follow or out of stock noted on it) and the second copy is retained by the stationery section.

Problems can arise, however, when senior staff do not follow the system. If the MD suddenly rings you for a new signature book you would be very unwise to respond that there will be a delay of two days before this can be supplied and that you must receive a requisition form first! A simple way around this is to have a requisition pad in your own drawer which you can use in response to verbal requests by senior staff. The top copy of the requisition can be sent to the person concerned, together with their order, and you have the second copy for your records. It is from all these second copies that the stock control cards can be updated (see Element 9.2). Copies which relate to orders as yet incomplete should be kept in a 'pending' tray and only the items which have actually been issued logged as such on the stock record cards.

CHECK IT YOURSELF

1   Find out the system in operation for both ordering goods from suppliers *and* for obtaining items from stock in your organisation.
2   Find out the degree to which computers are used in your organisation in relation to the acquisition of materials and equipment.

ACTIVITY SECTION

1   Visit your local library and look through the journal section to find some current office equipment magazines – including *What to Buy for Business*. Alternatively obtain a buyer's guide if that would be appropriate (see Did You Know on page 554).

Select one particular item of equipment which you think should be replaced or updated in your own office. Find out as much as you can about new models and their features together with prices. Write a memo to your boss, explaining your requirement and supporting your argument with the facts you have researched.

2   You work in a small organisation where four members of staff operate standalone PCs. All these are out-of-date and none will run the new integrated software you have used in your last company. You have already persuaded your boss about the benefits of these packages and he has now asked you to 'shop around' to obtain some quotes on computers.

After making enquiries you narrow your search down to three companies.
   –   Computalk, situated locally, is a new company. They want payment in full with the order. The price of each computer will be £1450 + VAT. They do not offer a discount but there are no delivery charges. Your boss has heard mixed reports about this company.
   –   Data Supplies is situated 200 miles away but has been in business for many years. They are quoting £1550 plus VAT. They offer 6 per cent discount on all orders over £3000. Delivery charges are £20 and you will have one month to pay if you order from them. You have no information at all on their reputation.
   –   Rainbow Computers is a large company situated 20 miles away. It has only been in business for the past three years but has an excellent reputation. Their quote is £1600 + VAT less 5 per cent cash discount. Delivery charges are £10. If you buy from them you must pay immediately to obtain the discount – otherwise you can pay in full at any time in the next three months.

Evaluate each of these companies and categorise them as A, B or C. Then write a memo to your boss explaining which offer you wish to accept, giving your reasons.

3   Contact a local supplier and find out about the maintenance/service arrangements available if you purchased

   a   a fax machine
   b   an answering machine

as a private individual.

Obtain information on *one* maintenance agreement in operation within your organisation and compare this with the information you have been given, in terms of both cost and service provided.

Element 9.2

Monitor the use of materials and equipment

You have already seen in Element 9.1 – and probably know from your own experience – that the type of systems in use for purchasing goods in organisations can vary tremendously from a very slapdash attitude to strict conformance with specified procedures. The dangers with the former are that there is no control over expenditure and no system in place for ensuring that the organisation obtains the best value for money. However, there is little point in instigating a sensible purchasing system and then forgetting all about goods once they have been ordered. Only if usage is constantly monitored can an organisation be certain that it is spending its money wisely.

Ways of monitoring the receipt, cost and usage of materials and equipment

Monitoring, as you saw in Unit 8, relates to obtaining information which can assist you in making informed decisions. In the case of materials and equipment, monitoring not only helps you to save money for your organisation but also enables you to fulfil the needs of staff more effectively. There is absolutely no point at all in continuing to buy something no-one uses whilst insisting that no new items are bought in order to keep costs down! This will irritate everyone. Yet only if you are monitoring usage can you be aware of the fact that staff needs have changed – what was required yesterday is no longer needed today and, to be really efficient, you should be thinking about what everyone will be using tomorrow!

Checking goods on receipt

When goods are received they must be checked carefully. If the goods have been despatched by the supplier's own transport a delivery note will be attached. If another method of transport has been used then you will receive an advice note with the goods and the delivery note will follow by post. Note that neither of these documents gives the amount due. In a large organisation the goods may be received (and even unpacked) in a central Stores section and be delivered to you with an internal goods received note attached.

You need to teach staff how to check incoming goods carefully, i.e. to check that:

- nothing is missing
- goods are not included which were never ordered
- the correct goods have been received
- no goods are faulty or damaged.

If any goods are missing then train staff to examine the delivery note or goods received note as the next basic step. It may be that the goods are temporarily out of stock and will follow later, in which case they will be marked as such. A note needs to be made of these items so that they can be followed up later, if necessary, and a careful check made of the invoice when it arrives in case it includes these items in error.

Some companies automatically substitute out-of-stock goods with other similar lines. If you do not want these then you are quite within your rights to return them.

If there is an obvious discrepancy, and either goods are missing or the wrong items are included, then check the order before you telephone the company – just to make sure. You may have a problem if a junior wrote out the order with the wrong item code and this wasn't noticed, as you will have to rely on the goodwill of your supplier to take the goods back – they have no legal obligation to do so.

If goods are faulty, damaged or not as described in the catalogue then under the Sale of Goods Act 1979/Trade Descriptions Act 1968 you are within your rights to return them (see also Element 4.2).

Once the goods have been checked they should be put into the store immediately to prevent loss, damage or accidents (e.g. if boxes are left lying around). The stock is then booked into the system against the delivery note or goods received note.

Monitoring the cost of materials and equipment

There are various ways in which the cost of materials and equipment should be monitored:

- by checking the prices quoted by suppliers at various periods and recording any price changes which may affect your choice of supplier
- by noting any special offers being marketed by new or existing suppliers
- by keeping records of usage and running costs (see next section)
- by undertaking a stock audit and using this to cost out usage over a specific period (see page 576)
- by monitoring faults and running costs.

You can assist in this process by:

- making sure you have up-to-date catalogues and price lists to hand
- making sure that you are on the mailing list to receive mail shots containing special offers
- devising a system for monitoring faults and problems, so that if there are any particular problems with the equipment you are aware of them. If you are ever in any doubt as to whether you will incur a call-out charge if you ring for help then check first –

and do make sure that you really need assistance and you cannot solve the problem yourself

- using your 'faults log' to ascertain the cost/benefits of possible maintenance agreements once the warranty expires.

DID YOU KNOW?

There are three systems of costing stock, of which FIFO is the most common for consumables. FIFO refers to 'first in, first out'. In this system not only is stock issued in this way (so that the oldest stock is used first) but stock is also valued on the same basis (Figure 9.2.1).

Monitoring the usage of materials and equipment

Monitoring the usage of materials is done either manually or by computer through the stock control system in operation and by carrying out stock checks, inventories and audits at regular intervals. This is essential if changes in usage are going to be noticed – which affects both ordering and storage procedures for that particular item.

Usage of equipment should be monitored when:

- the capacity of current equipment needs to be checked
- each time the equipment is used there is a direct and significant effect on running costs.

Therefore a network administrator may check usage of a computer network – not because of cost, but because he or she is checking whether the system still has spare capacity or is overloaded at certain times of the day. Monitoring of telephone usage, the number of items passing through a franking machine, the number of faxes sent or how many photocopies have been made by each person is carried out because of the effect on cost – as well as to prevent misuse or abuse by staff using the equipment for private purposes.

DID YOU KNOW?

Most modern office equipment incorporates a logging system or audit trail to assist monitoring procedures. Photocopier users may have a specific key number which is then shown on a printout of usage per person, digital switchboards incorporate call logging and monitoring facilities, every fax message is usually accompanied by a transmission statement and a full audit trail can be printed at the touch of a button, and so on.

However, the degree to which any significant use is made of this information varies greatly from one organisation to another.

Scope and limit of own authority relating to financial expenditure

Your own remit in relation to financial expenditure was discussed in Element 9.1. However, whilst the amount of money you can spend will vary from one organisation to another, the degree to which you

COSTING STOCK

There are three ways of costing stock for valuation purposes: FIFO, AVCO (average cost system) and LIFO (last in, first out). Only the first two are used for consumables, with FIFO being the most common.

- **FIFO** (first in, first out) means that stock is both costed and used in relation to when it was received.
- **AVCO** (average cost valuation) means that the cost of stock is averaged out over a given period, e.g. a year.

Two examples should suffice.

1 A company takes delivery of bond paper twice a year; on both occasions 100 reams are received. The first time the cost is £500 and the second time (because of inflation) it is £600.
2 The company also buys two laptop computers for executives travelling abroad. The first cost £2000 and the second (which is identical) £2500.

At the end of the year the stock left is 50 reams of bond paper and two laptop computers.

Under FIFO it is assumed that the cheaper paper was used first, so the 50 reams remaining were bought at the higher price. The stock valuation is therefore £300. If AVCO is used then the average cost for the year is calculated – in this case £1100 ÷ 200 = £5.50. The stock is therefore valued at £275.

With the laptop computers, neither of these is consumed in the same sense as the paper. The total cost was £4500 and this is therefore their valuation under either system. However, if one is damaged and written off then under FIFO it would be valued at £2000 and under AVCO it would be valued at £2250. If LIFO was used then the valuation would be the last amount spent, i.e. £2500.

On the basis that the Inland Revenue will not accept LIFO as a public method of accounting it is unlikely that this system would be adopted. Similarly it is also required that a company's system of valuation is consistent. You may therefore be instructed to follow the same system which is used for valuing any stocks of goods which are held by your company for resale.

Figure 9.2.1 Costing stock

try to control costs should not. It is the responsibility of anyone working at an administrative level to keep a close eye on expenditure on a regular basis – not just in relation to one-off items. You may appreciate the importance of this more fully if you realise that all items purchased – and their usage – are closely related to the profitability of the organisation.

The actual relationship with the company accounts depends upon whether the items are for resale or for use by the organisation itself. Office supplies clearly fall into the latter category but are important because they represent an expense and must be listed as such in the company's accounts. Capital expenditure (e.g. on office equipment) is also important. If equipment is bought outright, rather than leased, an allowance has to be made for depreciation because the machine will obviously wear out over a number of years and have to be replaced.

TEST YOURSELF

Imagine that you have started work in a small company which operates no recognisable stock control system. Working in groups, try to think of:

a   the type of problems which may result from this approach
b   the possible financial consequences for the organisation.

Compare your group's list with those made by others before you read further.

The importance of cost control

All organisations which wish to remain in business for any length of time monitor their costs very carefully in all areas – from raw materials for manufactured goods to the size of their electricity or telephone bill. To see why, you need to understand how an organisation's profit figure is calculated – and your contribution to this.

Profit can be worked out from the formula:

$$(P - C) \times V = \text{gross profit}$$

where

P = selling price of an item
C = cost price of the same item
V = volume

This much is easily understood. The only way gross profit can be increased is by the company:

a   increasing the selling price (but then customers may reject their goods in favour of those made by a competitor)
b   increasing the volume sold (easier said than done if the market is competitive – plus the additional costs attached to this option must be considered, e.g. advertising)
c   reducing the cost of making the item (e.g. by using cheaper components or re-evaluating the design).

Not only is the last option the only one which is under the direct control of the company, but a cost reduction will have a greater effect on profits than the same percentage rise in sales. For this reason a company will be very concerned about the cost of making a product or supplying a service.

Once the gross profit has been calculated, the accountants are concerned with working out the net profit made by the company. In order to do this, the expenses of running the company must be known:

Gross profit − expenses = net profit

The largest item by far is usually the wage bill, but every item counts − electricity, rent, depreciation, expenditure on stationery, telephone, fax line, etc. The higher the expenses then, obviously, the lower the net profit. In a small organisation which is struggling to survive in a competitive market the difference of only a few thousand pounds may be crucial. Therefore, in an area which may seem mundane, office materials and equipment, you are making a direct contribution to your organisation's profitability by your actions (or lack of them!).

The penalties of a lack of control

If a company has no system whatsoever, any of the following may result. (Check this list against the one you made earlier − note that the following is not an exhaustive list and you may have thought of some good points not shown below.)

- Wrong or damaged stock is delivered but not noticed and therefore paid for.
- The wrong stock is ordered in error − it must be paid for although it is of no use to the company.
- The company is paying too much for stock; there is no system to take advantage of discounts through bulk buying, special offers, etc.
- There is wastage through deterioration or poor storage; stock becomes obsolete yet it is neither used up nor written off correctly.
- Invoices are unchecked so may be incorrect when paid or invoices are not paid on time so that no advantage is taken of prompt payment discounts and all suppliers are hesitant to deal with the company in future.
- Haphazard storage and ordering procedures result in staff being unable to find the goods they need − so either they order unnecessarily or supplies run out at critical moments, thus endangering customer relations.
- Over-ordering and/or lack of control means more capital is tied up in stock than is necessary.
- Pilfering and misuse may be rife.

Every item listed above will add to the organisation's costs and it should be your aim to reduce these wherever possible.

Paying for goods and monitoring expenditure

If you have bought goods which are subject to cash discount for prompt payment then do make sure you process the invoices for these in time to gain the benefit! The invoice should be the same as the delivery note except that this time the price is included. Do check that the two match and that all the calculations are accurate. If you are honest you will notify your supplier of any errors – no matter which of you would benefit!

At this point it is worth bearing in mind that the invoice should show a similar total amount to that which you expected – if you did your homework correctly. If, say, you bought a new set of electronic postage scales and when the invoice arrived it was for a larger amount than you were quoted, then you may be within your rights to return these under the Consumer Protection Act 1987. This is particularly the case if you were misled over the price.

Payment now needs to be authorised, and again the policy for this will depend on the organisation for which you work. In a small company your next step may be to make out the cheque and present it to your boss for signing. In a large organisation only your boss may be able to authorise payment; the invoice is then passed to the Finance section. In this case they will also be responsible for posting this payment to the accounts and, from this information, would be able to give you the total expenditure with any one supplier as and when you asked. However, this will show the total organisational expenditure with this company – not just that of your own department.

If your boss wishes to keep track of your section's own expenditure against the allocated budget then you are advised to keep your own departmental records. Similarly, in a small organisation you will be expected to keep records of expenditure on consumables against budget, even if you are not doing the accounts work yourself.

Whether you track this expenditure by supplier or item is up to you and will depend very much on the type of information your boss requires. A good computer package may be able to do much of the work for you if there are sections on the computerised stock card where you include the cost price and the supplier of the individual goods. In this case you must ensure that your staff note down any differences in price which are shown on the invoice from the cost price currently held in the computer for that item.

If you keep up-to-date and comprehensive records of expenditure then you will find that much of the work which needs to be undertaken for the annual audit (see page 576) is already completed and the task is not as overwhelming as you first thought it would be.

Ways of making the best use of materials and equipment

You will only be able to make the best use of materials and equipment if you have a clear system of control. In relation to materials, this obviously means devising a good stock control system.

Devising a system

Firstly it is important to define the scope of your system, i.e. whether it should encompass purely ordering and storage procedures or be more comprehensive in its coverage. Only if the system is devised to operate as a whole, rather than everyone 'doing their own thing', can it be expected to function properly. Not only that, but a system which is effective will also incorporate elements for coping with the unexpected.

As an administrator you may be involved in collecting information on this aspect and making your recommendations in relation to:

- which supplies should be held in stock and which (if any) should be bought only as required
- the maximum levels and minimum quantities to be held in relation to budgeted allowance for stock, storage space available, projected usage and lead times for supply
- the method of stock control to be used, i.e. manual or computerised
- the range of goods to be encompassed by the system, e.g. whether to include equipment, special requirements at director level
- the method and frequency of audit and the costing procedure to be employed
- the degree to which emergencies may occur which could not be served by the planned system – and how these should be handled
- the frequency with which operational requirements should be reconsidered and updated.

Monitoring procedures

When a system is devised there must be some way in which it is controlled. In a comprehensive system this does not mean merely completing stock record cards, as this is only one aspect of a total control mechanism. To be effective the system should incorporate:

- the total stock control system operation and the details which must be recorded
- the scale of the operation and staffing requirements (bearing in mind the range/quantities of goods in stock, usage, etc.)
- the frequency of usage reports to be issued and the method of analysis to be employed
- the frequency of inventory reconciliation and audits

- the method of valuation – usually AVCO (average cost system) or FIFO (first in first out)
- other reporting procedures and frequency.

The proposed control system for stock needs to be discussed and costed. If you already operate a microcomputer then a stock control package can easily be purchased and installed; you may, however, like to note that these are often linked to accounts packages and much may depend on the accounting system currently operated by your organisation. Nevertheless, given that you can operate most stock control packages independently, there are many advantages to having your system on computer, rather than operated manually (see below for a comparison of both systems).

The major benefit of a computerised system is that of on-going management information at the touch of a key as reports on usage, cost etc. can be generated quickly and easily. This facility needs to be linked with the requirements of your organisation in relation to the following.

- Physical stock checks – how frequently must a stock inventory be undertaken and the quantities in stock compared to the stock records?
- How often will a full audit be carried out and what system of costing will be used – and who will carry this out?
  A full audit means working out exactly how much has been spent in a specified period (usually a year) by:
  - carrying out a stock inventory
  - calculating the value of the stock currently held
  - calculating the quantity of issued stock and its cost
  - noting any discrepancies or adjustments (e.g. between issued stock plus current stock and the total ordered over the year) and costing these.
- What system should be instigated for coping with – and making adjustments for – damaged, missing or obsolete stock? These are easy to record on any stock control system but what you need to establish are company procedures and reporting requirements, e.g.:
  - what level of damage or 'loss' must be reported to management and what level is 'acceptable' (e.g. minor damage through carelessness, mislaying small items)
  - the degree to which you will be consulted and/or informed if any stock is about to become obsolete (to enable you to use it up quickly). In many cases obsolete stock can be given an alternative use (e.g. out-of-date forms converted into scrap pads or resold cheaply to staff). You need to establish whether you can instigate such measures yourself or whether you would need to check with your boss beforehand.

Once basic procedures have been established, so that you know which areas are your specific responsibility, the final fact to ascertain is how often the system is going to be reviewed. Obviously the needs of the company will change over time and therefore stock evaluation should be ongoing. Your boss may suggest that you prepare a report on your system, together with your recommendations for changes, every six months. If you detail your views first, he or she can then think over your proposals before the two of you meet to agree on any changes which must be made.

Organisations' procedures for recording usage of materials and equipment

The most usual procedure for recording usage of materials is to set up either a manual or a computerised stock control system.

Manual stock control

With this system a series of record cards is created, one card for each item in stock (see Figure 9.2.2). These may be index cards, stored in a cabinet, or visible-edge record cards, stored in special visible-edge folders. The advantages are that they are easy to complete (and amend) and can be taken from place to place (which may also be a disadvantage!). However, it does mean that you could take them home to examine if you so wish.

Stock issued is booked out on the card and incoming stock is also recorded, so that a running balance is available for each item. You can obviously adapt the style of card shown in Figure 9.2.2 for your own use – for example, if you have three stock cupboards to monitor, it would be sensible to include a heading for 'location'. This can also include the shelf number if the storage area is large to guide the stock control clerk.

STOCK RECORD CARD					
Item A4 Bond paper (white)			**Max** 100 reams **Min** 20 reams		
Supplier Office Supplies Ltd			**Units** reams		
Date	Received	Issued	Department	Order No.	Balance

Figure 9.2.2 A stock record card

The difficulty starts when you want to analyse stock movements or usage, as the only way this can be done is by searching through all the cards methodically, noting down relevant facts. Other types of analysis such as the frequency with which you use certain suppliers, may be almost impossible from this source and more easily compiled by examining invoices over a given period.

Computerised stock control

A computerised stock control package is simply a database designed to record, calculate and report on stock. A stock card similar to the one in Figure 9.2.2 will appear on your screen. If the package is designed to record stock which will be resold (as most are) then you will have to ignore certain areas if you are using this purely for in-house consumable items. For instance, there are likely to be spaces where you can insert the cost price (useful), and the percentage mark-up required (not so useful). The latter column means that the computer can automatically calculate the selling price of each item – a feature which is irrelevant for your needs.

There are usually other useful headings, e.g. 'Quantity currently on order'. This stops the computer reminding you to re-order something when you are still waiting for it to be delivered.

The package is accessed to record outgoing and incoming stock and the current balance is automatically shown on each card. A report can also be generated which details usage further – though you might find that this goes under the heading of 'Sales analysis'! If your package has this facility then you must have an area on the stock card to nominate a department, person or office, as it is under these headings that usage will be grouped.

It is in the area of reports that a computerised package definitely has the edge for anyone who is trying to monitor and control stock. In addition to 'usage' reports you can also ask the computer to give you:

- a printout of all stock at cost price (i.e. an instant stock valuation)
- a list of all stock which needs to be re-ordered
- a list of all items and the number currently in stock with a blank column at one side. This column is completed during a physical stock check (inventory) and the number actually in stock is recorded for comparison against the stock shown by the computer
- an audit trail. This logs all the computer entries which have been made – and is useful if you want to analyse what your junior could possibly have done to end up with the balance currently showing of 5 million paperclips!

You should note that the computer will enable you to make adjustments to stock levels (though these too will be recorded on the audit trail). The computer will want to know why you want to make such adjustments (to satisfy your accountants at a later date). Valid reasons may include a correction of an incorrect entry or because stock is damaged, lost or now obsolete.

Reporting procedures

It is useful to discuss with your boss the reports you should generate, how frequently, and whether or not you should show them all to him or her or operate a system of 'management by exception'. On this basis it is a matter of 'Don't tell me if it's OK, just tell me if it's not.' Whilst this is normally much easier for both of you, some initial parameters need to be set as to what is meant by OK! If you consider that the Sales department are still operating normally if they use 20 per cent additional stock one month, but your boss does not, then you will be operating at cross-purposes.

Once agreement has been reached you can then operate by means of, say, monthly 'exception reports' which detail only differences in usage or expenditure.

DID YOU KNOW?

You will be wise to make sure that you, too, establish a clear system of 'management by exception'. In other words – junior staff don't tell you when things are going to plan but they do tell you when things aren't! This way, if they suddenly find that there has been a run on a certain item, or if something is missing, you will know in time to take the appropriate action. Do remember to avoid the 'shoot the messenger' syndrome. If staff interrupt you with bad but important news when you are busy, and you are obviously annoyed with them, don't be surprised if they opt not to disturb you next time!

Usage of equipment

The way in which this can be logged or recorded has already been discussed on page 570. However, some organisations are less than efficient in putting this information to good use – possibly because they are concerned about staff reactions to what may be perceived as 'Big Brother' tactics. In fact, provided that the information is issued sensibly and without undue threats, it is usually to everyone's benefit to have the issues of costs, usage and expense clearly on the table. Sometimes there may be good suggestions which can be made by staff for saving money which would never have been made had they not been consulted in the first place. Similarly, however, managers cannot expect their staff to be cost-conscious unless they set a good example themselves.

CHECK IT YOURSELF

Find out the logging systems in operation in your organisation in relation to the usage of equipment. Discuss as a group whether this information is made public in the organisation and the degree of cooperation sought by staff and compare your answers.

Ways of making recommendations for improvements in the use of materials and equipment

Any recommendations you make for improvements should be based on sound financial and economic principles and not because you are attracted by sales blurb, a colour photograph in a catalogue or a very persuasive sales person! Improvements can often be suggested because of new developments in materials or equipment which would be beneficial to the organisation in general and users in particular. If your ideas also enable the organisation to save money then you are likely to be twice as popular!

You can only make sensible suggestions if you are completely up to date on what is required and why it is needed. You first need a working knowledge of what is already in use, what it can do and what it can't. You then need to be aware of feedback from users and their comments. Finally you need to be well informed in terms of what is coming on the market.

As an example, think about one of the most commonly used materials in an office – paper. How much do you know about paper – how it is made, what it costs, its sizes and suitability? Did you know, for instance, that paper comes in different weights as well as different sizes? Paper thickness is expressed in microns, where 1 micron = 0.001 mm. This is usually shown in terms of gsm or grams per square metre. The higher the figure the heavier and thicker the paper. The lightest paper is about 45 gsm and is only suitable for copies. Bond paper starts at 60 gsm and ranges up to 85 gsm – the heaviest is watermarked quality for prestige work. Printer paper starts at 60 gsm and ranges up to 90 gsm.

Did you know, too, that different paper has special finishes or is specially treated for certain usage? For instance, copier paper is specially treated during manufacture to be impervious to the heat it encounters during the copying process. It is also specially treated to lie flat. You cannot normally, therefore, mix and match ordinary bond paper and copier paper with good results. Equally, if you use a laser printer you may find that premium bond paper is recommended but that any less than 80 gsm is too light.

Unless you know these facts you will be all too easily impressed the next time a sales person walks through the door and offers you a unique paper sample which will work on anything. This may be true – but you should ask the right questions to ascertain the accuracy of the claim first!

Once you have the facts to hand, you have several choices:

- if you have the authority, you can order some of the new materials yourself
- alternatively, you may persuade the sales person to let you have a trial pack – possibly for free
- you can ask staff for their views
- you can ask your boss for permission to change your normal order
- if the item is expensive, you can memo your boss with details for consideration.

The approach you use will depend largely upon your own area of responsibility and authority, the cost of the item concerned and the type of boss you work for!

DID YOU KNOW?

With all items of capital expenditure the time will come when it is actually cheaper to buy a new machine than it is to keep servicing and maintaining the old one. However, do let your own judgement (and the figures in your faults log) be your guide, rather than the service engineer. Whilst possibly very honest and honourable, he or she may also have a vested interest in persuading you to update your equipment. If you have kept accurate records then the situation is easy to clarify and you have the basis of a factual, objective request to your boss for the replacement that you need.

Organisations' procedures for disposal of unwanted or faulty materials and equipment

You have already seen the type of procedures which are in operation in organisations in relation to the receipt of faulty materials (see page 568), which should, of course, be identified on delivery. However, sometimes it is the case that items will not be identified as faulty until some time later, particularly if they have been kept in storage. Immediately the problem is discovered you should contact the supplier – with most reputable companies (and particularly ones you deal with frequently) you should have no problem returning such items at a later date.

However, procedures should also be in place for dealing with materials and equipment which:

- have been ordered in excess and are now surplus to requirements
- are now obsolete (e.g. pre-printed items showing telephone numbers that changed on Phone Day, old computers which will not run modern packages)
- have become faulty in use – from a stapler or a floppy disk to a fan heater or computer
- have been damaged during storage (through sunlight, heat, water or just carelessness).

These procedures need to be in force so that adjustments in relation to the valuation of stock can be carried out at the time the audit is prepared.

All staff need to be aware that they cannot simply throw things away if they don't like the look of them! This is particularly the case with expensive items of capital equipment – whether they work or not! Usually such items have to be officially 'written off' and the company's insurers informed before they can be disposed of. All items should be examined first to see if they could be:

● repaired quite easily and cheaply
● given an alternative use, e.g. made into scrap pads
● sold to staff at discount prices.

If none of these is a possibility then you may find that you will have the authority to dispose of small items provided that you record the necessary adjustments in the stock system, but you will have to inform the Finance section to arrange for capital items to be officially 'written-off'. Whatever you do, never discard (or resell!) anything without checking the official procedure first!

 ## ACTIVITY SECTION

1   You are about to teach a junior member of staff exactly how she should complete a standard stock record card and book stock in and out.

   a   Devise a clear list of instructions which she can use as a check list to help her to accomplish this task.
   b   Three weeks later, you notice that many of the cards are incomplete or illegible. State clearly the action you would take to try to solve the problem.

2   You work for a clothing company which started life five years ago as the brainchild of the owner, Jeff Tate. Since then it has gone from strength to strength – selling mainly overseas. A small fax machine has been installed in your section ever since you can remember and is now used almost constantly. Last year the old one 'died' and Jeff Tate, without consulting you at all, simply replaced it with the same make but a slightly updated model.

   Because the company operates in a competitive market Jeff Tate is also keen on keeping costs down. His biggest worry at present is the size of the phone bill – for the last quarter it was over £2500. He has tried everything he can think of to reduce it but nothing seems to make any difference.

   Yesterday you read a report which highlighted the fact that most managers do not associate additional fax use with increasing telephone costs. The report suggested that costs can be reduced if a fax machine has time-saving features such as multi-tasking, sequential broadcasting, relay broadcasting and delayed send. You consider that at least 25 per cent of faxes could be delayed to off-peak transmission times without difficulty or loss of business because of changes in time zones around the world.

Finally, the report concentrated upon hardware and argued that machines with the faster 14.4 kbps modem also cut transmission times, and therefore line costs, and are particularly valuable if a large number of international faxes are sent. You estimate that over 55 per cent of your faxes are sent abroad.

a State the ways in which you can obtain actual hard evidence of fax usage in relation to telephone charges for Jeff Tate.

b Obtain information on at least three different fax machines which offer time-saving features.

c Write a memo to Jeff Tate which sets out the reasons why you think he should upgrade his fax and the type and model you recommend, with reasons. In addition, support your argument with financial data and your proposed cost savings over the next year.

d Attach to the memo your proposed training plan for staff, to ensure that maximum benefits are gained from the installation of the new fax.

3 You have recently started work as office administrator for a relatively small company which has rapidly expanded over the past three years. One of your duties is to introduce a stock control system and to monitor expenditure on office supplies. The director to whom you are responsible, John Frankland, has given you a list of the items he knows the company used last year, although he doesn't think that this is exhaustive. The list does not include printed items such as letterheads, memo paper, printed forms, business cards and compliment slips and all quantities shown are approximate.

A4 bond paper (white)	50 reams
A4 bank paper	5 reams
paper clips	2000
brown manila file folders	200
A4 photocopying paper	200 reams
carbon paper	1 box
fax rolls	20
blue ballpoint pens	150
DL white envelopes (self-adhesive)	5000
C5 brown envelopes	2000
HB pencils	30
lever arch files	2
box files	15
envelope wallets	100
shorthand pads	500
punches	5

Sellotape (large rolls)	30
bulldog clips	2
toner cartridges (for laser printer)	8
continuous feed printer paper	20 boxes

a Divide the list into active and non-active stock and note down suggested maximum and minimum quantities to be stocked in each case.

b Examine a current office supplies catalogue and list any other items you feel should be included, and again add maximum and minimum quantities.

c From the price list which accompanies the catalogue calculate the cost of obtaining maximum stock levels for all the items you have listed.

d Analyse the list Mr Frankland has given you from the point of view of possible wastage, misuse or pilferage, i.e. note down any discrepancies in the quantities used which you think are suspicious or indicate that staff are not cost conscious.

e Detail all your findings and recommendations in a memo.

4 You are responsible for the ordering, recording and monitoring of all stock used by the Sales department for which you work. Although your organisation has a centralised Purchasing department and all accounts are settled by the Finance section, each department in the organisation is responsible for monitoring its own expenditure against budget for items such as consumables.

Because your department has a large requirement for stationery stock, especially when major events occur – exhibitions, presentations, seminars, etc. – you keep separate stock records of all the goods you order and use and of all expenditure by the department.

To help you in your task your boss, Ms Pamela Street, has agreed that the present manual system of stock control should be replaced with a software package you can run on your IBM-compatible computer which, at present, you use only for word processing.

She has asked you to investigate at least two suitable packages and to find out the features of each and the price.

Carry out the investigation she requires and detail your findings in a memo. Include details on the method you would use to transfer the information from one system to another and the timescale you think would be required for this. Include any disadvantages you consider there may be in operating the system on computer and the ways in which you think these might be overcome.

Organise and record meetings

Element 10.1

Arrange and prepare for meetings

You should note that this unit is an **option** unit. The fact that you have chosen to study and prove your comeptence in this area should mean that as part of your job you undertake duties which involve arranging and preparing for meetings in your workplace. If you do not, then you are advised not to select this option. If you only do part of the work outlined in the scheme then you will need to talk to your tutor or adviser about the best way to demonstrate competence in the remaining areas.

Organisations' procedures relating to the conduct and financial provision of meetings

Conduct of meetings

The conduct of a meeting depends very much on its purpose. Informal meetings, by their very nature, take place without any specified procedures or rules being followed. Formal meetings, on the other hand, tend to be very procedure conscious and there can be problems if the conduct of the meeting is such that these procedures are not followed.

Informal meetings can range from a discussion between two people on a specific topic to a regular series of discussions by a group (sometimes called a working party) to talk about ongoing matters which affect the work of that group. Formal meetings, on the other hand, are normally held:

- for a specific purpose
- at regular intervals.

The proceedings of those meetings are formally recorded.

The type of formal meeting in which you as an administrator or PA may be involved depends on the type of organisation in which you work and also at what level. Generally speaking, the higher the level, the more formal the meeting.

Whatever the level, however, you should expect at some stage in your career to have involvement in:

- a Board meeting
- various types of committee meeting
- an Annual General Meeting

- an Extraordinary General Meeting
- a class meeting (less frequently!)
- a meeting of creditors (possibly only once!)
- a statutory meeting (as above!).

Board meeting

A body such as a limited company must act through its Board of Directors, which is responsible for managing the company's affairs. The first Board meeting must be held as soon as possible after the appointment of the first directors and the receipt of the company's Certificate of Incorporation.

Business at subsequent meetings might include both policy-making and routine business transactions, such as:

- development of the company's business
- means of acquiring additional capital
- acquisition of another company
- receipt of reports from various committees
- sanctioning large amounts of capital expenditure
- the organisation of the company
- the appointment of senior staff.

Committee meeting

If allowed by the Articles of Association (the rules by which a company is governed under the Companies Acts 1948–1989), the Board of Directors can delegate powers and duties to a committee or committees which carry out certain tasks and report back to the Board.

The principal forms of committee are as follows.

Executive

A committee with plenary power, i.e. one which can make a binding decision provided it acts *intra vires* (within its terms of reference). If it acts *ultra vires* (outside its terms of reference) its decision will not be binding.

Advisory

A committee which gives advice and makes recommendations but which does not have the power to make binding decisions.

Standing

A committee which is permanently in existence with business conducted at regular intervals.

Ad hoc

A committee formed for a particular task. Having achieved its purpose it then ceases to exist.

Sub

A committee formed as part of another committee which can be either standing or ad hoc.

Joint

A committee formed for the purpose of coordinating the activities of two or more committees. Again it may be standing or ad hoc.

Annual General Meeting

Unless the company is a private company, it must hold an AGM each year to which all shareholders must be invited. The business transacted is that specified in the Articles of Association, e.g.:

- to receive the directors' and auditors' reports
- to examine the accounts and balance sheets
- to sanction the dividend
- to appoint or re-appoint directors
- to decide on the auditors' remuneration.

Other business may be transacted provided its nature is clearly stated.

Extraordinary General Meeting

An EGM is normally called to transact business which cannot conveniently be held over until the next AGM.

Other less frequent meetings include the following.

Class meetings

Held principally in connection with the variation of rights and privileges attached to different classes of share.

Meetings of creditors or classes of creditors

Held in connection with any form of reconstruction or on the winding up of the company.

Statutory meetings

Held between the directors of a company and its shareholders not earlier than one month or later than three months after a company commences trading.

Financial provision

Some forms of meeting are more elaborate and formal than others and consequently more time-consuming. If, for instance, the meeting is to be an Annual General Meeting many formalities have to be observed. Other meetings such as departmental meetings can be more informal as the number of members can be kept to a minimum, the amount of paperwork reduced and the order of business made more flexible. In business, time equals money and the more elaborate the meeting, the more expensive it is to operate. Consequently the benefits of having a meeting should also be balanced against the expense involved.

TEST YOURSELF

You are a keen runner and have become a member of the local athletics club. Unfortunately, however, someone has informed on you and the club chairman now knows that you can both take notes and use a word processor! He has therefore persuaded you to act as meetings secretary and to prepare for and take notes at the monthly committee meetings. The club treasurer has recently retired and, as yet, the chairman has had little success in finding a replacement.

You start to prepare for your first meeting but find that you have insufficient stationery – both typing paper and club letter-headed paper. The typewriter you are asked to use is on its last legs – and you have a feeling that to ask for its replacement with a word processor is a waste of time. You ask the chairman whether or not tea and biscuits are provided. He says they are.

The club house is kept open for two extra hours each month to allow these meetings to take place and the caretaker who normally locks up therefore stays on for those two hours. The bar is closed during that period as the bar steward is a member of the meeting.

Fortunately, however, all the committee members give their time voluntarily – which is just as well because there are 14 of them. You also give up your free time not only to attend the meeting but also to make arrangements for the meeting and to carry out a number of duties after it has ended (including typing up notes of the proceedings).

When a new club treasurer is appointed she is anxious to keep the books straight and asks you to give her some idea of the money spent on each meeting.

1   List the items of expenditure involved in running such a meeting. Are there any 'hidden' items which are not immediately apparent?
2   If you were asked to reduce costs, state how you would go about doing so.
3   Write a short paragraph on the additional expenditure which would have been incurred had the meeting been a work meeting rather than one attended by volunteers.
4   If you were asked to weigh the balance of having regular meetings against the expense which they incur, what arguments would you use?

Own role and responsibilities

Normally one of your duties as administrator is to act as the meeting secretary whenever a meeting is chaired by your boss. In this context – as in many others – you must be a good organiser. For best results you should work closely with your chairperson, but certain tasks will be your responsibility. Remember that there is a regular cycle of tasks for meetings and you must therefore keep a checklist of things to be done for each meeting you attend. You should also make certain that you have a first-class filing system to deal with all the paperwork.

(See page 608 for your specific responsibilities in arranging and preparing for meetings.)

Ways of determining the purpose and objectives of meetings

Purposes of meetings

The obvious question here is why a meeting is ever necessary given the rapid advances in telecommunications and the ease by which written and pictorial information can be transmitted by fax and E-mail. However, there are occasions when meetings need to be held – as the example below indicates.

You are administrator to the Chief Executive of a local borough council. It is your custom to spend the first hour each Monday checking diaries and planning appointments. This Monday you meet as usual and run through the events of the week.

- Your boss needs some updating on the progress being made in the implementation of new contracts for the cleaning staff.
- He feels that he should meet the cleaning staff to explain to them yet again the reasons for wanting to implement the new contracts.
- He wants to speak to the departmental managers to check on whether or not they are going to have difficulty in meeting their quarterly targets. He is anxious that the overall target of reducing expenditure by 5 per cent should be met.
- He also wants to hold a discussion with the Accounts and Computer Services Managers before he makes a decision as to what he should tell the next meeting of the Finance and General Purposes Committee about the progress being made towards the computerisation of the accounts system.

Obviously, when meeting the various groups of people, your boss wants to:

- be informed
- explain
- persuade
- pacify
- encourage
- motivate
- pressurise
- make a decision.

However, it could be argued that he could have done this in a number of other ways. He could, for instance, have written a memo to everyone; he could have asked for information over the telephone; or he could have seen everyone individually.

TEST YOURSELF

Discuss as a group or with your tutor or adviser why you think that, in each of the above cases, a meeting with the people concerned would be the most appropriate form of communication. Think, for instance, of:

- the advantages of oral rather than written communication in a situation where persuasion or encouragement is required
- the exchange of ideas and the generation of interest
- dispelling anxiety
- the achievement of a common objective.

Other purposes

Meetings are also frequently held to:

- identify, discuss and find a solution to a problem
- brief staff on new methods, procedures, policies, etc.
- assess progress
- negotiate agreement towards a joint decision
- conduct disciplinary proceedings.

DID YOU KNOW?

The main **objective** of any meeting is to achieve what it has set out to do, i.e. to achieve its purpose.

Ways of determining purpose and objectives

The ways in which you can determine both purpose and objectives include:

- your own knowledge – if you are working closely with your boss and he or she is chairing a particular meeting you should be quite clear as to its purpose and objective
- information given to you by your colleagues or other members of the meeting as to what they think are the purpose and objectives
- through reading
  - the terms of reference (normally included in the minutes of either the first meeting or in its standing orders (see page 593)
  - the last two or three sets of minutes to establish the general 'flavour' of what is being discussed and the reason for it.

Ways of evaluating and selecting venues

Most meetings are held on site either in a specially allocated meetings room, the Board Room or in a manager's office. If you are arranging such a meeting all you will be required to do is check:

- which room is going to be used and book it, if necessary
- that it is of a suitable size and that there is sufficient equipment and furniture available
- on the day of the meeting that it is not too hot/cold/dark/untidy etc.
- whether any refreshments are required.

If you do think the room unsuitable you can either book another room for succeeding meetings (if this is possible) or take steps to have the existing room improved.

More is expected of you if you are responsible for arranging meetings at an external venue. What you should do, first of all, is to establish the type and purpose of the meeting. The more important and high profile it is, the more likely it is that it will need to be held at a high quality venue – which is obviously going to add to the cost and which puts pressure on you when making your choice. However, even a small meeting with a client, or a staff development meeting deliberately held off the premises so that no one will be distracted by routine work activities, will need to take place in the most appropriate surroundings. Otherwise the objective is defeated.

It is useful to agree the following *general* points with your boss:

- the price range (some organisations specify how much should be spent on different types of meetings)
- the geographical location
- any specific preferences for particular hotels or conference centres in the area
- any specific standard facilities, e.g. video conferencing facilities to accommodate very large meetings, secretarial facilities such as access to photocopiers, etc.

Also to be established in relation to *specific* meetings is:

- the date (or dates)
- the type of meeting and the number of members involved
- what meal arrangements are required
- whether or not overnight accommodation is needed.

If you are an experienced administrator or PA you will have built up a file of suitable venues over a period of time. If you are less experienced you will have to start from scratch. In either case, however, you must be careful to update the information at regular intervals – remember the odd occasion when you returned to a hotel or restaurant which you thought was marvellous only to find to your huge disappointment that its standards had fallen!

DID YOU KNOW?

It is useful to make a special note of the different venues required by:

- your company as a whole or particular committees/working parties
- those organising meetings which require visiting speakers
- those organising special presentations
- overseas visitors who may be invited to attend
- any disabled members
- anyone with special dietary requirements.

Selecting the venue

Most hotels now offer a comprehensive business service to cater for almost any type of meeting or conference and will provide you with well-produced and highly professional brochures on the services they offer.

CHECK IT YOURSELF

a Check at your place of work whether meetings or conferences are ever held at external venues. If so, find out where and try to establish the reason for that choice.

b Obtain at least four brochures from hotels within a 20-mile radius of your place of work.

Discuss your findings with the rest of your group or your tutor or adviser and write a short paragraph on the different facilities offered by each venue. Be sure to make reference to the prices charged.

Evaluating the venue

No hotel or conference centre is going to point out to you any drawbacks in their services. It is up to you to find that out for yourself. Unless you have a completely reliable source of information, by far the best method of evaluating a venue is to go to see it. Bear in mind, however, that merely wandering around a hotel accompanied by a charming hotel manager isn't going to tell you everything you want to know – particularly if you are wined and dined at the same time.

It is good practice to prepare a small questionnaire beforehand and to complete it immediately after the visit. Not only will this force you to concentrate on certain basic requirements, it will enable you to make a comparison with other similar hotels and it will also act as an aide memoire for you or your colleagues in future.

TEST YOURSELF

Visit either two of the hotels from which you have already obtained information or two hotels used by your place of work. In each case complete a copy of the questionnaire given in Figure 10.1.1. Discuss your results with the rest of the group or with your tutor or adviser.

Types of facilities associated with meetings

Once having arranged suitable accommodation, you should then be able to check on the facilities required. Basic facilities include:

- suitable table and seating arrangements
- equipment such as overhead projectors, CCTV (for the showing of videos), laptop computers
- the provision of the necessary documentation (see below).

Range and sources of documentation for meetings

Most meetings are conducted in accordance with their Standing Orders – the rules which provide for the way in which the meeting should be run. In such circumstances it is important for you to be

NAME OF HOTEL/VENUE

Address:

Telephone Number: **Fax Number:**

Number and size of meetings rooms:

Facilities:

Number of bedrooms:

Dining/bar facilities:

Leisure facilities (swimming pool, sauna, etc.):Facilities for the disabled:

Car parking facilities:

Accessibility from airports, railway stations, motorways:

Price:

Contact:

Date:

Figure 10.1.1 Evaluation questionnaire

aware of the appropriate paperwork you may have to prepare in order to comply with those rules:

- Notice
- Agenda
- Chairperson's Agenda
- Supplementary papers
- Minutes

Notice

You must let the members of a meeting know when it is going to happen and where it is going to take place. If the meeting is informal all you may need to do is to type a brief memo or even make a telephone call (although cautious administrators rarely rely on verbal communication!). If the meeting is formal, however, certain procedures must be observed.

The notice must be sent to all members. If it is not this may affect the validity of the meeting, i.e. whether or not the decisions made at that meeting have any binding effect. However, if you do forget to send a notice to a member all may not be lost – your omission may be excused if:

- the rules provide for waiver, i.e. where the members of the meeting are allowed to overlook the mistake
- everyone entitled to be present is actually present – they may have heard about the meeting on the office grapevine! – and agrees to what is being done
- those to whom a notice has not been sent are 'beyond summoning distance', e.g. abroad or too ill to attend.

The length of notice required is normally provided for in the rules or Standing Orders of the meeting. If not, reasonable notice must be given. Unless otherwise provided, it is implied that the number of days stated are clear days – i.e. exclusive of the day of serving the notice and of the day of the meeting.

CHECK IT YOURSELF

Look at the example of a notice shown in Figure 10.1.2 and check that the following details are included:

- place of meeting
- date, day and time of meeting
- the kind of meeting, where applicable
- details of any special business (if appropriate)
- the date of notice

```
┌────────────────────────────────────────────────────────┐
│                        NOTICE                          │
│                                                        │
│  Derby Ceramics Ltd                                    │
│  King Street                                           │
│  DERBY                                                 │
│  DE3 1AA                                               │
│                                                        │
│  12 June 199_                                          │
│                                                        │
│  The next Board meeting will be held in Committee      │
│  Room No 1 at 1430 hours on Tuesday, 27 June.          │
│                                                        │
│  (Signed)                                              │
│                                                        │
│  Anne Davies                                           │
│  Secretary                                             │
│                                                        │
└────────────────────────────────────────────────────────┘
```

Figure 10.1.2 Notice of meeting

- the signature of the person convening the meeting (normally that of the meetings secretary and only included in formal notices).

Agenda

No-one should be expected to attend a meeting without having some clear idea of what is to be discussed at that meeting. Think of the agenda as a compass which is intended to indicate the direction the meeting must take.

The items on the agenda should therefore be arranged according to the rules of the meeting; if these do not specify the order it is up to you to arrange the items logically – normally with the routine business first so as to leave more time for the other more specific business of the meeting.

Fortunately there are a number of guidelines for you to follow.

CHECK IT YOURSELF

Look at the example of an agenda shown in Figure 10.1.3.

- **The heading** This must indicate what kind of a meeting it is and when and where it is to be held. It is usual to send the notice out with the agenda so that the information is not given twice. Only when time is short and an agenda is not yet completed is a separate notice sent out.
- **Apologies for absence** This item allows for the recording of the names of those people who have indicated that they cannot attend.

```
┌─────────────────────────────────────────────────────────┐
│                    NOTICE AND AGENDA                      │
│                                                           │
│  Derby Ceramics Ltd                                       │
│  King Street                                              │
│  DERBY                                                    │
│  DE3 1AA                                                  │
│                                                           │
│  12 June 199_                                             │
│                                                           │
│  The next Board meeting will be held in Committee Room No 1 at 1430 │
│  hours on Tuesday, 27 June.                               │
│                                                           │
│  (Signed)                                                 │
│  Anne Davies                                             │
│  Secretary                                                │
│                                                           │
│                                                           │
│  A G E N D A                                              │
│    1   Apologies for absence                              │
│    2   Minutes of the previous meeting                    │
│    3   Matters arising                                    │
│    4   Correspondence                                     │
│    5   Display of company's products at autumn exhibition │
│    6   Staff welfare                                      │
│    7   Any other business                                 │
│    8   Date and time of next meeting                      │
└─────────────────────────────────────────────────────────┘
```

Figure 10.1.3 Example of an agenda

- **Minutes of the previous meeting** This allows members the opportunity of pointing out any factual errors which may have been made in the minutes.
- **Matters arising** This enables members to comment on and query any action taken as a result of the discussions at that meeting.
- **Correspondence** This item can be used to draw the attention of the meeting to a communication of general interest, e.g. a request from a charity for volunteers for a flag day.
- **Specific item(s)** There can be as many items of specific business as you or the chairperson think fit into the meeting's terms of reference.
- **Any other business** This item allows members to ask for discussion to take place on a matter which has arisen too late to be included as a normal item on the agenda.

- **Date and time of next meeting** This is usually the final agenda item. However, it is often useful for the chairperson to discuss this item before the actual business of the meeting begins This overcomes the problem of members who have to leave before the end of the meeting.

DID YOU KNOW?

It is usual for the chairperson to ask members for items for 'Any other business' at the beginning of the meeting. It is then possible for a decision to be made as to their importance – whether they should be discussed immediately, whether time should be left at the end of the meeting for discussion, or discussion should be deferred until the next meeting, when the item may be given its own 'slot' on the agenda.

Chairperson's agenda

From the very beginning you will realise that your main role as the meetings secretary is to support and assist your chairperson. Of particular assistance to him or her is any quick and easy source of reference to use during the course of the meeting. The normal agenda is usually insufficient for this purpose and what you should therefore do is to provide the chairperson with an annotated or extended version (Figure 10.1.4).

DID YOU KNOW?

1 It is likely that your chairperson will use the chairperson's agenda to make notes as the meeting progresses and these notes may help you when you are preparing the minutes. Be careful, however! It is advisable that once the minutes have been prepared and accepted by the members that the chairperson's agenda is destroyed – otherwise there could be problems if the chairperson's notes (which may have been made in a hurry and not corrected at a later date) do not coincide with the actual minutes. This is one of the few occasions when you are actually encouraged not to keep a record.

2 At formal meetings you may be required to:
  – use the full notice heading instead of the abbreviated form used in Figure 10.1.4
  – provide the actual wording of the motions as the chairperson will announce them, e.g. 'I move that the Meeting accepts the report of the Auditors for the year under review.'

Supplementary papers

Most meetings require you to prepare additional documentation, depending on the items to be discussed. Try to avoid the following problems!

- It is common for too much paperwork to be produced, which deters all but the most determined member from reading it. How enthusiastic would you be about reading a

CHAIRPERSON'S AGENDA

Meeting: Board Meeting
Date/time: 1430 hours, 27 June 199_
Place: Committee Room No 1

AGENDA ITEM	NOTES
1 **Apologies for absence** John Brookes still in hospital – meeting's best wishes for a speedy recovery.	1
2 **Minutes of previous meeting**	2

3 **Matters arising**
Questions may be asked on:
a final cost of refurbishment
   to reception area – £27500
b progress on launch of new
   christening mug
   – Press conference 2/7 –
     information to follow
   – Article in *The Lady* 7/7
   – Advertising campaign
     10/7 onwards
	3

4 **Correspondence** Letter of thanks from local college for company's response to request for work-experience places	4

5 **Display of company's products at**
autumn exhibition
– to be held at NEC Birmingham
– Sales Manager to provide members
  with report. Information pack
  already circulated
	5

6 **Staff welfare** Staff Welfare Committee anxious to hold staff dinner dance. Advise Board to recommend that Committee be asked to provide further details at next meeting.	6
7 **Any other business** Comments on selling trip to USA	7
8 **Date and time of next meeting** Avoid 7–14 July – Conference in Brussels	8

Figure 10.1.4 Example of a chairperson's agenda

30-page document relating to just one item on a 10-item agenda?

- Equally annoying to members is receiving a document on the morning of the meeting – although this may provide a good excuse for some of them to give up even the pretence of having read it!
- Wherever possible try to avoid tabling papers (i.e. producing them at the time of the meeting) – given that your hands may be tied if you are waiting for your chairperson or another senior member of the organisation to produce the relevant documents.
- Remember, however, that if you send out too much documentation there is a danger that
  a   people will forget to bring it along to the meeting
  b   some will have read it and others not
  c   some confidential information will be accidentally passed on to others
  You're in a no-win situation!
- Try to adopt a layout for these papers which is easy to read and to which the members will become accustomed. Unlike the rest of the meetings documentation there is usually no set format for you to follow. Consider the use of
  –   headings and subheadings
  –   numbered paragraphs, sections and subsections for easy reference
  –   tables, graphs and illustrations.

Make sure that every paper is properly identified and linked to the relevant agenda item. Ensure too that the reproduction of the documents is of a high standard – you are trying to tempt members to read them.

Minutes

It is always wise to have a written record of any business transacted, even at an informal meeting. In some cases it is a legal requirement. Although the format to be followed can vary and often depends on 'house rules', the more formal a meeting is, the more likely it will be that you have to record the proceedings in a standardised manner.

CHECK IT YOURSELF

Look at the set of minutes in Figure 10.1.5 and check that the following information has been included.

- The name of the organisation, the type of meeting and the place, date and time of the meeting.
- The names of those present. It is usual to put the name of the chairperson first and that of the secretary last. It is also advisable to put

the names of the rest of the members in alphabetical order – thus avoiding problems of status! You should also indicate whether any member is a co-opted member (i.e. one invited for a special purpose as distinct from one who is a regular member of the meeting) or there ex officio (i.e. one who is entitled to attend by virtue of his or her position in the organisation).

Note that if the meeting is particularly large (such as a shareholders' meeting) you need record only the number present.

- A brief note of what has been discussed and decided using an acceptable form of wording. Items should be numbered, and, if possible, should follow the numbering of the Agenda.
- The date and time of the next meeting. From what you already know, how should this item have been dealt with – bearing in mind that the meeting might have lasted a long time?
- Space for the chairperson to sign and date the minutes once they are agreed as a correct record at the next meeting.

DID YOU KNOW?

1   Enclosures with minutes can present special problems unless you are very well organised. A good method is to abandon the usual procedure of typing 'Enc.' at the foot of the minutes and substitute a short line of four dots in the left margin each time an enclosure is mentioned. At the end you need simply check the number of times you have typed dots against the number of enclosures. If your word-processing package won't let you do this, list the enclosures at the end.

2   The more senior an administrator or PA you become the greater the possibility that you will be required to produce minutes which contain more formal language than that used in the illustration in Figure 10.1.5. Look, for example, at item 6 which summarises the discussion and the decision about the organisation's annual dinner dance. In a more formal context the item would have to be rewritten to include the word RESOLVED (because a decision was made) and to reduce the discussion, e.g.

'It was RESOLVED that the Staff Welfare Committee be asked to report back to the Board of Directors on the possibility of holding a staff dinner dance.'

3   Numbering systems for minutes vary – some organisations use the minute number followed by the year, e.g. 23/95 would be the 23rd item discussed and minuted for that committee during 1995.

4   Some organisations insist on the inclusion of an Action Column – to contain the initials of those who are given the responsibility to undertake certain tasks and report back at the next meeting. The aim is to focus on both responsibility and accountability.

MINUTES

Minutes of the Board Meeting held in Committee Room No 1 at 1430 hours on 27 June 199_.

PRESENT

Ms Gemma Fisher	Secretary
Mr Ernst Heilberg	Chair
Mrs Linda Hargreaves	Purchasing Manager
Mr David Jones	Sales Manager (Co-opted)
Miss Veronica Olonde	Secretary
Mr John Wright	HR Manager

1 APOLOGIES FOR ABSENCE
Apologies for absence were received from Mr John Brookes. The Chairperson was instructed by the meeting to send him best wishes for a speedy recovery.

2 MINUTES OF THE PREVIOUS MEETING
The minutes of the previous meeting were taken as read, agreed as a true and correct record and signed by the chairperson.

3 MATTERS ARISING
The chairperson reported that the final cost of the refurbishment of the reception area was £27500.
He also outlined the publicity arrangements made for the forthcoming launch of the new christening mug.
The Purchasing Manager confirmed that the maintenance contract for the computer equipment had been renewed for another year.

4 CORRESPONDENCE
The Secretary read out the letter of thanks from the college for the organisation's participation in its student work-experience scheme. It was agreed that this was a useful way of furthering industry/college links.

5 DISPLAY OF COMPANY'S PRODUCTS AT AUTUMN EXHIBITION
The Sales Manager referred to the report which had been circulated previously to members. The exhibition was to take place at the National Exhibition Centre, Birmingham, and involved a team of five members of staff who had received specific training in the techniques required for mounting such an exhibition. A full statement as to the cost would be presented at the next meeting.

6 STAFF WELFARE
The chairperson reported that the Staff Welfare Committee was anxious to hold a staff dinner dance. Discussion took place about the cost of such a proposal and it was agreed that the Committee should be asked to prepare a report for the Board's consideration at a later meeting to cover not only the question of cost but also that of venue.

7 ANY OTHER BUSINESS
The chairperson gave a brief outline of his recent visit to the USA. A return visit was being planned by representatives of several large departmental stores in New York when it was hoped that some new business would be generated.

8 DATE AND TIME OF NEXT MEETING
It was decided that the next meeting should be held at 1430 hours on Tuesday, 20 July 199_.

(Signed)   .... Chairperson

     .... Date

Figure 10.1.5 A set of minutes

Arrangements for attendance at meetings

In the case of a formal meeting, it is the notice sent out with the agenda which informs members that they are expected to attend a meeting at a certain date and time. In the case of a more informal meeting, you may send out a brief memo with the agenda or even E-mail all members with the date and time of the meeting. In an ideal world that would be the end of the matter. However, the business world is anything but ideal and you may find that in order to make sure that the meeting is quorate (see page 613) or that you have the key people there, you may have to sort out some problems.

TEST YOURSELF

Look at the following scenarios.

● Your boss is chairing an important managers' meeting at 2 pm this afternoon. However, he is also having lunch with an important client (an appointment he made without consulting you or the office diary) and you are anxious that he is back in the office in time to begin the meeting.
● Your boss is having a meeting with the departmental staff about the changeover to a new ordering system. The office manager is opposed to the new system and has said that she will be unable to attend because she is too busy. You know her attendance is vital but you would rather keep her on your side as she is an excellent worker in other ways.
● One of the directors misses an important meeting and later in the week telephones you saying that the reason for his non-attendance was non-receipt of the notice and agenda. All the rest of the Board members had received theirs.
● One absent-minded member of staff always forgets the time (and sometimes the date) of even the most important meetings.
● Another – senior – member of staff makes a point of arriving late and leaving early.

Discuss with the rest of your group or with your tutor or adviser the action you would take to try to resolve these problems.

Arrangements for the provision of facilities at meetings

Once you have established what facilities are needed, it is your job to see that they are available. One difficulty with a meeting is that there is no room for manoeuvre. If the members of a meeting have assembled and are expecting to be able to use an OHP or video recorder, it is of little use saying that the equipment will be available within a couple of hours. They are needed there and then. Consequently, a good administrator or PA checks and double-checks that what has been ordered is actually in the meetings room at the appropriate time.

Normally, if the meeting is taking place on-site, there is little problem as you will be able to make sure that the equipment is provided. It is less easy to be sure if the meeting is taking place off-site. Much depends, of course, on the care you have taken to choose a suitable venue, and your past experience should assist you to determine whether or not a particular hotel can be relied upon to supply the appropriate facilities at the right time.

Steps you can take to try to avoid any mishaps include:

- being there yourself (or sending a reliable member of staff)
- checking by telephone on the day of the event that all the facilities promised are available
- being readily available at the office so that, if necessary, you can carry out some emergency action
- having available, if possible, reserve equipment or documentation together with someone on standby to rush it to the venue should it be necessary
- briefing one of the members of the meeting to let you know immediately if there are any problems – preferably in sufficient time for you to try to do something about it!

Methods of agenda preparation

Look back to page 596 if necessary to remind yourself of the layout and purposes of an agenda. Preparing agendas normally becomes second nature to an administrator or PA and the more experienced he or she is, the fewer difficulties tend to arise. However, certain basic principles should always be observed.

1 Items for the agenda can be obtained from

   - the action column of the previous set of minutes, e.g. 'This item to be discussed at the next meeting'
   - the chairperson

- other members of the meeting (it is sometimes a good idea to telephone people if you or your boss want to 'encourage' them to supply an item for the agenda. Otherwise they may find it difficult to take the initiative).

2   An agenda should not be a miniature set of minutes – nor, however, should the headings be so brief as to be meaningless. If one item of business to be discussed is the new legislation relating to part-time staff, you should avoid the temptation to write a page of explanatory notes. Equally you want something more definite than the heading 'staffing'.

3   A word of warning! It is a common error, particularly for a new meetings secretary, to 'overload' the agenda. You will naturally want to clear as much business as possible, but do be realistic – you will probably know how long the meeting is scheduled to run so try to avoid the possibility of the discussion of important items being curtailed because of lack of time. In the early stages you should be able to rely on your chairperson to check the agenda with you to see whether you have achieved the right balance. (You may have to bear in mind, however, that the chairperson may have reasons of his or her own for curtailing a particular item or placing it at a particular stage on the agenda – and that decision rests with the chairperson alone!)

How to organise and collate documentation

Although much depends on the type of meeting, you will need to follow certain procedures as regards the organisation and collation of meetings documents.

- You must make certain that the notice, agenda, minutes of previous meetings and all supplementary papers are filed together in the appropriate date order so that they are easy to retrieve. Your filing system should stand you in good stead here.
- If you use a word-processing package make sure that the document headings in the directory are uniform. Otherwise you may find that you have difficulty in gathering together all the relevant documents.
- Remember that a meeting is an active situation and that papers are needed for immediate reference. They should therefore be easily recognisable. Some administrators use a colour coding system so that, for instance, notices, agendas and minutes are printed on different coloured paper for ease of reference. They also organise the papers into sets and place them into coloured folders, one for each member. Spare sets are similarly organised.
- In the case of supplementary papers, a system of cross-reference is needed to ensure that
  - the correct document is consulted at the meeting, and

- it is returned to its correct folder at the end of the meeting.
- A standard numbering system should be used throughout the whole series of documents so that, for instance, number 1 on the Agenda relates to number 1 on the Minutes, etc.

Legal and regulatory requirements related to meetings

Informal meetings are normally held in line with company policy and their procedures will therefore differ from organisation to organisation. Formal meetings, on the other hand, have to comply with various legal requirements. Examples include:

- the Annual General Meeting, the Extraordinary General Meeting and the statutory meeting, the regulations for which are laid down by the Companies Acts and must therefore be followed precisely
- statutory meetings of local government committees, whose establishment and operation is again laid down by various Acts of Parliament.

 TEST YOURSELF

As an administrator or PA you may have (or be expected in future) to organise both informal meetings which require no adherence to legal regulations and also formal meetings which must comply very carefully with such regulations. From an organisational point of view, discuss with the rest of the group or your tutor or adviser the advantages and disadvantages of arranging each type of meeting.

Consequences of inadequate preparation for meetings

One of the consequences of inadequate preparation for a meeting is that you look a complete idiot – which does not exactly enhance your promotion prospects! Other, even more serious, consequences include:

- having to postpone a meeting (if, for instance, the correct paperwork has not been completed, the required length of notice given or the meeting is not quorate (see page 613)
- making the business carried out at that meeting invalid (i.e. treating it as if it had never taken place) because an important procedure has not been followed
- upsetting the members of that meeting to such an extent that they are unwilling to waste time attending another one
- undermining the authority of your boss should he or she be the chairperson of the meeting
- creating the wrong atmosphere so that it becomes more difficult to carry on the business of the meeting effectively.

ACTIVITY SECTION

1   Barbara has recently been appointed to a post of administrator for the Stores Manager of a large departmental store. A meeting of the managers is held each month to discuss various operational issues. The agenda obviously differs each month but a standing item is always the departmental targets and whether or not they have been met. The next meeting is scheduled for October when a major item on the agenda will be the preparations for the Christmas shopping period. There will also be some discussion about staff hours during that period and – on a lighter note – what staff parties or celebrations should be organised. Barbara is an experienced administrator and feels there should be no problem in organising the meeting. However, she becomes a little over-confident and finds herself facing some problems.

–   She sends out an agenda to the managers but misses off one name.

–   She wrongly assumes that the last set of minutes has already been circulated.

–   She remembers to obtain the statistics required and has them ready for the managers as they sit down for the meeting.

–   She has booked the meetings room but, because there are some extra staff attending the meeting this month, there are insufficient chairs for everyone.

–   Her boss asks her for his agenda. She hands him one but since she has forgotten to go through it with him and to add notes and reminders for him, he has to struggle on from memory.

–   When the agenda item about the staff party is reached, Barbara is about to produce a list of possible venues but cannot find them amongst all the spare papers which are lying on the table. She has to agree to circulate them at a later date.

  a   Discuss as a group or with your tutor or adviser:
      i   what errors Barbara has made
      ii how her boss could have assisted her more – given that she was new to the job.

  b   Draw up a checklist for her for the November meeting to prevent her from repeating her mistakes.

2   Obtain samples of the meetings documentation you use at work – but remember to check to make sure that you do not take documents which include confidential or sensitive information. As a group, hold your own meeting to exchange information on the following:

–   the different types and styles of documentation in common use

–   venues and facilities for meetings held – on-site and outside the organisation

–   arrangements required for meetings

–   checklists for meetings.

Compile your own agenda including the above items and any others of common interest. Nominate a chairperson, a minute secretary and hold the meeting. Each member of the group should make a valid contribution based on his or her experiences of meetings to date. The minutes taken at the end should be circulated to all present after the event as a reminder of the main points discussed.

Element 10.2

Attend, support and record meetings

Role and responsibilities in providing administrative support

Hopefully, you have already seen that the preparation of a checklist means that an administrator is able to carry out his or her duties as meetings secretary much more effectively. A good administrator or PA normally plans what he or she should do:

- before the meeting
- during the meeting
- after the meeting.

Do not rely on memory!

Actions which are normally taken include the following.

Before the meeting

- Book the appropriate accommodation and make sure that you allow for sufficient time (at least 15 minutes) before and after the meeting.
- Prepare and circulate the necessary documents – notice, agenda, chairperson's agenda, minutes of previous meeting, supplementary papers (see page 595).
- If required, obtain any statements from members who cannot be present but who may wish to have their views made known about certain items to be discussed.
- If necessary, prepare a seating plan of the meeting for the chairperson and provide him or her with background notes on any new members. (He or she may chair a large number of different meetings and need a reminder as to who everyone is around the table.) It may be a good idea to prepare place-names, particularly at formal meetings.
- Prepare an attendance list so that members can sign it on the day of the meeting. It saves you a job and, in some cases, is a legal requirement.
- Check that the seating arrangements are appropriate and that there is a supply of pens, paper, etc.
- Have ready a supply of spare agendas, minutes of the previous

meeting and supplementary papers – someone always turns up without them.

- Check on any equipment which is to be used, e.g. cassette recorder or video equipment. If it is being moved to an external venue, list the serial numbers and check that it will be insured in transit and covered whilst in the hotel.
- Check on refreshments. If a buffet or full meal is being served take note of any special dietary requirements. Many people today are now vegetarian or vegan or may have to follow a certain diet because of their religious beliefs.
- Check on whether or not the area is 'no-smoking' and, if so, warn smokers beforehand. Otherwise provide ashtrays.
- If necessary, make the appropriate car parking arrangements.
- Check whether any interpreters are needed.
- Inform Reception of the date and venue of the meeting and make sure someone has been delegated to take phone messages on the day on behalf of those attending.

DID YOU KNOW?

Unless it is absolutely unavoidable do not put yourself in the position of having to serve tea or coffee during the meeting – you have too much else to do. On the odd occasion when you find that you have to do so, try tactfully to make sure your chairperson does not carry on with the meeting but calls a halt in the proceedings until refreshments have been served.

On the day of the meeting

- If the meeting is to be held on-site, confirm arrangements with reception and the switchboard. If the meeting is held off-site, confirm with the venue concerned.
- Nominate someone to take messages for those attending the meeting (the switchboard may be too busy). The person concerned should know how to handle requests that the meeting be interrupted to pass on an urgent message. If such a disturbance is inevitable, then the messenger should write down the message and hand it to the person concerned, rather than pass on the information verbally.
- Check on accommodation and cleanliness/heating/lighting/ seating arrangements.
- Arrange for the relevant papers, files and correspondence to be brought to the room.
- Be there first to welcome members.
- Check that the attendance list is being completed.
- Sit next to the chairperson (to be able to give reminders of certain points if necessary and to pass relevant papers).
- Take notes of the proceedings (trying, if possible, to keep a separate list of actions promised by the chairperson so that you can act as memory-jogger later).

After the meeting

It is easy to breathe a sigh of relief after a meeting and to turn your attention to the next job. Try to avoid this temptation and take follow-up action as soon as possible.

- Check your notes for any urgent action promised by your chairperson.
- Draft the minutes and check them with your chairperson and other relevant members of the meeting before arranging for their reproduction and circulation.
- Draft any letters of thanks if necessary (e.g. to people invited to a meeting for a particular purpose).
- Prepare any other correspondence arising from the meeting.
- Check that all papers used at the meeting have been returned to their original files.
- Enter the date of the next meeting in your diary and that of your chairperson.

Roles and responsibilities of participants at meetings

The meetings secretary is not the only person responsible for the smooth running and the success of a meeting. Equally important is the role and responsibilities of:

- the chairperson
- the other members of the meeting.

 DID YOU KNOW?

In some meetings, one of the participants will be the treasurer who keeps the accounts, presents financial statements and advises on suitable funding. He or she is normally a member of a very formal meeting, a specialist meeting such as the sports and social committee meeting or a meeting of a voluntary body such as a drama club.

The role of the chairperson

A good chairperson – one who is competent, tactful, impartial and firm – can make your life much easier. Such a person will:

- be fully conversant with the standing orders of the meeting
- start the meeting punctually
- insist that all who speak address the chair, i.e. talk to the meeting as a whole rather than to each other
- explain clearly the topic to be discussed and, having given the lead, then keep quiet and allow discussion to develop and ideas to be formulated
- see that everyone has the opportunity to speak and keep those who do speak to the point

- decide when the discussion has gone on long enough and ensure that a summary of the discussion is given before a decision is taken – this is particularly vital for your minutes!
- ensure that any motion is clear and worded in such a way as to stand the best chance of gaining general agreement. Try to avoid allowing a motion to be negative, i.e. it is more acceptable to propose that something be done than to propose that something should not be done (see page 613)
- leave no-one in doubt as to what has been agreed
- close the meeting promptly and formally so that everyone is clear that the business has been concluded.

In order to be able to carry out these duties efficiently the chairperson is likely to have been given certain powers by virtue of the standing orders of the meeting:

- to maintain order
- to decide points of order as they arise and to give rulings on points of procedure
- to give a casting vote, i.e. a second vote where there is an equality of votes. Although the Chairperson can vote either way he or she will normally vote to preserve the status quo, i.e. the existing state of affairs
- to adjourn the meeting.

DID YOU KNOW?

The best (or most experienced) chairperson recognises that there is often a 'hidden agenda' taking place during the course of a meeting and tries to handle it properly. Take, for instance, a situation in which two members of the meeting are both competing for promotion and are therefore set on showing how assertive they can be. A good chairperson does not comment openly on this competition but instead tries to create an atmosphere that is cooperative rather than competitive so that the two members concerned have little option but to try to work together.

The role of the participants

However good the chairperson and the secretary, the meeting will still not be successful if the other members of the meeting do not play their part.

An effective member of a meeting should be:

- knowledgeable (someone who arrives at a meeting and tries to catch up on the paperwork as the apologies are being read out cannot expect to contribute as effectively as someone who has prepared himself or herself beforehand)
- interested (someone who is lying back staring out of the window or surreptitiously looking at the clock is very irritating – and can distract the other members of the group)

- prepared to contribute, i.e. to put his or her point of view
- able to keep to the point
- able to listen to other points of view
- prepared to do some work outside the meeting, e.g. to carry out a task given to him or her by the chairperson.

DID YOU KNOW?

Much advice is now given to women members of a meeting on how to make themselves heard even though the meeting may be male dominated. If you are a woman member, suggestions include:

- never sitting at a corner of the table (which makes it easy for you to be ignored)
- making a contribution early in the proceedings – otherwise you may be inclined to sit back and say nothing
- being positive rather than self-effacing in approach and never prefacing any remarks by words such as 'I may not be expert but . . .', 'It may sound silly but . . .', 'Correct me if I'm wrong . . .' etc.
- wearing a colourful jacket to make yourself noticed!

Conventions in the conduct of meetings

The conduct of a meeting depends on the type of meeting it is. An informal meeting will rely less heavily on conventions than a formal meeting which may be bound by law to follow certain procedures.

Informal meetings

At an informal meeting the atmosphere tends to be relaxed (at least at the beginning!) and much depends on the way in which the chairperson wants to handle matters. However, it is always advisable to

- set a time limit or **guillotine** on the length of the meeting
- follow the agenda without too many diversions
- have a clear consensus of opinion as to what has been decided.

The meeting then proceeds as follows.

1   The chairperson will open the meeting, welcome new members and receive apologies for absence. He or she should then check on the items to raised under 'Any other business' to see whether any of them are so urgent that they must be dealt with immediately. Otherwise time might run out before that agenda item is reached.

2   The chairperson will then (unless the meeting is very small and informal) ask whether the minutes of the previous meeting can be 'taken as read' (otherwise you will have to read them aloud).

3   The chairperson then asks whether the minutes can be agreed 'as a true and correct record' – this is where you hold your breath. If there are any corrections you must note them and make reference to them in the next set of minutes.

4 The items of business, as listed on the agenda, will then be discussed in turn and the decisions taken will be noted for the minutes (see Figure 10.1.5).

Formal meetings

In more formal meetings, however, such as those held by Local Authorities, the Civil Service or the Trade Unions, there is normally a set procedure (sometimes known as the **order of business**).

1 Before the meeting actually begins you must check that a **quorum** exists, i.e. the minimum number of people required to be present in order for the business of the meeting to be validly transacted. If an insufficient number of people arrives the meeting cannot be held. Note that you must also be careful to check throughout the course of the meeting that a quorum remains. If some people leave in the middle of the meeting it is easy for it to become **inquorate** without anyone realising it at the time. Only when a quorum has been mustered can the chairperson open the meeting.

2 If a quorum is present, the chairperson will open the meeting, welcome new members and receive apologies for absence. He or she should then check on the items to be raised under 'Any other business' to see whether any of them are so urgent that they must be dealt with immediately.

3 The chairperson will then ask whether the minutes of the previous meeting can be 'taken as read'.

4 The chairperson then asks whether the minutes can be agreed 'as a true and correct record'. If there are any corrections you must note them and make reference to them in the next set of minutes.

5 Other business of the meeting will then be discussed, with each item possibly involving one or more of the following procedures.
  − Any proposals which are made at the meeting are normally referred to as **motions**.
  − The rules may expect each motion to have a **proposer** and a **seconder**, i.e. someone who puts forward the proposal and someone who supports him or her. If no-one is prepared to act as seconder the motion can go no further. (In most cases, however, you will find that the proposer of a motion has already asked someone to be its seconder before the meeting begins.)
  − Sometimes the proposer of a motion realises in the course of the discussion that the motion is not likely to be successful or has been overtaken by other suggestions. In this case it can be withdrawn and no further discussion need take place.
  − Once a motion has been discussed it may then be put to the vote and a **resolution** (i.e. a decision) reached which either

accepts or rejects it. Note that a difficulty for the secretary may be that during the discussion someone may propose an **amendment** to the motion in order to improve it. There is a set procedure to be followed which may confuse you at first if you are trying to follow a number of different arguments at the same time (see below). Note the difference between an amendment and a **rider**, which is an addition to a resolution after it has been passed.

6 During the discussion you may hear the chairperson or other member remind the meeting of a **point of order**. This normally means that one of the rules of the meeting has not been followed, that the discussion has become irrelevant or that the language used is unacceptable or open to innuendo or misrepresentation.

7 If, for some reason, the meeting cannot continue – because, for instance, some relevant information is not available or the meeting has become too unruly – the Chairperson can call a motion to **adjourn** the meeting. Normally the motion includes a time, date and place for its continuance. If it does not, it is said to be adjourned **sine die** (without another date having been arranged). Note the difference between postponing a meeting (which has not begun) and adjourning a meeting (which has begun, but has been discontinued).

8 After discussion has ended it is normal for the motion to be put to the vote. There are five main methods of voting:

a   by voice (in very small meetings)
b   by show of hands
c   by poll (by the marking of a voting paper where a member may have more than one vote, e.g. a vote for each share held)
d   by division (the procedure in Parliament and, in some cases, in local government where members go into separate rooms according to whether they are for or against the motion)
e   by ballot (where members mark their voting papers and deposit them in a box which is afterwards opened and the votes counted).

After the voting has taken place the chairperson normally declares the result. In formal meetings it is declared in formal terms, i.e.:

The motion is carried	It is agreed
The motion is lost	It has been rejected
The motion is carried unanimously	Everyone is in favour

| *The motion is carried* **nem con** | No-one voted against but some have abstained (i.e. not voted for or against). |

Suppose the original motion had been

> I propose that we hold the annual staff dinner dance on Saturday, 12 December, at the Royal George Hotel.

One of the younger members of the meeting might protest that there should be a visit to a night-club afterwards. A married member might want the start and finishing times included for the benefit of those who require baby-sitters. Someone else might object to the term 'dinner dance' and want it altered to 'get-together'.

How do you think the chairperson should deal with these suggestions? Three possibilities are:

a   by allowing general discussion to take place followed by a general agreement as to what changes should be made
b   by allowing discussion on one suggested amendment at a time, followed by a vote on each amendment in turn
c   by allowing discussion on one suggested amendment at a time, followed by a vote on each amendment as it affects the original motion.

Discuss your ideas with the rest of your group before reading on.

Correct procedure

What the chairperson should not do is to allow all the proposed amendments to be discussed at the same time. The procedure to be followed is (c) above. Each amendment is discussed in turn and then each amendment is voted on – in the order in which it affects the original motion. Therefore the suggested amendment from staff dinner dance to staff get-together would be voted on first, the insertion of the times second and the proposed visit to a night-club third.

Assuming that the amendment to include a visit to a night-club was rejected but the other two accepted, the motion (now known as a substantive motion) would read:

> I propose that we hold the annual staff get-together from 8 pm to 12 midnight on Saturday 12 December at the Royal George Hotel.

Some of the procedures given above may seem very confusing. The best way to clarify how these work is to see a formal meeting in action. Try to attend a

Trade Union or other formal meeting held in your organisation. If this is impossible, watch a televised union meeting (e.g. those held at the Trades Union Congress) to see the system in operation.

Scope and limit of own contribution

As the meetings secretary you will have to concentrate on making notes of the meeting and on liaising closely with the chairperson. However, you may find that on occasions you are both the meetings secretary and also a member of that meeting. In such circumstances, you should not be expected to undertake both roles – if you are taking notes, you may be listening to what is being discussed but you will find it difficult to contribute effectively. Consequently, wherever possible, you should try to make sure that, even though you are responsible for arranging the meeting, another member of staff is present to take the notes.

What you should also remember is that, as a member of the meeting, you have as much right to be heard as anyone else. It is easy to relegate yourself to the position of organiser and to forget that you can also make a valuable contribution in other ways. Unfortunately, it is sometimes easy for other members of the meeting also to forget that.

TEST YOURSELF

You are a member of the departmental management team and attend the weekly meetings. However, because you are also expected to make the arrangements for those meetings you find that one of the other members tends not to listen to you, to interrupt you when you begin to speak and to talk to other members of the meeting when you do have the opportunity to make your contribution. You do not want to complain to the chairperson (your boss) at this stage because you do not want to antagonise one of your colleagues. However, when you approach him, he expresses surprise at what you have said and denies trying to undermine you.

Discuss with the rest of the group or your tutor or adviser what other actions you could take to try to resolve the situation.

If all else fails and you have to approach your boss, discuss how you would do so and what you might avoid saying.

Methods of evaluating arrangements

The current emphasis on quality control requires that almost any arrangement or procedure should be evaluated to see:

● how effective it is
● how it can be improved.

In evaluating the success or otherwise of a meeting you should:

- rely upon your own judgement (and the evidence of your own eyes if you were present at the meeting)
- monitor the reactions of the chairperson and other members of the meeting.

You may also wish to follow the procedure of including in the meetings papers a questionnaire to be completed by the members. You have to be careful, however, not to overwhelm the members. Nowadays people are beset on all sides with requests for them to complete questionnaires – from banks, building societies and stores – and the tendency is for them to ignore many of these requests. You may therefore wish to get your boss on your side and ask him or her to 'encourage' members to complete the forms.

However, completion of the forms is only the first stage in evaluation. What you must do then is to analyse the responses and attempt to take action in those areas which are obviously causing concern. Remember also that you should always give feedback to those who have completed the questionnaire.

TEST YOURSELF

You have been working as an administrator for a year and have been responsible for arranging a series of meetings for the company's quality steering group. At the end of the twelve-month period you asked the members of the group to complete a questionnaire and received the following replies:

'I don't like the time of the meeting. I know 9 am suits everyone else but the meeting always tends to overrun and I don't get back to my department until nearly 11. Why can't we have the meeting at 4 pm?'

'The timing suits me fine – but I don't like the venue. That room is far too near my office and, as you know, I'm constantly being dragged out to solve a problem.'

'Why can't you stop the boss from rabbiting on for hours about nothing' (signed 'anonymous'!)

'The agenda and all the supporting papers are always sent out too late – I never have time to read through them.'

'As long as Joachim is a member of the group, we'll never get anything done. His contribution is non-existent.'

'Get rid of Joachim – he's a dead loss.'

'I hate filling in questionnaires!'

1 Discuss as a group or with your tutor how you will set about solving these problems.

2 Discuss also how you will let the members know that their comments have been read and acted upon.

Emergency procedures relating to meetings

Look back to Unit 3 in which ways of dealing with emergencies during the course of a working day were discussed. Emergencies occur even in the best planned meetings and, in dealing with them, you should rely upon your own self-control and ability to respond to the unexpected. Remember, however, that some emergencies can be anticipated:

- the unexpected absence or delay of the chairperson
- the non-arrival of an important or key member of that particular meeting
- an unexpectedly non-quorate meeting
- *your* absence through illness
- the disappearance of important documents
- the double-booking of the venue
- the non-appearance of refreshments
- a failure to inform the receptionist to book car parking spaces
- the sudden illness of a member of the meeting
- the calling of an unexpected meeting to discuss an emergency.

TEST YOURSELF

Discuss with the rest of your group or with your tutor or adviser

a   what action you would take to deal with such situations
b   what procedures you would put into operation to deal with them should they occur again.

Include your answers in a short report.

Purposes served by minutes and reports of meetings

Most meetings, however informal, are recorded in some way. Formal meetings require formal sets of minutes: informal meetings require a summary of what has been discussed and agreed. If you are an administrator or PA responsible for a group of junior staff you will probably not be surprised to learn that many staff will do almost anything rather than take the notes of a meeting and they have to be encouraged, persuaded or even threatened into doing so! If you do find yourself in such a position it may help your cause if you can point out the benefits there are in recording the proceedings of meetings.

- They are an excellent aide memoire to all the members – particularly if there is an action column against which the name of a member is put as a reminder that he or she should carry out some action (see page 601).
- They are proof that something has been said (that is why at the beginning of most meetings there is nearly always an agreement

that the 'minutes of the previous meeting are a true and correct record'). Not only does this prevent anyone at a future date from arguing about what was said, it also satisfies any legal requirements there may be.

- They can act as the basis for continuing discussion. If a clear account is given of what was discussed at the previous meeting, then the meeting can move on and no time is lost in going back over old ground.

- On a personal note, they serve to indicate how good the chairperson and the meetings secretary are! A well-presented and informative set of minutes can catch the eye of the managing director and can assist you in any promotion hopes you may have!

Ways of recording key issues and decisions

As already indicated, formal minutes are used to record the proceedings of formal meetings. The proceedings of informal meetings are normally recorded in a summarised form.

However, different versions of these two formats are used by different organisations.

Variations include:

- a pre-printed format sometimes put on to the computer network to be used for all meetings in a particular organisation (Figure 10.2.1)

- a set of minutes with an action column to the right-hand side. In this column is recorded the initials of each person who agreed to undertake a specific task, alongside where the task is mentioned in the minutes (see page 601).

Legal and regulatory requirements relating to meetings

Even though, where relevant, the requirements of the Companies Acts have been met (look back to page 586 if necessary to remind yourself of what they are), the minutes of meetings should also comply with the legal requirements imposed upon all written or computerised documents:

The Data Protection Act 1984

The Copyright, Designs and Patents Act 1985

(see pages 272 and 368 for further details).

In addition, you, as the meetings secretary, should be careful not to report any defamatory remarks. People can get very excited in meetings, tempers run high and allegations and accusations can be made in the heat of the moment. You cannot prevent a member

GREENTOWN CORPORATION
MEETINGS NOTES

Meeting: **Date:**

Circulation list: Chief Executive: Chief Accountant: Personnel Director: Others

....

....

Those present:

....

....

....

Apologies for absence:

....

....

AGENDA

1	5
2	6
3	7
4	8

MINUTES

Figure 10.2.1 A pre-printed format for meetings notes

making such comments – and he or she must take the responsibility for them. It is also the responsibility of the chairperson to try to control the making of 'unwise' comments. However, what you *must* avoid is reporting exactly what was said – otherwise you could be implicated in any legal action for defamation. If you are in any doubt at all either leave out the remarks or consult your chairperson. By the time of the next meeting, the members concerned will probably have calmed down and will be very grateful that you have not reported their remarks verbatim!

ACTIVITY SECTION

1 Although in most meetings voting is by a show of hands, why do you think:

   a many people prefer voting by means of a secret ballot
   b the 'voice' method of voting is only used at very small meetings?

2 Complete the following sentences with the appropriate word or phrase:

   a As only five people were present the meeting could not begin because of the lack of a . . . .
   b 'Although I support the motion in principle I should like to propose the following . . . .'
   c The . . . . . . Committee, formed to make arrangements for the Lord Lieutenant's visit, has now been disbanded.
   d Because possible redundancies were being discussed at the next meeting it was decided to invite the HR Manager to attend as a . . . . . . member.
   e 'I wish to . . . the motion and trust that someone will . . . it.'
   f As a suitable date and time could not be agreed the meeting was adjourned . . . .

3 A junior member of staff has been appointed as your assistant to help you organise and service the meetings in your company. The idea is that eventually he will be able to deputise for you when you are absent through illness or on holiday.

   a State
      – the duties you would give him initially to help you to prepare for a meeting
      – the duties you would allow him to undertake whilst the meeting is in progress
      – the duties you consider he should undertake once the meeting is over.
   b Draw up a schedule to show how you would extend his role over the next twelve months.

4 A colleague has been appointed as Chairperson of the Safety Committee of your organisation for the next twelve months. She is not familiar with meetings procedure.

   Bearing in mind that these meetings are relatively informal, with safety representatives from various departments present plus the Health and Safety Officer in an ex officio capacity:

   a draw up a schedule which will show her at a glance how each meeting should progress and her role in the proceedings
   b make out a list of 'Chairperson's do's and don'ts' which she can

read before her first meeting to enable her to run it more smoothly and cooperate fully with her meetings secretary.

5 There are certain personality traits which are very easy to identify during the course of a meeting, especially:
- the non-stop talker
- the digresser
- the mumbler
- the one who is slow on the uptake
- the silent one
- the one who persists with his or her viewpoint or idea despite lack of support or even despite active opposition from the other members
- the sycophant who always agrees with the boss
- the one who knows all the rules (down to the last page and paragraph number).

Discuss (if you are working with a group) and/or make notes on how a good chairperson would deal with each of these personalities at a meeting.

6 You work for Toptree Paper Products plc – a large company which makes paper for the office stationery market. The directors are concerned about the future of the industry in view of the volume of cheap imported paper currently flooding into Britain. They have decided to hold a planning meeting next weekend at a local hotel. The draft schedule is as follows:

- Friday evening, 6 pm start: welcome by both Chairman and MD. Overview of weekend. Dinner at 8 pm.
- Saturday 9 am–noon: video on paper industry plus follow-up slides on sales figures, competitors, etc. Presentation by Sales Director, Martin Broome, and guest speaker from local Business School – Arif Choudry.
- Lunch 12.30 pm–2 pm
- Saturday 2 pm–4 pm: Appraisal of Toptree Paper Products in terms of strengths and weaknesses plus presentations of pre-prepared papers by department.
- 4 pm–6 pm: Overview of findings, by MD. Dinner 8 pm.
- Sunday 9 am–noon: 'think tank' session by directors working in groups. Lunch as Saturday.
- Sunday 2 pm–5 pm – ideas brought together. Final plenary session hosted by Chairman and MD.

a Type up a draft programme for the weekend using the information given above.
b Note that Arif Choudry will attend for dinner on the Friday night and leave after Saturday lunch. Make out a comprehensive list of all the duties you will need to undertake before the weekend takes place and all the arrangements you will have to make with the hotel.
c Draft a letter to the hotel confirming the details.

d The MD has asked you to be present at the hotel for the final session on Sunday afternoon, to take notes. Why do you think you have been asked to attend this particular session, and not the others?

7 You have recently started work at JDP Information Systems Ltd – a small computer consultancy – as administrator to one of the (two) directors. Once a month sales meetings are held in the board room, to which all 12 sales representatives are invited. The aim of the meetings is to report on progress to date with prospective and actual customers, highlight and clarify queries, discuss new product development and sales techniques, identify areas of weakness in sales reporting methods (if any), and discuss future prospects.

You attended the first meeting with the 'outgoing' administrator and were horrified to find:

- On arrival at the board room everyone had to wait outside because the last meeting was over-running – not that this mattered very much as your director, who chaired the meeting, arrived ten minutes late.
- No notice or agenda had been issued so the discussion was something of a 'free for all'.
- Two reps didn't turn up – but nobody knew why not.
- Two errors in last month's minutes were never recorded – the administrator merely made a pencilled alteration on her set of papers.
- Representatives frequently talked amongst themselves – which made minute taking difficult, if not impossible.
- Most reps had forgotten to bring their copies of last month's sales report, which should have been discussed during the meeting. This item was therefore abandoned.
- The meeting ran out of time long before major items had been covered and the next group to use the board room were already waiting.
- There was a gap in the notes for the minutes where the administrator had to jump up to serve coffee.
- The meeting was interrupted four times for reps to take urgent telephone calls. Each time a junior member of staff simply opened the door and called across the room.
- Several belligerent members 'shouted down' the suggestions of the others and once the rep for North Wales started on his pet theme of Welsh language publicity material no-one could stop him talking.
- A fierce argument broke out between a non-smoker and a smoker when the latter lit a cigarette.
- Later that day you noticed that several confidential matters, brought up at the meeting, were being freely discussed by the other office staff.

After the meeting the director took you on one side. He said that he acknowledged that the meetings were chaotic but the company had grown very quickly in the past two years and none of the employees were knowledgeable about correct meetings procedure – including himself. He added that one of the reasons you were appointed to the job was because of your meetings expertise and he therefore thought that you could help to reorganise them!

a Outline for him the procedures he should follow – and why – to be an effective chairperson. He would like these particularly to relate to the present problems he is experiencing at sales meetings.

b Make out a brief checklist of your own responsibilities to ensure that subsequent meetings run more smoothly.

c Note down how meetings should be interrupted should this prove necessary.

d State the importance of confidentiality in terms of meetings and the ways in which this can be achieved (see also page 630).

e Draw up a draft notice and agenda for the next meeting – to be held four weeks from today at 1400 hours – from the topics usually discussed at these meetings.

f You are lucky in that the director is very honest about the situation and will be supportive of you in your efforts to bring about change. It is still important that you do not hurt his feelings by being tactless in the way that you present the problem and your suggested solutions. Make out a list of 'do's and don't's' – for yourself – in relation to the way in which to handle the situation in a diplomatic manner.

g If your director had been unaware that there was a problem what difference, if any, would this make to your approach?

Element 10.3

Produce and progress records of meetings

Own role and responsibilities

It is obviously your responsibility to see that the end product of the meeting, i.e. the record of what was said, is of a high standard. Not only will it enhance your image, it will also prevent any problems which may occur at a later stage if any queries arise about what was actually said at the meeting – either from one of the participants or someone who was not present at the meeting but who has an interest in what was decided. Even more important to remember is that minutes of a meeting can be produced as evidence during legal proceedings in a court.

You should therefore be prepared to spend time in ensuring that the minutes are:

- true, impartial and balanced
- written in clear, concise and unambiguous language
- as brief as is compatible with accuracy.

Role and responsibilities of participants

After what has just been said, it may cheer you up slightly to note that you are not expected to take *sole* responsibility for the accuracy of records of a meetings. The chairperson and the rest of the participants at a meeting have also to bear some of that responsibility. The chairperson, for instance, must make sure at the end of the meeting that no-one is left in any doubt about what decisions have been made and what agreements have been reached. The other participants must also ensure that they are clear about what has been decided and whether or not they have made known their agreement to or disagreement with that decision.

Given, however, that memories can be short, it is obviously a good idea for you, as the meetings secretary, to draft out the minutes and to check with the chairperson or any key members of the meeting that what you have written is correct. Members will have the opportunity at the following meeting to agree the minutes as a true and correct record but it is not normally wise to wait until then to correct all the errors which may have been made – it can cause a re-debate of the previous discussion and can leave you feeling and looking inefficient!

TEST YOURSELF

It can happen that a member of a meeting says something which he or she later regrets. You have recorded accurately what was said but when you approach that person to ask for confirmation, he or she either denies having said it or wants you to alter the minutes to omit those remarks. Discuss as a group or with your tutor or adviser what you would do in such circumstances.

Methods of preparing records of meetings

Look back to Figure 10.1.5 for an example of a set of minutes. The information they contain is normally required no matter what type of meeting is being held, although in more informal meetings you may not have to follow all the formalities and may be expected to record only:

- the heading
- the day, date and time
- those present
- a brief summary of what was discussed.

Note too that in *very* formal meetings only the decision is recorded – not the preceding discussions.

However, whatever the type of meeting, you will be expected to follow certain norms in relation to grammar and style. You may also find it helpful – no matter how experienced you may be – to follow a set routine when recording the proceedings at a meeting.

Taking notes

- Prepare your writing materials thoroughly beforehand. Have a supply of pens and pencils. Either use a shorthand notebook or A4 lined paper. The advantage of A4 paper is that you can write more on one sheet and can subdivide it into sections. You can also leave a wide margin (some secretaries draw a line down the middle of the page and use the left half only, leaving the right half for any alterations as the meeting progresses). If you are allowed to do so, consider the use of a cassette recorder as a back-up.

- If you are new, try to find a mentor. If you are lucky you will be working in an organisation where at first you will be taking minutes alongside another more experienced administrator who will compare notes with you afterwards. If not, there may be someone in the organisation who is willing to give you some assistance over layout or subject matter plus background information about what normally happens in the various meetings.

- Check the level of detail you are expected to record. Many minutes these days are merely summaries of the discussions which took place, rather than details of who said what.

- Be selective about what you write down while it is being said. This saves having to plough your way through pages of notes later to find the parts that matter. It is also less of a strain on your note-taking skills than trying to write down every word! The more familiar you are with the topic under discussion the better – you should at least know what the chairperson is going to say about it.

- If you lose the thread of the discussion, don't panic! Right at the beginning of the meeting make sure you know the names of all the members so that you can note who is contributing to a particular topic and, if necessary, query it with them after the meeting.

- If you are still unsure, do not risk recording inaccurate or confusing information. It is preferable to minute nothing at all rather than something which is incorrect.

 DID YOU KNOW?

Believe it or not it can actually be a disadvantage to have a very high shorthand speed for minute taking, as then the temptation to write down too much is tremendous! You can even train yourself to write down minutes without any shorthand skills at all, providing you have developed some foolproof method of abbreviating key words.

The basic points to remember are:

- Any note-taking or shorthand system is not an art form but a means to an end! Don't worry about your outline or symbol being technically correct – so long as you can read it.
- Write neatly and space it out.
- Know the terminology of your 'trade' and the outlines/symbols/abbreviations you can use for all the technical terms you hear.
- Be aware that during transcription it is the short, simple words which usually cause the most trouble!
- Take advantage of respites in the meeting – the break for coffee or informal or humorous discussion – to check through your notes.
- If necessary, make notes to yourself, either in a separate column or in square brackets so that they are easily identifiable.

Transcribing notes

It is equally important to have a set routine once you have left the meeting. Remember the longer you leave the task of converting your notes into draft minutes, the harder it will become. Try to arrange your diary so that you have a couple of hours free as soon as possible after the meeting has finished. Following the procedures set out below should also help.

- Draft the minutes as soon as possible after the meeting while the events are fresh in your mind. Check if your boss wants you to use an action column at the right-hand side of the minutes for the names or initials of anyone who has been asked to take action on any topic.
- Until you become experienced, and sometimes even throughout your career, you may find it preferable to submit your draft minutes to the chairperson for checking. Even if you have recorded the information accurately, it may be that the chairperson prefers a different emphasis at certain points (for a variety of reasons!). If you have typed up your minutes on a word processor it is then a simple matter to edit your text before printing out your final version.

Grammatical conventions

- Keep your sentences short and your wording simple. Use the third person (rather than 'I', 'we' or 'you') and the past tense – you are writing about something which is over and done with.
- There are several routine phrases which are often employed, e.g. 'After discussion it was decided that . . . .' Note that in very formal minutes you should always try to avoid using actual names. For instance, instead of saying 'Alison Lee proposed that . . .' you would use the term 'It was proposed that . . .'.
- Remember to avoid slang and colloquial expressions which are often used in everyday speech. Report unemotionally whenever possible. For instance, the chairperson of a budget meeting may have exploded about overspending in the previous financial

period but in the minutes this can be simply reflected by the following statement:

'The chairperson said that any budget overspending would not be tolerated in the future.'

DID YOU KNOW?

Writing in the third person and past tense becomes easier with practice. Most people have no difficulty converting a sentence such as '"I think we should increase the sales budget," said the Sales Director' to 'The Sales Director felt that the sales budget should be increased.' (Note the use of the word 'that' to introduce reported speech.)

Difficulties, however, may arise in the following cases.

'Always true' statements

Consider the following: '"Bloggs plc is a very large company," said the Chairman.' If you convert this to 'The Chairman said that Bloggs plc was a very large company' then you imply that Bloggs plc is no longer very large – which is (presumably) incorrect. Therefore the correct version should be 'The Chairman said that Bloggs plc is a very large company.'

Questions

It is fairly easy to convert a sentence such as '"Can we extend the advertising campaign?" asked Mrs Andrews' to 'Mrs Andrews asked whether they could extend the advertising campaign' or 'Mrs Andrews queried whether the advertising campaign could be extended.'

However, if the question is rhetorical then direct conversion is not suitable. In this case you need to show the meaning which was implied when the question was asked, e.g. '"Am I going to have another set of inaccurate calculations?" asked the Sales Manager, annoyed.' This statement obviously means that inaccurate figures are not acceptable and should be rephrased to reflect this, e.g. 'The Sales Manager commented that he did not expect to receive any more inaccurate calculations.'

Time

Remember that expressions of time change when reported speech is used:

- 'today' becomes 'that day'
- 'now' becomes 'then'
- 'tomorrow' becomes 'the next day' or 'the following day'
- 'yesterday' becomes 'the day before' or 'the previous day'.

Therefore 'I will be going there tomorrow' converts to 'He said that he would be going there on the following day.'

TEST YOURSELF

Convert each of the following statements correctly into reported speech. Try to use alternatives to words such as 'asked' and 'said', e.g.

queried, commented, suggested etc. Remember not to repeat slang expressions.

1 'It's all very well to make that suggestion,' said Susan Bolova, 'but do you honestly think the staff will respond?'
2 'I visited the company yesterday,' said Paul Jenkins, 'and they said that they wanted me to call again next Tuesday.'
3 'A six-month trip to Australasia – that's an expensive venture you're suggesting. Are you sure it would pay off?' asked Malcolm O'Leary.
4 'I know it is a three-hour flight from London to New York on Concorde,' said Imran Patel, 'and the flight departs from Terminal 4.'

Ways of obtaining approval of records

The first step you would take to obtain approval for what you have written is to check with your chairperson, whose responsibility it is to ensure that the minutes are a true and correct record and to sign them as such. The members of the meeting have the opportunity to record their approval at the following meeting when the item 'Minutes of the previous meeting' is discussed (although refer back to page 612 for the problems that can occur at this stage). If there is a call for an amendment to be made and it is agreed by the chairperson and the rest of those present, then the next set of minutes must contain the amendment.

Organisations' procedures for style and format of records

Look back to pages 385 and 442 for details of 'house style' in relation to the preparation of documents. Minutes of a meeting tend to be regarded as important documents both in relation to their content and also their circulation. It is highly likely therefore that the organisation in which you work has set procedures not only for the way in which the minutes of a meeting should be recorded but also for the way in which they should be displayed. (See Figures 10.1.5, 10.2.1 and page 601 for examples.) In most cases, this will benefit you as an administrator or PA not only because you have fewer decisions to make, but also when you train your junior staff.

CHECK IT YOURSELF

Check at your place of work to see the types of format used for meetings and discuss with your group or tutor or adviser any variations there may be on the standard systems of recording meeting proceedings. Include your answers in a short report.

Procedures for the issue of records

Once the minutes have been prepared and checked – and signed – by the chairperson they are ready for circulation. The traditional practice in some small meetings of merely asking the meetings secretary to read out the minutes at the start of the next meeting has all but disappeared and normally the members of a meeting can expect to receive a copy of the minutes well before the next meeting so that – hopefully – they can read them and arrive at the meeting prepared to discuss any issues.

It is essential, therefore, that you have an up-to-date circulation list of the people to whom the minutes should be sent. Remember that this list may include not only the members of the meeting but also other interested parties. For instance, the minutes of a weekly meeting of members of a department in a large organisation may be circulated to the senior management team, who may not be present at the meeting but who may wish to be kept informed of what is happening. In some organisations there is a rule that certain sets of minutes are made available to all members of staff.

One difficulty which may occur, particularly when minutes are to be circulated widely, is where they contain confidential information. Obviously you would check with your chairperson if you were unsure about any item but you should also be prepared to use your own initiative to avoid any possible breach of confidentiality.

TEST YOURSELF

1 One method used to avoid any possible breaches of confidentiality arising from the circulation of a set of minutes is for the meetings secretary to prepare two sets of minutes – one for the members and one for more general use. Discuss as a group or with your tutor the possible dangers of using such a method.

2 What actions do you think a chairperson could take should he or she become aware that some confidential information is being 'leaked' by one of the members of the meeting – although the identity of that person is merely suspected, not known!

Methods of identifying and monitoring agreed action plans

A widely used method of keeping a check on who has agreed to do what is by the inclusion of an action column normally positioned at the right-hand side of a set of minutes (see page 601). However, that is only the beginning of the process. As any experienced administrator or PA knows, the writing of a person's name against an action to be taken does not necessarily mean that that action will automatically be taken! Some members of a meeting can be relied upon: others need more persuasion.

In some cases, the members of the meeting themselves will act as monitors of the situation. If a meeting is held each week, the chairperson, under the item 'Matters arising', can query any action which has been promised but not taken – and normally the person concerned is eventually shamed into doing what he or she has promised. However, if the meeting is held less regularly and it is important that the action promised is taken before the next meeting takes place, a different strategy must be used. Persistence is the key here. A good administrator or PA will check through each set of minutes to note who has promised to do something and will make sure that he or she reminds that person of his or her promise well before the next meeting or the appropriate deadline.

TEST YOURSELF

It can be difficult if it is the chairperson or a very senior member of staff who fails to carry out the action promised. Discuss as a group or with your tutor or adviser what action you would take in each of those situations.

Legal and regulatory requirements relating to the production and issue of records

The legal implications of meetings records have already been discussed (see page 619). In any written record of a meeting, you must therefore avoid including any ambiguous, imprecise or – worse – defamatory statement.

Obviously you cannot afford the suggestion that a set of minutes has been tampered with or altered after it has been approved and it is therefore exceedingly important to make sure that the completed and signed minutes are filed away safely. Some sets of minutes are so confidential that they are always stored in a locked filing cabinet and any amendments made in ink and counter-initialled. Even less formal minutes are regarded as sufficiently important to warrant your looking after them with great care.

ACTIVITY SECTION

1 Whilst you were absent last week the sales meeting went ahead as usual. As no-one was free to take the minutes your boss, Martin Lewis, jotted down notes of what happened on his chairperson's agenda (Figure 10.3.1).

From these notes produce a summarised set of minutes.

2 You have acted as the secretary at the meeting of the Staff Welfare Committee held in the staff canteen at 1700 hours on Wednesday, 2 July, to discuss the arrangements for the staff dinner dance.

CHAIRPERSON'S AGENDA

Meeting: Sales Meeting

Date/time: 1000 hours, 14 March 199-

Place: Board Room

Sales Team: Martin Lewis (Chair), G Barton,
C Edwards, P Hinchcliffe, T
Marsden, F Paton, J Vines
(In attendance - Paul Bailey,
Technical Manager)

AGENDA ITEM	NOTES
1 Apologies for absence	1 Frank Paton (held up on M4)
2 Minutes of previous meeting	2 OK
3 Matters arising Questions may be asked on: • progress on McNaughton contract • date new advertising campaign starts on TV	3 ML reported - Meeting arranged with Jim Pascal Sales Dir of MCN a week on Tues. to finalise penalty clause. ML - starts Yorkshire on Anglia begins 21 March networked (national coverage) from 28/3
4 Customer reports • Tom Marsden just returned from trip to Paris • Check if problems at Micro Products solved	4 Saw Desseau & Cie - interested in new machine - 3 other bidders. Our prospects good. Board decision expected by 26/3. No - PB reported 2 technicians visiting next Mon.
5 Advertising campaign Report on progress to date	5 ML - Meeting with ad. agents last week. Some minor modifications still required to literature. Final proofs due next wk.
6 Technical modifications Report by Paul Bailey on model 48X	6 Re D report on technical modifications tabled. PB gave overview. To be discussed in depth at next meeting.
7 Forthcoming exhibition Olympia, London 14 - 21 October	7 CE- stand booked. CE/JV to organise/co-ordinate. ML's sec to book accomm. - check requirements with JV.

8 **Any other business**	8 Ph reported strike at Evans Electronic now over.
	Thl following up enquiry by Kent County Council
9 **Date and time of next**	9 23 March 10am
Avoid 28 March – 3 April	Board Room
(Easter)	

Figure 10.3.1

Other than you, those present included Mr William Sanderson (who chaired the meeting), Mrs Muriel French, Mr Henry Cartwright and Miss Barbara Atkinson. The agenda was as follows:

1 Apologies for absence
2 Minutes of the previous meeting
3 Matters arising
4 Correspondence
5 Proposed venue
6 Entertainment
7 Printing
8 Any other business
9 Date and time of next meeting.

Given below is an actual transcript of the meeting. From this, prepare a set of minutes, with a clear action column, for the chairperson to sign.

MEETING TRANSCRIPT

Chair   Good afternoon – thank you for coming. Might I give a special welcome to our new secretary who has taken over the job at rather short notice? Before we actually start the meeting can I take it that everyone has a copy of the agenda and the minutes of the previous meeting? If not, we have some spare copies available. Good. Next point. Have we any items for Any other business? Has anything urgent arisen since the agenda was sent out? No? Right. Let's get on. The first item on the agenda – Apologies – ah, yes – Frank Thomas is away on a selling trip and Angela Norman is on holiday this week. (*To you*) Can you make a note of that please.

The next item – the minutes of the previous meeting – can I take them as read and approve them as a correct record? (*All agree*)

Right – matters arising from the previous meeting. If I go through the Minutes page by page as usual, you can stop me if you wish to query an item.

Henry	Can I query item 5 on page 2? What has happened about getting the prices from the various hotels?
Chair	We have the prices listed and the secretary will pass a copy of them to all of you when we reach that item on the agenda
	Any other queries? Can we then start on the main business of the meeting?
Barbara	Is there any correspondence to be dealt with?
Chair	I'm sorry, I should have dealt with that item – no, there isn't.
	The next item is that of choice of hotels – remember we have to make a report to the Board giving our recommendations for the staff dinner dance and venue is something we must discuss. We have a list of prices from the various hotels. (*You circulate them to everyone*) One or two hotels were late in responding to our request so we didn't have time to circulate them beforehand.
Muriel	Could I make the point that I didn't like the hotel we went to last year – the 'Golden Hind' – the service was poor and the meal ordinary. Some of the girls in my office have asked me to say that they weren't too keen on it either.
Barbara	I didn't think it was too bad but I'm willing to try somewhere else – how about the 'Boar's Head'?
Henry	It's a bit far out – there may be transport problems.
Muriel	What about the 'Royal George'? I've been there recently and quite liked it. They seem quite used to catering for large numbers.
Henry	The new owner of the 'Imperial' is eager to expand his business and may be willing to give us good value for money
Chair	Any other ideas? Well, it seems a straight choice between the 'Royal George' and the 'Imperial'.
Barbara	Why don't we try the 'Royal George' this year and the 'Imperial' next year, when we have more of an idea whether the new venture will be a success?
Chair	Can we decide on that? Do you all agree the 'Royal George' this year, then? (*All nod*) OK, then it's agreed. (*To you*) Can you contact them to confirm the provisional booking? Tell them we'll confirm exact numbers and so on nearer the time.
	Next item. The entertainment. Henry – you were going to look into the matter, weren't you?
Henry	Yes, if you remember last time we had a small band which was popular with the older members of the staff but didn't go

down too well with the younger element. One girl has suggested that we have some disco music to be played during the intervals, which seems a good idea. If everyone is in favour of that then I can check with the hotel to see if it could be arranged.

Muriel	Wouldn't it be a bit difficult, trying to talk above that sort of music?
Henry	There is a separate bar at the 'Royal George' where anyone who wanted could sit during the intervals.
Muriel	If that's the case then I have no objections.
Chair	Has anyone else anything to say? Well, should Henry be authorised to go ahead and make the necessary enquiries? (*All agree*)
	Last item, as we have no items to discuss under AOB. The problem of printing. The in-house reprographics unit is under some pressure at the moment and may not be too willing to cooperate with us about the printing of menus, invitations, etc. Should we think about contacting local printers to see how much they will charge us?
Barbara	What do you think the Board's reaction will be?
Chair	I don't suppose they'll be too keen to spend a huge amount of money but they do look upon the dance as a good public relations exercise and of benefit to the staff, so they may be willing to pay a printer rather than risk the event looking as if it has been poorly organised.
Muriel	Why don't we obtain some prices as you suggest and let the Board decide – we can make it a strong recommendation from this committee but it is up to them eventually to decide what they want to pay.
Chair	Is that acceptable to everyone? (*Everyone agrees*) (*To you*) Will you get together some prices for the next meeting, please?
	Before you all go, let's fix a date and time for the next meeting – pretty soon, I suggest. How about 3rd August? The same time? 1700 hours?
	(*General agreement*)
	Well, it only remains for me to thank you for coming.

11 Arrange and monitor travel and accommodation

Element 11.1

Organise travel and accommodation arrangements

You should note that this unit is an **option** unit. The fact that you have chosen to study and prove your competence in this area should mean that as part of your job you undertake duties which involve arranging and monitoring travel and accommodation in your workplace. If you do not, then you are advised not to select this option. If you only do part of the work outlined in the scheme then you will need to talk to your tutor or adviser about the best way to demonstrate competence in the remaining areas.

Scope and limit of own authority for organising travel and accommodation

According to the World Tourism Organisation, 250 million people travel internationally on business every year and nearly 25 per cent intend to increase the amount they travel in the future despite the recession and the opportunities afforded by the advent of new technology and video-conferencing.

Given that you are involved in making arrangements for your organisation's business travellers – presumably both within the UK and worldwide – what is the scope of the role you undertake? Are you considered to be something of a specialist and asked for your advice? Do you choose and recommend the routes your travellers take and the hotels they stay in – or do you simply follow instructions and contact the local travel agent? Are you responsible for organising everything – from the planning of the trip onwards – and how many decisions can you make on your own?

Even if the scope of your responsibility is very limited, you still have some choice in how you plan travel. You can simply do just what is required or you can adopt a professional, well-organised approach. The difference lies in the detail. Anyone can ring a travel agent, but a good administrator will check the fine print, make sure the trip does not coincide with local holidays and have information to hand on climate, local customs and medical precautions. He or she will also be capable of coping with group bookings, liaising with those who are away and keeping the office well organised in their absence. Finally, by knowing the full range of services and alternatives available and who to contact for more information, a good administrator will keep the costs of business travel within or below budget.

To help you to do this, after each practical section of information in this element you will find a Hints and Tips section on organisation and costs. The aim of these sections is to give you some of the practical knowledge used every day by office administrators, PAs and secretaries experienced in planning travel. Because much of the information given in these sections also relates to Element 11.2, you will find that the second part of the unit is much shorter – mainly because you have already covered most of the material you need to know.

Ways of obtaining details of travel and accommodation requirements

There are many different ways in which you can obtain details of travel and accommodation:

- by telephone
- by fax
- by E-mail
- by memo
- by scribbled note
- in a meeting to pre-plan the trip
- on a special reservation request form.

You should note that receiving complicated and important instructions by telephone is always risky. If you mis-hear something then you will have to take the blame later. Therefore you would be wise to insist that all but the simplest requests are confirmed in writing – either by fax, E-mail, memo or brief (but legible) note.

If you are involved in any pre-planning sessions then, although these are verbal, there should be plenty of opportunity to clarify the details. You would probably be asked along to the session because of your expertise and the fact that you can offer sensible advice. Before you make any bookings, however, you should type out a report of the meeting as you understand it, and give everyone involved a copy with instructions to contact you immediately if they disagree with anything you have written.

To prevent misunderstandings and to ensure that all the important and necessary details have been included, some organisations ask staff to complete a pre-printed request form for travel and accommodation which is sent to the travel section or those people involved in making arrangements. An example is shown in Figure 11.1.1. The main advantage with using this system is that you get the important information you need first time round and, because the request is in writing and signed, no disputes can arise over what really was requested or required.

```
TRAVEL/ACCOMMODATION REQUEST FORM

Name .........................          Dept ...........................
PASSENGER DETAILS

Title           Surname         Initials        DOB
...............     .........................     ........................     ...........................
...............     .........................     ........................     ...........................
...............     .........................     ........................     ...........................
...............     .........................     ........................     ...........................


DEPARTURE DATE .............................          FROM ...............................

Cities to be visited    Length of stay      Accommodation preferred
........................     ..............................     ...........................................
........................     ..............................     ...........................................
........................     ..............................     ...........................................
........................     ..............................     ...........................................
........................     ..............................     ...........................................
........................     ..............................     ...........................................


PREFERRED FORM OF TRAVEL ...........................................................
PREFERRED DEPARTURE TIME ............... SMOKING/NON-SMOKING*

ITINERARY REQUIRED YES/NO*

SPECIAL REQUESTS



Signed.................................. Date ..........................

* Please delete as required
```

Figure 11.1.1 A travel/accommodation request form

Booking arrangements for travel and accommodation

There are various ways in which you can book travel and accommodation. The most obvious is to sit back, contact a travel agency, and let them do all the work. Indeed, organising business trips through a travel agent is the method which is most commonly used by large organisations with a business travel requirement. Most travel agents recognise the special needs of business travellers and you will probably have a special contact person to deal with who will give you useful help and advice.

However, the more times you contact your travel agent for details and the more often you want to change and amend your bookings the higher will be the cost for your organisation. Not only that, but even discussing the most basic requirements is going to mean yet another phone call. For that reason, most administrators involved in making travel arrangements try to sort out most of the details beforehand themselves – and simply contact the travel agent when the actual booking needs to be made. This not only saves money, but means that you are not just reliant on the advice which is given to you but have the ability to check things out yourself!

Booking travel

Before you make any bookings for travel you have to know the different methods of travel available, comparative costs and your company policy on travel. All these factors are dealt with later in this element.

Making the actual booking used to mean buying several travel guides – the *ABC World Airways Guide* being the most popular – to plan the trip. Today, as an alternative, you can obtain this information on disk by subscribing to the Official Airline Guide's FlightDisk. This runs on most PCs and is updated each month with a new disk. Alternatively, if you are linked to Internet you can use CompuServe to access several timetables and reservations systems which used to be solely available to travel agents. In either case you can custom-build a flight itinerary and then simply notify either your agent or the airline when you want the ticket issued.

For other methods of travel you can keep a range of timetables, e.g. for ferries and trains, and refer to them as required to make out a suggested itinerary. Again, you then have the choice as to whether to contact the company direct to make the booking or do this through your travel agent.

DID YOU KNOW?

An alternative to FlightDisk is TravelPlan. This provides a schedule of both air and rail travel plus information on hotels in Europe and foreign currency. Again the information is updated monthly. All you have to do is to select the combination of travel you want and the software will do the rest – providing you with a timetable of flights, hotels, costs and estimated journey times.

CHECK IT YOURSELF

Contact Practical Concepts at Airport House, Purley Way, Croydon, CR0 0XZ (phone 0181 781 1988) for further information on Travelplan software. Contact Reed Travel Group, Church Street, Dunstable, Bedfordshire LU5 4HB (phone 01582 695 050) for details of the OAG FlightDisk.

If you want a free trial of the latter you will need to say whether you would want this in Windows or DOS format.

Hints and tips on making travel bookings

- When the ticket arrives, check it carefully and if you have any queries do not be worried about asking for clarification. You will not be the first person to receive a wrongly issued ticket!
- Find out your boss's preferred methods of travelling and, where possible, stick to this unless some of his or her preferences go against company policy (see below).
- A fly/drive deal can be a good idea if your boss has a lot of appointments to keep. Ask your travel agent for details or contact British Airways.

Booking accommodation

Whether you are booking accommodation in the UK or abroad, for business travel you are better confining your choice to a hotel in one of the well-known hotel groups, e.g. Holiday Inn, Inter-Continental, Hilton, Trusthouse Forte, Sheraton, Marriott, Ramada and Best Western International. Standards are known and trusted, the services are designed for the business traveller and there are London-based reservations offices to handle bookings worldwide.

A list of hotel reservation offices, addresses and phone numbers can be found in *Travel Trade Gazette* – or you can phone a London hotel in the same group and ask for their international reservations number. You can also obtain information through your travel agent or on Prestel, and some airlines (e.g. British Airways) operate a hotel booking service. Another invaluable book, which gives details of hotels in a variety of towns and cities worldwide, is the *ABC Worldwide Hotel Guide*. Equally, Michelin Guides are indispensable for information on hotels and restaurants in Europe.

If your boss is going to a British town where there is no well-known hotel, then refer to the *AA Handbook or Hotels and Restaurants in Great Britain*; or ring the local Tourist Board. Most hotels are grouped by star categories – the more stars the better the facilities. Below three stars is not usually suitable for executive travel. In the same way you can contact the Tourist Boards of small towns abroad, e.g. the local Syndicate d'Initiative in France, to obtain a printed list of hotels in a particular area – although you may have to translate some of the information given about the facilities available!

Bear in mind that the needs of a business traveller are different from those of the holidaymaker. A swimming pool and gym are not as valuable as an 'any hour' check-in service, tea/coffee making facilities in the room, early morning breakfast facilities, fax machines and good dining/meeting rooms. Car parking may be essential – if your boss is travelling to the hotel by road do remember to check this! Many hotels are also waking up to the fact that more and more business travellers are now women – to whom a trouser press is less important than a good hairdrier!

DID YOU KNOW?

Expotel Hotels have launched a Woman Aware scheme to enable them to respond more effectively to the specific needs of the female business traveller in relation to security, facilities and service. If you have a female boss who travels on business or if you are female and travel yourself, contact Expotel on 0161 442 3535 and ask for a free Woman Aware membership pack.

CHECK IT YOURSELF

Contact Corporate Reservations Service Ltd, 30–32 Staines Road, Hounslow, Middlesex, TW3 3JS (Phone: 0181 577 2424) and ask for a copy of their brochure if you are regularly in the business of booking hotels. This gives a range of hotels both in the UK and around the world; bookings can be made easily by making one telephone call!

Hints and tips on making hotel bookings

- You will usually save money if you book a flight and hotel together. This is because many airlines or travel agents hold rooms at lower rates than the published price and will sell these off cheaply – particularly at off-peak periods. So ask the airline or your travel agent what is available at the same time as you request the flight ticket.
- Always confirm your reservation in writing – preferably by telex, not fax (there is no proof of receipt with a fax). If you do use fax, ask the hotel to fax back confirmation. This is particularly important in some parts of the world where hotels are far less careful about keeping reservations!
- Provide your boss with the names, addresses and phone numbers of alternative hotels in the area – just in case!
- Enquire if the hotel has no-smoking rooms if your boss is a non-smoker.
- Be aware that a twin room has twin beds and a double room has a double bed.
- Check if the rate is per room or per person and whether breakfast is included. (In the USA, for instance, there is one room rate regardless of the number of people the room holds and the price never includes breakfast.)
- If your boss will be arriving after 6 pm make sure the hotel knows, so that it won't re-let the accommodation.
- If the hotel is one you have not used before, check if credit cards are acceptable. If the hotel is abroad remember that the words

Barclaycard and Access mean nothing – you must use the terms Visa and Mastercard.

- Another American idea now being adopted in Europe is the 'all-suite' hotel – based on the idea that many business travellers need more space than is traditionally provided in a single room. The definition of a 'suite' can vary, from two (or more) spacious rooms to one main room with areas for working, sleeping and even eating.

Hints and tips on cost

- As a general rule, cut-price fares are unsuitable for business purposes. They either relate to a time for travelling which is inconvenient or mean that your boss ends up with an inflexible ticket (which cannot be changed even in an emergency) or a much longer journey than normal.
- Many international hotel chains (especially in the USA) operate special schemes for regular visitors, e.g. Honored Guest or Gold Pass. If your executive is in one of these privilege programmes try to make bookings at these hotels and give the membership number when making the reservation.
- If you are on the mailing list of hotel chains you will be sent details of their special offers.
- First-time business travellers should be aware that the cost of their stay will soar if they take advantage of the mini-bar in their rooms, as prices are frequently exorbitant.
- It is far cheaper to phone the office using an international telephone credit card (obtainable from Post Office Telecommunications) than to use a hotel phone, which is usually subject to a considerable surcharge.

Organisations' procedures and policies on travel and accommodation

Some organisations employ their own specialist travel planners or, if large enough, may have their own travel section which deals with all the enquiries and bookings. The vast majority employ the services of a local, reputable travel agent.

However, they are likely to have had in-depth discussions with the agent to make sure that their travel policies are followed by all staff. In addition, special negotiations may have taken place on 'frequently used' routes to reduce the price. This is particularly the case if your organisation has one or two offices overseas which are often visited by executives.

Travel policies will usually cover such areas as:

- which travel agent will handle company travel reservations

- which staff are authorised to make bookings on behalf of the organisation
- how much can be spent on tickets, e.g. whether first class, business class or economy reservations have to be made and over what distance
- which routes can be used for air travel and which carriers (airlines) can be used
- alternative methods of travel recommended or allowed
- the amount per night which can be spent on hotel accommodation
- the range of expenses allowable.

Even with a clearly specified policy, exceptions are almost bound to occur from time to time and these can cause problems for administrators and executives. For instance an executive may be offered the opportunity to collect 'bonus miles' as part of a frequent flyer programme. This may, or may not, be with one of the recommended airlines named in the travel policy. Whilst some organisations have no objection to their executives collecting free air miles and see this as one of the 'perks' of business travel, other organisations insist that their executives must fly with an airline such as Virgin, which, in addition to rewarding the traveller, also rewards the company!

 DID YOU KNOW?

Usually, the further the distance to be travelled the more willing is the employer to pay for an expensive ticket. A survey carried out by *Business Traveller* showed that on flights of between 5 and 10 hours 11 per cent of passengers held first-class tickets and 52 per cent held business class, whereas on long-haul flights of over 10 hours 19 per cent travelled first class and 51 per cent in business class.

The same survey also showed that, upon arrival at their destination, 33 per cent of business travellers chose a five-star hotel and 53 per cent opted for four-star accommodation.

Ways of preparing itineraries

There are basically two types of itinerary. One is a simplified list of travel arrangements which may be typed out on an A4 sheet or – summarised – on a small card (which is easier to keep handy). The second type is a more detailed schedule which covers events and functions being attended, contact names, etc.

There are a few simple, basic rules to follow when drawing up a standard itinerary.

- Type the dates covered, the destination and the names of those involved clearly at the top.
- List the arrangements in date and time order and always use the 24-hour clock.

- Include all important information, e.g. times of departure/arrival, flight numbers and terminals for airline reservations; name, address, telephone number and fax/telex numbers of hotels or car hire firms. Remember all travel arrangements must be covered, including getting from home/office to the airport and return.

An effective way of presenting this information is to paper-clip it to a wallet folder in which are placed all the confirmation documents – again in date/time order. Tickets should be kept separately. An example travel itinerary is shown in Figure 11.1.2.

Programme itineraries

These go under a variety of names – itineraries, detailed itineraries, programme itineraries, agendas or travel/visit programmes! Their style will also vary from one organisation to another, although the main features are usually the same:

- a detailed list of all travel arrangements from leaving home to returning home

---

ITINERARY FOR MS MARGARET SAHAMI

VISIT TO PARIS

26–28 February

Monday 26 February

0530	Company car from home to Birmingham airport
0615	Check-in for flight to Paris
0715	Depart Birmingham flight BA 968
0925	Arrive Paris (Charles de Gaulle) To be met by Mr Lefevre, Paris rep
	Accommodation booked at Hotel Sevigne, 6 Rue Belloy, Paris 75016. Tel: (010 331) 47.20.88.90 Tlx: 610219

Wednesday 28 February

1700	Depart Paris office for Charles de Gaulle airport (company car)
1825	Check-in for flight to Birmingham
1925	Depart Paris flight AF 962
1935	Arrive Birmingham To be met by company car for journey home

---

Figure 11.1.2 An example travel itinerary

- a list of all visits arranged, where, who with, contact names/numbers, documents provided
- additional notes re contacts/free days/entertainment/social functions, etc.
- notes within the programme relating to additional documents, e.g. meeting agendas, conference programmes, invitations, contracts, etc.
- notes on any possible alternatives requested plus alternative/emergency contact numbers.

An extract from a travel programme to the United States is given in Figure 11.1.3. Compare the level of detail in this against that shown in Figure 11.1.2.

Ways of evaluating cost in terms of routes and methods of travel

Because time is money in business, it is usual for business travellers to want to reach their destination the quickest way possible. For European and intercontinental journeys this usually means travelling by air. Within the UK, air travel may be less convenient as time has to be allowed for travelling from airport to city centre – and the cost is higher than by rail. Also within the UK, rail may be preferable to road travel for long journeys as it is quicker, less tiring and work can be done on the way. Sea travel is the least popular method of travel abroad unless, for some reason, your executive wants to take his or her car.

Air travel

Essential for planning air travel are either the *ABC World Airways Guide*, timetables from airlines you use regularly or one of the PC software travel planning packages mentioned on page 639. Alternatively, you can ring your travel agent for details, but you are then restricted to their choice and opinion on flights and not your own.

You must be able to read a timetable without difficulty, know your airlines (and the ones your boss loves/likes/detests), and understand the terms used, some of which are specific to the airline industry. You should also keep yourself informed about new developments and promotional offers.

Many airlines are currently considering installing laptop computers, telexes and faxes in onboard work stations on aeroplanes; while payphones, powerful enough to make calls worldwide, are already fitted in many planes. The phones are for outgoing calls only so you cannot consider this a quick and easy way of contacting your boss whilst in transit (unless the company has a corporate jet).

On the ground, airlines in Europe and North America are testing the use of smart cards and ticket-free flying in place of standard paper

TRAVEL PROGRAMME FOR JAMES TAYLOR

VISIT TO JAPAN   10–13 JUNE 199_

Monday 10 June

1300   Company car from office to airport

1430   Check in Heathrow, Terminal 3

1530   Depart flight VS900

Tuesday 11 June

1055   Arrive Tokyo
              To be met by Mr Kumagai, Tokyo Agent.

Hotel   For nights of 11 and 12 June only
              Rate 24 000 Yen (£105) approx. per night

              Palace Hotel, 1-1 Marunouchi 1-chome,
              Chiyoda-ku, Tokyo, Japan

              Tel: 010-8133-211-5211
              Fax: 010-8133-211-6987
              Confirmation No 182971 (attached)

1400   Meeting with Sumito Corporation
              Mr T Hirachi   Tel 010-8133-294-1611
              Re: Supply agreement (see contract attached)

1730   Dinner – to be confirmed by Mr Kumagai

Wednesday 12 June

All day   Meeting with Sukiyu AG (with J P Fisher)
              Mr G Kumagai   Tel 010-8133-5486-6206
              (Contact Dr T Suki)
              Re: Licensing contract (see customer file)

1730   Dinner at Oshaya Hotel. Black tie.
              Invitation attached.

Thursday 13 June

1055   Depart hotel for airport with Mr Kumagai

1155   Check in Tokyo airport

1255   Depart flight VS901

1730   Arrive Heathrow Terminal 3.
              Company car arranged for transport home.

£800 in US Travellers' Cheques
£100 cash in Yen

Figure 11.1.3 An example travel programme

documentation to speed up the check-in procedure. Airline carriers have spent millions of pounds investing in special VIP lounges designed to cater for the business traveller and offering everything from complimentary drinks to massage and showers to workstations with telephones.

DID YOU KNOW?

In London, BA opened the first arrivals lounge in the world in 1994 – having spent £1.6 million on the project. The area is situated in Terminal Four and comprises 23 showers, a suit-pressing, valeting and shoe-cleaning service as well as a complimentary buffet. Several other airlines have now followed suit. The aim is – to quote one user – 'to take the red out of red eye'. If you don't know what this means, read the information which follows carefully!

Facts you should know

Airport There is often more than one in a city (think of London with Gatwick, Heathrow, Stansted and City airports). Make sure your boss knows to which one he or she is travelling and try to use the one nearest to where he or she will be staying or visiting. Always check that connecting flights from a city arrive/leave from the same airport or allow plenty of time for the transfer (see also *Minimum connection times*). All airports are identified by a three-letter code, e.g. LHR = London Heathrow, JFK = New York, John F Kennedy airport. Be careful when there are two of the same name, e.g. Birmingham UK (BHX) and Birmingham (Alabama) USA (BHM).

Business class The class of travel most often used by business people – cheaper than first class and better than economy. Sometimes called Club Class.

Carrier The name of the airline, again identified by a letter code, e.g. BA = British Airways, AA = American Airlines.

Check-in time The time before a flight when the passenger must book in at the airline desk at the airport. For connecting flights travellers do not have to check in again at the next airport unless, for some reason, baggage has to be collected in transit.

Computerised booking system The most common system used by travel agents is the Travicom/Gallileo system which not only makes the booking but also issues the tickets.

Domestic flight A flight within one country.

Frequent flier programmes Virtually all airlines have a 'club' for their regular business travellers, though the names vary, e.g. Diamond Club (British Midland), Raffles Class (Singapore Airlines), Le Club (Air France). Rules for membership vary and may be based on miles flown or payment of a membership fee (check with the airline or your travel agent). There are many benefits from membership – valet car parking, priority check-in, business lounges (with fax, photocopiers, phones, etc.), plus discounts and special offers.

Jet lag The problems of tiredness and fatigue associated with travelling across several time zones, exacerbated by lack of sleep and short nights. Normally worse travelling from east to west, it can severely impair anyone's ability to do business for several hours (so do not time the first appointment immediately after arrival!).

Long-haul The term used for long intercontinental flights, e.g. UK to Australia. Long-haul flights have stop-overs for refuelling.

Minimum connection time The minimum amount of time which must be allowed between connecting flights. This will depend on whether the incoming/outgoing flight is from the same terminal or different terminals – or even different airports. You will not be allowed to make a booking that breaks the rules on this. Details are given in the *ABC World Airways Guide*.

Non-transferability Most airlines insist that tickets are non-transferable. Therefore if your boss is ill at the last minute you can't send along a substitute with the same ticket. The airline is likely to insist that the booking is cancelled and a new reservation made – if there is still space!

Open-dated return A pre-paid return ticket with no specified date for return travel. The traveller is then free to book the return flight when ready to do so.

Red eye The overnight flight from New York to London. So called because the time change means passengers lose a night's sleep.

Short-haul The opposite of long-haul, e.g. European flights.

Shuttle The walk-on domestic UK air service – no booking needed.

Terminal The specific airport building at which the flight arrives or from which it departs. In large airports there are often several, identified by number, i.e. Terminal 1, 2, etc. Always note down the number – both for the traveller and anyone meeting him or her.

Time zones The hourly segments into which the world is divided. West of Great Britain is earlier than GMT, east is later.

TOD Ticket on Departure system for last-minute bookings. Becoming more common as a service to business passengers.

Wait list The 'reserve' list for a scheduled flight; on European flights there is a high rate of cancellations so it is always worth booking on the wait list for the flight your boss prefers. Book a second choice alternative in case the wait list does not come up and cancel this option if it does.

Hints and tips on organisation

- Organise business appointments first then look to see which flights are the most convenient.
- Keep a 'rating' guide of airlines from your boss's experiences. Try a star system (5 stars = excellent, 0 = awful). Devise a simple scoring system based on food, in-flight service, delays, leg room on board and any other categories your boss thinks appropriate.
- Keep a similar 'rating' guide of airports and their facilities. One of the favourites is usually Schiphol (Amsterdam) which is rated highly because of fast baggage handling, lack of congestion and good duty-free areas. Frankfurt also does well in the ratings at 'processing' on-going passengers quickly. These factors may influence your choice of routing your executives if they have to break their journey somewhere.
- If allowed, register your boss with the frequent flier programme of the airline he or she likes best. When booking always remember to give the frequent flier registration number.
- Many flights today are non-smoking. If this will be a problem for your boss you may have to investigate alternative airlines/routes.
- Most seats on airlines are pre-bookable. Find out if your boss wants smoking (if available) or non-smoking, aisle or window. Bear in mind that these choices may vary with length/time of flight, e.g. an overnight choice may be for an aisle seat whereas for a short daytime flight a window seat may be preferable.
- If your boss is not a seasoned air traveller remind him or her that:
  - alcohol increases jet lag – mineral water prevents dehydration and therefore is much better
  - loose clothes should be worn as the body expands at high altitudes
  - long-haul travellers in first class are given oversocks (feet swell too), so that they can remove their shoes, and eyemasks. These items can be bought pre-flight (together with ear plugs if the noise might be disturbing)
  - a suitcase with jazzy stickers is easy to identify in a busy baggage hall
  - fountain pens leak at high altitude
  - some airlines still do not like laptop computers to be used in flight in case of interference with vital communications equipment, so check first – and make sure the batteries will last for the length of the trip!
  - baggage tags should be kept carefully (they should be attached to the ticket); the number on these is needed if baggage is lost.

Hints and tips to save money

Calculating fares is complicated and better left to the experts. If you make many bookings your company may send you on a special travel course to learn how to do this. Even without this information, though, you can save your company money.

- Watch out for special offers. During certain promotional periods frequent fliers may be able to upgrade a class – which can make all the difference on an overnight flight.
- Alternatively a special offer may be available if you re-route the trip, e.g. London to Boston via New York instead of direct.
- Some frequent flier programmes offer free trips after a certain number of miles travelled. Try to coordinate bookings to log up the miles required and, if the rules of membership allow for this, centralise offers received by the company so they can be used by all executives for the benefit of the company as a whole.
- The magazines *Business Traveller* and *Executive Travel* give recommended price lists for all classes of travel; check these against any prices you are quoted.
- Check your company's policy on this, but on long-haul flights some organisations prefer to pay for first-class travel (so the executive can get a fairly good night's sleep) rather than schedule a day off into the itinerary.

TEST YOURSELF

- Find out the name of the following airlines from their identification letters and state for which country they are the flag carrier. What is the capital city of each country you have listed?

    LH   SN   QF   KL   AZ   EI   OA   SR   PA   IB

- The following are all American airports. Can you name them?

    BOS   IND   LAX   SFO   SEA   PHL   LGA   LAS

Road travel

Bear in mind that your boss may want to travel by road abroad, either by taking a car to Europe or flying to the destination and then hiring a car. All travellers using their own car should be members of a motoring organisation, e.g. the AA or the RAC. These organisations not only offer breakdown and 'get you home' services in the UK but also advice and information on driving abroad. The AA also operates a computerised route planning service for both members and non-members, which can take the work and worry out of planning a trip to take in three cities in Germany, a visit to Belgium and an overnight stop in Holland by the best route possible.

Car ferries

The most usual method of transporting a car across the water is by ferry. Alternatives for passengers travelling from Dover are by hovercraft, Seacat and jetfoil – all of which are more expensive but halve the travelling time. (The jetfoil service is passenger-only.)

When you make the booking you will need to know the make/length/registration number of the vehicle. On ferries you can book a cabin – in some cases for day journeys as well as night crossings. You must specify if private facilities are required.

Some ferry companies, e.g. P&O, have now introduced an Executive Club class on some routes if the ticket holder pays a supplement. Members can use the Club class lounge which contains desks, telephones and fax facilities.

All travellers must check in at the Ferryport before sailing; times vary (the average is about one hour before sailing) so check the ticket or ask your travel agent. For last-minute bookings you can arrange for the ticket to be ready for collection on departure from the Ferryport.

Hints and tips

- Remember that it may be much easier and quicker for your boss to cross from the east coast if he or she is visiting northern Europe.
- It takes time to load and unload a ferry. You therefore need to take account of the waiting time for embarkation and disembarkation when planning the schedule.
- A longer ferry journey can often reduce the driving required. Although longer ferry journeys are more expensive they are cheaper per mile than short crossings.
- If you time arrival for early morning (and book a cabin overnight) driving time is maximised.
- If your boss regularly takes a car abroad then watch for off-peak reductions – especially if the day of travel is flexible. By planning the journey for a quiet day and time – and sometimes for a specified length of time – substantial reductions can be obtained out of season.

British cars abroad

The regulations for British cars taken to Europe vary from one country to another. Most countries require:

- headlamps which point towards the nearside to avoid blinding oncoming traffic (rather than adjusting the headlamps it is easier to fit temporary headlight converters)
- a spare set of headlamp bulbs
- a warning triangle to be displayed if the car breaks down.

The AA recommends that the driver takes a spare clutch/accelerator cable as these are different for right-hand drive cars and obtaining a spare on the Continent can therefore be very difficult.

All British cars should also carry an approved GB plate on the rear of the vehicle.

Documents required include the driver's licence (in Spain an International Driving Permit is required), the vehicle registration documents and a Green Card or International Motor Insurance Certificate. The latter extends the driver's insurance to cover European countries and is issued by his or her insurance company. In Spain a Bail Bond is also required which covers the driver if he or she is taken into custody after an accident. This is available from the AA, RAC and Europ Assistance – a company which specialises in comprehensive cover packages to Europe.

The quickest way to take a car a long distance is often by Motorail; the car travels by train and the driver can relax in a sleeper or couchette. Motoring organisations have full details for each country – which saves having to contact separate railway organisations. Note that you must notify the insurance company so that the car is covered for any damage during the rail journey.

Hints and tips

- Make sure the driver knows which roads are toll roads – and has some small change available in the relevant currency.
- Money can be saved by filling up with petrol on the cheaper side of the border.
- Keep a list of the main driving regulations per country on either a country fact sheet or on a card index file. Photocopy the card and give it to the driver before departure.

Hiring a car

First rule – beware unknown or backstreet companies which hire out cars which are unfit for the road. Quite apart from the problems of possible breakdowns, if a driver is stopped for driving a car which isn't roadworthy the police will charge the driver, not the hire company! Therefore insist on a relatively new vehicle with a low mileage. However, note that in the case of mechanical breakdown it is the hire company which is legally responsible, not the driver. To be on the safe side hire a vehicle from a member of the British Vehicle Renting and Leasing Association (BVRLA), whose members have to operate to a specific code of conduct.

The driver has to produce a current driving licence (and may be refused if the licence has been endorsed for a motoring offence) and will probably be asked for proof of identity. The driver must have been driving for a minimum of one year (often longer for more expensive cars) and must be at least 21 years of age (23 in some cases).

Cars are hired out either on an unlimited mileage basis – the most common method – or with an additional charge for mileage above a specified limit. The best way to pay is by credit card which means no deposit is required and there is no restriction on the choice of cars.

In Britain there are four multinational car companies – Avis, Budget Rent-a-Car, Europcar and Hertz – as well as independent large companies, e.g. British Car Rental, Kenning and Swan National. These companies offer one-way hire so that 'quick drop-offs' can be arranged at many airports and railway stations. From 1995 Hertz are offering hirers in Europe the facility to collect a car in one country and drop it off in another for a basic $50.

DID YOU KNOW?

To combat the increasing theft of hire cars, Europcar now fits Tracker units in some of its expensive models. These automatically alert the police if the car is stolen.

In Miami, where personal security is more of an issue, Avis has fitted vehicles with satellite navigation aids and panic buttons linked to the police.

Hints and tips

- When you book, check the procedure in case of an emergency breakdown or accident; has the company a 24-hour emergency call-out number?
- Although the standard of car-hire vehicles from local firms is more variable than from national firms it is well worth shopping around as often their prices are much lower.
- Always check whether or not the price you are quoted includes VAT.
- Many large car hire firms have their own credit cards which enable the user to claim up to 20 per cent discount. It may also enable him or her to collect in one place and drop off in another without any surcharges.
- If you find a good local firm, and hire cars often, try to negotiate a better deal. Even with national firms local branches are often allowed to set their own charges.
- Hiring a car in major cities and at airports is more expensive as 'national tariffs' are charged, as opposed to the out-of-town rates charged elsewhere. If cost is a major consideration it can be worth using a good rail link from an airport to get to a local depot.
- Although the basic hire charge includes insurance against passenger liability and third party risks, extra charges may be levied. Collision damage waiver covers damage done to the vehicle and there may be an additional charge for personal

accident insurance. Check the charges for both of these as rates can vary considerably.

- Car hire abroad can be much cheaper than in the UK and may be offered at premium rates and/or linked to frequent flier programmes and rail bookings (check with the airline, your travel agent or the rail company).
- Check the basics of the vehicle upon collection – tyres, fluid levels, lights, wipers and how much fuel is in the tank. Drive around the block and check that the brakes, instruments and clutch function properly. Make sure the handbook is in the car.

Coach travel

Coaches are rarely used for business travel but it is not inconceivable that you will have to book a coach journey at some stage – if only for a relative of your boss who wants to visit Europe but hates flying! The best people to contact are National Express at Eurolines, 52 Grosvenor Gardens, Victoria, London SW1. In addition National Express has enquiry centres all over the UK and will send you a timetable, answer your queries and accept credit card reservations. The fare includes coach travel, ferry crossings and additional charges such as road tolls. Note that insurance is not included – not even for passenger luggage or belongings.

Rail travel – Britain

Most business travellers in Britain use the InterCity service to go from one city centre to another and most main railway stations have a Travel Centre with staff who can deal with enquiries and reservations. In addition they stock maps, timetables and booklets on a variety of services. If your nearest station is too far away, then your local Rail Appointed Travel Agent can offer the same service.

British Rail operates a Business Travel Service which includes travel advice and reservations for rail and car-hire. Companies can open their own Rail Travel Account so that all reservations can be made by telephone. In addition they can arrange to issue a rail warrant to their staff which is presented at the booking office and exchanged for a ticket. British Rail then sends the company an account at the end of the month for the tickets/warrants issued.

There are two main categories of travel on British Rail – Standard and First Class. A variation is Silver Standard – offered in the specially marked coaches on main business trains. However, many executives prefer to travel First Class. Always look to see if a Pullman train is an option: the service is better, as are the facilities, which include an 'at-seat' catering service and a restaurant car offering an extensive menu. If you purchase an Executive ticket then in addition to the first-class ticket and seat reservations you also receive refreshment and car parking vouchers, a London underground Zone One ticket and the facility to add and pre-pay for meals and/or sleeper reservations. The Scottish Executive ticket includes sleeper travel in either direction and can be combined with the Motorail service. Both First Class and Executive ticket holders can use the Pullman Lounges at Edinburgh, London (Kings Cross and Euston), Leeds and Newcastle which are equipped with telephone, television/teletext, a photocopier and, in London, a fax machine.

Rail travel – Europe

The latest train to capture attention is, of course, Eurostar. From London the service provides six trains a day to Paris and three trains a day to Brussels travelling through the Channel Tunnel to reach their destination. Many business people prefer Eurostar – particularly if they live in or near central London. There is no longer the inconvenience of travelling to and from airports, it is reportedly far less tiring than flying and it is cheaper (about £195 by train, £250 by plane). SNCF, the French railway company, has spent large sums of money on the Lille Europe railway station where Eurostar meets the high-speed TGV network serving all the major destinations in France.

In general, in Europe, rail links are getting quicker – therefore narrowing the gap between rail and air travel. London to Lyon is 4 hours by plane and costs about £507, by Eurostar it takes 6.5 hours and costs £333. Paris to Geneva by rail takes 3.5 hours as compared to 65 minutes by air yet is less than half the price and takes you from city centre to city centre. In Germany, Lufthansa (the German airline) has started a fast rail service between the main German cities. Passengers are given boarding cards and are served by Lufthansa cabin staff. The change has helped to reduce the demand for domestic air flights as it means quicker and easier travel from one city centre to another.

Hints and tips

- Whether your boss travels First or Standard class always make a seat reservation. Check whether he or she prefers to travel in a smoking or non-smoking compartment and facing the front or rear of the train (or has no particular preference).
- Make sure your boss carries a phone card – most trains these days have card phones.
- Register with the British Rail Business Travel Service by dialling 0181 200 0200 and you will be sent a comprehensive guide to InterCity services and a new guide whenever timetables change.
- Keep a full set of British Rail timetables for the routes your boss uses or have your own copy of the British Rail Timetable or the *ABC Rail Guide*.
- If your boss is travelling to a major city by rail and staying a few days it may be worth checking if any company operates an inclusive short-break package – which can be much cheaper.

- Make sure you are on the mailing list of any rail company you use regularly, so that you are advised of special offers, e.g. rail rover information/car-hire discounts.
- If you need to refer to Continental train information on a regular basis it is worth buying a copy of the *Thomas Cook International Timetable*.

Types of documentation required for travel and accommodation

Before anyone can travel abroad they need a valid passport. For some countries a visa and/or a current vaccination certificate is required. In addition you will also need adequate insurance and foreign currency – or some means of paying for what you buy!

Passports

The style of British passports is now the same format as European passports. The words European Community are printed on the front cover and the passport itself is printed with machine readable characters. Eventually it is intended to mechanise passport control to reduce delays at frontiers.

Application forms for passports are available from the Post Office or travel agents as well as from passport offices in London, Liverpool, Glasgow, Peterborough, Belfast and Newport (Gwent). There are several different passport forms but the usual one is form A. Two photographs must accompany the form (those from photo booths are quite acceptable) and must be endorsed by a British subject who is of professional standing and has known the applicant for at least two years. In addition the applicant must enclose his or her birth certificate (and marriage certificate if the applicant is a woman who wants her passport in her married name). The passport is valid for ten years and an extra large version is available for people who travel frequently.

Whilst it is usual to apply for a passport by post, in an emergency you can visit the passport office in person and wait for the application to be processed. In some circumstances a business traveller may need two passports – e.g. if travelling to an Arab country which will refuse admittance to anyone whose passport contains evidence they have visited Israel, or if submitting a passport to obtain a visa for a future trip at the same time as a current trip abroad is being scheduled. In these circumstances the Passport Office will give you details of how to apply for a second passport.

Once the passport is received make a note of the number and date and place of issue and keep the information in a safe place. If your boss has credit cards insured by a 'card safe' company (see page 662) then the passport details can also be registered with them. If the passport is lost or stolen in the UK notify the card safe company, the police and the passport office. If it is missing abroad then notify the police and contact the nearest British Embassy or Consulate who will arrange for the necessary emergency travel documents to be issued for the return journey home.

Visas

Visas are required by many countries and are usually just a formality. They are obtained from the Embassy or Consulate of the country concerned. Staff there will give you details of the cost, how to apply, the length of time for which the visa is valid and how long it usually takes for one to be issued. Again in an emergency you can apply in person.

Your travel agent will make any visa arrangements for you; this means handing over the passport whilst the visa is issued. The visa is stamped on a page in the passport and states clearly the date of expiry. If your boss needs several valid visas on an almost permanent basis then keep a note of the date of expiry of each so that they can be renewed in good time.

DID YOU KNOW?

Vaccinations and medical requirements are dealt with on page 664.

Travel insurance

Two important points to note are, firstly, standard holiday cover is not sufficient for business travellers – a good ongoing policy is needed which covers any number of trips. Secondly, although EC countries now have reciprocal arrangements with Britain provided you have obtained form E111 (available from a Post Office), the medical care is provided by the state sector, and standards fall far short of the NHS in many countries. In addition costs have to be paid on the spot and reclaimed later. It is therefore wise to take out additional medical insurance for all countries.

Policies are available from insurance companies, banks, building societies, brokers, major travel agents and the AA. Cover should include the following.

Medical expenses To cover medical treatment (including hospitalisation), a special air ambulance home and an ambulance to and from the airport in both countries. £1 million is recommended for worldwide cover.

Personal liability £1 million, to cover accidental injury to people or property.

Cancelling or early return Should cover the full cost of the trip. Acceptable reasons should include illness or death of self or business associate/fellow traveller, redundancy, disasters at home/work (e.g. fire), being a police witness or on jury service.

Belongings and money To cover personal items and company equipment or samples taken abroad. 'Money' should include travellers cheques and tickets, not just cash.

Delayed luggage At least £75 to cover emergency purchases.

Delayed departure If delay is more than 24 hours through bad weather, strikes or transport failure then the full cost of the trip should be covered.

In addition, other features can include the expenses incurred in obtaining a duplicate passport and cover for legal expenses. Aim for a nil excess policy, which means the full amount of any claim will be paid, without deductions.

Hints and tips

- Obtain a copy of the policy document (not the advertising blurb) and read the exclusion clauses carefully before taking out the insurance. For instance, check the limit on individual valuables – and exactly what goods are classed as valuables.
- Photocopy the policy for the traveller to take with him or her.
- If your boss has a charge card or gold card, business travel insurance may be included. If so, check exactly what cover is given. Do not automatically assume it will be sufficient.
- If you cancel the trip and are claiming on the insurance policy, get a cancellation invoice from the travel agent plus written proof as to the reason.
- Make sure your boss knows it is important to keep all receipts of any extra travel/accommodation/medical costs incurred.
- Check the policy to ensure what events must be reported to the police immediately for claims to be valid. Get written confirmation from the police that this has been done.
- In some countries medical treatment will not be started until the insurance has been checked. Make sure your boss knows the emergency number to ring for help.
- If the trip is curtailed because of a delayed departure then you need the details confirmed in writing by the airline.
- If baggage is missing then the traveller should complete a Property Irregularity Report – obtainable from the airline. Ask the airline to confirm the loss.
- Make sure the insurance company is aware of any ongoing medical condition. If there is any doubt about cover ask for a doctor's letter to certify fitness to travel and send this, plus any other details, to the insurance company, so you cannot be accused of 'withholding material fact'.
- Bear in mind that if your boss is a woman who is pregnant, cover may not be provided at all – or only during the first six months of pregnancy.

- Many insurance policies insist that valuables must be kept in a hotel safe.

- Look through a copy of the latest *AA Guide* and note the facilities offered against the different star categories of hotels. What does the percentage figure quoted indicate?
- Call at a few of your local banks, building societies and insurance companies and obtain literature on travel insurance. Check the cover offered and work out which is the best value for money.

Ways of making monetary arrangements

Travellers abroad have a variety of methods of paying for goods. The first rule is to keep to a minimum the amount of cash taken – for obvious reasons. However, some currency is obviously required for small day-to-day needs. This should be ordered from the bank seven days in advance – especially if the currency is an unusual one. Note that for some countries, e.g. Morocco or Tunisia, you can obtain currency only upon arrival. In other cases the amount of cash that can be taken out of the country on departure is restricted. Alternatives to cash include Eurocheques, travellers' cheques, credit cards, gold cards and charge cards.

Eurocheques are only used in European and Mediterranean countries and to be of any use the traveller also needs a Eurocheque card which guarantees the cheques up to £100 (or more in some cases). If the traveller has a PIN number the card can also be used to obtain money from cash dispensers abroad which display the distinctive red and blue EC logo. The bank can supply a list of cashpoints in Europe in an illustrated booklet which also shows how to use the different types of cash machines found in different countries. Allow ten days to get a Eurocheque book and card and bear in mind that commission is paid on all cheques debited to the account.

Travellers' cheques are available in sterling and several other currencies as well. A commission charge is levied by the bank when you buy the cheques and, if they are sterling cheques, a further commission is charged when they are cashed. Both dollars and sterling are known as 'hard currencies' and are acceptable in many countries in the world. Travellers' cheques are ordered from the bank and the traveller must sign each one on receipt. On encashment the holder must produce his or her passport and sign the cheque(s) again. The list of cheque numbers and the cheques themselves must be kept safely in separate places for security and the list of numbers produced if the cheques are lost or stolen. In the case of loss or theft a refund can be obtained –

theoretically straight away but it may be more problematic in practice, especially in unusual places with no correspondent ('link') bank.

Today the most usual method of paying for items abroad is by using credit cards or charge cards. Indeed in some countries, e.g. the USA, this may be the only acceptable way to pay in some situations. Mastercard and Visa are the main credit cards and these usually offer better rates of exchange than the local tourist rates. The major problem with credit cards abroad – especially for business travellers – is the credit limit. In some countries hotels protect themselves by asking for the card on arrival and then processing it for a much larger amount than the quoted hotel bill (in case damage is caused or the guest runs up a tremendous restaurant bill). Whilst only the amount spent is actually charged to the card at the end of the stay, in the meantime the card will be useless for other purchases if it has reached its limit. It is therefore wise to take at least two cards – preferably one Visa and one Mastercard – so that one is always available to use.

Another way around this is to carry charge cards – and many business travellers subscribe to either Diner's Club or American Express. A charge card is different from a credit card in that the account must be paid in full at the end of a pre-set period (between 45 and 60 days) or a late payment penalty is levied. There is no pre-set spending limit. There is an annual fee and Diner's Club also charge a joining fee. Corporate cards can be purchased and issued under the name of the company. A breakdown account is issued to the company giving the expenditure for each charge card so that expenses can be checked.

The advantage of charge cards is that they can be used for air tickets and additional hotel stays if the trip is unexpectedly extended or the executive is re-routed halfway across the world. Other benefits include automatic travel insurance and automatic emergency replacement if the card is lost or stolen.

Another Corporate charge card is the Thomas Cook card, which can be used wherever Mastercards are acceptable and which gives the same service as other charge cards plus air travel, hotel and car savings. In addition, holders receive privileged treatment in any Thomas Cook office worldwide, including the use of their telex machines.

A gold card is similar to a charge card but often with more facilities, perks and higher fees. Many gold cards offer comprehensive travel benefits, e.g. travel insurance, emergency assistance and guaranteed hotel reservations. The holder has to earn at least £20 000 a year to qualify – more with some cards.

 ## DID YOU KNOW?

Whereas an organisation may make a direct payment in advance for British travel and accommodation (e.g. to the travel agent, to British Rail or to a hotel), it is unlikely to do the same with an overseas booking. Usually, business travellers who go abroad frequently are issued with credit cards or charge cards which are listed in the company name. All bills charged to these cards are recorded as that person's expenses. This allows more flexibility (in case arrangements have to be changed) as well as ensuring a competitive exchange rate (see below).

International monetary exchange rates

You can easily find out the current exchange rate for a country by reading the morning newspaper, ringing the bank or watching Ceefax or Teletext. All these rates fluctuate against sterling depending upon demand and supply. If sterling is strong you will receive more for each pound you exchange; if sterling is weak then you will receive less. However, you can do very little about this if you urgently need $400 for someone travelling to America tomorrow!

There are two facts that you should know, however.

- Banks charge a commission on the money they change – this is usually charged per transaction not as a percentage of the amount exchanged. Therefore, the more you can change at once the better.
- The best rate is usually that negotiated by credit card companies – so it is more cost-effective to buy on credit abroad than to pay cash.

Hints and tips

- Keep a note of currency regulations in countries your executives frequently visit, plus banking hours and other useful hints and tips about money.
- Always make sure your boss has some small change for tips, taxi fares or even a cup of coffee on arrival. You can do this by keeping in a safe place the small change he or she brings back and reissuing it on the next trip to the same country.
- Because it is usually cheaper to buy larger amounts of foreign currency at one time, try to 'batch' your orders and keep spare currency in the office safe.
- Make sure first-time travellers know they should avoid obtaining currency at airports and railway stations where rates are usually poor or commission charges high.
- No traveller abroad should ever be reliant on just one credit card. If the card company makes a mistake, or the limit is reached, then funds could be drastically curtailed!
- Shop around for exchange rates on currency and commission charges on currency and travellers' cheques. Do bear in mind that what seems to be a good buy may not be once the commission charges are included.
- Try to avoid selling back currency a business traveller comes

home with – otherwise you are losing money both ways. It is far better to keep it for next time.

- Make sure your boss has a BT Chargecard for making calls back to the UK.
- Remember that your boss may return with unused travellers' cheques. If these are sterling or dollar cheques they can be used anywhere on subsequent business trips. If you have purchased specific currency cheques they can only be used in the country to which the currency relates.
- Dollar travellers' cheques can be used as cash in the USA; therefore make sure your boss has some in small denominations, e.g. $10 and $20.
- Many airlines, petrol companies, hotels and car-hire firms issue their own charge cards. Holders of these are often eligible for discounts, so if your boss uses any of these services regularly it is worth obtaining more details.

 ## DID YOU KNOW?

An increasing number of companies are now offering a service, for a yearly premium, to cover the loss of credit cards at home or abroad. The service greatly simplifies the procedure involved if cards are lost or stolen, as only one phone call is required and the card agency does the rest. The facilities vary from one company to another. Check that you are offered:

- cover for fraudulent use before notification (though the owner is usually liable for the first £50)
- the facility to make reverse charge calls from all over the world (to notify the loss)
- an emergency cash advance worldwide
- a replacement airline ticket worldwide (repayable later).

Companies will also record details of other valuables – passports, share certificates, etc. – and keep these on computer so that the information is readily available in case of loss or theft.

Hints and tips

- Bear in mind that if a card protection policy is paid by credit card then the small print of the agreement will probably include automatic renewal. You have to notify them if you want to change – do not expect them to check with you every year before renewal.
- Keep a list of all emergency telephone numbers and give your boss a typed copy. If there is an emergency card safe number then put a copy of this in an unusual place so that if the wallet or handbag is stolen the number to ring hasn't disappeared too!

Ways of identifying and making arrangements for special requirements

Today virtually all travel organisations and hoteliers are very familiar with dealing with special requests. However, if you keep a record for even a short length of time, you will soon find that some can be trusted more than others – in which case you may start a 'preferred' list for certain travellers.

You will have to make special arrangements if:

- people have mobility difficulties – ranging from visual impairment to need for wheelchair access
- a traveller is on a special diet – from vegetarian to low fat or salt-free
- there is likely to be a language problem
- someone has a particular medical need or must take regular medication
- someone runs out of money!

You will normally be able to identify special requirements because someone will tell you. However, you do need to be sensitive to the fact that some people do not like to make a fuss or be seen to be a nuisance. In this case you would be well advised to bring your professional expertise to bear in making suitable arrangements – rather than always waiting to be asked! A few positive suggestions may be very welcome by all concerned.

The golden rule in all these cases is to *notify people as soon as you know.*

- Airlines make special arrangements for dealing with disabled passengers, special diets, unaccompanied children, etc. and are well used to doing so. Check with them if the problem is a medical one, however: in some cases flying may not be recommended.
- Hotels usually have a number of rooms where the spaces in the room are wide enough for wheelchair access and there are bathroom fittings for the disabled. Special diets are not seen as a problem in most large hotels.
- Your travel agent will also be able to give you advice and assistance in the case of special requirements – though if the problem is a monetary one the best source of help will be your bank!
- Don't forget that there are a whole range of societies in Britain which are supportive to those with special needs – examples are the RNIB, MENCAP and the British Diabetic Association. Any of these will gladly give you help and advice if you contact them.

International time zones

International time zones are the bane of the business traveller because, in many cases, the result is jet lag. This is always worse if the journey is east to west and lasts a long time, with the result that you can arrive at your destination at mid-day whilst your body clock is telling you it's 4 o'clock in the morning!

You need to allow for these problems both when making arrangements for your boss on arrival at his or her destination and when arranging meetings for people who have just landed. If you have a boss who regularly gets it wrong, then you could do worse than to buy him or her *Arrive in Better Shape* by Farrol Khan next Christmas! Or at least make sure that he/she knows that:

- alcohol makes things worse, not better
- pre-flight exercise helps
- comfortable clothing and footwear are essential – preferably with an elasticated waistband
- buying an economy seat is foolish if there is a meeting of prime importance upon arrival.

Incidentally, if you are unsure about international time zones, spend a few minutes studying your Phone Book. Together with the international dialling codes, you will find the time difference for each country listed. These are not always exact to the hour – Britain and several other countries change their clocks during the year to make the maximum use of daylight. In Australia, each state is apt to do this on different dates, just to add to the confusion! The best check is the air ticket – which is always made out to show the time of departure and arrival in each country. This is why a ticket from San Francisco to London will show about 18 hours difference between departure and arrival.

Medical requirements and arrangements for travel outside the United Kingdom

Frequent business travellers to foreign countries should be regularly checked by the company doctor who must be informed of the countries which have been or will be visited. More and more companies are operating preventative health care policies so that travellers are briefed on any health dangers endemic to the area they are visiting – and can also be counselled on the stress involved in making frequent trips.

Illness abroad can cause havoc to an important schedule as well as distress for the person involved. In addition, nearly 2000 people return to the UK each year with malaria, while others contract diseases such as hepatitis, typhoid and even AIDS. Companies which do not have their own doctor and which want expert advice can contact any of the

British Airways Travel Clinics, MASTA (the Medical Advisory Service for Travellers Abroad) or the Thomas Cook Medical Centre in London.

Inoculations and/or vaccinations are either essential or recommended for many countries and most can be administered by a GP. All GPs and travel agents should keep an up-to-date list of vaccination requirements but must be contacted in advance of the trip – it is several weeks before some vaccinations are completely effective. In addition the Department of Health produces an excellent leaflet called *Health Advice for Travellers* which you can obtain by ringing 0800 555 777.

All travellers should be aware of basic health rules whilst abroad and take basic precautions.

- Remember to take vaccination certificates. The best place is inside the back cover of the passport, fastened with a rubber band.
- Carry a small first aid kit which includes sterilisation tablets, antiseptic cream, plasters, insect repellent and remedies for travel sickness, headaches, stomach upsets, and insect bites and stings. Remember to take any medicine needed regularly. Visitors to more remote places should include anti-malaria drugs. In addition, special kits are available with sterilised and sealed items of equipment which may be required by a doctor or nurse in an emergency. There are also special AIDS kits, containing sterile syringes and dressings, for travellers to high AIDS-risk areas. If sexual contact is likely then condoms are essential.
- Do not drink the water (or use it for cleaning teeth) unless it is known to be safe – bottled water should be used instead.
- Avoid raw vegetables, salads, unpeeled fruit, shellfish, ice cream and ice cubes.
- Have a dental check-up before travelling as treatment can be difficult or costly abroad.
- Remember that a severe attack of diarrhoea or vomiting causes dehydration. Anti-diarrhoea medicines are not, in themselves, a cure. In addition the sufferer should stop drinking alcohol and eating solid food and replace body fluids by drinking a rehydration solution (e.g. one level teaspoon salt and four heaped teaspoons of sugar added to safe drinking water). If the attack lasts longer than three days see a doctor.
- Carry a medical card which states their blood group and any special medical condition from which they suffer.
- Make sure they have adequate health insurance in addition to the standard European cover (see page 657). This is vital for countries where treatment must be paid for and is expensive, e.g. the USA and Canada.
- On returning home, report any strange symptoms immediately to their doctor (and remember to say where they've been).

- Several organisations make up special medical kits, the most famous being the London School of Hygiene and Tropical Medicine. Details can be obtained by phoning their Medical Advisory Services for Travellers (MASTA) on 0171 631 4408.
- Ring the British Airways Travel Clinics information desk on 0171 831 5333 and find out where your nearest travel clinic is situated.

Security and confidentiality procedures

Whilst organising travel and accommodation is not, in itself, usually an activity which is classed as 'confidential', there are aspects of business trips which your boss may not want shouted around the organisation! Given that any administrator or PA worth his or her salt should always lean heavily towards the side of discretion, it is unlikely that you would discuss these anyway. You would be unwise, therefore, to make public knowledge:

- the price of travel or the cost of a particular ticket
- the reason for the trip – particularly if discussions are of a confidential or sensitive nature
- details of *anyone's* expense claims.

If the correct procedures have been carried out and company policy followed, then it is not the job of the general office to speculate about the wisdom of the trip or its cost!

Legal and regulatory requirements relating to travel and accommodation

There are several points to remember in relation to making bookings for travel or accommodation.

- When you make a travel booking your legal contract is between you and the supplier of the service – not with the travel agent. When you receive a ticket or booking confirmation look at the conditions carefully.
- Airlines are liable for losses, inconvenience and distress under the Warsaw Convention – an international legal agreement. This agreement also states the minimum amount of compensation an airline must pay if luggage goes astray or is damaged.
- Although you may be able to claim that a hotel giving poor service in the UK is not living up to its brochure promises – and therefore acting contrary to the Trade Descriptions Act or the Sale of Goods and Services Act – you will not be in the same position in the case of accommodation abroad unless you made the booking through the hotel's representative in this country.
- Reputable travel agents are bonded through the Association of

British Travel Agents to protect their clients if the firm experiences financial difficulties. Reputable airlines are bonded with the International Air Transport Association, although this is not compulsory.

● Although travellers abroad still have legal rights to expect what they have paid for, the situation is a bit different if you are sending foreign correspondents to war zones or countries where there is a severe political or military problem!

● The whole reason why you take out travel insurance is to gain compensation if something goes wrong! If the journey is an unusual one then make sure you have taken out a fully comprehensive policy which includes cover for the financial failure of the operator or carrier and check if you are covered in the case of war risk.

● If you have a problem and are not sure whether you have a claim in law then you should contact your solicitor or telephone the Office of Fair Trading for their advice.

DID YOU KNOW?

Passengers' rights on British Rail have improved since the publication of the Passenger's Charter in March 1992. If you have a problem ask for a copy of BR's Code of Practice for Customer Comments (at any station) and find out which Customer Service Manager you should contact. Finally, you can write to the Transport Users Consultative Committee for your region and ask them to take up your complaint for you.

ACTIVITY SECTION

1 Your boss has read that Royal Mail International has started a service to support British companies who are in the business of developing new overseas markets. They run an International Business Portfolio club for customers, issue a quarterly magazine and publish a Business Travel Guide with information on currency exchange rates, visa requirements and hints and tips on local culture and customs. He has asked you to contact RMI and find out more about the service and information they offer.

Write to them at Royal Mail International, Freepost, Export Clubs, 12–15 Fenton Way, Basildon, Essex, SS15 4BR.

2 You work for Jayne Shackleton, Sales Director of a large drug company. She is visiting the United States next week. From the information given below, design a comprehensive visit programme.

Extract from letter from travel agent

Flights have been confirmed as follows:

Sunday 9 June – Depart LHR 15.00, terminal 4 BA 185 – Arrive Newark at 17.45

Wed 12 June – Depart Newark 15.10, CO225
Arrive San Francisco 18.30
Please note that we have wait listed you on the earlier flight at 13.10, arriving at 16.30, as requested. Flight number CO223

Thurs 13 June – Depart San Francisco 18.30 BA286
Arrive LHR, terminal 4, 12.40 Fri 14 June.

Please note check-in is one hour for all flights.

Fax from New York office Fax No 0101-617-923-1982

Hotel booked for stay in New Jersey = Marriott, 105 Davidson Avenue, tel. 0101-908-560-0900, fax 0101-908-560-3118. Avis hire car available at Newark.

Fax from San Francisco office

Fax 0101-415-266-1092

Avis hire car reserved at airport. Dinner with Stanford confirmed – please collect Lisa Chowley at Sheraton hotel at 18.45. Your hotel Holiday Inn, 500 Airport Boulevard, Burlingame, San Francisco. Tel: 0101-415-340-8400, fax 0101-415-340-0199.

Note from Jayne

Please arrange $1200 in travellers' cheques (some in small denominations) and $500 cash.

Extract from diary

Mon 10 June	0930 Klineman Inc., Bloomfield – contact Dr Jack Glover – tel. 0101-215-704-2910. Re R & D programme
	1330 KWN Corp, Midway – tel. 0101-201-628-0110. Contact Dr Alfred Hubert. Re Licensing agreement
Tues 11 June	All day in NY office – meeting with Dan Williamson et al
Wed 12 June	0900 Glenby International Corp – contact Dr Simon Oates. Tel: 0101-201-831-3271 Re antibody research programme
Thurs 13 June	0900 Phila Inc, tel. 0101-415-340-8201. Contact Dr Peter Farthing – re anti-coagulant drugs
	1230 lunch at Stanford University – Prof Larry McDermott et al – tel. 0101-415-723-0198

Documents

1 Beatty's test report for Kline
2 Copy of licensing contract for KWN
3 Research papers for Glenby

Note from Jayne

Whilst you were at lunch the travel agent phoned – my wait list has come up! I've checked with San Francisco – the hire car will be available earlier.

Fax from New York

Have managed to arrange the plant tour you wanted of Technofusion Inc. Have arranged this for Tuesday am – starting at 0830. We can have lunch on site and return to the office by 1300 – should be no problem completing discussions by 1900 as planned as we can do most of the preliminary paper work before you arrive. Contact name at Technofusion is Warren Gallagher – tel. 0101-201-831-0014, fax 0101-201-831-8839.

Regards, Dan

3 Your organisation has recently decided that it can reduce the costs of travel substantially if planning trips becomes a centralised function within the company. You have been given the job of senior travel planner and a budget of £500 to set up your new office. You will have two junior assistants to help you.

Executives in your company travel mainly by rail in the UK and by air to overseas destinations.

a Make a comprehensive list of travel books or software you would like to buy to help you plan trips effectively.
b Make a comprehensive list of the contents of each for your two assistants.
c Contact your local travel agent and obtain details of its business travel service. Summarise these in a memo to your new staff.
d Obtain as much information as possible on different travel insurance policies. Select the one you think would be most suitable and notify your boss, with the reasons for your recommendation.

Element 11.2
Monitor and verify travel and accommodation arrangements

Throughout this unit we have been concerned with the costs of business travel – and for very good reasons. A recent survey revealed that nine out of ten companies considered that their travel costs were increasing faster than their turnover. Of these costs about 46 per cent are on air fares and 24 per cent on accommodation – therefore any savings in these areas can help considerably.

No organisation can keep its spending on travel and accommodation within reasonable limits if staff concerned in making bookings and reservations do not take the appropriate action to check the amounts of money involved and if there is no systematic method of monitoring expenditure.

Methods of monitoring travel and accommodation arrangements

Imagine a company with absolutely no controls over spending on travel and accommodation. The temptation to travel first class, stay in the finest hotels, take a trip for no justifiable reason, eat in the most expensive restaurants – and take a friend as well – would be far too strong for most people to resist. For quite obvious reasons, therefore, it is important that spending on travel and accommodation is monitored regularly. A good way to do this is to check the type of arrangements which have been made, and by whom. If the arrangements are not substantially different from previous requests, and if frequency of travel has not changed, then it is likely that total expenditure will be much the same as before. It is only when there is a substantial change that costs are affected, for example when:

- more journeys are made
- different hotels are used
- journeys are made to new places
- different people are included on trips abroad.

It is therefore sensible and cost-effective to operate a 'management by exception' monitoring system. This means that where arrangements stay roughly the same or very similar then you do not need to take note. Where arrangements are different then you need to know *what* is different and *why*. It is this last point which is most important. There can be many good reasons for travelling more often, staying in new places or going for longer. However, if you are not satisfied with the reason given, then you may wish to note this on an exception report for the attention of your boss.

 ## DID YOU KNOW?

You should always make sure that people are aware of the type of flight and the type of accommodation you have reserved for them. They should also know to tell you if anything goes wrong and they are downgraded for any reason as you can then make a claim for a refund. They will doubtless be less keen to tell you when they suddenly find they are upgraded by the airline or hotel – although this can happen because of pressure on space!

Ways of dealing with changes to arrangements

Business arrangements normally have to be far more fluid than social travel arrangements – simply because there are so many reasons why they may have to be changed at the last minute. Airlines are used to business people changing their bookings – and so are hotels. It is one very good reason why you should use a reputable and understanding travel agent to make these changes for you.

Cancellations are relatively easy to do – but may cost your organisation money unless a suitable rearrangement can be made. The airline has the right to charge for an unsold seat and the hotel for an unsold room – although your organisation may have suitable insurance to cover for this. However, nobody can *stop* you making a cancellation. What somebody can do is to refuse to take an extra booking because they are full. Therefore you may have a problem if you suddenly find that a trip for four people has to become a trip for eight or if you need to extend the first booking for a couple of days.

On scheduled flights you may not have a problem – not everyone needs to travel on the same plane. Similarly, people can stay at neighbouring hotels, rather than all at the same one. In case of queries about return flights you are wiser if you arrange for open-dated return tickets to be issued – your colleagues can then organise their own return flights when they are ready to do so.

DID YOU KNOW?

If you need to cancel at the last moment, bear in mind that the hotel cannot charge you immediately for the cost. It has to try to re-let the room first. Unless the rate was clearly quoted as room only, then if it fails to re-let it can bill you for only two-thirds of the account. It must deduct one-third, which is the amount officially allowed for food.

Methods of monitoring financial allocations

To keep an eye on costs properly, it is important that every organisation operates a well-organised expenses system, especially in relation to cash advances to business travellers. Company credit cards or charge cards can reduce this need and enable expenditure by type, department or individual to be checked. However, day-to-day expenses may still be required and extra allowances granted, e.g. for clothing required for very hot or very cold countries, and these should be monitored closely.

Monitoring can be done on a basis of average cost per country or city. Any expense claims which are much higher than this figure should be investigated. According to a survey undertaken by *Business Traveller*, the dearest city in the world in which to stay is Tokyo, where almost

£290 a day is required just to eat, sleep and do a small amount of entertaining. Paris is the next most expensive at £240 a day, whilst London is close behind at £236 a day. Inflation must also be taken into account – remember that this varies from one country to another. At present prices in the Far East are rising rapidly and therefore any 'league table' of countries must be updated regularly.

Finally you should be aware that your company can claim tax relief on travel expenses which their employees incur 'necessarily' and 'in the performance of their duties'. Either dispensation for deductible items on specific trips has to be arranged in advance with the tax office or your boss has to enter deductible benefits on his tax form P11D every year. All travellers should keep a record of expenses and benefits received.

 DID YOU KNOW?

You can reduce the cost of hotel bills by:

- haggling with reception if you are trying to make a last-minute booking. After 2 pm hotels are desperate to fill up empty rooms – even at discount prices
- booking through a discount agency, e.g. the London Hotels Discounted Reservations, which acts as an agent for unsold beds in the city (tel. 0171 454 5099)
- contacting a tourist office or National Tourist Board. Scottish, Irish and Welsh tourist boards all have lists of bargain breaks and you can often make bookings for the Continent in the same way, e.g. through the Belgium Tourist Reservations Centre in London.

Methods of checking and verifying expenditure

You will usually receive two types of claims for expenditure:

- invoices from your travel agent, airline or hotels
- expense claims from individuals for whom you have made travel arrangements.

The first are easier to check than the second, and are less contentious. If you have a query over a bill you can simply ring and check the amount. Quite obviously basic checks should be made that the accommodation or travel is as agreed and covers the appropriate dates and that the addition is correct! Items to look for are those for which you may have been quoted 'all-in' and then have been billed separately – such as breakfast or a hire car.

Slightly more difficult are expense claims. These must be completed and submitted in line with company policy and you have every right to query items which contravene this policy – for instance an expense claim with no receipts attached. However, do be aware that to challenge someone's expense claim can be a serious issue – particularly if you seem to be a considerable sum of money adrift. Unless you have specific responsibility for this area, therefore, you would be well advised to double-check your calculations carefully and refer the matter to your own manager before taking action. Needless to say, if you can't read the handwriting or have just received an expense claim from a new representative who can't add up, then you are quite within your rights to have a gentle word to make sure that you receive properly completed documents in future.

International monetary exchange rates

Do bear in mind that you may find foreign currency entries on expense claims or invoices and these will need converting into sterling. If you telephone the bank to find the rate of exchange, do be aware that they have one rate at which they sell currency and another at which they buy!

You will save yourself a lot of work – and the organisation some money – if travellers pay foreign bills by credit card. They then give you the bill which you can match to the credit card statement when this is received. Not only will the credit card company have converted the money for you, but also the commission charge is less. However, do dissuade people from drawing out cash on their credit card whilst abroad as most card issuers charge interest from the date the cash is withdrawn.

Procedures for dealing with problems

No matter how well organised you are, or how many instructions you have given to people or how much care you have taken, things can still go wrong. Often knowing the legal rights of people involved in travel and knowing who to speak to if something goes wrong is all that is needed. We think that this unit has given you a considerable amount of assistance for dealing with problems already – and we would like to challenge you to see how you would cope. Below are ten problems which could occur, at home and abroad. For each one write down the action you think you should take immediately and any action you could take to prevent the problem occurring again. Try to complete the quiz before you read any further. The answers are given after the Activity Section.

TRAVEL PROBLEMS QUIZ

1   Your boss rings you from Orly airport to say that at the Hertz desk they have no record of the car you reserved.
2   Just as your boss's car is about to collect him to take him to the airport you discover you can't find the flight tickets.
3   A young representative with your company rings you from Rome to say he has lost his passport and air ticket home.

4   Your boss has her handbag stolen in New York – it contains credit and charge cards, travellers' cheques and foreign currency.

5   You are asked to collect the hire car you ordered for your boss. Five minutes later you are involved in a crash. You are uninjured but the car is badly damaged.

6   Your boss was attending a meeting in Shrewsbury then travelling to London by train and finally flying to Paris. She rings you from Heathrow airport to say that her train was delayed and she has missed her flight.

7   Your boss telephones you from his hotel in Geneva to say that he is expecting to take delivery of his hire car at any moment but has just discovered that he has left his driving licence in his desk drawer.

8   Your boss rings you from the Ambassador hotel in Karlsruhr, 70 miles from Frankfurt airport. On her arrival in Frankfurt on the afternoon BA flight her baggage was missing but an identical case was left on the carousel. Assuming that her case had been taken in error by the person whose suitcase was left, she reported the situation to the BA desk and handed over the case. She was assured that BA would contact the person concerned, exchange cases and deliver her case to her hotel. That was five hours ago. Despite constantly phoning Frankfurt airport she is getting no reply. She has an important dinner to attend that evening and has arrived wearing a casual outfit.

9   Your boss is taken ill the day before an important trip abroad. At the last minute the MD agrees to go in his place.

10 Your boss rings from the airport to say that the airline has overbooked the flight for which he has a reservation and he is being transferred onto the next flight three hours later. He is furious with the airline and worried that he will not be able to meet your company's representative at Vienna airport as arranged, nor be in time to attend an important meeting that evening.

Legal and regulatory requirements relating to the parties involved in travel and accommodation arrangements

When you are travelling or staying in a hotel it is useful to know what rights you have if things go wrong, what regulations you need to follow and who can help if you are completely stuck. However, it is impossible in this book to give you an example of everything that could happen or details of every regulation which may affect you, or your colleagues, when you are travelling. Do remember that if you are booking through an agency they should be a very useful source of help and advice – as should some of the other organisations mentioned in the keys to the questions.

ACTIVITY SECTION

1   You work for a small computer consultancy in Leeds. One director, Dave Wilkinson, frequently makes trips abroad and tries to combine

these into an overall business visit to save money. His one insistence is that, as he is a relatively heavy smoker, you keep domestic US flights as short as possible because no smoking is allowed on them. He also refuses to travel by British Airways on UK domestic flights for the same reason.

Six weeks from next Tuesday he wants to travel by rail to London, for a meeting with your distributor. After staying overnight he then wants to fly to Rome where he will stay for two days. His next stop is in Denver, USA, where he will be for the next week, before moving on to Melbourne for six days. He will then return home via Singapore where he will be staying for four days. He knows that it can be cheaper to book a 'round the world' ticket (i.e. to keep travelling in the same direction) and has therefore decided that he could take advantage of this by breaking his trip and staying in Hawaii for the weekend.

a   Plan his journey to London using a current British Rail timetable. If possible try to find a suitable Pullman train.
b   Plan his flights, being aware of his requests. Make sure you are clear on days and dates, bearing in mind the time zones he will travel through. Submit your plan for his approval.
c   Assuming he agrees with your plan, draw up a comprehensive itinerary with dates and times. Clearly state terminals, names of airports and check-in times.
d   Assuming this is the first trip he has made to these particular countries, find out what visas are required and whether he needs any vaccinations or inoculations before he leaves – and the timescale which must be allowed for these. Detail this information in a memo.

2   You are tired of the number of telephone calls you keep receiving from representatives who have left essential items at home when they are travelling. You have decided to minimise problems in future by issuing a checklist which states everything they need for a possible sales presentation.

Starting at 'A' and working through the alphabet, list as many useful items as you can think of which begin with each letter. Compare your list with ours below.

3   Your boss has recently arrived back in the office in a fury after a trip abroad. On arrival in the UK she was stopped by customs officials. She claims she was chosen at random, had her luggage searched and then had to repack all the items herself. She is also certain that a small vase she had carefully wrapped in her case was damaged during the search. The delay meant that she missed her ongoing connection and could only get a Shuttle nearly two hours later. She is talking about asking for compensation from customs officials for the delay.

You calm her down and promise you will investigate to find out more details about her rights.

   a Obtain a copy of the Travellers' Charter which gives information on what you rights are when you pass through customs.

   b Can your boss claim for compensation
     i if customs officers damaged her vase
     ii for missing her connection?

   c If your boss had been searched personally she should have been told her rights of appeal beforehand. In case this happens next time she is travelling, find out
     i what she should be told beforehand
     ii what to do to stay within the law if she does not agree to a personal search.

KEY TO 'TRAVEL PROBLEMS QUIZ' (PAGE 673)

1 *Immediately* – your boss should have a copy of the reservation confirmation detailing the type of car and the telephone number of the office where the arrangement was made. Otherwise fax this through to the Hertz desk at Orly. If arrangements were made through a travel agent you could contact them or, for speed, contact Hertz headquarters and ask them for help. In the meantime your boss could enquire at other car-hire desks at the airport or ask the airline for help – particularly if travelling First or Business Class. Have you a Paris agent or Paris office who could help? Final resort – taxi to hotel/company/city centre and make different arrangements, e.g. through hotel or French Tourist Office.

In future – check that executives always carry a copy of the confirmation with them, plus a list of emergency telephone numbers.

2 *Immediately* – you should have noted the ticket number. If not, you still have the travel details on the itinerary. Ring the airline (at the airport) or travel agent and explain. A duplicate ticket can be issued for collection at the airport against a computer reservation. You may have to pay for this until the airline knows that the original ticket has not been presented for use.

In future – design a better system for ticket storage, and stick to it. If your boss has lost it then change the arrangements; only hand it over at the last minute.

3 *Immediately* – advise him to contact the local airline office (or you contact the UK office). The replacement procedure will be similar to that given under question 2. He should report the loss of the passport to the local police and obtain a police statement. Then take this and three passport photos and some identification to the nearest British Consulate or Embassy or High Commission. Claim the cost of the replacement and the charge for the emergency passport back from your travel insurance company.

In future – why not type out a list of 'What to do in an emergency' for all your company's travellers?

4 *Immediately* – tell her to report the loss to the local police and obtain a copy of the statement. This will be needed for insurance claims. Cancel the cards by ringing the card issuers' emergency numbers or by contacting your card protection agency. Check with each card company their procedure for sending replacement cards abroad (if you don't know this already). Charge card companies are often better at this than credit card companies.

The booklet given with travellers' cheques states the nearest bank; contact them to report the loss and give the cheque numbers. Until replacements arrive your executive is without funds. Ring your bank and ask them to express funds to her; if you give the address of her hotel they will be able to send them to their nearest correspondent bank. Tell her where the bank is: she should take her passport for identification. In a dire emergency – no funds, no ID, etc. – head for the British Embassy.

In future – as for question 3.

5 *Immediately* – presumably the car was covered for both drivers: you and your boss. Take the names, addresses and car numbers of those involved and details of witnesses. If anyone is injured call the police. Keep an accurate record of the accident and notify the company immediately. You should be able to obtain a replacement car, but may have to pay additional insurance charges.

6 *Immediately* – she should go to the airline desk and tell them the situation. They will usually do all they can to get her on the next flight out, especially if she belongs to their frequent-flyer programme. If this is completely impossible you may have to investigate alternatives, e.g. rail/hovercraft links. In a real emergency, with a top executive and a very valuable contract at stake, it may mean chartering a plane! Notify contacts at the other end of the revised travel plans. Check your insurance policy for cover – note that at present British Rail's Condition 25 absolves them from responsibility, though this may change in the future.

In future – little you can do unless you didn't allow enough time in the schedule for possible (reasonable) delays.

7 *Immediately* – fax a copy to the hotel. Providing he shows ID (e.g. his passport) then this should be sufficient. Alternatively you could use Datapost to send it to him overnight. This means it will arrive quickly and you will be covered if it is lost in the post.

In future – design a checklist of everything he will need for his trips and go through this methodically with him before he leaves (see also Activity Section).

8 *Immediately* – check all travel details and make sure you have the bag tag number(s). Ring the airline office at your nearest airport, explain the problem and give all travel details and other relevant information. Ask them to chase up Frankfurt and keep you informed. They can telex their baggage handling office direct. Keep your boss informed. Check the travel insurance – she can probably buy a replacement outfit but she must keep her receipts and her check-in baggage tags. She will also need a letter from the airline confirming the loss.

In future – if her suitcase is a common make she could put on some jazzy stickers to personalise it and make this less likely to happen.

9   *Immediately* – notify your travel agent or the airline. Don't just send the MD along with the same ticket without checking – usually it is non-transferable.

In future – if 'switching' people is a regular feature of your organisation, check if the airline operates a ticket on departure system. You reserve the seat in the company's name, they make out the ticket on departure and issue this at the airport in the name of the traveller. Or ask your travel agent for help.

10 *Immediately* – reassure him that you will contact the representative with the revised information. Action on the meeting depends on whether your boss's presence is crucial, and if so could the start be delayed/could the meeting be rescheduled – could the rep help? If your boss was going for information purposes only, the rep could go on ahead and they could meet up later. Your boss could get a taxi from the airport. Note that by directing your boss to the Executive lounge he should be able to contact your rep direct (which would be best).

In future – note that a confirmed reservation gives a traveller a legal entitlement to a seat, but not necessarily on the flight booked. Only if the delay is 'unreasonable' is the airline liable, and three hours wouldn't be considered unreasonable for a flight from London to Vienna (whatever your boss thinks!).

It is therefore sensible to allow enough time between the arrival time of a flight and the start of an event if attendance at the latter is vital. Alternatively, you should make a 'contingency plan' – which includes giving your executive a list of emergency numbers to contact and knowing what action he would want you to take in an emergency such as this.

KEY TO QUESTION 2 (PAGE 675)

A   Audio tapes

B   Batteries (spare – for razor, dictating machine, etc.)
    Briefcase
    Baggage labels (spare)

C   Calculator
    Car keys
    Car documentation

Credit/charge cards
Confirmation documents

D   Diary

E   Electrical current adaptor
Emergency phone numbers
Eye mask
Eurocheque book and card

F   Foreign currency
Flight bag
Floppy disks

G   Guide books

H   House keys

I   Insurance documents
International driving licence
Itinerary

L   Lap-top computer

M   Maps
Medical packs

P   Passport
Phrase book
Phone card

S   Sunglasses
Sterling
Spectacles (and spares!)
Sales literature
Speeches
Samples
Suitcase

T   Tickets
Travellers' cheques

V   Vaccination certificates
Visa
Visiting cards

12 Contribute to the acquisition and control of financial provision

---

Element 12.1

Contribute to the acquisition of financial provision

You should note that this unit is an **option** unit. The fact that you have chosen to study and prove your competence in this area should mean that as part of your job you undertake duties which involve the acquisition and control of financial provision in your workplace. If you do not, then you are advised not to select this option. If you only do part of the work outlined in the scheme then you will need to talk to your tutor or adviser about the best way to demonstrate competence in the remaining areas.

Own role and responsibilities

Today, more than ever before, greater numbers of staff in a wider range of organisations are involved in the financial aspects of business. Financial accountability has become a 'buzz-phrase' in the 1990s for people involved in a variety of enterprises and activities. No longer is it just the entrepreneur or management accountant who is expected to understand estimating, costing and financial calculations, but now also administrators and staff in organisations ranging from fund-holding general medical practices to trust hospitals, from locally managed schools to formula-funded colleges or universities. Local authorities, government departments and newly privatised organisations have all been charged with greater accountability for the resources they use and the finances they need.

This, of course, has long been a requirement in private organisations which, faced with competitive environments, difficult economic circumstances and changing technologies have had to keep a very sharp eye indeed on the resource requirements of their business. In the long run only the fittest survive and no organisation wants to contract or make workers redundant.

To avoid this, most businesses have a strong framework of financial management and reporting systems which incorporate:

● systematic organisational planning to achieve stated objectives
● estimating and calculating resource requirements to meet these objectives

- financial monitoring and budgetary control to ensure that plans are adhered to and variances noted and investigated
- the use of financial information and procedures to support and inform decision-making.

Finance and decision-making

A variety of decisions have to be made in business every day and which rely on accurate financial forecasting. Whereas many of these will be concerned with day-to-day operations, others will include assessing and evaluating current practices or planning for the future, e.g.:

- whether to undertake certain types of work in-house or contract it out
- whether improvements and renovations can be carried out and paid for out of current funds
- whether to obtain some new equipment and, if so, whether it should be rented, bought or leased
- whether an item is profitable to make – and, if so, in what quantities
- whether the organisation can afford additional staff – on either a temporary or a permanent basis, or a full-time or part-time basis
- what the pricing strategies should be for particular products or services to cover the fixed and variable costs of production
- what the general levels of expenditure can be afforded on materials and equipment.

Whilst the decision-making itself is likely to be carried out at management level, it is essential that these decisions are based on sound calculations from data which may have been assembled by administrative staff.

Administration and finance

The role of an administrator in relation to financial requirements is likely to vary tremendously from one organisation to another and from one job to another. One administrator may assist his or her line manager to control a multi-million pound budget, obtain estimates and costings and attend regular resource meetings. A second may have little to do with budgets or costings but may run a large section and control the cashflow for that area. A third may operate a section designated as a cost centre which provides an administrative or central service for the rest of the organisation and charges for specific jobs on an individually costed basis. A fourth may have a particular area of responsibility which includes a financial remit. For instance, a marketing assistant may be charged with planning and costing a particular direct mail or advertising campaign and asked to submit estimates of proposed expenditure to his or her boss, and run that budget when agreed. Finally, any administrator can be called upon to cost out potential new developments or refurbishments – for instance, if the reception area is being reorganised or the offices are moving to a new location.

Your ability to obtain accurate estimates of resource requirements and expenditure on any of these occasions are essential attributes of this part of your job.

DID YOU KNOW?

The degree to which financial justification for action is required can vary enormously from one organisation to another. In one organisation your boss may simply enjoy challenging you – when you ask if you can have a new computer he tells you to 'prove that you need it'. At the other extreme you may work in a section where individual jobs are costed and set against specific budgets and where there is a strict system of budgetary control, cost control and the identification of specific cost centres.

Budgets

A budget is a financial plan which identifies the financial targets of the organisation over a stated period. The master budget is a compilation of many different budgets, prepared by different sections of the organisation based on their forecasts of costs and revenue.

- The sales budget will include the number of units forecast to be sold and the selling price of each. The total will give the expected total revenue for the period. However, against the revenue must be set the cost of selling the goods or service, e.g. advertising, promotion and distribution, and separate budgets will be prepared for each of these.
- The production budget must obviously take into account the planned sales for the period. Separate budgets will also be prepared to take into account current and planned future stock levels, work-in-progress and raw material requirements.
- Budgets for services are budgets prepared by departments not directly involved in the production or selling of goods, e.g. administration, human resources and computer services.
- Budgets for policy areas are budgets prepared by top management and are often calculated over a longer period than normal operating budgets. Examples would be budgets for Research and Development or Capital Expenditure. They will take into account long-term strategies for the business.
- The cash budget is extremely important as this shows the proposed effects of all the other budget activities on the cashflow of the organisation. If a deficit is projected, then either the budgets would have to be redrawn and spending curtailed or an overdraft or loan would have to be arranged. If a surplus is indicated, then plans can be made to use this money wisely, e.g. by investment, rather than leave it lying idle in a current account.

The aim of preparing a budget is that, for all current activities, the organisation knows the level of expenditure and revenue required and can then monitor this to check that it is 'on target' for the time period in question, and take appropriate action if it isn't.

DID YOU KNOW?

In most commercial organisations the principal factor affecting all budgets is the level of sales. This would be known as the **limiting factor**, and in such cases the sales budget must be calculated first. All the other subsidiary budgets would then be prepared and the targets adjusted to take the forecast sales level into account. If a different limiting factor is identified, e.g. a scarcity of a certain raw material, then this becomes the limiting factor and must be done first.

Degree of budget devolution

It is easy to think of a large master budget being comprised of smaller budgets, one per department, each the responsibility of the departmental manager. However, in many organisations budgets are devolved beyond this level with many members of staff being designated as 'budget holders'. For instance, each stock clerk may become a budget holder for his or her own area. If the organisation is structured into geographical units or divisions then each of these may be allocated its own budget – and so on. The greater the degree of devolution, the greater the financial accountability of each member of staff.

Consider the following example. Tree of Knowledge is the educational arm of Oak Tree Publishing PLC. Each Managing Editor at Tree of Knowledge is responsible for the sales and costs budgets of his or her books. For each new book project, a pre-set spreadsheet like the one below is completed.

Tree of Knowledge Publication Plan

Title	Pages	Price	Discount	Fixed cost	Royalty	Direct unit cost	Units printed	Sales/yr
New History	96	£4.95	20%	£25 000	10%	£1.00	10 000	15 000

CHECK IT YOURSELF

Find out the system in operation in your organisation for preparing budgets and the degree to which devolution of budgets takes place.

Anticipated work programme

Financial planning and forecasting takes place within a financial cycle, which is normally a period of twelve months. This means that anticipated activities and resource requirements for that period have to be predicted and costed. However, this does not mean to say that you may not have to undertake other planning activities which have a shorter or longer time horizon. What is essential, however, is that both the routine workload and special requirements (e.g. for seasonal demands) are identified for the period in question.

It is easier to forecast the work programme in some organisations and departments than in others. In many organisations demand fluctuates according to the season – obvious examples include ice cream and firework manufacturers. A large car dealership, for example, may know that its busy times are early August and early January – when new registrations and new models are released. A publisher of textbooks will have a plan for book sales for the year and a schedule when these are due to take place. The marketing department in both organisations is likely to have a 'calendar' of events linked to the products made and the demand for goods at different times of the year. The marketing manager can use this to predict the resources required throughout the year to finance the planned activities.

Even with something as basic as forecasting your need for petty cash, you would need to have some indication of current work activity and proposed events. Whilst this may be achieved by using historic costs this will not take account of changes to the way in which the section operates, new developments, increases in costs and so on. On one side you need emergency funds for contingencies, on the other you do not want to bid for an increase in your float which you don't really need.

DID YOU KNOW?

Your organisation's strategic plan gives its long-term goals over the next 3 to 5 years. The thinking behind the formulation of a strategic plan is that, if you don't know where you are going, you can hardly find out when you've arrived.

The operational plan translates the strategic plan into operational objectives – i.e. what must be done, when and by whom. The key part here is to find where your initials or your section appears and how often!

Methods of estimating requirements for financial provision

Estimating your requirements for financial provision means identifying the resources needed to fulfil your work programme or the operational objectives for which you are responsible, then finding the costs involved.

There are four different types of resources you may require:

- **services** – from other people, departments or organisations
- **materials** – physical goods, from paper to computer disks
- **equipment** – from computers to photocopiers
- **people** – members of staff or external contractors who will need to be paid.

Producing estimates

If you have to provide formal estimates for required resources, and particularly if you have to justify these in terms of your budget, then you are likely to be involved in **costing**. All resources used in business are made up of a number of cost elements and calculating, recording and monitoring these is an important part of financial planning.

It is usual to divide costs into **direct** and **indirect costs**. Let us assume that you are responsible for a large reprographics section in your organisation. You undertake printing for each department and then 'bill' them for the work you have done. You can only decide how much to charge if you know how much it costs you to carry out a particular request.

Direct costs are those which are directly affected by undertaking a job. To produce 1000 reports of 20 pages, for instance, has an immediate direct cost of 20 000 pieces of paper. This would be a **direct material** cost. The operator of the machine would be a direct **labour cost** and any additional **direct expenses** involved would also be added (e.g. royalties paid for the use of copyright in the report). The total of direct costs is often referred to as the **prime cost**.

The **indirect costs** are normally those **overheads** which cannot be directly identified with what is being produced. In this example, rent, rates, heating, lighting, machine maintenance and depreciation would all be involved.

The total cost of producing the report is therefore the sum of prime cost and overheads. To this you may be expected to add a profit element.

Cost centres

Many organisations are divided into a number of defined cost centres. The cost centres may be identified on a functional, geographical or operational basis but, broadly, each is a subdivision of the organisation where costs can be grouped for the purpose of monitoring and controlling expenditure. The direct costs are easy to allocate, but indirect costs have to be shared or **apportioned** on some basis which reflects usage of the service or facility.

TEST YOURSELF

1   A factory making jeans has the following direct and indirect costs.

Materials
Direct – often called raw materials, e.g. denim, zips, fasteners
Indirect – often called factory overheads, e.g. oil for machinery, spare parts

Labour
Direct – piece-work operatives in the production area
Indirect – stores, administration, personnel and other service departments

Expenses
Direct – e.g. royalty charge for using a designer logo on each garment
Indirect – overheads such as rent, rates and electricity which cannot be attributed directly to the product

With reference to your own organisation, draw up a similar table giving examples of each type of cost incurred.

2   Decide as a group the fairest way for the following indirect costs to be apportioned between departments in a company:
   a   operating the canteen
   b   insurance premiums
   c   paying security guards
   d   the electricity bill
   e   depreciation of equipment.

3   Find out whether cost centres operate in your organisation and the way in which different costs are coded for recording purposes. Compare your findings with other members of your group.

Costing systems

The aim of costing is to be able to calculate the cost of one unit of production or one unit of service. However, there is a considerable difference between working out the cost of producing a litre of milk and that of providing one passenger-mile on an InterCity train! For that reason, different costing methods are used depending upon the type of unit being calculated.

● **Process costing** is generally used when identical products are being manufactured through a continuous production process, e.g. litres of milk, tins of baked beans or reams of paper. The total cost can be calculated over a certain period and then divided by the number of units produced. This gives an average cost per unit of production.

● **Job costing** is used when the costs must be calculated for an individual job – such as the builder who says he will put up a wall in your garden and goes off to calculate the quantity of bricks and mortar required, or the specialist or manufacturer who quotes for a sports car with tinted windows and bullet-proof glass made for an oil sheikh! In the case of job costing, the direct costs are worked out for each stage of production and then the indirect costs are added.

● **Batch costing** is used when a quantity of identical articles is produced as a batch. The procedure used is similar to job costing except that on completion the total batch cost is divided by the number of articles produced to give the average cost of each one. Batch costing is often used in the paint, clothing, footwear and engineering industries.

- **Contract costing** is similar to job costing but is more complex. It is used when the work will be complex or will last a long time – for instance, building a leisure centre or a motorway. In this case specialist estimators are employed to obtain quotations and estimates and to calculate the costs involved over the duration of the contract – which may last several years.
- **Operating costing** is used when a combination of two factors must be considered. A haulage company needs to take into account distance and the amount of freight (or tonnage) carried. InterCity would cost a train journey in relation to both the distance and the number of passengers. A hotel or hospital would cost in terms of number of beds and frequency of use.

Only when the costs have been calculated can people in business start to make decisions about the price to charge.

DID YOU KNOW?

If an organisation needs to use more than one system of costing (e.g. process costing in one department and batch costing in another) then this is called **multiple costing**.

TEST YOURSELF

Jan and James set up a sandwich bar in the middle of town. They successfully made and sold a selection of sandwiches every day. James decided that they could do better if they also delivered sandwiches according to people's orders. He arranged for leaflets to be printed and delivered to organisations in the area telling them about the delivery service.

After six weeks Jan and James had started to have arguments. Coping with the delivery side of the business had become a headache, with James missing most of the morning. Jan felt the price they charged for the delivered sandwiches didn't reflect their time cost.

You are their accountant – can you help them untangle their problem?

1   Identify the direct and indirect costs of making sandwiches to sell in the sandwich bar.
2   Given the competitive nature of the sandwich business, and based on reasonable costs of sandwich production, what do you consider would be a reasonable range of selling prices for their goods?
3   What additional costs are involved in the delivery service?
4   When costing the delivered sandwiches, should Jan and James reallocate the fixed costs already carried by the shop-bought sandwiches?
5   Do you think the delivery service will affect the sales in the sandwich bar?

6 Are there any factors, other than cost, that you might take into account when pricing the sandwiches?

7 Do you consider the selling price of the delivered sandwiches should be
a higher than in the shop
b the same price as in the shop
c cheaper than in the shop?

Give a reason for your answer.

Activity-based costing

This is a recent approach to costing which attempts to allocate costs more precisely than the usual system of apportioning costs for a service or activity. It operates through examining more closely the requirements for the service or activity by identifying the specific factors which cause (or 'drive') the costs in the first place. These factors are called **cost drivers** and are crucial to the apportioning of costs using this system. Examples of typical cost drivers are given below.

Service area or activity	Example of cost driver
Publicity	Number of advertisements placed
Sales	Number of invoices produced
Despatch	Number of deliveries made
Personnel	Number of hours worked per week/vacancies filled
Purchasing	Number of orders produced

The way in which this affects the apportionment of costs is shown in the example below. Assume a Purchasing department buys goods on behalf of a bicycle manufacturing company which is structured in two different divisions. One division is responsible for mass-producing bicycles which are sold to shops around the country. A large number of bicycles are produced each year and the design rarely changes. The other division specialises in making custom-built bicycles to customers' own specifications. Under traditional systems of costing, the costs of ordering the raw materials through the Purchasing department would be apportioned in relation to volume of production. Therefore, the mass production division would be apportioned more costs than the custom bicycle division. However, in reality, the custom bicycle division causes far more work for the Purchasing department. This is because it generates a larger number of individualised purchasing orders (i.e. the cost driver) than the mass production division – which simply orders standard items. Under activity-based costing, the custom bicycle division would be apportioned more overheads than the mass production division. This will therefore produce more realistic product costs because the overheads are spread over cost units in relation to the factors which cause the costs in the first place, i.e. the cost drivers.

DID YOU KNOW?

There are many different ways to calculate a budget. The method used often depends upon the type of organisation or department:

- standard costs are usually calculated for production costs. These take the overall cost of producing each individual item and are revised each year
- administrative or selling costs are often based on the level of spending in the previous year plus adjustments
- zero-based budgeting is an alternative whereby the assumption is nil expenditure and every item which is to be spent must be justified
- flexible budgeting allows for differences in sales or costs throughout the year and does not necessarily penalise managers when there is a change, *provided* that such changes can be justified in terms of additional revenue or it can be proved that the manager cannot be held responsible for the changes.

TEST YOURSELF

In some organisations it is common practice to submit a budget which is the same as last year plus an additional percentage to allow for inflation. Some argue that this system is essential if the organisation is to keep pace with increasing costs. Others say that this type of budget favours the high spender and disadvantages the manager wanting to keep close control of departmental spending.

a What are your views on this subject?
b How are budgets calculated in your organisation or department?

Organisations' financial procedures

Your Finance section has two main responsibilities:

- to make sure that the organisation has sufficient funds for any capital expenditure which is required, e.g. for new equipment, buildings or vehicles
- to make sure that the organisation has enough working capital available to meet its regular expenses, e.g. salaries, stationery and electricity bills.

Basically all the procedures which are followed relate to these two key objectives.

- Capital budgets will be prepared in order to check availability of funds.
- If additional funds are required then decisions have to be made about suitable sources and whether loans are needed in the long term, medium term or short term.
- Cashflow forecasts and cash budgets will be prepared to make sure there is always sufficient working capital.

Both the capital and cash budgets must be strictly controlled (see Element 12.2). A common reason for failure of small and medium sized companies is not the fact that they do not have adequate capital reserves each year but that they have **insufficient working capital** for their needs. If you work for a small business and regularly pay all the bills but do little about the fact that your customers are not paying *you* then you are working hard to put yourself out of a job!

Dangers can arise, too, when the requirement for working capital is growing so quickly that the business cannot generate profit rapidly enough. This is known as 'overtrading' or operating beyond the financial capacity of the business.

If, therefore, you need resources to achieve planned work, the Finance department needs procedures in place to ascertain:

- whether your plans should be financed from capital expenditure or working capital
- the viability and profitability of your proposal
- what alternative uses could be made of the money.

Your organisation is likely to have different procedures for you to follow depending upon whether you are:

- seeking to resource a planned activity from working capital
- seeking to resource a new development from the capital budget. In this case you are more likely to be bidding for a 'one-off' payment.

In addition, the degree to which details have to be submitted and the person responsible for making the decision will vary – usually depending upon the quantity and value of resources you require!

CHECK IT YOURSELF

Find out the correct procedure to be followed in your organisation if:

- a member of staff wants to use the photocopier to do a personal job. He estimates he will take approximately 10 000 photocopies
- your clerical section is asked to help another department during a busy period by keying in some urgent documents. You estimate it will take three word-processor operators about two days each to complete the work
- a member of staff wants a salary advance because of a personal emergency
- you urgently need to hire a temporary member of staff to cover for staff illness
- you read about an electronic filing system which will revolutionise the

work in your offices. You know it will be a huge asset for the
organisation – but you will need to get your hands on £16 500 to buy it!

Organisations' requirements for the presentation and format of estimates

The type of estimates to be produced and their format can vary
tremendously. Today most are produced on spreadsheet packages
because this means they are simple to amend. Some organisations have
a recommended format to be followed for financial or resource
requests or 'bids'. Others have a format for costings on a spreadsheet
so that it is not the responsibility of the individual operator to enter
formulae to undertake the calculations. This is usually the case if you
are following a specified formula for job, batch or process costing. The
spreadsheets will have been planned, designed and set up in advance.
All you do is to enter the relevant figures.

If there are no required layouts or formats to follow then you have to
use your common sense. Quite obviously a complex costing exercise
including a variety of direct and indirect costs and subdivided into
services, materials, equipment and labour should lead you to consider
using a spreadsheet; a bid for new equipment required for a particular
purpose (such as an electronic filing system) may require a brief report
with figures showing the outlay offset by labour savings.

At Tree of Knowledge, the educational arm of Oak Tree Publishing
PLC, before the directors make any publishing decisions a spreadsheet
is always compiled combining different possible costs for a book
together with market shares. This helps the directors to decide the
likely market share they can win, and how much they should be
investing in each book.

Title: ECONOMICS FOR STARTERS

Gross margin % by varying market share % and fixed cost per page	Market share %	Fixed per page £					
		70	75	80	85	90	100
	40%	60.25%	59.84%	59.44%	59.03%	58.62%	57.81%
	50%	62.40%	62.07%	61.75%	61.42%	61.09%	60.44%
	60%	63.59%	63.32%	63.05%	62.78%	62.51%	61.96%
	70%	64.74%	64.51%	64.28%	64.05%	63.81%	63.35%
	80%	65.16%	64.95%	64.75%	64.55%	64.34%	63.94%
	90%	65.98%	65.80%	65.62%	65.44%	65.26%	64.89%

TEST YOURSELF

1   Obtain examples of the type of estimates used in your workplace and
    compare the formats with those provided by other members of your
    group.

2   You and a friend have set up in business providing a reprographic, fax
    and text-production service. You have been asked to quote for the

typing of a 500-page dissertation from manuscript which must then be carefully checked before five copies are printed and bound.

a List the direct costs involved in the production of the dissertation.

b List the indirect costs involved.

c Devise a suitable format to estimate the total costs and project a price for the job which is calculated on total costs plus 40 per cent profit.

Sources of information on which to base estimates

In the above example, you would now have to complete all the numerical information in relation to the direct and indirect costs of producing the dissertation. Where would you get this information, and how could you ensure that it is accurate?

Obviously, if you had done a similar job before it would be a simple matter to look back to see what you charged previously. If not, then you would have rather more homework to do!

- Your direct costs should be relatively easy to calculate. You can estimate the amount of paper, the number of disks and the number of binders you need easily enough. Operator time is more difficult to assess – you may have to do this by noting the average length of time to produce an A4 page of manuscript but the style of writing, the number of tables and the complexity of the content will all be factors which would influence this aspect of the job. For that reason you may have to build in a 'contingency plan' which enabled you to charge more if the task was particularly difficult. The final factor in this, of course, is how much it will cost you to pay the operator for his or her time.

- Your indirect costs can only be calculated if you know the running costs of your business and then can apportion these over the time it will take to do the job. This means collecting together actual bills received for rent, electricity, heating etc, *or* projecting the amount you will spend on these items.

As a final check, when you have finished, you could find out the price that other organisations charge for the same service – to see if you are close. If you were very much cheaper then this would indicate either that you have missed out something important or that you can afford to include more for your profit.

Ways of interpreting source information

You have just seen the importance of cross-checking one set of information against a different set to check that you are on the right lines. This is often advisable because not only are there different sources from which you can receive information but also different ways in which you can interpret it.

The most obvious example is that of historical data. If you are calculating the price for a job – as above – but taking into account last year's overheads or last year's costings, how might that affect the accuracy of your estimate?

When information is being sought it is normally obtained by reference to past costs. This is because there is usually a record of costs which have already been incurred. However, you are trying to make an estimate in relation to future costs and revenue. In this case, therefore, past costs are helpful because they give you a guide, but must be adjusted taking into account factors such as inflation before they can be used for future projections.

Equally, you should also query why a set of figures is structured in a certain way. It may be that last time you carried out a costing exercise there was a need for it to be end- or front-loaded in a certain way. The earlier proposed cost may contain inaccuracies or allow for overspending in a way which would not be appropriate on this occasion. Unless you attached notes to your estimate to state your reasoning then this time you may be using the data without realising the significance of particular figures or calculations.

Finally, you need to check the unit of output or service you are calculating and make sure you are comparing like with like. If your last quotation for preparing a report was £15 you may get rather a shock if you repeat this amount and then find out that whereas the last report contained 12 pages this one contains 200!

DID YOU KNOW?

Many budgets or expenditure estimates contain both an estimates and an actuals column so that the final amount actually spent is also recorded as evidence for later information and checking. This is discussed in Element 12.2.

TEST YOURSELF

Identify the possible outcome(s) in each of the following cases.

- A new administrator is asked to submit an estimate for temporary staff over the next six months. When she refers to last year's actual figures she notes that these were considerably higher than the estimate. She does not realise that this figure included emergency cover during a 'flu epidemic and calculates a 10 per cent increase for this year.
- An estimate is required for moving all the computer equipment to a new building half a mile away. The administrator requests two quotations – one from an outside company and one from Computer Services. The first gives a full breakdown of the service required and the recabling requirements; the inside quotation is a 'one-liner' but is less than half the price! With the move only a few days away, the administrator quickly accepts the 'internal' estimate and arranges for the job to be completed as quickly as possible.

Organisations' financial timescales

All organisations have a variety of financial timescales. The one which will concern you will depend upon the area in which you are operating:

- the financial accountants will prepare the accounts at the end of the financial year. This may, or may not, coincide with the fiscal year or the calendar year
- budgets are usually prepared initially on a twelve-month cycle, although they may be reviewed each quarter or at some fixed period. The cash budget is usually a 'rolling budget' which is updated weekly or monthly
- actual spending against projected spending is monitored more frequently – often monthly (see Element 12.2)
- the cashflow cycle operates over a relatively short timescale. This is the process of issuing invoices, obtaining payments, buying stock and paying bills – including wages!
- petty cash may be balanced and the float restored on a weekly or monthly basis.

Figure 12.1.1 shows an example of a possible financial timescale.

Throughout the year the financial staff will be monitoring company finances. A variety of factors can mean that, in reality, things go better or worse than expected. If expenditure is lower than planned or revenue higher than forecast then further bids may be acceptable. In this case there can be a sudden 'call' for bids against the capital budget with a specific deadline. Equally, if the organisation is bidding for outside funding or for an outside contract there may be a specific deadline date by which time you must have submitted any estimate of expenditure for your own section.

DID YOU KNOW?

In some public sector organisations it used to be the case that if there was a budget surplus at the end of the year very little money from one year could be carried over to the next. This used to lead to a mad scramble each March as staff bought almost anything to use up the spare money! Today the situation isn't *quite* as bad but there are still some anomalies. One factor which helps is the ability to 'vire' (or 'move') money from one budget to another. Another is the ability to carry savings forward from one year to

| FINANCIAL TIMESCALE |
| ABC CORPORATION PLC |

FINANCIAL TIMESCALE
ABC CORPORATION PLC

Date	Event
May	Update of 5-year strategic plan by department and submission to Board.
June	Approval of strategic plan by Board. Corporate profit objectives agreed.
July	Guidelines for writing operational plans issued to line managers.
August	Update of operational plan for next twelve months completed by department and section
September	Approval of operational plans by Board. Guidelines for budget preparation issued to departments.
October	Draft budgets prepared by departments. Checked by Finance section for comparisons with current budget and last year's actual results. Returned to line managers with comments.
November	First draft of master budget prepared by Finance and submitted to directors and line managers for consultation process
December	Second draft of master budget prepared by Finance. To incorporate any feedback/new assumptions from first draft.
January	Master budget finalised and submitted to Board for approval. Revised departmental budgets to be completed.
February	Departmental budgets finalised and submitted to Board for approval.
March	Departmental budgets approved for implementation from April.

Figure 12.1.1 Example of a financial timescale

another, although the amount is still likely to be very low as a percentage of overall spending.

ACTIVITY SECTION

1   You have been administrator in the sales office of a large organisation for the past two years. At present you are responsible for two word-processor operators, a database operator and a junior clerk. However, staffing levels in the office are the same as they were two years ago – despite the fact that sales (and the corresponding workload) have increased by 22 per cent in the same period. Your staff are struggling to cope with the increased work yet when you lobby your boss for an extra full-time member of staff he simply says that the organisation is working to tighter margins and there isn't enough slack in the budget for additional staff.

Last week the whole section was overjoyed when, against intense competition, the organisation secured a large export order worth several million pounds. Your staff have since been to see you to reiterate their request for extra help and told you, quite firmly, that unless some assistance is forthcoming they will be far less cooperative in future when quotations and estimates need producing quickly to secure a major contract.

You feel that to pass these threats on to your boss would be counterproductive but consider that this could be an opportune moment to ask him to reconsider the staffing position.

a   What sources of information would you use to establish the level of activity in the office now, as compared with two years ago?

b   What sources of information would you use to estimate the cost of hiring and retaining an additional full-time member of staff?

c   In what ways could you use the section's anticipated work programme to substantiate your case?

d   What alternative courses of action could you suggest in order to pacify the staff if your ideal solution was unaffordable?

2   You and your friend have both worked for the health service for a number of years. You are employed as assistant administrator in the medical records section of a large hospital. Your friend has just started work as assistant to the practice manager of a large fund-holding general practice.

When you talk to her about her new job you are amazed to find that she appears to be more involved in finance than anything else. The practice has to formulate its own budget for staff wages, drugs prescribed to patients, hospital treatment and referrals to consultants and home visits by locums on call between 11 pm and 7 am. Indeed, everything used by the practice has to be costed. Revenue is allocated to the practice by the FHSA on a 'per patient' basis with top-up payments for patients with special medical requirements, e.g. diabetics, pregnant women, epileptics and so on.

a   If you were listing the resources required for the practice under the headings of 'services', 'materials', 'equipment' and 'people', state two items you would enter under each heading.

b   To estimate treatment costs required this year your friend has looked in the files to find out how much was charged by the local hospital for blood tests, X-rays and other services last year.
   i   What other sources of information should be accessed to obtain a more accurate picture?
   ii In what ways could you suggest the information should be adjusted to obtain a more accurate estimate for the current year?

c   Your friend is all in favour of this method of running a general practice but you strongly disagree. She considers that the method is far more efficient and doctors are less extravagant in issuing expensive drugs or making home visits when they are not necessary. She believes that the money saved can be better used in obtaining services from a variety of hospitals in the region for patients in need, so enabling the GP to shop around for the best service. Your view is that few patients are consulted about which hospital they want to use, GPs will be tempted to use the cheapest to save money and if distant hospitals are used then this will be very inconvenient for families making visits.

As a group, debate this issue further – preferably after having obtained more detailed information about the budgeting requirements of a fund-holding general practice – and draw up a list of advantages and disadvantages of this type of financial planning in a service industry.

Element 12.2
Contribute to the control of financial provision

You have already learned about the role of budgets in an organisation, why estimates for expenditure are prepared and the importance of correct interpretation of information.

However, writing a budget or an estimate is only one part of the financial accountability exercise. The key element in effective financial management is *control*. Budgets must be carefully monitored and any variances recorded and then investigated. If the petty cash tin isn't checked and balanced at regular intervals, the contents are likely to be misused before too long. As you are probably only too well aware, from your personal life, it doesn't matter what your plans are, it's the ability to see them through which matters – particularly in relation to money!

Own work role and responsibilities

If you are responsible for submitting estimates for financial provision, then it is likely that you also have the job of recording actual expenditure against your planned schedule.

In some cases your estimated costs may be completely accurate. This would be the case, for instance, where you had asked a supplier to quote for equipment and/or materials and the account you receive is the same as the quotation – which it should be. If you were given an estimate then the total amount may be slightly different, but only by a small, acceptable, percentage. This is often the case if you were instructed only to submit your estimate in whole numbers or to the nearest hundred or thousand.

In other cases, however, there may be a difference between your proposed cost and the actual cost. In a budget this is called a **variance** and must be recorded as either adverse (A) or favourable (F). If you are spending more than forecast, this is an adverse variance; if you are spending less than you thought, this is a favourable variance. Check the methods of presentation used in your organisation. Plus and minus signs or brackets may be used to indicate variances.

At Tree of Knowledge, the publishing company in our example, a variance sheet like the one below is produced for each title published.

Final costs on new titles: spring quarter

Title	Fixed cost			Paper, print and bind			Notes
	Est	Actual	Variance	Est	Actual	Variance	
Contemporary Religion	28421	31788	3367	2500	2503	503	Higher photo fees and origination
Understanding RE	2076	2406	330	3752	1648	−2104	Higher photo fees. PPB lower because of use of wallet

The degree to which you will be held responsible for the variance will depend upon the degree of control you had over the reason for the difference. If, for instance, you underestimated the amount of paper used for photocopying because you ignored the fact that some paper is likely to be spoiled in a large job, then you could be criticised for not estimating your requirements properly and ignoring important factors. If, however, you underestimated the total job because there was an unexpected increase in the cost of the maintenance contract on the photocopying machine, then you can hardly be held responsible.

TEST YOURSELF

You work as administrator in a large hotel which is controlled by a national chain. Your manager has been to a regional meeting at which he was reprimanded because his budget forecast proved inaccurate in several respects. He claims several of the factors which influenced these variations were outside his control and he can hardly be expected to take responsibility for these. As a group, which of the following costs do you consider are under his control and which not?

- An increase in wages paid to all hotel staff in the group.
- An increase in advertising because of fierce local competition.
- An increase in pilferage by guests.
- Redecoration costs for the new bar area.
- Training costs for new bar staff.
- An increase in the insurance premium.

- An increase in the number of bad debts (i.e. people leaving the hotel without paying their bills in full).

Scope and limit of own authority in expending finance

Even if you have submitted an estimate for expenditure and followed all the requirements for requesting additional resources, this does not mean that you should start writing large cheques the second you find that you have been successful! There will still be a limit to the amount you can authorise on a particular order or the amount you can sanction on a particular payment. However, if you have been allocated a particular expenditure code, then you can normally pass invoices for payment against this code until the limit of the agreed expenditure has been reached.

In other cases, it may not be the individual item cost which determines whether or not you are allowed to buy it, but the type of item! You may be allowed to purchase consumables such as stationery up to quite a large sum but not be allowed to buy any capital equipment without specific authorisation.

The first point to bear in mind is that you cannot make assumptions, particularly with a new employer, in relation to what you are allowed to spend and what you are not. You must check and, if necessary, ask for agreement in writing.

Secondly, whatever you spend, you must ensure that you keep accurate records. This is not just because someone will have to match up your spending to the company accounts, the budget or other financial documents. It is also a safeguard for yourself and for your own peace of mind on the day the auditors appear!

Thirdly, it is your responsibility to make sure that your staff follow the systems laid down. *Never* be tempted to turn a blind eye to malpractice or even simple carelessness in relation to financial records or expenditure.

TEST YOURSELF

The maximum amount allowed for petty cash purchases in your organisation is £30. Everyone knows this, including the junior staff. Yesterday you were away on a course. When you return today you are amazed to find a voucher in the tin for £65 clipped to a receipt for a meal for three at a local restaurant. When you investigate you find that the newest member of staff was harangued into giving out the money by a representative who had clients to entertain and had forgotten his credit card.

What action would you take:

a   immediately, to make sure that you are not held responsible if there is an investigation
b   to prevent the situation recurring in the future?

Ways of monitoring financial expenditure

The way in which you monitor financial expenditure is likely to vary depending upon the amount being spent, the source of the funds and the method of payment used. Ironically, it is usually much more difficult to monitor small, frequent payments than large, infrequent sums. You probably know this from your personal life. If you had a savings account with money put by for special occasions, and only drew out large amounts for good reasons, e.g. holidays or a special treat for yourself, you are unlikely to forget what you have spent. You will probably find it a simple matter to keep a close eye on the account and on your total spending from it.

However, to take the opposite extreme, keeping track of loose change in your pocket can be almost impossible and there are always times when your salary seems to disappear almost as soon as you have received it!

In business, it is essential that all expenditure is recorded and monitored. Whether this is through the completion of petty cash vouchers, a computer program recording invoice payments or manual entries into a cash book is irrelevant. Only if the amount and reason for spending has been noted can the expenditure then be recorded in the correct account or against the appropriate budget or estimate. Only then, too, is the information of value to you when you are making future decisions or having to prepare future estimates. Make it a habit to keep copies of all invoices that you either check or authorise. Then you will be able to check exactly how much was spent on toner, or on leaflet artwork, for example.

Ways of dealing with deviations to planned expenditure

As you saw at the beginning of this element, even with careful planning and budgeting not all expenditure will be as forecast. In that case you are normally in a situation where you have to make a decision in relation to:

a   the degree of acceptable variance, and
b   what to do about it.

Bear in mind, of course, that variances can be favourable as well as adverse and you may be in what seems to be the rather pleasant position of having saved money. However, the issues to consider now are:

● is an adverse variance always bad
● is a favourable variance always good?

The answer to both is 'no'! It is important to look at why the variance occurred. Only if the reason is known and analysed can corrective action be taken. For that reason, it is always critical that you:

- report any variance promptly (never try to fudge or hide it)
- identify whether the variance is favourable or adverse
- identify the reason for the deviation.

You can then go one stage further and identify whether the reason is:

a one which can be controlled by your own department or organisation

b one which is likely to have overall favourable or unfavourable results.

A practical example

Suppose you are in charge of producing a staff newsletter. This is issued each week to all staff in the organisation and you are allowed a budget for the materials required. When you submitted your budget this year you looked at the amount spent last year and simply added about 5 per cent. You work for quite a strict manager who becomes annoyed if spending goes over budget in any particular area.

After three months you have decided to work out how much you have spent on the newsletter to date. To your horror you find that the cost of producing the newsletter for the period is 15 per cent higher than expected.

You then investigate to find the reasons why. Your findings are shown in Figure 12.2.1.

In this case you may be criticised for not foreseeing that paper may increase in price and for not holding to your budgeted number of pages. However, the main reason for the increase would appear to be that you have improved the quality of the newsletter and that this has meant that its popularity has increased with staff. If the newsletter is going to serve its purpose as a communications instrument then it is

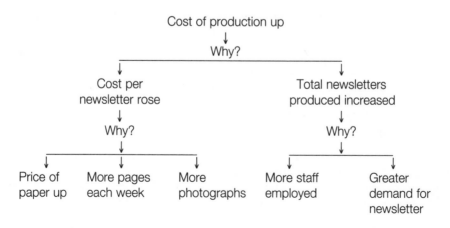

Figure 12.2.1 Analysing variances when producing a newsletter

useless if staff do not read it. The manager in question is therefore likely to be less negative in relation to the variance in costs. Equally, you can hardly be held responsible for the increase in staff numbers.

It is therefore sensible to attach a note to any variance or deviation stating exactly what has happened and why the differences occurred. Only by doing that can you give your line manager the information necessary for the correct decisions to be taken in each case.

Organisations' styles and format for recording expenditure

The precise way in which the expenditure is recorded for a department or section or in a particular organisation can vary from a computerised record to a manual system of accounting. Small items of expenditure are still likely to be logged through the petty cash system and then analysed under headings which link with the main cash book. Larger items of expenditure may be linked to cost codes so that, in a computerised system, total expenditure in a particular area from travel to entertaining and from stationery to raw materials can be displayed at the touch of a key (or two!)

CHECK IT YOURSELF

Draft a brief report on the different methods used for recording expenditure in your organisation. Try to establish the different methods used to record large and small amounts and expenditure on both consumable and capital items.

Identify the methods of recording expenditure with which you are personally involved as part of your job.

Organisations' reporting procedures

Financial reporting procedures usually include:

- the preparation of budget statements showing actual as well as planned expenditure
- management reports on variances and exceptions
- financial statements showing budgeted profit and loss accounts and budgeted balance sheets (i.e. the adjusted master budget)
- reports on performance in relation to targets.

In this case the planned and actual figures have been used to prepare an analysis of the situation for which the line manager or budget holder is usually held accountable. This may be you, or it may be your boss. In either case you should be operating as a team and supporting each other – particularly if any report highlights something with which you would take issue or feel is unjust.

If you have kept accurate records and files yourself then it is a fairly straightforward task to check that the information recorded is accurate. If it is not, the first step is obviously to ask for it to be adjusted.

If appropriate action has been taken to remedy a potentially problematic situation or adverse variance then this should also be recorded.

Finally, of course, there is always the situation where you can celebrate because you have not only controlled your expenditure but achieved your objectives at less cost than you estimated. Ironically this can sometimes be simply because of a pure stroke of luck – but if your boss sees this as the time to tell everyone how good you are, why should you spoil the moment?

ACTIVITY SECTION

1   You are monitoring expenditure in your own section when you identify each of the following changes which could affect your budget substantially by the end of the year. What action would you take in each case?

   a   A substantial increase in the price of envelopes from your usual supplier.
   b   An increase in the rate charged by the employment agency for temporary staff.
   c   A reduction in the amount of photocopier paper wasted since the new machine was installed.
   d   An increase in the amount of petty cash claims being made each week for travel and entertainment.

2   Your organisation is moving offices and you have been asked to help to plan the new reception area. You have been told that you can bid for a specific amount from the capital expenditure budget but that, once the amount has been allocated, no further sums will be available.

   a   What sources of information would you use to prepare your initial estimate?
   b   As a group, prepare a basic cost sheet and decide the type of fixtures and fittings required and the expenditure you would consider realistic to decorate and furnish the area.
   c   Six weeks after submission you find that your estimate has been approved for 10 per cent less than your initial planned figure. What steps would you take to prune the costs to allow for this reduction?
   d   How would you record the amounts spent as the area is completed?
   e   Two companies have contacted you to say that unfortunately they will have to increase the price of their goods because of an unexpected increase in price by their own suppliers. What action would you suggest could be taken to try to keep the project as near to budget as possible?

f Two days before the area is due to open you are visited by the company's health and safety officer. He insists that a number of plants you bought are moved from the area because they are situated in a hazardous position and informs you that a much larger, anti-slip mat must be positioned at the entrance. You know that you haven't enough money left to cover this item. What would you do?

3 The expense claims regularly submitted by one representative are far higher than those submitted by the other four reps employed by your organisation. However, this particular representative consistently sells more than anyone else – in some cases beating all previous records! Your boss continues to pass all his claims because he is so pleased with the results. However, you know that word is getting around and other members of staff disagree with this policy.

Discuss as a group what you would do if you were his boss and the factors which would influence your decision.

Index